Analysis of Variance for One Within-Subjects Factor

16-4 Sum of squares

$$SS_{between} = n_S \Sigma(\bar{X}_i - \bar{X}_T)^2$$

$$SS_{subjects} = n_A \Sigma(\bar{X}_k - \bar{X}_T)^2$$

$$SS_{subjects \times treatment} = \Sigma(X - \bar{X}_i)(X - \bar{X}_k)$$

$$SS_{total} = \Sigma(X - \bar{X}_T)^2$$

16-4 Degrees of freedom

$$df_{between} = n_A - 1$$

$$df_{subjects} = n_S - 1$$

$$df_{treatment \times subjects} = (n_A - 1)(n_S - 1)$$

$$df_{total} = n_A n_S - 1$$

16-4 Mean square

$$MS_{between} = \frac{SS_{between}}{df_{between}}, \quad MS_{subjects} = \frac{SS_{subjects}}{df_{subjects}}$$

$$MS_{treatment \times subjects} = \frac{SS_{treatment \times subjects}}{df_{treatment \times subjects}}$$

16-4 F ratio

$$F = \frac{MS_{between}}{MS_{treatment \times subjects}}$$

16-3 Planned posttest

$$t = \frac{\bar{X}_j - \bar{X}_k}{\sqrt{\dfrac{2MS_{treatment \times subjects}}{n_S}}}$$

Analysis of Variance for Two Between-Subjects Factors

17-2 Sum of squares

$$SS_A = n_B n_S \Sigma(\bar{X}_{A_i} - \bar{X}_T)^2$$

$$SS_B = n_A n_S \Sigma(\bar{X}_{B_j} - \bar{X}_T)^2$$

$$SS_{A \times B} = n_S \Sigma(\bar{X}_{A_i B_j} - \bar{X}_{A_i})(\bar{X}_{A_i B_j} - \bar{X}_{B_j})$$

$$SS_{within} = \Sigma(X_{A_i B_j} - \bar{X}_{A_i B_j})^2$$

$$SS_{total} = \Sigma(X - \bar{X}_T)^2$$

17-2 Degrees of freedom

$$df_A = n_A - 1, \quad df_B = n_B - 1$$

$$df_{A \times B} = (n_A - 1)(n_B - 1)$$

$$df_{within} = n_A n_B(n_S - 1), \quad df_{total} = n_A n_B n_S - 1$$

17-2 Mean square

$$MS_A = \frac{SS_A}{df_A}, \quad MS_B = \frac{SS_B}{df_B},$$

$$MS_{A \times B} = \frac{SS_{A \times B}}{df_{A \times B}}, \quad MS_{within} = \frac{SS_{within}}{df_{within}}$$

17-2 F ratio

$$F = \frac{MS_A}{MS_{within}}, \quad F = \frac{MS_B}{MS_{within}}, \quad F = \frac{MS_{A \times B}}{MS_{within}}$$

17-3 Posttest of main effects of A

$$t = \frac{\bar{X}_{A_j} - \bar{X}_{A_k}}{\sqrt{\dfrac{2MS_{within}}{n_B n_S}}}$$

17-4 Posttest of main effects of B

$$t = \frac{\bar{X}_{B_j} - \bar{X}_{B_k}}{\sqrt{\dfrac{2MS_{within}}{n_A n_S}}}$$

17-5 Posttest of effect of A at one level of B

$$t = \frac{\bar{X}_{A_j B_i} - \bar{X}_{A_k B_i}}{\sqrt{\dfrac{2MS_{within}}{n_S}}}$$

17-6 Posttest of effect of B at one level of A

$$t = \frac{\bar{X}_{A_i B_j} - \bar{X}_{A_i B_k}}{\sqrt{\dfrac{2MS_{within}}{n_S}}}$$

Chi Square

18-1 Chi square

$$\chi^2 = \Sigma \frac{(O - E)^2}{E}$$

18-2 Phi' coefficient (Cramer's statistic)

$$\phi' = \sqrt{\frac{\chi^2}{n(L - 1)}}$$

For my mother,

Jeanne K. Andriot,

whose courageous example inspired
me to go back to school,

and for

Alyssa and Zack Quiroz,

whose joy in learning new things
inspires me still.

Contents

Preface   xi

CHAPTER 1   **Why Study Statistics?** 1

The Causes of and Cure for Math Phobia   2

The Use, Misuse, and Abuse of Statistics   5

The Role of Research in Psychology and the Role of Statistics
    in Research   6

Summary   9   *Exercises   10*

CHAPTER 2   **Research and Measurement** 13

The Structure of an Experiment   14

Measurement   18

Scales of Measurement   26

Summary   33   *Exercises   33*

CHAPTER 3   **Frequency Tables and Graphs** 37

Distributions   38

Constructing Frequency Tables   39

Constructing Graphs of Frequency Distributions   44

Constructing Grouped Frequency Tables   55

Characteristics of Distributions   65

Summary   67   *Exercises   68*

CHAPTER 4   **Measures of Central Tendency** 73

Statistical Procedures   74

The Mean   79

The Median   84

The Mode   92

Comparing the Mean, Median, and Mode   96

    Summary   99   *Exercises   100*

CHAPTER 5 **Measures of Variability** 107

The Range   108

Measures of Variability Based on Deviations   110

Measures of Variability Based on Quartiles   121

Describing a Distribution of Scores   126

    Summary   129   *Exercises   130*

CHAPTER 6 **Measures of Relative Standing** 135

Standard Scores   137

Percentiles   150

    Summary   160   *Exercises   161*

CHAPTER 7 **The Normal Distribution** 167

What Is a Normal Distribution?   168

Using the Normal Distribution   173

The Relevance of Theoretical Distributions   186

    Summary   187   *Exercises   188*

CHAPTER 8 **Measures of Linear Correlation** 191

The Concept of Correlation   192

Measuring the Correlation between Interval or Ratio Variables:
    Pearson's Product-Moment Correlation   198

Measuring Correlation between Ordinal Variables:
    Spearman's Rank-Order Correlation   206

Measuring Correlation between Nominal Variables:
    The ϕ Coefficient   212

Correlation and Causation   213

    Summary   215   *Exercises   216*

CHAPTER 9 **Regression and Prediction**... 223
Prediction   224
Graphing the Relationship between Two Variables   229
Regression   238
Regression, Correlation, and Causation   248
          Summary   249   *Exercises   250*

CHAPTER 10 **Probability and the Binomial Distribution**........ 255
Basic Concepts in Probability   256
The Binomial Distribution   265
The Relevance of Theoretical Distributions   272
          Summary   273   *Exercises   274*

CHAPTER 11 **Sampling Distributions**... 277
Constructing a Distribution of Sample Proportions   279
Distributions of Sample Means   285
The Exactness of Parameter Estimates   295
          Summary   301   *Exercises   302*

CHAPTER 12 **Hypothesis Testing**.. 307
Research Hypotheses   309
The Logic of Hypothesis Testing   314
Unidirectional and Bidirectional Hypothesis Tests   323
Conducting the z Test for a Sample Mean   327
Decision Making in Statistical Tests   332
          Summary   337   *Exercises   339*

CHAPTER 13 **Parametric Tests for One Sample** 343
Student's t Test for a Sample Mean   345
The z Test for a Sample Proportion   352
The Power of a Statistical Test   357
Testing Hypotheses about a Population   368
          Summary   371   *Exercises   372*

CHAPTER 1 4 **Parametric Tests for Two Samples** 375

Between-Subjects and Within-Subjects Tests   377

The *t* Test for a Difference between Means:
   A Between-Subjects Test   378

The *t* Test for a Mean Difference: A Within-Subjects Test   389

A Parametric Test of the Strength of a Relationship:
   Pearson's Product-Moment Correlation   395

Parametric Tests Revisited   401

   Summary   403   *Exercises   404*

CHAPTER 1 5 **Nonparametric Tests for Two Samples** 411

A Sampling Distribution of Ranks   413

The Mann-Whitney *U* Test: A Between-Subjects
   Nonparametric Test   419

The Wilcoxon Signed-Ranks Test: A Within-Subjects
   Nonparametric Test   430

A Nonparametric Test of the Strength of a Relationship:
   Spearman's Rank-Order Correlation   436

Hypothesis Testing Revisited   439

   Summary   441   *Exercises   442*

CHAPTER 1 6 **A Statistical Test for More than Two Samples:
The One-Factor Analysis of Variance** 447

Analyzing the Variance among Scores   449

The Analysis of Variance for a Between-Subjects Factor   457

Posttests for the Analysis of Variance   466

The Analysis of Variance for a Within-Subjects Factor   468

Comparing Between- and Within-Subjects Tests   476

   Summary   478   *Exercises   479*

CHAPTER 1 7 **A Statistical Test Comparing More than
Two Samples: The Two-Factor Analysis
of Variance** 485

The Interaction between Factors   486

The Analysis of Variance for Two Between-Subjects Factors 488
Computing the Values of F 495
Posttests for a Two-Factor Analysis of Variance 506
Other Analyses of Variance 515
Summary 517 *Exercises 517*

CHAPTER **18** **Chi Square** 523
Calculating χ^2 524
Using χ^2 to Measure the Correlation between Two Variables 530
The χ^2 Test of Association 535
The χ^2 Test for Goodness of Fit 543
Summary 546 *Exercises 547*

CHAPTER **19** **Deciding Which Statistic to Use** 551
Consider the Characteristics of the Distribution 552
Consider the Purpose the Statistic Serves 554

Appendix A: Statistical Tables 559
Appendix B: Answers to Exercises 581
Glossary of Statistical Terms 603
Glossary of Statistical Symbols 615
Index 619

Preface

This text began as a small manual prepared for my students, describing step-by-step how to use each of the statistical formulas covered in class. Throughout the course of my teaching career, I have found that the most effective way to help students understand a statistical formula measure is to have them compute the statistic on a variety of sets of data. However, many of the students that I teach have difficulty understanding how to use statistical formulas, and none of the statistics texts available provided a description of all the steps involved in using each formula. To meet my students' needs, I wrote a step-by-step procedures manual to use as a supplement to the textbook for the course.

I soon found that too many of my students were relying solely on this manual and had stopped referring to the textbook because of the difficult wording and complex examples. To help my students understand why we use statistics and what information each statistic provides, I added explanations, demonstrations, and examples to the manual, and an early version of this text evolved.

Features That Help Students Understand Statistical Concepts

Understanding Statistics is designed particularly for students who lack extensive mathematical experience. It is written for students studying in any of the areas of the behavioral sciences, a fair proportion of whom find all mathematics, including statistics, intimidating.

Understanding Statistics places equal emphasis on understanding what statistics measures and on learning to calculate those statistics. To help students understand what each statistic measures, this text stresses the following fundamentals of statistics:

Emphasis on basic statistics   The statistics covered in this text are the most basic and commonly used, the ones most likely to be encountered by students in both their readings and outside research.

A minimum of technical jargon   *Understanding Statistics* is written in a clear, easy-to-read style, using a minimum of technical terminology.

In-text definitions of statistical terms   Each statistical term is formally defined when it is first introduced and then redefined when used in later chapters. The term also appears in the glossary provided at the end of the text. To help students understand the meanings of statistical terms, common English words are used as synonyms for the statistical term (e.g., "center point" for central tendency).

Explanation of concepts through demonstrations   Rather than explain statistical concepts through algebraic proofs, which many students find confusing and unconvincing, statistical concepts are demonstrated empirically. For example, the concept that the mean is sensitive to changes in the scores is demonstrated by calculating the means of two sets of scores that differ only in the value of one score. A very small sampling distribution is constructed empirically to demonstrate the concept of theoretical sampling distributions.

Examples based on simple research designs   The research studies used as examples in the text and in the end-of-chapter exercises are fictitious and based on simple designs. At the introductory level, students often have difficulty understanding research designs drawn from the behavioral science literature, which increases their difficulty in understanding the statistics those examples are used to illustrate. In concert with the very basic level of the research examples used in this text, all of the researchers depicted in these examples are students.

On-going research examples used throughout text   Two on-going research studies are used as examples throughout the text: Joe Johnson's research on math anxiety and Jane Jeffers's research on psychology alumni's incomes. Using these on-going examples reduces the need for students to understand new and different research designs for each example presented and also demonstrates the wide variety of ways in which data can be analyzed.

Conceptual and computational exercises   The exercises included at the end of each chapter are divided into those focused on conceptual understanding and on those focused on computational practice. Many of the conceptual exercises lead students through demonstrations of statistical concepts similar to those used in the text to explain those concepts.

Features That Help Students Calculate Statistics

To provide help to students in learning to calculate statistics, *Understanding Statistics* includes several distinctive aids:

Step-by-step procedures   The method for using each statistical formula included in the text is described in sidebars, step by step, when the formula is first introduced. These sidebars also include an explanation of all of the symbols used in the formula.

Abundance of completely worked examples Each statistical procedure is illustrated with one or more completed examples, showing all of the computational steps.

In-text explanations of mathematical terms and operations This text assumes students are able to perform the basic mathematical operations of addition, subtraction, multiplication, and division, as well as finding the squares and square roots of numbers. All other mathematical terms and operations are explained in the text as they occur rather than in a separate appendix.

End-of-chapter summaries Each chapter includes a summary of the main concepts covered, providing a study aid for students.

Sidebars on "Checking Your Answers." Included at the end of each chapter are sidebars with hints for solving the exercises. These hints include ways to assess whether the answers are reasonable, as well as caution against the most commonly made errors.

Appendix containing answers to all computational exercises The answers to all exercises involving computations are included at the end of the text. In addition, fully worked solutions to all of the exercises are provided in the instructor's manual.

Focus and Organization of the Text

To prevent students from feeling overwhelmed by the amount of information presented, each chapter focuses on one main statistical concept and presents just a few statistical techniques. For example, the concepts of central tendency and variability, presented together in many texts, are presented here in separate, consecutive chapters.

In addition to statistics used with data measured on interval and ratio measurement scales, *Understanding Statistics* covers statistics appropriate for data measured on ordinal and nominal measurement scales, which are often given little coverage in introductory texts. Throughout my teaching experience, I have found that students are better able to grasp, for example, the concept of central tendency when we explore the mean, median, and mode. Similarly, relative standing is better understood when both standard scores and percentiles are explored. In this text, measures for interval and ratio data are presented first in each chapter, followed by measures for ordinal and nominal data. Instructors who wish to skip those latter measures may do so without adverse consequences.

The first half of *Understanding Statistics* focuses on descriptive statistics. Chapter 1 describes the crucial role of statistics in research and also gives students concrete tips to overcoming math anxiety and focus on learning. Chapter 2 describes the nature of measurement, including a description of the four scales of measurement, while Chapter 3 describes methods for constructing frequency tables and graphs of sets of data, including the exploratory technique of stem-and-leaf display.

Chapters 4 through 7 focus on descriptive statistics used with one set of data, including measures of central tendency, variability, relative standing, and the normal distribution. For the median and related concepts, both a simple method and the more precise method based on interpolation are presented, allowing instructors to cover the method they prefer, or both. The concepts of standard scores and the normal distribution are presented in separate chapters to help preclude students from erroneously assuming that the normal distributions can be used with any data set converted to standard scores.

Chapters 8 and 9 focus on linear correlation and regression, respectively. Both Pearson's product-moment correlation and Spearman's rank-order correlation are included, as well as the *phi* (ϕ) coefficient as a measure appropriate for nominal data. Chi square (χ^2), the correlational technique used much more frequently with nominal data, is covered separately in Chapter 18. These chapters examined the concepts of correlation and regression as descriptive techniques. The use of Pearson and Spearman's correlations in inferential testing are described later in Chapters 14 and 15.

The second half of *Understanding Statistics* focuses on inferential statistics. Chapter 10 presents basic concepts of probability, including a description of the binomial distribution. The concept of sampling distributions is introduced in Chapter 11, as well as the concept of confidence intervals. The basic concepts of hypothesis testing are presented in Chapter 12, which also provides a discussion of decision making, including Type I and Type II errors and a brief introduction to the concept of power. Chapter 13 continues a discussion of hypothesis testing, presenting inferential tests that can be used with one sample of scores, as well as a further exploration of power and effect size.

The remaining chapters of *Understanding Statistics* explore the most commonly-used inferential tests. For each test, the text first describes the sampling distribution that forms the basis of the test, then describes how the test should be conducted. Chapter 14 covers parametric tests for two samples; Chapter 15 presents nonparametric tests. Chapters 16 presents the one-factor ANOVA for both a between-groups factor and a within-groups factor, while Chapter 17 describes the two-factor ANOVA for between-groups factors. Both chapters include descriptions of posttests, and Chapter 17 includes an exploration of the concept of interactions. Finally, Chapter 18 explores chi square, both as a measure of correlation and as an inferential test appropriate for nominal data.

The last chapter in the text presents several flow charts to be used in analyzing data. Throughout the use of these charts, students first determine what purpose the statistic serves, and then, based on considering the characteristics of the data, including the scale of measurement and shape of distribution, determine which statistic to use. This chapter serves as a review and integration of the main concepts explored in all of the previous chapters.

Ancillaries

An array of ancillary materials is available to complement *Understanding Statistics in the Behavioral Sciences: Step by Step*. Contact your local Wadsworth representative for instructor's copies of these items and for packaging options.

Computerized Test Bank

All of the items in the test bank are present in a computerized version. A cross-platform CD, Examview, is available to adopters on request.

Instructor's Manual/Test Bank

In this helpful aid you will find teaching tips, sample syllabi, and fully worked solutions to all exercises in the book. Multiple-choice test items are also included.

Study Guide

Conscientious use of this invaluable ancillary will help students make the most of their statistics course. Each chapter of this guide contains a fill-in-the-blank review of all the major concepts, along with additional exercises. Solutions to the study guide questions and exercises are provided in the concluding chapter.

Web Site

On-line quizzes and annotated links to outside sources can be found on the Web at http://www.wadsworth.com/psychology_d.

Acknowledgments

As John Donne wrote, "No man is an Island, entire of itself." This also holds true for anyone who has endeavored to write a textbook. I am indebted to many people who have provided valuable insight in the creation of this text. I wish to thank Sue Carlisle, who patiently helped me through many revisions and also aided in shipping manuscript parts out of Montana at a rate considerably faster than our normal Pony Express. I also wish to thank Beal Mossman, Emeritus Professor of Psychology, Montana State University—Billings, for his help, support and encouragement, including testing an earlier version in his class. I am grateful to Lisa Hensley, who first saw the promise in this text, as well as Roz Sackoff and Brad Potthoff, who have brought that promise to fruition. In addition, I am grateful to Gretchen Otto and Karen Boyd for their patient and prodigious work in bringing the manuscript to printed form.

A considerable number of reviewers have critiqued various portions of this text. Their comments were enormously helpful in directing me to issues that I had overlooked and their concrete suggestions for improving the text clearly reflected their own dedication to the teaching of statistics. I am indebted to them and wish to acknowledge their substantial contributions: Bryan C. Auday, Gordon College; Barney Beins, Ithaca College; Gary Forbach, Washburn Institute for the Study and Practice of Leadership; Charles A. Levin, Baldwin-Wallace College; Robert Pasnak, George Mason University; Donald Schniff, State University of New York at New Paltz; Anna Smith, Troy State College; Mary Tallent-Runnels, Texas Tech University; Bruce Warner, Kutztown State University, and Evangeline Wheeler, Towson University.

I want to express my deep gratitude to my sister, Laurie Andriot, for volunteering to compile the index for this text and for doing an outstanding job. No other book has been as exquisitely indexed. I also want to thank the students in my classes who used an earlier version of this text. I have learned as much from them as they ever have from me. Finally, and most important, I wish to acknowledge my incalculable debt to my daughter, Beth. She was, and is, unendingly patient, supportive, and encouraging. She most certainly is Sunday's child. To borrow from Jo March in Louisa May Alcott's *Little Women,* "What do women do who haven't any daughters to help them through their troubles?"

Why Study Statistics?

1

The Causes of and Cure for Math Phobia
Why Are Students Afraid of Statistics?
How to Learn Statistics

The Use, Misuse, and Abuse of Statistics

The Role of Research in Psychology and the Role of Statistics in Research
Psychology and the Scientific Method

Psychology, Research, and Theories
Research, Numbers, and Statistics
Types of Statistics
SUMMARY
EXERCISES
Conceptual Exercises
ENDNOTE

▶ Statistics is one of the courses most frequently required of students majoring in psychology. The vast majority of students enroll in statistics courses only because they are required to complete the course in order to graduate. Many students dread taking the statistics course, so much so that one very common nickname for statistics courses is "Sadistics."

There are three reasons why many students resist the idea of taking a course in statistics. One is that statistics involves mathematics. Students who dislike mathematics often think that they will also dislike statistics, just as students who fear mathematics also fear statistics. A second reason is that many people, students and nonstudents alike, distrust statistics. We have so often seen statistics used in a manipulatory and self-serving manner that many people distrust all uses of statistics. The third reason is that often students do not understand the purpose for using statistics in psychology. Not understanding that statistics play an essential role in psychological research, students are likely to see statistics as being irrelevant and worthless. These three reasons stem from a misunderstanding of the nature of statistics and the role they play in the discipline of psychology. We will take a closer look at these three reasons and examine the integral role that statistics do play in psychology.

The Causes of and Cure for Math Phobia

Why Are Students Afraid of Statistics?

There is an abundance of research about students' fear of mathematics, or math anxiety, so much that it has its own moniker: math phobia. One obvious conclusion permeates this research: students are anxious about math because they firmly believe that they cannot do math. Some students put off taking math courses as long as possible, and as each term passes, their anxiety increases. They are afraid that math will keep them from ever getting a degree. That's a lot of stress to be under as you sit in class on the first day of a course in statistics!

Many students believe that some people can do math and some people can't, and, furthermore, that people are born that way. Students who think they can't do math feel doomed, believing that there is nothing that they can do to fix the problem. As long as they feel that way, their anxiety can only increase, making it even more difficult to pass a math course. In order to overcome math phobia, you have to change the belief that you do not have the ability to do math. Note the key word is *belief*. Math phobia is fundamentally a belief that you have low math ability, that you can't learn math. It is a belief, not a fact.

The scientific evidence for differences in math ability comes primarily from scores on standardized math tests. But standardized test scores reflect math *achievement,* not math *ability.* Low standardized test scores show only that students have not yet learned the math skills tested, not that they lack the ability to learn. There is a big difference between not *having learned* math and not *being able to learn* math.

Virtually all college students have the ability to learn statistics. You wouldn't be in college if you weren't capable of learning. Of course, some students have an easier time learning statistics than others. If you are one of the students who find math difficult, remember that you have the ability to learn statistics but that you might need to put in more time keeping up. If you are willing to invest the time and effort, you can succeed!

How to Learn Statistics

First and foremost, it is important to realize that a course in statistics is more than just learning how to compute them. In fact, knowing how to compute statistics is meaningless unless you understand what those statistics measure. A statistics course is about understanding statistical concepts, just as a course in development is about understanding developmental concepts. In that way, a statistics course is no different than any other course in psychology.

In addition, it may help to know that while statistics does involve the use of mathematics, the only mathematics used in the statistical formulas described in this text is simple arithmetic. In these statistical formulas, you will be asked to add, subtract, multiply, and divide numbers, as well as square numbers and find the square root of numbers. None of the mathematics involved in statistics is more complicated than that.

To succeed in learning statistics, the most important thing you can do is to keep trying. Most students fail simply because they get frustrated and give up. You can't succeed in learning statistics if you give up. If you absolutely refuse to quit trying, no matter how frustrated you get, you can succeed in understanding statistics.

Here are some specific suggestions to help you master statistics:

▶ *Attend class.* When students have difficulties in a class, they often feel uncomfortable and begin skipping. This is one of the worst things you can do. Missing class won't help you learn. Make a resolution that, barring illness, you'll attend every class.

▶ *Sit near the front of the class.* Students who feel anxious and uncomfortable in a class often choose to sit in the back. Nonetheless, there are several good reasons to choose a seat near the front. One is that it is easier to pay attention sitting in the front because there are fewer distractions. Students in the front also tend to participate more actively, which helps learning.

▶ *Ask questions.* Some students are embarrassed to ask questions in class. They are afraid that they will be a bother or that others will think that they are stupid. But if you don't understand something, chances are good that there are other students who are confused, too. Asking a question could well be a favor to everyone in the class!

▶ *Read the text.* The concepts that your instructor explains in class are also described in your textbook. If you don't completely understand a concept in class, reading the text can provide clarification. Read for understanding, not just to get through. Books about math and statistics are meant to be read slowly. Each paragraph presents one main idea. Make sure you understand that idea before going on.

▶ *Take notes on all problems your instructor works in class.* Your instructor will probably work problems on the board, demonstrating how to use each statistical formula. Make sure you write down all of the work so that you can go over it later. You can practice working the same examples, and then if you don't get the same answer, you can compare your work to your notes to see where you erred. You can do the same thing with the examples shown in the text.

▶ *Practice working problems!* The key to most learning is practice. You don't learn tennis by stopping after you hit the ball over the net once, saying, "Okay, I can do that now." You get good at tennis by hitting the ball, over and over again. It's the same with statistics. You get good by working problems over and over again. You can gain speed and confidence through practice—lots of practice! The goal is not to be able to use a formula correctly one time; the goal is to be able to use it correctly every time.

▶ *Get a study buddy.* It is very helpful to study in a group or with another member of your class. It is rare that everyone will make exactly the same mistake in working exercises, and so the members of a study group can help each other track down errors and mistakes. In addition, finding out that everyone in the group is having difficulty with a concept can give you confidence to ask the instructor for clarification in class.

▶ *If there is anything you don't understand, get help.* Learning statistics is cumulative. The concepts in each chapter build on the concepts presented earlier. If you have difficulty with a concept, you will inevitably have trouble understanding all of the concepts that build on it. It is crucial to get help as soon as you run into difficulty. Instructors are glad to help students who are actively trying to learn. But that means you must do your part. Try working the problems on your own first, and then, if you have trouble, show your work to your instructor. Usually the trouble is something simple to clarify.

All of these suggestions can help you succeed in learning statistics. They may seem to be common sense, things you've heard many times before. In fact, they are common sense, because they do work. If you go to class, read the text, practice problems, and seek help when you run into difficulties, you can conquer statistics!

The Use, Misuse, and Abuse of Statistics

We all use statistics: to illustrate a point, to make a case for our point of view. It is perfectly appropriate for people to use statistics to advocate for their viewpoints. What is not appropriate is for anyone to misuse statistics, to use them in deceptive, manipulatory ways. And there are occasions in which statistics are misused—by businesses, the media, politicians, bureaucrats, and by scientists. Sometimes the misuse of statistics is not intentional but rather is the result of misunderstanding or error. Nonetheless, the misuse of statistics is always inappropriate.

The American Psychological Association, in its *Ethical Principles of Psychologists and Code of Conduct,*[1] has established ethical guidelines to govern the activities of psychologists, including research. These *Ethical Principles* describe ethical and humane standards for the use of both animal and human subjects, including the right of human participants to give informed consent. In addition, the *Ethical Principles* specifically state that "psychologists plan their research so as to minimize the possibility that results will be misleading" (Section 6.06b) and that in reporting the results of research, "psychologists do not fabricate data or falsify results" (Section 6.21a). Furthermore, the *Ethical Principles* require that researchers make their original data available to other professionals for the purpose of reanalyzing that data. Thus, a reader who has a question about how a researcher analyzed the data in an experimental report can request the original data from the researcher and reanalyze on their own. All of these standards help to minimize the misuse of statistics in psychological research.

Whether statistical misuse is unintentional, caused by lack of understanding, or intentional chicanery, the only protection is to understand enough about statistics to be aware of that misuse. It is a case of caveat emptor—let the buyer beware. Ignoring all statistics because some statistics are misused is like throwing out the baby with the bath water. Not all uses of statistics are inappropriate. Not all uses of statistics are deceptive. To ignore all statistics would mean to ignore all the information that the valid use of statistics provides. We need to be able to understand statistics when they are used appropriately as well as identify when they are misused. One important reason to study statistics is that when you understand statistics, you will be able to see through any deception and misuse.

The Role of Research in Psychology and the Role of Statistics in Research

Psychology and the Scientific Method

Psychology is a science. Often, we think of science as a subject we take in school, such as biology or chemistry. Just as students take a course in French to learn French, so they take a science course in order to learn science. However, science is more than a subject to be learned. Fundamentally, science is one method of increasing our knowledge about the world. What all of the subjects that we think of as "the sciences" have in common is that they all use the same method—the scientific method—to increase our knowledge.

Most of us have learned the four steps in the scientific method:

1. Observe a phenomenon;
2. Form a tentative explanation (a hypothesis) of the phenomenon;
3. Conduct an experiment to test the tentative explanation; and
4. If the results of the experiment do not support the tentative explanation, revise the explanation.

The definitive step, the step that makes this method scientific, is Step 3. It is experimental research that makes science scientific. Scientists add to the body of knowledge by conducting experiments, by making observations in the real world. The fact that psychologists conduct experiments in order to test their hypotheses or theories is what makes psychology a science. It is research that enables us to test the validity of psychological theories. It is through research that psychology as a discipline and an area of knowledge has grown over the past century. What we know about psychology today has come through research.

Psychology, Research, and Theories

In introductory psychology classes, one of the most frequently asked questions is, "Why are there so many theories?" Students in introductory psychology often take the class because they want information to help them make their lives better and improve their relationships with others. They want concrete facts, not theories. The problem is that psychologists do not have all the facts explaining why we humans behave as we do. Psychologists construct theories to try and explain what we do not know for certain.

Some psychological theories have an enormous amount of facts supporting them. For example, B. F. Skinner's theory of operant conditioning and

Jean Piaget's theory of cognitive development both have a wealth of supporting research. However, there are other theories that have very little or no support from research. Many of the "theories" propounded in books found in the psychology and self-help sections of bookstores fall in this category. Many of these books fail to report any supporting evidence from research. These "theories" are little more than just the opinion of people who have simply set themselves up as experts. One of the problems with these "pop psych" theories is that we have no way of determining their validity other than just accepting the claims of the authors.

Some people might ask, "What's wrong with that? If it helps people to read pop psych books, what's the problem?" The problem is that we have no evidence to determine whether or not these theories are helpful. In fact, some of these theories may be harmful. We can look at history to see examples of false beliefs that were harmful to people. Just remember the twenty people hanged as witches in seventeenth century Salem, Massachusetts. In the twentieth century, Adolf Hitler held the false and definitely harmful belief that society would be improved by the elimination of millions of people. If a theory is worth believing, then it is worth testing with research. If "experts" don't bother to show us any concrete evidence in support of their theories, how much are their theories worth?

We have two choices in psychology. The first is to accept people's ideas and theories without any supporting evidence from research. The problem with this choice is that we would have no way of knowing which theories are valid and which are nonsense. Our other choice is to accept only those theories that are supported by research evidence. Research provides us a means of evaluating the validity of theories. Research is our protection against so-called "experts," charlatans, and flimflam artists.

Research, Numbers, and Statistics

Numbers are an integral part of doing research. When conducting an experiment, a researcher essentially measures a series of events. In psychology, the events could be a person's responses on an intelligence test or a rat's behavior in a maze. In order to provide evidence in support of a theory, researchers need concrete records of the events they have observed. It isn't enough for a researcher to say, "Well, it seemed to me that the rats ran faster when given reinforcement than not." They must provide concrete, verifiable measurements of their observations, such as the time in seconds it takes rats to run a maze or the IQ scores of the participants tested. And these measurements mean numbers.

In a psychological experiment, researchers collect scores from every subject tested. However, when reporting the results of the experiment, researchers generally do not list all of the scores they have collected. Instead of

FIGURE 1-1 Converting Scores to a Numeric Summary

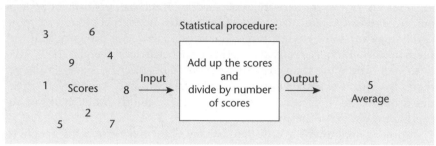

reporting hundreds of scores, researchers usually use just a few numbers to de-scribe the entire group of scores. For example, they might use the average score as a way of describing the center of the group. There are also ways to use a single number to describe how spread out a group of scores is and whether the group is fairly balanced or is lopsided. With just a few numbers, re-searchers can give their readers a pretty fair description of the scores they have collected in their research without having to list all of those scores. To find these numbers that describe a group of scores, researchers use a statistical pro-cedure. This can be illustrated graphically, as shown in Figure 1-1.

A statistical procedure is like a machine: you put all of the scores in the machine, process them, and the machine outputs a single number represent-ing all of the scores that you originally put in. In essence, a statistical proce-dure is a series of mathematical steps used to summarize a group of scores with a single number. In Figure 1-1, the statistical procedure is the steps used to convert the nine scores shown into a single number, the average. The statis-tical procedure for finding the average has two mathematical steps: (1) adding up the scores and then (2) dividing by the number of scores.

The numeric summaries generated by statistical procedures are usually called statistics. In order to understand what a statistic represents, we need to understand the statistical procedure used to generate it. That is the subject matter of this book. Each chapter examines one type of statistical procedure and explains how that type of procedure is used to summarize scores. By un-derstanding these statistical procedures, you will understand what the statis-tics measure.

Imagine what the world would be like if scientists did not collect mea-surements or calculate statistics. If scientists did not collect measurements, we would have to rely on their impressions of the results of their experiments. Imagine a cancer researcher testing a new form of chemotherapy, rather than giving us concrete evidence of the effectiveness of the drug, simply saying, "Well, it sure seemed to me to work." Without measurements, researchers have no way to show us the results of their experiments except to give us their subjective impressions. Statistics in turn are a way of summarizing measurements, which scientists use as evidence to support or refute arguments. When you understand statistics, you will be able to evaluate how valid those arguments are.

Types of Statistics

There are two main branches of statistics that we will examine in this text. One branch is called **descriptive statistics**, which are used to describe a group of scores or the relationship between groups of scores. Suppose you collect the ages of all the students in your statistics class. You could use the average age as a way of describing the center point of all the ages. If you collect both the ages and IQs of your classmates, you can use descriptive statistics to depict whether there is any relationship between age and IQ.

The other branch of statistics is called **inferential statistics.** Sometimes, rather than test an entire group of subjects, researchers will test only a small subgroup. For example, a researcher studying the vocabulary size of two-year-old children probably would test only a group of 20 or 30 two-year-olds rather than test every two-year-old child in the United States. The subgroup is then used as an estimate of how the entire group would perform, if they were all tested. In essence, researchers use a subgroup to make *inferences* about how the entire group could be expected to perform, and inferential statistics are used to evaluate how valid those inferences are.

In the first part of this text, we examine several types of descriptive statistics. In the latter part of the text, we examine the use of inferential statistics. In examining both of these branches of statistics, this text has two goals. One is to help you learn to calculate the statistics most frequently used in psychology. Just as important is the second goal: to help you understand what these statistics tell us.

Descriptive statistics are procedures used to describe the characteristics of a set of scores or to describe the relationship between sets of scores.

Inferential statistics are procedures used to make an inference about a larger group of scores from a subgroup of those scores.

Σ *S U M M A R Y*

▶ To overcome a fear of learning statistics, remember that basic statistics involves nothing more than arithmetic computations, that understanding what statistics measure is as important as computing them, and that active effort and resolving difficulties as they arise leads to success.

▶ While there can be misuse and abuse of statistics, nearly all psychological researchers adhere to the *Ethical Principles of Psychologists and Code of Conduct* of the American Psychological Association, which advocates for fair and open research practices.

▶ The best defense against the abuse of statistics is knowledge of what those statistics measure.

▶ Psychology is a science because psychological research follows the scientific method. The validity of psychological theories is tested through research.

▶ Psychological research provides measurements that can be used to support or refute theories. Statistics are numerical summaries of those measurements.

▶ Descriptive statistics are used to describe a group of scores or the relationship between groups of scores. Inferential statistics are used to make an inference about a larger group of scores from a smaller subgroup of those scores.

E X E R C I S E S

Conceptual Exercises

1. Describe how a fear of mathematics can lead a student to not succeed in understanding statistics and how the inability to understand statistics can lead to an increased fear of mathematics.

2. Describe five things that you can do to improve your chances of succeeding at understanding statistics.

3. Describe how a lack of understanding of statistics allows people to be fooled by the misuse and abuse of statistics.

4. Find an example from real life in which statistics are misused in order to fool the public.

5. Find an example from real life in which two opposing sides of a controversy quote different, conflicting statistics, each in support of their side of the controversy. (One example might be the Republicans and Democrats citing different statistics about Medicare increases.)

6. Find an example in a newspaper or magazine in which the writer makes an argument without giving research evidence. What does the writer use to support the argument? How convincing is this support, compared to research evidence?

7. Explain why psychology is considered a science.

8. Describe the four steps in the scientific method.

9. Construct an example of a hypothesis of your own and a way to test that hypothesis. Identify the four steps of the scientific method in your example.

10. Describe the problems that would arise for psychologists if we did not conduct experiments or use statistics.

11. Describe the two branches of statistics, and explain how each branch is used to help meet one of the goals of scientific research.

12. Look for three references to the term *statistics* in the newspaper or a magazine. Describe the context in which the term is used.

13. Look for an example of a sports statistic in the newspaper. Explain how the statistic is computed.

14. A television commercial states that 6 out of 10 physicians recommend "Nuke-It" for headache relief. How valid is the use of this statistic?

E N D N O T E

1. *Ethical Principles of Psychologists and Code of Conduct* (Washington, D.C.: American Psychological Association, 1992).

Research and Measurement

The Structure of an Experiment

Populations and Samples

STEP-BY-STEP PROCEDURE 2-1: How to Differentiate Populations and Samples

Parameters and Statistics

Variables and Constants

STEP-BY-STEP PROCEDURE 2-2: How to Differentiate Variables and Constants

Measurement

Characteristics and Number Lines

The Unit of Measurement

Continuous and Discrete Variables

STEP-BY-STEP PROCEDURE 2-3: How to Differentiate Continuous Variables and Discrete Variables

Degree of Precision

Identifying the Unit of Measurement

STEP-BY-STEP PROCEDURE 2-4: How to Identify the Unit of Measurement

Intervals

Real Limits

STEP-BY-STEP PROCEDURE 2-5: How to Find the Real Limits of an Interval

Scales of Measurement

Nominal Scales of Measurement

Ordinal Scale of Measurement

Interval Scales of Measurement

Ratio Scales of Measurement

Comparing the Measurement Scales

STEP-BY-STEP PROCEDURE 2-6: How to Identify the Scale of Measurement

CHECKING YOUR ANSWERS

S U M M A R Y

E X E R C I S E S

Conceptual Exercises

Computational Exercises

E N D N O T E

▶ Statistics are computed using scores collected from subjects. Before we begin to examine the procedures for calculating those statistics, it is important to examine the nature of the scores on which they are based. In conducting an experiment, researchers make decisions about how the subjects' performance will be measured and how scores will be collected and recorded. These decisions affect which statistics the researchers can later legitimately use to analyze those scores. To understand the effect of researchers' decisions about scores, we will first look at the structure of the experiments that psychological researchers conduct.

The Structure of an Experiment

Populations and Samples

A **subject** is a person or animal observed or tested in an experiment.

When psychologists do research, they are trying to find evidence to support their ideas about the behavior of a particular group of people or animals, called **subjects.** The American Psychological Association recommends that we acknowledge the active role of human volunteers participating in psychological research by calling them *participants* rather than *subjects,* a recommendation that is followed in this text whenever it is clear that the subjects are humans.

Suppose that Joe Johnson, a student majoring in psychology, has a hypothesis about what causes college students to feel anxious while taking math tests. If he were to conduct an experiment to test his hypothesis, Joe would have two choices in selecting participants: either he could test the entire group of math-anxious college students or he could test a subgroup. The entire group of interest is called the **population;** if only a subgroup is tested, that subgroup is called a **sample.**

A **population** is a group of subjects or events that have a common set of characteristics of interest in an experiment.

A **sample** is a subgroup of a population. If not all members of the population are observed in the experiment, the subgroup that is observed is a sample.

Researchers use samples as a labor-saving device. In the best of all possible worlds, researchers would test every subject in the population. If Joe wants to measure college students' level of math anxiety, the most accurate way would be to test every math-anxious student in existence. This, of course, is impossible. Researchers usually do not have the time or resources to test every member of the population they are interested in studying, and so they test a subgroup or sample of the population.

In order to use a sample as an example of how the entire population would perform, if tested, it is important that the sample be representative of the population. We must have every reason to believe that the sample will perform essentially as the entire population would perform. One way to ensure that a sample is representative of the population is to select the sample randomly. A **random sample** is a group in which every member of the population in question has an equal chance of being selected. Pragmatically, this means that chance alone determines which members of the population are included in the sample. This ensures that there is no bias in the way that the sample is chosen and that the sample is representative of the population.

A **random sample** is a subgroup of a population in which each member of the population has an equal chance of being included.

When reading a research report, it is important to be able to determine whether the group of subjects described is a population or a sample. To do this, follow the steps listed in Step-by-Step Procedure 2-1.

Suppose that Joe believes that students who have trouble working math problems quickly will feel more anxious when time limits are placed on testing. He decides to test a group of 20 math-anxious students under two conditions, once with time limits and once without time limits, to see if removing the time limits reduces their anxiety. To decide whether the group of participants in Joe's experiment is a population or sample, we can use Procedure 2-1.

Answering the question in Step 1, Joe's hypothesis pertains to reducing math anxiety in college students. There are two characteristics defining the population. The characteristic, "college student," is stated explicitly in the hypothesis, so it is easy to identify. The characteristic, "math-anxious," is implicit in the hypothesis. Joe is attempting to reduce math anxiety in college students, and implicit in that attempt is that the students must initially have math anxiety in order for it to be reduced in the experiment. Thus, the characteristics defining the group that is the focus of the study are "math-anxious" and "college student." In Step 2, answer the question, "Is every single math-anxious college student tested in this study?" Since Joe tested only twenty math-anxious college students, which certainly is not the entire population of math-anxious college students, the group of students who were actually tested were a sample of the population.

Note that whether a group of subjects is a population or a sample depends entirely upon the experimenter's intent. In fact, a particular group might be a population in one experiment but a sample in another. When the instructor of your statistics class reports the average grade that students earned on the last test, the members of your class constitute a population.

STEP-BY-STEP PROCEDURE 2-1

How to Differentiate Populations and Samples

1. Identify the group of subjects that is the target of the researcher's hypothesis. What characteristics define that group of people or animals?

2. Is every person with those characteristics tested in the study? If yes, the group of subjects tested is the population. If no, the group of subjects tested is a sample.

Your instructor is not using your class as an example of some larger group but rather is concerned only with how the members of your class performed on the test. On the other hand, a researcher might ask your class to participate in an experiment on psychology majors' understanding of statistics. In this case, your class would be a sample, because the experimenter is interested in all psychology majors, not just the students in your class.

Parameters and Statistics

In Chapter 1, we looked at how a researcher will first use an experimental procedure in order to collect scores and then use a statistical procedure in order to generate a single number that summarizes those scores. When the entire population is tested in the experiment, so that there is a score from every member of the population, any numeric summaries of those scores are called **parameters.** Any numeric summaries of the scores collected from a sample of subjects are called **statistics.** Generally, parameters are represented by Greek letters, such as μ (pronounced "mew") and σ ("sigma"), while statistics are represented by roman letters (the letters in our alphabet, such as X and Y). Thus, if you see a Greek symbol, generally you can know that the number represents a population parameter, while if you see a roman letter, the number represents a sample statistic.

A **parameter** is a numeric summary calculated from the scores of a population. Parameters are represented by Greek letters.

A **statistic** is a numeric summary calculated from the scores of a sample. Statistics are represented by roman letters.

Researchers use samples as an example of how the entire population would have scored if tested. This means that statistics can be used as *estimates* of population parameters. Researchers use the numeric summaries calculated from samples (statistics) in order to estimate what the numeric summaries of a population (parameters) would be if the entire population were tested.

Researchers ultimately are interested in describing or estimating the parameters of populations. Joe is interested in showing that the math test scores of the entire population of math-anxious college students improve when the test time limits are removed. He is not interested solely in the twenty students tested. Rather, he is using the scores of his sample as an estimate of what the scores of the entire population would be if tested. Note that sample statistics are good estimates of population parameters *only if* the sample is representative of the population. If the sample differs in essential characteristics from the population, we cannot expect the sample statistics to be at all similar to parameters of that population.

Although sample statistics estimate population parameters, it is important to note that a statistic will not always have exactly the same value as the population parameter that it estimates. For example, we could find the highest score in a sample and use it as an estimate of the highest score in the population from which that sample comes. But we cannot expect the sample's highest score to be exactly equal to the population's highest score. The highest score in a sample is only an estimate of the population's highest score, not an exact duplicate. It is important to remember that sample statistics are *estimates* of population parameters.

Variables and Constants

In discussing the concept of populations, we have already looked at the characteristics that define a population. In Joe's experiment, the characteristics that defined his population were "math-anxious" and "college student." The population in Joe's study has many other characteristics in addition to the ones that define the group as a population. For some of those characteristics, the members of the population are all alike. For example, the population of math-anxious college students share the characteristic of disliking math classes and, to state the obvious, the characteristics of being human and being alive. If all of the members of a population are the same on a characteristic, that characteristic is a **constant.**

There are also numerous characteristics on which the population of math-anxious college students differ. For example, they probably differ in hair color, eye color, age, sex, state of residence, level of intelligence, place of birth, and a host of other characteristics. If the members of a population differ on a characteristic, then that characteristic is a **variable.**

To determine whether a characteristic is a variable or a constant in a particular study, we must determine whether or not there is only one value of that characteristic in the population under study. In Joe's study, the characteristic, species, has only one value, human. Therefore, the characteristic, species, is a constant. On the other hand, the characteristic, sex, can have two values in the population of Joe's study (male or female). Presumably, both male and female college students can be math anxious. Thus, the characteristic, sex, is a variable in Joe's study. Step-by-Step Procedure 2-2 describes one method for differentiating between variables and constants.

Note that it is whether one or more values of a characteristic occurs *in the population* that determines whether that characteristic is a constant or a variable. It does not matter how many values of the characteristic occur in the sample. For example, in the population of Brownie Girl Scouts in the United

A **constant** is a characteristic of a population for which only one value occurs in that population. Because only one value occurs, the value of the characteristic *remains constant* in the population.

A **variable** is a characteristic of a population for which more than one value occurs in that population. Because more than one value occurs, the value of the characteristic *varies* in the population.

STEP-BY-STEP PROCEDURE 2-2

How to Differentiate Variables and Constants

1. Identify the population being studied. (Note: Be careful to identify the population and not the sample.)

2. Identify the characteristic of interest. Note that when you are considering constants, it is easy to confuse the value and the characteristic. If everyone in a population is male, then the characteristic is sex and the value is male.

3. Consider the population to determine whether one value or more than one value of the characteristic occurs in that population. If only one value of the characteristic occurs, that characteristic is a constant. If more than one value occurs, that characteristic is a variable.

States, the characteristic, sex, is a constant, because all Brownies are girls. However, in the population of 4-H Club members in the United States, sex is a variable, because both boys and girls can be members of 4-H Clubs. It is possible that all of the members of a particular 4-H Club are girls, but that doesn't make sex a constant. Sex is a constant *only if* all of the members of the *population* are the same sex, not just because all of the members of a sample are.

Measurement

When conducting an experiment, researchers measure the subjects' performance on one or more variables. Those measurements constitute the subjects' scores in the experiment. For example, in Joe's study, he measured the students' level of math anxiety and their performance on a math test. Each measurement of one subject on one variable is a **datum.** More than one datum are **data.** Thus, the outcome of an experimental procedure is data, a set of scores.

A **datum** is a measurement of one subject on a given variable. The plural of *datum* is *data.*

Data are a set of measurements obtained from a group of subjects on a given variable.

In experiments, researchers establish procedures for measuring the desired characteristics. It is crucial that the same procedure be used when measuring all subjects in the experiment. If the researcher allows the procedure to vary, then we cannot validly compare the results. Suppose Joe uses a ten-question math test for half his participants, and a twenty-question math test for the rest. It would be nonsensical to compare these results. The procedure that the researcher uses is a rule for how to assign subjects values on the characteristic being observed. This then is the core of **measurement.**

Measurement is the process of using a rule to assign values to subjects on the characteristic being observed.

In an **operational definition,** a variable is defined by the procedures or operations used to measure the variable.

In an experiment, researchers define variables operationally. In an **operational definition**, a variable is defined by the procedures (or operations) that are used to measure the variable. An operational definition is not the same as a dictionary definition. For example, a dictionary definition of intelligence is "the capacity to acquire and apply knowledge,"[1] while an operational definition of intelligence might be "the person's score on the Stanford-Binet IQ test." In this experiment, administering the Stanford-Binet IQ test is the procedure used to measure intelligence, and thus the operational definition defines intelligence in terms of the procedure used to measure it. The advantage of operational definitions is that they enable other researchers to replicate the procedure used in an experiment.

Characteristics and Number Lines

A number line is a picture of the values of a characteristic. We will see in the next chapter that number lines are the basis of constructing graphs representing groups of scores. The points on the number line represent the values of scores that theoretically could occur when a researcher observes a characteristic. Note that the number line does not contain just the values that *do*

FIGURE 2-1 Number Line Representing Number of Children in a Family

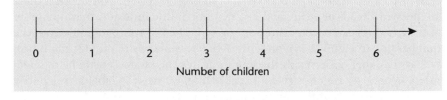

Number of children

FIGURE 2-2 Number Line Representing Scores on Twenty-Question Math Test

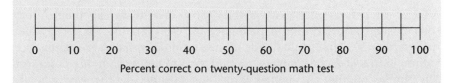

Percent correct on twenty-question math test

occur in a group, but all the values that *might occur.* Figure 2-1 shows the values that might occur when we measure the number of children in a family. It is possible for families to have zero children, one child, two children, or three children, so all of these values are shown on the number line in Figure 2-1. A sample of families studied in an experiment may contain no families that have three children, but it is still possible for a family to have three children, and so that value is included in the number line. However, it is impossible for a family to have −5 children, and so the number line in Figure 2-1 does not include the value, −5. The arrowhead on the right side of the number line indicates that higher values could occur when measuring the number of children in a family.

Because a number line represents all the values that could occur when measuring a characteristic, we can construct the number line before we actually observe and measure the subjects in a sample. For example, let's construct a number line for the math test scores in Joe's study of math anxiety. Suppose that Joe intends to give students a twenty-question math test, and score the percent of questions that each student answers correctly. When Joe gives the test, a student might get twenty questions correct, or nineteen correct, or eighteen, and so on, all the way down to the possibility that a student might get no questions correct. Converting these values to percents, we find that the values that could occur are 100 percent, 95 percent, 90 percent, and so on. We can represent these values on a number line as shown in Figure 2-2.

There are several things to note about the number line in Figure 2-2. First, although there is a tick mark for each of the values, not all of the tick marks are labeled. Even though the tick mark for 5 percent is not labeled, the value 5 percent is still represented on the number line by a tick mark. The number line begins at 0, the lowest percent that could possibly occur on Joe's test, and ends at 100, the highest percent that could possibly occur. The fact that there are no arrowheads at either end of the number line indicates that no higher or lower values can occur than those shown. The last thing to note about the number line in Figure 2-2, representing the possible scores on Joe's math test, is that the label underneath the line indicates the characteristic being measured. Whenever we construct a number line, we need to label it to identify the characteristic that the number line represents.

The Unit of Measurement

The **unit of measurement** is the quantity selected to serve as the unit with which to measure a variable. When constructing a number line, the unit of measurement forms the divisions of the line.

After researchers decide what variables to observe in an experiment, they then must decide what unit to use to measure each variable. For the variable, height, the researcher could decide to measure in feet, half feet, quarter feet, inches, tenths of inches, meters, centimeters, millimeters, or any of an infinite number of other possibilities. If the researcher decides to measure height in inches, then inches is the **unit of measurement.** For the variable, annual income, a researcher could measure each participant's income to the nearest cent, to the nearest dollar, to the nearest hundred dollars, or to the nearest thousand dollars. If the researcher decides to measure income to the nearest thousand dollars, then the unit of measurement is a thousand dollars.

Continuous and Discrete Variables

Some characteristics that we can measure occur in discrete units. Discrete characteristics are those composed of separate, distinct, unconnected, indivisible parts. The number of children in a family is a discrete characteristic because children are separate, distinct, unconnected beings. Generally, we measure discrete characteristics in whole numbers. There might be three children in a family, or four children, but it is impossible for a family to have 2.37 children. Children do not come in partial units. The number of trees is another example of a discrete variable. Perhaps we could divide a tree in half and still say that the thing being measured is a unit of a tree, but if we continue dividing the unit of measurement, at some point the thing is no longer a tree. We would have a pile of lumber, not a tree. A **discrete variable** is a discrete characteristic for which there is more than one value in a population.

A **discrete variable** cannot be infinitely divided into smaller units. For a discrete variable, the thing being measured occurs in discrete units, which, if they were divided, would no longer be the thing originally measured.

While some characteristics occur in discrete units, other characteristics are continuous in nature. Continuous characteristics do not have distinct units but occur in one continuous, uninterrupted quantity. Time is a continuous characteristic. We can divide time into units, such as years or days or minutes, but time itself occurs in one continuous, uninterrupted flow. Consider also all of the water in an ocean. The water is one continuous mass. We can separate the water, cup by cup, but water does not come in natural units, such as cups or gallons. Water itself is continuous, not discrete. A **continuous**

variable is a continuous characteristic of a population for which there is more than one value.

While discrete variables occur in whole units, there are no natural units for continuous variables. The units in which we measure continuous variables are constructs of the human mind. We humans came up with the idea of measuring time in days and minutes and the idea of measuring liquids in cups and gallons. When measuring continuous variables, we select the unit to use. In fact, for continuous variables, there are an infinite number of choices for the unit of measurement. We can measure height in inches, half inches, quarter inches, tenths of a inch, hundredths of an inch, and so on. For these variables, the unit of measurement can be subdivided into smaller and smaller units, infinitely. Theoretically, when we measure height, we could continue dividing the unit of measurement into smaller and smaller units forever. No matter how small the unit, we can still measure height with it. Thus, for continuous variables, the unit of measurement can be subdivided infinitely. Discrete variables, on the other hand, cannot be infinitely divided without changing the nature of the thing being measured.

Thus far, the examples given have not been psychological in nature. This is in part because researchers in psychology often disagree about the nature of psychological variables. Consider, for example, the question of whether IQ scores represent a continuous or discrete variable. IQ scores themselves only occur in whole numbers, and in that sense they are discrete. However, the underlying characteristic being measured is intelligence, and some psychologists argue that there is infinite variability in human intelligence, so that it is a continuous variable.

It is important to be able to distinguish between continuous and discrete variables because the type of statistical procedure we may use depends in part upon the type of variable being measured. Step-by-Step Procedure 2-3 gives one method for distinguishing between continuous and discrete variables.

> For a **continuous variable**, the unit of measurement can be infinitely divided into smaller and smaller units.

STEP-BY-STEP PROCEDURE 2-3

How to Differentiate Continuous Variables and Discrete Variables

1. Identify the characteristic being measured.

2. Identify the unit in which the characteristic is being measured.

3. Divide the unit of measurement in half. In the study under consideration, could the characteristic be measured in that half-unit? Divide the unit in half again and again. Is it possible to continue dividing the unit indefinitely and still use those units to measure the characteristic? If so, the variable is continuous. If not, the variable is discrete.

Degree of Precision

If we can measure the variable, height, with a unit as small as millimeters and with a unit as large as miles, there is obviously considerable variation in the size of the unit of measurement that a researcher might select. The smaller the unit of measurement, the more precise that measurement will be. In order to determine the **degree of precision** of a measurement, we need only know the unit of measurement. If we measure height to the nearest inch, we know the measurement is accurate to the nearest inch.

When the unit of measurement is an indivisible quantity, as is characteristic of discrete variables, the measurement will be absolutely precise. For example, if we are measuring the number of children in a family and select one child as the unit of measurement (a quantity which is indivisible), then all the measurements of that variable will be absolutely precise. There can never be a fraction over one child or a fraction under one child.

This is not the case, however, for continuous variables, when the unit of measurement is a quantity that is divisible. The measurement of continuous variables is never absolutely precise. Consider the example of measuring the length of a pencil, as shown in Figure 2-3. If we are measuring to the nearest inch, this pencil is 4 inches long. However, this measurement is not absolutely precise because in fact the pencil is a little over 4 inches long. If we measured the length of the pencil to the nearest quarter inch, we would say that the pencil is 4¼ inches, but this too would not be absolutely precise. Generally, when we measure continuous variables, the actual measurement is a little over or a little under what we say it is.

For continuous variables, the degree of precision is the unit of measurement. When we measure height in inches, then our measurements are precise to the nearest inch. Similarly, when we measure age in years, our measurements are precise to the nearest year.

If researchers have the choice of the unit of measurement, how do they decide which unit to use? How do they decide how precisely to measure a

> The **degree of precision** of a measurement is the degree of accuracy in measuring a variable. A measurement is accurate to the unit of measurement.

FIGURE 2-3   Measuring a Continuous Quantity

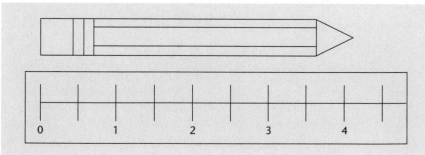

variable? Pragmatically, researchers are limited in how precisely they can measure by the equipment they use. If I am using a stopwatch that measures in seconds, I cannot measure any more precisely than in seconds. The measuring equipment a researcher uses will always put a limit on how precise the measurements can be.

As a general rule, a researcher needs to choose a unit of measurement that will result in scores that vary between the things being measured. We could select a unit of measurement that was so large that every subject received the same score. For example, we could measure adults' heights to the nearest yard. This would be rather meaningless, as virtually all the adults we measured would be 2 yards tall. There is little purpose in showing that nearly all adults are 2 yards tall. Generally, when we take measurements in psychological research, we are hoping to examine differences between subjects. To examine those differences, we have to use a unit of measurement precise enough so that there are differences in the scores. The more precise the unit of measurement, the more likely we are to find differences in scores among the subjects.

Identifying the Unit of Measurement

One of the things that you will need to be able to do is to identify in which unit a characteristic is measured. Sometimes this is a simple task. Frequently a researcher will state the unit in which characteristics are measured. However, there are times when the unit of measurement is not stated, and in those cases, you need to be able to identify the unit of measurement from a list of scores. Look at the list of salaries below:

$12,300
$11,000
$9,400
$7,900
$5,200

To identify the unit of measurement, look for the lowest place where the digits are not all zeros. In this list of salaries, the digits in the ones' place and in the tens' place are all zeros. However, the digits in the hundreds' place are not all zeros. Therefore, these scores were measured to the nearest hundred dollars. Step-by-Step Procedure 2-4 gives one method for determining the unit of measurement.

Intervals

As we examined previously, with continuous variables, measurements are not absolutely precise. When we say that a rat ran a maze in 12 seconds, that doesn't mean that the rat ran the maze in exactly 12 seconds. If we measured the time to the nearest second, in fact the time taken could have been

---

STEP-BY-STEP PROCEDURE 2-4

How to Identify the Unit of Measurement

1. Write the scores in a list, so that each place forms a vertical column. This makes it easier to identify which places contain all zeros.

2. Begin at the smallest place in the scores (i.e., the place the farthest to the right). Consider each place in turn, from right to left:

▶ If any of the scores in the list have a digit other than zero in that place, then that place is the unit of measurement.

▶ If all of the scores in the list have a zero in that place, it is not the unit of measurement.

Note: This procedure only works when the unit of measurement is a power of 10 (e.g., whole numbers, tens, hundreds, thousands, and so on, or tenths, hundredths, and so on).

---

anywhere from 11.5 seconds up to 12.5 seconds. Thus, the measurement of 12 seconds doesn't represent just the point 12 on the number line. In this case, the measurement, 12 seconds, actually represents the section of the number line from 11.5 seconds up to 12.5 seconds, a segment that is called an **interval**.

> An **interval** is the segment of a number line represented by a single value of a continuous variable.

All of us have been rounding measurements up and down since we first started measuring. To understand the concept of intervals, simply remember that on a continuous variable, a subject's score has probably been rounded up or down, that the score value represents not just a point on the number line but a segment of the number line. If a subject gets a score of 12 on a continuous variable, that score initially may have been anywhere in the interval between 11.5 and 12.5.

Real Limits

> The **real limits** of an interval are the upper and lower edges of the interval on the number line represented by a given value. The **lower real limit** of a score value is the lowest point on the number line that can be assigned that value. The **upper real limit** is equal to the lower real limit of the next higher score value. The real limits are always one-half unit of measurement from the point on the number line representing a score value.

The **real limits** are the edges of the segment on the number line that represents a given value. The lowest point on the number line that could be assigned to a score value is called the **lower real limit** of that value's interval. The lower limit of one interval is also the **upper real limit** of the interval immediately below it. As shown in Figure 2-4, when measuring in whole inches, the lowest point on the number line that could be given the value of 4 is 3.5, and thus 3.5 is the lower real limit of the score value, 4. The lower real limit of the next score value, 5, is 4.5, and therefore 4.5 is also the upper real limit of the value, 4.

> The **interval size** is the width of the segment on the number line represented by a score value. The interval size is always equal to the unit of measurement.

The **interval size** is the distance on the number line covered by an interval. It is the distance from the lower real limit of the interval to the upper real limit, and that distance is always equal to the unit of measurement. The lower real limit is always half the unit of measurement below the score value, and the upper real limit is always half the unit of measurement above. Thus,

FIGURE 2-4 Segment of Points Included in the Interval of 4 inches

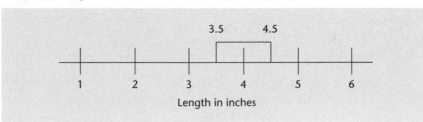

FIGURE 2-5 Comparison of the Interval Sizes of 2 and 2.0

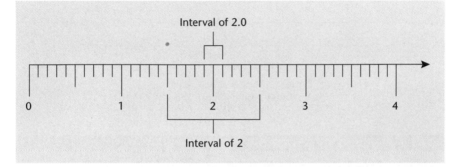

the distance between the lower and upper real limits equals the unit of measurement.

Thus far, all of our examples have used whole numbers. To understand the concept of intervals, we need to examine other unit sizes. For example, suppose we measured the length of objects to the nearest tenth of an inch. Figure 2-5 shows the interval of 2 (measured to the nearest inch) and the interval of 2.0 (measured to the nearest tenth inch) marked on a ruler. Looking at the ruler, it is evident that the interval of 2 and the interval of 2.0 are not the same thing. The interval of 2.0 represents all the points from 1.95 up to 2.05, while the interval of 2 represents all the points from 1.5 up to 2.5. The interval of 2 is a wider segment of the number line than the interval of 2.0.

We can also have intervals larger than the integer, 1. For example, we might measure income to the nearest thousand dollars. The value of $12,000 would represent everyone who had incomes between $11,500 and $12,500, as shown in Figure 2-6. In this case, the interval size is $1,000.

All of the examples we have seen thus far have been based on the decimal system, with intervals of multiples of ten. There can be good reasons why researchers select other interval sizes. For example, in the field of developmental psychology, researchers often measure the age of children to the nearest half year. Figure 2-7 shows a portion of the number line for this variable,

FIGURE 2-6   Example of Intervals Larger than 1

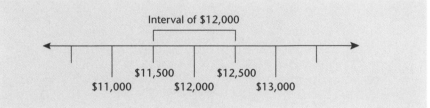

FIGURE 2-7   Example of Number Line Not Based on Decimal System

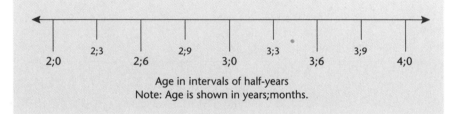

Age in intervals of half-years
Note: Age is shown in years;months.

STEP-BY-STEP PROCEDURE 2-5

How to Find the Real Limits of an Interval

1. Identify the unit of measurement. The size of the interval will be equal to the unit of measurement.

2. Divide the unit of measurement in half.

3. To find the lower real limit of an interval, subtract one-half the unit of measurement from the score value of that interval.

4. To find the upper real limit of an interval, add one-half the unit of measurement from the score value of that interval.

---

with the score values indicated in large digits and the real limits in small digits.

Step-by-Step Procedure 2-5 lists the steps for finding the real limits of an interval. We will use the concepts of intervals, interval size, and real limits to understand many of the statistical concepts we will examine in the following chapters of this book. Taking the time to understand the these concepts now will help you understand the statistical concepts to come.

Scales of Measurement

Measurements in science are concrete. The measurement is never simply "4." It is always "4 'something.'" When the variable is "number of children," the value for 4 is "4 children." When the variable is "length in inches," the value for 4 is "4 inches." The meaning of "4" depends on the variable being measured.

The meaning behind the numbers used to represent variables is not the same for all variables. For example, with the variable of the number of children in a family, we know that a family with six children has twice as many children as a family with three children does. Thus, we can make ratio comparisons with the variable, number of children. We cannot make ratio comparisons with other variables such as IQ scores. We cannot say that someone with an IQ of 100 is twice as smart as a person with an IQ of 50. The reason that we can make ratio comparisons with one variable and not the other is that the two variables represent different measurement systems. There are, in fact, four different types of measurement systems, called scales of measurement. These four are the nominal, ordinal, interval, and ratio measurement scales. We will look at each of these different types of measurement scales to see how they differ.

Nominal Scales of Measurement

In a **nominal scale of measurement**, numbers are used solely to label, classify, identify, or otherwise differentiate values of the characteristic being measured. Social Security numbers are one example of a nominal measurement scale. Another example is "type of religion." A researcher might assign different numbers to each of the religions, to code them, but the numbers serve only to categorize the religions. Each religion is given a unique number solely to differentiate it from the other religions. If one person has a score of "2" and another person a score of "4" on the variable, type of religion, the only information we can derive is that the two people have different religious affiliations.

The order in which numbers are assigned to nominal categories is completely arbitrary. For example, Figure 2-8 shows two ways that a researcher might assign numbers to values of different religions. We could just as easily represent the values in one order as the other. The numbers serve only to differentiate the values. A higher score on this variable does not mean that the person has more religion. Because the order of the numbers means nothing, nominal scales of measurement do not have magnitude.

Ordinal Scale of Measurement

In **ordinal measurement scales**, the order of the numbers is meaningful. A higher number means more of the thing being measured. An example of an ordinal scale is letter grades: A, B, C, D, and F. Letter grades are frequently converted to numeric grades, with 4 representing an A and 0 representing an F. The order of these numbers is meaningful, not arbitrary. It would certainly change the meaning of the grade of A if it were assigned a value of 2, rather than 4!

In a **nominal scale of measurement**, numbers are used solely to label, classify, identify, or otherwise differentiate values of the characteristic being measured. The order of numbers in the scale is not meaningful. A greater number indicates a different value of the characteristic but not a larger value.

In an **ordinal scale of measurement**, numbers are used to indicate the rank order of values of the characteristic being measured. In an ordinal scale, a greater number indicates more of the thing being measured but does not indicate how much more.

FIGURE 2-8   Assigning Numbers to Values on a Nominal Scale of Measurement

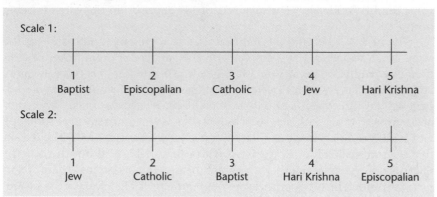

FIGURE 2-9   Five-Point Rating Scale

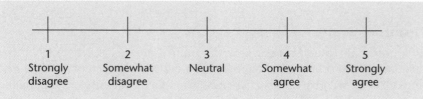

The order of the numbers is not arbitrary in an ordinal scale, as it is in a nominal scale. This, then, is the fundamental difference between nominal scales and ordinal scales. In a nominal scale, the order of the numbers assigned has no meaning. For the variable, sex, we could assign the number 1 to represent men and 2 to represent women, or we could represent men with 2 and women with 1. However, the order of the numbers assigned in an ordinal scale is meaningful. A larger number in an ordinal scale means more of the thing being measured, and thus ordinal scales have magnitude.

While for an ordinal scale, we know that a larger number represents more of the thing being measured, we can never know exactly how much more. For example, suppose we asked participants to respond to a series of questions with a rating scale such as that shown in Figure 2-9. If a participant responds with 5 to the first question and with 4 to the second question, we know that the participant agrees more strongly with the first question than with the second. However, we do not know how much stronger that agreement is. Exactly how much difference is there between "somewhat agree" and "strongly agree"? There is no way to know.

Similarly, if we know that one golfer is in first place and another is in second place, we know that the first golfer is ahead in the rankings, but we have no way of knowing how far ahead. The first golfer may lead by one stroke or by twenty. The rankings of first and second place simply do not tell us how far apart the two golfers are. The reason that we cannot tell is we do not know the size of the interval between first and second place. In ordinal scales, generally we do not know the interval size.

Variables that are ranked (i.e., designated as first, second, third, etc.) are always measured on an ordinal scale of measurement. Variables that are measured as ratings are also ordinal, as are developmental stages and levels. In fact, some researchers in psychology believe that nearly all measurements of psychological characteristics are ordinal.

Interval Scales of Measurement

In an **interval scale of measurement,** both the order of the numbers and the distance between numbers is meaningful. Thus, a larger number indicates more of the thing being measured and also how much more. An example of an interval scale is Fahrenheit temperature. When measuring temperature, the order of the numbers is meaningful. The larger the number representing temperature, the more heat there is.

Not only does a higher number mean more of the thing being measured, the higher number indicates exactly how much more. We not only know that there is more heat at 90° than at 70°, we know exactly how much more: 20° more. The reason that we know exactly how much more is because the intervals in the Fahrenheit scale are equal. One degree is the same amount of heat, whether it is the difference between 20° and 21° or between 100° and 101°.

While interval scales have meaningful order and equal intervals, they do not have an absolute zero. A scale has an absolute zero when the number, zero, represents the absence of the thing being measured. The Fahrenheit scale measures amount of heat, but 0°F does not mean the absence of all heat. Even though 0°F is cold, there still is some heat present. The same is true for the Celsius scale. There is a third temperature scale, the Kelvin scale, that does have an absolute zero. In the Kelvin scale, 0°K, which is the same as −273.16°C, is the temperature at which all molecular movement ceases and absolutely no heat is generated. Thus, at 0°K, there is absolutely no heat, so the zero in the Kelvin scale is an absolute zero.

Another example of an interval scale is calendar years, such as the years 1965 and 1990. The order of numbers for calendar years is meaningful, so that the fact that 1990 is a larger number than 1965 tells us that 1990 occurred later in time than 1965 did. The scale of measurement for calendar years also has equal intervals (ignoring the fact of the day added in leap years), so the length of time between 1960 and 1965 is the same as the length of time between 1980 and 1985. However, the scale of measurement for calendar years does not have an absolute zero. In fact, in our system, there was no year zero. The year before 1 A.D. was the year 1 B.C. Even if there had been a year 0 between 1 B.C. and 1 A.D., it would not represent the absence of the thing being

An **interval scale of measurement** has equal distances between adjacent numbers (equal intervals), as well as ordinality. Both the order of numbers and the distances between them are meaningful. The difference between numbers indicates how much larger one value is than another.

measured, because 0 in fact would represent a year. Therefore, calendar years are measured on an interval scale of measurement.

Ratio Scales of Measurement

A **ratio scale of measurement** has an absolute zero point, as well as equal distance between adjacent numbers and ordinality. The order of numbers, the distances between them, and the distance from the zero point are all meaningful. A number that is twice as far from the zero point than another number indicates a value that is twice as great.

Ratio measurement scales have all of the characteristics of interval scales. The order of the numbers in a ratio scale is meaningful, and the scale has equal intervals. In addition, ratio scales have an absolute zero, so that the number zero represents the absence of the thing being measured. An example of a ratio scale is the distance that a person can jump, measured in feet. If someone gets a score of 0, that means that person jumped 0 feet, or no feet at all. Note that the person might have actually jumped 2 inches, but when measuring in feet, a score of 2 inches would be recorded as 0 feet. Thus, to the nearest foot, that person jumped no distance at all.

One consequence of having an absolute zero is that ratios are meaningful. For example, if Joe jumps 6 feet and Ted jumps 3 feet, then we can form a ratio of their distances:

$$\frac{6 \text{ feet}}{3 \text{ feet}} = 2.$$

Joe jumped twice as far as Ted jumped. With a ratio scale, we can use ratios to compare scores meaningfully. This is not true for interval scales. We can divide 40° by 20°, with a result of 2, but that does not mean that 40° is twice as hot as 20°. Ratio scales of measurement are the only scales with an absolute zero and therefore are the only scales for which it is meaningful to make ratio comparisons.

Comparing the Measurement Scales

You may have noted that the names of the four scales of measurements give an indication of what types of information the numbers in each scale convey to us. In a **nominal** scale, numbers are used to *name* values, thus to differentiate them. In an **ordinal** scale, numbers are used to *order* values, and thus to indicate which values have more of the thing being measured. An **interval** scale has *equal intervals* that enable us to compare the distance between scores. And because a **ratio** scale has an absolute zero, it is possible to make *ratio* comparisons.

You may also have noticed that the four scales of measurement form a hierarchy, with each succeeding scale having all the characteristics of the scales below it, plus one additional characteristic. Table 2-1 shows this relationship. Step-by-Step Procedure 2-6 shows the steps in identifying scales of measurement.

TABLE 2-1 Characteristics of the Four Scales of Measurement

Characteristic	Nominal Scale	Ordinal Scale	Interval Scale	Ratio Scale
Names and differentiates values	Yes	Yes	Yes	Yes
Meaningful order	No	Yes	Yes	Yes
Equal intervals	No	No	Yes	Yes
Absolute zero	No	No	No	Yes

STEP-BY-STEP PROCEDURE 2-6

How to Identify the Scale of Measurement

1. Identify the variable; that is, identify the thing that is being measured. If you were to draw a number line of the variable, what would you label it?

2. Is the order of the numbers on the number line meaningful? Would it be nonsense to randomly reassign the numbers? Does a larger number mean more of the thing being measured?

▶ If the answer to these questions is no, then the order is not meaningful and the scale is nominal.

▶ If the answer to these questions is yes, then continue to Step 3.

3. Are there equal intervals? If you subtract one score from another, does the result tell exactly how much more one score has of the thing being measured? Is one unit of what is being measured the same amount everywhere on the scale?

▶ If the answer to these questions is no, then the intervals are not equal and the scale is ordinal.

▶ If the answer to these questions is yes, then continue to Step 4.

4. Is there an absolute zero? Does the number 0 represent the complete absence of the thing being measured? Can you make ratio comparisons between scores (that is, does it make sense to say that one score is twice as large)?

▶ If the answer to these questions is no, then there is not an absolute zero and the scale is interval.

▶ If the answer to these questions is yes, then there is an absolute zero and the scale is ratio.

After reading about the differences between the four measurement scales, you might say, "So what?" Why does it matter which scale a researcher is using? There are two reasons. The first is that by understanding the differences between these four scales, you will be aware of when those scales are misused. For example, if Bill has an IQ of 120 and Sue an IQ of 100, does that mean that Bill is 20 percent smarter than Sue? IQ scores represent an interval scale, and it is meaningless to make ratio comparisons with interval scores. It is important to be able to recognize when such statements are meaningless. The second reason that the scales are important is that there are different statistical procedures for each of the measurement scales. In order to know which statistical procedures are appropriate to use for a particular set of scores, we need first to identify the set's scale of measurement. Understanding the concept of measurement scales, as well as the other concepts of measurement discussed in this chapter, is fundamental to a further understanding of statistics.

CHECKING YOUR ANSWERS

1. A frequent mistake is to think that large groups must be populations and small groups must be samples. What makes a group a population or a sample is not the size of the group but the researcher's intentions.

2. One error that students make in deciding whether a characteristic is a variable or a constant is that they consider only the sample and not the population. All of the members of the entire population must have the same value for a characteristic to be a constant.

3. To check your answer in deciding whether a variable is continuous or discrete, select one of the values on the number line representing the variable. For example, 7 may be such a value. Add a decimal to the value, such as .43, to get 7.43. Ask yourself if this possibly could be a legitimate value of the thing being measured. If it could be a legitimate value, the variable is continuous; if not, the variable is discrete. For example, 7.43 could be a possible value of age (a person can be 7.43 years old), but 7.43 cannot be a possible value of number of children (no one can have 7.43 children). Thus, age is continuous, number of children is discrete.

4. When finding the unit of measurement, check your answer by picking two adjacent values on the number line representing the variable being measured. Subtract the smaller value from the larger value. The difference is the unit of measurement.

5. To check your answer when finding the real limits between two adjacent values, add the two values together and divide by two. The result will be the point exactly half-way between the two values, which is the real limit.

6. To check your answer when deciding whether a scale of measurement is nominal, select any two values from the number line representing the thing being measured. Ask yourself whether the larger number means the subject has more of the thing being measured. More of what? If the answers to these questions are nonsensical, then order is not meaningful and the scale of measurement is nominal.

7. To check your answer when deciding whether a scale of measurement is ordinal, select any two values from the number line and ask yourself how much more of the thing being measured is in the larger value than in the smaller value. If you cannot give a specific quantity as an answer, the scale is ordinal. If you can give a specific quantity, the scale is either interval or ratio.

8. To check your answer when deciding whether a scale of measurement is interval or ratio, first ask yourself whether it is even possible for a subject to receive a score of 0. If not, the scale is interval. If a score of 0 is possible, ask yourself if it means the subject has none of the thing being measured. If it does, the scale is ratio; if not, interval.

S U M M A R Y

▶ A population is a group of subjects or events in an experiment that have a common set of characteristics of interest. A sample is a subgroup selected from a population. A random sample is one in which every member of the population has an equal chance of being selected.

▶ A parameter is a numeric summary of a population characteristic, while a statistic is a numeric summary of a sample characteristic. Generally, parameters are represented by Greek letters and statistics are represented by roman letters. Sample statistics can be used to estimate the parameters of the population from which the sample was drawn.

▶ A variable is a characteristic on which the members of a population differ. Thus, for a variable, more than one value of the characteristic occurs in the population. A constant is a characteristic on which all of the members of a population are the same and thus for which only one value of the characteristic occurs.

▶ Measurement is the process of using a rule to assign values to subjects on the characteristic being observed.

▶ The unit of measurement is the quantity selected by the experimenter to serve as the unit with which to measure a variable.

▶ Discrete variables occur in separate, distinct, indivisible units, while continuous variables occur in an unbroken mass or quantity, which can be arbitrarily divided into infinitesimally small units.

▶ The degree of precision is the degree of accuracy with which a variable is measured and is determined by the unit of measurement.

▶ An interval is the segment of the number line represented by a single value of a continuous variable. The lower real limit and upper real limit of an interval are respectively one-half the unit of measurement below and above the stated value. The interval size is the distance between the lower and upper real limits and is equal to the unit of measurement.

▶ In a nominal scale of measurement, numbers are used solely to classify or differentiate values of the characteristic being measured. In an ordinal scale, numbers are used to rank the values of a characteristic. Interval scales are based on equal intervals, and so we can determine exactly how much larger one value is than another. Finally, ratio scales have an absolute zero, such that a value of zero represents the complete absence of the characteristic being measured. The absolute zero of ratio scales allows us to make ratio comparisons.

E X E R C I S E S

Conceptual Exercises

1. Define the following terms:

population	data	lower real limit
sample	measurement	upper real limit
random sample	operational definition	interval size

parameter	continuous variable	nominal scale
statistic	discrete variable	ordinal scale
variable	unit of measurement	interval scale
constant	degree of precision	ratio scale
datum	interval	

2. Differentiate between each of the following:
   A. population vs. sample
   B. parameter vs. statistic
   C. variable vs. constant
   D. continuous vs. discrete variable
   E. nominal scale vs. ordinal scale
   F. ordinal scale vs. interval scale
   G. interval scale vs. ratio scale

3. In each of the following, identify whether the italicized group of people is a population or a sample.
   A. A researcher observes a *group of 100 infants* individually to find the mean age at which infants in the United States begin to talk.
   B. The registrar of a college reported that the mean age of the *incoming freshman class* was 19.1 years old.
   C. The electric company reported that the average monthly electric bill for all of *its utility customers* was $40.17.
   D. Based on the responses of *252 readers* to a survey, the local newspaper reported that the horoscope column was its readers' favorite feature.
   E. The County Clerk reported that among all of the *county's registered voters,* the majority registered as independents.
   F. The local television station conducted a telephone poll of *1,000 state residents* to report that a majority of people in the state did not support an increase in the state's sales tax.

4. Explain why a random sample can be used to estimate the values of population parameters, but a nonrandom sample cannot.

5. Get a package of M&Ms. Count the total number of M&Ms in the package. Then count the number of yellow ones (or any color of your choice), and divide by the total number of candies to find the proportion of yellow M&Ms in the package. Next, draw a sample of ten M&Ms at random (i.e., draw the candies with your eyes closed), and calculate the proportion of yellow candies in the sample. Replace the M&Ms, and repeat the process of drawing a sample of ten candies four more times, each time calculating the proportion of yellow candies. How good are the samples at estimating the proportion of yellow M&Ms in the entire package?

6. Consider the group of people who comprise the congregation of a church. Identify whether each of the following would be a variable or a constant in that group of people:
   A. sex
   B. religious affiliation
   C. age in years
   D. socioeconomic level
   E. biological species
   F. political persuasion

7. Consider your statistics class as a population.
   A. Identify three dimensions that would be variables in that population. For each variable, list two values that actually occur in your statistics class.

B. Identify three dimensions that would be constants in the population of your statistics class. For each constant, list the one value that actually occurs in your statistics class.

8. Consider all of the six-year-old children in the United States as a population. Suppose a researcher draws a sample of twenty six-year-old children, and in that sample, all of the children happen to be boys. In this example, is sex a variable or a constant? Why?

9. Identify whether each of the following is a variable or a value:

   A. sex   E. ten years old
   B. ID number 12-345-6789   F. 75 percent correct
   C. sophomore   G. temperature in degrees Fahrenheit
   D. grade point average   H. IQ

10. Following is a list of measurable dimensions: *(a)* sex; *(b)* running speed; *(c)* religion; *(d)* years of schooling; *(e)* grade point average; *(f)* letter grades; *(g)* IQ scores; *(h)* whether a person has a college degree; and *(i)* whether a person voted in the last election.

    A. For each dimension, identify at least two different values that could occur when measuring that dimension.
    B. Construct a number line to represent each of the dimensions. Note that you will need to assign number values to the dimensions. Be sure to label the dimension being measured.
    C. For each of the dimensions, identify the scale of measurement and explain the criteria on which you based your decision for each dimension.

11. Identify the scale of measurement for each of the variables described below:

    A. A university administrator surveys students' assessment of the quality of several educational programs, asking students to rate each program on a seven-point scale, from "very poor" to "excellent."
    B. An instructor randomly assigned numbers to students to be used as secret codes in posting grades.
    C. A school administrator records the year of birth for each child in the school.
    D. An instructor gave students a ten-question true-false quiz and assigned grades as the percent of questions answered correctly.
    E. As a measure of vocabulary size, a researcher had preschool children wear tape recorders for one day in order to count the number of different words each child used.
    F. A school administrator asked elementary school teachers to indicate whether each child in their classes were either hyperactive or not hyperactive.
    G. To compare the effect of the season of birth, a hospital administrator recorded the birth weight of infants born in the summer and winter.

12. Explain the relationship of the lower real limit and upper real limit to the unit of measurement and the interval size.

13. Construct an operational definition for each of the following concepts:

    A. intelligence of rats   C. infants' love for their caretakers
    B. morality level of preschool children   D. final grade earned in general psychology

Computational Exercises

14. Listed below are three sets of scores:

Set I	Set II	Set III
250	4,000	3.45
248	3,800	3.40
245	3,500	3.37
242	3,400	3.33
241	3,100	3.30
238	3,000	3.27
237	2,800	3.23
235	2,700	3.21

    A. Identify the unit of measurement for each of these sets of scores.

    B. Identify the lower real limit and upper real limit for each of the following scores selected from Set I: 241, 250.

    C. Identify the lower real limit and upper real limit for each of the following scores selected from Set II: 3,400; 4,000.

    D. Identify the lower real limit and upper real limit for each of the following scores selected from Set III: 3.30, 3.37.

15. Each of the scores below are listed with the interval size with which the score was measured. Identify the lower real limit and upper real limit for each score.

    A. interval size = 1, score = 47   E. interval size = .1, score = 3.6

    B. interval size = 10, score = 590   F. interval size = .1, score = 15.0

    C. interval size = 100, score = 6,500   G. interval size = .01, score = 0.19

    D. interval size = 100, score = 10,000   H. interval size = .01, score = 1.00

E N D N O T E

1. Excerpted from *The American Heritage Dictionary of the English Language.* 3d ed. (Boston: Houghton Mifflin Company, 1996).

Frequency Tables and Graphs

3

Distributions

Constructing Frequency Tables

Frequency Tables

Relative Frequency Tables

STEP-BY-STEP PROCEDURE 3-1: Converting the Frequency of Scores to a Proportion

Cumulative Frequency Tables

Relative Cumulative Frequency Tables

STEP-BY-STEP PROCEDURE 3-2: Constructing a Frequency Table

Constructing Graphs of Frequency Distributions

Basic Structure of Graphs

Bar Graphs

Frequency Histograms

Frequency Polygons

STEP-BY-STEP PROCEDURE 3-3: Constructing a Graph

An Exploratory Technique: Stem-and-Leaf Displays

STEP-BY-STEP PROCEDURE 3-4: Constructing a Stem-and-Leaf Display

Constructing Grouped Frequency Tables

Why Use Grouped Frequency Tables?

Number of Groups

STEP-BY-STEP PROCEDURE 3-5: Determining the Number of Score Values in a Distribution

STEP-BY-STEP PROCEDURE 3-6: Determining the Number of Group Intervals

Group Interval Size

STEP-BY-STEP PROCEDURE 3-7: Calculating the Size of a Group Interval

Lowest Group Interval

STEP-BY-STEP PROCEDURE 3-8: Identifying the Lowest Score Value of First Group Interval

Constructing the Grouped Frequency Distribution

STEP-BY-STEP PROCEDURE 3-9: Constructing a Grouped Frequency Distribution

Stated Limits, Real Limits, and Midpoints

STEP-BY-STEP PROCEDURE 3-10: Calculating the Lower Real Limit, Upper Real Limit, and Midpoint of a Group Interval

Characteristics of Distributions

CHECKING YOUR ANSWERS

SUMMARY

EXERCISES

Conceptual Exercises

Computational Exercises

ENDNOTE

▶ In Chapter 2, we examined how researchers collect scores and
determine what characteristics those scores have. The next
step is to compile the scores in a meaningful way. Remember
that researchers collect the scores in an experimental
procedure in order to support an argument. However, listing
page after page of scores collected from subjects won't
convince anyone that the researcher's argument is valid.
Researchers need to summarize the scores in some fashion
that can then be used to support their hypotheses.

This and the next several chapters focus on the branch of statistics called descriptive statistics. Recall from Chapter 1 that descriptive statistics are used to
describe a group of scores or the relationship between groups of scores. One
simple way to describe a group of scores is to construct a summary table; another way is to construct a graph pictorially representing the group of scores.
That is the focus of this chapter. In addition, in this chapter we examine the
concept of distributions and the way in which tables and graphs can be used
to examine differences between distributions. These concepts will build a
foundation for the other descriptive statistics we will examine in the following chapters.

Distributions

As we saw in Chapter 2, a scale of measurement consists of all the values that
possibly *could* occur when measuring a variable. For example, the scale shown
in Figure 3-1 represents the variable math test scores in the math anxiety research of our hypothetical student, Joe Johnson. This scale shows the possible
scores that students could receive; it does not show us how many students received each score value.

> A **distribution** is a set of
> score values and the fre-
> quency with which those
> values occur.

A **distribution** is the set of scores that either actually did occur or that
theoretically would occur when a set of observations are made. A distribution
has two components: the score values and the frequency that those values
occurred. Suppose that Joe tested twenty students, who received the scores
shown in the graph in Figure 3-2. Note that each box represents one student's

FIGURE 3-1   Scale of Measurement for Twenty-Question Math Test

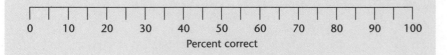

| 0 | 10 | 20 | 30 | 40 | 50 | 60 | 70 | 80 | 90 | 100 |

Percent correct

FIGURE 3-2 Distribution of Scores on Twenty-Question Math Test

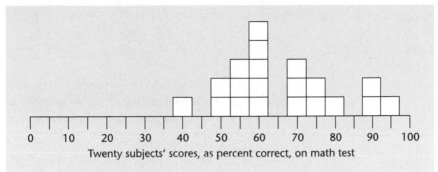

Twenty subjects' scores, as percent correct, on math test

score. The scale at the base of the graph is the same scale of measurement in Figure 3-1. Thus, both the measurement scale in Figure 3-1 and the base of the graph in Figure 3-2 show the score values that possibly could occur in Joe's study. However, Figure 3-2 also shows the number of students who actually did receive each of the score values. For instance, the distribution shows that five students got scores of 60 percent correct. This additional information, the frequency that each score value occurs, is what differentiates a distribution from a scale of measurement.

There are two types of distributions. A **theoretical distribution** is the set of scores that *would* occur if a set of observations were made, as predicted by a theory. In theoretical distributions, rather than collect scores from actual subjects, researchers make a prediction based on some theory about how subjects would perform if they were tested. A **frequency distribution** is the set of scores that result from researchers actually observing and measuring the performance of real subjects.

For example, students in a class often have ideas about what the final grade distribution should be (i.e., how many A's, B's, C's, D's, and F's there should be). This is a theoretical distribution in which the frequencies of grades are predicted by the students' idea or "theory" of the ideal grade distribution. On the other hand, the frequencies of grades actually given out by the instructor is a frequency distribution, the set of grades that actually occurred. We will examine theoretical distributions more thoroughly in Chapter 7. In this chapter, we will concentrate on frequency distributions, sets of scores that have actually been collected.

A **theoretical distribution** is the set of scores that would occur if a set of observations were made, based on theoretical predictions.

A **frequency distribution** is a set of scores that actually did occur when a set of observations was made.

Constructing Frequency Tables

Frequency Tables

A **frequency table** is a tabular presentation of a frequency distribution. The simplest frequency tables have two columns. The first column shows the

A **frequency table** is a tabular presentation of a frequency distribution. A frequency table shows the number of subjects who receive each score value.

TABLE 3-1 Students' Scores on Twenty-Question Math Test (Percent)

60	75	90	80	60	40	70	55	70	60
50	95	55	70	55	60	90	50	60	75

TABLE 3-2 Frequency Distribution for Math Test Scores in Table 3-1

Percent Correct	Frequency
95	1
90	2
85	0
80	1
75	2
70	3
65	0
60	5
55	3
50	2
45	0
40	1
	$n = 20$

score values that occur in the set of scores; the second column shows the frequency or number of times each score value occurred in the set of scores. In Joe's experiment, there were the twenty scores, which are listed in Table 3-1.

We can compile these scores in a frequency table, as shown in Table 3-2. The first column lists the score values that the twenty students in Joe's study received, from a high of 95 percent to a low of 40 percent. Note that the convention in constructing frequency tables is to list score values from highest to lowest. Also note that the score values, 85, 65, and 45 percent, are listed, although none of Joe's students actually received scores with those values. They are included so that the values listed in the table will be consecutive, which makes reading the table easier. The column of score values is labeled with the name of the variable being measured, "percent correct."

The second column in Table 3-2 shows the number of times that each score value occurred. For example, it shows that one student received a score of 95 percent and that five students received scores of 60 percent. If you add up the frequencies, the sum will equal the total number of scores in the set. In this example, the sum of the frequencies adds up to twenty, indicating that there were twenty scores in the set. It is important to remember that the numbers in the first column are *score values* and not scores. In Joe's study, five students received scores of 60 percent, but 60 percent is listed only once in the first column.

Using frequency tables has several advantages over just listing the scores. Frequency tables organize the scores and present them in a concise format, so they are easier to understand. We can see at a glance in Table 3-2 that scores ranged from 95 percent to 40 percent. In addition, the information in a frequency table allows us to see the shape of the distribution. In Table 3-2 we can see that more students received a score of 60 percent than any other value, that most students received scores in the middle of the distribution, and that very few students received the highest or lowest score values. Thus, just by compiling the scores into a frequency table, we have made the scores more understandable and have begun to analyze them.

Relative Frequency Tables

Another way to tabulate a frequency distribution is to show the **relative frequency** instead of the frequency. Frequency is the *number* of times that a score value occurs in a set; relative frequency is the *proportion* of times that value occurs. We find proportions by dividing the number of times a score value occurred by the total number of scores in the set, as shown in Step-by-Step Procedure 3-1.

Figure 3-3 shows how to construct a relative frequency table for the scores from Joe's study. Since there are a total of twenty scores, to convert each frequency to its relative frequency, we simply divide the frequency by 20, the number of scores, which is symbolized by n.

A **relative frequency table** shows the proportion of subjects who receive each score value.

STEP-BY-STEP PROCEDURE 3-1

Converting the Frequency of Scores to a Proportion

$$\text{proportion of scores} = \frac{\text{frequency of scores}}{n}$$

where n is the total number of scores.

FIGURE 3-3 Calculating Relative Frequencies for the Math Scores Shown in Table 3-1

Percent Correct	Frequency	Computations	Relative Frequency
95	1	1/20 =	.05
90	2	2/20 =	.10
85	0	0/20 =	.00
80	1	1/20 =	.05
75	2	2/20 =	.10
70	3	3/20 =	.15
65	0	0/20 =	.00
60	5	5/20 =	.25
55	3	3/20 =	.15
50	2	2/20 =	.10
45	0	0/20 =	.00
40	1	1/20 =	.05
	$n = 20$		1.00

Note that final table would not show these two columns. They are shown here to demonstrate how to construct the table.

The only difference between a frequency table and a relative frequency table is the way in which the frequencies are shown. The first column remains unchanged. The second column in a relative frequency table shows the proportion of times a score value occurs rather than the number of times. Note that the proportions should add up to 1.00. It is sometimes easier to see the shape of a distribution when relative frequencies are given instead of simple frequencies. For example, in Figure 3-3, it is easy to see that the highest proportion occurred at the score value, 60 percent.

Cumulative Frequency Tables

A **cumulative frequency table** shows the number of subjects who score at or below each score value.

A third way to tabulate a frequency distribution is to show the **cumulative frequency**, which is the total number of subjects who had scores equal to or less than a given score value. We can find the cumulative frequency for each score value by adding the number of subjects receiving that score value to the number of subjects who received all values lower than that value. Because it is conventional to list the score values from highest to lowest, we need to begin counting cumulative frequencies with the lowest score value, at the bottom of the table. Figure 3-4 shows this process. Note that the cumulative frequency for the highest score value, 95 percent, equals the total number of

FIGURE 3-4   Calculating Cumulative Frequencies for Math Scores Shown in Table 3-1

Percent Correct	Frequency	Computations	Cumulative Frequency
95	1	1 + 19 = 20	20
90	2	2 + 17 = 19	19
85	0	0 + 17 = 17	17
80	1	1 + 16 = 17	17
75	2	2 + 14 = 16	16
70	3	3 + 11 = 14	14
65	0	0 + 11 = 11	11
60	5	5 + 6 = 11	11
55	3	3 + 3 = 6	6
50	2	2 + 1 = 3	3
45	0	0 + 1 = 1	1
40	1	1 = 1	1
	$n = 20$		

Note that final table would not show these two columns. They are shown here to demonstrate how to construct the table.

students, twenty. That is because all twenty students received scores of 95 percent or below.

Cumulative frequency tables are very useful for showing the rate of learning. For example, suppose you are studying a foreign language and record the number of new words that you learn each week. The scores are listed in Table 3-3, showing both frequency and cumulative frequency. We can tell from the frequency column that you learned from seven to twenty new words a week. But the frequency column gives no indication of the total number of words you had learned by any given week, which is what the cumulative frequency column shows. For example, it shows that by week 7, you had learned a total of eighty-four words. The cumulative frequency column also shows it took you five weeks to learn the first fifty words, but that it only took you three weeks to learn the second fifty words, so that your rate of learning increased.

TABLE 3-3 Frequency Distribution of Words Learned per Week

Week	Frequency	Cumulative Frequency
8	16	100
7	20	84
6	14	64
5	13	50
4	10	37
3	12	27
2	8	15
1	7	7

Frequency tables and cumulative frequency tables each give the reader slightly different information. Which type of table researchers use depends on the type of information that the researchers want to convey to their readers.

Relative Cumulative Frequency Tables

The last type of frequency table is a **relative cumulative frequency table**, which shows the proportion of subjects who received scores at or below a given score value. This is similar to a cumulative frequency table, which shows the *number* of subjects who receive scores at or below a given score value, except that the relative cumulative frequency table shows the proportion, rather than the number, of subjects.

A **relative cumulative frequency table** shows the proportion of subjects who score at or below each score value.

To construct a relative cumulative frequency table, first construct a cumulative frequency table, and then convert each cumulative frequency into a proportion by dividing the cumulative frequency by the total number of subjects. For the scores collected in Joe's study on math anxiety, a relative cumulative frequency table would be constructed as shown in Figure 3-5.

In a relative cumulative frequency table, the highest relative cumulative frequency will always be 1.00, which represents 100 percent of the students' scores. In Figure 3-5, the relative cumulative frequency of the score value, 95 percent, is 1.00, indicating that 100 percent of the students had scores of 95 percent or lower. Like a cumulative frequency table, the relative cumulative frequency table is useful for showing changes in the rate of learning. In our hypothetical math anxiety experiment, the relative cumulative frequency

FIGURE 3-5 Calculating Relative Cumulative Frequencies

Percent Correct	Cumulative Frequency	Computations	Relative Cumulative Frequency
95	20	20/20 = 1.00	1.00
90	19	19/20 = .95	.95
85	17	17/20 = .85	.85
80	17	17/20 = .85	.85
75	16	16/20 = .80	.80
70	14	14/20 = .70	.70
65	11	11/20 = .55	.55
60	11	11/20 = .55	.55
55	6	6/20 = .30	.30
50	3	3/20 = .15	.15
45	1	1/20 = .05	.05
40	1	1/20 = .05	.05

Note that final table would not show these two columns. They are shown here to demonstrate how to construct the table.

table shows that over half of the students scored 60 percent correct or lower on the math test.

The examples of the frequency tables shown thus far have included the computations, so that you can see how the frequencies or relative frequencies were compiled. Of course, these computations are not included in the final version. In finished form, each table consists of two columns, one listing the score values and the second listing the rate at which each score value occurred. We have examined four different ways to show those rates: frequencies, relative frequencies, cumulative frequencies, and relative cumulative frequencies. There is nothing to prevent us from listing more than one of these in a single table, or even all four of them, if doing so provides meaningful information to the reader. Step-by-Step Procedure 3-2 describes the general steps involved in constructing a frequency table.

Constructing Graphs of Frequency Distributions

Researchers use frequency tables in order to present sets of scores in an understandable and concise fashion. Another way that researchers can present scores is in graphs. Graphs and frequency tables present the exact same information, just using different formats. Frequency tables present the information

---

STEP-BY-STEP PROCEDURE 3-2

Constructing a Frequency Table

1. Arrange the scores in a list, from highest value to lowest value.

2. For each score value, tally the number of subjects who received that score value.

3. List the score values in order, from highest value to lowest value. If the variable is nominal, list the score values alphabetically. Label the column at the top with the name of the variable.

4. For a frequency table, in a second column list the number of times that each score value occurred. Label the column, "frequency."

5. For a relative frequency table, calculate the proportion of times that each score value occurred by dividing the frequency for each score value by n, the total number of scores. List the proportions in a column and label the column, "relative frequency."

6. For a cumulative frequency table, beginning with the lowest score value, calculate the cumulative frequency for each score value by adding the frequency for that value to the frequencies for all lower score values. List the cumulative frequencies in a column and label the column, "cumulative frequency."

7. For a relative frequency table, first calculate the cumulative frequency for each score value, as described in Step 6. Then divide each cumulative frequency by n, the total number of scores. List the relative cumulative frequencies in a column and label the column, "relative cumulative frequency."

---

in lists, while graphs present information in a picture. Tables and graphs both have their unique advantages. In a table, we can clearly see exactly how frequently each score value occurred. However, in a graph, it is sometimes difficult to read the exact frequency of each score value, although we can usually read a close approximation to the frequency. On the other hand, it is often easier to see the overall shape of a distribution and any peculiarities from a graph of the distribution than from a frequency table.

Basic Structure of Graphs

A graph is a picture of a distribution of scores. As shown in Figure 3-6, the structure of the graphs described in this section consists of two number lines, the X-axis and Y-axis. Both the X- and Y-axes are number lines. The X-axis, located horizontally at the base of the graph, is a number line representing the scale of measurement of the variable being measured. If we were to construct a graph of the scores from Joe's study, the X-axis would represent the measurement scale for the students' math test scores, the same scale shown in Figure 3-1. The Y-axis, located vertically on the left side of the graph, is a number line representing frequencies or relative frequencies. Thus, the X-axis

FIGURE 3-6 Constructing the *X*- and *Y*-Axes
for Graph to Represent Scores in Math-Anxiety Study

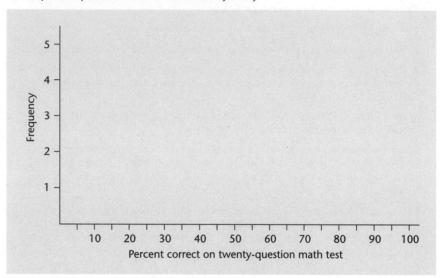

represents the information contained in the first column of a frequency table, and the *Y*-axis represents the information contained in the second column.

By convention, the intersection of the *X*-axis and *Y*-axis (where the two lines meet in the lower left corner) represents the value of zero on both number lines. Having both lines begin at 0 allows us to make fair comparisons. For example, Figure 3-7 shows two graphs, representing the number of men and women in two classes. In both graphs, the bar representing women is twice as high as the bar representing men, making it appear that there are twice as many women as men. This, in fact, is true for class A, as there are four women and two men. However, it is not true for class B. Even though the bar representing women is twice as high as the bar representing men, there are not twice as many women as men in class B. In the graph for class B, the heights of the bars is misleading because the *Y*-axis does not begin at zero. To keep from misleading readers, whenever either the *X*-axis or *Y*-axis does not begin at 0, it is conventional to indicate that a segment of the number line has been removed by making two diagonal marks, such as those shown on the graph for class B.

We can change the graph of a frequency distribution graph to show relative frequency simply by changing the values on the *Y*-axis. Figure 3-8 shows two segments of graphs of the same scores. The segment of the graph on the left shows the frequencies of scores, while the segment of the graph on the right shows the relative frequencies for the same scores. Both graphs represent twenty students' scores. Four students had a score of 30, which is 20 percent of the students, as shown in the graph on the right. Notice that the two graphs are identical, except for the labels on the *Y*-axis.

FIGURE 3-7 Comparison of *Y*-Axes that Do and Do Not Originate at Zero

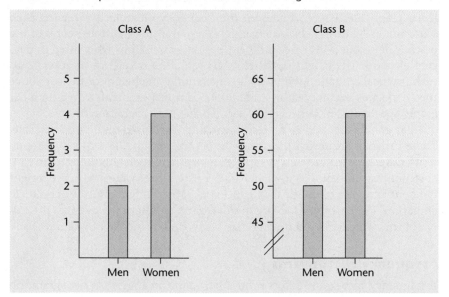

FIGURE 3-8 Comparison of *Y*-Axes
Representing Frequencies and Relative Frequencies

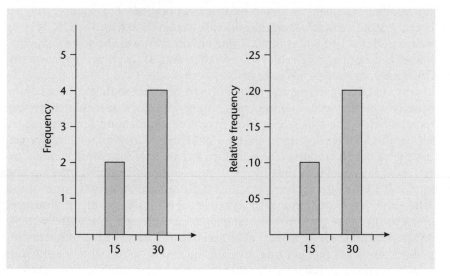

The concepts described thus far are the basic structures of a graph, the *X*-axis and *Y*-axis. All graphs of frequency distributions contain an *X*-axis and a *Y*-axis. What remains is to represent the actual scores on the graph. There are three ways to do this: the bar graph, the frequency histogram, and the frequency polygon.

Bar Graphs

A bar graph uses bars to represent the frequency of subjects receiving each score value. Figure 3-9 shows a bar graph representing fictitious scores of the percent of people with three different political affiliations who voted in a recent election. The height of the bar represents the frequency of voters with each political affiliation who voted. For example, the height of the bar above the Democrats category shows that 80 percent of Democrats voted. In a bar graph, spaces are left between the bars representing each category.

Bar graphs are used to represent variables measured on a nominal scale. These variables are always qualitative in nature, in that different values represent a difference in kind or type rather than a difference in amount. In the variable, political affiliation, shown in Figure 3-9, the three values do not represent different amounts of political affiliation but rather different kinds of political affiliation. The bars not touching in a bar graph represent the fact that the values of the variable represented on the X-axis do not increase in amount.

Frequency Histograms

A frequency histogram differs from a bar graph in that, in a histogram, no spaces are left between the bars representing the frequencies of scores. Figure 3-10 shows a completed frequency histogram for the math test scores from our hypothetical math anxiety study. The height of the bars indicates the number of students who received each score value. For example, the bar over the score value of 60 reaches the height of "5" on the Y-axis, indicating that 5 students had scores of 60. There are no bars over the score values below 40 or over the score values of 45, 65, 85, and 100, indicating that no students received those score values.

In a frequency histogram, the bars are constructed so that the sides of the bars for adjacent values are touching, representing the fact that the values represented on the X-axis increase in magnitude or amount. Thus, frequency histograms are appropriate to use for quantitative variables, which have values that differ in amount. These include variables measured on ordinal, interval, or ratio scales of measurement. Recall that for ordinal, interval, and ratio scales, the order of the score values is meaningful, that both interval and ratio scales have equal intervals, and that a ratio scale has an absolute zero.

A further qualification for using frequency histograms is that the variable represented on the X-axis be discrete. Recall from Chapter 2 that discrete variables have values representing distinct, indivisible parts, while continuous variables represent characteristics that do not occur naturally in distinct parts. A frequency histogram is used to represent the results of Joe's math test in Figure 3-10, because on that test, the students' scores of percent correct is a discrete variable. Frequency histograms are used for discrete quantitative variables, while frequency polygons, which we will examine next, are used for continuous quantitative variables.

FIGURE 3-9 Bar Graph of Percent of Democrats, Republicans, and Independents Voting in Recent Election

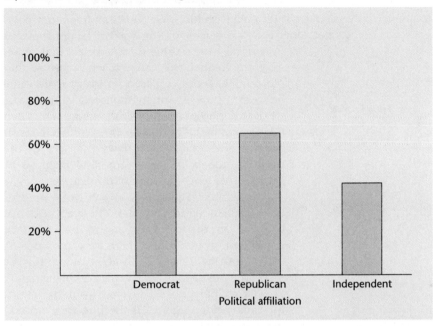

FIGURE 3-10 Frequency Histogram of Distribution of Math Test Scores Shown in Table 3-2

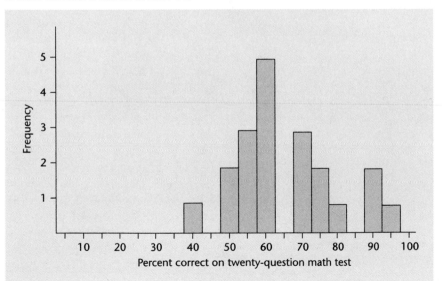

Frequency Polygons

While frequency histograms and bar graphs use bars to represent the scores, frequency polygons are constructed with lines. We construct frequency polygons by placing a dot above each score value on the X-axis. The dot is placed horizontal to the value on the Y-axis that represents the frequency of subjects who received that score value. A dot is placed for every score value between the lowest and highest score values in the set of scores, even if some of those score values had frequencies of 0. The dots are then connected with straight lines. Table 3-4 shows the ages of the twenty students in Joe's study, and Figure 3-11 shows a frequency polygon of those ages.

Notice that Figure 3-11 shows two score values not included in Table 3-4. The graph extends to age 17 on the lower end and to age 26 on the upper end, even though there were no students with those ages in Joe's study. We do this to make the frequency polygon a complete figure. The term "polygon" is derived from the Greek for "many-sided figure." If the line were not extended down to the X-axis, we would have a floating line rather than a many-sided figure.

TABLE 3-4   Frequency Distribution for Ages of Students in Joe's Study

Age	Frequency
25	1
24	0
23	1
22	2
21	3
20	7
19	4
18	2
	$n = 20$

FIGURE 3-11   Frequency Polygon of Students' Ages in Joe's Study

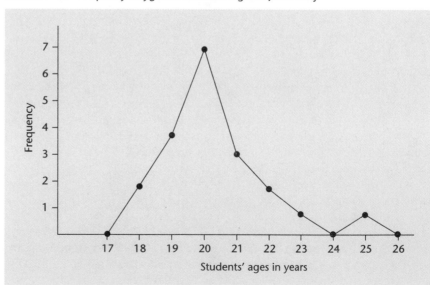

FIGURE 3-12 Cumulative Frequency Polygon of Students' Ages in Joe's Study

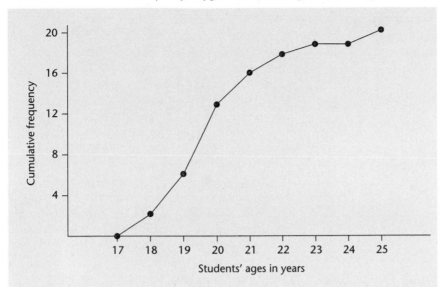

We can also construct graphs representing cumulative frequency distributions. Figure 3-12 is such a graph, representing the relative cumulative frequency distribution of the ages of students in Joe's study. Note that this graph is brought down to the *X*-axis on the left side but not on the right side. This particular graph is called a *frequency ogive* rather than a frequency polygon because the graph does not depict a complete polygonal figure.

Figure 3-13 shows two graphs, a frequency polygon and a frequency histogram. Suppose that the frequency polygon represents the number of minutes that it took a group of participants to solve a puzzle. The graph shows us the proportion of participants who solved the puzzle in 1, 2, 3, and 4 minutes. Because number of minutes is a continuous variable, we could ask what percentage of participants we might expect to solve the puzzle in 3½ minutes, even though the time was not measured to the half second. The frequency polygon in Figure 3-13 shows that we can estimate that 20 percent of the participants could have solved the puzzle in 3½ minutes.

Now suppose that the frequency histogram, on the right side of Figure 3-13, represents the number of children per family. This graph shows us the proportion of families with one, two, three, and four children. Because number of children is a discrete variable, it is impossible for any family to have 3½ children. Obviously, it would be nonsensical to try to estimate the proportion of families with 3½ children. The bars of the frequency histogram prevent us from making these kinds of estimates for discrete variables. This is the reason that histograms are used to represent discrete variables, while

FIGURE 3-13   Comparison of Frequency Polygons and Frequency Histograms

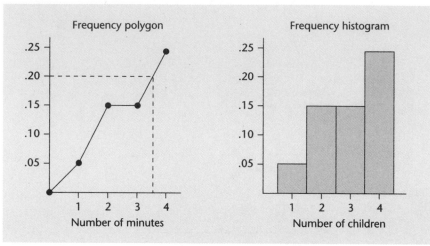

continuous variables can be represented by a line graph, such as a frequency polygon.

In summary, bar graphs are used to represent nominal variables. Ordinal, interval, and ratio variables are represented by frequency histograms for discrete variables or by frequency polygons for continuous variables. Step-by-Step Procedure 3-3 summarizes the steps used to construct a graph.

An Exploratory Technique: Stem-and-Leaf Displays

The graphs we have examined thus far are designed to present information about a distribution in finished form, to help readers understand the nature of the distribution. Generally, by the time these graphs are constructed, all of the data analysis has been completed. When beginning to analyze a set of data, researchers often like to make a quick sketch of the distribution for their own understanding. One technique that quickly and effectively shows the shape of a distribution, for preliminary data analysis, is the **stem-and-leaf display**.[1]

Figure 3-14 shows a group of twenty scores and a stem-and-leaf display of those scores. In a stem-and-leaf display, each score is divided into two parts: the stem and the leaf. In Figure 3-14, each score contains two digits, and so the tens' digit is the stem and the ones' digit is the leaf. Note that in Figure 3-14, the scores range from 25 to 63 and so the stems range from 2 to 6. These stems are listed on the left side of the stem-and-leaf display. To the right of each stem is listed the ones' digit for all of the scores that have that stem. For example, the first line represents the scores of 25, 26, and 27, all of which are in the 20s and thus have a stem of 2. In the display, to the right of the stem

A **stem-and-leaf display** is a way of depicting a distribution of scores by separating the digits of each score into two parts: a stem composed of the leftmost digit(s) and a leaf composed of the rightmost digit(s). The scores are then placed in groups by the value of the stems.

STEP-BY-STEP PROCEDURE 3-3

Constructing a Graph

1. *Decide what kind of graph to make.* Identify the type of variable to be graphed. For nominal variables, construct a bar graph; for other discrete variables, construct a frequency histogram; and for continuous variables, construct a frequency polygon. Decide whether the graph will show frequencies, cumulative frequencies, relative frequencies, or relative cumulative frequencies. Construct a frequency table of the distribution.

2. *Draw the X-axis.* Construct the X-axis of the graph by drawing a line horizontally at the bottom of the graph. Draw tick marks vertically down from the X-axis, equally spaced, one tick mark for each score value or group interval in the table constructed in Step 1. If the graph will be a frequency polygon and will display frequencies or relative frequencies, the graph will be extended down to the X-axis at each end, so include one extra tick mark at each end. Omit the extra tick mark at the lower end if it would represent the value of zero. Label the tick marks with the score values or the midpoints of the group intervals they represent. Label the X-axis with the name of the variable.

3. *Draw the Y-axis.* Construct the Y-axis by drawing a line vertically up from the left end of the X-axis. Draw tick marks horizontally out from the Y-axis, equally spaced, one tick mark for each frequency or relative frequency to be shown. If the Y-axis does not represent a continuous line number, starting at 0, mark the segment that has been left out by making two small diagonal lines across the Y-axis. Label each tick mark with the frequency or relative frequency that it represents. In the left margin, label the Y-axis with the name of the type of frequencies shown in the graph.

4. *Draw bars or lines representing frequencies in the distribution.* For bar graphs, construct a bar over each score value so that the height of the bar corresponds to the frequency of that score value in the distribution. Leave spaces between bars representing the various score values.

For frequency histograms, construct a bar over each score value so that the height of the bar corresponds to the frequency of that score value or group interval in the distribution. The width of the bar should equal the distribution's interval width or group interval width. The bar should be centered over the score value or the midpoint of the group interval, so that the edges of the bar are at the real limits. There should be no space between bars of adjacent score values or group intervals.

For frequency polygons, place a dot over each score value or the midpoint of each score value at a height that corresponds to the frequency of that score value or group interval in the distribution. Connect the dots with straight lines. If the graph represents frequencies or relative frequencies, extend the line down to the X-axis at the next score value beyond both ends of the distribution. If the graph represents cumulative frequencies or relative cumulative frequencies, the line will extend down to the X-axis on the left end of the distribution.

5. *Title the graph to indicate what the graph represents.* The title of a graph of a frequency distribution identifies the variable measured.

FIGURE 3-14 Example of a Stem-and-Leaf Display

Scores					Stem-and-leaf display							
25	26	27	32	35	2	5	6	7				
35	36	38	39	39	3	2	5	5	6	8	9	9
41	42	44	47	48	4	1	2	4	7	8	9	
49	53	57	58	63	5	3	7	8				
					6	3						

FIGURE 3-15 Comparing Frequency Distributions and Stem-and-Leaf Displays

Stem-and-leaf display	Frequency histogram

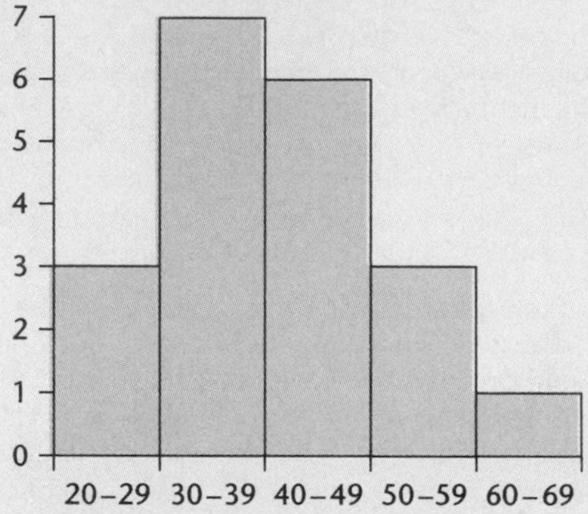

of 2 is listed the digits 5, 6, and 7, which are the ones' digits of the scores, 25, 26, and 27.

Stem-and-leaf displays present information in a way similar to a frequency histogram. Figure 3-15 shows a frequency histogram and a stem-and-leaf display for the set of scores listed in Figure 3-14. In this figure, the stem-and-leaf display is rotated so that the leaves are listed vertically above each stem. Notice that the heights of the columns in the stem-and-leaf display form the same pattern as the bars in the histogram.

If scores contain more than two digits, the researcher determines how to divide the number of digits in the scores into stems and leaves. For example, when scores contain three digits, the researcher can use stems of either one or two digits. With stems of one digit, the researcher would have a maximum of ten stems, while with two digits there could be up to 100 stems. It is also possible to list a stem value more than once, as shown in Figure 3-16.

FIGURE 3-16 Example of a Stem-and-Leaf Display

Scores					Stem-and-leaf display						
365	378	390	401	423	6	08	13	22			
427	438	454	462	471	5	69	74	86	93		
485	496	501	511	519	5	01	11	19	27	38	44
527	538	544	569	574	4	54	62	71	85	96	
586	593	608	613	622	4	01	23	27	38		
					3	65	78	90			

STEP-BY-STEP PROCEDURE 3-4

Constructing a Stem-and-Leaf Display

1. Count the number of digits in the scores. Decide how many digits to include in the stems and in the leaves representing the scores. The more digits the stems contain, the larger the number of stems that there will be. The fewer digits the stems contain, the larger the number of leaves there will be for each stem.

2. List the scores, from smallest to largest.

3. In a column on the left side of the paper, list the values of the stems in ascending order (from smallest to largest). Note that each value of stem is listed only once.

4. Draw a vertical line to the right of the column of stems.

5. In a row to the right of each stem, list the leaf values for all of the scores that have that stem.

If each one-digit stem were listed only once, the display would have only four stems, which may be too few to depict a pattern in the distribution. However, if two-digit stems were used, from thirty-six to sixty-two, there would be twenty-seven stems, far too many for this relatively small set of scores. Step-by-Step Procedure 3-4 describes the steps in constructing a stem-and-leaf display.

Constructing Grouped Frequency Tables

Why Use Grouped Frequency Tables?

Frequency tables are a more efficient way of displaying scores than simply listing all of the scores individually. However, if there are a very large number of score values, frequency tables may not be efficient enough. For example, a frequency table of IQ scores, say from an IQ of 145 down to an IQ of 20, would have 126 rows and would be several pages long. Just as it is difficult to glean much information about a distribution from a long list of scores, so it is from a frequency table that lists hundreds of score values.

The solution is to compile the score values into groups, so that rather than listing hundreds of score values, the table shows a dozen or so groups of score values. These groups are called **group intervals**. A frequency table that uses group intervals rather than score values is called a **grouped frequency distribution**.

Suppose Jane Jeffers conducted a survey of the current income of State University alumni who graduated at least ten years ago with a bachelor's degree in psychology. The information from this survey could be useful in giving you an idea of what income you could expect after you are established in

A **group interval** is a segment of a scale of measurement that contains more than one score value.

A **grouped frequency distribution** is a set of groups of score values and the frequencies of the score values in each group. A grouped frequency distribution is also called a **class interval frequency distribution**.

TABLE 3-5   Annual Incomes for 180 Psychology Alumni

$117,000	$79,000	$61,000	$50,000	$39,000	$27,000
$114,000	$79,000	$61,000	$49,000	$39,000	$27,000
$113,000	$78,000	$60,000	$49,000	$38,000	$27,000
$111,000	$77,000	$60,000	$49,000	$37,000	$26,000
$109,000	$77,000	$60,000	$48,000	$37,000	$25,000
$107,000	$76,000	$59,000	$48,000	$37,000	$25,000
$105,000	$75,000	$59,000	$47,000	$36,000	$25,000
$104,000	$75,000	$58,000	$47,000	$36,000	$24,000
$104,000	$75,000	$58,000	$47,000	$36,000	$24,000
$102,000	$73,000	$58,000	$46,000	$35,000	$22,000
$99,000	$72,000	$57,000	$46,000	$35,000	$22,000
$97,000	$71,000	$57,000	$45,000	$35,000	$21,000
$96,000	$71,000	$57,000	$45,000	$35,000	$20,000
$96,000	$70,000	$56,000	$45,000	$34,000	$19,000
$94,000	$69,000	$56,000	$45,000	$34,000	$18,000
$93,000	$68,000	$55,000	$45,000	$32,000	$18,000
$93,000	$68,000	$55,000	$44,000	$32,000	$18,000
$91,000	$68,000	$55,000	$44,000	$32,000	$17,000
$89,000	$67,000	$54,000	$44,000	$31,000	$17,000
$88,000	$67,000	$53,000	$43,000	$31,000	$15,000
$88,000	$66,000	$53,000	$43,000	$30,000	$15,000
$87,000	$66,000	$53,000	$42,000	$30,000	$15,000
$86,000	$65,000	$52,000	$42,000	$30,000	$13,000
$85,000	$65,000	$52,000	$41,000	$30,000	$12,000
$84,000	$65,000	$51,000	$41,000	$29,000	$10,000
$84,000	$65,000	$51,000	$41,000	$29,000	$10,000
$82,000	$64,000	$50,000	$40,000	$28,000	$9,000
$81,000	$64,000	$50,000	$40,000	$28,000	$9,000
$80,000	$63,000	$50,000	$40,000	$28,000	$7,000
$80,000	$62,000	$50,000	$40,000	$27,000	$6,000

your career. Suppose Jane collected information from 180 alumni, measured in thousands of dollars, as shown in Table 3-5. Even though arranged in order, this list is much too long to be understandable. However, putting the scores into a frequency table doesn't help much, as can be seen in Table 3-6. The solution to this problem is to combine score values into groups so that there are fewer components in the table, which makes the table easier to understand.

TABLE 3-6 Frequency Distribution for Annual Incomes in Table 3-5

Income	Frequency	Income	Frequency	Income	Frequency	Income	Frequency
$117,000	1	$89,000	1	$61,000	2	$33,000	0
$116,000	0	$88,000	2	$60,000	3	$32,000	3
$115,000	0	$87,000	1	$59,000	2	$31,000	2
$114,000	1	$86,000	1	$58,000	3	$30,000	4
$113,000	1	$85,000	1	$57,000	3	$29,000	2
$112,000	0	$84,000	2	$56,000	2	$28,000	3
$111,000	1	$83,000	0	$55,000	3	$27,000	4
$110,000	0	$82,000	1	$54,000	1	$26,000	1
$109,000	1	$81,000	1	$53,000	3	$25,000	3
$108,000	0	$80,000	2	$52,000	2	$24,000	2
$107,000	1	$79,000	2	$51,000	2	$23,000	0
$106,000	0	$78,000	1	$50,000	5	$22,000	2
$105,000	1	$77,000	2	$49,000	3	$21,000	1
$104,000	2	$76,000	1	$48,000	2	$20,000	1
$103,000	0	$75,000	3	$47,000	3	$19,000	1
$102,000	1	$74,000	0	$46,000	2	$18,000	3
$101,000	0	$73,000	1	$45,000	5	$17,000	2
$100,000	0	$72,000	1	$44,000	3	$16,000	0
$99,000	1	$71,000	2	$43,000	2	$15,000	3
$98,000	0	$70,000	1	$42,000	2	$14,000	0
$97,000	1	$69,000	1	$41,000	3	$13,000	1
$96,000	2	$68,000	3	$40,000	4	$12,000	1
$95,000	0	$67,000	2	$39,000	2	$11,000	0
$94,000	1	$66,000	2	$38,000	1	$10,000	2
$93,000	2	$65,000	4	$37,000	3	$9,000	2
$92,000	0	$64,000	2	$36,000	3	$8,000	0
$91,000	1	$63,000	1	$35,000	4	$7,000	1
$90,000	0	$62,000	1	$34,000	2	$6,000	1

Number of Groups

In constructing a grouped frequency distribution, the first question is how many groups to use. If we use too many groups, the table will be so large that it will still be difficult to discern any patterns among the scores. There are 112 score values in Jane's data. We could arrange the 112 score values into fifty-six groups of two score values each, such as Table 3-7. However, this table, with fifty-six groups, is still very long and unwieldy.

TABLE 3-7   Grouped Frequency Distribution with Too Many Classes

Income	Frequency	Income	Frequency	Income	Frequency
$116,000–117,000	1	$78,000–79,000	3	$40,000–41,000	7
$114,000–115,000	1	$76,000–77,000	3	$38,000–39,000	3
$112,000–113,000	1	$74,000–75,000	3	$36,000–37,000	6
$110,000–111,000	1	$72,000–73,000	2	$34,000–35,000	6
$108,000–109,000	1	$70,000–71,000	3	$32,000–33,000	3
$106,000–107,000	1	$68,000–69,000	4	$30,000–31,000	6
$104,000–105,000	3	$66,000–67,000	4	$28,000–29,000	5
$102,000–103,000	1	$64,000–65,000	6	$26,000–27,000	5
$100,000–101,000	0	$62,000–63,000	2	$24,000–25,000	5
$98,000–99,000	1	$60,000–61,000	5	$22,000–23,000	2
$96,000–97,000	3	$58,000–59,000	5	$20,000–21,000	2
$94,000–95,000	1	$56,000–57,000	5	$18,000–19,000	4
$92,000–93,000	2	$54,000–55,000	4	$16,000–17,000	2
$90,000–91,000	1	$52,000–53,000	5	$14,000–15,000	3
$88,000–89,000	3	$50,000–51,000	7	$12,000–13,000	2
$86,000–87,000	2	$48,000–49,000	5	$10,000–11,000	2
$84,000–85,000	3	$46,000–47,000	5	$8,000–9,000	2
$82,000–83,000	1	$44,000–45,000	8	$6,000–7,000	2
$80,000–81,000	3	$42,000–43,000	4		

TABLE 3-8   Grouped Frequency
Distribution with Too Few Classes

Income	Frequency
$62,000–$117,000	60
$6,000–$61,000	120

On the other hand, if we use too few groups, we will lose most of the differences among the scores that form the pattern in the distribution. Table 3-8 shows the scores from Jane's study of psychology alumni, arranged in only two groups. There are far too few groups in Table 3-8 to show any pattern among the incomes.

Thus, having too many groups is confusing and too few groups, uninformative. How many groups should we have to condense the data enough to be understandable but still have enough groups so that the pattern among the scores is evident? By convention, when forming groups, researchers generally use between ten and twenty, which results in a grouped frequency distribution that is small enough for the reader to be able to discern the pattern among the scores but still large enough that the pattern is still discernible.

An additional convention is that there should be 2, 3, 5, or a multiple of 5 score values in each group interval. This convention is used to avoid having an awkward number of score values per group interval. For example, if we had

> ### STEP-BY-STEP PROCEDURE 3-5
>
> ## Determining the Number of Score Values in a Distribution
>
> **1.** Calculate the distance the distribution covers on the number line:
>
> $$\text{distance} = \text{largest score value} - \text{smallest score value} + i,$$
>
> where i is the interval size, which equals the unit of measurement.
>
> **2.** Divide this distance by the interval size, i, to find an estimate of the number of score values to include per group interval:
>
> $$\text{number of score values} = \frac{\text{distance}}{\text{interval size}}.$$

7 or 13 score values per group interval, the grouped frequency table would be very awkward to read. Because we are used to dealing with multiples of 2, 3, and 5, grouping score values in those quantities makes the table easier to read.

The first step in deciding how many groups to use is to determine the number of score values in the distribution. Step-by-Step Procedure 3-5 shows one method, to divide the distance covered by the distribution on the number line by the original unit of measurement. Recall that the unit of measurement is the quantity that was used as a unit with which to measure the original variable. To find the distance that the distribution covers on the number line, we subtract the lowest score value from the highest score value and then add the interval size. The interval size is added to ensure that we find the entire distance covered by the distribution. This distance is called the range, which we will examine in Chapter 5. In Jane's study, the highest score is $117,000, the lowest score is $6,000, and the interval size was $1,000:

$$\text{distance} = \text{highest score} - \text{lowest score} + i$$
$$= \$117{,}000 - \$6{,}000 + \$1{,}000 = \$112{,}000.$$

Then, to find the number of score values, we divide this distance by the interval size:

$$\text{number of score values} = \frac{\text{distance}}{\text{unit of measurement}} = \frac{\$112{,}000}{\$1{,}000} = 112.$$

There are 112 score values in the distribution from Jane's study. We need to arrange these 112 score values into 10 to 20 groups, with 2, 3, 5, or a multiple of 5 score values per group interval. In order to decide how many groups to use and how many score values to include in each group interval, we simply use trial and error. Step-by-Step Procedure 3-6 shows the general method for determining the number of groups that would result by dividing the total number of score values into groups of 2, 3, 5, or a multiple of 5 score values per group interval.

STEP-BY-STEP PROCEDURE 3-6

Determining the Number of Group Intervals

$$\text{number of class intervals} = \frac{\text{total number of score values}}{\text{number of score values per class interval}}$$

Note: Round fractional answers up to nearest whole number.

FIGURE 3-17   Deciding Number of Score Values
Per Group Interval in a Grouped Frequency Distribution

Score values per group interval	
2	number of groups = $\frac{112}{2}$ = 56 groups
3	number of groups = $\frac{112}{3}$ = 37.3 groups, 37.3 groups rounded up → 38 groups
5	number of groups = $\frac{112}{5}$ = 22.4 groups, 22.4 groups rounded up → 23 groups
10	number of groups = $\frac{112}{10}$ = 11.2 groups, 11.2 groups rounded up → 12 groups
15	number of groups = $\frac{112}{15}$ = 7.5 groups, 7.5 groups rounded up → 8 groups

Figure 3-17 shows the computations using Step-by-Step Procedure 3-6 to divide the 112 score values in Jane's study into equal-size groups. From the computations in Figure 3-17, we can see that if we put incomes into groups of two, three, or five, there will be over twenty groups, which is too many. If we put incomes into groups of fifteen, there will only be eight groups, which is too few. However, if we put incomes into groups of ten, there will be twelve such groups, which is within the conventions.

Group Interval Size

In Chapter 2, we saw that an interval is the segment of the number line represented by a single score value. The size of the interval is the distance between the lower real limit and the upper real limit of the score value, a distance which always equals the unit of measurement. In Jane's study, the

STEP-BY-STEP PROCEDURE 3-7

Calculating the Size of a Group Interval

$$\text{size of class interval} = (\text{unit of measurement}) \times \left(\begin{array}{l}\text{number of score values} \\ \text{per class interval}\end{array}\right)$$

STEP-BY-STEP PROCEDURE 3-8

Identifying the Lowest Score Value of First Group Interval

1. Divide lowest score in the distribution by the group interval size. Round the result *down* to the next lower integer.

2. Multiply the result of Step 1 by the group interval size to identify the lowest score value of the first group interval.

incomes were measured to the nearest thousand dollars and so the interval size was $1,000.

In constructing a grouped frequency distribution, we are combining intervals into groups. For Jane's study, we are putting incomes into groups of ten. We will combine ten number line segments of $1,000 each into one group interval of $10,000. Therefore, the group interval size is equal to the original interval size times the number of intervals included in each group interval. Step-by-Step Procedure 3-7 shows this formula for finding the group interval size.

Lowest Group Interval

The next step in constructing a grouped frequency distribution is to decide the location of the lowest group interval. There are two rules. First, the lowest group interval must include the lowest score value in the original set of scores. In Jane's study of psychology alumni's incomes, the lowest score value was $6,000, and so our lowest group interval must include the score value of $6,000.

The second rule is that the lowest score value in each group interval must be a multiple of the group interval size. In Jane's study, the group interval size is $10,000, and thus the lowest score value in each of our twelve groups must be a multiple of $10,000. Step-by-Step Procedure 3-8 describes one way to identify the lowest score value that will satisfy both of these rules for the first group interval. The lowest income in Jane's study is $6,000. According to Step-by-Step Procedure 3-8, we divide this income by the group interval size, $10,000:

$$\text{Step 1:} \frac{\text{lowest score}}{\text{group interval size}} = \frac{\$6,000}{\$10,000} = 0.6.$$

Step 2 is to round this result down to the next lower whole number: 0.6 rounds down to 0. Step 3 is to multiply this result by the group interval size to find the lowest score value included in the first group interval:

$$\text{lowest score value} = 0 \times \$10,000 = 0.$$

Thus, we can begin the lowest group interval with an income of $0.

Constructing the Grouped Frequency Distribution

We are now ready to construct the grouped frequency distribution. We are going to construct twelve groups, with ten score values in each group interval. The size of each group interval will be $10,000, and the lowest score value in the lowest group interval will be $0. The results are shown in Table 3-9. Note that the highest income in Jane's study was $117,000, but the grouped frequency distribution goes up to $119,000. If we stopped at $117,000, then the highest group interval would not be the same size as the others.

Once the groups are constructed, the final step is to tabulate the frequencies. For each group interval, from the scores in Table 3-5, count the number of scores that fall within the lowest and highest score values for that group interval. Table 3-9 shows the frequency of scores in each group interval in Jane's psychology alumni's income study. Step-by-Step Procedure 3-9 describes all of the steps involved in constructing a grouped frequency distribution. In addition to frequencies, we can also use relative frequencies, cumulative frequencies, and relative cumulative frequencies in group interval distributions. They are computed in the same way as described previously.

TABLE 3-9 Grouped Frequency Distribution for Psychology Alumni's Incomes in Table 3-5

Group Interval	Frequency
$110,000–$119,000	4
$100,000–$109,000	6
$90,000–$99,000	8
$80,000–$89,000	12
$70,000–$79,000	14
$60,000–$69,000	21
$50,000–$59,000	26
$40,000–$49,000	29
$30,000–$39,000	24
$20,000–$29,000	19
$10,000–$19,000	13
$0–$9,000	4

Stated Limits, Real Limits, and Midpoints

The **lower stated limit of a group interval** is the lowest score value in the group interval.

The **upper stated limit of a group interval** is the highest score value in the group interval.

In the grouped frequency table for Jane's study, there are two incomes listed for each group interval. The lower income listed is called the **lower stated limit** of that group interval, while the upper income listed is the **upper stated limit.** Thus, in Table 3-9, for the group interval, $40,000–$49,000, the lower stated limit is $40,000 and the upper stated limit is $49,000. The stated limits are the ones "stated" in the grouped frequency table, but they are not the real limits of each group interval.

If we marked a number line between the lower and upper stated limits of each group interval, there would be gaps between the groups. Figure 3-18 shows an example of one gap, between the group interval representing

STEP-BY-STEP PROCEDURE 3-9

Constructing a Grouped Frequency Distribution

1. Follow Step-by-Step Procedure 3-5 to determine the total number of score values in the distribution.

2. Using Step-by-Step Procedure 3-6, divide the number of score values by 2, 3, 5, and multiples of 5 (e.g., 10, 15, 20, . . .), until the result, rounded up to the next whole number, is a number between 10 and 20. That result will be the number of group intervals to form. The number used as a divisor (2, 3, 5, or a multiple of 5) is the number of score values to include in each group interval.

3. Using Step-by-Step Procedure 3-7, calculate the group interval size by multiplying the unit of measurement by the number of score values in each interval.

4. Follow Step-by-Step Procedure 3-8 to identify the lowest score value of the first group interval.

5. Construct the group interval frequency distribution by first listing the lowest score value of each group interval from highest to lowest. These values will be multiples of the group interval size, with the lowest value being the one determined in Step 4. The number of values listed will equal the number of group intervals, as found in Step 2.

6. Place a dash after each of the values listed in Step 5, and then list the highest score value in each group interval, which can be found by subtracting the unit of measurement from the lowest score value in the group interval immediately above. At the end of this step, you will have constructed a column of group intervals, each consisting of the lowest value and highest value in the group interval. Label the column with the name of the variable.

7. For each group interval, count the number of scores in the set of scores that have values in that group interval. List these frequencies in a second column, labeled "Frequency."

incomes of \$30,000–\$39,000 and the group interval of incomes of \$40,000–\$49,000. The gap is between the upper stated limit, \$39,000, of the lower group interval and the lower stated limit, \$40,000, of the higher group interval. The real limit between these two groups is actually halfway between \$39,000 and \$40,000.

The **lower real limit** of a group interval is the lowest point on the number line included in that group interval. The lower real limit of a group interval is always one-half the original interval size below the lower stated limit. In Jane's study, the original interval size was \$1,000, and one-half of that is \$500. So the lower real limit of the \$40,000–\$49,000 group interval is \$500 less than the lower stated limit of \$40,000, or \$39,500. Step-by-Step Procedure 3-10 shows the formula for finding the lower real limit from the lower stated limit. Caution! In the formula, be sure to use the original interval size and *not* the group interval size.

The **lower real limit (LRL) of a group interval** is equal to the lower real limit of the lowest score value in the group interval. The LRL is one-half the original interval size below the lower stated limit.

FIGURE 3-18   Gap Between Stated Limits in Grouped
Frequency Distribution of Psychology Alumni's Incomes

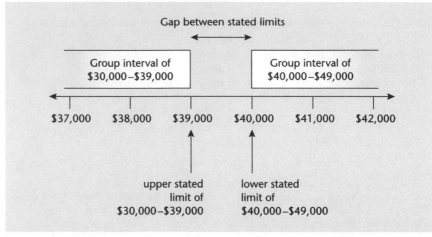

S T E P - B Y - S T E P   P R O C E D U R E   3 - 1 0

Calculating the Lower Real Limit, Upper Real Limit, and Midpoint of a Group Interval

$$\text{lower real limit} = \text{lower stated limit} - \frac{\text{interval size}}{2}$$

$$\text{upper real limit} = \text{upper stated limit} + \frac{\text{interval size}}{2}$$

$$\text{midpoint} = \frac{\text{lower stated limit} + \text{upper stated limit}}{2}$$

1. To find the lower real limit, divide the interval size by 2 and subtract that result from the lower stated limit.

2. To find the upper real limit, divide the interval size by 2 and add that result to the upper stated limit.

3. To find the midpoint, add the lower stated limit to the upper stated limit and then divide that result by 2.

The **upper real limit of a group interval** is equal to the upper real limit of the highest score value in the group interval. The upper real limit is one-half the original interval size above the upper stated limit. It is also equal to the lower real limit of the next higher group interval.

The **upper real limit** of a group interval is equal to the lower real limit of the next higher group interval. The upper real limit of a group interval is also always one-half the original interval size above the upper stated limit. Step-by-Step Procedure 3-10 also shows the formula for finding the upper real limit. For the $40,000–$49,000 group interval in Jane's study, the upper real limit is $500 (one-half the interval size of $1,000) above the upper stated limit of $49,000, or $49,500.

The **midpoint of a group interval** is the point on the number line that is halfway between the lower stated limit and the upper stated limit. This point is also halfway between the lower real limit and the upper real limit of the group interval. Procedure 3-10 shows how to find the midpoint of a group interval. Using this procedure to calculate the midpoint of the $40,000–$49,000 group interval, we find:

$$\text{Midpoint} = \frac{\$40,000 + \$49,000}{2} = \frac{\$89,000}{2} = \$44,500.$$

As a way of checking your answer, if there are an odd number of score values in each group interval, the midpoint will always be a score value. If there are an even number of score values per group interval, the midpoint will be exactly halfway between two score values. In the example above, the midpoint is $44,500, exactly halfway between the score values of $44,000 and $45,000. If, when calculating midpoints, your answer is neither a score value nor halfway between score values, you've made an error somewhere.

Characteristics of Distributions

This chapter has focused on constructing tables and graphs of frequency distributions. From the graphs shown in this chapter, we can see that distributions can be very different. Three of the characteristics that we can use to compare distributions are central tendency, variability, and skewness.

The first characteristic of a distribution is its center point. What value represents the center of the distribution or a typical score in the distribution? There are several ways of measuring the center of a distribution numerically, which we examine in Chapter 4. These methods are called **measures of central tendency.** If we know the center point of a distribution, then we can compare it to other distributions. Is the center of one distribution lower than, higher than, or just the same as the center point of another distribution? In Figure 3-19, because the distribution in graph B is farther up the number line, it has a higher center point than the distribution in graph A.

The second characteristic of a distribution is its variability, or how spread out the scores are. Some distributions have scores that are clustered very closely around the center point. In other distributions, the scores are more spread out. Ways of measuring the spread of a distribution are called **measures of variability,** which we examine in Chapter 5. How much do the scores vary from the center point? In Figure 3-19, the scores in the distribution in graph A are more spread out, more disperse, than the scores in the distribution in graph B.

The third characteristic is a distribution's skewness, or how balanced the distribution is. If we took the graph of a distribution and folded it in half at the center point, would the two halves be identical? Or would the two halves

The **midpoint of a group interval** is the point on the number line that is halfway between the lower and upper stated limits. That point is also the point that is halfway between the lower and upper real limits.

Measures of central tendency are descriptive statistics that describe the center point(s) of a set of scores, indicating where on a number line a set of scores is centered.

Measures of variability are descriptive statistics that describe the degree to which a set of scores is spread out over the number line.

FIGURE 3-19   Comparison of Characteristics of Distributions

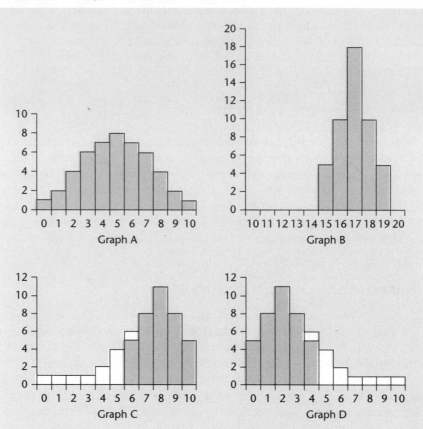

Graph A

Graph B

Graph C

Graph D

Measures of skewness are descriptive statistics that describe the degree to which a set of scores is not symmetrical about the center point of the set. A distribution is skewed when there are more scores at one end of the distribution than at the other. If the lower tail of the distribution is the longer one, the distribution is **negatively skewed.** If the upper tail is the longer one, then the distribution is **positively skewed.**

be different shapes? Is the graph symmetrical or not? In Figure 3-19, both the distributions in graphs A and B are balanced, while the distributions in graphs C and D are skewed.

The distribution in graph C has a negative skew. If that distribution contained only the darkly hatched cases, it would be balanced. It is the lightly hatched cases at the lower end that unbalance the distribution. These cases, at the left or negative side of the graph, are the ones causing the negative skew. Similarly, it is the cases at the right or positive side of the distribution in graph D that cause it to be positively skewed. In the graphs shown in Figure 3-19, the ends of the distributions are called the tails. To decide whether a distribution is positively or negatively skewed, remember that the longer tail of the graph points in the direction of the skew.

There are statistical **measures of skewness** that give a numerical index of the degree that a distribution is skewed. Examining these measures is beyond the scope of this book. If you are interested in learning more about these measures of skewness, they are described in more advanced statistics texts.

CHECKING YOUR ANSWERS

1. When constructing a frequency table, be sure to list the values from highest at the top to lowest at the bottom. If you start with the lowest values at the top of the table, then the cumulative frequencies will not add up correctly.

2. When constructing a frequency table, check your answer by adding up all of the frequencies. The total should equal the number of subjects, *n*. Relative frequencies should add up to 1.00.

3. In a cumulative frequency table, remember to begin finding the cumulative frequencies with the lowest score value, at the bottom of the table.

4. In a grouped frequency table, first check to make sure that there are from 10 to 20 groups. Then check to make sure that the lower stated limit of the lowest group interval is exactly divisible by the unit of measurement. Check to make sure that you included 2, 3, 5, or a multiple of 5 intervals in each group interval. Then, multiply the unit of measurement by the number of intervals in each group interval. Check to make sure that the lower stated limit of each group interval is exactly that distance above the lower stated limit of the class below and, similarly, with the upper stated limits. Finally, look at your grouped frequency table to see if it makes sense and is easy to read!

5. When constructing a graph, make sure that you label the tick marks on the *X*-axis with the values being represented, and then label the entire *X*-axis with the name of the variable being measured. Make sure that you label the tick marks on the *Y*-axis with the frequencies or relative frequencies being represented. Be sure that you title the graph to show what the graph represents. Check to make sure you use the correct type of graph for the variable being measured: bar graphs for nominal data, frequency histograms for discrete ordinal, interval, or ratio data, and frequency polygons for continuous interval or ratio data.

$\sum$ SUMMARY

▶ A distribution is a set of score values together with the frequency those values occur. The set of scores that results from actual observations of subjects is called a frequency distribution, while a set of scores derived from theoretical predictions is called a theoretical distribution.

▶ A frequency table presents a set of scores in tabular form. It lists the score values and then the frequency, relative frequency, cumulative frequency, and/or cumulative relative frequency of each of those score values.

▶ In graphs of frequency distributions, the *X*-axis represents score values and the *Y*-axis represents either the frequency or the relative frequency that the score values occur. It is assumed that both axes originate at zero. Axes that do not originate at zero are so indicated by tick marks.

▶ Bar graphs are used to depict nominal variables, which are qualitative in nature. The bars representing the frequency that each score value occurs do not touch each other in bar graphs.

▶ Frequency histograms are used to depict discrete quantitative variables, which may be measured on an ordinal, interval, or ratio scale of measurement. The bars representing the frequencies of score values touch each other in histograms.

▶ Frequency polygons are used to depict continuous quantitative variables, which may be measured on either an interval or a ratio scale of measurement. Graphs of the cumulative frequencies of these variables are called ogives, as they do not form a complete polygonal figure.

▶ A stem-and-leaf display is a way of depicting a distribution of scores by separating each score into two parts, the stem and the leaf, then listing all of the stems in increasing order, together with the leafs associated with each stem.

▶ If there are a large number of score values, a grouped frequency distribution, which combines score values into from ten to twenty groups, may provide a more understandable way in which to present the information.

▶ In a grouped frequency distribution, the lower and upper stated limits of a group interval are the lowest and highest score values in that group interval, respectively. The lower and upper real limits of a group interval are one-half unit of measurement beyond the respective stated limit. The midpoint of the group interval is halfway between the stated limits.

▶ Measures of central tendency describe the center point(s) of a distribution of scores. Measures of variability describe the degree to which scores are spread out in a distribution. Measures of skewness describe the degree to which a distribution of scores is not symmetrical about the center point of the distribution.

E X E R C I S E S

Conceptual Exercises

1. Define the following terms:

distribution	upper stated limit of a group interval
frequency distribution	midpoint of a group interval
theoretical distribution	X-axis
frequency table	Y-axis
relative frequency table	bar graph
cumulative frequency table	frequency histogram
relative cumulative frequency table	frequency polygon
stem-and-leaf display	measures of central tendency
group interval	measures of variability
grouped frequency distribution	measures of skewness
lower real limit of a group interval	negatively skewed
upper real limit of a group interval	positively skewed
lower stated limit of a group interval	

2. Describe how to differentiate between the following:
   A. frequency distribution and theoretical distribution
   B. scale of measurement and distribution
   C. frequency, relative frequency, cumulative frequency, and relative cumulative frequency

3. What are the advantages of arranging a distribution of scores in a frequency table? Construct your own example to illustrate your points.

4. What advantages are there in arranging a distribution of scores in a grouped frequency table? What are the disadvantages? Construct an example to illustrate your points.

5. Compare a stem-and-leaf display and a frequency table. What are the advantages of each?

6. How do bar graphs, frequency histograms, and frequency polygons differ? What type of data is appropriate for each?

7. For each of the following, construct two distributions that demonstrate:
   A. a difference in central tendency
   B. a difference in variability
   C. a difference in skewness

Computational Exercises

8. Toss ten pennies twenty-five times, each time recording the number of heads out of the ten pennies. Construct a table that shows the following: (*a*) frequency, (*b*) relative frequency, (*c*) cumulative frequency, and (*d*) relative cumulative frequency.

9. Buy a bag of M&M candies. Count the number of each color M&M in the bag. Construct a table showing the following: (*a*) frequency, (*b*) relative frequency, (*c*) cumulative frequency, and (*d*) relative cumulative frequency. Explain why it isn't appropriate to use cumulative frequencies for this table.

10. Jennifer recorded the number of patients visiting a rural emergency room each day during a one-month period. The results are listed below. Construct a table showing the following: (*a*) frequency, (*b*) relative frequency, (*c*) cumulative frequency, and (*d*) relative cumulative frequency.

23	27	20	26	21	31
30	25	25	32	23	26
20	27	30	25	24	23
26	24	26	21	26	23
25	27	29	20	25	30

11. Construct a graph of the frequency distribution from Exercise 10.

12. Joshua conducted a study of the satisfaction of students majoring in psychology at State University with the psychology program. The students were asked to rate their satisfaction on a scale from 1 to 7, where 1 was very unsatisfied; 2, moderately unsatisfied; 3, slightly unsatisfied; 4, neutral; 5, slightly satisfied; 6, moderately satisfied; and 7, very satisfied. Listed below are the students' ratings. Construct a table showing

the following: (*a*) frequency, (*b*) relative frequency, (*c*) cumulative frequency, and (*d*) relative cumulative frequency.

5	3	7	6	5
4	3	6	7	4
5	5	6	5	4
4	5	6	6	7
4	1	3	5	6

13. Construct a graph of the relative frequency distribution from Exercise 12.

14. Jacques recorded the ethnic origins of twenty-five students in the Student Senate at State University, which are listed below, with 1 representing African-Americans; 2, Native Americans; 3, Asian-Americans; 4, Hispanics; 5, Caucasians; 6, multiracial; and 7, others. Construct a table showing the following: (*a*) frequency, and (*b*) relative frequency. Explain why it isn't appropriate to use cumulative frequencies for this table.

1	5	2	6	4
7	5	5	4	2
5	1	4	5	6
2	3	6	2	5
2	5	5	4	1

15. Construct a graph of the frequency distribution from Exercise 14.

16. James recorded the ages of fifty children enrolled in judo classes. The ages of the children are listed below. Construct a table showing the following: (*a*) frequency, (*b*) relative frequency, (*c*) cumulative frequency, and (*d*) relative cumulative frequency.

7	8	9	8	9	8	10	8	9	8
8	11	6	10	7	6	9	7	10	8
8	12	8	7	8	9	8	8	7	11
7	8	9	6	9	8	10	8	12	9
8	9	8	9	10	8	11	9	8	6

17. Construct a graph of the cumulative frequency distribution from Exercise 16.

18. Josephine recorded the SAT verbal scores of fifty high school seniors at Middletown High School, as listed below. Organize this distribution, using a stem-and-leaf plot with nine stems.

681	764	462	510	607	582	619	711	424	523
790	638	495	524	583	679	594	529	613	702
613	492	540	475	591	642	694	582	483	703
459	590	355	512	399	573	710	420	537	632
370	438	710	625	555	440	667	416	386	550

19. Jonas recorded the IQ scores of forty students as listed below. Use a stem-and-leaf plot to organize this distribution.

93	92	107	131	120	112	144	124	115	135
127	104	101	119	98	103	118	121	96	119
130	104	142	113	98	126	84	109	106	117
102	87	108	106	119	105	128	110	122	90

20. Jena decided to arrange three distributions of scores into grouped frequency tables. Listed below are the lowest score, highest score, and original interval size for each distribution of scores. Using the guidelines for forming a grouped frequency distribution, identify the most appropriate group interval size that the researcher should use in arranging each distribution in a grouped frequency table.

    A. lowest score = 37, highest score = 100, original interval size = 1
    B. lowest score = 0.87, highest score = 4.00, original interval size = .01
    C. lowest score = 1,430, highest score = 1,700, original interval size = 10

21. Jarrett decided to arrange three distributions of scores into grouped frequency tables. Listed below are the lowest score, the original interval size, and the grouped interval size selected by the researcher. Identify the stated limits for the lowest group interval of each distribution.

    A. lowest score = 67, original interval size = 1, grouped interval size = 5
    B. lowest score = 5.3, original interval size = .1, grouped interval size = 2.0
    C. lowest score = 1,700, original interval size = 100, grouped interval size = 300

22. Jillian also decided to arrange three distributions of scores into grouped frequency tables. Listed below are the stated limits of one of the grouped intervals and the original interval size. Identify the real limits and midpoint of this grouped interval.

    A. stated limits: 70–79; original interval size = 1
    B. stated limits: 1.00–1.04; original interval size = .01
    C. stated limits: 13,000–14,000; original interval size = 1,000

23. The children at Washington Elementary School had IQ scores that ranged from 79 to 137.

    A. Construct group intervals for these IQ scores.
    B. Identify the lower real limit, lower stated limit, and midpoint for each group interval.

24. Jules surveyed the ages at which 100 graduate students received their doctoral degrees in the psychology program at State University. These ages are listed below. Construct a grouped frequency table for these data. Identify the stated limits, frequency, real limits, and midpoint of each group.

45	38	36	35	34	33	32	31	30	29
42	37	36	35	34	33	32	31	30	29
41	37	36	35	34	33	32	31	30	29
41	37	35	35	34	33	32	31	30	29
40	37	35	34	33	33	32	31	30	28
40	37	35	34	33	33	32	31	30	28
39	36	35	34	33	32	32	31	30	28
39	36	35	34	33	32	31	31	30	28
38	36	35	34	33	32	31	31	29	27
38	36	35	34	33	32	31	31	29	27

25. Construct a graph of the relative cumulative frequency distribution from Exercise 24.

26. Jamila recorded the GPAs of fifty psychology majors as listed below. Construct a grouped frequency table for these GPAs. Identify the stated limits, frequency, real limits, and midpoint of each group.

3.98	3.69	3.50	3.32	3.51
3.91	3.67	3.47	3.31	3.15
3.89	3.66	3.46	3.30	3.49
3.85	3.54	3.44	3.29	3.41
3.81	3.63	3.42	3.27	3.10
3.79	3.62	3.41	3.25	3.08
3.59	3.61	3.38	3.23	3.43
3.75	3.57	3.37	3.20	3.46
3.72	3.56	3.36	3.57	3.24
3.70	3.54	3.34	3.18	3.01

27. Construct a graph of the grouped frequency distribution from Exercise 26.

E N D N O T E

1. The technique of stem-and-leaf displays was first developed by J. W. Tukey and is described in *Exploratory Data Analysis,* by J. W. Tukey (Reading, MA: Addison Wesley, 1977).

Measures of Central Tendency

4

Statistical Procedures

The Summation Sign, Σ

How to Use a Formula

Rounding

The Mean

Calculating the Mean of a Distribution

STEP-BY-STEP PROCEDURE 4-1: Calculating the Mean of a Distribution of Scores

How to Interpret the Mean

The Median

How to Compute the Median

STEP-BY-STEP PROCEDURE 4-2: Calculating the Median of a Distribution of Scores

How to Interpret the Median

The Mode

STEP-BY-STEP PROCEDURE 4-3: Finding the Mode in a Distribution

Comparing the Mean, Median, and Mode

CHECKING YOUR ANSWERS

SUMMARY

EXERCISES

Conceptual Exercises

Computational Exercises

▶ In the last chapter, we saw that Jane Jeffers collected information on the annual incomes of psychology alumni ten or more years after graduating. Looking at the results of this study, you might ask, "So, what can I expect to earn with a degree in psychology?" From the analysis we've done thus far, the most we can predict is that you might earn anywhere from $6,000 to $117,000 a year. That's not very specific. Of course, this prediction does tell you something. For example, it tells you that you aren't likely to earn $1 million a year working in psychology. However, giving you only the range of incomes you might earn isn't very precise. You could demand, "Give me just one number. Exactly how much can I expect to earn?"

There are several ways that we could answer that question. First, we could report that the greatest number of alumni had incomes in the range of $40,000–$49,000, which, in statistical terms, is the *modal* income. We could also report that half of psychology alumni earned incomes over $49,900, which is the *median* income in statistical terms. Finally, we could report that the average income of psychology alumni is $52,600, which, in statistics, is the *mean* income.

"But," you might ask, "which is the correct one? Which one really tells me how much I can expect to earn?" The answer is "all of them." All three statistics tell you how much you can expect to earn. Each indicates, in its own way, what a typical income for psychology alumni might be. Each gives an indication of the center of the distribution of psychology alumni's incomes.

Measures of central tendency are numbers used to describe the center of a distribution of scores. In this chapter, which is the first of several chapters on calculating descriptive statistics, we explore the concepts of the mean, median, and mode, examining both how these statistics represent the center of a distribution and how to compute them. We will also look at when it is appropriate to use each statistic and when it is not. Before examining these measures of central tendency, we should look at a special notation used in many statistical formulas.

A **measure of central tendency** is a number that describes the center of a distribution of scores. The number can be thought of as the typical score or the score that best represents the distribution. The three most commonly used measures of central tendency are the mean, median, and mode.

Statistical Procedures

The Summation Sign, Σ

Many of the math symbols that we will find in statistical formulas are symbols with which you are already familiar, such as + and −. There is one

FIGURE 4-1 Example of Using the Summation Sign, Σ

1. Finding ΣX

Student	IQ (X)	
Alice	130	
Bill	110	
Carol	100	Add these together to find ΣX.
Dave	120	
Esther	+ 115	
	$\Sigma X = 575$	

2. Finding ΣX^2

Student	IQ (X)		X^2		
Alice	130		$130^2 =$	16,900	
Bill	110	First square each	$110^2 =$	12,100	Then add these
Carol	100	person's score, X.	$100^2 =$	10,000	together to find ΣX^2
Dave	120		$120^2 =$	14,400	
Esther	115		$115^2 = +$	13,225	
			$\Sigma X^2 =$	66,625	

3. Finding $(\Sigma X)^2$

First find ΣX as shown in Part 1 above: $\Sigma X = 575$.

Then square this number to find $(\Sigma X)^2$: $(\Sigma X)^2 = 575^2 = 330,625$.

symbol, however, that we often find in statistical formulas that you may not have seen before. The summation sign, Σ, means to sum or add up. (Σ is the Greek capital letter for "S" and is called "sigma," pronounced "sig-muh.") The summation sign is always followed by one or more letters representing scores, such as ΣX and ΣXY. The letters following Σ represent the values that are to be added together. Instead of using the names of variables, such as IQ scores and GPA, variables are represented in formulas by letters. The letter X represents one variable in the formula, and the letter Y represents a second variable in a formula.

Because the summation sign is used in many statistical formulas, it is important to understand what it tells us to do. Three of the more common uses of the summation sign are shown in Figure 4-1, which lists the IQ scores of five students. Note that the IQ scores have been labeled X.

Figure 4-1, Part 1, shows that to find ΣX, the sum of X, we simply add up the five students' IQ scores, the scores that are labeled X. In this case, ΣX equals 575. Part 2 of Figure 4-1 shows that there are two steps to finding ΣX^2, the sum of X^2: first we square each of the scores labeled X, and then we add up these squared values. In Figure 4-1, ΣX^2 is 66,225. Part 3 shows that there are also two steps to finding $(\Sigma X)^2$, the square of the sum of X: first we find ΣX by adding up the scores labeled X, and then we square that value. In Figure 4-1, $(\Sigma X)^2$ is 575^2 or 330,625.

It is important to note that ΣX^2 is not the same thing as $(\Sigma X)^2$. In Figure 4-1, ΣX^2 is 66,225, while $(\Sigma X)^2$ is 330,625. ΣX^2 tells us to first square each score, and then to sum the squared scores. $(\Sigma X)^2$ tells us to sum the scores first and then to square the total. Although ΣX^2 and $(\Sigma X)^2$ look very similar, they represent very different values. Getting them confused can lead to serious errors! So, remember:

$$\Sigma X^2 \text{ means first square then sum,}$$

$$(\Sigma X)^2 \text{ means first sum then square.}$$

All of the expressions discussed thus far are found in statistical formulas designed to be used with scores arranged in a simple list. There are additional expressions that we encounter in formulas designed to be used with scores arranged in a frequency table. Figure 4-2, Part 1, demonstrates how to find ΣXf.

FIGURE 4-2 Example of Using the Summation Sign, Σ, with Scores Arranged in a Frequency Table

1. Finding ΣXf

IQ (X)	f		Xf	
130 × 10			1,300	
110 × 20		Multiply each score value by its frequency.	2,200	Add these products together to find ΣXf.
100 × 30			3,000	
120 × 20			2,400	
115 × 10			+ 1,150	
			$\Sigma Xf = 10{,}050$	

2. Finding ΣX^2f

IQ (X)		X^2	f		X^2f	
130^2		16,900 × 10			169,000	
110^2		12,100 × 20			242,000	
100^2	Square each score value.	10,000 × 30		Multiply each square value by its frequency.	300,000	Add these products together to find ΣX^2f.
120^2		14,400 × 20			288,000	
115^2		13,225 × 10			+ 132,250	
					$\Sigma X^2f = 1{,}131{,}250$	

3. Finding $(\Sigma Xf)^2$

First find ΣXf as shown in Part 1 above: $\Sigma Xf = 10{,}050$.

Then square this number to find $(\Sigma Xf)^2$: $(\Sigma Xf)^2 = 10{,}050^2 = 101{,}002{,}500$.

First, each score value is multiplied by its frequency, and then these products are summed. Part 2 of Figure 4-2 shows how to find $\Sigma X^2 f$, by first squaring each score value, then multiplying that squared value by its frequency, and finally summing the resultant products. Finally, Part 3 of Figure 4-2 illustrates how to find $(\Sigma X f)^2$, by first finding $\Sigma X f$ as shown in Part 1, and then squaring this result.

These expressions are the ones we will encounter in the statistical techniques in this and the following few chapters. We will find other expressions using the summation sign in later chapters of this text. Rather than examine every possible case here, these other expressions will be explained in detail when we encounter them.

In this section, we have looked at how to use the summation sign, Σ, a math symbol frequently found in statistical formulas. Armed with this knowledge, we are ready to take a more general look at how to use statistical formulas.

How to Use a Formula

A statistical formula is a procedure used to convert one or more groups of scores into a single number. The key word is "procedure." According to the dictionary, a procedure is a method of accomplishing something, a method that is composed of steps. Thus, a statistical formula is a series of steps used to compute a statistic. For example, the formula for the mean is a procedure that summarizes the center point, or average, of a group of scores. If we put the set of scores, 3, 4, 6, 7, and 9, into the formula for the mean, the result will be a single number, 5.8, the mean of that set of scores:

$$3, 4, 6, 7, 9 \rightarrow \text{formula} \rightarrow 5.8.$$

Every formula is written in symbols, such as X, N, and the Greek letter μ. For example, one formula for the mean, which will we examine in more depth later in this chapter, is

$$\mu = \frac{\Sigma X}{N}.$$

The symbol on the left, μ, represents the mean. Every statistic we examine will be represented by a symbol. In statistical formulas, the symbol representing that statistic is always shown on the left.

The right side of the formula shows the mathematical procedure that we follow to calculate the statistic. Note that the right side of the formula contains letters and mathematical symbols. The formula for the mean shown above contains the letters X and N. The letters on the right side of the formula always represent numbers that we need to insert in the formula before we can begin to actually calculate the formula. The letters may be either Greek letters (such as μ and σ) or roman letters (the letters in our alphabet). For each statistical formula, what each of the letters in the formula represents will be explained immediately following the formula.

After we have substituted numbers for each of the letters on the right side of the formula, we then carry out the mathematical operations shown. In the formula for the mean, there is one operation, dividing ΣX, the sum of the scores, by N, the number of scores. In this text, the mathematical procedure for calculating each statistic will be described step by step. These step-by-step procedures are included in case you have difficulty understanding how to use the formulas. When calculating any statistical formula, work carefully, following the procedure step by step, and you will have no difficulty finding the correct value.

Rounding

When you use a calculator to compute the value of a statistic, the calculator display will show a string of digits as the answer. For example, when calculating the mean of the numbers, 2 inches, 3 inches, and 6 inches, a calculator may show the answer as 3.6666667. However, when calculating statistics, it is appropriate to show the answer one place more precisely than the scores used to calculate the statistics. If we were to give the mean to the same degree of precision as the scores, to the nearest inch, the mean would be 4 inches. Saying that the mean is 3.7 inches not only tells us that the mean is in the interval of 4 inches (remember that the interval of 4 inches contains all the points from 3.5 inches up to 4.5 inches), it also tells us where the mean lies in that interval. The mean 3.7 inches is near the lower end of the interval of 4 inches.

Suppose we change the set of scores slightly, to 2, 3, and 8 inches. One calculator might show that the mean of these three numbers is 4.3333333. If we round to the original unit of measurement, the mean would be 4 inches, the same as the mean for the three scores, 2, 3, and 6 inches. (Recall that the unit of measurement is the quantity selected as a unit with which to measure the variable.) However, if we round one place more precisely than the original unit of measurement, the mean of 2, 3, and 8 inches would be 4.3 inches, which is at the higher end of the interval of 4 inches. The means of both sets of numbers are in the interval of 4 inches, but by rounding one place more precisely, we gain the additional information of where in that interval the means lie. We know that the mean of 2, 3, and 8 inches is a little higher on the number line than the mean of 2, 3, and 6 inches.

The rule to round one place more precisely than the scores applies to statistics and parameters that are measured in the same scale as the scores. For example, if the scores represent length measured in inches, the mean will also be in inches. In these cases, round the value of the statistic one place more precisely than the scores.

There are some statistics and parameters whose values will not be in the same scale of measurement as the scores. For example, percentiles, which we will examine in Chapter 6, are not in the same scale of measurement as the scores. An IQ score of 100 is at the 50th percentile, but saying that someone has an IQ at the 50th percentile is not the same as saying that person has an IQ of 50. The value, 50th percentile, is not in the same measurement scale as IQ scores. When the statistic or parameter is no longer in the original scale of measurement, the general convention in this text will be to round to two decimal places.

Finally, some of the procedures we examine in this text will result in values that represent scores. For example, we might want to find the IQ score that lies at the 95th percentile. In Chapter 6, we will study a procedure that enables us to make this conversion to show that the score at the 95th percentile is an IQ of 124.75. However, there is no such IQ score as 124.75. IQ scores are given only in whole numbers. When the result of a statistical procedure gives us a score value, it makes sense to report that score in the original unit of measurement. Thus, we should report the IQ score at the 95th percentile as 125, a whole number, which is the original unit of measurement.

In summary, we have three rules to follow in deciding to which place to round the result of a statistical procedure:

1. When the result of a statistical procedure is a score, round to the original unit of measurement.
2. When the result of a statistical procedure is a statistic or parameter that is in the original measurement scale, round the value one place more precisely than the unit of measurement of the scores.
3. When the result of a statistical procedure is a statistic or parameter that is not in the original measurement scale, round the value to two decimal places.

The Mean

Calculating the Mean of a Distribution

The **mean** is the arithmetic average of a group of scores. It is what we calculated to get a grade point average. Step-by-Step Procedure 4-1 shows the formulas to calculate the mean of a distribution of scores from both a simple list of scores and from scores listed in a frequency table. We will look first at the formulas for a simple list. Suppose we want to find the mean of a population of five scores, 2, 3, 5, 6, and 8 inches. Step-by-Step Procedure 4-1 tells us to first add these scores together and then to divide by N, the number of scores. In this case, there are five scores, so N is 5:

$$\mu = \frac{\Sigma X}{N} = \frac{2 + 3 + 5 + 6 + 8}{5} = \frac{24}{5} = 4.8 \text{ inches.}$$

The mean of this set of five scores is 4.8 inches. Note that the mean is rounded one place more precisely than the original scores. The original scores were

The **mean** is the arithmetic average of a distribution. It is the balance point of a group of scores, the value for which the sum of the distances of scores from the mean is zero.

Calculating the Mean of a Distribution of Scores

The mean of a population

For a simple list of scores	For scores listed in a frequency table
$$\mu = \frac{\Sigma X}{N}$$	$$\mu = \frac{\Sigma Xf}{N}$$

where μ = the mean of the population
X = the scores in a simple list or score values in a frequency table
f = the frequency of each score value in a frequency table
N = the number of scores in the population

The mean of a sample

For a list of scores	For scores listed in a frequency table
$$\bar{X} = \frac{\Sigma X}{n}$$	$$\bar{X} = \frac{\Sigma Xf}{n}$$

where $\bar{X}$ = the mean of a sample
X = the scores in a simple list or score values in a frequency table
f = the number of scores with each value in a frequency table
n = the number of scores in the sample

How to calculate the mean:

1. *For a list of raw scores:* Add up all the scores in the population or sample to find ΣX. *For scores listed in a frequency table:* Multiply each score value, X, by its frequency, f. When completed for each score value, add up all the products to find ΣXf.

2. Count the number of scores in the population to find N, or the number of scores in the sample to find n.

3. Divide the results of Step 1 by the results of Step 2 to obtain the mean. The mean of a population is symbolized by μ, and the mean of a sample is symbolized by $\bar{X}$.

---

measured to the nearest whole inch; the mean is given to the nearest tenth of an inch.

Procedure 4-1 shows that the formulas for the mean of a population and the mean of a sample use different symbols. Recall that a population is the entire group of subjects or events in which the experimenter is interested, while a sample is a subgroup of the population. Recall also that numeric summaries of populations are called parameters, while numeric summaries of samples are called statistics. The calculations in the formulas for the mean of a population and a sample are the same. In both, we add together the scores in the set and then divide by the number of scores. The only difference is in the symbols used. The Greek letter μ (called "mu" and pronounced "mew") represents the mean of a population, while the symbol $\bar{X}$ represents the mean of a sample.

FIGURE 4-3 Calculating the Mean of the Math Test Scores from Joe's Study, Using a Simple List

X (%)

95	60
90	60
90	60
80	60
75	55
75	55
70	55
70	50
70	50
60	40

Step 1: Add all the scores together: $\Sigma X = 1{,}320$.

Step 2: Count the number of scores in the set to find n. There are 20 scores in this set, so $n = 20$.

Step 3: Divide the ΣX found in Step 1 by the number of scores, n, found in Step 2:

$$\bar{X} = \frac{\Sigma X}{n} = \frac{1{,}320}{20} = 66.0\%.$$

Thus, the symbol used to represent the mean tells us whether it is the mean of a population or a sample.

The scores in Figure 4-3 are from the hypothetical study of math anxiety, conducted by Joe Johnson, the same scores shown in Table 3-1 in the previous chapter. Figure 4-3 shows how to calculate the mean of these math test scores. Because these scores represent a sample, we use the formula for the mean of a sample. Figure 4-3 shows that the mean math test score is 66.0 percent.

It is quick to calculate the mean for a small number of scores from a simple list but could be time consuming if there are many scores in the group. When the number of scores is large, it is quicker to calculate the mean from scores listed in a frequency table. Procedure 4-1 shows the formulas for calculating the mean from a frequency table. Figure 4-4 shows an example of calculating the mean of a frequency distribution, again using the scores from Joe's math anxiety study. In Figure 4-4, the scores are arranged in the frequency table constructed in the previous chapter. Note that, for the same group of scores, the formula for calculating the mean from a frequency table gives us the same value for the mean as the formula for calculating the mean from a simple list did. The mean math score in Joe's study is 66.0 percent no matter which formula we use to do the computations.

By using the midpoints of the groups for the values of X, we can also use the formula for calculating the mean from a frequency table to estimate the mean of a grouped frequency distribution. Figure 4-5 shows an example of calculating the mean of a grouped frequency distribution using the incomes earned by psychology alumni in Jane Jeffers's study. Based on the midpoints

FIGURE 4-4 Calculating the Mean of the Math Test Scores from Joe's Study, Using a Frequency Table

Math Scores X (%)	Frequency f		Xf	
95	1		$95 \times 1 =$ 95	
90	2		$90 \times 2 =$ 180	
85	0		$85 \times 0 =$ 0	
80	1		$80 \times 1 =$ 80	
75	2		$75 \times 2 =$ 150	
70	3	Step 1: Multiply each X by its frequency, f.	$70 \times 3 =$ 210	Then add all of these products together: $\Sigma Xf = 1{,}320$.
65	0		$65 \times 0 =$ 0	
60	5		$60 \times 5 =$ 300	
55	3		$55 \times 3 =$ 165	
50	2		$50 \times 2 =$ 100	
45	0		$45 \times 0 =$ 0	
40	$+ 1$		$40 \times 1 = + 40$	
	$\Sigma f = 20$		$\Sigma Xf = 1{,}320$	

Step 2: Find the number of scores by adding together all the frequencies: $n = \Sigma f = 20$.

Step 3: Divide the result of Step 1, ΣXf, by the number of scores, n, found in Step 3:

$$\overline{X} = \frac{\Sigma Xf}{n} = \frac{1{,}320}{20} = 66.0\%.$$

of the grouped frequency distribution, Figure 4-5 shows that an estimate of the mean of the psychology alumni's incomes is $52,600.

We saw from the example of the scores on Joe's math test that the mean calculated from a frequency table is the same value as the mean calculated from a list of scores. This is not true for means calculated using midpoints. The mean calculated with midpoints will not always be exactly the same as the mean calculated from the scores themselves. Thus, when we calculate a mean from a grouped frequency table, the value we get is an *estimate* of what the mean would be if we calculated it from the scores themselves.

How to Interpret the Mean

The mean is one way to measure central tendency. The mean tells us where a distribution is centered on the number line. By finding the means, we know that the math test scores in Joe's study centered around 66.0 percent and that the incomes of the psychology alumni Jane surveyed centered around $52,600. The mean also enables us to compare two sets of scores. Is one set higher or lower on the number line than the other set? If we surveyed accounting alumni, would we find that their mean income was higher than psychology alumni's or lower? Because the mean shows us the center of a distribution of

FIGURE 4-5 Calculating an Estimate of the Mean of the Psychology Alumni's Incomes

Income Midpoint	Frequency *f*		(Midpoint)*f*	
$114,500	4		114,500 × 4 = 458,000	
104,500	6		104,500 × 6 = 627,000	
94,500	8		94,500 × 8 = 756,000	
84,500	12		84,500 × 12 = 1,014,000	
74,500	14		74,500 × 14 = 1,043,000	Then add all of these
64,500	21	Step 1: Multiply each	64,500 × 21 = 1,354,500	products together:
54,500	26	midpoint by its frequency, *f*.	54,500 × 26 = 1,417,000	Σ (midpoint)*f*
44,500	29		44,500 × 29 = 1,290,500	= $9,460,000.
34,500	24		34,500 × 24 = 828,000	
24,500	19		24,500 × 19 = 465,500	
14,500	13		14,500 × 13 = 188,500	
4,500	+ 4		4,500 × 4 = + 18,000	
$\Sigma f = 180$			Σ(midpoint)*f* = $9,460,000	

Step 2: Find the number of scores by adding together all the frequencies: $n = \Sigma f = 180$.

Step 3: Divide the result of Step 2, Σ(midpoint)*f*, by the number of scores, *n*:

$$\bar{X} = \frac{\Sigma(\text{midpoint})f}{n} = \frac{\$9,460,000}{180} = \$52,600.$$

scores, we can make these comparisons. If we change even one score in the distribution, the mean will change. Of course, we could use either of the other measures of central tendency to make these comparisons, too. How does the mean differ from the other two measures of central tendency, the median and the mode?

The unique characteristic of the mean is that it is the balance point of a distribution. In Figure 4-6, Set A is a group of four scores with a mean of 5.0. Imagine that we have balanced the number line on a fulcrum, represented by a triangle. Recall that a fulcrum is the point on which a line will balance when the weight on one side of the fulcrum equals the weight on the other side. Now imagine that each of the boxes representing scores has the same weight. The way the scores are arranged, the number line balances perfectly with the fulcrum at 5.0. Thus, the weight of the scores is evenly balanced around the mean of 5.0.

Now, suppose we moved two of the scores down to a value of 1, as shown in Set B in Figure 4-6. There are still four scores in the set, but now three of those scores have a value of 1. To get Set B to balance on a fulcrum, we have to move the fulcrum down to 3.0, which is the mean. The mean is the fulcrum, the balance point of a set of scores.

Why does a set of scores balance exactly at the mean? Remember when you were a kid and played on a seesaw? If you put two kids who weighed the same on the seesaw, and they sat the same distance away from the middle, the

FIGURE 4-6   The Mean as the Balance Point of a Distribution

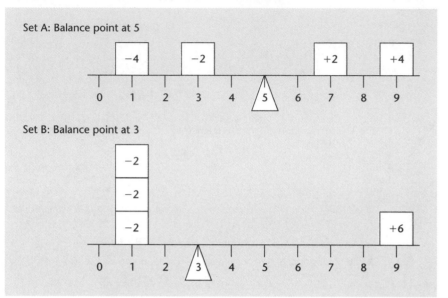

seesaw would balance. But if one of the kids moved back to the very edge of the seesaw, it would tip down toward that side. Given that the two kids were the same weight, trying to get a seesaw to balance depends on how far they sit from the center. Balancing scores on a number line is the same thing. All the scores have the same weight, and therefore, balancing scores on a number line depends entirely on how far the scores are from the center. The mean is *sensitive* to any change in the scores. This is not always true for the median, which we will examine next.

The Median

The **median** is the value on the number line for which half of the scores in the distribution have lesser values and half of the scores have greater values. It is the halfway point in a group of scores, such that half the scores are below it on the number line and half the scores are above it.

The **median** is the value on the number line that half the scores in the distribution lie below and half the scores lie above. If all the scores are arranged in order, the median is the value that will divide the distribution exactly in half, so that 50 percent of the scores have values less than the median, and 50 percent have values greater than the median.

How to Compute the Median

There are two methods for determining the median, a simplified method and a more precise method. Some statistics books, computer programs, and researchers use only the simplified method, while others use the more precise method. Both methods will be examined here, so that you can understand these statistics when you encounter them. Step-by-Step Procedure 4-2 describes both methods for finding the median.

STEP-BY-STEP PROCEDURE 4-2

Calculating the Median of a Distribution of Scores

A. Preliminary Steps

For scores in a simple list

1. Arrange the scores in order, from highest to lowest.

2. Count the number of scores in the distribution to find the number of scores *n*. Multiply *n* by .5.

3. Draw an arrow so that half of the scores (.5*n*) are below the arrow and half are above. The arrow will point between two scores if *n* is even and directly at one score if *n* is odd.

For scores in a frequency table

1. Construct a frequency table, listing both frequencies and cumulative frequencies.

2. Add up the frequencies, *f*, to find the number of scores, *n*. Multiply *n* by .5.

3. Identify the lowest score value with a cumulative frequency equal to .5*n* or greater than .5*n*.

B. Simplified Method of Finding the Median

For scores in a simple list

▶ If the arrow points directly at one score then the median is the value of that score.

▶ If the arrow points between two scores, add the values of the two scores on either side of the line together, and divide by 2 to find the median.

For scores in a frequency table

▶ If the score value identified in Step A has a cumulative frequency greater than .5*n*, then that score value is the median.

▶ If the score value identified in Step A has a cumulative frequency equal to .5*n*, then the median is the upper real limit of that score value.

C. More Precise Method of Finding the Median

Note: This method described gives a more precise value for the median. It can always be used for frequency tables. For scores in a simple list, it is used if the arrow in Step A points between two scores of the same value or directly at a score for which there are other scores with the same value. Draw a box around all of these scores with the same value.

$$\text{median} = \text{LRL} + i\left(\frac{.5n - f_b}{f_w}\right)$$

where LRL = the lower real limit of the interval containing the median
  i = interval size of the distribution
  n = number of scores in the distribution
  f_b = number of scores below the interval containing the median
  f_w = number of scores in the interval containing the median

1. Count the number of scores that have values lower than the interval containing the median to find f_b (frequency below). *For a simple list:* This is the number of scores below the box. *For a frequency table:* This is the cumulative frequency of the score value immediately below the score value identified in Step A.

2. Subtract the results of Step 1 from the results of Step A.

3. Count the number of scores in the interval containing the median to find f_w (frequency within). *For a simple list:* This is the number of scores within the box. *For a frequency table:* This is the frequency of the score value identified in Step A.

4. Divide the results of Step 2 by the results of Step 3. Round this value to one decimal place.

5. Multiply the results of Step 4 by the interval size, *i*. Remember that the interval size is equal to the unit of measurement.

6. Find the lower real limit, LRL, of the interval containing the median.

7. Add the results of Steps 5 and 6 together to find the median.

To illustrate the specified method for calculating the median, we will first use this procedure to find the median of several small groups of scores. Suppose we want to find the median of the scores below:

$$1 \quad 3 \quad 4 \quad 7 \quad 9$$

These scores are already listed in order, thus completing Step A1. Doing Step A2, we find there are five scores in the group, and multiplying 5 by .5 we get 2.5. Step A3 tells us to draw an arrow so that there are 2.5 scores above the median and 2.5 scores below the arrow. Since there are an odd number of scores in this set, the arrow will point directly at a score:

$$1 \quad 3 \quad 4 \quad 7 \quad 9$$
$$\uparrow$$

The arrow points directly at the score of 4. Step B says that if the arrow points directly at one score, then the median is the value of that score. This is the case here, and thus 4 is the median of this group of scores. Half of the scores have values lower than 4; half have values greater than 4.

Now, we will add one score to the group, so that there are now six scores:

$$1 \quad 3 \quad 4 \quad 7 \quad 8 \quad 9$$
$$\uparrow$$

Because there are an even number of scores, the arrow now points between two scores, so that there are three scores below the arrow and three above. Step B says that if the arrow points between two scores, as in this case, then the median is the value midway between those two scores. To find the midway point, we simply add 4 and 7, which equals 11, and then divide by 2, to get 5.5. The value of 5.5 is exactly halfway between the scores of 4 and 7 and thus is the median. Half of the scores have values less than 5.5; half have values greater.

In the next example, there are three scores of 4 in the middle of the group:

$$1 \quad 3 \quad \boxed{4 \quad 4 \quad 4} \quad 7 \quad 8 \quad 9$$
$$\uparrow$$

There are eight scores in this set, so the arrow is drawn with four scores on either side of the arrow. According to the simplified method, to find the median we add the two scores on either side of the arrow and divide by 2:

$$\text{median} = \frac{4 + 4}{2} = \frac{8}{2} = 4.$$

Because the two scores on either side of the arrow have the same value of 4, we can use the more precise method to find the median for this group of scores. In the example, there is a box drawn around the three scores of 4, which will help in using the more precise formula, described in Procedure 4-2.

To use the formula, we need to find several values. First, we need the lower real limit, LRL, of the interval containing the median, which in this set of scores is the interval of 4. Remember from Chapter 2 that the interval of 4 is not just the score, 4, but all the points on the number line that would round to 4. As the scores are whole numbers, the interval size, i, is 1. The LRL is one-half of the unit of measurement below 4, or 3.5. There are eight scores in the set, and so n is 8. We also need to find f_b, which represents "frequency below," the number of scores below the interval containing the median (i.e., the number of scores below the box). In the set of scores shown above, there are two scores below the box (the scores of 1 and 3), and so f_b is 2. Finally, we need to find f_w, which represents "frequency within," the number of scores in the interval containing the median (i.e., the number of scores in the box). There are three scores of 4 in the box, and so f_w is 3.

These are the values we need in order to calculate the formula given in Procedure 4-2:

$$\text{median} = \text{LRL} + i\left(\frac{.5n - f_b}{f_w}\right) = 3.5 + 1\left[\frac{.5(8) - 2}{3}\right] = 3.5 + 1\left(\frac{4 - 2}{3}\right)$$

$$= 3.5 + 1\left(\frac{2}{3}\right) = 3.5 + 1(.7) = 3.5 + .7 = 4.2.$$

Thus, the more precise value of the median of the set of eight numbers shown above is 4.2.

The medians generated by the simplified and more precise methods differ in precision. The simplified median is reported in the same unit of measurement as the scores themselves. In the example above, the scores are measured in whole numbers and the median is reported as a whole number, 4. The more precise median is reported one place more precisely than the original unit of measurement. In this case, the more precise value of the median is reported to one decimal place, 4.2. If we rounded this to a whole number, the result would be 4, the same as the simplified version. The simplified method indicates that the median is in the interval of 4; the more precise method indicates precisely where in the interval the median lies.

The examples thus far have used fairly small sets of scores. We can compute the median for larger sets, such as the scores from Joe's math anxiety study. To compute the median for larger sets of numbers, it is easier to start with the scores arranged in a frequency table. Procedure 4-2 shows how to find the median using a frequency table.

Figure 4-7 shows the frequency distribution of the scores in Joe's math-anxiety study. In finding the median from a frequency table, it is useful to compute both the frequencies and the cumulative frequencies of the scores. Figure 4-7 shows how to find the values needed for the formula shown in Procedure 4-2, as well as the steps in computing the formula. As shown in Figure 4-7, the precise value of the median of the math test scores from Joe's

FIGURE 4-7 Calculating the Median of Math Test Scores from Joe Johnson's Study

Precise Method

Percent Correct	Frequency	Cumulative Frequency	
95	1	20	The cumulative frequency of the highest score is n.
90	2	19	
85	0	17	
80	1	17	The frequency of the score in the interval containing the median is f_w.
75	2	16	
70	3	14	
65	0	11	The first score to have a cumulative frequency of $.5n$ or greater is the interval containing the median.
60	5	11	
55	3	6	
50	2	3	The cumulative frequency of the score below the interval containing the median is f_b.
45	0	1	
40	1	1	

The lower real limit, LRL, is halfway between the score in the interval containing the median and the score immediately below:

$$LRL = \frac{60 + 55}{2} = 57.5.$$

The interval size, i, is the difference between any two adjacent score values, such as 60 and 55:

$$i = 60 - 55 = 5.$$

To calculate the median, insert the values found above into the formula:

$$\text{Median} = LRL + i\left(\frac{.5n - f_b}{f_w}\right) = 57.5 + 5\left[\frac{.5(20) - 6}{5}\right] = 57.5 + 5\left(\frac{10 - 6}{5}\right)$$

$$= 57.5 + 5\left(\frac{4}{5}\right) = 57.5 + 5(.8) = 57.5 + 4 = 61.5\%.$$

Simplified Method: The score value with the lowest relative cumulative frequency over .50 is 60, and thus 60 is the simplified version of the median.

study is 61.5 percent. In the simplified method, the median is the score value, 60 percent.

We can also use Procedure 4-2 to calculate the median for a grouped frequency distribution by finding the lower real limit and interval size of the group instead of the score value. Figure 4-8 shows the frequency and cumulative frequency distributions for the psychology alumni's incomes from Jane's study. Also identified in Figure 4-8 are the values needed in the formula described in Procedure 4-2 to find the median. For Jane's survey of psychology alumni's incomes, Figure 4-8 shows that the precise value of the median income is $49,900. This shows that half of the alumni reported incomes of less than $49,900, and half reported incomes over that amount. According to the simplified method, the median is the midpoint, $54,500, of the group, $50,000–$59,000.

Just as with the mean, the median calculated from a frequency table is the same value as the median calculated from a list of scores. However, as we also found with the mean, this is not true for medians calculated using midpoints. The median calculated with midpoints will not always be exactly the same as the median calculated from the scores themselves. Thus, when we calculate a median from a grouped frequency table, the value we get is an *estimate* of what the median would be if we calculated it from the scores themselves.

How to Interpret the Median

The median, like the mean, is a measure of central tendency. It represents the center of a distribution of scores. While the mean is the balance point of a distribution, the median is the halfway point, the value that has 50 percent of the scores below it and 50 percent of the scores above it. This value is also called the 50th percentile. We will examine percentiles in Chapter 6.

To understand what the formula for the median measures, let's look at it graphically. Figure 4-9 shows two graphs of the same set of 16 numbers. Each score is represented by a box. According to the simplified method of finding the median, for this set of 16 scores the median is 5. This is shown in the first graph on Figure 4-9. The dotted line divides the set of boxes at the value of 5 on the number line. Note that when the line is set at 5, there are 9 whole boxes below the line and 7 whole boxes above it. Thus, the point, 5, on the number line does not divide the set of scores precisely in half.

As shown in Figure 4-9, the formula for the more precise method of calculating the median indicates that the median for the set of 16 scores is 4.75. The second graph in Figure 4-9 has a dotted line at 4.75. Note that this line divides the set of 16 boxes exactly in half. Eight of the boxes are below the line (seven whole boxes and four quarter boxes) and eight of the boxes are above the line (five whole boxes and four three-quarter boxes). Thus, the point on the number line that divides the set of scores precisely in half is 4.75. The simplified method of finding the median divides a set of scores approximately in half; the precise method divides every set exactly in half.

FIGURE 4-8 Calculating the Median for the Grouped Frequency Distribution of Psychology Alumni's Incomes

Precise Method

Group	Frequency	Cumulative Frequency	
$110,000–$119,000	4	180	The cumulative frequency of the highest score is *n*.
100,000–109,000	6	176	
90,000–99,000	8	170	The frequency of the score in the interval containing the median is f_w.
80,000–89,000	12	162	
70,000–79,000	14	150	
60,000–69,000	21	136	The first score to have a cumulative frequency of .50*n* or greater is the interval containing the median.
50,000–59,000	26	115	
40,000–49,000	29	89	
30,000–39,000	24	60	The cumulative frequency of the score below the interval containing the median is f_b.
20,000–29,000	19	36	
10,000–19,000	13	17	
0–9,000	4	4	

The lower real limit, LRL, is halfway between the lower stated limit of the interval containing the median and the upper stated limit of the interval immediately below:

$$\text{LRL} = \frac{50{,}000 + 49{,}000}{2} = 49{,}500.$$

The interval size, *i*, is the difference between the lower stated limits of any two adjacent groups, such as 50,000 and 40,000:

$$i = 50{,}000 - 40{,}000 = 10{,}000.$$

To calculate the median, insert the values found above into the formula:

$$\text{Median} = \text{LRL} + i\left(\frac{.5n - f_b}{f_w}\right) = \$49{,}500 + \$10{,}000\left[\frac{.5(180) - 89}{26}\right]$$

$$= \$49{,}500 + \$10{,}000\left(\frac{90 - 89}{26}\right) = \$49{,}500 + \$10{,}000\left(\frac{1}{26}\right)$$

$$= \$49{,}500 + \$10{,}000(.04) = \$49{,}500 + \$400 = \$49{,}900.$$

Simplified Method: The group with the lowest cumulative frequency over .50*n* is the group, $50,000–59,000. The midpoint of this group, $54,500, is the simplified version of the median.

FIGURE 4-9 Calculating the Median Graphically

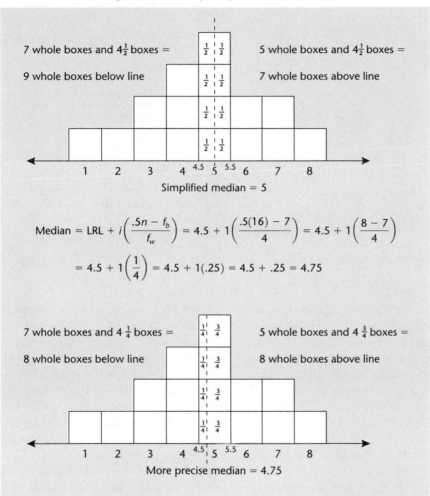

In our examination of the mean, we saw that the mean is the balance point in a distribution, the point in which the distances of scores above and below the mean are the same. Suppose we have three children, all weighing the same, on a seesaw, two children on one side and one child on the other. To get the seesaw to balance, the single child will have to sit twice as far from the center of the seesaw as the two children on the other side. If the two children are sitting three feet from the center, the single child will have to sit six feet from the center for the seesaw to balance. This is the essence of the mean. There often are more scores on one side of the mean than the other, but the sums of the distances from the mean of scores on both sides of the mean will always be equal. With the median, it is the number of scores that matter, not their distances from the center.

FIGURE 4-10   Effect of Changing Score Values on the Median

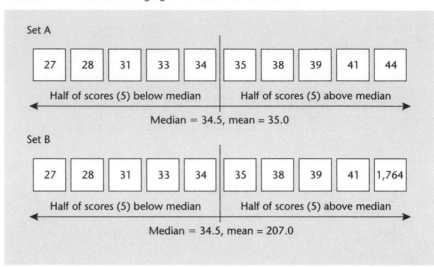

In addition, in our examination of the mean, we found that the mean is sensitive to changes in scores. If we increase the value of any one score, the mean will also increase. If we decrease the value of a score, the mean will decrease. On the other hand, the median is not always sensitive to changes in scores, particularly changes in "outlying" scores, scores at the edges of a distribution. To demonstrate, Figure 4-10 shows two sets of scores. The only difference between these two sets is the value of the highest score: In Set A, the highest score is 44, while in Set B, it is 1,764. Note that this does not affect the value of the median. For both sets, the median is 34.5. In both sets, exactly half the scores are below 34.5 and half are above, regardless of the value of extreme scores. Thus, in this case, changing the value of an outlying score did not change the value of the median because the median is not sensitive to a change in the value of an outlying score. However, the mean is sensitive to changes in the scores. For Set A, the mean is 35.0; for Set B, 207.0. Changing the value of one score changed the value of the mean dramatically.

The Mode

The **mode** is the score value that occurs most often in a distribution. In a frequency table, the mode is the score value that has the highest frequency. For example, Figure 4-4 shows that five students scored 60 on Joe's math test, the highest frequency listed in Figure 4-4. Since the score value of 60 has the highest frequency in the distribution, 60 is the mode. Note that the mode in

The **mode** is the score value that most frequently occurs in a distribution. In a grouped distribution, the mode is the most frequently occurring group in the distribution.

FIGURE 4-11 Examples of Unimodal, Bimodal, and Multimodal Distributions

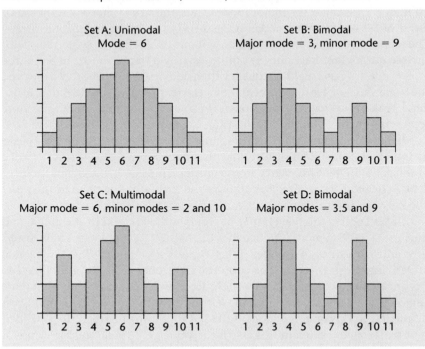

Figure 4-4 is 60, the score value, and not the frequency, 5. The mode is always a score value, not a frequency.

We can also find the mode of a grouped distribution, as shown in Figure 4-5, which shows the groups that we constructed for the scores in Jane's psychology alumni's income study. In Figure 4-5, the group with the highest frequency is \$40,000–\$49,000, which therefore is the mode of the distribution. It would also be appropriate to say that the mode of this distribution is \$44,500, the midpoint of the group that has the highest frequency.

Figure 4-11 shows graphs of four sets of scores. In Set A, the score value of 6 has the highest frequency. Thus, 6 is the mode. In Set B, the highest bar represents the score of 3, and so 3 is the mode of Set B. Notice that there is one peak in the graph of Set A, but that the graph of Set B has two peaks, one over the score value of 3 and the other over the score value of 9. Thus, the graph of Set B shows that there are two clusters of scores in the distribution. Distributions that have two clusters of scores, such as Set B, are called **bimodal** and have two peaks. Distributions in which there is only one apparent cluster of scores, and thus only one peak in the graph, are **unimodal**. Distributions in which there are more than two clusters of scores and thus more than two peaks in their graphs, such as Set C in Figure 4-11, are called **multimodal**.

A **bimodal distribution** has two clusters of scores and thus two peaks in its graph.

A **unimodal distribution** has only one apparent cluster of scores and thus only one peak in its graph. In a bimodal or multimodal distribution, the score value with the highest frequency in each cluster is a mode.

A **multimodal distribution** has more than two clusters of scores and thus more than two peaks in its graph.

The major mode is the mode(s) that have the highest frequency. Any other modes are called **minor modes.**

In a distribution such as Set B in Figure 4-11, the score value with the highest frequency is called the **major mode.** Thus, the score value of 3 is the major mode of Set B. Any other modes in the distribution are called **minor modes.** The score value of 9 in Set B is the minor mode. Note that the score value with the second highest frequency is not necessarily a minor mode. In Set B, the score value of 4 has a higher frequency than does the score value of 9. However, the score value of 4 is not the center of a cluster of scores and does not lie under a peak in the graph. Even though the graph shows that there were more scores of 4 than of 9 in the set, the score value of 4 is not a mode in Set B.

In Set C in Figure 4-11, there are three clusters of scores, with three peaks in the graph. The middle cluster has the highest peak, and the score value of 6 has the highest frequency in the cluster, and so 6 is the major mode of Set C. The score values of 2 and 10 have the highest frequencies in the other two clusters, and so 2 and 10 are minor modes in Set C.

In Set D, there are two clusters of scores and two peaks in the graph, and thus Set D has two modes. Notice that the highest frequency in both clusters is 5, and so both of the modes in Set D are major modes. The score value underlying the peak in the cluster on the right side of the graph is 9, and so 9 is one of the major modes in Set D. Notice, however, that two adjacent score values, 3 and 4, in the cluster on the left side of the graph are tied for highest frequency. In this case, the mode is the point midway between the two adjacent score values, which in this case is the value, 3.5. Therefore, the values of 3.5 and 9 are major modes in Set D. Step-by-Step Procedure 4-3 describes how to identify the mode or modes in a distribution of scores.

STEP-BY-STEP PROCEDURE 4-3

Finding the Mode in a Distribution

1. Draw a graph of the distribution of scores.

2. Identify the number of peaks in the graph (i.e., the number of times that the graph rises and falls in frequency). If there is one peak, the distribution is **unimodal.** If there are two peaks, the distribution is **bimodal.** If there are more than two peaks, the distribution is **multimodal.**

3. Identify the score value under the highest point of each peak in the graph. That score value will be a mode. If two adjacent score values are tied for the highest frequency (if the highest point of a peak in the graph covers two adjacent score values), then the mode will be the midpoint between those two score values (i.e., the real limit between the score values).

    A. If the distribution is unimodal, then the score value under the highest point in the graph is called the **mode.**

    B. If the distribution is bimodal, there will be two score values identified. If the frequencies of these two score values are equal (if the two peaks in the graph are exactly the same height), then both score values are called **modes.** However, if the frequency of one score value is greater than the frequency of the other (if one of the peaks in the graph is higher than the other), then the score value with the greater frequency is called the **major mode** and the other score value is called the **minor mode.**

    C. If the distribution is multimodal, there will be three or more score values identified. The score value with the greatest frequency is called the **major mode**; all the remaining score values identified are called **minor modes.** However, if two of the score values are tied for the greatest frequency and are not adjacent on the number line, both are called **major modes.**

Constructing a grouped frequency distribution can be a useful tool to help you interpret a set of scores meaningfully and to identify the modes. When there are a great number of minor fluctuations in frequencies in a distribution, constructing a grouped distribution will help to smooth out the graph. This will help you identify the changes in frequencies that can be meaningfully interpreted. Whether to form a grouped distribution is fundamentally a judgment call. Remember that one purpose of analyzing scores is to examine the characteristics of the variable being measured. When deciding which unit of measurement to use, select the one that will best show those characteristics.

If the unit of measurement is very precise, there can be many minor fluctuations in the frequencies of scores, and the graph of a distribution may have many peaks and valleys. For example, Figure 4-12A shows that the graph of the incomes from Jane's study of psychology alumni has 38 peaks. It would be meaningless to identify all the score values under those peaks as modes in the distribution. Figure 4-12B shows the grouped frequency distribution we

FIGURE 4-12 Comparing Graphs of Frequency Distribution and Grouped Frequency Distribution for Incomes in Table 3-11

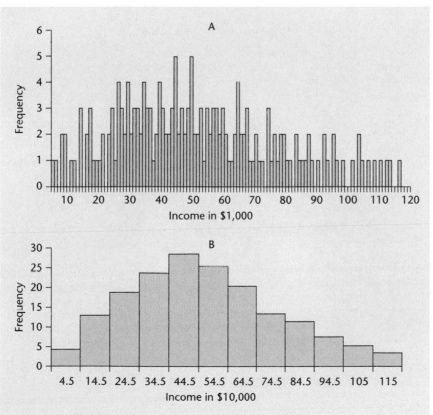

constructed in Chapter 3. The graph of the grouped distribution (in units of ten thousands) shows only one peak, with the mode at $44,500. By making the unit of measurement less precise, we smooth out the graph, collapsing the minor fluctuations in frequency, making it easier to describe the distribution.

Comparing the Mean, Median, and Mode

Each of the three measures of central tendency is a way of describing the center of a group of scores. The mean is the balance point of a distribution, with the sums of the distances of scores below the mean and above the mean being equal. The median is the halfway point of a distribution, with half of the scores having lower values than the median and half having higher values. The mode is the most frequently occurring score value in the distribution. Each of these is one way of describing the center point of a group of scores.

Even though the mean, median, and mode all describe the center point, they are not always the same value. In fact, only if the distribution is unimodal and balanced will these measures of central tendency all have the same value. In Figure 4-13, Set A is unimodal and balanced, with the mean, median,

FIGURE 4-13   Comparison of the Mean, Median, and Mode

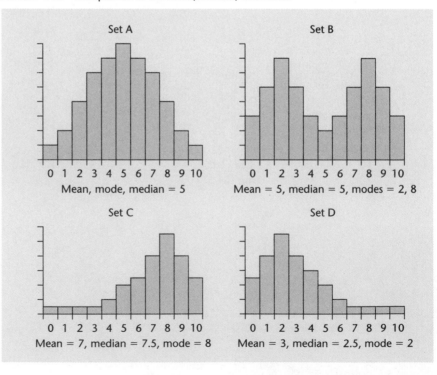

and mode all at the score value of 5. Set B is balanced, but is not unimodal. Because Set B is balanced, the mean and median are both at the score value of 5. But because there are two clusters of scores, there are two modes, at 2 and 8. Whenever a set of scores is balanced, the mean and median will be at the same score value. However, if a balanced set is not unimodal, the mode will not be at the same score value as the mean and median.

When the distribution is not balanced, the mean, median, and mode will all differ. Set C in Figure 4-13 has more scores at the higher end of the number line than at the lower end. In distributions with this shape, the mean will always be lower than the median, which in turn will be lower than the mode. Set D is the mirror image of Set C, with more scores at the lower end of the number line than at the higher end. The relationship between the mean, median, and mode in Set D is the reverse of the relationship in Set C. In Set D, the mean is higher than the median, which is higher than the mode.

When the mean, median, and mode have different values, how do we decide which one to use? In general, when the distribution is not unimodal, the best measure of central tendency is the mode. In Set B of Figure 4-13, it would be difficult to say that 5 is the most typical score. The modes, 2 and 8, are more typical. When the distribution is unimodal but not balanced, the median is the best measure of central tendency. In Jane's study of psychology alumni's incomes, the mean income was $52,600. If we found one additional alumnus who had an income of $2,000,000, the mean would increase to $63,400. When there are extreme scores that unbalance the distribution, the mean may not be the most typical score. On the other hand, the median is not sensitive to changes in outlying scores. In the psychology alumni study, the median income was $49,900, which better represents the center of the distribution. When the distribution is both unimodal and relatively balanced, the mean is the best measure of central tendency. Of course, it is appropriate to use two or all three measures of central tendency to describe a set of scores.

In addition to considering the shape of the distribution when deciding which measure of central tendency to use, it is also important to consider the scale of measurement that the scores represent. For example, it is meaningless to use the mean or median to describe nominal scores. Zip codes are a nominal scale of measurement. Recall that in a nominal scale, numbers are used only to differentiate or categorize values of the variable being measured. It would be nonsensical to calculate the mean zip code of a group of people. What information could the mean zip code tell us? However, finding the most frequent zip code, the mode, is meaningful. Thus, no matter what shape the distribution, with nominal scores use the mode.

For ordinal scores, it is appropriate to use either the median or the mode. Recall that for an ordinal scale of measurement, the order of the score values is meaningful, but the interval size does not remain equal. Players on the pro golf circuit could calculate the modal place that they finished in tournaments one year, or the median place. A player might note that her modal finish was fifth place, that she finished fifth more often than any other place. She could also note that her median finish was sixth place, that half the time she finished under sixth place and half the time over sixth place. However, it would not be meaningful to calculate the mean place that she finished. When determining the finish places in a golf tournament, the scale of measurement does not have equal intervals. The distance between first and second place may not be the same as the distance between second and third. Additionally, the distance between first and second may not be the same in one tournament as in another. Since the interval size is not constant, it is meaningless to calculate the mean of ordinal scores because the mean is based on the idea of equal intervals. So, for ordinal scores, use either the median or the mode, even if the shape of the distribution is balanced.

Finally, for interval or ratio scores, it is appropriate to use any of the measures of central tendency. Because interval and ratio scores are based on equal intervals, it is meaningful to calculate the mean. While it doesn't make sense to calculate the mean place that golfers finish in tournaments, it would be meaningful to calculate the mean number of strokes they used per game. Thus, the mean is only appropriate for interval or ratio scores with a distribution that is unimodal and relatively balanced. A summary of which statistic is appropriate, considering both the shape of the distribution and the scale of measurement, is shown in Table 4-1.

Obviously, for some distributions, there is more than one measure of central tendency that can be meaningfully used. In this case, we should use the measure that conveys the most information about the distribution of scores. In general, the mean conveys more information than the median, and in turn, the median conveys more information than the mode does.

TABLE 4-1 When to Use the Mean, Median, and Mode

Scale of Measurement	Shape of Distribution		
	Unimodal Balanced	Unimodal Unbalanced	Not Unimodal
Interval or ratio	Mean Median Mode	Median Mode	Mode
Ordinal	Median Mode	Median Mode	Mode
Nominal	Mode	Mode	Mode

CHECKING YOUR ANSWERS

1. The mean of a set of scores should be near the center. As an approximate check, add the highest and lowest score values together and divide by 2. The mean should be near this value.

2. When calculating the mean from data in a frequency table, be sure to use the appropriate formula. When the data are in a frequency table, you must multiply each score by its frequency.

3. Like the mean, the median is usually near the center of the distribution. If you add the highest and lowest score values together and divide by 2, the median usually is close to that value.

4. You should also consider the shape of the distribution when checking your answers. If the distribution is balanced (or nearly so), the mean and median will be close in value. If the distribution is skewed, the mean will be greater than the median if there is a positive skew, while the mean will be less than the median if there is a negative skew.

5. As a check on the median, count the number of scores that have values less than the median. This should be half of the scores in the set.

6. The mode is usually the easiest of the measures of central tendency to find, a fact which may lull you into carelessness. Be sure that your answer is the *score value* with the highest frequency and not the highest frequency itself. Then be sure that you have located any minor modes. The surest way to find the mode(s) is to graph the distribution. The score value under the highest point of each "hump" in the distribution is a mode. If the graph has three "humps," then there are three modes (major and minor).

7. To make sure that your answer is correct, do all the computations a second time. It may seem like extra work, but it is the surest way to find computational errors.

Σ SUMMARY

▶ Measures of central tendency are descriptive statistics that indicate the center point of a distribution of scores.

▶ The summation sign, Σ, represents the arithmetic operation of adding a group of values together. ΣX means "add all the values of X (or scores) together." It also means "the sum of all the values of X (or scores)."

▶ The left side of a statistical formula contains a symbol that represents the statistic being measured. The right side of the formula consists of the mathematical steps used to calculate the statistic.

▶ When rounding, carry the value of statistics that remain in the original unit of measurement one place more precise than the scores. Carry the value of all other statistics two decimal places.

▶ The mean is the average of a group of scores. It is the balance point of the distribution, where the sum of the distances of scores from the mean is the same for the scores below the mean as for the scores above the mean. Thus, $\Sigma(X - \mu) = 0$. The mean is sensitive to any change in the scores.

▶ The median is the value that has 50 percent of the scores below it and 50 percent of the scores above it. The simplified procedure for finding the median finds the score value that is closest to having 50 percent of the scores below it. The more precise procedure finds the value on the number line below which are exactly 50 percent of the scores.

▶ The mode is the score value that occurs most often in a distribution. A bimodal distribution has two clusters of scores, indicated by two peaks in the graph drawn of the distribution. A unimodal distribution has only one peak in its graph. Distributions with graphs having more than two peaks are called multimodal. If there is more than one peak in the graph of a distribution, the score value under the highest peak is the major mode, while the score value under the remaining peaks are all minor modes.

▶ The mean is appropriate to use only for distributions that are approximately balanced in shape and are measured on an interval or ratio scale. The median may be used for the same distributions as the mean and may also be used for distributions that are skewed and distributions that are measured on an ordinal scale. The only measure of central tendency appropriate for distributions measured on a nominal scale is the mode, which is also the most appropriate measure for bimodal and multimodal distributions.

E X E R C I S E S

Conceptual Exercises

1. Define the following terms:

measure of central tendency	bimodal
mean	multimodal
median	major mode
mode	minor mode
unimodal	

2. Assume that the following sets of scores represent populations. For each set, find the mean, rounding to the appropriate place. Then answer the questions below.

Set I	Set II	Set III	Set IV	Set V	Set VI	Set VII
0.317	3.17	31.7	317	3,170	31,700	317,000
0.312	3.12	31.2	312	3,120	31,200	312,000
0.301	3.01	30.1	301	3,010	30,100	301,000
0.297	2.97	29.7	297	2,970	29,700	297,000
0.291	2.91	29.1	291	2,910	29,100	291,000
0.284	2.84	28.4	284	2,840	28,400	284,000
0.273	2.73	27.3	273	2,730	27,300	273,000

A. In what way are these seven sets of scores the same? In what way are they different?

B. In what way are the seven means the same? In what way are they different?

C. Explain how the rules for rounding lead to these results.

3. Each of the following sets of scores represents a population. Calculate the mean for each set, and then answer the questions below.

Set I	Set II	Set III	Set IV
10	15	15	100
9	9	9	90
8	8	8	80
7	7	7	70
6	6	1	60

A. Explain why the mean of Set II is larger than the mean of Set I.

B. Explain why the mean of Set III is the same as the mean of Set I, even though the scores in Sets I and III are not exactly the same.

C. Explain why the mean of Set IV is exactly ten times the size of the mean of Set I.

4. Calculate the median for the following three sets of scores, using the precise method, and then answer the questions below.

Set I	Set II	Set III
3.1	31	310
2.9	29	290
2.9	29	290
2.8	28	280
2.7	27	270
2.7	27	270
2.7	27	270
2.5	25	250
2.4	24	240

A. Compare the values of f_b, f_w, and n for these three sets of scores. Why are these values the same for all three sets, and what effect does this have on the value of the median?

B. Compare the values of i and LRL for the three sets of scores. How do these values differ, and what effect does this have on the value of the median?

5. Calculate the median for the following four sets of scores, using the precise method, and then answer the questions below.

Set I	Set II	Set III	Set IV
3.1	3.1	3.1	3.1
2.8	2.9	2.9	2.9
2.7	2.8	2.9	2.9
2.7	2.7	2.8	2.8
2.7	2.7	2.7	2.8
2.6	2.7	2.7	2.7
2.5	2.6	2.7	2.7
2.5	2.5	2.6	2.7
2.4	2.5	2.5	2.5
2.4	2.4	2.4	2.4

A. Compare the values of i and LRL for the four sets of scores. Explain why these values are the same for all three sets and what effect this has on the values of the median.

B. Compare the values of f_b for these four sets of scores. How do these values differ for the three sets, and what effect does this have on the value of the median?

6. Draw a graph of each of the distributions below, demonstrating the characteristics listed:
   A. A distribution for which the mean, mode, and median are all the same value.
   B. A distribution in which the value of the mean is greater than the value of the median.
   C. A distribution in which the value of the mean is less than the value of the median.
   D. A distribution in which the mean and median have the same value, but the value of the mode is different.

7. Describe the characteristics of distributions for which the mean, median, and mode would each be the most appropriate measure of central tendency. Construct an example of a distribution for each measure of central tendency to illustrate your answer.

8. Describe how each measure of central tendency (the mean, median, and mode) can be considered to indicate the center of a distribution.

Computational Exercises

9. Six sets of scores are listed below. The mean of each set is also given, as it would appear as first computed on a typical calculator. Round each of these means to the appropriate place.

Set I	Set II	Set III
7	29	300
6	31	600
8	37	400
5	26	700
9	43	900
6	36	500
4	28	200
mean = 6.428571429	mean = 32.85714286	mean = 514.2857143

Set IV	Set V	Set VI
129,000	1.69	0.031
131,000	1.53	0.072
124,000	1.72	0.047
136,000	1.58	0.063
142,000	1.61	0.045
127,000	1.77	0.059
133,000	1.64	0.064
mean = 131,714.2857	mean = 1.648571429	mean = 0.05442857143

10. Two sets of scores are listed below. Use these sets to calculate the indicated sums.

X	Y
5	8
3	6
6	4
0	5
4	7

A. ΣX D. ΣY^2

B. ΣY E. $(\Sigma X)^2$

C. ΣX^2 F. $(\Sigma Y)^2$

11. Two sets of scores are listed below. Use these sets to calculate the indicated sums.

X	Y
3.2	0.47
4.1	0.79
2.6	0.84
4.8	0.91
7.5	0.38
2.7	0.29
3.9	0.16
2.7	0.22
5.4	0.35
3.7	0.65

A. ΣX D. ΣY^2

B. ΣY E. $(\Sigma X)^2$

C. ΣX^2 F. $(\Sigma Y)^2$

12. Calculate the sums indicated for the frequency distribution listed below.

X	f
10	9
9	14
8	20
7	16
6	11

A. ΣXf B. $\Sigma X^2 f$ C. $(\Sigma Xf)^2$

13. Calculate the mean for the frequency distribution in Exercise 13. Assume that the distribution is a sample.

14. The following sets of scores all represent samples. Calculate the mean for each set. **Be** sure to round appropriately.

Set I	Set II	Set III	Set IV	Set V	Set VI
5	8	40	500	3.2	0.38
3	5	10	500	4.1	0.45
6	4	60	800	2.6	0.84
0	5	40	700	4.8	0.91
4	7	30	200	7.5	0.38
	5	50	700	2.7	0.29
		10	500	3.2	0.16
			300	2.7	0.22
				5.4	0.35
					0.65

15. Calculate the median for each of the sets of scores in Exercise 14, using the simplified method.

16. Calculate the median for each of the sets of scores in Exercise 14, using the more precise method. Compare these results to the results you found for Exercise 15. Explain why any differences occurred.

17. Each of the three sets of scores below represents a sample. Calculate the mean for each set, using the procedure for a simple list of scores.

Set I: Students' IQs		Set II: Students' GPAs		Set III: Students' Incomes	
115	110	3.5	3.1	$20,000	$14,000
113	110	3.5	3.1	20,000	14,000
113	110	3.4	3.0	19,000	12,000
112	110	3.4	2.9	19,000	12,000
112	109	3.4	2.9	19,000	12,000
112	109	3.4	2.9	17,000	10,000
111	109	3.3	2.8	17,000	10,000
111	109	3.3	2.8	15,000	10,000
111	108	3.3	2.7	15,000	9,000
110	106	3.2	2.5	14,000	8,000

18. Construct a frequency distribution for each of the sets of scores shown in Exercise 17. Calculate the mean for each set, using the procedure for frequency distributions. Verify that the results are the same as found in Exercise 17.

19. Using the simplified method, find the median for each of the sets of scores in Exercise 17. Then, again using the simplified method, find the medians again, using the frequency distributions constructed in Exercise 18. Compare these results.

20. Using the more precise method, find the median for each of the sets of scores in Exercise 17. Then, again using the more precise method, find the medians again, using the frequency distributions constructed in Exercise 18. Compare these results to those found in Exercise 19.

21. The grouped frequency distribution on the right was constructed from the data shown in the frequency table on the left. These scores represent a sample. Calculate the mean of both distributions. Compare the results, and explain why the means differ.

Age	f	Age	f	Age	f
40	1	30	7	39–41	3
39	2	29	10	36–38	12
38	5	28	6	33–35	19
37	4	27	5	30–32	25
36	3	26	7	27–29	21
35	8	25	4	24–26	13
34	6	24	2	21–23	7
33	5	23	4		
32	10	22	2		
31	8	21	1		

22. Calculate the median for the frequency distribution and for the grouped frequency distribution in Exercise 21, using the simplified method. For the grouped frequency distribution, use the midpoints as the score values. Compare the results.

23. Calculate the median for the frequency distribution and for the grouped frequency distribution in Exercise 21, using the more precise method. For the grouped frequency distribution, use the midpoints as the score values. Compare the results with the medians found in Exercise 22.

24. Find the median for the following five distributions, using both the simplified method and the precise method:

    A. 4, 6, 8, 10, 12
    B. 4, 6, 7, 8, 8, 8, 10, 11
    C. 10, 30, 40, 40, 40, 40, 50, 50, 80, 90
    D. 1.3, 1.4, 1.6, 1.8, 1.8, 1.9, 2.0
    E. 0.01, 0.04, 0.04, 0.05, 0.05, 0.06, 0.06, 0.07, 0.08, 0.08, 0.09

25. Six sets of scores are listed below. Sets I, II, and III represent intelligence scores; Sets IV and V represent students' ratings of faculty on a 7-point scale (7 = excellent, 1 = very poor); and Set VI represents religious affiliation. Determine the mode(s) for each set of scores:

Set I			Set II			Set III	
IQ	f		IQ	f		IQ	f
135	1		135	1		135	5
130	3		130	5		130	3
125	5		125	8		125	1
120	6		120	8		120	2
115	8		115	6		115	4
110	7		110	4		110	8
105	5		105	3		105	6
100	2		100	2		100	2
95	1		95	1		95	1

Set IV			Set V			Set VI	
Rating	f		Rating	f		Religion	f
7	1		7	3		Baptist	1
6	3		6	6		Catholic	4
5	6		5	1		Jewish	5
4	8		4	6		Lutheran	8
3	6		3	8		Methodist	6
2	3		2	3		Presbyterian	3
1	1		1	1		Other	1

26. Consider both the shape of the distribution and the scale of measurement for each set of scores shown in Exercise 25; determine whether the mean, median, or mode is the most appropriate measure of central tendency. Justify your answer.

Measures of Variability

5

The Range

STEP-BY-STEP PROCEDURE 5-1: Calculating the Range of a Distribution

Measures of Variability Based on Deviations

Measuring the Deviation from the Mean

The Variance and Standard Deviation: Definitional Formulas

STEP-BY-STEP PROCEDURE 5-2: Calculating the Standard Deviation of a Distribution: Definitional Formula

The Variance and Standard Deviation: Computational Formulas

STEP-BY-STEP PROCEDURE 5-3: Calculating the Standard Deviation of a Distribution: Computational Formula

Some Characteristics of the Variance and Standard Deviation

Measures of Variability Based on Quartiles

Quartiles

STEP-BY-STEP PROCEDURE 5-4: Calculating the Quartiles of a Frequency Distribution

The Semi-Interquartile Range

STEP-BY-STEP PROCEDURE 5-5: Calculating the Semi-Interquartile Range

Describing a Distribution of Scores

CHECKING YOUR ANSWERS

SUMMARY

EXERCISES

Conceptual Exercises

Computational Exercises

A **measure of variability** is a number that indicates the degree to which the scores in a distribution vary from the center point.

▶ The measures of central tendency that we have examined only tell us where on the number line the center of a distribution lies. In describing a distribution, we may also want to describe how spread out the scores are around that center point. For instance, in our study of psychology alumni's incomes, we might ask if most of the alumni had incomes near the mean of $52,600 or if there was a large spread in incomes, with some alumni earning very small incomes and others, very large incomes. In statistical parlance, these are questions of **variability.** How far did the incomes vary from the center point? Did most of them vary just a little, so that they clustered around the center? Or were they more spread out?

In this chapter, we will examine several ways to measure variability. Like the measures of central tendency we explored in Chapter 4, there is no one measure of variability that is best to use in all cases. Each measure of variability serves a unique function.

The Range

The **range** is the distance that a distribution of scores covers on the number line; that is, the distance between the lower real limit of the lowest score value and the upper real limit of the highest score value.

The simplest way to describe the spread in a group of scores is to measure the distance the group covers on the number line, the **range.** Step-by-Step Procedure 5-1 describes how to find the range.

Let's find the range of the set of scores below:

4 feet   5 feet   7 feet   8 feet   10 feet

The lowest score in this set is 4 feet, and the highest score is 10 feet. Recall that the interval size, i, is the same as the unit of measurement. As these scores

---

STEP-BY-STEP PROCEDURE 5-1

Calculating the Range of a Distribution

range = highest score value − lowest score value + i

where i = the interval size

1. Identify the lowest score value and the highest score value in the distribution.
2. Subtract the lowest score value from the highest score value.
3. Add the interval size to the result of Step 2 to obtain the range.

FIGURE 5-1 Example of Calculating the Range

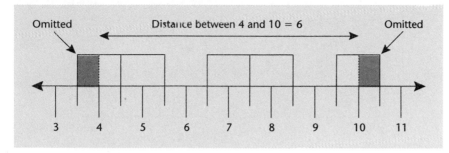

were measured in whole feet, the interval size is 1 foot. We can use these values in the formula shown in Procedure 5-1 to find the range:

$$\text{range} = \text{highest score} - \text{lowest score} + i = 10 - 4 + 1 = 7 \text{ feet.}$$

One question you might ask is, why do we need to add the interval size, *i*? Why not just subtract the lowest score from the highest? To answer this question, let's consider a picture of these five scores, as shown in Figure 5-1. These scores are measured in feet, which is a continuous variable. Remember that the score of 4 feet does not represent just a point on the number line but represents the segment from 3.5 feet up to 4.5 feet. As can be seen in Figure 5-1, if we just measured the distance between 4 feet and 10 feet, we would be omitting half a foot at each end of the range: from 3.5 feet up to 4 feet and from 10 feet to 10.5 feet. To include these segments, we need to add 1 foot, the interval size, to the distance between the highest and lowest score values.

We can use Procedure 5-1 to measure the range of incomes in Jane's study. The lowest income reported by a psychology alumnus was $6,000, and the highest income was $117,000. The incomes were measured to the nearest thousand dollars; thus, the interval size is $1,000. We can put these values in the formula to find the range:

$$\text{range} = \$117,000 - \$6,000 + \$1,000 = \$112,000.$$

The range is a simple and quick way in which to describe how spread out a distribution is. The disadvantage of the range is that it tells us nothing about what is happening to the scores in between the highest and lowest values. Are the rest of the scores clustered together, or are they spread out evenly? Knowing the distance the set of scores covers on the number line tells us nothing about how the scores are arranged within that distance.

Figure 5-2 shows two sets, each with 40 scores. Although the two sets of scores have the same range, the scores in Set B are spread out more between the endpoints than are the scores in Set A. The range doesn't show this difference in variability. Suppose these sets represent quiz scores for two classes. For both classes, the mean is 6 and the range is 11. However, a majority of the students in class A answered 5, 6, or 7 questions correctly, while the grades in

FIGURE 5-2   Comparing Two Distributions with the Same Range

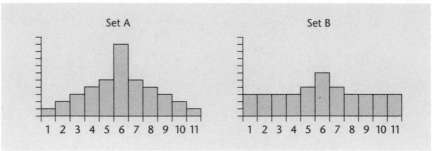

class B were more spread out. More students in class B than in class A did very well on the quiz, scoring at the upper end of the distribution. This information, while very relevant, is not revealed by the range. Thus, while the range tells us how much the highest and lowest score vary, it doesn't tell us much about the variability among the rest of the scores in the set.

Measures of Variability Based on Deviations

Measuring the Deviation from the Mean

A **deviation** is the distance that a score lies from a given point. A **deviation from the mean** is the distance that a score lies from the mean of the distribution.

If we want to measure how spread out all of the scores in a set are, we could simply measure how far each score is from the center. The distance of a score from any given point is a **deviation.** If we measure how far each score is from the mean, then we would be measuring the **deviation from the mean.** The concept of statistical deviation is comparable in ways to the concept of deviants in society. If we were to measure moral sensibility, most of us would have scores near the mean and would be considered average or the norm. There would be some people, such as serial murderer Ted Bundy, who would have low scores that deviate far below the mean and hence would be considered deviant. Of course, there would also be some people, such as the late Mother Teresa, who would have scores far above the mean and who would also be considered deviant. In this sense, a deviant is simply someone who differs from the norm or average. In the same way, statistical deviation is a measure of how far scores differ from the mean of a distribution.

You may have already heard of one method for measuring the deviation from the mean, the standard deviation. The formula for calculating the standard deviation of a population is shown below:

$$\sigma = \sqrt{\frac{\Sigma(X - \mu)^2}{N}}.$$

Do not worry right now about how to use this formula. We will go through the procedure for how to use it in the next section. It is included here because

FIGURE 5-3   Examples of Calculating the Average Absolute Deviation

	Set X			Set Y		
X	**X − μ**	**|X − μ|**	**Y**	**Y − μ**	**|Y − μ|**	
8	8 − 6 = +2	2	10	10 − 6 = +4	4	
7	7 − 6 = +1	1	8	8 − 6 = +2	2	
6	6 − 6 = 0	0	6	6 − 6 = 0	0	
5	5 − 6 = −1	1	4	4 − 6 = −2	2	
4	4 − 6 = −2	2	2	2 − 6 = −4	4	
Sum of deviations from mean	0	6		0	12	

$$\text{AAD} = \frac{\Sigma|X - \mu|}{n} = \frac{6}{5} = 1.2, \qquad \text{AAD} = \frac{\Sigma|Y - \mu|}{n} = \frac{12}{5} = 2.4$$

many students at first find it confusing. The formula does contain the term, $(X - \mu)$, which represents the distance or deviation of each score from the mean. But then, in the formula, each of these deviations is squared, the average of these squared deviations is found, and then the square root is found. What purpose do these squares and square roots serve? How do they help us measure deviation? This is the question that this section addresses.

The simplest way to measure these deviations would be to first find the deviation of each score from the mean and then to find the average of those deviations:

$$\text{average deviation} = \frac{\Sigma(X - \mu)}{N}.$$

Figure 5-3 shows the deviations from the mean for two sets of scores. Both sets have 5 scores and both have a mean of 6. To find the deviation of each score from the mean, we simply subtract the mean from the score. If we add up these deviations in order to find the average deviation, a problem becomes quickly apparent. For both sets, the sum of the deviations is zero. This is a characteristic of the mean. Because the mean is the balance point, the sum of the deviations from the mean will always be zero for any set of scores. Thus, we cannot use the sum of the deviations as a measure of how spread out the scores are because the sum will always be zero.

One solution to this difficulty is to take the absolute value of each deviation. When we find the absolute value, we drop any minus signs and make all the deviations positive. The formula for finding the average absolute deviation is

$$\text{average absolute deviation} = \frac{\Sigma|X - \mu|}{N}.$$

Figure 5-3 shows the absolute deviations for both sets of scores. We can sum these absolute deviations and find that in Set *X*, the scores deviate a total of 6 points from the mean, while the scores in Set *Y* deviate a total of 12 points. To find the average we divide each of these sums by 5, the number of scores. The average absolute deviation for Set *X* is 1.2 and for Set *Y*, 2.4. Thus, the average absolute deviation is twice as large from Set *Y* as for Set *X*, reflecting the fact that the scores in Set *Y* are twice as spread out as the scores in Set *X*.

The **average absolute deviation from the mean** is the average of the absolute distance of each score from the mean.

What we have computed is the **average absolute deviation from the mean.** This perhaps is a complicated name for a statistic, but it describes exactly what the statistic measures.

The Variance and Standard Deviation: Definitional Formulas

In the average absolute deviation, the purpose of using the absolute value is to change the negative deviations to positive values, to get around the problem that the sum of the deviations of scores from the mean is zero. However, because the average absolute deviation uses the absolute value, it cannot then be used in higher order statistical procedures. Thus, the solution to one problem causes another problem. There is another way of changing negative deviations into positive values: by squaring them. Whenever we multiply a number by itself, the result is always a positive number. If we square each deviation, the result is always positive.

Figure 5-4 shows the same two sets of scores we examined above. Instead of finding the absolute value of each deviation, in Figure 5-4 the deviations are squared. For Set *X*, the total of these squared deviations is 10, and dividing by 5, the number of scores, we find the average squared deviation is 2.0. For Set *Y*, the total of the squared deviations is 40, and dividing by 5, the number of scores in Set *Y*, the average squared deviation is also 2.0. What we have computed is the average squared deviation from the mean. Rather than use this lengthy description as a name for this statistic, it is called the **variance.**

The **variance** is the average of the squared deviations of scores from the mean.

There is one (easily resolved) difficulty with the variance. In squaring the deviations, we changed the unit of measurement. Suppose the scores in Figure 5-4 were measured in feet. The deviations are also measured in feet: 8 feet deviates 2 feet above the mean. However, the squared deviations are measured in square feet. The average of these squared deviations is still in squared feet. Thus, the variance is 2.0 squared feet for Set *X* and 8.0 squared feet for Set *Y*. We need the measure of variability to be in the original unit of measurement, in this case, in feet rather than squared feet.

The **standard deviation** is the square root of the variance and is thus the square root of the average squared deviation of scores from the mean.

The simple way to resolve this difficulty is to find the square root of the variance. Figure 5-4 shows that the square root of the variance is 1.4 feet for Set *X* and 2.8 feet for Set *Y*. We have thus returned to the original unit of measurement. This statistic, the square root of the variance, is called the **standard deviation.** Note that the formulas for the average absolute deviation and the

FIGURE 5-4 Examples of Calculating the Variance and Standard Deviation

Set X			Set Y		
X	**X − μ**	**(X − μ)²**	**Y**	**Y − μ**	**(Y − μ)²**
8	8 − 6 = +2	4	10	10 − 6 = +4	16
7	7 − 6 = +1	1	8	8 − 6 = +2	4
6	6 − 6 = 0	0	6	6 − 6 = 0	0
5	5 − 6 = −1	1	4	4 − 6 = −2	4
4	4 − 6 = −2	4	2	2 − 6 = −4	16
Sum of squared deviations	0	10		0	40

$$\text{variance} = \frac{\Sigma(X - \mu)^2}{n} = \frac{10}{5} = 2.0 \qquad \text{variance} = \frac{\Sigma(Y - \mu)^2}{n} = \frac{40}{5} = 8.0$$

$$\text{standard deviation} = \sqrt{\text{variance}} \qquad \text{standard deviation} = \sqrt{\text{variance}}$$
$$= \sqrt{2.0} = 1.4 \qquad\qquad = \sqrt{8.0} = 2.8$$

standard deviation do not give us exactly the same values. For Set X, the average absolute deviation measured the average spread as 1.2 feet, while the standard deviation measures it as 1.4 feet. The average absolute deviation and standard deviation do not measure exactly the same thing, but both are measures of the degree to which scores are spread out from the mean.

Step-by-Step Procedure 5-2 shows the way to calculate the standard deviation for scores collected from both a population and a sample. Remember that the variance is always the square of the standard deviation. By convention, we use the symbols σ^2 and σ to represent the variance and standard deviation of a population, respectively. For a sample, we use the symbols, s^2 and s.

Note that the formulas for a population and a sample are different. In the denominator, we divided by the number of scores, N, for a population, but by $n - 1$ for a sample. Remember that the reason we calculate statistics from samples is solely to estimate what the population parameters would be if we tested the entire population. The population standard deviation is a measure of how spread out the scores in the population are, and thus the sample standard deviation is an *estimate* of the spread in a population of scores.

There is a problem, though, in that scores in samples tend not to be quite as spread out as the scores in the population from which the sample was drawn. When we select a small group of subjects from a large population, the scores of the small group will tend not to be as spread out as all of the scores in the population. Thus, the amount of variability in a sample is smaller than the amount of variability in the population; that is, the sample standard deviation tends to be smaller than the population standard deviation. But we

---

Calculating the Standard Deviation
of a Distribution: Definitional Formula

For a population

For a simple list of scores   For scores listed in a frequency table

$$\sigma = \sqrt{\frac{\Sigma(X - \mu)^2}{N}} \qquad\qquad \sigma = \sqrt{\frac{\Sigma(X - \mu)^2 f}{N}}$$

where σ = the standard deviation of a population
   X = the scores, for a simple list, or score values, for a frequency table
   μ = the mean of the population
   f = the frequency of each score value in a frequency table
   N = the number of scores in the population

For a sample

For a simple list of scores   For scores listed in a frequency table

$$s = \sqrt{\frac{\Sigma(X - \bar{X})^2}{n - 1}} \qquad\qquad s = \sqrt{\frac{\Sigma(X - \bar{X})^2 f}{n - 1}}$$

where s = the standard deviation of a sample
   X = the scores, for a simple list, or score values, for a frequency table
   $\bar{X}$ = the mean of the sample
   f = the frequency of each score value in a frequency table
   n = the number of scores in the sample

1. Calculate the mean of the set of scores.

2. Subtract the mean from every score in the set of scores.

3. Square each of the deviations found in Step 2. *For a simple list:* Add up all the squares. *For a frequency table:* Multiply each squared deviation by its frequency. Then add up all the squares.

4. For a population, divide the result of Step 3 by *N*, the number of scores, to find σ^2, the population variance. For a sample, first subtract 1 from *n*, the number of scores, and then divide the result of Step 3 by $n - 1$, to find s^2, the sample variance.

5. Find the square root of the result of Step 4 to find the standard deviation, σ for a population and *s* for a sample.

---

want the sample standard deviation to be a good estimate of the population standard deviation. Statisticians have found that if we divide the sum of the squared deviations by $n - 1$, rather than *n*, the result is a good estimate of the population variance.

Some texts introduce a third form of the standard deviation, which is

$$S = \sqrt{\frac{\Sigma(X - \bar{X})^2}{n}}.$$

This formula measures the standard deviation of a sample when it is *not* to be used as an estimate of the population standard deviation, σ. The value of the standard deviation generated by this formula tends to underestimate the value of σ and thus is a biased estimator. When we examine the concept of hypothesis testing, we will need an unbiased estimator for σ, and as we will see, the value of s (which has a divisor of $n - 1$, rather than n) serves this function. So as to not overcomplicate this discussion of measures of variability, in this text we are examining only σ and s.

We can use Procedure 5-2 to find the variance and standard deviation of the students' math test scores from Joe's study. Because the students in Joe's study represent a sample rather than a population, we use the formulas for a sample. Figure 5-5 shows the steps involved in these computations and that the variance of the math test scores, s^2, is 217.37, and the standard deviation, s, is 14.7 percent.

FIGURE 5-5 Calculating the Standard Deviation of the Math Test Scores from Joe's Study, Using the Definitional Formula

Step 1: Calculate the mean, which we previously found to be 66 percent.

$(X - \bar{X})$		$(X - \bar{X})^2$	
$95 - 66 =$	29	$29^2 = 841$	
$90 - 66 =$	24	$24^2 = 576$	
$90 - 66 =$	24	$24^2 = 576$	
$80 - 66 =$	14	$14^2 = 196$	
$75 - 66 =$	9	$9^2 = 81$	
$75 - 66 =$	9	$9^2 = 81$	
$70 - 66 =$	4	$4^2 = 16$	
$70 - 66 =$	4	$4^2 = 16$	
$70 - 66 =$	4	$4^2 = 16$	
$60 - 66 =$	-6	$-6^2 = 36$	
$60 - 66 =$	-6	$-6^2 = 36$	
$60 - 66 =$	-6	$-6^2 = 36$	
$60 - 66 =$	-6	$-6^2 = 36$	
$60 - 66 =$	-6	$-6^2 = 36$	
$55 - 66 =$	-11	$-11^2 = 121$	
$55 - 66 =$	-11	$-11^2 = 121$	
$55 - 66 =$	-11	$-11^2 = 121$	
$50 - 66 =$	-16	$-16^2 = 256$	
$50 - 66 =$	-16	$-16^2 = 256$	
$40 - 66 =$	-26	$-26^2 = 676$	

Step 2: Subtract the mean from each score.

Step 3: Square each deviation and then add up these squares to find $\Sigma(X - \bar{X})^2 = 4{,}130$.

Step 4: For a sample, divide the result of Step 3 by $n - 1$ to find the variance:

$$s^2 = \frac{\Sigma(X - \bar{X}^2)}{n - 1} = \frac{4{,}130}{19} = 217.37.$$

Step 5: Calculate the square root of the result of Step 4 to find the standard deviation:

$$s = \sqrt{s^2} = \sqrt{217.37} = 14.7.$$

FIGURE 5-6   Calculating the Standard Deviation for the Incomes in Jane's Study, in Thousands of Dollars, Using the Definitional Formula

Step 1: Calculate the mean, which we already found to be $52.6 thousand.

$(midpoint - \bar{X})$

$114.5 - 52.6 =$	61.9		
$104.5 - 52.6 =$	51.9		
$94.5 - 52.6 =$	41.9		
$84.5 - 52.6 =$	31.9		
$74.5 - 52.6 =$	21.9		
$64.5 - 52.6 =$	11.9	Step 2: Subtract the	
$54.5 - 52.6 =$	1.9	mean from each score.	
$44.5 - 52.6 =$	-8.1		
$34.5 - 52.6 =$	-18.1		
$24.5 - 52.6 =$	-28.1		
$14.5 - 52.6 =$	-38.1		
$4.5 - 52.6 =$	-48.1		

$(X - \bar{X})^2$

$61.9^2 =$	$3,831.61$	
$51.9^2 =$	$2,693.61$	
$41.9^2 =$	$1,755.61$	
$31.9^2 =$	$1,017.61$	
$21.9^2 =$	479.61	
$11.9^2 =$	141.61	Step 3, first part: Square each
$1.9^2 =$	3.61	deviation from in Step 2.
$-8.1^2 =$	65.61	
$-18.1^2 =$	327.61	
$-28.1^2 =$	789.61	
$-38.1^2 =$	$1,451.61$	
$-48.1^2 =$	$2,313.61$	

$3831.61 \times 4 =$	$15,326.44$	
$2693.61 \times 6 =$	$16,161.66$	
$1755.61 \times 8 =$	$14,044.88$	
$1017.61 \times 12 =$	$12,211.32$	
$479.61 \times 14 =$	$6,714.54$	
$141.61 \times 21 =$	$2,973.81$	Step 3, second part: Multiply each of the squared deviations by its
$3.61 \times 26 =$	93.86	frequency and then add up these results: $\Sigma(X - \bar{X})^2 f = 120,419.80$.
$65.61 \times 29 =$	$1,902.69$	
$327.61 \times 24 =$	$7,862.64$	
$789.61 \times 19 =$	$15,002.59$	
$1451.61 \times 13 =$	$18,870.93$	
$2313.61 \times 4 =$	$9,254.44$	

Step 4: For a sample, divide the results of Step 4 by $n - 1$ to find the variance:

$$s^2 = \frac{\Sigma(X - \bar{X})^2 f}{n - 1} = \frac{120,419.80}{180 - 1} = \frac{120,419.80}{179} = 672.74$$

Step 5: Find the square root of the result of Step 4 to find the standard deviation:

$$s = \sqrt{s^2} = \sqrt{672.74} = \$25.9 \text{ thousand} = \$25,900.$$

Thus far, we have examined how to calculate the standard deviation from a list of scores. If the list of scores is very long, calculating the standard deviation can be very time consuming. To save time and effort, we can calculate the standard deviation of scores arranged in a frequency table. This procedure is also shown in Procedure 5-2.

We can use this procedure to estimate the standard deviation of a grouped frequency distribution by using the midpoints of the groups as the score values. Figure 5-6 shows the midpoints of the groups we constructed for the survey of psychology alumni's incomes. Those incomes were recorded to the nearest thousand dollars. The squares of numbers in the thousands are very large and cumbersome to work with. To simplify our work, the midpoints in Figure 5-6 are listed in thousands (e.g., $4,500 is listed as $4.5 thousand). This will make the computations less cumbersome. This is a legitimate conversion, as long as we remember to convert back when we are done. Figure 5-6 shows the steps in computing the variance and standard deviation of the psychology alumni's incomes, using Procedure 5-2. The variance is 672,740,000 squared dollars, and the standard deviation is $25,900.

The Variance and Standard Deviation: Computational Formulas

The formula for the variance and standard deviation that we have used so far is called the **definitional formula** because it is written the way the variance and standard deviation are defined. The variance is defined as the average of the squared deviations from the mean, and that is exactly how the variance is computed using the definitional formula. The formula based on the definition of the variance and standard deviation was introduced first here so that you would get a sense of what those statistics measure. However, they can be cumbersome to calculate with the definitional formula.

There is another set of formulas for the variance and standard deviation, called the **computational formulas,** which are simpler to compute. Step-by-Step Procedure 5-3 shows the computational formulas for the standard deviation of a population and a sample. Both the definitional and the computational formulas compute the same values. The definitional and computational formulas for the variance of a population are shown below:

$$\frac{\Sigma(X - \mu)^2}{N} = \frac{\Sigma X^2 - \dfrac{(\Sigma X)^2}{N}}{N}.$$
$$\text{definitional} \quad \text{computational}$$

The numerators (the top part) of these two formulas look very different, but they in fact compute exactly the same value. The one on the right is simpler to compute because it eliminates the necessity of first calculating the mean and then subtracting the mean from each score in the set, which can be very time consuming.

In order to show that the computational formula computes the same value as the definitional formula, let's find the standard deviation of the math test scores in Joe's study. Remember that by using the definitional formula we already found that the standard deviation was 14.7 percent. Figure 5-7 shows the steps for finding the variance and standard deviation of Joe's math test scores, using the computational formulas in Procedure 5-3. As Figure 5-7 shows, the variance is 217.4 and the standard deviation is 14.7 percent. These are the same results we found using the definitional formulas in Procedure 5-2. Thus, the computational and definitional formulas for the variance and standard deviation produce the same answers.

STEP-BY-STEP PROCEDURE 5-3

Calculating the Standard Deviation
of a Distribution: Computational Formula

For a population

For a simple list of scores

$$\sigma = \sqrt{\dfrac{\Sigma X^2 - \dfrac{(\Sigma X)^2}{N}}{N}}$$

For scores listed in a frequency table

$$\sigma = \sqrt{\dfrac{\Sigma X^2 f - \dfrac{(\Sigma X f)^2}{N}}{N}}$$

where σ = the standard deviation of a population
   X = the scores, for a simple list, or score values, for a frequency table
   f = the frequency of each score value in a frequency table
   N = the number of scores in the population

For a sample

For a simple list of scores

$$s = \sqrt{\dfrac{\Sigma X^2 - \dfrac{(\Sigma X)^2}{n}}{n - 1}}$$

For scores listed in a frequency table

$$s = \sqrt{\dfrac{\Sigma X^2 f - \dfrac{(\Sigma X f)^2}{n}}{n - 1}}$$

where s = the standard deviation of a sample
   X = the scores, for a simple list, or score values, for a frequency table
   f = the frequency of each score value in a frequency table
   n = the number of scores in the sample

1. *For a simple list:* Add up all the scores to find ΣX. *For a frequency table:* Multiply each score value by its frequency; then add all these products together to find $\Sigma X f$.

2. Square each score or score value. *For a simple list:* Add up all the squared scores to find ΣX^2. *For a frequency table:* Multiply each squared score value by its frequency, then add up these products to find $\Sigma X^2 f$.

3. Square the result of Step 1 to find $(\Sigma X)^2$ for a simple list or $(\Sigma X f)^2$ for a frequency table.

4. Divide the results of Step 3 by the number of scores in the set.

5. Subtract the results of Step 4 from the results of Step 2.

6. For a population, divide the result of Step 5 by N, the number of scores to find σ^2, the population variance. For a sample, first subtract 1 from n, the number of scores, and then divide the result of Step 5 by $n - 1$ to find s^2, the sample variance.

7. Find the square root of the result of Step 6 to find the standard deviation, σ for a population and s for a sample.

Procedure 5-3 also describes the computational formulas for the standard deviation for use with frequency distributions. We can use Procedure 5-3 to compute the standard deviation of the psychology alumni's incomes from Jane's study, replacing the score values in the formula with the group midpoints. This procedure is shown in Figure 5-8. Again, to simplify calculations,

FIGURE 5-7 Calculating the Standard Deviation for the Math Test
Scores from Joe's Study, using the Computational Formula

X		X^2	
95		$95^2 = 9{,}025$	
90		$90^2 = 8{,}100$	
90		$90^2 = 8{,}100$	
80		$80^2 = 6{,}400$	
75		$75^2 = 5{,}625$	
75		$75^2 = 5{,}625$	
70		$70^2 = 4{,}900$	
70		$70^2 = 4{,}900$	Step 2: Square
70		$70^2 = 4{,}900$	each of the scores,
60	Step 1: Add up all the	$60^2 = 3{,}600$	then add up
60	scores to find $\Sigma X = 1{,}320$.	$60^2 = 3{,}600$	all the squared
60		$60^2 = 3{,}600$	scores to find
60		$60^2 = 3{,}600$	$\Sigma X^2 = 91{,}250$.
60		$60^2 = 3{,}600$	
55		$55^2 = 3{,}025$	
55		$55^2 = 3{,}025$	
55		$55^2 = 3{,}025$	
50		$50^2 = 2{,}500$	
50		$50^2 = 2{,}500$	
40		$40^2 = 1{,}600$	
$\Sigma X = 1{,}320$		$\Sigma X^2 = 91{,}250$	

To calculate the variance and standard deviation, insert the values from Steps 1
and 2 into the formula, and carry out the calculations:

$$s^2 = \frac{\Sigma X^2 - \frac{(\Sigma X)}{n}}{n-1} = \frac{91{,}250 - \frac{1{,}320^2}{20}}{20-1} = \frac{91{,}250 - \frac{1{,}742{,}400}{20}}{19}$$

$$= \frac{91{,}250 - 87{,}120}{19} = \frac{4{,}130}{19} = 217.37$$

$$s = \sqrt{s^2} = \sqrt{217.37} = 14.7.$$

the midpoints have been listed in thousands of dollars. Just as we found with
Procedure 5-2, the formula in Procedure 5-3 shows that the variance of the
psychology alumni's incomes is 672.74 thousand squared dollars, and the
standard deviation is $25,900.

Some Characteristics of the Variance and Standard Deviation

We have already examined some of the characteristics of the variance and
standard deviation that make them effective measures of variability. One
important characteristic is that both the variance and the standard deviation can be used as elements in other statistical procedures. We will see the

FIGURE 5-8 Calculating the Standard Deviation for the Incomes in Jane's Study, in Thousands of Dollars, Using the Computational Formula

midpoint	f	(midpoint)f
114.5 × 4 =		458.0
104.5 × 6 =		627.0
94.5 × 8 =		756.0
84.5 × 12 =		1,014.0
74.5 × 14 =		1,043.0
64.5 × 21 =		1,354.5
54.5 × 26 =		1,417.0
44.5 × 29 =		1,290.5
34.5 × 24 =		828.0
24.5 × 19 =		465.5
14.5 × 13 =		188.5
4.5 × 4 =		18.0

Step 1: Multiply each score by its frequency, then add the results to find $\Sigma Xf = 9,460.0$.

$\Sigma f = 180$

midpoint	midpoint^2
$114.5^2 =$	13,110.25
$104.5^2 =$	10,920.25
$94.5^2 =$	8,930.25
$84.5^2 =$	7,140.25
$74.5^2 =$	5,550.25
$64.5^2 =$	4,160.25
$54.5^2 =$	2,970.25
$44.5^2 =$	1,980.25
$34.5^2 =$	1,190.25
$24.5^2 =$	600.25
$14.5^2 =$	210.25
$4.5^2 =$	20.25

Step 2, first part: Square each score.

(midpoint)^2	f	(midpoint)^{2}f
13,110.25 × 4 =		52,441.00
10,920.25 × 6 =		65,521.50
8,930.25 × 8 =		71,442.00
7,140.25 × 12 =		85,683.00
5,550.25 × 14 =		77,703.50
4,160.25 × 21 =		87,365.25
2,970.25 × 26 =		77,226.50
1,980.25 × 29 =		57,427.25
1,190.25 × 24 =		28,566.00
600.25 × 19 =		11,404.75
210.25 × 13 =		2,733.25
20.25 × 4 =		81.00

Step 2, second part: Multiply each squared score by its frequency, and add up the results to find $\Sigma X^2f = 617,595$.

Recall that *n* represents the number of scores. We can find the value of *n* by summing the frequencies in the frequency table. For this set, *n* is 180. To calculate the variance and standard deviation, insert the values from Steps 1 and 2 and the value of *n* into the formula, and carry out the calculations:

$$s^2 = \frac{\Sigma X^2f - \dfrac{(\Sigma Xf)}{n}}{n-1} = \frac{617,595 - \dfrac{9,460^2}{180}}{180-1} = \frac{617,595 - \dfrac{89,491,600}{180}}{179}$$

$$= \frac{617,595 - 497,175.76}{179} = \frac{120,419.44}{179} = 672.74$$

$$s = \sqrt{s^2} = \sqrt{672.74} = \$25.9 \text{ thousand} = \$25,900.$$

importance of this characteristic when we examine hypothesis testing. A second characteristic is that, because squared values are always positive, both the variance and the standard deviation are positive values. This overcomes the difficulty found in using the average deviation, that the sum of deviations from the mean is always zero.

Another characteristic is that the sum of the squared deviations from the mean, the quantity that forms the numerator in the formulas for the variance and standard deviation, is less than the sum of the squared deviations from any other value. This is one justification for preferring the standard deviation over other measures of variability. This characteristic is of particular importance to the concept of regression, which we will examine in Chapter 9.

A consequence of squaring the deviations is that a large deviation has a comparatively larger impact. Consider, for example, scores that are 1 point and 10 points from the mean. These scores would contribute 1 point and 10 points, respectively, to the sum of absolute deviations but would contribute 1 point and 100 points (10^2) to the sum of the squared deviations. Thus, the variance and standard deviation are particularly sensitive to very large deviations from the mean.

A final characteristic is that when there is absolutely no variability among the scores, both the variance and the standard deviation are zero. A set of scores can have absolutely no variability only if all of the scores have the same value, in which case the mean would also be that same value. If all of the scores have the same value as the mean, then there is absolutely no deviation among the scores. Thus, the value of zero represents the absence of variability, which makes intuitive sense.

Measures of Variability Based on Quartiles

Because the mean is used in computing the variance and standard deviation, we can use those measures of variability only with data measured on an interval or ratio scale. Furthermore, as it is not appropriate to use the mean for distributions that are seriously skewed, it would also not be appropriate to use the variance and standard deviation for those distributions. We may have occasion to measure variability in situations such as these, in which the standard deviation is not appropriate. In these cases, we could use a measure of variability based on quartiles.

Quartiles

Recall from the last chapter that the median is the point on the number line that has 50 percent of the scores below it and 50 percent of the scores above it. We can use a similar concept to measure how spread out the scores are. For example, we could find the point on the number line that has 25 percent of the scores below it and also the point that has 25 percent of the scores above it. Together with the median, these points, called **quartiles** (symbolized Q_k, where k is the quartile number), divide the range into quarters.

Figure 5-9 shows two sets of scores, divided by quartiles. Notice that both sets have eight scores and that the only difference between the two sets is the scale on which they are measured. In Set A, the values 6, 12, and 16 divide the

A **quartile** is one of three points that divide a distribution into fourths. The **first quartile,** Q_1, is the point on the number line that has 25 percent of the scores below it. The **second quartile,** Q_2, is the same as the median and has 50 percent of the scores below it. The **third quartile,** Q_3, is the point that has 75 percent of the scores below it.

FIGURE 5-9   Dividing a Set of Scores in Quarters

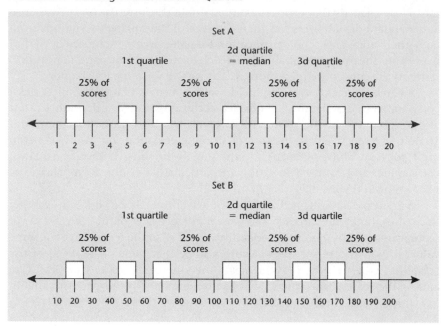

set into four groups of two scores each. In Set B, these values are 60, 120, and 160, and are the first quartile, second quartile (median), and third quartile, respectively. The first quartile is the score value below which lie 25 percent (or one-fourth) of the scores in a distribution. The second quartile is the score value below which lie 50 percent (or two-fourths) of the scores, and similarly, the third quartile is the score value below which lie 75 percent (or three-fourths) of the scores. The procedure for finding the values of quartiles is an extension of the procedure for finding the median. As with the median, we can use a simplified method or a more precise method for finding quartiles. Both these methods are shown in Step-by-Step Procedure 5-4.

We will use the simplified method described in Procedure 5-4 to find the quartiles for the incomes from Jane's study, as shown in Figure 5-10. As can be seen, 25 percent of the incomes lie below the first quartile, $34,500; 50 percent of the incomes lie below the second quartile, $54,500, which is also the median; and 75 percent of the incomes lie below the third quartile, $64,500. Note that using the simplified method, the values of the three quartiles for Jane's study are all midpoints of the grouped intervals. This is because the simplified method indicates only which interval contains a given quartile and not precisely where in that interval the quartile lies. To find the exact location in the interval, we need to use the more precise method described in Procedure 5-4.

STEP-BY-STEP PROCEDURE 5-4

Calculating the Quartiles of a Frequency Distribution

Note that these steps are followed separately for each quartile. In these steps, the value of q is .25 for the first quartile, .50 for the second quartile, and .75 for the third quartile.

A. Preliminary Steps

1. Construct a frequency table, listing both frequencies and cumulative frequencies.

2. Add up the frequencies, f, to find the number of scores, n. Multiply n by q.

3. Identify the lowest score value with a cumulative frequency equal to or greater than the value of qn found in Step A2.

B. Simplified Method of Finding Quartiles

▶ If the score value identified in Step A has a cumulative frequency greater than qn, then that score value is the specified quartile.

▶ If the score value identified in Step A has a cumulative frequency equal to qn, then the specified quartile is the upper real limit of that score value.

C. More Precise Method of Finding Quartiles

$$Q_k = \text{LRL} + i\left(\frac{qn - f_b}{f_w}\right)$$

where LRL = the lower real limit of the interval containing the specified quartile
    i = interval size of the distribution
    q = .25 for Q_1, .50 for Q_2, and .75 for Q_3
    n = number of scores in the distribution
    f_b = number of scores below the interval containing the specified quartile
    f_w = number of scores in the interval containing the specified quartile
    k = quartile number

1. Count the number of scores that have values lower than the interval containing the specified quartile to find f_b (frequency below). This is the cumulative frequency of the score value immediately below the score value identified in Step A.

2. Subtract the results of Step 1 from the results of Step A.

3. Count the number of scores in the interval containing the specified quartile to find f_w (frequency within). This is the frequency of the score value identified in Step A.

4. Divide the results of Step 2 by the results of Step 3. Round this value to one decimal place.

5. Multiply the results of Step 4 by the interval size, i. Remember that the interval size is equal to the unit of measurement.

6. Find the lower real limit (LRL) of the interval containing the specified quartile.

7. Add the results of Steps 5 and 6 together, to find the specified quartile.

FIGURE 5-10   Calculating Quartiles and the Semi-Interquartile
Range Using Simplified Method for Incomes from Jane's Study

Midpoint	Frequency	Cumulative Frequency
$114,500	4	180
104,500	6	176
94,500	8	170
84,500	12	162
74,500	14	150
64,500	21	136
54,500	26	115
44,500	29	89
34,500	24	60
24,500	19	36
14,500	13	17
4,500	4	4

For Q_3 qn is .75(180) or 135. The lowest group with a cumulative frequency of 135 or greater is the group with midpoint $64,500, which is thus Q_3.

For Q_2 qn is .50(180) or 90. The lowest group with a cumulative frequency of 90 or greater is the group with midpoint $54,500, which is thus Q_2.

For Q_1 qn is .25(180) or 45. The lowest group with a cumulative frequency of 45 or greater is the group with midpoint $34,500, which is thus Q_1.

To calculate the semi-interquartile range, insert the values for the first and third quartiles into the formula, and carry out the calculations:

$$\text{semi-interquartile range} = \frac{\text{third quartile} - \text{first quartile}}{2}$$

$$= \frac{\$64,500 - \$34,500}{2} = \frac{\$30,000}{2} = \$15,000.$$

Figure 5-11 shows the steps in using the more precise method to find the first and third quartiles for the incomes from Jane's study. The second quartile is the same as the median, which we found in Chapter 4 to be $49,900. Figure 5-11 indicates that the first quartile is $33,300, and thus 25 percent of the psychology alumni participating in Jane's study had incomes of $33,300 or less. The third quartile is $69,000, below which are 75 percent of the alumni's incomes.

The Semi-Interquartile Range

The first, second, and third quartiles indicate the three points on the number line that divide the number of scores in the set into fourths. We can use these values to construct a way of measuring how spread out the scores are. For

FIGURE 5-11 Calculating Quartiles and the Semi-Interquartile Range Using Precise Method for Incomes from Jane's Study

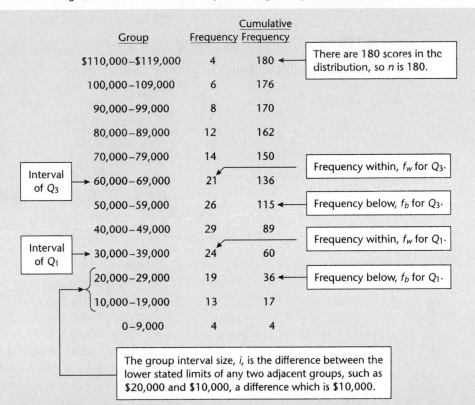

The lower real limit of the interval containing Q_1, $30,000–39,000, is $29,500. To calculate the first quartile, insert the values found above for Q_1 into the formula:

$$Q_1 = LRL + i\left(\frac{qn - f_b}{f_w}\right) = \$29,500 + \$10,000\left[\frac{.25(180) - 36}{24}\right] = \$29,500 + \$10,000\left(\frac{45 - 36}{24}\right)$$

$$= \$29,500 + \$10,000\left(\frac{9}{24}\right) = \$29,500 + \$10,000(.38) = \$29,500 + \$3,800 = \$33,300.$$

The LRL of the interval containing Q_3, $60,000–69,000, is $59,500. To calculate the third quartile, insert the values found above for Q_3 into the formula:

$$Q_3 = LRL + i\left(\frac{qn - f_b}{f_w}\right) = \$59,500 + \$10,000\left[\frac{.75(180) - 115}{21}\right] = \$59,500 + \$10,000\left(\frac{135 - 115}{21}\right)$$

$$= \$59,500 + \$10,000\left(\frac{20}{21}\right) = \$59,500 + \$10,000(.95) = \$59,500 + \$9,500 = \$69,000.$$

To calculate the semi-interquartile range, insert the values for the first and third quartiles into the formula, and carry out the calculations:

$$\text{semi-interquartile range} = \frac{\text{third quartile} - \text{first quartile}}{2}$$

$$= \frac{\$69,000 - \$33,300}{2} = \frac{\$35,700}{2} = \$17,850.$$

STEP-BY-STEP PROCEDURE 5-5

Calculating the Semi-Interquartile Range

$$Q = \frac{Q_3 - Q_1}{2}$$

where Q = the semi-interquartile range
       Q_1 = the first quartile
       Q_3 = the third quartile

1. Using Step-by-Step Procedure 5-4, find the value of the third quartile.

2. Using Step-by-Step Procedure 5-4 again, find the value of the first quartile.

3. Subtract the results of Step 2 from the results of Step 1.

4. Divide the results of Step 3 by 2 to find the semi-interquartile range.

---

example, in Set A of Figure 5-9, the distance between the first quartile and second quartile is 6, and the distance between the second and third quartiles is 4. The average of these two distances is 5. Therefore, 50 percent of the scores in Set A are within 5 points of the median. In Set B, the distance between the first and second quartiles is 60; between the second and third quartiles, 40. The average of these two distances is 50, and thus 50 percent of the scores in Set B lie within 50 points of the median.

The **semi-interquartile range** is the average of the distance between the first and second quartiles and between the second and third quartiles. It represents the distance from the median within which 50 percent of the scores in a distribution lie.

This measure is called the **semi-interquartile range** (symbolized Q). It is the distance from the median within which 50 percent of the scores in a distribution lie. The semi-interquartile range is a measure of variability. It tells us that the spread in the scores in Set B is ten times the size of the spread among Set A scores. The semi-interquartile range is useful for measuring variability when the variance and standard deviation are inappropriate. Because the scores must be listed in order to find the semi-interquartile range, it can be used only for variables in which the order of scores is meaningful and thus cannot be used with nominal data.

Step-by-Step Procedure 5-5 shows the method for calculating the semi-interquartile range. The semi-interquartile range for the incomes in Jane's study is calculated in Figure 5-10 using the simplified values of the first and third quartiles, and in Figure 5-11 using the more precise values of the quartiles. As indicated in Figure 5-11, the precise value of the semi-interquartile range for the incomes in Jane's study is $17,850.

Describing a Distribution of Scores

So far, in these first five chapters, we have examined quite a few statistical concepts. It would be helpful to pause here and review why researchers use

FIGURE 5-12 Frequency Polygon of Psychology Alumni's Incomes, Shown in Table 3-12

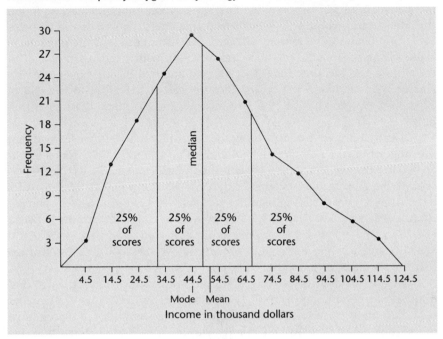

these concepts in conducting experiments. Remember that researchers conduct experiments in order to find evidence to support their arguments. Joe wanted to find evidence to support his idea that time pressure when taking math tests causes math-anxious students to score poorly. In conducting experiments, researchers observe and measure events. Joe observed and measured the accuracy of twenty students on a math test. Measurements provide the evidence that researchers use to support their arguments. If Joe simply observed the students taking the math test without measuring their performance, all he could give to support his argument would be his own impressions: "Well, the students certainly seemed less anxious when taking the math test without time limits!" Having measurements is a little more convincing!

We have examined several ways that researchers can arrange scores in tables and graphs, as well as the technique of forming grouped intervals to summarize data. The fundamental reason that researchers arrange data in tables and graphs is to present the data in a way that will be understandable to the reader and to make it clear how the measurements support the researcher's arguments. Figure 5-12 shows the incomes of psychology alumni, collected in Jane's study, reprinted from Chapter 3. This graph is much more understandable than the list of incomes from 180 psychology alumni.

We then examined several ways that researchers can describe a set of scores statistically. In Jane's study of psychology alumni's incomes, we found that the mean income was $52,600 and that the distances of the incomes above and below $52,600 were balanced. We also found that the median income (using the precise method) was $49,900, which tells us that half of the alumni had incomes under $49,900 and half had incomes over $49,900. Finally, we found that the modal income was in the grouped interval of $40,000–$49,000. More alumni had incomes in that range than any other range.

In examining ways of measuring the variability in scores, we learned that the range of incomes among psychology alumni was $112,000, from a low of $6,000 to a high of $117,000. The semi-interquartile range told us that 50 percent of the alumni had incomes within $17,850 of $49,900. The quartiles tell us that ten years after graduation, a psychology alumni has a 25 percent chance of earning less than $33,300, a 25 percent chance of earning between $33,300 and $49,900, a 25 percent chance of earning between $49,900 and $69,000, and a 25 percent chance of earning over $69,000. We also learned that the standard deviation was $25,900.

These statistics provide us a great deal of information about the distribution of incomes among psychology alumni. It is unlikely that a researcher would use all of these various statistics to describe a single set of scores. Most of the time, researchers will select one measure of central tendency and one measure of variability to describe a distribution. We have analyzed the incomes from Jane's study with all of these statistical techniques to show you the variety of ways we have to describe a set of scores and the amount of information that we can get from those statistics.

CHECKING YOUR ANSWERS

1. When computing statistics, it always helps to have some idea of what constitutes a reasonable answer. For small sets of data, both the standard deviation and the semi-interquartile range are usually somewhere near one-fourth of the range. Subtract the lowest score value from the highest score value, and then divide by 4. The standard deviation and the semi-interquartile range should be somewhere near this value. If the distribution has a large number of scores and is approximately bell-shaped, then the standard deviation will be close to one-sixth of the range. Thus, if you multiply the standard deviation by 6, the result should be close to the range. Remember that these checks are only approximate!

2. As a check on the quartile range and semi-interquartile range, count the number of scores between the first quartile and the median and the number of scores between the median and the third quartile. Each of these values should represent exactly one-fourth of the scores in the set. To check the semi-interquartile range, subtract the median from the third quartile, and then, separately, subtract the first quartile from the median. The semi-interquartile range should be between these two values.

3. When computing the standard deviation, if you get a negative number under the radical sign (the square root sign), it is certain that you made an error. The variance and the standard deviation are *never* negative numbers. One possible source of the error is that you may have mixed up ΣX^2 and $(\Sigma X)^2$. Remember that ΣX^2 means to square the scores first and then sum, while $(\Sigma X)^2$ means to sum up the scores first and then square.

4. When calculating the standard deviation from data in a frequency table, be sure to use the appropriate formula (Step-by-Step Procedure 5-2 or 5-3). When the data are in a frequency table, you must multiply each score by its frequency. If you simply add up the score values without first multiplying by the frequency, the answer you get will *not* be the standard deviation.

5. The more times you calculate these measures of dispersion for various sets of data, the more you will get a feel for what is an appropriate answer. And remember, the best way to check your computations is to do them over a second time.

Σ S U M M A R Y

▶ Measures of variability are numerical summaries that indicate the degree to which the scores in a distribution vary.

▶ The range is the distance that a distribution of scores covers on the number line. While it is easy and convenient to use, it reflects only the degree to which the end points of the distribution differ and gives no information about the variation among the scores between these end points.

▶ A deviation is the distance a score lies from a given point. A deviation from the mean is the distance that a scores lies from the mean.

▶ The average deviation of a set of scores from the mean of the set is always 0 because the sum of the deviations of scores from the mean is 0.

▶ The average absolute deviation is an average of the absolute distances of scores from the mean.

▶ The variance is a measure of deviation based on finding the average of the squared deviations of scores from the mean. The standard deviation is the square root of the variance.

▶ The definitional formula for the standard deviation is expressed in terms of the squared deviations from the mean. The computational formula does not require the computation of the deviation of individual scores from the mean and, as a consequence, is more convenient to use for large groups of scores.

▶ There are several characteristics that give the variance and standard deviation an advantage in use. The sum of the squared deviations from the mean, which is the basis of both the variance and standard deviation, is less than the sum of the squared deviations from any other value. Large deviations have a comparatively greater impact on the variance and standard deviation than do small deviations, which makes both measures very sensitive to large deviations from the mean. Finally, the values of both the variance and standard deviation are zero when there is absolutely no variation among the scores.

▶ Because the variance and standard deviation are based upon deviations of scores from the mean, these measures of variability should be used only when it is appropriate to use the mean, which is when the scores are measured on an interval or ratio scale of measurement and when the distribution is approximately balanced in shape.

▶ Quartiles are the three values on the number line that divide a distribution into fourths. The first quartile is the value that has 25 percent of the scores less than it. The second quartile is the value that has 50 percent of the scores less than it. The second quartile is equal to the median. The third quartile is the value that has 75 percent of the scores less than it.

▶ The semi-interquartile range is a measure suitable for measuring variability in distributions of scores measured on an ordinal scale or that are skewed. The semi-interquartile range is one-half the distance between the first and third quartiles.

E X E R C I S E S

Conceptual Exercises

1. Define the following terms:

measure of variability	quartile
range	first quartile
deviation	second quartile
average absolute deviation	third quartile
variance	semi-interquartile range
standard deviation	

2. Calculate the range of each of the following sets of scores. What is the similarity among these seven ranges? What is the difference? Why do these results occur?

Set I	Set II	Set III	Set IV	Set V	Set VI	Set VII
0.317	3.17	31.7	317	3,170	31,700	317,000
0.312	3.12	31.2	312	3,120	31,200	312,000
0.301	3.01	30.1	301	3,010	30,100	301,000
0.297	2.97	29.7	297	2,970	29,700	297,000
0.291	2.91	29.1	291	2,910	29,100	291,000
0.284	2.84	28.4	284	2,840	28,400	284,000
0.273	2.73	27.3	273	2,730	27,300	273,000

3. Calculate the range and the average absolute deviation for each of the following three sets of scores, which represent samples. Explain why the range is the same value for all three sets, but the average absolute deviation differs.

Set I: X	Set II: X	Set III: X
36	36	36
20	29	35
19	22	34
18	15	3
17	8	2
1	1	1

4. Calculate the average deviation and the average absolute deviation for each of the three sets of scores below, which represent samples. Explain why the average deviation always equals zero and why the average absolute deviation does not.

Set I	Set II	Set III
9	9	9
8	8	9
7	7	9
6	6	9
5	2	8
4	1	4
3	1	3
2	1	2
1	1	1

5. Calculate the average absolute deviation for each of the following sets of scores:

Set I	Set II	Set III
7	14	70
6	12	60
5	10	50
4	8	40
3	6	30
2	4	20
1	2	10

   A. One point separates each score in Set I, while two points separate each score in Set II. How is this reflected in the average absolute deviations of the two sets of scores?

   B. While one point separates each score in Set I, ten points separate each score in Set III. How is this reflected in the average absolute deviations of the two sets of scores?

6. Assume that the three sets of scores shown in Exercise 5 are populations (albeit very small populations). Calculate the standard deviation of each distribution.

   A. One point separates each score in Set I, while two points separate each score in Set II. How is this reflected in the standard deviations of the two sets of scores?

   B. While one point separates each score in Set I, ten points separate each score in Set III. How is this reflected in the standard deviations of the two sets of scores?

   C. Compare the value found for the standard deviation of each sample with the value of the average absolute deviation found in Exercise 5. Why do these values differ?

7. Describe the strengths and weaknesses of the range, average absolute deviation, and standard deviation.

8. Describe the characteristics of distributions for which the semi-interquartile range is more appropriate than the standard deviation.

9. Buy a bag of regular M&Ms. Assign number values to each color as follows: brown = 1, red = 2, orange = 3, yellow = 4, green = 5, blue = 6.

   A. Count the number of each color M&M in the bag and construct a frequency table, listing the assigned numbers as the score values. For example, if there are twelve blue M&Ms, then in the frequency table, for the score value 6, the value of f is 12. Compute the standard deviation of this distribution using one of the formulas for a population.

B. Draw a sample of ten M&Ms and list their colors with the assigned number value. Compute the standard deviation of these ten score values, using one of the formulas for a sample. Return the ten M&Ms to the bag. Repeat this process five times, each time returning the sample to the bag, so that you have calculated the standard deviation for six samples.

C. Compare the standard deviations of the six samples to the standard deviation of the population. How close are the sample standard deviations as estimates of the population standard deviation?

Computational Exercises

10. Calculate the range of the following sets of scores, which represent samples:

Set I	Set II	Set II
7	29	300
6	31	600
8	37	400
5	26	700
9	43	900
6	36	500
4	28	200

Set IV	Set V	Set VI
129,000	1.69	0.031
131,000	1.53	0.072
124,000	1.72	0.047
136,000	1.58	0.063
142,000	1.61	0.045
127,000	1.77	0.059
133,000	1.64	0.064

11. Calculate the range of each of the following sets of scores, which represent samples:

Set I: Students' IQs		Set II: Students' GPAs		Set III: Students' Incomes	
115	110	3.5	3.1	$20,000	$14,000
113	110	3.5	3.1	20,000	14,000
113	110	3.4	3.0	19,000	12,000
112	110	3.4	2.9	19,000	12,000
112	109	3.4	2.9	19,000	12,000
112	109	3.4	2.9	17,000	10,000
111	109	3.3	2.8	17,000	10,000
111	109	3.3	2.8	15,000	10,000
111	108	3.3	2.7	15,000	9,000
110	106	3.2	2.5	14,000	8,000

12. Use the three sets of scores from Exercise 11 to complete the following:
    A. Calculate the standard deviation of each set, using the definitional formula for scores arranged in a simple list.
    B. Calculate the standard deviation of each set, using the computational formula for scores arranged in a simple list. Compare the results to the values found with the definitional formula.

13. Construct a frequency table for each of the sets of scores in Exercise 11. Use these frequency tables to complete the following:
    A. Calculate the standard deviation of each set, using the definitional formula for scores in a frequency table. Compare the results to the values found in Exercise 12.
    B. Calculate the standard deviation of each set, using the computational formula for scores arranged in a frequency table. Compare the results to the values found with the definitional formula and with the values found in Exercise 12.

14. The following sets of scores all represent samples.

Set I	Set II	Set III	Set IV	Set V	Set VI
5	8	40	500	3.2	0.38
3	5	10	500	4.1	0.45
6	4	60	800	2.6	0.84
0	5	40	700	4.8	0.91
4	7	30	200	7.5	0.38
	5	50	700	2.7	0.29
		10	500	3.2	0.16
			300	2.7	0.22
				5.4	0.35
					0.65

A. Calculate the standard deviation of each sample, using the definitional formula.
B. Calculate the standard deviation of each sample, using the computational formula. Compare these results with the values found using the definitional formula.

15. The following sets of scores represent intelligence scores from three different populations.

Set I		Set II		Set III	
IQ	f	IQ	f	IQ	f
135	1	135	1	135	5
130	3	130	5	130	3
125	5	125	8	125	1
120	6	120	7	120	2
115	8	115	6	115	4
110	7	110	4	110	8
105	5	105	3	105	6
100	2	100	2	100	2
95	1	95	1	95	1

A. Calculate the standard deviation of each distribution, using the definitional formula.
B. Calculate the standard deviation of each distribution, using the computational formula. Compare these results to the results found in Part A.

16. The following is a distribution of the ages of a population of nontraditional students:

Age	f	Age	f
40	1	30	7
39	2	29	10
38	5	28	6
37	4	27	5
36	3	26	7
35	8	25	4
34	6	24	2
33	5	23	4
32	10	22	2
31	8	21	1

A. Calculate the standard deviation of the population, using first the definitional formula and then the computational formula.

B. Calculate the first, second, and third quartiles for the distribution, using the simplified method. Then calculate the semi-interquartile range.

C. Calculate the first, second, and third quartiles for the distribution, using the more precise method. Then calculate the semi-interquartile range. Compare these results to those found in Part B.

17. The distribution below represents the intelligence test scores of a population of students:

IQ	f
135–139	5
130–134	7
125–129	9
120–124	13
115–119	15
110–114	22
105–109	27
100–104	33
95–99	29
90–94	25
85–89	21
80–84	10
75–79	4

A. Calculate the standard deviation of the population, using first the definitional formula and then the computational formula.

B. Calculate the first, second, and third quartiles for the distribution, using the simplified method. Then calculate the semi-interquartile range

C. Calculate the first, second, and third quartiles for the distribution, using the more precise method. Then calculate the semi-interquartile range. Compare these results to those found in Part B.

Measures of Relative Standing

6

Standard Scores

Transformed Scores and the Effect of Changing the Unit of Measurement

STEP-BY-STEP PROCEDURE 6-1: Effect on the Mean of Changing Scores by a Constant

STEP-BY-STEP PROCEDURE 6-2: Effect on the Standard Deviation of Changing Scores by a Constant

Converting Scores to Standard Scores

STEP-BY-STEP PROCEDURE 6-3: Converting Scores to Standard Scores

The Mean and Standard Deviation of Standard Scores

Standard Scores as Measures of Relative Standing

Converting Standard Scores Back to the Original Unit of Measurement

STEP-BY-STEP PROCEDURE 6-4: Converting Standard Scores to Scores in the Original Unit of Measurement

Using Standard Scores in Psychological Testing

To Use or Not to Use Standard Scores: What's Appropriate?

Percentiles

The Simplified Method for Finding Percentiles

STEP-BY-STEP PROCEDURE 6-5: Calculating Percentiles and Percentile Ranks: The Simplified Method

The Simplified Method for Finding Percentile Ranks

The Precise Method of Finding Percentiles

STEP-BY-STEP PROCEDURE 6-6: Calculating Percentiles and Percentile Ranks: The More Precise Method

The Precise Method of Finding Percentile Ranks

Percentiles as a Way of Comparing Relative Standing

CHECKING YOUR ANSWERS

SUMMARY

EXERCISES

Conceptual Exercises

Computational Exercises

▶ All of the statistical techniques that we have examined thus far are used to describe the characteristics of a single distribution of scores. There are many situations in which we also might want to describe where a particular score lies in a given distribution. The statistical techniques that enable us to do this are called **measures of relative standing.** The relative standing of a particular score is a measure of where that score lies compared to the other scores in the distribution.

A **measure of relative standing** is a transformation of a distribution of scores resulting in score values that indicate the location of each score relative to the other scores in the distribution.

Transformed scores are scores that have been changed by one or more mathematical operations from the original measurement scale to a new scale that has a different center point or degree of variability, or both.

Raw scores are scores expressed in the measurement scale that was originally used to measure and record the scores.

Suppose you get a grade of 34 correct on a 40-question history test. How did you do compared to the other students in the class? Was your grade of 34 correct at the top of the distribution, or was it near the center or the bottom? In addition, you might ask how your score on this history test compared to tests you have taken in other classes. Is your history grade the same as the grades in your other classes, or is it higher or lower than those other grades? These are all questions of relative standing.

Measures of relative standing are **transformed scores,** scores that have been converted from the original measurement scale to a new scale. Scores that are expressed in the scale in which they were originally measured in an experiment are called **raw scores.** In Joe Johnson's experiment, the students' performance was originally measured as the number of test questions answered correctly, and thus these raw scores were "number correct." Joe converted or transformed these raw scores from "number correct" to "percent correct." To transform scores, the same mathematical operation is performed on every score in the distribution. To transform scores from "number correct" to "percent correct," Joe divided each student's raw score by the total number of questions on the math test.

Scores expressed as percentages, such as "percent correct," measure relative frequency. We examined relative frequency in Chapter 2 in the context of constructing frequency tables. The scale, "percent correct," does not tell us the *actual* number of questions a student answered correctly but rather tells us the number answered correctly *relative to* the total number of questions in the test. Measures of relative standing are analogous to measures of relative frequency, such as "percent correct." Scores expressed as relative standing tell us the location (or standing) of a particular score *relative to* the other scores in the distribution. In this chapter, we examine two measures of relative standing: standard scores and percentiles.

Standard Scores

Transformed Scores and the Effect of Changing the Unit of Measurement

Before examining the concept of standard scores, we are going to take a brief detour and examine the effects of changing the unit of measurement. Looking at what happens when we change the unit in which scores are measured will help explain the concept of standard scores.

In Chapter 2, we examined the concept of measurement and saw that researchers frequently have a choice of unit with which to measure scores. For example, we could decide to measure people's heights in feet, in inches, in centimeters, or any other unit that measures the height of objects. If we decided to measure height in centimeters, we might later decide to convert those measurements to inches. Table 6-1 shows the heights of a sample of nine students selected from the Peel Junior High cricket team, originally measured in centimeters.

When we do the same mathematical operation on every score in a distribution, we are changing the scores by a constant. Table 6-1 shows the cricket players' heights converted from centimeters to inches, accomplished by dividing each player's height in centimeters by the constant, 2.54. Note that the scores remain in the same order. Multiplying or dividing every score in a distribution by a constant (other than zero) does not change the order of the scores. Similarly, adding or subtracting a constant to every score in a distribution leaves the order unchanged. Table 6-1 shows the heights of the nine cricket team members, all wearing two-inch shoes. We converted the heights

TABLE 6-1 Converting Scores

Student	Height (cm)	Height (inches)	Height in Inches with 2-Inch Heels
Aloysius	190	75	77
Brian	186	73	75
Carl	182	72	74
David	180	71	73
Ernie	170	67	69
Fred	160	63	65
Gertrude	158	62	64
Harry	154	61	63
Igor	150	59	61
$\bar{X}$	170	67	69
s	15	5.9	5.9

by adding two inches to each score but again this did not change the order of the scores.

When we change every score in a set by adding, subtracting, multiplying by or dividing by a constant, we are simply changing the unit of measurement. Dividing the heights in centimeters by 2.54 changes the unit of measurement from centimeters to inches. As long as we change every score in the set in the same way, the order of the scores does not change. Igor remains the shortest whether his height is measured in centimeters, inches, or feet. Note that for this to hold true, we must use the same unit of measurement for all the scores. If we measure Carl as 182 cm tall and David as 71 inches tall, it is difficult to compare their heights and decide who is taller!

In addition to the cricket players' heights, Table 6-1 lists the means $(\overline{X})$ and standard deviations (s) of those heights for each unit of measurement we have examined. (Note that since these nine students are a sample from the cricket team, the standard deviation was calculated using the formula for a sample.) When the heights are measured in centimeters, the mean was 170 cm, with a standard deviation of 15 cm:

$$\overline{X}_{cm} = \frac{\Sigma X}{n} = \frac{1,530}{9} = 170 \text{ cm}$$

$$s_{cm} = \sqrt{\frac{\Sigma X^2 - \frac{(\Sigma X)^2}{n}}{n-1}} = \sqrt{\frac{261,900 - \frac{1,530^2}{9}}{9-1}} = 15 \text{ cm.}$$

We can use the same formulas to calculate the mean and standard deviation of the cricket players' heights measured in inches, as shown below:

$$\overline{X}_{inches} = \frac{\Sigma X}{n} = \frac{603}{9} = 67 \text{ inches}$$

$$s_{inches} = \sqrt{\frac{\Sigma X^2 - \frac{(\Sigma X)^2}{n}}{n-1}} = \sqrt{\frac{40,683 - \frac{603^2}{9}}{9-1}} = 5.9 \text{ inches.}$$

Of course, using these formulas to find the mean and standard deviation every time that we change the unit of measurement can be a time-consuming process! There is an easier method for finding the mean and standard deviation when the unit of measurement is changed. To convert heights in centimeters to inches, we divided each student's height in centimeters by 2.54. In the same way, we can find the mean and standard deviation in inches by dividing the mean and standard deviation in centimeters by 2.54, as shown below:

$$\overline{X}_{inches} = \overline{X}_{cm} \div 2.54 = 170 \text{ cm} \div 2.54 = 67 \text{ inches}$$

$$s_{inches} = s_{cm} \div 2.54 = 15 \text{ cm} \div 2.54 = 5.9 \text{ inches.}$$

STEP-BY-STEP PROCEDURE 6-1

Effect on the Mean of Changing Scores by a Constant

Adding a constant: If every score in a distribution is converted by adding a constant, the converted mean is equal to the mean of the original scores plus the constant:

$$\mu_{X+C} = \mu_X + C.$$

Subtracting a constant: If every score in a distribution is converted by subtracting a constant, the converted mean is equal to the mean of the original scores minus the constant:

$$\mu_{X-C} = \mu_X - C.$$

Multiplying by a constant: If every score in a distribution is converted by multiplying by a constant, the converted mean is equal to the mean of the original scores multiplied by the constant:

$$\mu_{CX} = C\mu_X.$$

Dividing by a constant: If every score in a distribution is converted by dividing by a constant, the converted mean is equal to the mean of the original scores divided by the constant:

$$\mu_{X/C} = \frac{\mu_X}{C}.$$

These are the same values we found using the formulas for the mean and standard deviation. Thus, we need to calculate the mean and standard deviation from the actual scores only once. If we then change the unit of measurement, we can convert the mean and standard deviation by using the same procedure used to convert the scores themselves. Step-by-Step Procedure 6-1 shows the formulas for converting the mean when the unit of measurement is changed by adding, subtracting, multiplying by, or dividing by a constant.

When we change the unit of measurement, we are simply moving the scores up or down on the number line. For instance, when, measuring in inches, we changed from measuring the cricket players' heights bare-footed to measuring them in 2-inch heels, the entire set of heights moved 2 inches up on the number line, as shown in Figure 6-1. The mean also moved 2 inches up on the number line, from 67 inches when the students were bare-footed to 69 inches when they wore 2-inch heels. In the same way, when we subtract a constant from every score, the entire set moves down on the number line, and the mean moves down as well. Multiplying or dividing every score in a set similarly moves the entire set on the number line. Thus, when we convert scores, we are shifting the set of scores on the number line, and the mean moves as well.

FIGURE 6-1   The Effect of Adding a Constant on the Mean and Standard Deviation

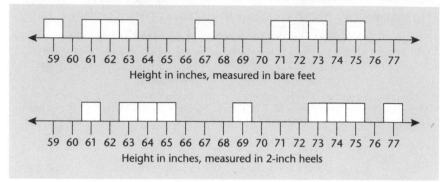

Step-by-Step Procedure 6-2 shows the formulas for converting the standard deviation when the unit of measurement is changed by adding, subtracting, multiplying by, or dividing by a constant. Note that when we change the unit of measurement by adding or subtracting a constant, the standard deviation does not change. In Figure 6-1, we can see that measuring the cricket players in 2-inch heels moved the entire set of scores up 2 inches on the number line but did not change how spread out the heights were. The standard deviation of the cricket players' heights is 5.9 inches, whether the cricket players were measured in bare feet or in 2-inch heels.

However, changing the unit of measurement by multiplying or dividing by a constant does change the standard deviation. Multiplying every score in a distribution by a constant increases the standard deviation by that constant. In a similar fashion, dividing every score in a distribution by a constant decreases the standard deviation by that constant. The standard deviation of the cricket players' heights is 15 cm or 5.9 inches. Of course, this is actually the same distance. What is changed is the number of measurement units, from 15 for cm to 5.9 for inches.

In summary, whenever each of the scores in a distribution is changed by a constant, the mean is changed in the same way by the constant. The standard deviation is also changed whenever each score is either multiplied by or divided by a constant. However, the standard deviation does not change when a constant is either added to or subtracted from each score. Finally, if each score in the set is changed in the same way by a constant, the order of the scores does not change. The highest score remains highest; the lowest score remains lowest.

Converting Scores to Standard Scores

Because changing a score by adding, subtracting, multiplying, or dividing by a constant does not change the order of the scores, we can use these operations to develop a measure of relative standing. First, we can convert the

---

STEP-BY-STEP PROCEDURE 6-2

Effect on the Standard Deviation of Changing Scores by a Constant

Adding a constant: If every score in a distribution is converted by adding a constant, the converted standard deviation is equal to the standard deviation of the original scores:

$$\sigma_{X+C} = \sigma_X.$$

Subtracting a constant: If every score in a distribution is converted by subtracting a constant, the converted standard deviation is equal to the standard deviation of the original scores:

$$\sigma_{X-C} = \sigma_X.$$

Multiplying by a constant: If every score in a distribution is converted by multiplying by a constant, the converted standard deviation is equal to the standard deviation of the original scores multiplied by the constant:

$$\sigma_{CX} = C\sigma_X.$$

Dividing by a constant: If every score in a distribution is converted by dividing by a constant, the converted standard deviation is equal to the standard deviation of the original scores divided by the constant:

$$\sigma_{X/C} = \frac{\sigma_X}{C}.$$

---

scores by subtracting the mean from every score to find the deviation of each score from the mean. Table 6-2 shows the heights in centimeters of the nine cricket players again. The second column in Table 6-2 shows the results of subtracting the mean, 170 cm, from each student's height. This result is the deviation of the students' heights from the mean. (Recall that we encountered the concept of deviations from the mean in Chapter 5, when examining the concept of variance and standard deviation.) Aloysius is 20 cm taller than the mean (deviation = 20), while Igor is 20 cm shorter than the mean (deviation = −20). Note that subtracting the mean from each student's height does not change the order of heights: Aloysius is still tallest; he has the greatest deviation above the mean. And Igor is still shortest, with the greatest deviation below the mean. The deviation of Ernie's height from the mean is 0, which shows that Ernie's height is equal to the mean.

Converting scores to deviations from the mean gives us a measure of where the scores stand, relative to other scores in the same distribution. A negative deviation indicates that the score is lower than the mean, and a positive deviation indicates the score is higher than the mean. Thus, we know that Aloysius's height, which has a positive deviation, +20 cm, is taller than average, and Igor, who has a negative deviation of −20 cm, is shorter than

TABLE 6-2 Converting Scores to Standard Scores

Student	Height (cm)	$X - \mu$	$(X - \mu)/\sigma$
Aloysius	190	20	1.33
Brian	186	16	1.07
Carl	182	12	0.80
David	180	10	0.67
Ernie	170	0	0.00
Fred	160	−10	−0.67
Gertrude	158	−12	−0.80
Harry	154	−16	−1.07
Igor	150	−20	−1.33
$\bar{X}$	170	0	0
s	15	15	1.00

average. In addition, we can tell that Aloysius, whose height is 20 cm above the mean, is certainly taller than David, whose height is only 10 cm above the mean. We do not even have to know what their actual heights are. We can make this comparison directly from the information provided by the deviations from the mean.

Deviations from the mean enable us to compare the relative standing of scores *within* a distribution, as the examples just discussed show. However, they do not give us a way to compare the relative standing of scores *between* two distributions measured on different scales. This is because the deviations from the mean are still expressed in the scores' original unit of measurement. For example, Aloysius's height deviates from the mean by 20 cm, while Brian's deviates by 6 inches. Which one is farther from the mean? We cannot tell, because one deviation is measured in centimeters and the other in inches.

In order to make comparisons between two sets of scores, the two sets have to be on the same scale of measurement. It would be simple to compare Aloysius's and Brian's heights just by measuring either both in centimeters or both in inches. However, comparing scores from two different distributions is not always this simple, because it frequently is not possible to convert one distribution to the scale of measurement used for the other distribution. Consider, for example, the case of comparing the cricket players' heights to their IQ scores. We can't measure heights in IQ points or IQ scores in centimeters or inches. The solution to this difficulty is to convert both scales—IQ scores and heights—to a third scale, using the standard deviation as a measurement unit. While it may seem odd to think of a standard deviation as a unit of measurement, in the previous section we saw that we can transform a set of scores with any unit of measurement as long as we change every score in the same way.

FIGURE 6-2 The Standard Deviation as a Unit of Measurement

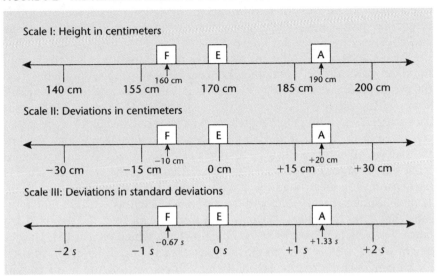

Figure 6-2 shows three scales of measurement used to measure the heights of the cricket players. Three of the cricket players are represented on each scale: Aloysius (A), Ernie (E), and Fred (F). Scale I is the original measurement scale, in which the players' heights are measured in centimeters. Aloysius's height is 190 cm, Fred's height is 160 cm, and Ernie's height is 170, the same as the mean. Scale II shows the deviations of the players' heights from the mean in centimeters. Aloysius's height is 20 cm above the mean; Fred's is 10 cm below the mean; and Ernie's height is exactly at the mean. Finally, Scale III shows these deviations measured in standard deviation units rather than centimeters. Aloysius's height is 1.33 standard deviations above the mean, Ernie's height is 0.67 standard deviations below the mean, and Ernie's height does not deviate from the mean at all.

Recall that to convert the players' heights from centimeters to inches, we divided each height in centimeters by 2.54, because there are 2.54 cm per inch. Aloysius's height is converted from centimeters to inches below:

$$\frac{\text{Aloysius's height in centimeters}}{\text{centimeters per inch}} = \frac{190 \text{ cm}}{2.54 \text{ cm}} = 75 \text{ inches.}$$

To convert the player's heights from centimeters to a unit of a standard deviation, we divide each height in centimeters by 15 because the standard deviation is 15 centimeters. For Aloysius, these computations are

$$\frac{\text{deviation of Aloysius's height in centimeters}}{\text{standard deviation in centimeters}} = \frac{20 \text{ cm}}{15 \text{ cm}} = 1.33 \text{ standard deviations.}$$

Thus, Aloysius's height is 1.33 standard deviations above the mean, which is 20 cm.

A **standard score** is a measure of relative standing in which a score's location in a distribution is indicated as a ratio between the score's deviation from the mean and the standard deviation. This ratio expresses a score's deviation from the mean in units of the standard deviation.

This is the concept of a **standard score**, which uses the standard deviation as a unit of measurement to express the deviation of each score from the mean. Standard scores are also called z scores. The standard scores for all the cricket players are shown in Table 6-2.

Each standard score gives us two pieces of information. First, the sign of the standard score tells us whether the score has a value lower or higher than the mean. Standard scores with negative signs lie below the mean; standard scores with positive signs lie above the mean. Second, the value of the standard score, disregarding the sign, tells us how far the score lies from the mean, compared to the standard deviation. The standard deviation is a measure of the average or standard distance of scores from the mean. When a standard score has an absolute value greater than 1 (ignoring the sign), the score is farther from the mean than the standard distance of scores from the mean. Table 6-2 shows that the standard score of Igor's height is -1.33, which indicates that Igor's height is 1.33 times as far from the mean as the standard distance. The standard score of David's height is .67, which tells us that David's height is not quite as far from the mean as the standard distance.

Step-by-Step Procedure 6-3 shows how to convert a score to a standard score. In effect, standard scores use the standard deviation as a unit of measurement. In Table 6-1, we changed the measurement unit from centimeters to inches. Thus, we changed Aloysius's height of 190 cm to 75 inches. Remember that a unit of measurement is a quantity. A centimeter is a certain quantity of length, as is an inch. A standard deviation is also a quantity. In the sample of cricket players, the standard deviation is a quantity of 15 cm. The standard scores in Table 6-2 tell us how many of those units of 15 cm each score lies from the mean. Gertrude's height is .80 standard deviations under the mean, and Aloysius's height is 1.33 standard deviations above the mean.

The Mean and Standard Deviation of Standard Scores

When a set of scores is converted to standard scores, the mean of the standard scores will always be zero:

$$\bar{X}_z = \frac{\Sigma z}{n} = \frac{(-1.33) + (-1.07) + (-.80) + (-.67) + 0 + .67 + .80 + 1.07 + 1.33}{9} = 0.$$

The standard deviation of a set of standard scores will always be 1.00, as we can see when we compute the standard deviation of the standard scores of the cricket players' heights:

$$s_z = \sqrt{\frac{\Sigma(z - \bar{X}_z)^2}{n - 1}}$$

$$= \sqrt{\frac{(-1.33)^2 + (-1.07)^2 + (-.80)^2 + (-.67)^2 + 0^2 + .67^2 + .80^2 + 1.07^2 + 1.33^2}{9 - 1}}$$

$$= \sqrt{1.00} = 1.00.$$

STEP-BY-STEP PROCEDURE 6-3

Converting Scores to Standard Scores

For scores from populations

$$z = \frac{X - \mu}{\sigma}$$

where X = a score
  μ = the population mean
  σ = the population standard deviation
  z = the standard score

For scores from samples

$$z = \frac{X - \bar{X}}{s}$$

where X = a score
  $\bar{X}$ = the sample mean
  s = the sample standard deviation
  z = the standard score

1. Calculate the mean and standard deviation of the set of scores.

2. Subtract the mean from the given score.

3. Divide the result of Step 2 by the standard deviation to find the standard score for the given score.

When we convert a set of scores to standard scores, we are transforming the scores to a scale of measurement with a mean of 0 and a standard deviation of 1.00. The unit of measurement for standard scores is one standard deviation. A standard score of 1.00 indicates that the score is one standard deviation above the mean. A standard score of -2.00 indicates that the score is two standard deviations below the mean. The standard score tells us how many standard deviations the score is from the mean.

Standard Scores as Measures of Relative Standing

The fact that the mean of a distribution of standard scores is always 0 and the standard deviation is always 1.00 enables us to compare the location of scores in a distribution. A score that has a z of 2.00 is twice as far above the mean as a score that has a z of 1.00 in that distribution. A score that has a z of -1.00 is just as far below the mean as a score with a z of $+1.00$ is above the mean.

Because every set of standard scores has the same mean (0) and the same standard deviation (1.00), we can make comparisons between two distributions of scores. When Aloysius's height was measured in centimeters and Brian's in inches, we were unable to determine which player's height was greater because the two heights were measured on different scales. When both boys' heights are converted to standard scores, we can make this comparison. Aloysius's and Brian's heights convert to standard scores of +1.33 and +1.07, respectively. Thus, Aloysius's height is 1.33 standard deviations above the mean, while Brian's is only 1.07 standard deviations above the mean. By converting both scores to standard scores, we can compare them, even though they were converted from different scales of measurement.

Thus, standard scores enable us to compare scores between distributions. Suppose that Charlie has an IQ of 140, and he scored 450 on the SAT verbal test. Is Charlie's score on the SAT up to the level we'd expect based on his IQ score? It is difficult to compare an IQ of 140 and verbal SAT score of 450 because the two scores come from different distributions. However, we could compare these two scores if we first convert them to standard scores. Most IQ tests have a mean of 100 and a standard deviation of 15, so we could use these values to convert an IQ score of 140 to a standard score:

$$z_{IQ} = \frac{140 - 100}{15} = 2.67.$$

Charlie's IQ is 2.67 standard deviations above the mean IQ. The SAT verbal test theoretically has a mean of 500 and standard deviation of 100, values we can use to convert Charlie's verbal SAT score to a standard score:

$$z_{SAT} = \frac{450 - 500}{100} = -0.50.$$

Charlie's verbal SAT score is half a standard deviation below the mean. Thus, while Charlie's IQ is considerably above average, his verbal SAT score was below the average. It doesn't appear that his SAT performance is at the same level as his IQ.

As another example of converting the original scale of measurement to standard scores, recall from Chapter 2 that Jane Jeffers surveyed psychology alumni to find their incomes ten years after graduating. The distribution of psychology alumni's incomes, from this study, is shown in Figure 6-3, with two scales of measurements. The first scale is the original measurement scale, in which incomes were measured in thousands of dollars. The second scale shows those incomes converted to standard scores. Note that the shape and size of the graph doesn't change. All that changes is the ruler underneath the graph. We can measure income in cents or dollars or thousand dollars. A person whose income is one million cents has the same income as a person who earns $10,000. The amount of money earned hasn't changed. All that has changed is the unit in which we are measuring that income. Similarly, a psychology alumnus with an income of $78,500 earns exactly the same amount of money as an alumnus whose income is one standard deviation above the mean. All that changes is the unit in which we measure that money.

FIGURE 6-3 Converting the Incomes Shown in Table 3-12 to Standard Scores

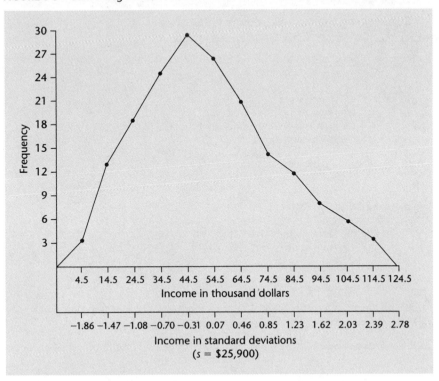

Converting Standard Scores Back to the Original Unit of Measurement

In addition to changing scores into standard scores, we can also convert standard scores back into the original unit of measurement. Step-by-Step Procedure 6-4 shows the steps to accomplish this. Suppose we want to find out what income is two standard deviations above the mean in Jane's study. Recall that the mean is $52,600 and the standard deviation is $25,900. A score two standard deviations above the mean is a standard score of 2.00. Putting these values in the formula from Procedure 6-4, we find:

$$X = zs + \bar{X} = (2.00)(\$25{,}900) + \$52{,}600 = \$51{,}800 + \$52{,}600 = \$104{,}400.$$

An income of $104,400 is two standard deviations above the mean income of psychology alumni in Jane's study.

We could also find the income that is 1.5 standard deviations below the mean:

$$X = zs + \bar{X} = (-1.50)(\$25{,}900) + \$52{,}600 = -\$38{,}850 + \$52{,}600 = \$13{,}750.$$

An income of $13,750 is 1.5 standard deviations below the mean.

STEP-BY-STEP PROCEDURE 6-4

**Converting Standard Scores to Scores
in the Original Unit of Measurement**

For scores from populations

$$X = z\sigma + \mu$$

where z = a standard score
    μ = the population mean
    σ = the population standard deviation
    X = the score value corresponding to z

For scores from samples

$$X = zs + \bar{X}$$

where z = a standard score
    $\bar{X}$ = the sample mean
    s = the sample standard deviation
    X = the score value corresponding to z

1. Calculate the mean and standard deviation of the set of scores.

2. Multiply the standard score by the standard deviation.

3. Add the mean to the results of Step 2, to find the score value that corresponds to z.

Using Standard Scores in Psychological Testing

Standard scores are frequently used in scoring psychological and educational tests. On an intelligence test, for example, the number of questions someone answers correctly doesn't really tell us anything. What is important, as a measure of intelligence, is how many questions someone answers correctly *compared to the other people taking the test*. That is why for intelligence tests and achievement tests, such as the SAT and ACT, and for a majority of psychological tests, measures of relative standing, particularly standard scores, are used as the basis of scoring.

When developing the scoring system for an intelligence test, test developers first construct a set of test items and verify that those items measure intelligence. They then test a sample of people on that set of test items and record the number of test items each person answers correctly. They calculate the mean and standard deviation of these scores and then convert the scores to standard scores. For example, suppose the test contains 100 questions and the mean number of questions answered correctly is 54, with a standard deviation of 14. Then, everyone who answers 54 questions correctly has a standard score of 0.00 (the mean), and everyone who answers 68 questions correctly has a standard score of 1.00 (i.e., one standard deviation above the mean).

The test developers next convert those standard scores to a new scale of measurement. In constructing intelligence tests, the most common convention is to use a mean of 100 and a standard deviation of 15. Using this new mean and standard deviation, the standard score of 0.00 is converted to an IQ score of 100 (the new mean) and the standard score of 1.00 is converted to an IQ score of 115. When the test developers publish their new intelligence test, they include a table that lists all possible values of the number of questions answered correctly and the corresponding IQ score that the participants in their sample received. Then, whenever psychologists give a client the intelligence test, they score the test by looking up the number of questions answered correctly, find the corresponding IQ score received by people in the original sample, and assign that IQ score to the client.

Some achievement tests, such as the SAT and GRE, use a mean of 500 and standard deviation of 100. Thus, if the test constructed above was an achievement test rather than an intelligence test, a person who answered 82 questions correctly would have a score of 700, the score that is two standard deviations above the mean of 500. A score of 700 tells us the person answered as many questions correctly as did the people in the original SAT sample who scored two standard deviations above the mean. As with intelligence tests, scores on achievement tests such as the SAT and GRE tell us how a person scored compared to the scores of the people in the original sample.

The majority of psychological tests use measures of relative standing as scores in order to compare that person's performance to the performance of the people in the original sample. This comparison is valid only if the person taking the test is similar in essential characteristics to the people in the original sample. This provocative question, which is beyond the scope of a statistics text, is addressed in courses on psychological testing. However, it is apparent that the statistical concept of measures of relative standing is an essential component of psychological testing.

To Use or Not to Use Standard Scores: What's Appropriate?

Because the mean and standard deviation of a distribution are used to convert the scores in that distribution to standard scores, we should use standard scores only for those distributions for which it is appropriate to calculate the mean and standard deviation. As we saw in Chapter 4, it is not appropriate to calculate the mean for distributions measured on ordinal and nominal scales. Consequently, it is not appropriate to convert ordinal and nominal data to standard scores. Similarly, we saw in Chapter 4 that it is more appropriate to use the median than the mean to describe the center point of distributions that are considerably skewed (that is, distributions that are not balanced around the center point). It would be useful to have a measure of relative standing that does not depend on the mean and standard deviation for use with those distributions for which these statistics are not appropriate. The next section examines one such measure of relative standing, percentiles.

Percentiles

In Chapter 4, we saw that the median is the point on the number line below which lie 50 percent of the scores in a distribution. The concept of quartiles, which we examined in Chapter 5, extended the concept of the median to divide the distribution into quarters. Recall that the first quartile is the point on the number line below which 25 percent of the scores lie, the second quartile is the same value as the median and has 50 percent of the scores less than it, and the third quartile has 75 percent of the scores less than it. We can extend this concept further to find the point on the number line that has any given percent of scores below it.

The *kth* **percentile** is the score value that has *k* percent of the scores in a distribution below it.

This is the concept of **percentiles**. The *kth* percentile is the point on the number line below which lie *k* percent of the scores in a distribution. The 90th percentile is the point on the number line that has 90 percent of the scores lower than it. The median is thus the 50th percentile, the first quartile is the 25th percentile, and the third quartile is the 75th percentile.

The Simplified Method for Finding Percentiles

As we saw with the median, there are two methods for finding percentiles, a simplified method and a more precise method. The simplified method identifies the score value of the interval containing the specified percentile (or the midpoint of the grouped interval, for group frequency distributions). The more precise method indicates specifically where in the interval the percentile lies. First, we will examine the simplified method for finding percentiles, which is described in Step-by-Step Procedure 6-5.

Table 6-3 shows the grade point averages of 650 honors students at State University. We can use Procedure 6-5 to find any percentile, from the 1st percentile to the 99th. Let's use Procedure 6-5 to first find the 50th percentile, which is also the median (as well as the second quartile). These are all the same point on the number line, the point below which lie 50 percent of the scores in this distribution. The preliminary step in Procedure 6-5 is to construct a frequency table of the distribution, listing both frequencies and cumulative frequencies. This has already been done, as seen in Table 6-3.

In Procedure 6-5, the symbol *k* represents the chosen percentile. As we want to find the 50th percentile, *k* is 50. The first step is to divide the value of *k* by 100 and then multiply that result by the total number of scores. Remember that the cumulative frequency of the highest score value equals the

---

STEP-BY-STEP PROCEDURE 6-5

Calculating Percentiles and Percentile Ranks:
The Simplified Method

To find both percentiles and percentile ranks, the preliminary step is to construct a frequency table of the distribution of scores, showing table frequency and cumulative frequency. Note that the sum of the frequencies is the total number of scores, n.

Finding the kth Percentile

1. Divide k by 100 and then multiply by the number of scores, n.

2. Identify the lowest score value with a cumulative frequency equal to or greater than the result of Step 1.

3. Identify which of the following two cases fits, to determine the score value at the kth percentile.
   A. Case 1: If the score value identified in Step 2 has a cumulative frequency equal to the result of Step 1, add that score value and the score value immediately higher than it, and divide that result by 2, to find the kth percentile.
   B. Case 2: If the score value identified in Step 2 has a cumulative frequency greater than the result of Step 1, that score value is the kth percentile.

Finding the percentile rank of a selected score value

$$\text{percentile rank} = 100\left(\frac{f_b + .5f_w}{n}\right)$$

where n = number of scores in the distribution
f_b = number of scores below the interval containing the kth percentile
f_w = number of scores in the interval containing the kth percentile

1. Find the frequency of the specified score value. Multiply that frequency by .5.

2. Find the cumulative frequency of the score value immediately below the specified score value. Add this cumulative frequency to the results of Step 1.

3. Divide the result of Step 2 by n, the total number of scores in the distribution.

4. Multiply the result of Step 3 by 100 to find the percentile rank of the given score value.

---

total number of scores in the distribution, and thus for this distribution n is 650:

$$(k/100) \times n = (50/100) \times 650 = .50 \times 650 = 325.$$

The 50th percentile is the point on the number line below which lie the values of 325 scores.

The next step in the simplified method of finding percentiles is to identify the lowest score value with a cumulative frequency of 325 or more scores,

TABLE 6-3   Frequency Distribution of Grade Point Averages for Honors Students at State University

GPA	f	Cumulative Frequency	GPA	f	Cumulative Frequency	GPA	f	Cumulative Frequency
4.00	1	650	3.83	10	562	3.65	20	339
3.99	1	649	3.82	11	552	3.64	19	319
3.98	2	648	3.81	12	541	3.63	18	300
3.97	3	646	3.80	11	529	3.62	30	282
3.96	4	643	3.79	10	518	3.61	20	252
3.95	4	639	3.78	12	508	3.60	29	232
3.94	3	635	3.77	13	496	3.59	21	203
3.93	4	632	3.76	12	483	3.58	22	182
3.92	4	628	3.75	13	471	3.57	20	160
3.91	7	624	3.74	12	458	3.56	22	140
3.90	7	617	3.73	14	446	3.55	21	118
3.89	6	610	3.72	14	432	3.54	23	97
3.88	7	604	3.71	15	418	3.53	25	74
3.87	8	597	3.70	17	403	3.52	24	49
3.86	8	589	3.69	16	386	3.51	11	25
3.85	9	581	3.68	16	370	3.50	14	14
3.84	10	572	3.67	15	354			

which in Table 6-3 is a GPA of 3.65. If this score value has a cumulative frequency equal to 325, then the 50th percentile would be the upper real limit of 3.65. The cumulative frequency of the GPA of 3.65 is 339, and so this case does not apply. As indicated in Procedure 6-5, if the score value of 3.65 has a cumulative frequency greater than 325, then that score value itself is the 50th percentile. Therefore, the 50th percentile in the distribution shown in Table 6-3 is a GPA of 3.65.

As another example, let's find the 96th percentile in the distribution shown in Table 6-3. For the 96th percentile, k is 96. The calculations for Step 1 of the simplified method are

$$(k/100) \times n = (96/100) \times 650 = .96 \times 650 = 624.$$

Thus, we are looking for the point on the number line below which lie 624 scores. The next step is to identify in the frequency distribution the lowest score value that has a cumulative frequency of 624 or more. We can see that the GPA of 3.91 has a cumulative frequency of exactly 624 scores. Procedure 6-5 indicates that if the cumulative frequency of the indicated score is equal to the number of scores calculated in Step 1, then the specified percentile is the upper real limit of that score value. To find the upper real limit, we simply add together the identified score value and the score value immediately above it, and then divide by 2:

$$90\text{th percentile} = \frac{3.91 + 3.92}{2} = 3.915.$$

The 96th percentile is thus 3.915. In the distribution shown in Table 6-3, 95 percent of the GPAs have values less than 3.915.

Note that percentiles are *score values,* not percentages. In this distribution, the 50th percentile is a GPA of 3.65 and the 96th percentile is a GPA of 3.915. Note also that for the simplified method, the value identified as the *k*th percentile will be either a score value or its upper real limit.

The Simplified Method for Finding Percentile Ranks

Using Procedure 6-5, we can find the value of any percentile, from the 1st percentile to the 99th percentile. The ordinal values, from 1st to 99th, are called the **percentile ranks.** Using the examples we have already calculated, a GPA of 3.65 is at the 50th percentile rank and a GPA of 3.915 is at the 96th percentile rank. Thus, saying that a given score value is the *k*th percentile is the same as saying that score value is at the *k*th percentile rank. Note that the percentile ranks of 0 and 100 are never found. If they were, the lower real limit of the lowest score value would have a percentile rank of 0 and the upper real limit of the highest score value would have a percentile rank of 100.

The **percentile rank** of a score value is the percent of scores in a distribution at or below that score value.

In addition to the simplified method for finding percentiles, Procedure 6-5 also describes the simplified method for finding percentile ranks. Suppose that we want to find the percentile rank of a GPA of 3.60. Procedure 6-5 indicates that we need to identify only three quantities to find this percentile rank. We need to identify the total number of scores in the distribution, which in the distribution shown in Table 6-3 is 650. Next, we need to identify the value of f_w, which is the frequency of the specified GPA, 3.60. Table 6-3 shows that 19 honor students had a GPA of 3.60, and thus f_w is 19. Finally, we need to identify the value of f_b, which is the cumulative frequency of the score value immediately below the identified score value of 3.60. Table 6-3 shows that the cumulative frequency of a GPA of 3.59, which is the GPA immediately below our specified GPA of 3.60, is 203. This means that 203 honor students had GPAs less than 3.60. These are the values we need to use the formula in Procedure 6-5 to find the percentile rank of the GPA of 3.60:

$$\text{percentile rank} = 100\left(\frac{f_b + .5f_w}{n}\right) = 100\left[\frac{203 + .5(19)}{650}\right] = 100\left(\frac{203 + 9.5}{650}\right)$$

$$= 100\left(\frac{212.5}{650}\right) = 100(.3269) = 32.69 \rightarrow 33\text{d percentile rank.}$$

Thus, in this distribution a GPA of 3.60 is at the 32.69th or 33d percentile rank. This is the same as saying that the 33d percentile is a GPA of 3.60 and indicates that 33 percent of the honor students had GPAs lower than 3.60.

When examining the simplified method of finding percentiles, we saw that the 50th percentile is a GPA of 3.65. To compare the results given by the simplified methods of finding percentiles and percentile ranks, we will find the percentile rank of a 3.65 GPA. The total number of scores, *n,* is still 650. There were 20 students who had a GPA of 3.65, and so f_w is 20. The cumulative frequency of a GPA of 3.64, the score value immediately below our specified value of 3.65, is 319, and thus f_b is 319. These are the values we need to find the percentile rank of a GPA of 3.65:

$$\text{percentile rank} = 100\left(\frac{f_b + .5f_w}{n}\right) = 100\left[\frac{319 + .5(20)}{650}\right] = 100\left(\frac{319 + 10}{650}\right)$$

$$= 100\left(\frac{329}{650}\right) = 100(.5062) = 50.62 \rightarrow 51\text{st percentile rank.}$$

Thus, the simplified method of finding percentile ranks indicates that a GPA of 3.65 is at the 51st percentile rank.

Note that the simplified methods of finding percentiles and percentile ranks give us slightly different values. The simplified method of finding percentiles indicates that the GPA of 3.65 is the 50th percentile, while the simplified method of finding percentile ranks indicates that the GPA of 3.65 is the 51st percentile. This is a consequence of simplifying these methods. While these two methods do not always give exactly the same values, the values they do give are very close and are adequate for most purposes. The more precise method of finding percentiles and percentile ranks, which we examine next, will not give us this discrepancy.

The Precise Method of Finding Percentiles

Step-by-Step Procedure 6-6 describes the precise method of finding percentiles and percentile ranks. To compare the results given by the simplified and precise methods, let's find the score value at the 50th percentile again, this time using the precise method. We already found some of the values that we need in order to calculate the formula shown in Procedure 6-6: $k = 50$, $n = 650$, $f_b = 319$, and $f_w = 20$. We also need the interval size, *i.* The GPAs listed in Table 6-3 are measured to the hundredths place (.01), and so *i* is .01. Finally, we need the lower real limit, LRL, of the GPA, 3.65. Recall that the lower real limit is one-half the interval size below the score value: LRL = 3.65 − .005 = 3.645. These are the values we need to calculate the formula given in Procedure 6-6:

$$50\text{th percentile} = \text{LRL} + i\left(\frac{.01kn - f_b}{f_w}\right) = 3.645 + .01\left[\frac{.01(50)(650) - 319}{20}\right]$$

$$= 3.645 + .01\left(\frac{325 - 319}{20}\right) = 3.645 + .01\left(\frac{6}{20}\right) = 3.645 + .01(.3)$$

$$= 3.645 + .003 = 3.648.$$

Calculating Percentiles and Percentile Ranks: The More Precise Method

To find both percentiles and percentile ranks, the preliminary step is to construct a frequency table of the distribution of scores, showing table frequency and cumulative frequency. Note that the sum of the frequencies is the total number of scores, n.

Finding the kth Percentile

1. Divide k by 100, and then multiply by the number of scores, n. Identify the lowest score value or grouped interval with a cumulative frequency equal to or greater than this result.

$$k\text{th percentile} = LRL + i\left(\frac{.01kn - f_b}{f_w}\right)$$

where k = the desired percentile rank
  LRL = the lower real limit of the interval containing the kth percentile
  i = interval size of the distribution
  n = number of scores in the distribution
  f_b = number of scores below the interval containing the kth percentile
  f_w = number of scores in the interval containing the kth percentile

2. Multiply k by .01, then multiply that result by the number of scores, n.

3. Subtract f_b from the result of Step 2. Note that f_b is the cumulative frequency of the interval immediately below the interval containing the kth percentile.

4. Divide the result of Step 3 by f_w, which is the number of scores in the interval containing the kth percentile.

5. Multiply the result of Step 4 by i, the interval size.

6. Add the result of Step 5 to the LRL of the interval containing the kth percentile. (Note that the lower real limit is one-half the interval size below the stated score value.) The value found in this Step 6 is the kth percentile.

Finding the percentile rank of a selected score value

$$\text{percentile rank} = \frac{100\left[f_b + f_w\left(\dfrac{X - LRL}{i}\right)\right]}{n}$$

where X = the selected score value
  LRL = the lower real limit of the interval containing the score value X
  i = interval size
  n = number of scores in the distribution
  f_b = number of scores below the interval containing the score value X
  f_w = number of scores within the interval containing the score value X

1. Find the lower real limit, LRL, of the selected score value or grouped interval containing that score value. Subtract the LRL from the score value.

2. Divide the result of Step 1 by the interval size, i.

3. Multiply the result of Step 2 by the number of scores with the selected score value, f_w. (For a grouped frequency distribution, f_w is the number of scores in the grouped interval containing the selected score value.)

4. To the result of Step 3 add the number of scores with values less than the selected score value, f_b. (For a grouped frequency distribution, f_b is the cumulative frequency of the grouped interval immediately below the grouped interval containing the selected score value.)

5. Multiply the result of Step 4 by 100.

6. Divide the result of Step 5 by the total number of scores in the distribution, n, to find the percentile rank of the selected score value.

The simplified method indicated that the 50th percentile was a GPA of 3.65, while the precise method gives us a GPA of 3.648 for the 50th percentile. Recall that the GPA of 3.65 does not just represent a single point on the number line but rather is all of the points from the lower real limit of 3.645 up to the upper real limit of 3.655. The GPA of 3.65 is an interval of the number line, not just a single point. The actual value of the kth percentile might be anywhere in the interval. We saw that the precise method indicated that the

50th percentile is the value, 3.648. However, the simplified method does not give this degree of precision. The simplified method will indicate the location of the kth percentile as the midpoint of an interval, which is the score value. In special cases, when the cumulative frequency of the identified score interval is equal to k percent of the total scores, the simplified method indicates the upper real limit of the interval as the kth percentile. Thus, the simplified method indicates which interval contains the kth percentile, but does not indicate precisely where in that interval the kth percentile lies.

As another example to compare the simplified and precise methods of finding percentiles, we will find the 80th percentile in the grouped frequency distribution of psychology alumni's incomes collected by Jane Jeffers. Recall that Jane surveyed psychology alumni to find out how much they were earning 10 years after graduation. The 80th percentile is the income below which were 80 percent of these alumni's incomes.

Figure 6-4 shows both the simplified and precise methods for finding the 80th percentile in the grouped frequency distribution of psychology alumni's incomes. The simplified income indicates that the 80th percentile is $74,500, which is the midpoint of the grouped interval, $70,000–$79,000. The precise method indicates that the 80th percentile is $75,200. Thus the simplified method tells us which interval contains the 80th percentile; the precise method indicates exactly where in that interval the 80th percentile lies.

The Precise Method of Finding Percentile Ranks

Procedure 6-6 also shows the precise method of finding the percentile rank of any score value. When scores are arranged in a simple list or a frequency table, the simplified and precise methods of finding percentile ranks give us exactly the same value for the percentile rank of a given score. As both methods will give the same value, and, in addition, the simplified method is faster to use, it makes sense to use the simplified method for distributions arranged in a simple list or a frequency table.

However, when the scores are arranged in a grouped frequency table, the two methods usually indicate different values for the percentile rank of a given score. Figure 6-5 shows the steps involved in using both methods to find the percentile rank of an income of $62,000 in the grouped frequency distribution of psychology alumni's incomes.

The precise method indicates that the income $62,000 is at the 67.34th or 67th percentile rank, while the simplified method indicates the same income is at the 70th percentile rank. The reason that these two methods give different values is that the simplified method is actually just an estimate.

Percentiles as a Way of Comparing Relative Standing

Percentiles are one way to measure where a score lies in a distribution compared to the other scores. Saying that an income of $75,200 in Jane's study is

FIGURE 6-4 Calculating the 80th Percentile for the Grouped Frequency Distribution of Psychology Alumni's Incomes

Group	Frequency	Cumulative Frequency	
$110,000–$119,000	4	180 ←	The cumulative frequency of the highest score is *n*.
100,000–109,000	6	176	
90,000–99,000	8	170	
80,000–89,000	12	162	The first score to have a cumulative frequency of .80*n* or greater is the interval containing the 80th percentile.
70,000–79,000	14 ←	150 ←	
60,000–69,000	21	136 ←	
50,000–59,000	26	115	The frequency of the interval containing the 80th percentile is f_w.
40,000–49,000	29	89	
30,000–39,000	24	60	The cumulative frequency of the interval below the interval containing the 80th percentile is f_b.
20,000–29,000	19	36	
10,000–19,000	13	17	
0–9,000	4	4	

The lower real limit, LRL, is halfway between the lower stated limit of the interval containing the 80th percentile and the upper stated limit of the interval immediately below:

$$LRL = \frac{70,000 + 69,000}{2} = 69,500.$$

The interval size, *i*, is the difference between the lower stated limits of any two adjacent groups, such as 50,000 and 60,000:

$$i = 60,000 - 50,000 = 10,000.$$

To calculate the 80th percentile, insert the values found above into the formula:

$$\text{80th Percentile} = LRL + i\left(\frac{.01kn - f_b}{f_w}\right) = \$69,500 + \$10,000\left[\frac{.01(80)(180) - 136}{14}\right]$$

$$= \$69,500 + \$10,000\left(\frac{144 - 136}{14}\right) = \$69,500 + \$10,000\left(\frac{8}{14}\right)$$

$$= \$69,500 + \$10,000(.57) = \$69,500 + \$5,700 = \$75,200.$$

Simplified Method: The group with the lowest cumulative frequency over .80*n* is the group, $70,000–$79,000. The midpoint of this group, $74,500, is the simplified version of the 80th percentile.

FIGURE 6-5 Calculating the Percentile Rank for the Income of $62,000 in the Grouped Frequency Distribution of Psychology Alumni's Incomes

Group	Frequency	Cumulative Frequency	
$110,000–$119,000	4	180 ←	The cumulative frequency of the highest score is n.
100,000–109,000	6	176	
90,000–99,000	8	170	
80,000–89,000	12	162	
70,000–79,000	14	150	
60,000–69,000	21 ←	136 ←	The interval containing the specified score value.
50,000–59,000	26	115 ←	
40,000–49,000	29	89	The frequency of the interval containing the specified score value is f_w.
30,000–39,000	24	60	
20,000–29,000	19	36	The cumulative frequency of the interval below the interval containing the selected score value is f_b.
10,000–19,000	13	17	
0–9,000	4	4	

The lower real limit, LRL, is halfway between the lower stated limit of the interval containing the specified score value and the upper stated limit of the interval immediately below:

$$LRL = \frac{60,000 + 59,000}{2} = 59,500.$$

The interval size, i, is the difference between the lower stated limits of any two adjacent groups:

$$i = 60,000 - 50,000 = 10,000.$$

To calculate the percentile rank of $62,000, insert the values found above into the formula:

$$\text{percentile rank} = \frac{100}{n}\left[f_b + f_w\left(\frac{X - LRL}{i}\right)\right] = \frac{100}{180}\left[115 + 21\left(\frac{62,000 - 59,500}{10,000}\right)\right]$$

$$= .56\left[115 + 21\left(\frac{2,500}{10,000}\right)\right] = .56[115 + 21(.25)] = .56[115 + 5.25]$$

$$= .56[120.25] = 67.34 \rightarrow 67\text{th percentile rank}$$

Simplified Method

$$\text{percentile rank} = 100\left(\frac{f_b + .5f_w}{n}\right) = 100\left[\frac{115 + .5(21)}{180}\right] = 100\left(\frac{115 + 10.5}{180}\right)$$

$$= 100\left(\frac{125.5}{180}\right) = 100(.6972) = 69.72 \rightarrow 70\text{th percentile rank}$$

at the 80th percentile tells us where that income stands compared to the other incomes in the distribution. It tells us that an income of $75,200 stands above 80 percent of all the incomes in the distribution and below 20 percent of those incomes. Percentiles tell us where a particular score stands relative to the other scores in the distribution; thus, percentiles are a way of measuring relative standing.

Some psychological tests use percentiles rather than standard scores. Educational tests are frequently scored with percentiles. Suppose ten-year-old Mario participates in standardized testing at the end of fourth grade. The report of his performance indicates that he was at the 95th percentile in reading and the 40th percentile in math achievement. These percentiles indicates that he did better on the reading test than 95 percent of the fourth graders taking the test, but that he did better than only 40 percent of the fourth graders taking the math test. These percentile scores give us no indication of how many questions Mario answered correctly on the tests. We only know how well he did *as compared to* the other children taking the same tests. Thus, percentiles tell us where each score stands relative to the other scores in the distribution.

Like standard scores, percentiles tell us how someone did on the test compared to the people in the original sample. Both standard scores and percentiles measure the relative standing of scores, but they measure relative standing in different ways. Standard scores measure the size of a score's deviation from the mean compared to the standard deviation. Percentiles measure the percent of scores in a distribution that have values lower than a specified score. In the next chapter, we examine a method we can use to convert standard scores to percentiles and percentiles to standard scores. With this method, we can better examine the relationship between standard scores and percentiles.

CHECKING YOUR ANSWERS

1. When computing standard scores, first make an estimate of what the answer will be. If the score you are converting is above the mean, you can expect the standard score to be positive. If it is below the mean, the standard score will be negative. Estimate how many standard deviations the score is above or below the mean. This will give you an estimate of the absolute value of the standard score.

2. When converting standard scores back to the original unit of measurement, again first make an estimate of what is a reasonable answer. If the standard score is negative, the answer will be less than the mean of the original distribution. If the standard score is positive, the answer will be more than the mean. Look at the size of the standard score. The larger the standard score, the farther above or below the mean the answer will be.

3. When converting standard scores back to the original unit of measurement, be sure to round the answer to the unit of measurement. For example, if your answer was an IQ score of 116.32, it would be wrong. IQ scores never have decimals; they come only in whole numbers.

4. One common error that students make is confusing percentiles and percentile ranks. Remember that a percentile is a score value. In the distribution of IQ scores, the 90th percentile is the IQ *score* that has 90 percent of the scores lower than it. A percentile rank is similar to a percentage. The percentile rank of an IQ of 100 is 50, because an IQ of 100 has 50 percent of IQ scores below it (theoretically).

5. Before computing percentiles and percentile ranks, look at the distribution to make an estimate of what the answer will be. When finding the percentile rank of a given score, estimate what percentage of the scores lie below it. Then after doing the actual computations, check your answer with these estimates. If your answer is way off, you'll notice it!

S U M M A R Y

▶ Measures of relative standing are numbers that indicate where a particular score lies relative to the other scores in a distribution. They enable us to compare the location of a score to other scores in the same distribution and to scores in other distributions.

▶ When we change the unit of measurement of a distribution of scores by adding, subtracting, multiplying by, or dividing by a constant, we do not change the order of the scores within the distribution.

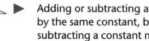 ▶ Adding or subtracting a constant to every score in a distribution, the mean is changed by the same constant, but the standard deviation remains unchanged. Thus, adding or subtracting a constant moves the distribution up or down on the number line but does not change how spread out the distribution is.

▶ Multiplying or dividing every score in a distribution by a constant changes both the mean and the standard deviation by the same constant. Thus, multiplying or dividing by a constant moves the distribution up or down on the number line and also changes the spread of the distribution.

▶ A standard score (*z* score) shows how far a score is from the mean of a distribution compared to the standard deviation. The sign of a standard score indicates whether the score is above or below the mean. A positive sign indicates the score lies above the mean; a negative sign indicates the score lies below the mean. The absolute value of a standard score indicates how many standard deviations above or below the mean the score lies.

 ▶ When any distribution of scores is converted to a set of standard scores, the mean is always 0 and the standard deviation, 1.00.

▶ A percentile is the score value that has a given percentage of scores in a distribution less in value to it. A percentile rank indicates the percentage of scores in a distribution that are less in value to a given score value. In the distribution of IQ scores, an IQ of 100 is at the 50th percentile, thus an IQ of 100 is at the 50th percentile rank.

▶ Many psychological tests use measures of relative standing as a means of reporting subjects' performance on the tests. Thus, when given a psychological test score based on relative standing, we know how the test taker did compared to other people who took the test, but we do not know how the test taker performed in any absolute sense.

E X E R C I S E S

Conceptual Exercises

1. Define the following terms:

   raw score   standard score

   transformed score   percentile

   measure of relative standing percentile rank

2. Suppose that an instructor gives a 25-question true-false test, on which the class scored a mean of 15, with a standard deviation of 5.

   A. What would the mean and standard deviation be if the instructor "raised the curve" by adding 3 points to each score?

   B. What would the mean and standard deviation be if, without "raising the curve," the instructor converted the scores to percentages by multiplying each score by 4?

   C. What would the mean and standard deviation be if the instructor first "raised the curve" by adding 3 points to each score and then converted the scores to percentages by multiplying each score by 4?

   D. Why does the mean change in all three cases above?

   E. Why does the standard deviation change in Parts B and C but not in Part A?

3. Assume that each of the four sets of scores below represent a population. Convert each set to standard scores

Set I	Set II	Set III	Set IV
7	9	9	70
6	7	8	60
5	5	7	50
4	3	6	40
3	1	5	30

   A. Explain why the score of 7 in Set I has a different value of z than the score of 7 in Set II.

   B. Explain why the score of 6 in Set I has a positive value of z, while the score of 6 in Set III has a negative value of z.

   C. Explain why the score of 5 has the same value of z in Sets I and II but a different value in Set III.

   D. Explain why the score of 7 in Set I has the same value of z as the score of 70 in Set IV.

   E. Despite differences in the value of the raw scores between the four distributions, the standard scores for the four distributions are identical. Explain why.

4. Assume that the ten scores below comprise a population:

   8 8 8 8 6 6 6 4 4 2

   A. Calculate the mean and standard deviation of this distribution. Remember to use the formulas for a population.

   B. Convert each score in the distribution to a standard score.

C. Calculate the mean and standard deviation of this distribution of standard scores.

D. Explain why the mean of this distribution of standard scores is 0 and the standard deviation is 1.00.

5. Three sets of scores are shown below. The interval size for Sets I and II is 5. The interval size for Set III is 10. For each of these distributions, find the percentile rank for each score value, using the simplified method.

Set I		Set II		Set III
50	50	25	100	50
45	50	25	100	50
40	45	20	90	40
35	45	20	90	40
30	40	15	80	30
25	40	15	80	30
20	35	10	40	20
15	35	10	40	15
10	30	5	40	10
5	30	5	35	5

A. The score of 40 is at the same percentile rank in Sets I and II, despite the fact that Set II has more scores than Set I. Explain why.

B. Explain why the score of 40 is at a different percentile rank in Set II than in Set III.

C. Explain why the score of 40 in Set II is at the same percentile rank as the score of 80 in Set III.

6. Explain why standard scores and percentiles are considered measures of relative standing.

Computational Exercises

7. For a population with $\mu = 75$, $\sigma = 10$, and raw scores measured with an interval size of 1:

A. Convert each of the following raw scores to a standard score:

(i) $X = 89$ (ii) $X = 67$ (iii) $X = 75$ (iv) $X = 54$ (v) $X = 93$ (vi) $X = 74$

B. Convert each of the following standard scores to the nearest raw score value:

(i) $z = 1.00$ (ii) $z = -1.70$ (iii) $z = 1.90$ (iv) $z = 2.50$ (v) $z = -1.90$
(vi) $z = 0.00$

8. For a population with $\mu = 400$, $\sigma = 25$, and raw scores measured with an interval size of 10:

A. Convert each of the following raw scores to a standard score:

(i) $X = 440$ (ii) $X = 460$ (iii) $X = 370$ (iv) $X = 420$ (v) $X = 340$
(vi) $X = 410$

B. Convert each of the following standard scores to the nearest raw score value:

(i) $z = 1.05$ (ii) $z = -1.99$ (iii) $z = 1.64$ (iv) $z = 2.54$ (v) $z = -1.64$
(vi) $z = 0.00$

9. For a population with $\mu = 12.5$, $\sigma = 1.5$, and raw scores measured with an interval size of .1:

   A. Convert each of the following raw scores to a standard score:

   (i) $X = 12.6$ (ii) $X = 13.4$ (iii) $X = 10.9$ (iv) $X = 15.7$ (v) $X = 11.0$
   (vi) $X = 9.9$

   B. Convert each of the following standard scores to the nearest raw score value:

   (i) $z = -1.00$ (ii) $z = 1.59$ (iii) $z = -1.65$ (iv) $z = 2.38$ (v) $z = 2.00$
   (vi) $z = 0.00$

10. Recall that IQ scores typically have a mean of 100, standard deviation of 15, and are measured with an interval size of 1:

    A. Convert each of the following IQ scores to a standard score:

    (i) 65   (ii) 78   (iii) 92   (iv) 106   (v) 126   (vi) 142

    B. Convert each of the following standard scores to the nearest IQ score value:

    (i) $z = -2.00$ (ii) $z = -1.65$ (iii) $z = -0.50$ (iv) $z = 0.00$ (v) $z = 1.65$
    (vi) $z = 2.00$

11. Recall that the SAT verbal test theoretically has a mean of 500, standard deviation of 100, and is measured with an interval size of 1:

    A. Convert each of the following SAT scores to a standard score:

    (i) 325   (ii) 465   (iii) 499   (iv) 501   (v) 633   (vi) 700

    B. Convert each of the following standard scores to the nearest SAT score value:

    (i) $z = -2.55$ (ii) $z = -1.96$ (iii) $z = -0.75$ (iv) $z = 0.00$ (v) $z = 1.50$
    (vi) $z = 2.33$

12. Recall that IQ scores typically have a mean of 100 and standard deviation of 15 and that the SAT verbal test theoretically has a mean of 500 and standard deviation of 100.

    A. Find the SAT verbal score that would have the same standard score as each of the following IQ scores:

    (i) 100   (ii) 115   (iii) 70   (iv) 112   (v) 87   (vi) 139

    B. Find the IQ score that would be closest to having the same standard score as each of the following SAT scores:

    (i) 400   (ii) 650   (iii) 375   (iv) 770   (v) 500   (vi) 505

13. Assume that the following ten scores constitute a population:

    36   36   36   36   32   32   32   28   28   24

    A. Calculate the mean and standard deviation.
    B. Convert each of the following scores to a standard score: (i) 36 (ii) 32 (iii) 28 (iv) 24.
    C. Transform each of these standard scores to a distribution with a mean of 50 and standard deviation of 10.

14. Assume that the three sets of scores below represent samples:

Set I: Students' IQs		Set II: Students' GPAs		Set III: Students' Incomes	
115	110	3.5	3.1	$20,000	$14,000
113	110	3.5	3.1	20,000	14,000
113	110	3.4	3.0	19,000	12,000
112	110	3.4	2.9	19,000	12,000
112	109	3.4	2.9	19,000	12,000
112	109	3.4	2.9	17,000	10,000
111	109	3.3	2.8	17,000	10,000
111	109	3.3	2.8	15,000	10,000
111	108	3.3	2.7	15,000	9,000
110	106	3.2	2.5	14,000	8,000

   A. Convert the following IQ scores to standard scores: (i) 112 (ii) 110 (iii) 108.
   B. Convert the following GPAs to standard scores: (i) 3.4 (ii) 3.1 (iii) 2.8.
   C. Convert the following incomes to standard scores: (i) $19,000 (ii) $15,000 (iii) $12,000.
   D. Find the IQ scores for which the standard scores are (i) 1.19, (ii) 0.24, (iii) -2.14.
   E. Find the GPAs for which the standard scores are (i) 1.31, (ii) -0.41, (iii) -1.45.
   F. Find the incomes for which the standard scores are (i) 0.69, (ii) -0.08, (iii) -1.62.

15. For the three samples shown in Exercise 14, use both the simplified and precise methods to:
   A. Find the IQ scores at the following percentiles: (i) 90th, (ii) 37th, (iii) 20th.
   B. Find the GPAs at the following percentiles: (i) 90th, (ii) 37th, (iii) 20th.
   C. Find the incomes at the following percentiles: (i) 90th, (ii) 37th, (iii) 20th.

16. For the three samples shown in Exercise 14, use the simplified method to find:
   A. The percentile rank of an IQ of (i) 112, (ii) 110, (iii) 108.
   B. The percentile rank of a GPA of (i) 3.4, (ii) 3.1, (iii) 2.8.
   C. The percentile rank of an income of (i) $19,000, (ii) $15,000, (iii) $12,000.

17. A distribution of the IQs of a population of 220 people is shown below:

IQ	f
135–139	5
130–134	7
125–129	9
120–124	13
115–119	15
110–114	22
105–109	27
100–104	33
95–99	29
90–94	25
85–89	21
80–84	10
75–79	4

A. Find the percentile rank, to the nearest whole number, of the following midpoints: (i) 137, (ii) 132, (iii) 127, (iv) 122, (v) 117, (vi) 112, (vii) 107, (viii) 102, (ix) 97, (x) 92, (xi) 87, (xii) 82, (xiii) 77.

B. Find the IQ scores that are at the (i) 90th, (ii) 80th, (iii) 70th, (iv) 60th, (v) 50th, (vi) 40th, (vii) 30th, (viii) 20th, and (ix) 10th percentiles in this set of scores.

18. Using the distribution of scores shown in Exercise 17:

A. Convert the midpoint of each class interval to a standard score.

B. Find the IQ scores, to the nearest whole number, that correspond to the following standard scores: (i) 2.00, (ii) 1.50, (iii) 1.00, (iv) 0.50, (v) 0.00, (vi) −0.50, (vii) −1.00, (viii) −1.50, (ix) −2.00.

C. Find the standard score of the IQ scores in Exercise 17 found to be at the following percentiles: (i) 90th, (ii) 80th, (iii) 70th, (iv) 60th, (v) 50th, (vi) 40th, (vii) 30th, (viii) 20th, (ix) 10th.

The Normal Distribution

What Is a Normal Distribution?

Characteristics of the Normal Distribution

The Normal Distribution as
a Theoretical Distribution

Using the Normal Distribution

The Normal Distribution Table

Determining the Proportion of Scores
under the Normal Curve

*STEP-BY-STEP PROCEDURE 7-1: Determining the
Proportion of Scores under the Normal Curve*

Determining the Scores that
Correspond to a Given Proportion
under the Normal Curve

*STEP-BY-STEP PROCEDURE 7-2: Determining the
Scores that Correspond to a Given Proportion
under the Normal Curve*

**The Relevance of
Theoretical Distributions**

CHECKING YOUR ANSWERS

S U M M A R Y

E X E R C I S E S

Conceptual Exercises

Computational Exercises

▶ In Chapter 3, we examined the concept of a distribution. Remember that a distribution is a set of score values and the frequencies that those values occurred. In that chapter, we looked at frequency distributions, which are the set of scores that a researcher actually observed and measured in an experiment. The hypothetical scores collected by Joe Johnson in his study on math anxiety and the incomes recorded by Jane Jeffers in her study of psychology alumni are both frequency distributions.

A **theoretical distribution** is a set of score values and the frequencies that would occur, as predicted by a theory.

In this chapter, we will examine the concept of a **theoretical distribution**, which is a set of score values and the frequencies that those values *would* occur, according to some theory. In a frequency distribution, the scores actually are collected from subjects. In a theoretical distribution, a theory is used to predict what scores would occur, assuming that the theory is true. In this chapter, we will primarily examine the normal distribution, on which many of the statistical techniques we will examine in the following chapters are based. In Chapter 10, we will examine another theoretical distribution, the binomial distribution.

What Is a Normal Distribution?

The normal distribution is a theoretical distribution that has a bell-shaped graph. It is frequently known as the "bell curve" and is also called the Gaussian distribution, after Karl Friedrich Gauss (1777–1855), who first defined it. Many physical characteristics, such as height and weight, and psychological characteristics, such as IQ and other tests of cognitive achievement, have distributions shaped like this bell curve. In these distributions, the majority of scores is in the middle of the distribution and is considered "normal." Relatively fewer scores lie in the tails of the distribution, and as these scores deviate far from the center, these scores are sometimes considered "deviant," in the sense of being untypical or unusual.

The normal distribution is actually a family of distributions. For example, both distributions shown in Figure 7-1 are normal distributions, but they differ in where they are located on the number line and in how spread out the distributions are. The shape of a normal distribution depends solely on the values of two parameters, the mean and standard deviation. In Figure 7-1, Distribution B is higher on the number line than Distribution A because Distribution B has a higher mean than does Distribution A. Distribution A is broader than Distribution B, because Distribution A has the larger standard deviation.

FIGURE 7-1 Examples of the Normal Distribution

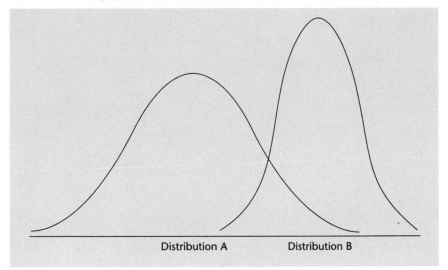

Distribution A   Distribution B

The graph of a normal distribution can be drawn by using the formula:

$$f(X) = \frac{1}{\sqrt{2\pi\sigma^2}}\, e^{-(X-\mu)^2/2\sigma^2},$$

where $\pi = 3.1416$ and $e = 2.7183$. Using this formula is complicated, requiring an understanding of calculus, and is far beyond the scope of this text. Note, though, that if we inserted the values of π and e in the formula, there are only three variables remaining: X (a score value) and the two parameters, μ and σ. Thus, the graph of a normal distribution over a range of score values depends on the mean and standard deviation of the distribution.

Characteristics of the Normal Distribution

While the graphs of **normal distributions** can differ in where they are located on the number line and in how spread out they are, there are several characteristics that all normal distributions have in common. First, all normal distributions are symmetrical. This means that the upper and lower halves of the distribution are always mirror images. Second, normal distributions are always unimodal. There is only one hump in the graph. A third characteristic of normal distributions is that, because they are symmetrical and unimodal, the mean, median, and mode are all the same value. The fourth characteristic that all normal distributions share is that they have the characteristic bell shape, which occurs because more of the scores are clustered around the

The **normal distribution** is a symmetric, unimodal bell-shaped probability distribution, used as a theoretical distribution to describe many physical and psychological variables.

FIGURE 7-2 Proportion of Cases under the Normal Curve

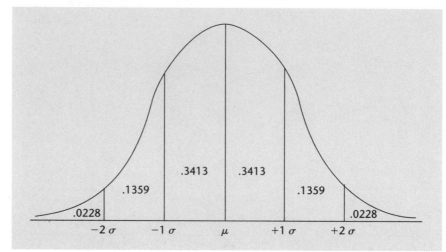

mean, causing a bulge in the graph at the mean. There are fewer scores at either end, which causes the descending tails of the bell shape. A fifth characteristic of normal distributions is that theoretically the tails extend toward infinity. The farther from the mean, the closer the graph gets to the *X*-axis, but the graph never actually touches the *X*-axis.

Figure 7-2 shows the proportion of cases under the normal curve. In every normal distribution, there is a total of .6826 or 68.26 percent of the cases within one standard deviation of the mean. Figure 7-2 shows that there are .2718 or 27.18 percent of the cases between one and two standard deviations from the mean (both above and below the mean). Finally, we can expect .0456 or 4.56 percent of the cases to be more than two standard deviations from the mean. These proportions hold true, no matter what the mean and standard deviation of the distribution are. If the distribution is normal, then we can expect to find these proportions under the curve.

The graph in Figure 7-2 shows the proportions of cases between only a few points in the normal distribution. It would be useful if we had a way to find the proportion of scores occurring between other points in the normal distribution, such as between the mean and one-half standard deviation. Statisticians have provided these proportions for us in tables, such as the table shown in Appendix A-1. If we can assume that a distribution is normal, then we can use this table to find the proportion of scores that would occur between any two score values. For instance, if we can assume that IQ scores are normally distributed, we could use the normal distribution tables to find the proportion of people with IQs between, say 110 and 120, or any other two values. Because the normal distribution table is so useful, it is crucial to remember that we have to know that a distribution is normal before we use the table.

The Normal Distribution as a Theoretical Distribution

Many IQ tests, such as the Wechsler Scales, have a mean, μ, of 100 and a standard deviation, σ, of 15. If we assume that the distribution of the population of IQ scores is normally distributed, from the proportions shown in Figure 7-2, we can expect that .6826 or 68.26 percent of people have IQ scores between 85 and 115 (i.e., within one standard deviation of the mean). By using the normal distribution table in Appendix A-1, we could find the proportion of people we could expect to have IQs between any two values, such as between 70 and 75 or between 93 and 122. Because we use the proportions listed in the normal distribution table to construct the distribution of IQ scores, this distribution is a theoretical distribution. We do not test any actual subjects to collect these scores and construct the distribution, as we would with an empirical frequency distribution. Rather, the distribution of IQ scores is based on the theoretical model of the normal distribution.

The normal distribution is based on the assumption that the underlying characteristic being measured is continuous rather than discrete. Psychologists assume that the distribution of IQ scores is normal in part because they assume that the underlying characteristic being measured, intelligence, is continuous. Recall that a continuous variable can theoretically have an infinite number of possible values. In actuality, IQ tests are scored in discrete whole numbers, such as 112 and 113. Theoretically, though, we could construct an IQ test to measure performance more precisely, so that scores such as 112.4 and 112.789 might occur. In fact, we might argue that no two persons have exactly the same degree of intelligence, that there are as many levels of intelligence as there are people. Of course, it is either impossible or impractical to measure intelligence with that degree of precision. Thus, in practice, IQ tests yield only a finite number of IQ score values.

That we obtain only a finite number of score values is true for all of the continuous variables that we measure. Thus, while the underlying characteristic being measured may have an infinite number of possible score values, our actual measurements are finite. Consequently, any distribution of measurements only approximates the normal distribution. This can be seen in Figure 7-3. Distribution A has 10 score values. We can see that this distribution is roughly the shape of the normal distribution but not precisely the same shape. Similarly, Distribution B, with 20 score values, also approximates the normal distribution but not exactly. However, Distribution B is closer to the shape of the normal distribution than is Distribution A. In general, given that all other things are equal, if the underlying characteristic is normally

FIGURE 7-3   Examples of Finite Distributions Approximating the Normal Distribution

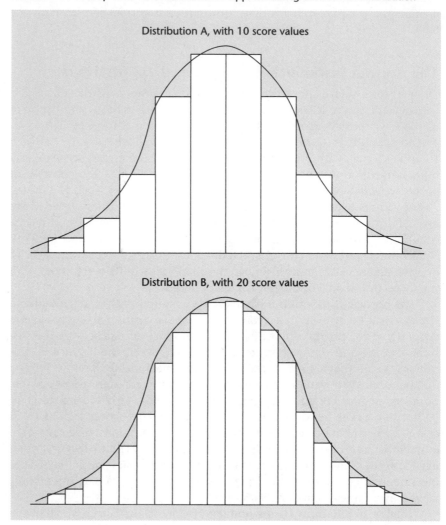

distributed, the more precise our measurements (i.e., the greater the number of score values), the more closely the distribution will approximate the normal distribution.

How do researchers know whether the underlying characteristic is normally distributed? In truth, we can never know for sure. All we know about the underlying characteristic comes from our measurements of it, and those measurements are always finite. Researchers make the assumption that the underlying characteristic is normally distributed if the empirical measurements of that characteristic approximate the normal distribution, as shown in Figure 7-3, and if the more precisely those measurements are made, the closer that approximation is.

Using the Normal Distribution

The Normal Distribution Table

Appendix A-1 is a normal distribution table listing the proportion of scores under the normal curve. In order to use Appendix A-1, we need to first convert the scores to standard scores (z scores). The reason that the normal distribution table lists z scores is that otherwise there would have to be a separate table for every possible combination of means and standard deviations. By converting the scores to z scores, we need only one table. However, only if we know or can assume that the scores come from a normal distribution is it appropriate to use the information in Appendix A-1.

There are many different ways we can ask questions about the proportion of scores that occur in the normal distribution. Before examining these questions, it will be helpful first to look at the way in which the normal distribution table in Appendix A-1 is set up. Figure 7-4 shows a small segment of that table representing the values of z from 0.90 to 1.00. The entire table in Appendix A-1 lists the values of z from 0.00 to 4.00. As seen in Figure 7-4, these values of z are listed in the first column of the table.

For each value of z, the second column lists the proportion of scores in the normal distribution between the mean and that value of z. For example, Figure 7-4 shows that .3413 or 34.13 percent of the scores in a normal distribution lie between the mean and a z of 1.00. Note that the small picture of the normal distribution at the top of the second column shows that the proportions listed are in the center of the graph between the mean and the value of z.

Finally, the third column lists the proportion of scores that lie above each value of z. Figure 7-4 indicates that .1587 (or 15.87 percent) of the scores in a normal distribution lie above a z of 1.00. Again, the small picture at the top of the third column shows that the proportions listed are in the tail of the distribution.

The normal distribution table, Appendix A-1, shows only positive values of z. Because the normal distribution is symmetrical (i.e., the two halves of the normal graph are mirror images), the proportions for a negative value of z are the same as for the corollary positive value of z. Thus, if 34.13 percent of the scores lie between the mean and a z of $+1.00$, there are also 34.13 percent of the scores between the mean and a z of -1.00.

When working problems involving the normal distribution table, it is particularly helpful to first draw a picture of the graph, similar to those shown in Figure 7-4. Draw a vertical line at the center of the graph, and label this position with the value of the mean, 0. Mark the left side of the graph as

FIGURE 7-4   Example from the Normal Distribution Table

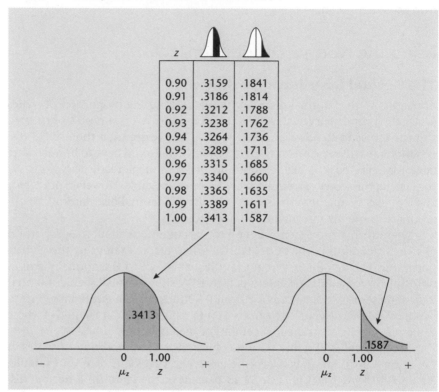

negative and the right side as positive. Then draw a vertical line to indicate the position of the *z* involved. If there is more than one value of *z*, indicate the position of each. Shade in the area on the graph of the proportion that you are seeking. Then it will be simple to use the normal distribution table in Appendix A-1 to find the relevant proportion(s).

Determining the Proportion of Scores under the Normal Curve

Step-by-Step Procedure 7-1 describes the general procedure for finding the proportion of scores under various segments of the normal curve. There are five types of questions about the proportion of scores under the normal curve. We will look at the way of answering each of these five questions, using the distribution of IQ scores as an example. IQ scores are assumed to be normally distributed, so it is appropriate to use Appendix A-1 to determine the proportion of scores that would occur. Recall that for many IQ tests, such as the Wechsler scales, the distribution of IQ scores has a mean of 100 and a standard deviation of 15.

STEP-BY-STEP PROCEDURE 7-1

Determining the Proportion of Scores under the Normal Curve

1. Before using Appendix A-1, convert all scores to standard scores by using the following formula:

$$z = \frac{X - \mu}{\sigma}$$

where X = a score in a normal distribution
   μ = the mean of the distribution
   σ = the standard deviation of the distribution

2. Draw a graph of the normal curve. Draw a vertical line down the middle of the graph to represent the mean, and label this point with the value of the mean, 0. Label the left side of the graph as negative and the right side as positive. Then draw a vertical line to represent each *z* score, to the right of the mean for positive *z* scores, and to the left of the mean for negative *z* scores. Shade in the portion of the graph being searched for.

3. Use Appendix A-1 to fill in the proportion of scores in each segment of the graph you have constructed.
   A. Find the value of each *z* score found in Step 2 in the first column of Appendix A-1. The second column of Appendix A-1 lists the proportion of scores between the mean and that *z* score. The third column of Appendix A-1 lists the proportion of scores from that *z* score outward, in the tail of the graph.
   B. For negative *z* scores, use the proportions in Appendix A-1 for the positive *z* score with the same absolute value. The normal curve is symmetrical, so the proportions for negative and positive *z* scores are equal.
   C. If there are two *z* scores on one side of the graph, use Appendix A-1 to find the proportion of scores between the mean and the *z* score nearer to the mean. Then use Appendix A-1 to find the proportion of scores in the tail of the graph, beyond the *z* score farther from the mean. Add those two proportions together, and then subtract from .5000 to find the proportion of scores between the two *z* scores.
   D. If there are no *z* scores on one-half of the graph, and thus that half is not divided into segments, then list the proportion of scores in that half of the graph as .5000.

4. Check the graph you have constructed to make sure that the proportions on each side of the mean add up to .5000, and that all of the proportions in the graph add up to 1.0000.

5. You should now be able to find the answer to the question you are solving directly on your graph.

Determining the proportion of scores between the mean and a z score.   In this first type of normal curve question, there are two possible outcomes: either the *z* score will be above the mean or it will be below the mean. In this first example, the *z* score will be above the mean. Suppose we want to find the proportion of IQ scores that we could expect between the mean and an IQ of

FIGURE 7-5   Finding the Proportion of IQ Scores between the Mean and 120

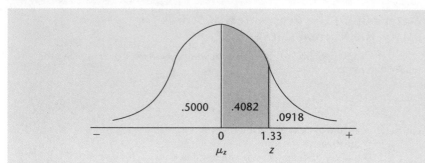

120. Following Procedure 7-1, the first step is convert the IQ score of 120 to a z score:

$$z = \frac{X - \mu}{\sigma} = \frac{120 - 100}{15} = 1.33.$$

The second step of Procedure 7-1 is to construct a graph, dividing the normal curve into segments and then using Appendix A-1 to identify the proportion of scores in each segment. Figure 7-5 shows a graph of the normal curve, with the z score of 1.33 marked to the right of the mean. The proportions of scores in the three segments of the graph come from Appendix A-1. We can read directly from this graph that we can expect .4082 of IQ scores, or 40.82 percent, between the mean of 100 and an IQ score of 120. Thus, if we had a normally distributed group of 100 IQ scores, we would expect 40 or 41 scores to have values between 100 and 120.

In the problem above, we found the proportion of scores between the mean and a positive z score. The other possible outcome is that the z score will be negative. For example, we could find the proportion of IQ scores between the mean and an IQ of 80. Again, the first step is to convert the IQ score of 80 to a z score:

$$z = \frac{X - \mu}{\sigma} = \frac{80 - 100}{15} = -1.33.$$

Note that an IQ score of 120 converts to a z score of 1.33, and an IQ score of 80 converts to a z score of −1.33. The fact that both of these z scores have an absolute value of 1.33 tells us that they are exactly the same distance away from the mean.

The second step in determining the proportion of scores between the mean and an IQ of 80 is to construct a graph. Figure 7-6 shows a graph of the normal curve, with the z score of −1.33 marked to the left of the mean. Note that this graph is the mirror image of the graph we constructed in Figure 7-5.

FIGURE 7-6   Finding the Proportion of IQ Scores between the Mean and 80

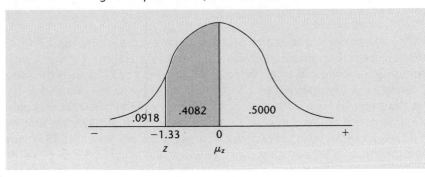

Because the normal curve is symmetrical, there is exactly the same proportion of scores between the mean and a z score of -1.33 and between the mean and a z score of $+1.33$. We can read directly from this graph that we can expect .4082 of IQ scores, or 40.82 percent, between the mean of 100 and an IQ score of 80. In a distribution of 100 IQ scores, 41 scores would have values between 80 and 100.

Finding the proportion of scores above a given z score.   The second type of question asks for the proportion of scores above a given z score. We can use the same two examples to illustrate how to solve these questions. For example, let's find the proportion of scores we could expect above an IQ of 120. Again, the first step would be to convert the IQ score of 120 to a z score, which we have already done. An IQ of 120 converts to a z score of 1.33. The second step is to construct the graph, which has already been shown in Figure 7-5. The proportions in Figure 7-5 show that .0918, or 9.18 percent, of IQ scores will be above 120.

   We could also find the proportion of scores we could expect above an IQ of 80. Remember that we converted the IQ score of 80 to a z score of -1.33. In the graph we constructed in Figure 7-6, there are two segments above the z score of -1.33. The graph shows that .4082, or 40.82 percent, of the scores fall between a z score of -1.33 and the mean, and that .5000, or 50.00 percent, of the scores fall above the mean. In order to determine the proportion of scores above a z score of -1.33, we need to add these two proportions together:

   proportion of scores above z of -1.33 = .4082 + .5000 = .9082.

Thus, .9082, or 90.82 percent, of IQ scores will be above a score of 80.

   These are the two forms that a question determining the proportion of scores above a given z score will take. If the z score is positive, you will be able to read the proportion directly on the graph you construct. If the z score is negative, you will need to add together two proportions from your graph in order to answer the question.

Finding the proportion of scores below a given z score.   The third type of question about the proportion of scores under the normal curve is to ask what proportion of scores can be expected below a given *z* score. This is the same as asking for a given percentile. Like the two types we have examined so far, this third type has two outcomes, depending on whether the *z* score is positive or negative. For example, let's find the proportion of IQ scores that we could expect below an IQ of 80, which converts to a *z* score of −1.33. Figure 7-6 shows that .0918, or 9.18 percent, of scores will be less than an IQ of 80. When asked to find the proportion of scores below a negative *z* score, you will be able to read the proportion directly from the graph you construct.

When the *z* score is positive, you will need to add two proportions together in order to find the proportion below that *z* score. For example, we can find the proportion of IQ scores expected below an IQ of 120. Recall that an IQ of 120 converts to a *z* score of 1.33. Figure 7-5 shows that there are .4082, or 40.82 percent, of the scores between the mean and a *z* score of 1.33, and there are .5000, or 50.00 percent, of the scores below the mean. We need to add these two proportions together in order to find the proportion of scores below a *z* score of 1.33:

proportion of scores below *z* of 1.33 = .4082 + .5000 = .9082.

Determining the proportion of scores between two z scores.   For this fourth type of question, there are again two possible outcomes. First, there can be one positive and one negative *z* score, such as the proportion of IQ scores between an IQ of 90 and an IQ of 130. Remember that the first step is to convert both of these IQ scores to *z* scores:

$$z = \frac{90 - 100}{15} = -.67, \qquad z = \frac{130 - 100}{15} = 2.00.$$

An IQ score of 90 has a *z* score of −.67, and an IQ score of 130 has a *z* score of 2.00. We are thus looking for the proportion of scores between a *z* score of −.67 and a *z* score of 2.00. Figure 7-7 shows a graph of the normal curve divided into four segments. Figure 7-7 shows that .2486, or 24.86 percent, of the scores lie between a *z* score of −.67 and the mean, and that .4772, or 47.72 percent, of the scores lie between the mean and a *z* score of 2.00. In order to find the proportion of scores between a *z* score of −.67 and a *z* score of 2.00, we need to add these two proportions together:

proportion of scores between *z* of −.67 and *z* of 2.00 = .2486 + .4772 = .7258.

Thus, we can expect .7258, or 72.58 percent, of IQ scores between an IQ of 90 and an IQ of 130.

FIGURE 7-7   Finding the Proportion of IQ Scores between 90 and 130

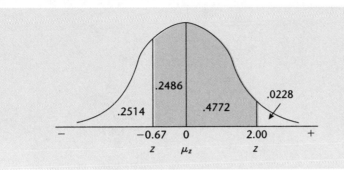

FIGURE 7-8   Finding the Proportion of IQ Scores between 120 and 130

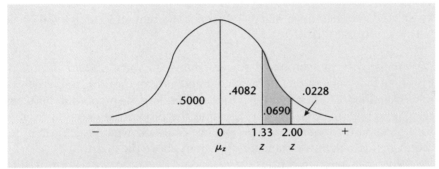

The other possible outcome to the question asking the proportion of scores between two z scores is that both z scores are on the same size of the mean (either both positive or both negative). For example, we could ask what proportion of IQ scores we could expect between an IQ of 120 and an IQ of 130. Note that we have used both of these IQ scores before, and that an IQ score of 120 converts to a z score of 1.33, while an IQ score of 130 converts to a z score of 2.00. These are shown in Figure 7-8.

In finding the proportions in the four segments of the graph in Figure 7-8, start first with the proportion of scores between the mean and a z score of 1.33, which Appendix A-1 shows is .4082. Then find the proportion of scores above a z score of 2.00, which Appendix A-1 shows is .0228. To find the proportion of scores between a z score of 1.33 and a z score of 2.00, we need to add these two proportions together and then subtract from .5000:

proportion of scores between z of 1.33 and z of 2.00 = .5000 − (.4082 + .0228)

$$= .5000 - .4310$$

$$= .0690$$

FIGURE 7-9 Finding the Proportion of IQ Scores within One Standard Deviation of the Mean

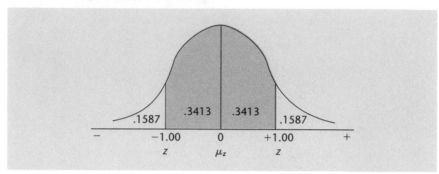

Thus, we have determined that .0690, or 6.90 percent, of IQ scores will occur between 120 and 130.

Determining the proportion of scores relative to the standard deviation. This final type of question is somewhat different than the other four types we have examined. The first four types involved finding the proportion of scores relative to a given score. We can also find the proportion of scores relative to the standard deviation. For example, we could ask what proportion of IQ scores are more than two standard deviations above the mean.

When the question concerns the standard deviation, we do not need to convert it to a z score. Remember that a z score tells us how many standard deviations from the mean a score lies. Two standard deviations above the mean is the same thing as a z score of 2.00. Thus, when we ask what proportion of scores are more than two standard deviations above the mean, we are asking what proportion of scores will be above a z score of 2.00. We can use the graph we constructed in Figure 7-8 to answer this question. Figure 7-8 shows that .0228, or 2.28 percent, of IQ scores will be more than two standard deviations above the mean.

We have not yet encountered two particular forms that questions about standard deviations can take. First, we could ask what proportion of scores lie within a given number of standard deviations from the mean. For example, we could ask what proportion of IQ scores lie within one standard deviation of the mean. One standard deviation is the same as a z score of 1.00. All of the IQ scores between the mean and a z score of 1.00 are within one standard deviation of the mean. In addition, all of the IQ scores between the mean and a z score of -1.00 are also within one standard deviation of the mean. Thus, asking what proportion of IQ scores lie within one standard deviation of the mean is the same as asking what proportion of IQ scores lie between a z score of -1.00 and a z score of $+1.00$. These values are shown in the graph in Figure 7-9. There is .3413, or 34.13 percent, of the scores between the mean and a z score of $+1.00$, and the same proportion of scores lies between the mean and a z score of -1.00. To find the proportion of scores within one standard deviation of the mean, we need to add these two proportions together:

proportion of scores within 1 σ of μ = .3413 + .3413 = .6826.

Thus, .6826, or 68.26 percent, of IQ scores lie within one standard deviation of the mean.

The other particular form that questions relative to standard deviations can take would be to ask what proportion of scores are more than a given standard deviation from the mean. The question above, asking the proportion within a given standard deviation, asks for the proportion of scores in the center segments of the graph. This form, asking the proportion that is more than a given standard deviation from the mean, asks for the proportion of scores in the tails of the graph.

For example, let's find the proportion of IQ scores that are more than one standard deviation from the mean. All of the IQ scores that are above a z score of $+1.00$ are more than one standard deviation from the mean. In addition, all of the IQ scores that are below a z score of -1.00 are also more than one standard deviation from the mean. Figure 7-9 shows that .1587, or 15.87 percent, of the scores fall above a z score of $+1.00$, and the same proportion falls below a z score of -1.00. In order to find the proportion of scores more than one standard deviation from the mean, we need to add these two proportions together:

proportion of scores more than 1 σ from μ = .1587 + .1587 = .3174.

Thus, .3174, or 31.74 percent, of IQ scores lie more than one standard deviation from the mean.

All of the questions examined in this section involve finding the proportion of scores in a normal distribution relative to one or more given scores. Thus, we can find the proportion of scores above a given score, below a given score, or between two scores. You do not need to memorize all of the different formats that these questions can take. To solve any of these problems, make sure that you draw a graph, using the mean of zero and the value(s) of z for the score(s) in the problem to divide the graph into segments, and then using Appendix A-1 to fill in the proportion of scores found in each segment. From this graph, you should be able to find the answer to any question about the proportion of scores under the normal curve.

Determining the Scores that Correspond to a Given Proportion under the Normal Curve

In the problems in the previous section, we began with a score (or standard deviation) and found the proportion under the normal curve that corresponded to that score. In this section, we will reverse that procedure. We'll

---

STEP-BY-STEP PROCEDURE 7-2

Determining the Scores that Correspond to a Given Proportion under the Normal Curve

1. First, draw a graph of the normal distribution. Draw a vertical line down the middle, and label it with the value of the mean, 0. Label the left side of the graph as negative and the right side as positive. Draw one or two lines, dividing the graph into segments, as follows:

   A. If the question asks for the score that has a given proportion above it, draw one line, to the right of the mean if the proportion is more than .5000 and to the left of the mean if the proportion is less than .5000.

   B. If the question asks for the score that has a given proportion below it, draw one line, to the left of the mean if the proportion is less than .5000 and to the right of the mean if the proportion is more than .5000.

   C. If the question asks for the scores that cut off a given proportion in the center of the distribution, draw two lines, one to the left and one to the right of the mean.

   D. If the question asks for the scores that cut off a given proportion in the tails of the distribution, draw two lines, one to the left and one to the right of the mean.

2. Divide the proportion given in the question into the segments of the graph.

   A. If the question asks for the score that has a given proportion above it and if the given proportion is less than .5000, write the given proportion in the upper tail. If the given proportion is more than .5000, subtract .5000 from the proportion, and write the remainder in the segment between the line in the left half of the graph and the mean.

   B. If the question asks for the score that has a given proportion below it and if the given proportion is less than .5000, write the given proportion

in the lower tail. If the given proportion is more than .5000, subtract .5000 from the proportion, and write the remainder in the segment between the line in the right half of the graph and the mean.

   C. If the question asks for the scores that cut off a given proportion in the center of the graph, divide the given proportion in half, and write that result in both segments on either side of the mean.

   D. If the question asks for the scores that cut off a given proportion in the tails of the distribution, divide the given proportion in half, and write that result in both tails.

3. Fill in the proportions in the remaining segments of the graph, so that the proportions in each half of the graph total .5000, and so that all of the proportions in the graph total 1.000.

4. If the question asks for one score, find the *z* score in Appendix A-1 that corresponds to the proportions in the graph you have drawn. Remember that if the *z* score is on the left of the mean, it is negative. If the question asks for two scores, find both of those *z* scores in Appendix A-1 that correspond to the proportions in the graph you have drawn. The two scores will have the same absolute value, and one will be positive, the other negative.

5. Convert the *z* score(s) back to the original unit of measurement, using the following formula:

$$z = \mu + z\sigma$$

where z = the *z* score found above
  μ = the mean of the distribution
  σ = the standard deviation of the distribution

---

begin with a proportion and then find the score under the normal curve that corresponds to that proportion. Step-by-Step Procedure 7-2 shows the general procedure for finding the scores that correspond to a given proportion under the normal curve.

There are four types of questions about finding scores that correspond to a given proportion under the normal curve. We will examine each type of question, again using the distribution of IQ scores as an example.

FIGURE 7-10   Finding the IQ Score that Has 20 Percent of the Scores above It

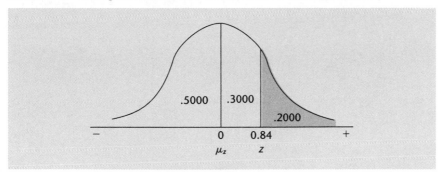

Finding the score that has a given proportion above it.   An example of this first type of question is to find the IQ score that has 20 percent of the scores above it. The first step in solving this problem is to draw the graph, as shown in Figure 7-10. Because the proportion in the question, 20 percent or .2000, is less than .5000, we draw the line to the right of the mean. We want the IQ score that cuts off .2000 in the upper tail. There is no z score in Appendix A-1 that has exactly .2000 above it. However, a z score of .84 has .2005 above it and a z score of .85 has .1977 above it. When we cannot find the exact proportion in the normal distribution table, we take the nearest value to it, which in this case is .2005, the proportion of scores above a z of .84.

The final step is to convert this z score back to the original unit of measurement, using the formula in Procedure 7-2:

$$X = \mu + z\sigma = 100 + (.84)(15) = 100 + 12.6 = 112.6 \rightarrow 113.$$

An IQ score of 113 has 20 percent of the scores above it. Note that the IQ score is 113, not 112.6. IQ scores only come in whole numbers. There is no IQ score of 112.6. It is important to report the score in the original unit of measurement.

Another example of a question asking for the score that has a given proportion above it is to ask for the IQ score that has 90 percent of the scores above it. The score with 90 percent above it will be in the left-hand portion of the graph. The mean has 50 percent of the scores above it, so any score with more than 50 percent above it has to be less than the mean. Again, the first step is to draw a graph, as shown in Figure 7-11. Note that we have divided 90 percent, or .9000, into two segments, .5000 above the mean and .4000 between the score we are seeking and the mean. Appendix A-1 shows that a z score of −1.28 has proportions closest to those shown in Figure 7-11. Using the formula in Procedure 7-2, we convert this z score to an IQ score:

$$X = \mu + z\sigma = 100 + (-1.28)(15) = 100 - 19.2 = 80.8 \rightarrow 81.$$

An IQ score of 81 has 90 percent of the IQ scores above it.

FIGURE 7-11　Finding the IQ Score that Has 90 Percent of the Scores above It

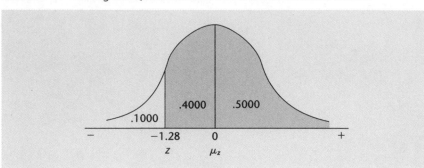

FIGURE 7-12　Finding the IQ Score that Has 95 Percent of the Scores below It

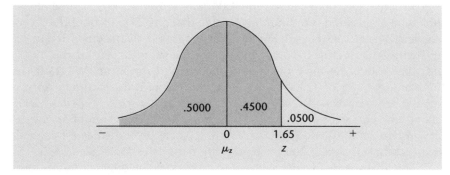

Finding the score that has a given proportion below it.　The procedure for solving this type of problem is very similar to finding a score that has a given proportion above it. For example, we could find the score that has 10 percent of the scores below it. This, in fact, is the same as the last problem we worked because the score that has 10 percent below it is also the score that has 90 percent above it.

To illustrate the procedure for finding the score that has a given proportion below it, we'll find the IQ score that has 95 percent of the scores below it. This is the same as finding the IQ score that has 5 percent above it, as shown in Figure 7-12. Appendix A-1 shows that a z score of 1.65 has proportions closest to those in Figure 7-12. Using the formula in Procedure 7-2, we convert the z score of 1.65 back to an IQ score, as follows:

$$X = \mu + z\sigma = 100 + (1.65)(15) = 100 + 24.75 = 124.75 \rightarrow 125.$$

An IQ of 125 has 95 percent of IQ scores below it.

Finding the scores that cut off a given proportion in the center.　Suppose we want to find the IQ scores that cut off the center 75 percent. To have

FIGURE 7-13 Finding the IQ Scores that Cut off the Center 75 Percent of Scores

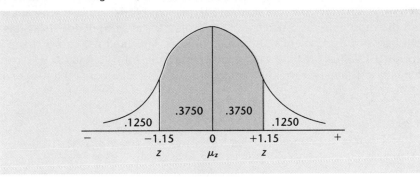

FIGURE 7-14 Finding the IQ Scores that Cut off the Most Extreme 5 Percent of Scores

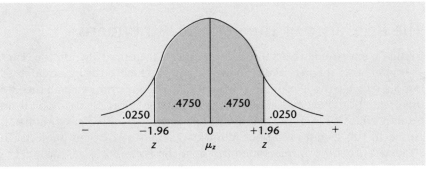

75 percent of the scores exactly in the center, we need to divide 75 percent in half, so that 37.5 percent of the scores are on each side of the mean, as shown in Figure 7-13. We are looking for two z scores, both with the same absolute value, one positive and one negative. Appendix A-1 shows that a z of ±1.15 has the proportions closest to those shown in Figure 7-13. We need to convert each z score separately:

$$X = \mu + z\sigma = 100 + (+1.15)(15) = 100 + 17.25 = 117.25 \rightarrow 117,$$

$$X = \mu + z\sigma = 100 + (-1.15)(15) = 100 - 17.25 = 82.75 \rightarrow 83.$$

The IQ scores, 83 and 117, cut off the center 75 percent of IQ scores.

Finding the scores that cut off a given proportion in the tails. In addition to finding a given proportion of scores in the center of the normal curve, we can also find a given proportion at the ends of the curve. For example, we could find the most extreme 5 percent of IQ scores. The 5 percent of IQ scores that are the farthest from the mean are the scores that are in the two tails of the normal curve, as shown in Figure 7-14.

Note that we do not put 5 percent of the scores in each of the tails, as then we would have the most extreme 10 percent of the scores. If we want to find the most extreme 5 percent of the scores, we need to divide that 5 percent between the two ends of the distribution. Appendix A-1 shows that a z score of ± 1.96 has the proportions shown in Figure 7-14. To find the IQ scores that cut off the most extreme 5 percent of the scores, we convert a z score of ± 1.96 to IQ scores:

$$X = \mu + z\sigma = 100 + (+1.96)(15) = 100 + 29.4 = 129.4 \rightarrow 129,$$

$$X = \mu + z\sigma = 100 + (-1.96)(15) = 100 - 29.4 = 70.6 \rightarrow 71.$$

The IQ scores, 71 and 129, cut off the most extreme 5 percent of the scores in the IQ distribution.

The Relevance of Theoretical Distributions

In this chapter, we have extensively examined the normal distribution. There are many other theoretical distributions, one of which is the binomial distribution, which we will examine in Chapter 10. The one thing that all theoretical distributions have in common is that the scores in the distribution are not actually collected from subjects in an experiment. All of the proportions discussed in this chapter were not found by actually testing any subjects. Instead, the proportions were found based on the assumption or "theory" that the distributions were normal in shape and then finding the proportions in the normal distribution table. It is in this sense that these distributions are theoretical. We are saying that, in theory, if we tested an infinitely large population, the distribution would have the shape of a normal distribution.

Theoretical distributions are important in the study of statistics. There are many attributes studied in psychology that are normally distributed. We have already examined at length the usefulness of the normal distribution in analyzing IQ scores. Many physical traits, such as height and weight, appear to be normally distributed. Similarly, many psychological traits, particularly those in the cognitive realm, including achievement test scores such as the SAT and GRE, are assumed to be normally distributed. An understanding of the normal curve enables us to analyze and make predictions about those attributes.

In addition, the normal distribution is particularly useful because many statistics are normally distributed. For example, suppose that we took many samples from a given population and calculated the mean of each sample. Under certain conditions, the graph of all of those means is shaped like the normal distribution. We can use that fact to make predictions about what value a sample mean from that population is likely to be. We will look at how to use the normal distribution to make predictions about sample statistics in

Chapter 11. The fact that many statistics are normally distributed gives us an important way to make predictions and to test hypotheses in psychology.

CHECKING YOUR ANSWERS

1. In working with the normal distribution, one common source of errors is rushing your work. Take the time to draw a picture of the problem you are trying to solve. Draw the shape of the normal distribution, labeling the *X*-axis with the values you have or you are trying to find. Divide the graph into sections according to these values, and then, using the normal distribution table in Appendix A-1, fill in the proportion of scores to be found in each section.

2. Remember that any *z* score below the mean is negative. When you find a *z* score that bounds a specified proportion of scores in Appendix A-1, you have to remember to insert the negative sign if it is below the mean.

3. Beware of making any of the proportions you find in Appendix A-1 negative. Sometimes students think that because a *z* score is negative, its corresponding proportion will be negative, also. The proportions listed in Appendix A-1 are always positive, even for negative *z* scores. Proportions are never negative.

4. When the question asks you to find a score that cuts off a given proportion in the normal distribution, be sure to work the problem completely. Some students stop after they have found the *z* score, which is incomplete. Be sure to convert the *z* score back to the original unit of measurement.

5. In order to use the table in Appendix A-1, you first must know that the distribution of scores is normally distributed. Just because you can change a set of scores to *z* scores does not mean that you can use Appendix A-1. If you know the mean and standard deviation, you can change any set of scores to *z* scores, but it is legitimate to use Appendix A-1 *only* if the distribution is normally distributed.

Σ SUMMARY

▶ A theoretical distribution is a set of score values and the frequencies that those values would occur, as predicted by a theory. In a frequency distribution, scores are actually collected from subjects. In a theoretical distribution, a theory is used to predict what scores would occur if the theory is true.

▶ The normal distribution is a theoretical distribution that has a bell-shaped curve. Many physical and psychological characteristics are normally distributed (or are assumed to be).

▶ Normal distributions are symmetrical around the mean and unimodal. The mean, median, and mode of a normal distribution are all at the same value. Only continuous variables can be normally distributed.

▶ A table of the proportion of scores under the normal curve can be used to find the proportion of scores in a normal distribution that would occur above a given score, below a given score, or between two given scores. The table can also be used to find the score values that would have a given proportion above or below it.

▶ The normal distribution is useful in the study of psychology because many physical and psychological characteristics can be assumed to be normally distributed. In addition, many statistics are normally distributed under specific conditions, a fact which is useful in testing hypotheses in psychological research.

E X E R C I S E S

Conceptual Exercises

1. Define the following terms:

   theoretical distribution

   normal distribution

2. Construct the following two distributions representing the students in your statistics class: (i) the distribution of the proportion of male and female students actually in your class; (ii) the distribution of the proportion of male and female students that would be in your class if the probability of being either male or female was equal.

   A. Which of these two distributions is an empirical distribution? Which is a theoretical distribution? Explain your answer.

   B. What is the difference in the way these two distributions are constructed?

3. Describe the characteristics of a normal distribution.

4. Describe when it is legitimate to convert a set of scores to z scores. Explain when it is legitimate to use the normal distribution. Explain the difference between these two uses.

5. Suppose that a math test has a mean of 75, with a standard deviation of 5 and that a history test has a mean of 80, with a standard deviation of 10. You received an 85 on both tests. On which test did you perform better? Explain your answer.

6. Explain what the area under the curve of a normal distribution represents.

Computational Exercises

7. Find the percent of cases that would occur in a normally distributed population:

   A. above a z of 1.00

   B. above a z of −2.00

   C. above a z of 2.00

   D. above a z of −1.67

   E. above a z of 1.67

   F. between a z of −1.00 and +1.00

   G. below a z of 1.00

   H. between a z of −1.67 and +1.67

   I. below a z of 2.00

   J. between a z of 1.00 and 2.00

   K. below a z of 1.67

   L. between a z of −1.67 and the mean

   M. above a z of −1.00

   N. between a z of 2.00 and the mean

8. Find the percent of cases that would occur in a normally distributed population:

   A. within 1 standard deviation above the mean

   B. within 1.5 standard deviations below the mean

   C. within 1.75 standard deviations of the mean

   D. more than 1.65 standard deviations above the mean

    E. more than 1.96 standard deviations below the mean

    F. within 2.58 standard deviations of the mean

9. Find the standard score(s) in a normally distributed population that would have

    A. 15 percent of the cases above it

    B. 5 percent of the cases above it

    C. 20 percent of the cases below it

    D. 90 percent of the cases above it

    E. 50 percent of the cases between it and the mean (two values)

    F. 5 percent of the cases farther from the mean than it (two values)

10. The population of IQ scores is normally distributed, with a mean of 100 and a standard deviation of 15. What percent of IQ scores could we expect to be

    A. greater than an IQ of 120?

    B. between an IQ of 110 and 120?

    C. less than an IQ of 120?

    D. between an IQ of 75 and 85?

    E. greater than an IQ of 87?

    F. between an IQ of 90 and 110?

    G. less than an IQ of 72?

11. Remember that the distribution of IQ scores is normal, with a mean of 100 and standard deviation of 15. Find the IQ score(s) that would have

    A. 25 percent of the cases above it

    B. 75 percent of the cases above it

    C. 90 percent of the cases below it

    D. 5 percent of the cases above it

    E. 15 percent of the cases above it

    F. 5 percent of the cases below it

12. Again, remember that IQ scores are normally distributed, with a mean of 100 and standard deviation of 15. What percent of IQ scores would be

    A. within one standard deviation of the mean?

    B. more than two standard deviations from the mean?

    C. between one and two standard deviations from the mean?

    D. more than 1.5 standard deviations above the mean?

    E. more than 2.5 standard deviations below the mean?

    F. more than 1.75 standard deviations from the mean?

13. The SAT math scores theoretically are normally distributed, with a mean of 500 and standard deviation of 100. What proportion of students could we expect to have SAT math scores:

    A. greater than 500?

    B. greater than 300?

    C. greater than 650?

    D. between 450 and 500?

    E. greater than 727?

    F. between 425 and 525?

    G. less than 450?

    H. between 550 and 575?

    I. less than 367?

14. Remember that SAT math scores are theoretically normally distributed, with a mean of 500 and standard deviation of 100. What SAT math score(s) would have

    A. 25 percent of the scores above it?

    B. 90 percent of the scores below it?

    C. 20 percent of the scores below it?

    D. 5 percent of the scores above it?

    E. 60 percent of the scores above it?

    F. 10 percent of the scores below it?

15. John measured the reaction time of a very large group of students and found that the mean reaction time was 1.5 seconds, with a standard deviation of 0.5 seconds. Assume

that these values represent a population that is normally distributed. What proportion of students would we expect to have reaction times:

A. greater than 2.0 seconds?   E. less than 2.1 seconds?

B. greater than 1.8 seconds?   F. between 1.2 and 1.6 seconds?

C. greater than 1.1 seconds?   G. between 1.8 and 2.0 seconds?

D. less than 1.4 seconds?   H. between 0.8 and 1.0 seconds?

16. In the population described in the above exercise, what reaction time(s) would have

    A. 25 percent of the scores above it?   C. 95 percent of the scores above it?

    B. 10 percent of the scores below it?   D. 50 percent of the scores below it?

17. The distribution of IQ scores has a mean of 100, with a standard deviation of 15, and is normally distributed. Find the IQ score that would lie at each of the following percentile ranks:

    A. 50th percentile   C. 25th percentile

    B. 95th percentile   D. 12th percentile

18. In the normally distributed population of IQ scores, with a mean of 100 and standard deviation of 15, find the percentile rank of the following IQ scores:

    A. 130   D. 89

    B. 120   E. 75

    C. 100   F. 62

Measures of Linear Correlation

8

The Concept of Correlation

The Direction of the Relationship

The Magnitude of the Relationship

Null Correlations

Linear and Curvilinear Relationships

Measuring the Correlation between Interval or Ratio Variables: Pearson's Product-Moment Correlation

Interpreting Pearson's Product-Moment Correlation

The Direction of the Relationship

The Magnitude of the Relationship

Calculating Pearson's Product-Moment Correlation

STEP-BY-STEP PROCEDURE 8-1: Calculating Pearson's Product-Moment Correlation (r)

Factors that Affect the Size of *r*

Measuring Correlation between Ordinal Variables: Spearman's Rank-Order Correlation

Calculating Spearman's Rank-Order Correlation

STEP-BY-STEP PROCEDURE 8-2: Calculating Spearman's Rank-Order Correlation (r_S)

Interpreting Spearman's Rank-Order Correlation

Measuring Correlation between Nominal Variables: The ϕ Coefficient

STEP-BY-STEP PROCEDURE 8-3: Calculating the ϕ Coefficient

Correlation and Causation

CHECKING YOUR ANSWERS

S U M M A R Y

E X E R C I S E S

Conceptual Exercises

Computational Exercises

▶ In the preceding chapters, we examined several ways that we can summarize and describe a single group of scores. We can describe where the group is centered on the number line and how spread out the scores in the group are. We can describe the shape of the group of scores, including whether the shape is balanced or lopsided. We also examined ways to indicate where particular scores lie in a group of scores. All these statistical techniques that we have examined thus far are called **univariate descriptive statistics,** in that they are used to describe a group of scores measured on one variable. In this chapter and the next, we examine **bivariate descriptive statistics,** which are statistical techniques that measure the relationship between two groups of scores representing two different variables.

Univariate descriptive statistics are statistics that are used to describe a group of scores measured on one variable.

Bivariate descriptive statistics are statistics that are used to describe the relationship between two groups of scores, representing two variables.

The Concept of Correlation

In the present chapter, we examine ways to measure the strength of the relationship between two groups of scores, each set representing a different variable. Suppose we gather a group of 100 children, ranging in age from infancy through adolescence, and measure each child's height and age. We could expect that the two variables, age and height, would be related. We could expect that the older the child, the taller that child would be. Now suppose we measured the IQ and shoe size of 100 college students. Would we expect the variables, IQ and shoe size, to be related? Would it be reasonable to expect that students with bigger feet would have higher IQs? Probably not! These questions are about **correlation,** the degree to which two groups of scores are related. We will examine three methods of measuring the correlation between two variables. Each of these methods gives us a number, called a **correlation coefficient,** which is an index of the strength of the relationship between the two variables.

Correlation is a description of the relationship between scores representing two different variables. It is a description of the degree to which the values of those two variables are related or covary.

A **correlation coefficient** is a number that measures the strength of the relationship between two variables.

Originally, back in the 1890s, the term *correlation* was written "co-relation." Correlation measures whether two variables are "co-related," the degree to which they are related to each other. Let's examine the relationship between the number of children families have and the number of bedrooms in their houses. Table 8-1 shows six groups of families. In the first group, there is a very strong relationship between the number of children and the number of bedrooms. The Adams family has five children and six bedrooms, while the

TABLE 8-1   Number of Children and Number of Bedrooms in Five Families

Group A	Number of children	Number of bedrooms		Group D	Number of children	Number of bedrooms
Adams	5	6		Pekovich	5	3
Brown	4	5		Quigley	4	2
Carey	3	4		Roberts	3	4
Davidson	2	3		Smith	2	6
Eastman	1	2		Taylor	1	5

Group B	Number of children	Number of bedrooms		Group E	Number of children	Number of bedrooms
Feldman	5	2		Underwood	5	5
Giardo	4	3		Vincent	4	2
Hoffmeyer	3	4		Wright	3	4
Ingolls	2	5		Xavier	2	6
Johannson	1	6		Young	1	3

Group C	Number of children	Number of bedrooms		Group F	Number of children	Number of bedrooms
Kurz	5	5		Jones	5	2
Long	4	6		Johns	4	4
Meyers	3	4		Jensen	3	6
North	2	2		Johnson	2	4
Olsen	1	3		Jepson	1	2

Eastman family has only one child and two bedrooms. In this group, the more children the family has, the more bedrooms.

We can also see this relationship in the graph in Figure 8-1. This graph is called a **scatterplot.** In previous graphs we have examined, the *X*-axis represented the score values of a variable, while the *Y*-axis represented the number of times that those score values occurred. A scatterplot represents two variables. In the scatterplots shown in Figure 8-1, the *X*-axis represents the number of children and the *Y*-axis represents the number of bedrooms. Each dot on the scatterplot represents one of the families. For example, in Group A, the dot in the upper right corner of the scatterplot represents the Adams family, who has five children and six bedrooms, while the dot in the lower left corner represents the Eastman family, with one child and two bedrooms. The scatterplot for Group A again shows a strong relationship between the number of children and number of bedrooms. In fact, all of the dots representing

A **scatterplot** is a graph of the relationship between two variables. The *X*-axis represents the values of variable *X*, the *Y*-axis represents the values of variable *Y*, and paired values of *X* and *Y* are represented on the graph by dots.

FIGURE 8-1   Scatterplots of the Relationship
between Number of Children and Number of Bedrooms

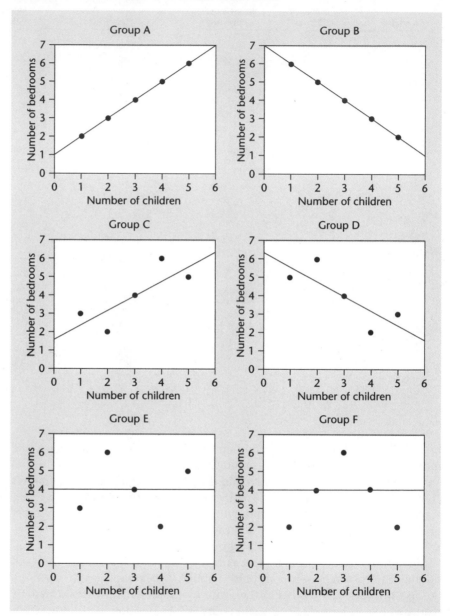

the families fall on a straight line, moving upward from left to right. The more children the family has, the more bedrooms.

The Direction of the Relationship

As in Group A in Table 8-1, there is also a relationship between the number of children and number of bedrooms in Group B, but this relationship is the opposite of the one seen in Group A. In Group B, the more children the family has, the *fewer* bedrooms. The Feldmans have the most children (five) but the fewest bedrooms (only two) while the Johannsons have the fewest children (one) but the most bedrooms (six). As we can see in the scatterplot of Group B, shown in Figure 8-1, the dots representing the families fall on a straight line, as in Group A, but for Group B the dots move downward from left to right. The more children a family has, the fewer bedrooms.

In both Groups A and B, there is a relationship between the number of children and bedrooms, but they are opposite relationships. The relationship demonstrated in Group A is called a **positive correlation.** In a positive correlation, high scores on one variable tend to be paired with high scores on the other variable, and, likewise, low scores on one variable tend to be paired with low scores on the other variable. This is the case in Group A: the more children a family has, the more bedrooms. On the other hand, the relationship demonstrated in Group B is called a **negative correlation.** With a negative correlation, high scores on one variable tend to be paired with low scores on the other variable, and vice versa. This is true of Group B: the more children a family has, the fewer the number of bedrooms.

Because one type of correlation is called "positive" and the other, "negative," does not mean that there is anything necessarily good about a positive correlation or bad about a negative correlation. The terms "positive" and "negative" come from the correlation coefficients used to measure these correlations. A positive correlation has a correlation coefficient with a positive sign, while the coefficient for a negative correlation has a negative sign. Thus, the terms "positive" and "negative" simply refer to the sign (+ or −) of the correlation coefficient. These positive and negative signs indicate the direction of the relationship between the two variables. On a scatterplot, the line fitting the dots slants upward from left to right in a positive relationship but downward in a negative relationship.

The Magnitude of the Relationship

The relationship between children and bedrooms among the families in Group C also shows a positive relationship. Over all the families, there is a definite trend for the larger families to have more bedrooms. However, the scatterplot for Group C in Figure 8-1 shows that the dots representing the families do not all fall on a straight line, as did the dots representing families

In a **positive correlation,** positive or large values on one variable tend to go with positive or large values on the other variable, while negative or small values on one variable tend to go with negative or small values on the other variable.

In a **negative correlation,** positive or large values on one variable tend to go with negative or small values on the other variable.

in Group A did. The relationship in Group A is called a **perfect positive correlation.** In Group A, in every case, the more children, the more bedrooms. The relationship in Group C is not perfect. For example, The Kurz family has five children and five bedrooms, while the Long family has four children and six bedrooms. Across all of the families, the relationship is positive. The scatterplot does show an overall trend for the families with a greater number of children to have a greater number of bedrooms. However, that trend is not perfect. In the same way, the relationship between children and bedrooms among the families in Group D shows a negative correlation, but not a perfect one, while our families in Group B exhibit a **perfect negative correlation.** In general, the closer all of the dots in a scatterplot are to a straight line plotted through them, the stronger the correlation will be.

In the correlation coefficient, the strength of the relationship is indicated by the magnitude or size of the coefficient, irrespective of the sign (i.e., by the absolute value of the coefficient). A correlation coefficient of $\pm.80$ indicates a stronger relationship than a coefficient of $\pm.60$ does. A coefficient of $-.80$ indicates a relationship that is just as strong as a coefficient of $+.80$ does. A coefficient of ±1.00 indicates the strongest possible relationship, a perfect correlation. The sign (positive or negative) indicates the direction of the relation, while the absolute value indicates the magnitude.

Null Correlations

Another type of relationship is demonstrated among the families in Group E in Table 8-1, in which there is no apparent relationship at all between number of children and number of bedrooms. One family with a lot of children has few bedrooms, while the other has many. Similarly, one family with few children has many bedrooms, while the other has few. In the scatterplot for Group E, the dots representing the families are all over the graph. There is not an overall trend among the dots moving upward from left to right, nor an overall trend moving downward. There simply is no relationship between children and bedrooms among the families in Group E. This is called a **null correlation.**

Linear and Curvilinear Relationships

A final critical distinction must be made. In evaluating the correlation between number of children and number of bedrooms in the five groups of families examined thus far, we have been judging the strength of the correlation by how well the points on the scatterplot fit on a straight line. Thus, we have been assessing the **linear relationship** between the two variables. A linear correlation is measured by the degree to which the relationship between two variables can be described by a straight line. There are other types of relationships between variables, one of which is a **curvilinear relationship.** A

In a **zero** or **null correlation,** there is no relationship between the values of two variables, so that positive or high values on one variable occur just as frequently with positive, high values as with negative, low values on the other variable.

A set of pairs of scores representing two variables have a **linear relationship** to the degree that the pairs of scores can be described by a straight line on a scatterplot.

A set of pairs of scores representing two variables have a **curvilinear relationship** to the degree that the pairs of scores can be described by a curved line on a scatterplot.

curvilinear correlation is measured by the degree to which a curved line can be used to describe the relationship.

In Table 8-1, the families in Group F exhibit a curvilinear relationship between the number of children and the number of bedrooms. As the number of children in the families increases, the number of bedrooms increases, up to a point. Then, for the families with the greatest number of children, the number of bedrooms decreases. As can be seen in the scatterplot of Group F shown in Figure 8-1, this relationship does not fit a straight line. In fact, if we calculated a correlation coefficient for these data, the coefficient would by zero, indicating a null linear correlation. The relationship between number of children and number of bedrooms in Group F is curvilinear rather than linear.

Many relationships between variables studied in psychology have both a linear component and a curvilinear component. In this chapter, we are examining only ways to measure the strength of a linear relationship. There are methods that can be used to measure the strength of a curvilinear relationship, but those methods are beyond the scope of this book. However, it is important to keep in mind that when we measure correlation in this chapter, a correlation coefficient of zero indicates only that there is no linear relationship between the two variables, but that there well may be a curvilinear relationship present. Also, the strength of the relationship between two variables may actually be stronger than a linear correlation coefficient indicates because that coefficient doesn't express any curvilinear relationship that may exist.

A final caution is warranted here. In this chapter, we are examining measures of linear correlation as descriptive statistics. We can measure the strength of a linear relationship between two variables either in an entire population or in a sample drawn from that population. As a descriptive statistic, we are here concerned only with the strength of the relationship among the set of scores we are examining. Consequently, a correlation coefficient of zero indicates that there is no linear relationship in the group of scores used to calculate the coefficient. If we find a null correlation for a sample, that indicates that there is no linear relationship *in the sample*. A null correlation for a sample does not necessarily mean that there is no relationship between the variables in the population from which the sample was drawn. We will examine this issue more fully in Chapters 14 and 15, when we use these correlation coefficients to test hypotheses.

In the following sections, we are going to look at three different ways of measuring correlation. The first method, Pearson's product-moment correlation, is used when both variables are either interval or ratio. The second method, Spearman's rank-order correlation is used when at least one of the variables is measured on an ordinal scale. The third method, the ϕ (the Greek letter *phi*, pronounced "fie") coefficient, is used when both variables are nominal. For each of these methods of measuring correlation, we are going to look both at what the formula actually measures and at the mechanics of computing the formula.

Measuring the Correlation between Interval or Ratio Variables: Pearson's Product-Moment Correlation

Interpreting Pearson's Product-Moment Correlation

Pearson's product-moment correlation coefficient (*r* for a sample, ρ for a population) is a measure of the degree of relationship between two interval or ratio variables. The value of *r* ranges from -1.00 to $+1.00$. The value ± 1.00 represents a perfect relationship, while a value of 0 represents the absence of any relationship.

Pearson's product-moment correlation is used to measure the linear relationship between two interval or ratio variables. Recall that for both interval and ratio scales of measurement, the size of the interval remains constant across the whole scale. The computations involved in Pearson's formula require that each variable is measured on a scale with equal intervals, and thus Pearson's formula can be legitimately used only with interval or ratio variables.

To illustrate this idea, let's look again at five of the groups of families, with their children and bedrooms. Table 8-2 shows the same information given in Table 8-1. In addition, in Table 8-2 the number of children and number of bedrooms is converted to standard scores. Recall that standard scores are a way of measuring the distance of a score from the mean. Thus, the number of children in the Feldman family is 1.41 standard deviations *above* the mean, but the number of bedrooms is 1.41 standard deviations *below* the mean.

The definitional formula for Pearson's product-moment correlation is shown below:

$$r = \frac{\Sigma z_X z_Y}{n}.$$

The letter *r* is used to represent Pearson's product-moment correlation. Note that this definitional formula is based on standard scores, which we are using to help examine what Pearson's *r* measures. In the section that follows, in which we examine how to calculate Pearson's *r*, the formula we will use does not involve standard scores.

The Direction of the Relationship

In the definitional formula, the value of *r* is the result of dividing the sum of the standard score cross products, $\Sigma z_X z_Y$, by *n*, the number of subjects. Table 8-2 lists the value of $\Sigma z_X z_Y$ and the value of *r* for each of the five groups of families. First, let's examine the direction of the relationship. Recall from the previous section that the direction of the relationship is indicated by the sign of the correlation coefficient. A coefficient greater than zero indicates a positive relationship and a coefficient less than zero indicates a negative relationship. In Table 8-2, note that the value of *r* is positive when the value of $\Sigma z_X z_Y$ is positive and that the value of *r* is negative when the value of $\Sigma z_X z_Y$ is negative. Thus, the sign of *r* is determined by whether $\Sigma z_X z_Y$ is positive or negative.

TABLE 8-2 Examples of the Strength of the Relationship between Two Variables, as Measured by *r*

Group A	Children (*X*)	Bedrooms (*Y*)	z_X	z_Y	$z_X z_Y$
Adams	5	6	1.41	1.41	2.00
Brown	4	5	.71	.71	.50
Carey	3	4	.00	.00	.00
Davidson	2	3	−.71	−.71	.50
Eastman	1	2	−1.41	−1.41	2.00
					$\Sigma z_X z_Y = 5.00$

$$r = \frac{\Sigma z_X z_Y}{n} = \frac{5.00}{5} = 1.00$$

Group B	Children (*X*)	Bedrooms (*Y*)	z_X	z_Y	$z_X z_Y$
Feldman	5	2	1.41	−1.41	−2.00
Giardo	4	3	.71	−.71	−.50
Hoffmeyer	3	4	.00	.00	.00
Ingolls	2	5	−.71	.71	−.50
Johannson	1	6	−1.41	1.41	−2.00
					$\Sigma z_X z_Y = -5.00$

$$r = \frac{\Sigma z_X z_Y}{n} = \frac{-5.00}{5} = -1.00$$

Group C	Children (*X*)	Bedrooms (*Y*)	z_X	z_Y	$z_X z_Y$
Kurz	5	5	1.41	.71	1.00
Long	4	6	.71	1.41	1.00
Meyers	3	4	.00	.00	.00
North	2	2	−.71	−1.41	1.00
Olsen	1	3	−1.41	−.71	1.00
					$\Sigma z_X z_Y = 4.00$

$$r = \frac{\Sigma z_X z_Y}{n} = \frac{4.00}{5} = .80$$

Group D	Children (*X*)	Bedrooms (*Y*)	z_X	z_Y	$z_X z_Y$
Pekovich	5	3	1.41	−.71	−1.00
Quigley	4	2	.71	−1.41	−1.00
Roberts	3	4	.00	.00	.00
Smith	2	6	−.71	1.41	−1.00
Taylor	1	5	−1.41	.71	−1.00
					$\Sigma z_X z_Y = -4.00$

$$r = \frac{\Sigma z_X z_Y}{n} = \frac{-4.00}{5} = -.80$$

continues

TABLE 8-2   *(continued)*

Group E	Children (X)	Bedrooms (Y)	z_X	z_Y	$z_X z_Y$
Underwood	5	5	1.41	.71	1.00
Vincent	4	2	.71	−1.41	−1.00
Wright	3	4	.00	.00	.00
Xavier	2	6	−.71	1.41	−1.00
Young	1	3	−1.41	−.71	1.00
					$\Sigma z_X z_Y = 0.00$

$$r = \frac{\Sigma z_X z_Y}{n} = \frac{0.00}{5} = .00$$

Generally, $\Sigma z_X z_Y$ will be positive when the majority of the cross products $z_X z_Y$ are positive. If you look at the cross products in Table 8-2 for Groups A and C, you may note that the cross products are positive either when both of the z scores are positive or when both of the z scores are negative. Both of the z scores are positive when the number of children and the number of bedrooms are both greater than average. Both of the z scores are negative when the number of children and the number of bedrooms are both less than average. Thus, when high scores on one variable tend to go with high scores on the other variable and when low scores on one go with low scores on the other, the cross products will tend to be positive, resulting in a positive value of $\Sigma z_X z_Y$ and a positive r.

Again generally, $\Sigma z_X z_Y$ will be negative when the majority of the cross products $\Sigma z_X z_Y$ are negative. If you look at the cross products in Table 8-2 for Groups B and D, note that the cross products are negative when one of the z scores is positive and the other z score is negative. A pair of z scores will have different signs when the score on one variable is above the mean and the score on the other variable is below the mean. Thus, when high scores on one variable tend to go with low scores on the other variable, the cross products will tend to be negative, resulting in a negative value of $\Sigma z_X z_Y$ and a negative r.

These examples demonstrate that for Pearson's r, the sign of the coefficient indicates the direction of the relationship between the two variables. When in the pairs of scores, both scores are above the mean in their respective distributions or both scores are below the mean, the value of r is positive. On the scatterplot, the direction of the dots representing the pairs of scores is generally upward from left to right, indicating a positive relationship. On the other hand, if the pairs of scores tend to consist of one score above the mean of its distribution and the other score below the mean, then the value of r is negative. On the scatterplot, the direction of the dots is generally downward from left to right, indicating a negative relationship.

The Magnitude of the Relationship

In Pearson's product-moment correlation, the strength of the relationship between the two variables is indicated by the magnitude of the absolute value of r (i.e., the size of r, irrespective of the sign). In Table 8-2, Groups A and B represent perfect correlations. Both have an absolute value of 1.00. Looking at the z scores for these two groups, note that the scores that are farthest from the mean on one variable are paired with scores that are farthest from the mean on the other variable. The scores that are next farthest from the mean on each variable are also paired, and finally the scores that are at the mean on both variables are paired. This is a perfect relationship.

The relationship between the two variables is not perfect in Groups C and D. In these groups, the scores that are farthest from the mean are paired with scores that are not as far from the mean. The absolute value of r for both of these groups is .80. This is a strong relationship but not a perfect one.

Finally, in Group E, there is no correlation at all between the number of children and bedrooms. Look at the z scores for Group E, shown in Table 8-2. Two families have a high number of children. One of those families, the Underwoods, also had a high number of bedrooms, but the other family, the Vincents, had a low number of bedrooms. Thus, for the Underwoods, both z scores were positive, resulting in a positive value of $z_X z_Y$, while for the Vincents, one z score was positive and the other, negative, resulting in a negative value of $z_X z_Y$. The same is true for the two families who had low numbers of children, the Xaviers and the Youngs. In effect, these cross products cancel each other out, resulting in a sum, $\Sigma z_X z_Y$, of zero and an r of .00. Keep in mind that Pearson's r is a measure of the linear relationship between the variables. A zero correlation means that there is no linear relationship present, not that there is no relationship at all. As seen in Group F, there well can be a curvilinear relationship present that is not reflected in Pearson's r.

Calculating Pearson's Product-Moment Correlation

To demonstrate how to calculate Pearson's product-moment correlation, r, we will turn again to the results of Joe Johnson's study on math anxiety. Recall that Joe gave students a twenty-question math test and recorded the percent each student answered correctly. Suppose that Joe also recorded the systolic blood pressure of ten of the students as a way of measuring their level of anxiety. (Presumably, the greater the anxiety, the greater the students' systolic blood pressure.) Figure 8-2 shows the scores on the math test and systolic blood pressure for these ten participants. We might ask whether there in fact is any linear relationship between how well students did on the math test and their blood pressure. If Joe's ideas are right, then students with high anxiety would have high blood pressure. Their high level of anxiety would cause them to do poorly on the math test, resulting in low scores. Thus, we should

FIGURE 8-2 Calculating the Correlation between Students' Math Test Performance and Systolic Blood Pressure in Joe's Math Anxiety Study

Subject (1)	Percent Correct on Math Test (X) (2)	X^2 (3)	Systolic Blood Pressure (Y) (4)	Y^2 (5)	XY (6)
1	95	$95^2 =$ 9,025	120	$120^2 =$ 14,400	$95 \cdot 120 =$ 11,400
2	80	$80^2 =$ 6,400	130	$130^2 =$ 16,900	$80 \cdot 130 =$ 10,400
3	75	$75^2 =$ 5,625	140	$140^2 =$ 19,600	$75 \cdot 140 =$ 10,500
4	75	$75^2 =$ 5,625	130	$130^2 =$ 16,900	$75 \cdot 130 =$ 9,750
5	70	$70^2 =$ 4,900	150	$150^2 =$ 22,500	$70 \cdot 150 =$ 10,500
6	60	$60^2 =$ 3,600	140	$140^2 =$ 19,600	$60 \cdot 140 =$ 8,400
7	60	$60^2 =$ 3,600	150	$150^2 =$ 22,500	$60 \cdot 150 =$ 9,000
8	60	$60^2 =$ 3,600	170	$170^2 =$ 28,900	$60 \cdot 170 =$ 10,200
9	50	$50^2 =$ 2,500	180	$180^2 =$ 32,400	$50 \cdot 180 =$ 9,000
10	40	$40^2 =$ 1,600	200	$200^2 =$ 40,000	$40 \cdot 200 =$ 8,000
	$\Sigma X = 665$	$\Sigma X^2 = 46,475$	$\Sigma Y = 1,510$	$\Sigma Y^2 = 233,700$	$\Sigma XY = 97,150$

$$r = \frac{\Sigma XY - \dfrac{\Sigma X \Sigma Y}{n}}{\sqrt{\left(\Sigma X^2 - \dfrac{(\Sigma X)^2}{n}\right)\left(\Sigma Y^2 - \dfrac{(\Sigma Y)^2}{n}\right)}} = \frac{97,150 - \dfrac{(665)(1,510)}{10}}{\sqrt{\left(46,475 - \dfrac{(665)^2}{10}\right)\left(233,700 - \dfrac{(1,510)^2}{10}\right)}}$$

$$= \frac{97,150 - 100,415}{\sqrt{(46,475 - 44,222.5)(233,700 - 228,010)}} = \frac{-3,265}{\sqrt{(2,252.5)(5,690)}} = \frac{-3,265}{\sqrt{128,167.25}} = \frac{-3,265}{3,580.05}$$

$$= -.91$$

expect a negative correlation between math test scores and systolic blood pressure.

The definitional formula for Pearson's product-moment correlation that we have used thus far, based on standard scores, is very cumbersome to compute. In order to use this formula, we need to convert every score to a standard score, which can be very time consuming. There is another version of the formula for Pearson's product-moment correlation, a computational formula, which uses the original scores, rather than standard scores. This formula is shown in Step-by-Step Procedure 8-1.

We can use Procedure 8-1 to calculate the linear correlation between students' math test scores and systolic blood pressure in Joe's study. In order to prevent errors, it is helpful to make a table, like that shown in Figure 8-2, listing in columns the students' scores on the math test, their blood pressure measurements, the squares of these scores, and the cross products. Figure 8-2

STEP-BY-STEP PROCEDURE 8-1

Calculating Pearson's Product-Moment Correlation (r)

$$r = \frac{\Sigma XY - \frac{\Sigma X \Sigma Y}{n}}{\sqrt{\left[\Sigma X^2 - \frac{(\Sigma X)^2}{n}\right]\left[\Sigma Y^2 - \frac{(\Sigma Y)^2}{n}\right]}}$$

where X = the scores on one variable
       Y = the scores on the other variable
       n = the number of pairs of scores

1. Sum the subjects' scores on variable X to find ΣX.

2. Sum the subjects' scores on variable Y to find ΣY.

3. Square each subject's score on variable X, and sum up these squares, to find ΣX^2.

4. Square each subject's score on variable Y and sum up these squares, to find ΣY^2.

5. Multiply each subject's score on variable X by that subject's score on variable Y, and then sum these cross products, to find ΣXY.

6. Multiply the result of Step 1 by the result of Step 2, and then divide by n, the number of subjects.

7. Subtract the result of Step 6 from the result of Step 5.

8. Square the result of Step 1, and then divide by n. Subtract this result from the result of Step 3.

9. Square the result of Step 2, and then divide by n. Subtract this result from the result of Step 4.

10. Multiply the result of Step 8 by the result of Step 9, then find the square root.

11. Divide the result of Step 7 by the result of Step 10, to find r.

shows the steps in calculating the value of Pearson's *r*. The numbers can get rather large, so it is important to work carefully and methodically.

Figure 8-2 shows that the value of Pearson's product-moment correlation, *r*, is −.91. This indicates that there is a very strong negative linear correlation between students' math test scores and systolic blood pressure in Joe's study. Thus, there is a tendency among the students Joe tested for those with higher blood pressure, and presumably greater anxiety, to have lower scores on the math test.

Factors that Affect the Size of *r*

One factor that can affect the size of *r* is the occurrence of one or more *extreme scores* in the sample. Consider Set I in Table 8-3. (This is the same set of scores

TABLE 8-3   Effect of an Extreme Score on the Size of *r*

Set I						Set II				
X	*Y*	z_X	z_Y	$z_X z_Y$		*X*	*Y*	z_X	z_Y	$z_X z_Y$
5	4	1.41	.71	1.00		5	4	.00	−.21	.00
4	1	.71	−1.41	−1.00		4	1	−.21	−.86	.18
3	3	.00	.00	.00		3	3	−.43	−.43	.18
2	5	−.71	1.41	−1.00		2	5	−.64	.00	.00
1	2	−1.41	−.71	1.00		1	2	−.86	−.64	.55
						15	15	2.15	2.15	4.62

$$\Sigma z_X z_Y = 0.00$$

$$\Sigma z_X z_Y = 5.53$$

$$r_{\text{Set I}} = \frac{\Sigma z_X z_Y}{n} = \frac{0}{5} = 0.00$$

$$r_{\text{Set II}} = \frac{\Sigma z_X z_Y}{n} = \frac{5.53}{6} = 0.92$$

as in Group E of families, in Table 8-2.) In Set I, the sum of the cross products of the standard scores is 0, and thus the correlation between the two variables is 0.

Set II is exactly the same as Set I, except that one pair of extreme scores has been added. Because there is an additional score in each set, the standard scores have been recalculated. The sum of the cross products is now 5.53, and Table 8-3 shows that the value of *r* is no longer anywhere near 0. With the addition of one pair of extreme scores, the value of *r* has increased from 0 to .92. With the inclusion of the pair of extreme scores, there is a very strong correlation between the two variables. Is it reasonable to say that Set II in Table 8-3 has a very strong correlation, when that relationship is due entirely to one pair of extreme scores? We need to be careful in accepting the validity of correlations when the sample contains a few extreme scores. If the extreme scores occurred legitimately in the group measured, then the strong correlation is valid. However, if the extreme scores are spurious, we may fairly question the validity of the strength of the correlation.

Another way that the size of a correlation can be affected is by combining *groups from two distinct populations* into one sample. For example, the correlation between height and weight would be considerably stronger in a group composed of infants and adult men than if measured with infants and adult men separately. Table 8-4 shows three sets of scores. In Set I, the scores range from 11 to 15 on both variables. Set I is arranged so that there is no correlation between the two variables, Pearson's *r* = .00. In Set II, the scores are 10 points less than in Set I. However, Set II also has no correlation between variables *X* and *Y*. Thus, separately, Set I and Set II both have zero correlations.

TABLE 8-4 Effect of Combining Groups on the Size of r

Set I						Set III				
X	Y	z_X	z_Y	$z_X z_Y$		X	Y	z_X	z_Y	$z_X z_Y$
15	14	1.41	.71	1.00		15	14	1.35	1.15	1.55
14	11	.71	−1.41	−1.00		14	11	1.15	.58	.67
13	13	.00	.00	.00		13	13	.96	.96	.92
12	15	−.71	1.41	−1.00		12	15	.77	1.35	1.04
11	12	−1.41	−.71	1.00		11	12	.58	.77	.45
				$\Sigma z_X z_Y = 0.00$		5	4	−.58	−.77	.45
						4	1	−.77	−1.35	1.04
Set II						3	3	−.96	−.96	.92
X	Y	z_X	z_Y	$z_X z_Y$		2	5	−1.15	−.58	.67
5	4	1.41	.71	1.00		1	2	−1.35	−1.15	1.55
4	1	.71	−1.41	−1.00						$\Sigma z_X z_Y = 9.26$
3	3	.00	.00	.00						
2	5	−.71	1.41	−1.00						
1	2	−1.41	−.71	1.00						
				$\Sigma z_X z_Y = 0.00$						

$$r_{\text{Set I or II}} = \frac{\Sigma z_X z_Y}{n} = \frac{0}{5} = 0.00 \qquad\qquad r_{\text{Set III}} = \frac{\Sigma z_X z_Y}{n} = \frac{9.26}{10} = 0.926$$

The third set was created simply by combining the first two sets into one. Thus, we have combined two groups of scores, both of which have zero correlations, into a single group. The standard scores were recalculated for this combined set. Note that in Set III, all of the scores that were originally in Set I have positive standard scores, while all of the scores that were originally in Set II have negative standard scores. The sum of the cross products for Set III is 9.26, which yields an r of .926. This is a very strong positive correlation.

There are two ways to look at the evidence demonstrated in Table 8-4. It is possible that the two groups in Table 8-4 represent two different, distinct populations, such as infants and adult men, so that the correlation found for the combined groups is spuriously high. It is also possible that these two groups represent different ranges within the same population, so that the correlations found for the separate groups are spuriously low. The factor of restricted range is examined next.

A third factor that affects the size of Pearson's r is the *size of the range of scores*. In Table 8-5, Set I has nine pairs of scores, ranging in value from 1 to 9.

TABLE 8-5　The Effect of Restricting the Range on the Size of r

Set I					Set II				
X	Y	z_X	z_Y	$z_X z_Y$	X	Y	z_X	z_Y	$z_X z_Y$
9	9	1.55	1.55	2.40					
8	8	1.16	1.16	1.35					
7	6	.78	.39	.30	7	6	1.41	.71	1.00
6	3	.39	−.78	−.30	6	3	.71	−1.41	−1.00
5	5	.00	.00	.00	5	5	.00	.00	.00
4	7	−.39	.78	−.30	4	7	−.71	1.41	−1.00
3	4	−.78	−.39	.30	3	4	−1.41	−.71	1.00
2	2	−1.16	−1.16	1.35				$\Sigma z_X z_Y$ =	.00
1	1	−1.55	−1.55	2.40					
			$\Sigma z_X z_Y$ =	7.50					

$$r_{Set\ I} = \frac{\Sigma z_X z_Y}{n} = \frac{7.50}{9} = 0.83 \qquad\qquad r_{Set\ II} = \frac{\Sigma z_X z_Y}{n} = \frac{.00}{5} = 0.00$$

As can be seen in Table 8-5, the value of Pearson's r for Set I is .83. Set II was constructed by eliminating the two highest pairs of scores and the two lowest pairs of scores from Set I, so that the scores range in value only from 3 to 7. Note that the pairs of scores in Set II are exactly the same as the middle five pairs of scores in Set I. However, the value of Pearson's r for Set II is zero. Thus, by using scores from only a portion of the original range, we have eliminated the correlation entirely. It is important, when interpreting a value of Pearson's r, to consider whether any of these factors may have had an effect.

Measuring Correlation between Ordinal Variables: Spearman's Rank-Order Correlation

Spearman's rank-order correlation coefficient (also called *rho*, for Greek letter ρ and denoted r_S for a sample, ρ_S for a population) is a measure of the degree of relationship between two variables that can be ordered by rank. The value of r_S ranges from −1.00 to +1.00. The value ±1.00 represents a perfect relationship, while a value of 0 represents the absence of any relationship.

The measure of correlation that we have looked at thus far, Pearson's r, is used only with interval or ratio variables. There may be occasions when we want to measure the linear correlation between ordinal variables. **Spearman's rank-order correlation coefficient** (called rho, for Greek letter ρ, pronounced "row" and denoted r_S for a sample, ρ_S for a population) measures the linear correlation between two variables that are at least ordinal. Recall from Chapter 2 that in an ordinal variable, the order of the values of the variable is meaningful. A larger value means more of the thing being measured. The conventional system used to represent letter grades, where an A is a 4, a B is a 3, and so on, is an ordinal variable. A grade of 4 is greater than a grade of 3. This is the scale of measurement for which Spearman's coefficient was designed. Spearman's coefficient can also be used to measure the correlation between one ordinal variable and another variable that is either interval or ratio.

Calculating Spearman's Rank-Order Correlation

Step-by-Step Procedure 8-2 shows the method for calculating Spearman's rank-order correlation coefficient. There are two phases in calculating r_s. The first phase is to rank-order the scores on each of the variables. The second phase is to find the correlation between those ranks. Because r_s is computed on ranks, Spearman's rank-order correlation coefficient can be computed only for variables that can be rank-ordered. Thus, we can use Spearman's coefficient to find the correlation between variables that are ordinal, interval, or

---

STEP-BY-STEP PROCEDURE 8-2

Calculating Spearman's Rank-Order Correlation (r_s)

$$r_s = 1 - \frac{6\Sigma D^2}{n(n^2 - 1)}$$

where D = the difference between paired ranks

n = the number of pairs of scores, which is the same as the number of subjects

1. For each variable separately, rank the subjects' scores:
   A. Give the rank of 1 to the score with the lowest value. Give the rank of 2 to the score with the next-lowest value. Continue until you give the rank of n to the score with the highest value.
   B. If two scores have the same value, give both of those scores the average of the next two ranks to be assigned. If three scores have the same value, give all three of those scores the average of the next three ranks to be assigned. In general, if k scores have the same value, give each of those k scores the average of the next k ranks to be assigned.
   C. As a check, the sum of the ranks will equal $.5n(n + 1)$.

2. For each subject, subtract the rank of that subject's score on variable Y from the rank of that subject's score on variable X to find D, the difference between that subject's ranks on the two variables. Square the value of D.

3. Sum the squares of D across all subjects. Multiply that sum by 6.

4. Square n, the number of subjects. Subtract 1 from that result.

5. Multiply the result of Step 4 by n.

6. Divide the result of Step 3 by the result of Step 5.

7. Subtract the result of Step 6 from 1, to find r_s, Spearman's rank-order correlation coefficient.

TABLE 8-6   Examples of Assigning Ranks to IQ Scores

	Set A				Set B	
Subject	**IQ**	**Rank**		**Subject**	**IQ**	**Rank**
1	125	7		1	130	9
2	119	6		2	121	7
3	113	5		3	121	7
4	108	4		4	121	7
5	105	3		5	117	5
6	103	2		6	109	3.5
7	100	1		7	109	3.5
				8	105	2
				9	102	1

ratio. However, we cannot use Spearman's coefficient to measure the correlation between two variables when one or both variables are nominal, because nominal variables cannot be rank-ordered.

The trickiest part of calculating r_S is the first step, assigning the ranks. Table 8-6 shows two sets of IQ scores. In Set A, there are no duplicate scores. None of the people have the same score as another person. This is the simplest case for assigning ranks. We start by assigning the lowest score the rank of 1. In Set A, participant 7 has the lowest IQ, 100, and so we give participant 7 the rank of 1. Participant 6 has the next lowest IQ, 103, and so we give participant 6 the rank of 2, and so on. Note that the highest rank, 7, is equal to the number of participants in the set. As a check, we can calculate $.5n(n + 1)$, which for Set A is $.5(7)(7 + 1)$, or 28. The sum of the ranks assigned in Set A, $1 + 2 + 3 + 4 + 5 + 6 + 7$, is also 28.

Set B in Table 8-6 contains two sets of tied scores. Participants 2, 3, and 4 all have IQ scores of 121, while participants 6 and 7 both have IQs of 109. As with Set A, we begin assigning ranks by giving the lowest score, which in this case is an IQ of 102, the rank of 1. The second-lowest IQ, 105, is given the rank of 2. The next-lowest IQ is 109, a score which is held by two participants. The next two ranks to be assigned are the ranks of 3 and 4, and so we find the average of these two ranks, which is 3.5, and assign that rank to both participants whose IQ is 109. Because we have used the ranks of 3 and 4, the next rank to be assigned is the rank of 5, which is given to the next higher IQ score, 117. The next highest IQ score, 121, is held by three participants. The next ranks to be assigned are the ranks of 6, 7, and 8, which average to 7, and so the three participants with IQs of 121 are each given the rank of 7. Finally, the highest rank, 9, is assigned to the participant with the highest IQ score, 130.

Note that as in Set A, that the highest rank in Set B is equal to *n*, the number of subjects. To check, we can calculate $.5n(n + 1)$, which for Set B is $.5(9)(9 + 1)$, or 45. The sum of the ranks for Set B is $1 + 2 + 3.5 + 3.5 + 5 + 7 + 7 + 7 + 9$, which is also 45. If the sum of the ranks did not equal 45, we would know that we had made an error.

Now that we have examined how to assign ranks, we will examine all of the steps in calculating Spearman's r_S, using the example of Joe Johnson's math anxiety study. Recall again that Joe gave students a twenty-question math test and recorded the percent each student answered correctly. In the previous section, we measured the correlation between these math test scores and the students' systolic blood pressure using Pearson's *r*. Suppose that instead of measuring blood pressure, Joe asked ten of the students to rate their level of math anxiety while taking the test, on a scale of 1 to 10 (with 1 being no anxiety and 10 being extremely high anxiety). Figure 8-3 shows the percent that each student answered correctly on the math test, and Figure 8-4 shows the students' self-rating on math anxiety.

We can use the formula for Spearman's rank-order correlation to calculate if there is any relationship between the students' math anxiety and their performance on the math test in Joe's study. The first step is to rank the students' scores on the math test, and separately, on their anxiety ratings. Figure 8-3 shows the steps in assigning these ranks. The students' math test scores were originally listed in order, from highest to lowest, and this simplified the process of assigning ranks. To also simplify the process of assigning ranks to the students' anxiety ratings, in the second part of Figure 8-3, those ratings have been listed in order from highest to lowest. Note that the numbers in the

FIGURE 8-3 Assigning Ranks to Math Test Performance in Joe's Math Anxiety Study

Student	Percent Correct on Math Test	Rank to Be Assigned		Rank on Math Test
1	95	10		10
2	80	9		9
3	75	8	There are 2 tied scores of 75, so we assign them the average of the ranks of 7 and 8, or 7.5.	7.5
4	75	7		7.5
5	70	6		6
6	60	5	There are 3 tied scores of 60, so we assign them the average of the ranks of 3, 4, and 5, or 4.	4
7	60	4		4
8	60	3		4
9	50	2		2
10	40	1		1

Sum of ranks = 55

FIGURE 8-4   Assigning Ranks to Self-Ratings on Anxiety in Joe's Math Anxiety Study

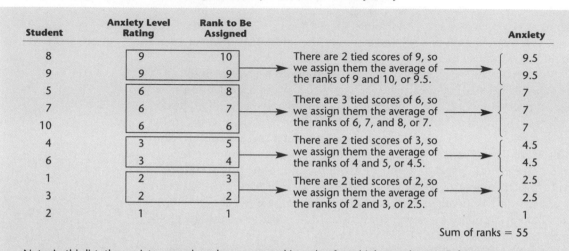

Student	Anxiety Level Rating	Rank to Be Assigned		Anxiety
8	9	10	There are 2 tied scores of 9, so we assign them the average of the ranks of 9 and 10, or 9.5.	9.5
9	9	9		9.5
5	6	8	There are 3 tied scores of 6, so we assign them the average of the ranks of 6, 7, and 8, or 7.	7
7	6	7		7
10	6	6		7
4	3	5	There are 2 tied scores of 3, so we assign them the average of the ranks of 4 and 5, or 4.5.	4.5
6	3	4		4.5
1	2	3	There are 2 tied scores of 2, so we assign them the average of the ranks of 2 and 3, or 2.5.	2.5
3	2	2		2.5
2	1	1		1

Sum of ranks = 55

Note: In this list, the anxiety scores have been arranged in order, from highest to lowest. Before computing Spearman's r_S, they must be put back in order by subject.

column headed "Student" no longer are in order. When we are ready to compute Spearman's r_S, we will need to put these anxiety ratings and their ranks back in order by student number, so that they are in the same order as the math scores. To check the accuracy of the ranks assigned to the math test scores and to the anxiety ratings, we first sum each set of ranks separately. Figures 8-3 and 8-4 show that the sum for each set of ranks is 55. Then we compare these sums to the result of the formula, $.5n(n + 1)$, which is $.5(10)(11)$, or 55.

Figure 8-5 shows the steps in calculating r_S. The ranks assigned in Figure 8-5 on math test scores and anxiety ratings are listed in order by student. Compare the order of the anxiety rating ranks in Figures 8-4 and 8-5. In Figure 8-4, the anxiety ratings are listed in order from highest to lowest. In Figure 8-5, they are listed in order by student number. And remember, as with Pearson's r, it is important to work carefully and methodically when calculating Spearman's r_S. Figure 8-5 shows that the correlation between Joe's math test scores and anxiety ratings for these students is $-.74$, which is a strong negative correlation. That indicates that the more anxious students rate themselves to be, the lower their math test scores.

Interpreting Spearman's Rank-Order Correlation

Spearman's rank-order correlation for ordinal data is equivalent to Pearson's r for interval and ratio data. Remember that Spearman's formula measures the relationship between *ranks* rather than the relationship between the scores di-

FIGURE 8-5   Calculating the Correlation between Math Test Performance and Anxiety Level

Subject	Rank on Math Test	Rank on Anxiety	D	D²
1	10	2.5	7.5	56.25
2	9	1	8.0	64.00
3	7.5	2.5	5.0	25.00
4	7.5	4.5	3.0	9.00
5	6	7	−1.0	1.00
6	4	4.5	−0.5	0.25
7	4	7	−3.0	9.00
8	4	9.5	−5.5	30.25
9	2	9.5	−7.5	56.25
10	1	7	−6.0	36.00

The boxes above the table read: "Subtract each student's anxiety rank from his/her math rank to find the difference, *D*." and "Square each of the differences to find *D²* for each subject."

Handwritten notes: "Subtraction of both Spearman Data 1 - 2"

$$\Sigma D^2 = 287.00$$

Sum all the squared differences, to find ΣD^2.

Insert the value of ΣD^2 in the formula for Spearman's r_s, and compute:

$$r_s = 1 - \frac{6\Sigma D^2}{n(n^2 - 1)} = 1 - \frac{6(287)}{10(10^2 - 1)} = 1 - \frac{1{,}722}{10(100 - 1)}$$

$$= 1 - \frac{1{,}722}{10(99)} = 1 - \frac{1{,}722}{990} = 1 - 1.74 = -0.74.$$

rectly. In fact, Spearman's formula will give the exact same correlation coefficient as Pearson's formula would if Pearson's formula were calculated on the ranks rather than on the scores. (Note that Pearson's and Spearman's formulas will *not* generate the same correlation coefficients if there are any tied ranks.)

Like Pearson's, the value of Spearman's correlation coefficient ranges from −1.00 to +1.00. A coefficient of +1.00 indicates a perfect positive linear correlation, and a coefficient of −1.00 indicates a perfect negative linear correlation. Like Pearson's, a Spearman's coefficient of zero indicates a null correlation, the absence of any linear correlation between the two variables being measured.

Measuring Correlation between Nominal Variables: The ϕ Coefficient

The ϕ **(phi) coefficient** is a measure of the correlation, or degree of relationship, between two dichotomous nominal variables.

Thus far, we have examined methods that can be used to measure correlation between variables that are ordinal, interval, or ratio. For the sake of completeness, in this section we will briefly look at one method that can be used to measure correlation between nominal variables, the ϕ (*phi*) **coefficient** (pronounced "fie"). In Chapter 18, we will examine another more frequently used method to measure the correlation between nominal variables, χ^2 (chi square).

For nominal variables, the numbers or names assigned to values are used solely to differentiate those values. The variable, sex, is a nominal variable. The terms *male* and *female* serve only to differentiate the two sexes. There is no implication that one sex is more of anything than the other; the two sexes are simply different. Similarly, if we assign code numbers to different majors, we are simply using the numbers as a way to differentiate between majors.

The ϕ coefficient is used to measure the correlation between two dichotomous nominal variables. A dichotomous variable is a variable that has only two values. Sex is a dichotomous variable because it has only two values, "male" and "female." Performance on a test can be measured dichotomously as "pass" or "fail." In fact, nearly all variables can be reduced to a dichotomous variable. For example, we could make the variable "age" dichotomous by recording only whether the person is an adult or child.

Suppose we survey a group of 100 students in a general psychology class on two questions: whether they read the assigned chapter and whether they passed the pop quiz on that chapter. We could display the results in a 2×2 contingency table (so called because it has two columns and two rows), as shown in Table 8-7.

As the variables shown in Table 8-7 are dichotomous and mutually exclusive, we can use the ϕ coefficient to measure the correlation between them. The ϕ coefficient can be used only on dichotomous variables, if only because variables that are not dichotomous have too many values to fit into the formula for ϕ. The procedure for calculating ϕ is shown in Step-by-Step Procedure 8-3.

TABLE 8-7 Number of General Psychology Students Who Did and Did Not Read Chapter and Who Did and Did Not Pass Quiz

Passed quiz?	Read? Yes	No
Yes	40	10
No	5	45

STEP-BY-STEP PROCEDURE 8-3

Calculating the ϕ Coefficient

$$\phi = \frac{AD - BC}{\sqrt{(A + B)(C + D)(A + C)(B + D)}}$$

where A, B, C, and D are the frequencies of subjects in the four cells of a 2 × 2 table representing two dichotomous variables:

A	B
C	D

1. Multiply A by D.

2. Multiply B by C. Subtract this result from the result of Step 1.

3. Add A and B. Add C and D. Add A and C. Add B and D.

4. Multiply the four sums found in Step 3 together. Find the square root of the result.

5. Divide the result of Step 2 by the result of Step 4 to find the ϕ coefficient.

[handwritten note: If equals 0 No CORRELATION]

Using the formula shown in Procedure 8-3, we can calculate the correlation between whether students read the chapter and whether they passed the quiz, as follows:

$$\phi = \frac{(40)(45) - (10)(5)}{\sqrt{(40 + 10)(5 + 45)(40 + 5)(10 + 55)}} = \frac{1800 - 50}{\sqrt{(50)(50)(45)(55)}}$$

$$= \frac{1750}{\sqrt{6,187,500}} = \frac{1750}{2487.47} = .70.$$

Thus, Procedure 8-3 shows that the correlation between reading the chapter and passing the quiz in the data shown in Table 8-7 is .70.

As with Pearson's r and Spearman's r_S, a positive value of ϕ indicates a positive correlation, a negative coefficient indicates a negative correlation, and a coefficient of zero indicates the absence of any correlation. Thus, the sign of the coefficient, + or −, indicates the direction of the relationship. The strength of the relationship is shown by the absolute value of the coefficient. A correlation of −1.00 is just as strong (in fact, perfectly so) as a correlation of +1.00. The weakest relationship is represented by zero, the absence of any correlation at all.

Correlation and Causation

In this chapter, we have examined several methods used to measure correlation. Each of these techniques is a way of measuring the strength of the relationship between two variables. It is important to note that a strong correlation between two variables, either positive or negative, does not mean that one of the variables caused the other. For example, in Joe's study of math anxiety, the fact that there was a correlation of −.93 between math test scores and systolic blood pressure does not prove that high blood pressure causes poor math test performance or that poor math test performance causes high blood pressure. The correlation of −.93 shows that there is a very strong relationship between math test scores and systolic blood pressure, but that correlation tells us nothing about what *causes* that relationship.

It is easy, when there is a high correlation between two variables, to assume that one of the variables is causing changes in the other variable. Nonetheless, correlation coefficients do not allow us to make any assumption about the cause of the relationship. For example, over the past 100 years, there has been an increase in the United States both in the number of refrigerators and in the cancer rate. If we calculated the correlation between the number of refrigerators and number of cancer deaths per year, there certainly would be a positive correlation. However, we cannot conclude from this correlation that either refrigerators cause cancer or that cancer leads to a greater number of refrigerators. A correlation only indicates that there is a relationship between two variables, but does not explain why that relationship occurs. Remember: *Correlation does not prove causation!*

CHECKING YOUR ANSWERS

1. When calculating any correlation coefficient, remember that the value can range from −1.00 to +1.00. When you calculate a correlation coefficient, if the value that you get is outside this range, it is certain that there is an error somewhere in your calculations.

2. When calculating Pearson's r, be careful identifying ΣX^2 and $(\Sigma X)^2$. If either of the terms in brackets inside the square root sign in the denominator is negative, you probably switched ΣX^2 and $(\Sigma X)^2$.

3. For both Spearman's r_S and Pearson's r, one way to check your answer is to make a scatterplot before beginning calculations. Using the scatterplot, estimate whether the correlation will be positive or negative and estimate the strength of the relationship. Then, after doing the calculations, compare your answer to this estimate.

4. When computing both Spearman's r_S and Pearson's r, remember that n represents the number of subjects, which is the same as the number of pairs of scores.

5. When calculating Spearman's rank-order correlation, some students forget to rank-order the scores and try to use the scores directly in the formula for r_S. Before using the formula, you must rank-order the scores. In addition, remember to rank-order each set of scores, those for X and those for Y, separately.

6. When calculating the formula for Spearman's r_S, be careful with the first part of the equation, the "1." In doing the calculations, some students let the "1" slip into the numerator of the fraction, so that they subtract ΣD^2 from 1, rather than first dividing by $n(n^2 - 1)$. In order to get the correct answer, you must reduce the fraction down to a single number *before* you subtract it from 1. On the other hand, don't forget to subtract the result of the fraction from 1. Some students get so involved in calculating the fraction that they simply forget to subtract that result from 1.

$\sum$ S U M M A R Y

▶ Correlation is a measure of the degree to which two variables are related. A correlation coefficient is a number between $+1.00$ and -1.00 that expresses that degree of relationship.

▶ A scatterplot is a graph that shows the relationship between two variables. The score values of one variable are shown on the *X*-axis, the score values of the second variable, on the *Y*-axis, and dots are used to represent the location of pairs of scores, one from each variable.

▶ In a positive correlation, scores on one variable tend to increase as scores on the other variable increase. A correlation coefficient with a positive sign $(+)$ indicates a positive correlation. In a negative correlation, scores on one variable tend to decrease as scores on the other variable increase. A correlation coefficient with a negative sign $(-)$ indicates a negative correlation. In a null correlation, indicated by a coefficient of zero, there is no relationship between scores on the two variables.

▶ In a correlation coefficient, the sign of the coefficient $(+$ or $-)$ indicates the direction of the relationship, while the absolute value of the coefficient indicates the strength of a relationship. A coefficient of ± 1.00 indicates a perfect relationship. A correlation of -1.00 is just as strong as a correlation of $+1.00$.

▶ Pearson's product-moment correlation, denoted by the symbol r, is a measure of the correlation between two interval and/or ratio variables. Pearson's r measures the similarity between the distances above or below the mean of pairs of scores collected from subjects.

▶ The size of Pearson's r can be affected spuriously by extreme scores in one or both distributions by combining groups of scores from two different populations and by restricting or expanding the range of the score values.

▶ Spearman's rank-order correlation coefficient, denoted ρ_s or r_s, is a measure of the correlation between two ordinal variables or between one ordinal variable and an interval or ratio variable. Spearman's r_s measures the similarity between the ranks of pairs of scores collected from subjects.

▶ The ϕ coefficient is a measure of the correlation between two nominal variables or between one nominal variable and one variable that is ordinal, interval, or ratio. The ϕ coefficient can be computed only on dichotomous variables (variables that have only two score values, such as A or $-$A and B or $-$B). The ϕ coefficient is a comparison of the probability that A occurs with B to the probability that A occurs without B.

▶ A correlation only indicates that there is a relationship between two variables. It does not explain why that relationship occurs. *Correlation does not prove causation.*

EXERCISES

Conceptual Exercises

1. Define the following terms:

correlation	null correlation
correlation coefficient	ϕ (*phi*) coefficient
positive correlation	Spearman's rank-order correlation
negative correlation	Pearson's product-moment correlation
zero correlation	

2. Jim studied marital satisfaction in several groups of couples by asking husbands and wives to rate their level of marital satisfaction on a scale from 1 (completely dissatisfied) to 10 (completely satisfied). The results for each group are shown below.

   Group I: Engaged Couples

Couple	Husband	Wife
1	10	10
2	8	8
3	6	6
4	4	4
5	2	2

   Group II: Newlyweds

Couple	Husband	Wife
1	10	8
2	8	10
3	6	6
4	4	2
5	2	4

   Group III: Cohabitating

Couple	Husband	Wife
1	10	8
2	8	2
3	6	6
4	4	10
5	2	4

   Group IV: Separated

Couple	Husband	Wife
1	10	4
2	8	2
3	6	6
4	4	10
5	2	8

   Group V: Divorced

Couple	Husband	Wife
1	10	2
2	8	4
3	6	6
4	4	8
5	2	10

   A. Calculate the value of Spearman's rank-order correlation coefficient for each of the groups of couples.

   B. Which group had the lowest sum of squared ranks? What value of ρ did that group receive?

   C. Which group had the largest sum of squared ranks? What value of ρ did that group receive?

   D. What is the relationship between the size of the sum of squared ranks and the value of ρ that you observed across all five groups?

   E. What is the relationship between the size of the sum of ranks and the value of the sample size, *n,* that you observed for these five groups?

   F. In regular English, use ρ to help describe the type of relationship present in each of the five groups.

3. Assume that the data in the previous exercise represent an interval scale of measurement, so that it is appropriate to use Pearson's product-moment correlation to measure the relationship between men's and women's marital satisfaction. Assume also that each group is a population.

   A. Convert each set of data to standard scores. Note that the same five scores are used for both the husbands and wives in each group, so that you only have to compute the mean and standard deviation once.

   B. Calculate the value of Pearson's r for each of the groups of couples, using the formula for standard scores.

   C. Which group had the highest sum of the cross products? What value of r did that group receive?

   D. Which group had the lowest sum of the cross products? What value of r did that group receive?

   E. What is the relationship between the size of the sum of cross products and the value of r that you observe across all five groups?

4. Josh studied the relationship between exercise and weight loss in several groups of people, with the following results. Examine the data in each 2×2 table, but do not calculate a correlation coefficient. Answer the questions below.

Set I

Exercise	Weight Loss Yes	No
Yes	40	0
No	0	40

Set V

Exercise	Weight Loss Yes	No
Yes	0	40
No	40	0

Set II

Exercise	Weight Loss Yes	No
Yes	30	10
No	10	30

Set VI

Exercise	Weight Loss Yes	No
Yes	40	0
No	20	20

Set III

Exercise	Weight Loss Yes	No
Yes	20	20
No	20	20

Set VII

Exercise	Weight Loss Yes	No
Yes	20	20
No	0	40

Set IV

Exercise	Weight Loss Yes	No
Yes	10	30
No	30	10

Set VIII

Exercise	Weight Loss Yes	No
Yes	20	20
No	40	0

Set IX

Exercise	Weight Loss Yes	No
Yes	0	40
No	20	20

   A. Which of the groups appear to have a positive correlation between exercise and weight loss, so that those who exercised lost weight and those who didn't exercise didn't lose weight?

   B. Which of the groups appear to have a negative correlation between exercise and weight loss, so that those who exercised did not lose weight, while those who didn't exercise did lose weight?

   C. Which of the groups appear to have no correlation, so that those who exercised weren't any more likely to lose weight than those who didn't exercise?

   D. Which of the groups appear to have the strongest correlation?

5. Calculate the correlation in each of the groups shown in the previous exercise, using the ϕ coefficient. How accurate were your estimates?

6. Suppose you have a group of 90 men and 60 women, for a total of 150 people. In the whole group, 50 people are registered as Democrats and 100 people are registered as Republicans.

   A. Construct a 2 × 2 table with the cell frequencies of Democrat men, Democrat women, Republican men, and Republican women such that there is absolutely no relationship between sex and party affiliation.

   B. Construct a 2 × 2 table with the cell frequencies of Democrat men, Democrat women, Republican men, and Republican women such that there is the strongest possible relationship between sex and party affiliation.

   C. Calculate the value of the ϕ coefficient for each 2 × 2 table you constructed. Do these values confirm the strength of the relationships you predicted?

7. Consider the correlation coefficients generated by Pearson's, Spearman's, and the ϕ formulas.

   A. What information does the sign (+ or −) of the coefficient tell us?

   B. What information does the size of the absolute value of the coefficient (disregarding the sign) tell us?

   C. What correlation coefficient indicates the strongest possible relationship? What coefficient indicates the weakest possible relationship?

Computational Exercises

8. Josiah was interested in exploring the relationship between the amount of time that students spend studying the night before a test, the amount of time they use to take an exam, and the grades they receive on the exam. He collected this information from eight students:

Student	Minutes Spent Studying	Minutes Spent Taking Test	Test Grade
A	85	39	85
B	135	55	98
C	90	47	81
D	115	59	92
E	45	43	70
F	60	40	68
G	105	37	89
H	70	51	76

A. Calculate the value of Pearson's product-moment correlation coefficient for each pair of variables: (i) time studying and test grade, (ii) time on test and test grade, and (iii) time studying and time on test.

B. In this group of eight students, which pair of variables shows the strongest relationship? Which pair of variables shows the weakest relationship?

9. Justine examined parents' opinions on the importance of three factors in child rearing: strict discipline of the child, nurturing the child, and amount of time spent with child. She surveyed nine parents, asking each parent to rate each of these factors on a scale of 1 (of least importance) to 10 (of extreme importance):

Parent	Strict Discipline	Nurturing Child	Time Spent with Child
A	5	10	8
B	10	4	9
C	5	8	7
D	9	6	2
E	6	8	6
F	9	6	5
G	3	10	9
H	7	6	4
I	4	9	5

A. Calculate the value of Spearman's rank-order correlation coefficient for each pair of variables: (i) strict discipline and nurturing child, (ii) strict discipline and time spent with child, and (iii) nurturing child and time spent with child.

B. In this group of nine parents, which pair of variables shows the strongest relationship? Which pair of variables shows the weakest relationship?

10. Jenetta studied the relationship between college grades and SAT scores by recording high school seniors' SAT scores and then, one year later, their first-year college grade point average. The results are shown below.

Student	SAT Score	GPA
1	1160	2.52
2	1250	3.14
3	1470	3.52
4	1020	2.31
5	1220	3.15
6	1390	3.76
7	1140	2.93
8	1280	2.76
9	1070	2.68
10	1190	3.39

A. What is the appropriate technique to use to measure the correlation in these data? Why?

B. Compute the correlation in these data.

C. What does the correlation coefficient you found say about the relationship between SAT scores and college GPA?

11. Joni studied the relationship between time spent studying and test scores among students in her statistics class by recording the number of problems that the students turned in as homework and their test scores. The results are shown below.

Student	Number of Problems	Test Score (%)
1	17	85
2	23	93
3	15	81
4	24	90
5	10	78
6	18	89
7	13	78
8	21	94
9	12	70
10	19	87
11	15	80
12	20	96

A. What is the appropriate technique to use to measure the correlation in these data? Why?

B. Compute the correlation in these data.

C. What does the correlation coefficient you found say about the relationship between the number of problems students work and their test scores?

12. Justin studied the relationship between the amount of exercise and perceived difficulty of exercise by having ten men record the number of hours they exercised in one week and then having them rate the difficulty of that exercise on a scale of 1 (very easy) to 10 (very difficult), with the following results.

Participant	Hours of Exercise	Perceived Difficulty
1	2.0	4
2	3.5	3
3	1.0	8
4	5.0	3
5	2.0	6
6	3.0	5
7	4.5	4
8	7.0	2
9	4.0	6
10	5.0	4

A. What is the appropriate technique to use to measure the correlation in these data? Why?

B. Compute the correlation in these data.

C. What does the correlation coefficient you found say about the relationship between the amount and perceived difficulty of exercise?

13. Some people believe that children do better in kindergarten if they start later. Jocelyn studied this belief by recording 16 kindergarten children's ages at the end of the school year and then compiling their grades into a class rank, with the child receiving the highest marks ranked as 1 and the child receiving the lowest marks ranked as 16. The results are shown below.

Child	Age	Rank on Grades
1	6.8	2
2	6.6	10
3	6.0	14
4	6.9	3
5	5.8	13
6	6.4	9
7	5.9	6
8	6.6	5
9	6.1	15
10	6.5	8
11	6.8	7
12	6.2	16
13	6.6	1
14	6.4	11
15	6.0	12
16	6.7	4

A. What is the appropriate technique to use to measure the correlation in these data? Why?

B. Compute the correlation in these data.

C. What does the correlation coefficient you found say about the relationship between kindergartners' ages and grades?

14. There is a common belief that children who watch violence on TV are more aggressive than children who do not watch TV violence. Jonah tested this belief by observing a group of children and noting whether or not they watched violent TV programs and whether or not they were aggressive on the playground, with the following results.

Watch TV Violence	Aggressive: Yes	No
Yes	41	9
No	17	33

A. What is the appropriate technique to use to measure the correlation in these data? Why?

B. Compute the correlation between TV violence and aggression in these data.

C. What does the correlation coefficient you found say about the relationship between TV violence and aggression?

15. Professors often have the suspicion that those who are regarded as easy graders receive higher student evaluations than those who are regarded as hard graders. Jack tested

this suspicion by asking students to rate eighty professors as either easy or hard graders. He then verified whether those professors were above or below average on student evaluations, with the following results.

Student Evaluations	Type of Grader: Easy	Hard
Above average	20	20
Below average	25	15

A. What is the appropriate technique to use to measure the correlation in these data? Why?
B. Compute the correlation in these data.
C. What does the correlation coefficient you found say about the relationship between whether students see professors as being easy or hard graders and the student evaluations those professors receive?

Regression and Prediction

Prediction

Blind Guessing

Using Information on One Variable
to Predict Scores on Another Variable

**Graphing the Relationship
between Two Variables**

Graphing a Straight Line

Graphing the Regression Line:
Predicting *Y* from *X*

STEP-BY-STEP PROCEDURE 9-1: Finding the
Value of the Slope of the Regression Line Using
X to Predict Y

STEP-BY-STEP PROCEDURE 9-2: Alternate
Method of Finding the Value of the Slope of
the Regression Line

STEP-BY-STEP PROCEDURE 9-3: Finding the
Y-Intercept and Constructing the Regression
Line Using X to Predict Y

The Second Regression Line

Regression

Regression as a Predictor of the Mean

Regression to the Mean

Regression and the Least-Squares Criterion

Standard Error of Estimate

STEP-BY-STEP PROCEDURE 9-4: Calculating the
Standard Error of Estimate

Coefficients of Determination
and Nondetermination

Regression, Correlation, and Causation

CHECKING YOUR ANSWERS

SUMMARY

EXERCISES

Conceptual Exercises

Computational Exercises

▶ In the last chapter, we examined the concept of correlation, the measure of the relationship between two variables. We can use our knowledge of the correlation between two variables to make predictions. There are many situations in which it would be useful to have the kind of knowledge that would help us make more accurate predictions. For example, college admissions officers want to be able to predict which applicants are the most likely to succeed in college. Suppose a college receives 2,000 applications for admission but can accept only 500 new students. How does the college decide which students to accept?

One method that college admissions officers could use would be to randomly accept students without any consideration of the students' prior records. For example, the college could accept every fourth student who applied. The problem with this method is that the college may accept students who may have very little chance of succeeding in college in preference over students who have a much higher chance of succeeding. If a college is unable to accept all its applicants, the admissions officers certainly want to select those students who are most likely to succeed.

An alternative to randomly accepting students would be to use information in the students' applications to help make predictions about who is and is not likely to succeed in college. For example, the admissions officers could use the students' high school grade point averages (GPAs) to help predict who will succeed in college. A student who had a 3.95 GPA in high school is probably more likely to succeed in college than a student who had a high school GPA of 1.75. This, of course, assumes that there is a relationship between high school grades and college grades, such that students who did well in high school are also likely to do well in college. Thus, if there is a correlation between high school and college grades, we can use that correlation to help predict from knowledge of students' high school grades who will succeed in college. Decisions that are based on relevant correlations are likely to be more accurate than decisions made randomly. Using information from correlations to make predictions is the focus of this chapter.

Prediction

We make predictions every day. When we look at the sky in the morning to decide whether we need to take an umbrella, we are making a prediction about the likelihood of rain. Predictions are a part of everyday life. Predictions are also a part of psychology. When a school psychologist uses an IQ score as the basis for assigning a child to a gifted program, the psychologist is making a prediction about the child's future performance in school. When a counselor uses a personality test as the basis for recommending career choices to a client, the counselor is making a prediction about the client's success and satisfaction in that career.

In essence, a **prediction** is a guess about which value of a variable a given event will have. For the school psychologist, the variable is school performance, and the psychologist is guessing that a child with a high IQ will perform better in a gifted program than in a regular school program. The employment counselor is making guesses about two variables, career success and career satisfaction. The counselor is guessing that the value the client will show on those two variables, the level of success and level of satisfaction, will be higher in the recommended career than in other careers.

In the statistical techniques that we have examined so far, we have collected actual measurements of events. Joe Johnson observed students taking a math test and measured their actual performance. Jane Jeffers measured the actual incomes of psychology alumni. When making predictions, however, we are not actually measuring events that we observe. Instead, we are making a guess about what value the score would be if we did actually measure it.

> A **prediction** is a guess about what value an event drawn from a specified population will have on a given variable.

Blind Guessing

Sometimes we make predictions without having any information to help us. In these cases, we are making a **blind guess.** When you pick heads or tails at a coin toss, you are making a blind guess. There is no information you could have to help you predict whether the coin will come up heads or tails (assuming that the coin is fair). If a college admissions officer selects every fourth applicant for admission, without examining any of the information in the application, the admissions officer would be making blind guesses.

> A **blind guess** is a prediction made without the aid of any relevant information.

Suppose you are paid for the task of guessing people's heights. You are seated in a room and are blindfolded. A person is brought into the room, and you are asked to guess that person's height. You have no information about the person. You do not even hear the person's voice to give you a clue whether the person was a male or female. This task captures the essence of blind guessing. You would have no information at all to help you make a prediction.

What height would you guess? Your best guess depends on the conditions for payment. Suppose you guess the heights of the fifteen people listed in Table 9-1. Also suppose that you are paid $1.00 only if you guess the height correctly, to the nearest inch. In that case, your best guess is the mode. In Table 9-1, the modal height is 72 inches. If you guess each person's height as 72 inches, you will be correct 5 out of 15 times, or 33 percent of the time, and earn $5.00. If you guess 71 inches, you will be correct only 3 times, or 20 percent of the time, and earn only $3.00. If you guess any other height, you will

TABLE 9-1 Comparing Errors in Prediction,
When an Error Is Defined as |Actual Height − Predicted Height|

Person	Actual Height (inches)	Mean: 68 Inches	Median: Predicted Height, 71 Inches	Mode: 72 Inches
Abe	74	6	3	2
Bob	72	4	1	0
Cal	72	4	1	0
Don	72	4	1	0
Erv	72	4	1	0
Fred	72	4	1	0
Gus	71	3	0	1
Hal	71	3	0	1
Ike	71	3	0	1
Jack	68	0	3	4
Ken	63	5	8	9
Lou	62	6	9	10
Moe	61	7	10	11
Ned	60	8	11	12
Opy	59	9	12	13
Total error		70	61	64
Total winnings		$11.50	$11.95	$11.80

be correct even less. Thus, if you are paid $1.00 only if you guess correctly, your best prediction would be the mode. Guessing the mode will not make you correct every time, but you will be correct more often guessing the mode than any other value.

Now suppose that you get paid $1.00 for every guess, but 5¢ is subtracted for every inch that you are off in either direction. If you are correct on every guess, you could win a total of $15.00. However, you would be penalized for errors. For instance, if a person is 70 inches tall and you guess 67 inches, then you will be paid $0.85, rather than $1.00. In this situation, the size of the error is defined as the absolute distance between the actual height and the height you predicted, |actual height − predicted height|. You want to earn as much money as possible. What is your best guess? Under these conditions, your best guess is the median. Table 9-1 shows the error in inches for three different predictions, the mean, the mode, and the median. If you predict all 15 men's heights as 72 inches, which is the mode, your total error is 64 inches, and you earn $11.80. If you predict the mean for every man, 68 inches, your total error is 70 inches, and you earn $11.50. However, if you predict all 15 men's heights as 71 inches, the median, your total error is only 61 inches, and you earn $11.95. Given the penalty of 5¢ per inch, the total error is lowest when your prediction is the median.

Thus far, we have seen that if you are paid only for correct guesses, your best prediction is the mode, but if you are paid more the lower your total error rate, then your best prediction is the median. Now suppose that again you are paid $1.00 a guess. An amount is deducted for each error, but this time the amount deducted depends on the size of the error. If your prediction is off by 1 inch, you lose 1¢. If your error is 2 inches, your loss is 2¢ per inch, or a total of 4¢. If your error is 3 inches, you lose 3¢ per inch, or a total of 9¢. If your error is 10 inches, you lose 10¢ per inch, or a total of $1.00. The amount you lose is the square of the size of the error. In this system, you are penalized more for large errors than for small errors. Your penalty is defined by (actual score − predicted score)^2, the square of the difference between the actual and predicted scores.

Under these conditions, your best prediction is the mean. Table 9-2 shows the penalties you would pay out of your winnings for the same predictions as

TABLE 9-2 Comparing Errors in Prediction, When an Error Is Defined as (Actual Height − Predicted Height)^2

Person	Actual Height (inches)	Mean: 68 Inches (in square inches)	Median: Predicted Height, 71 Inches (in square inches)	Mode: 72 Inches (in square inches)
Abe	74	36	9	4
Bob	72	16	1	0
Cal	72	16	1	0
Don	72	16	1	0
Erv	72	16	1	0
Fred	72	16	1	0
Gus	71	9	0	1
Hal	71	9	0	1
Ike	71	9	0	1
Jack	68	0	9	16
Ken	63	25	64	81
Lou	62	36	81	100
Moe	61	49	100	121
Ned	60	64	121	144
Opy	59	81	144	169
Total loss in square inches		398	533	638
Total winnings		$11.02	$9.67	$8.62

shown in Table 9-1. If you predict all of the heights as the mode, 72 inches, your losses are $6.38, and you earn $8.62. If you predict all of the heights as the median, 71 inches, your losses are slightly less, $5.33, and you earn $9.67. On the other hand, if you use the mean, 68 inches, as your prediction, your total losses are only $3.98, and you make $11.02. The cost of errors under these conditions would be the lowest when your prediction is the mean.

Most of the time, when we make predictions, there is no way to guarantee absolute accuracy. Our goal is not to guess perfectly, which is impossible, but to minimize errors and maximize accuracy. The best method to achieve this goal depends on our definition of error. If we define error simply as an incorrect guess, our best prediction is the mode. If we define error as the absolute deviation of the prediction from the score, our best guess is the median. However, if we penalize large errors proportionally more than small errors, our best guess is the mean. Thus, the best prediction depends on how errors are penalized.

Using Information on One Variable to Predict Scores on Another Variable

When we are making a blind guess, even when we are making the best prediction, there still is considerable error. We can reduce the size of the error if we have relevant information about the subject of our prediction. For example, suppose we are trying to predict the height of children in grade school. If we know nothing about the individual children, we can only make blind guesses. However, knowing the child's age can improve our prediction. We are likely to predict a shorter height if we know the child is six years old than if we know the child is ten years old.

Table 9-3 shows the heights of twenty-five fictitious children. The mean of the entire group of children is 49 inches. If we know nothing about a child selected from this group, our best blind guess of that child's height would be 49 inches, the mean. Of course, making this guess blind, our prediction could

TABLE 9-3 Mean Heights of a Distribution of Twenty-Five Children, by Age, in Inches

	6 Years	7 Years	8 Years	9 Years	10 Years
	45	48	51	54	57
	44	47	50	53	56
	43	46	49	52	55
	42	45	48	51	54
	41	44	47	50	53
Mean	43	46	49	52	55

err by as much as 8 inches. If we know the child's age, we could reduce this error. Suppose we know that the child is six years old. Our best prediction, then, would be the mean height of the six-year-old children, which is 43 inches. With this information about the child's age, the most that our prediction could err in this group of children is by 2 inches. We have reduced the maximum error from 8 inches when blind guessing to 2 inches when basing the guess on the child's age.

We can thus increase the accuracy of our predictions by using information about a relevant variable. Of course, the variable must be relevant to the prediction. A child's age is relevant to a prediction about the child's height because children's heights increase with age. It wouldn't make sense to use information about a child's IQ to predict height. We wouldn't necessarily expect taller children to have higher IQs. There isn't any relationship between IQ and height (at least, theoretically), and thus information about IQ isn't relevant to predictions about height.

A variable is relevant in making predictions about another variable if there is a correlation between the two variables. Age is relevant to predictions about height because age and height are correlated. IQ is not relevant to predictions about height because IQ and height are not correlated. If there is a relationship between two variables, we can use information from one variable to make predictions on the other variable. Thus, we can use information about a correlation to improve the accuracy of our predictions. And, as we shall see, the stronger the correlation, the more that accuracy will be improved.

When we use information from one variable to help predict scores on another variable, the variable about which we have information is called the **predictor variable.** If we use a child's age to help predict that child's height, age is the predictor variable. The predictor variable is conventionally designated as variable X. The variable to be predicted is called the **predicted variable.** In our example, we are trying to predict the child's height, and so height is the predicted variable. Conventionally, the predicted variable is designated as variable Y. The symbol X is used to represent a subject's actual score on variable X, and the symbol Y is used to represent the actual score of a subject on variable Y. To differentiate between actual scores and predicted scores, we use the symbol, Y', to represent a predicted score on variable Y. Thus, Y represents an actual measurement, while Y' represents a prediction.

The **predictor variable** is the variable in a regression equation that gives relevant information to help predict a value on another variable. The predictor variable is labeled X.

The **predicted variable** is the variable that a regression equation predicts. The predicted variable is labeled Y. A predicted score is designated as Y'.

Graphing the Relationship between Two Variables

Graphing a Straight Line

As we saw in the previous chapter, we can graph the relationship between two variables in a scatterplot. In scatterplots representing regression, the X-axis

FIGURE 9-1   Relationship between Age and Height among Twenty-Five Children

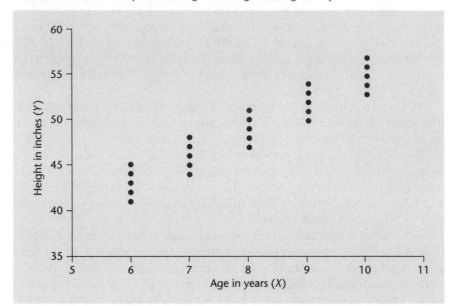

The **slope** of a straight line in a graph is the degree to which the line varies from horizontal and reflects the degree of change in the values on the *Y*-axis relative to changes in the values on the *X*-axis.

The **Y-intercept** is the point that a line on a graph crosses the *Y*-axis.

represents the values of the predictor variable, while the *Y*-axis represents the values of the predicted variable. The scatterplot shown in Figure 9-1 represents the heights of the children listed in Table 9-3. Suppose you wanted to use the information from the scatterplot in Figure 9-1 to predict the height of a six-year-old child. There are five heights shown for the six-year-old children in Figure 9-1. Which height would you predict? In order to make predictions, we need one value of *Y* for each value of *X*. Thus, we need a single line, rather than a mass of dots.

Figure 9-2 shows a single line, which we can use for prediction. To predict the height of an eight-year-old child from this graph, we first draw a line vertically from eight years old on the *X*-axis to the point where it intersects the line in the graph. Then we draw a line horizontally to the left to find the point it intersects on the *Y*-axis. Using this method, we find that the height of 49 inches on the *Y*-axis corresponds to the value of eight years old on the *X*-axis. From this graph, we predict that an eight-year-old child is 49 inches tall. Thus, if there is a straight line in the graph, rather than a mass of dots, we can find the value of *Y* that corresponds to each value of *X*.

There are only two things that we need to know in order to draw a graph of a straight line, the **slope** and the **Y-intercept**. Figure 9-3 shows examples of straight line graphs. One way that these graphs differ is the slopes of the lines. Line A has an upward slope, line B has a downward slope, and line C is

FIGURE 9-2 Predicting Height from Age

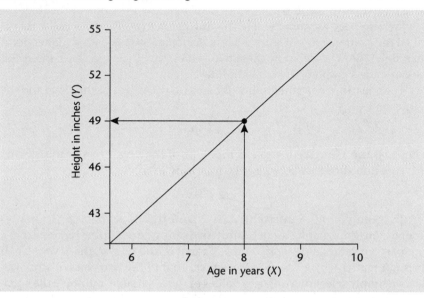

FIGURE 9-3 Graphs of Straight Line Equations

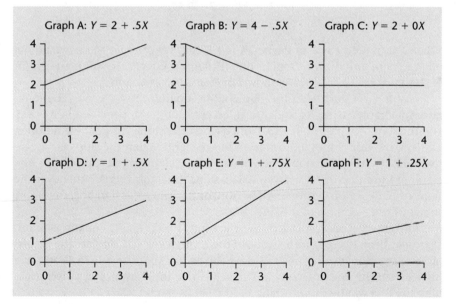

horizontal. Line E has a very steep slope, while line F has a more gradual slope. In order to draw a graph of a line, we need to know the slope of the line.

We also need to know where the line crosses the *Y*-axis, a point that is called the *Y*-intercept. In Figure 9-3, line A crosses the *Y*-axis at a higher point than line D does. If we know these two values, the slope and the *Y*-intercept, we can draw a graph of any straight line.

The equation for a straight line is based on the values of the slope and the *Y*-intercept:

$$Y = a + bX,$$

where *a* is the *Y*-intercept and *b* is the slope of the line. In order to see what this equation shows us, let's plot the following example:

$$Y = 2 + .5X.$$

In this example, the *Y*-intercept, *a*, is 2, and the slope, *b*, is .5. To draw a straight line on a graph, we need only two points, each point representing a pair of score values, one score on the *X* variable and one on the *Y* variable. It does not matter which two points we pick. To find the two pairs of score values, we simply select two different values of the *X* variable and solve the equation for the value of *Y*. Again, we can pick any two values of *X*. Let's try the values, *X* = 0 and *X* = 4:

$$Y = 2 + .5(0) = 2 + 0 = 2,$$
$$Y = 2 + .5(4) = 2 + 2 = 4.$$

When *X* is 0, then *Y* is 2, and when *X* is 4, *Y* is 4. We can plot these two points on the graph and draw a straight line through them. The result is the graph of the equation, $Y = 2 + .5X$, shown in Figure 9-3 as Graph A.

Graph B in Figure 9-3 is the graph of the equation, $Y = 4 - .5X$. The equations for Graphs A and B are identical, except that the slope of Graph A is +.5 and the slope of Graph B is −.5. Notice when the slope is a positive number, like +.5, the line slopes upward from left to right. When the slope is a negative number, the line slopes downward from left to right. Graph C is the graph of the equation, $Y = 2 + 0X$. The slope in Graph C is 0. Whenever the slope of a line is zero, the line will be horizontal. Thus, the sign of *b*, the slope, shows us the direction of the line.

In Figure 9-3, Graph D is of the equation, $Y = 1 + .5X$. Equations A and D are identical, except for the value of the *Y*-intercept, *a*. Compare the graphs of these two equations. They are identical, except that the line in Graph A is higher than the line in Graph D. The value of *a*, the *Y*-intercept, tells us how high the line will be on the graph.

Equations E and F are modifications of Graph D. For all three graphs, the *Y*-intercept, *a*, is 1, and thus all three graphs cross the *Y*-axis at 1. All three graphs have positive slopes, and so the lines all slope upward from left to right. The graphs differ in the values of the slope. Graph D has a slope of .5, Graph E has a slope of .75, and Graph F has a slope of .25. Notice that the line in Graph E is steeper than the line in Graph D, while the line in Graph F is not as steep. Therefore, the value of the slope, *b* (disregarding the sign), tells us how steeply the line will slope.

In summary, there are two characteristics that differentiate graphs of a straight line, the *Y*-intercept and the slope. First, the value of the *Y*-intercept, *a*, tells us where the line crosses the *Y*-axis and thus how high the line will be on the graph. Second, the sign of the slope, *b*, tells us in what direction the line will slope. If *b* is positive, the line will slope upward; if *b* is negative, the line will slope downward; and if *b* is zero, the line will be horizontal. The value of the slope (disregarding the sign) tells us how steeply the line will slope. The greater the value of *b*, the more steeply the line slopes. We will use these characteristics to help understand the line representing the correlation between two variables.

Graphing the Regression Line: Predicting *Y* from *X*

In Figure 9-1, we constructed a scatterplot of the relationship between age and height among 25 children. In order to make predictions from the information in the scatterplot, we need to draw a single line through the dots, called the regression line. As with all graphs of all straight lines, to construct a regression line through a scatterplot, we need only two values: the value of the *Y*-intercept, *a*, and the value of the slope, *b*. First we will find the value of the slope, *b*, and then use that value to find the value of the *Y*-intercept, *a*.

Step-by-Step Procedure 9-1 describes one method for finding the slope, based on the value of Pearson's product-moment correlation coefficient, *r*.

In order to find the slope of the regression line for the scatterplot shown in Figure 9-1, we need to know the standard deviations for variables *X* and *Y*, as well as the value of Pearson's product-moment correlation coefficient for variables *X* and *Y*. Recall that the scores for this scatterplot are listed in Table 9-3. The standard deviation of the children's ages shown in Table 9-3 is 1.44, the standard deviation of the children's heights is 4.56, and the correlation between the children's ages and heights is .95. These are the values that we need to use Procedure 9-1 to find the slope of the regression line:

$$b = \frac{s_Y}{s_X} r_{XY} = \frac{4.56}{1.44}(.95) = 3.$$

Thus, for the regression line predicting children's heights from their ages, the slope, *b*, is 3.

Step-by-Step Procedure 9-2 describes an alternate method of finding the value of the slope, which does not require knowing the value of Pearson's coefficient, *r*. In Procedure 9-2, we need the values of ΣX and ΣX^2, again with *X* representing the predictor variable, in this case, the children's ages. For the

A **regression equation** expresses the relationship between the known value of a predictor variable, *X*, and the predicted value of variable *Y*, based on the correlation between the two variables. A linear regression equation has the form, $Y' = a + bX$.

The **slope** of a regression line reflects the degree to which the predicted variable, *Y'*, increases or decreases as the predictor variable, *X*, increases. In the regression equation, $Y' = a + bX$, the value *b* represents the slope.

The **Y-intercept** of a regression line is the predicted value of *Y'* when the value of the predicted variable *X* is 0. In the regression equation, the value *a* represents the *Y*-intercept.

STEP-BY-STEP PROCEDURE 9-1

Finding the Value of the Slope of the Regression Line Using *X* to Predict *Y*

$$\text{Slope of the line: } b = \frac{s_Y}{s_X}r_{XY}$$

where b = the slope of the regression line
        s_Y = the standard deviation of variable Y
        s_X = the standard deviation of variable X
        r_{XY} = the correlation between variables X and Y

1. Calculate the sample standard deviation for variable X.

2. Calculate the sample standard deviation for variable Y.

3. Calculate Pearson's product-moment correlation coefficient for the relationship between variables X and Y.

4. Divide the standard deviation of Y, found in Step 2, by the standard deviation of X, found in Step 1. Multiply the result by the correlation coefficient found in Step 3. The result is b, the slope of the regression line.

STEP-BY-STEP PROCEDURE 9-2

Alternate Method of Finding the Value of the Slope of the Regression Line

$$\text{Slope of the line: } \quad b = \frac{n\Sigma XY - (\Sigma X)(\Sigma Y)}{n\Sigma X^2 - (\Sigma X)^2}$$

where b = the slope of the regression line
        X = the scores on the predictor variable
        Y = the scores on the predicted variable
        n = number of pairs of scores

1. Add up the scores for the predictor variable, X, to find ΣX.

2. Add up the scores for the predicted variable, Y, to find ΣY. Multiply this result by the result of Step 1.

3. Multiply each pair of scores together. Then add up all of these products, to find ΣXY, and multiply this sum by the number of pairs of scores, n. Subtract the result of Step 2 from this result.

4. Square the result found in Step 1.

5. Square each score for the predictor variable, X, and then add up these squared values, to find ΣX^2. Multiply this sum by n, and then subtract the result of Step 4.

6. Divide the result of Step 3 by the result of Step 5, to find the value of b, the slope of the regression line.

STEP-BY-STEP PROCEDURE 9-3

Finding the Y-Intercept and Constructing the Regression Line Using X to Predict Y

$$Y\text{-intercept:} \quad a = \bar{Y} - b\bar{X}$$

$$\text{Regression line:} \quad Y' = a + bX$$

where a = the Y-intercept
$\bar{Y}$ = the mean of variable Y
$\bar{X}$ = the mean of variable X
b = slope

1. Find the mean of the scores for the predictor variable, X.

2. Multiply the value of the slope, b, found using Step-by-Step Procedure 9-1 or 9-2, by the mean of variable X, found in Step 1.

3. Find the mean of the scores for the predicted variable, Y.

4. Subtract the result of Step 2 from the result of Step 3. The result is a, the Y-intercept.

5. Insert the value of b, found using Step-by-Step Procedure 9-1 or 9-2, and the value of a, found in Step 4, into the equation for the regression line.

---

children's ages shown in Table 9-3, the value of ΣX is 200, while ΣX^2 is 1,650. We also need the value of ΣY, which in this case is the sum of the children's heights, 1,225 inches. Finally, we need the value of ΣXY, the sum of the cross product of each child's age and height. For the heights listed in Table 9-3, ΣXY is 9,950. These are the values we need for the formula shown in Procedure 9-2:

$$b = \frac{n\Sigma XY - (\Sigma X)(\Sigma Y)}{n\Sigma X^2 - (\Sigma X)^2} = \frac{25(9,950) - (200)(1,225)}{25(1,650) - 200^2} = \frac{248,750 - 245,000}{41,250 - 40,000} = \frac{3,750}{1,250} = 3.$$

Using this formula, we find that the value of the slope is 3, the same value that we found using Procedure 9-1. Thus, Procedures 9-1 and 9-2 give the same value for the slope of the regression line.

The next step in constructing the regression equation is to use the value of the slope to find the value of the Y intercept, as shown in Step-by-Step Procedure 9-3. To do so, we need the means of the predictor variable, X, and the predicted variable, Y. For the regression line predicting height from age, the predictor variable is age, and the mean age of the children shown in Table 9-3 is 8. The predicted variable is height, and the mean height is 49 inches. Finally, for the formula shown in Procedure 9-3, we need the value of the slope, b, which we previously found to be 3:

$$a = \bar{Y} - b\bar{X} = 49 - (3)(8) = 49 - 24 = 25.$$

We now have the values of *a* and *b* that we need to construct the equation for the regression line:

$$\text{height}' = 25 + 3(\text{age}).$$

This equation says that the predicted height, *Y'*, will be three times the child's age, *X*, plus 25. To plot this regression line on the scatterplot in Figure 9-1, we need to use this equation to find the predicted values of *Y* for two values of *X*. We'll use the ages of six and ten years old:

$$Y' = 25 + 3X = 25 + 3(6) = 25 + 18 = 43,$$

$$Y' = 25 + 3X = 25 + 3(10) = 25 + 30 = 55.$$

The predicted height for a six-year-old child is 43 inches and the predicted height for a ten-year-old child is 55 inches. To draw the regression line, we find these two points on the scatterplot and draw a straight line through them, as shown in Figure 9-4.

We can now use the regression equation to predict the heights of children who were not part of the original sample of children. For example, we could predict the height of a child who is six-and-a-half years old:

$$Y' = 25 + 3X = 25 + 3(6.5) = 25 + 19.5 = 44.5 \text{ inches.}$$

According to the regression equation, we predict that a child who is six-and-a-half years old will be 44.5 inches tall.

FIGURE 9-4   Regression Line Predicting Children's Heights from Their Age

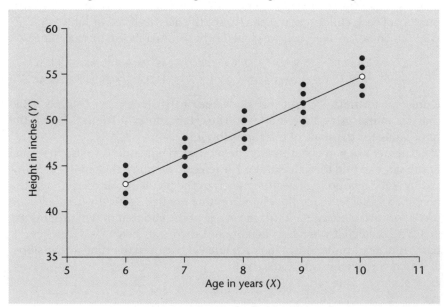

The Second Regression Line

Thus far, we have constructed the regression line using the child's age to predict height. We could reverse this process, to use the child's height to predict age. In this case, height is the predictor variable, X, and age is the predicted variable, Y. As before, the mean age of the 25 children was 8.0 years, with a standard deviation of 1.44. The mean height of children was 49.0 inches, with a standard deviation of 4.56. The correlation between age and height, r_{XY}, was .95.

We will again use Procedures 9-1 and 9-3 to construct the regression equation. The first value we will find is the slope of the regression line. Note that the standard deviation of the children's ages is now in the numerator, as age is now variable Y:

$$b = \frac{s_Y}{s_X}r_{XY} = \frac{1.44}{4.56}(.95) = 0.3.$$

We then use this value of b to find the Y-intercept, a. Remember again that age is now the predicted variable, Y:

$$a = \bar{Y} - b\bar{X} = 8 - (0.3)(49) = 8 - 14.7 = -6.7.$$

We now have the values of a and b that we need to construct the equation for the regression line:

$$\text{age}' = -6.7 + 0.3(\text{height}).$$

We can use this equation to predict the age of a child who is 45 inches tall:

$$\text{age}' = -6.7 + 0.3(45) = 6.8 \text{ years.}$$

It is important to note that we have constructed two different regression equations expressing the relationship between age and height. In one equation, we are predicting height from age. In the other equation, we are predicting age from height:

predicting height from age: $\text{height}' = 25 + 3(\text{age})$,

predicting age from height: $\text{age}' = -6.7 + 0.3(\text{height})$.

Figure 9-5 shows the regression line predicting the children's ages from their heights. Note that this is a different graph than the regression line predicting height from age, shown in Figure 9-4. Note also that the slopes of the two equations differ, as do the values of the Y intercepts. It is very important in constructing the regression equation to clearly identify which variable is the predictor and which is the predicted.

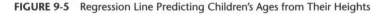

FIGURE 9-5   Regression Line Predicting Children's Ages from Their Heights

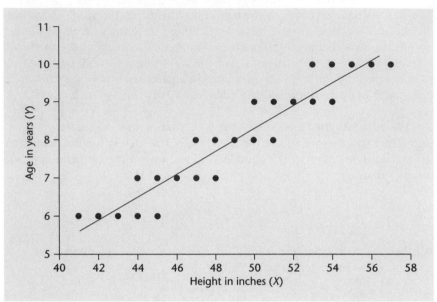

Regression

Regression as a Predictor of the Mean

For all subjects with a given value on the predictor variable, X, the regression equation will predict the same value on variable Y. Thus, using the regression equation we have constructed, the predicted height for all six-and-a-half-year-old children will be 43.5 inches. Similarly, this regression equation will predict that any eight-year-old child is 49 inches tall. Thus, the regression equation predicts one single value of variable Y for all the subjects who have the same value of variable X.

What value of variable Y does the regression equation predict? Table 9-4 shows the mean heights of the twenty-five children whose heights are listed in Table 9-3. The mean height of the six-year-old children in our study was 43 inches. What height would our regression equation predict for another six-year-old child, one who was not actually measured in our study? Table 9-4 shows that the regression equation would predict that another six-year-old child would be 43 inches tall, the mean height of six-year-old children in our original sample. In fact, the regression equation predicts the mean height of an age group for any child in that age group.

Remember that when making a blind guess, the best prediction can be the mean. Among all of the children in our sample, the mean height was

TABLE 9-4 Mean Heights and Predicted Heights of Children Shown in Table 9-3

Age (years)	Mean Height (inches)	Regression Equation	Predicted Height (inches)
6	43	$\hat{Y} = 25 + 3(6) =$	43
7	46	$\hat{Y} = 25 + 3(7) =$	46
8	49	$\hat{Y} = 25 + 3(8) =$	49
9	52	$\hat{Y} = 25 + 3(9) =$	52
10	55	$\hat{Y} = 25 + 3(10) =$	55

49 inches. If we do not know a child's age, our best prediction of the child's height by blind guessing would be that mean, 49 inches. However, if we know the child's age, we can improve the accuracy of our prediction. Given the child's age, the regression equation will predict the mean height of children in that age group. Of course, not every six-year-old child will be exactly 43 inches tall. In fact, only one of the five six-year-old children in our sample was actually 43 inches tall. Thus, the predictions we make using the regression equation will not be absolutely accurate. Nonetheless, those predictions will be the best guess, given the information available.

The distribution of children's heights shown in Table 9-3 was constructed so that the mean height for each age group would fall exactly on the regression line. In the real world, this usually will not occur. For example, Figure 9-6 shows a scatterplot of the math test scores and blood pressures that Joe Johnson collected in his study of math anxiety. The mean blood pressure found for students scoring each percentage correct on the math test does not always fall exactly on the regression line in Figure 9-6. The solid line in Figure 9-6 shows the regression line predicting blood pressure from math test performance. The dotted line connects the mean blood pressure for the students who scored each percent correct, from 40 percent to 95 percent. In effect, the regression line straightens out the zigzag line that connects the means of the groups.

Regression to the Mean

Thus far, we have been exploring regression lines without actually examining what the term *regression* means. To see what this term means, it is helpful to examine the regression equation based on standard scores. The formulas that we have been using to find the values of the slope, b, and Y-intercept, a, shown in Procedures 9-1 to 9-3, are based on raw scores. When we use standard scores in the regression equation, the formulas for a and b are simplified. The standard deviation of any distribution of z scores is 1.00. If the scores on both variable X and variable Y are converted to standard scores, then the

FIGURE 9-6   Scatterplot of Relationship between
Math Test Scores and Systolic Blood Pressure in Joe's Study

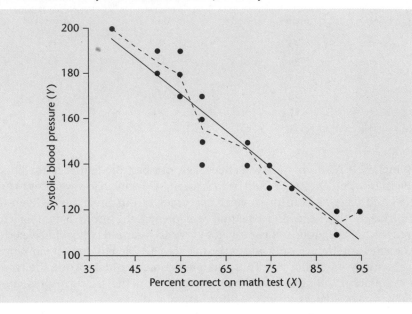

standard distributions of both variables equal 1.00, reducing the value of the slope, *b*, to r_{XY}:

$$b = \frac{s_{z_Y}}{s_{z_X}} r_{z_X z_Y} = \frac{1.00}{1.00} r_{z_X z_Y} = r_{z_X z_Y}.$$

When converted to *z* scores, the means of both distributions are equal to zero, and thus the value of the *Y*-intercept, *a*, is always zero:

$$a = \bar{Y} - b\bar{X} = 0 - r_{XY}(0) = 0 - 0 = 0.$$

Thus, the regression equation for standard scores is

$$z'_Y = r_{XY} z_X.$$

To predict a subject's standard score on variable *Y*, we simply multiply that subject's standard score on variable *X* by the correlation between *X* and *Y*.

Suppose we are predicting the IQ scores of three people at age 30. At age 20, Zach's IQ is 120, Yolanda's is 100, and Xavier's is 80. Table 9-5 shows their predicted IQs at age 30 for several values of *r*. If the correlation between IQ scores at ages 20 and 30 is perfect (*r* = 1.00), then the regression equation predicts that these three people will have the same IQ at 30 as at 20. Note that the predicted score remains the same as the predictor score.

TABLE 9-5 Effect of the Size of the Correlation, *r,* on Predicted Scores

IQ at Age 20; z		Predicted IQ at Age 30				
		r = 1.00	*r* = .75	*r* = .50	*r* = .25	*r* = 0
IQ:	120	120	115	110	105	100
z:	1.33	1.33	1.00	0.67	0.33	0.00
IQ:	100	100	100	100	100	100
z:	0.00	0.00	0.00	0.00	0.00	0.00
IQ:	80	80	85	90	95	100
z:	−1.33	−1.33	−1.00	−0.67	−0.33	0.00

When there is a less-than-perfect correlation between IQ scores at ages 20 and 30, the regression equation no longer predicts that the IQ scores at age 30 will be the same as at age 20. Zack has an IQ of 120 at age 20, but his predicted IQ at age 30, with an *r* of .75, is only 115. His IQ apparently will go down 5 points. On the other hand, Xavier's IQ increases when *r* is .75. Xavier's IQ at age 20 is 80, but his predicted IQ at age 30 is 85, which is up 5 points. In fact, what is happening is that the predicted IQs for both Zack and Xavier are 5 points closer to the mean. Note that with an *r* of .50, the predicted IQs at age 30 for both Zack and Xavier are 10 points closer to the mean than their IQs at age 20, and with an *r* of .25, the predicted IQs at age 30 are 15 points closer to the mean.

Let's examine the standard scores for the predicted IQs in Table 9-5. When the correlation is perfect and *r* is 1.00, for Zack, the predicted *z* score at age 30 is 1.33, the same as the *z* score for age 20. However, with an *r* of .75, the predicted *z* score is only 1.00, which is 75 percent of the *z* score at age 20. Similarly, with an *r* of .50, the predicted *z* score, 0.67, is 50 percent of the original *z* score, and with an *r* of .25, the predicted *z* score, 0.33, is only 25 percent of the original *z* score. When there is no relationship at all between predictor and predicted variables (i.e., when *r* = 0), the regression equation predicts that all three people in Table 9-5 will have IQs of 100 at age 30, no matter what their IQs are at age 20.

Remember that standard scores are a measure of how far scores lie from the mean. The scores in Table 9-5 show that the weaker the correlation, the closer the predicted scores are to the mean. In statistical terms, this relationship is called **regression to the mean**. The term *regression* means falling back or returning. Predicted scores tend to fall back or return closer to the mean than the scores from which they were predicted. The degree to which predicted scores are closer to the mean is determined by the value of *r*. The

When the correlation between the predictor and predicted variables is less than perfect, the value of the predicted variable will be closer to the mean, measured in standard deviations, than the corresponding value of the predictor variable. Thus, compared to predictor values, predicted values tend to **regress toward the mean**.

smaller the correlation, the closer the predicted scores will be to the mean. In fact, if there is no correlation at all, so that r is 0, the predicted scores will be the mean. It is because predicted scores tend to be closer to the mean, to regress toward the mean, that the term *regression* is used in statistical prediction.

Regression and the Least-Squares Criterion

For each value of the predictor variable, X, the regression equation will predict just one value on the predicted variable, Y. The regression equation predicts that every eight-year-old child would be 49 inches tall. Obviously, not every eight-year-old child actually will be 49 inches tall. The value generated by the regression equation is a prediction, an estimate of what the subject's score would be if it were measured. Unless the correlation between predictor and predicted variables is perfect, the predictions generated by the regression equation will not be perfect.

Given this inherent imperfection of the predictions generated by the regression equation, it would be useful to measure the degree of error in these predictions. In order to achieve this goal, we first need to define what we mean by error. To illustrate the logic of measuring the degree of error, examine the grade levels and reading levels of the ten children shown in Figure 9-7. Also shown in Figure 9-7 are the computations needed to construct the regression equation predicting reading level from the children's grade levels. This regression equation is

predicted reading level = 1.8 + 0.8(grade level).

Using this regression equation, we predict that any child in grade 1 is at a reading level of 2.6 and that any child in grade 4 is at a reading level of 5.0. The predicted reading level for each of the 10 children is shown in the third column of Figure 9-7.

In the notation we have been using, Y represents an actual score received by a subject, and Y' represents a predicted score generated from a regression equation. The difference between these two values, $(Y - Y')$, is a measure of the error in prediction. If there is a perfect correlation between X and Y, then the regression equation will predict scores perfectly, and there will be no difference between Y and Y' for any of the subjects. The more that the predicted score Y' deviates from the actual score Y, the larger the error in prediction.

The value $(Y - Y')$ measures the error involved in a single prediction. To measure the error of a regression line, we need to measure this difference for all of the values of Y, which is $\Sigma(Y - Y')$, the sum of the deviation between true and predicted scores for all of the scores. In Figure 9-7, we can see that this sum is zero. To circumvent this difficulty, we square the deviations. Figure 9-7 shows that the sum of the squared deviations between actual and predicted scores, $\Sigma(Y - Y')^2$, is 12.64.

FIGURE 9-7   Predicting Reading Levels from Grade Level

Person	Grade Level (X)	Reading Level (Y)	Predicted Reading Level (Y')	Deviation Due to Error (Y − Y')	(Y − Y')²
Abe	7	7	7.4	−0.4	0.16
Bob	6	8	6.6	1.4	1.96
Cal	6	5	6.6	−1.6	2.56
Dee	5	6	5.8	0.2	0.04
Eve	4	7	5.0	2.0	4.00
Flo	4	4	5.0	−1.0	1.00
Gig	3	5	4.2	0.8	0.64
Hal	2	3	3.4	−0.4	0.16
Ina	2	2	3.4	−1.4	1.96
Jim	1	3	2.6	−0.4	0.16
				$\Sigma(Y - Y') = 0.0$	$\Sigma(Y - Y')^2 = 12.64$

$$\bar{X} = \frac{\Sigma X}{n} = \frac{40}{10} = 4.0 \qquad\qquad \bar{Y} = \frac{\Sigma Y}{n} = \frac{50}{10} = 5.0$$

$$s_X = \sqrt{\frac{\Sigma(X - \bar{X})^2}{n - 1}} = \sqrt{\frac{36}{9}} = 2.0 \qquad s_Y = \sqrt{\frac{\Sigma(Y - \bar{Y})^2}{n - 1}} = \sqrt{\frac{36}{9}} = 2.0$$

$$r = \frac{\Sigma XY - \dfrac{(\Sigma X)(\Sigma Y)}{n}}{\sqrt{\left(\Sigma X^2 - \dfrac{(\Sigma X)^2}{n}\right)\left(\Sigma Y^2 - \dfrac{(\Sigma Y)^2}{n}\right)}} = \frac{229 - \dfrac{(40)(50)}{10}}{\sqrt{\left(196 - \dfrac{40^2}{10}\right)\left(286 - \dfrac{50^2}{10}\right)}} = 0.8$$

$$b = \frac{s_Y}{s_X} r_{XY} = \frac{2.0}{2.0}(0.8) = 0.8 \qquad\qquad a = \bar{Y} - b\bar{X} = 5.0 - (0.8)(4.0) = 1.8$$

Regression equation: $Y' = 1.8 + 0.8X$

This sum, $\Sigma(Y - Y')^2$, is a measure of the amount of error in the predictions. The smaller this sum, then the smaller the amount of error and the more accurate the predictions. Ideally, we want to make predictions so that this sum is as small as possible. The regression equation that we have been using in fact generates predicted scores for which this sum, $\Sigma(Y - Y')^2$, is the least possible. Of course, theoretically the smallest possible value that $\Sigma(Y - Y')^2$, could be is zero, but this will occur only if there is a perfect correlation. Given a less than perfect correlation, there will be some error present in the predictions. Our goal is to have this error as low as possible, and the regression line contains the predicted scores that produce the lowest or least sum of squared deviations from the actual scores. This is sometimes abbreviated as "least-squares." The term **least-squares** indicates that the sum of the squared

The **least-squares criterion** defines the accuracy of prediction as the sum of the squared differences between true scores and predicted scores. That sum will be the lowest when the predicted scores are on the regression line.

difference between actual and predicted scores is smallest when the predicted scores are on the regression line. The regression line produces the lowest rate of error in prediction and thus is the most accurate, as measured by the squared difference between actual and predicted scores.

Standard Error of Estimate

As we saw in the previous section, the sum, $\Sigma(Y - Y')^2$, reflects the error in the predictions made using a regression equation. We can use this sum to construct a measure of error in prediction:

$$s_{Y|X} = \sqrt{\frac{\Sigma(Y - Y')^2}{n - 1}}.$$

This formula is called the **standard error of estimate,** symbolized $s_{Y|X}$.

Compare the formula for the standard error of estimate to the formula for the standard deviation:

The **standard error of estimate** is a measure of the degree to which the true value of scores will vary from the predicted values generated by a regression equation. It is a measure of the accuracy of those predicted scores.

$$s_Y = \sqrt{\frac{\Sigma(Y - \bar{Y})^2}{n - 1}}.$$

The standard deviation is a measure of how far each actual score deviates from the mean of the distribution. The standard error of estimate is a measure of how far each actual score deviates from the predicted score. Where the standard deviation measures the spread in a group of scores, the standard error of estimate measures how far predicted scores lie from the values of the true score.

Because the standard error of estimate is based on $\Sigma(Y - Y')^2$, it is a measure of the degree of error in prediction. Remember that we use regression equations in order to increase the accuracy of our predictions over blind guessing and thus to reduce error. The standard error of estimate is a measure of how much error remains in those predictions.

In order to understand how the standard error of estimate measures error in prediction, let's examine first the degree of error in prediction when we make blind guesses. As we have seen, the best blind guess is the mean. Thus, when blind guessing, the predicted score, Y', will be the mean for every prediction. Therefore, in the formula for the standard error of estimate, we can insert the value of the mean for the predicted score, Y':

$$s_{Y|X} = \sqrt{\frac{\Sigma(Y - Y')^2}{n - 1}} = \sqrt{\frac{\Sigma(Y - \bar{Y})^2}{n - 1}} = s_Y.$$

Thus, if we are making blind guesses, the standard error of estimate will be the same as the standard deviation in the scores on variable Y.

As an example, for the ten children shown in Figure 9-7, if we are blind guessing their reading levels, the standard error of estimate is the same as the

---

STEP-BY-STEP PROCEDURE 9-4

Calculating the Standard Error of Estimate

$$s_{Y|X} = s_y \sqrt{1 - r^2}$$

where $s_{Y|X}$ = the standard error of estimate in predicting the value of *Y* from the value of *X*

s_Y = the standard deviation of variable *Y*

r = the correlation between variables *X* and *Y*

1. Calculate the standard deviation of the scores on the predicted variable, *Y*.

2. Calculate the value of Pearson's product-moment correlation, *r*, between the predictor variable, *X*, and the predicted variable, *Y*.

3. Square the value of *r* found in Step 2. Subtract that result from the number, 1. Find the square root of that result.

4. Multiply the result of Step 3 by the standard deviation of *Y*, found in Step 1, to find the standard error of estimate.

---

standard deviation of the reading levels, which is 2.0. However, if we use the predicted reading levels generated by the regression equation, the standard error of estimate is

$$s_{Y|X} = \sqrt{\frac{\Sigma(Y - Y')^2}{n - 1}} = \sqrt{\frac{12.64}{9}} = 1.2.$$

Thus, there is less error in prediction when we use the regression equation than when we are simply guessing blindly.

As we have seen, the regression equation is based on the correlation between predictor and predicted variables. We are using information about the relationship between two variables in order to reduce error in prediction. Consequently, the standard error of estimate is related to that correlation. The stronger the correlation between two variables, the more we reduce the error in prediction. In fact, we can calculate the value of the standard error of estimate from the value of *r*, as shown in Step-by-Step Procedure 9-4.

In this formula for the standard error of estimate, the degree of error is influenced by two factors: the value of the correlation, *r*, between the predictor and predicted variables and the standard deviation of the predicted variable. Table 9-6 shows the value of the standard error of estimate for several values of *r* and several standard deviations of *Y*. First, notice that the size of the standard error of estimate depends in part on the size of the original standard deviation. For each value of *r*, the standard error of estimate is larger when s_Y is 100 than when s_Y is 80. The larger the size of the standard deviation of the predicted variable, the larger the size of the standard error of

TABLE 9-6   Standard Error of Estimate for Various Values of r and s_y

r	s_y 100	80	60	40	20
.00	100.0	80.0	60.0	40.0	20.0
.10	99.5	79.6	59.7	39.8	19.9
.20	98.0	78.4	58.8	39.2	19.6
.30	95.4	76.3	57.2	38.2	19.1
.40	91.7	73.3	55.0	36.7	18.3
.50	86.6	69.3	52.0	34.6	17.3
.60	80.0	64.0	48.0	32.0	16.0
.70	71.4	57.1	42.8	28.6	14.3
.80	60.0	48.0	36.0	24.0	12.0
.90	43.6	34.9	26.2	17.4	8.7
1.00	0.0	0.0	0.0	0.0	0.0

estimate. Thus, the more spread out the original scores, the greater the error in prediction.

The degree of error in prediction is also affected by the strength of correlation between predictor and predicted variables. When r is 0, and thus when there is no correlation between variables X and Y, then the standard error of estimate is the same as the standard deviation. When there is no correlation, then the regression line does not reduce the errors in prediction at all. Thus, when the predictor variable, X, has no correlation to the predicted variable, Y, the effect is the same as blind guessing.

When r is .10 or .20, there is a very small reduction in the rate of error. However, when r is as large as .60, there is a 20 percent reduction in the rate of error. For example, when the standard deviation is 100, the standard error of estimate is 100 when r is 0 but is 80 when r is .60, a 20 percent reduction in error. When r is as large as .90, there is over 50 percent reduction in the rate of error. With a standard deviation of 100 and r of .90, the standard error of estimate is only 43.6. Thus, the larger the correlation between predicted and predictor variables, the smaller will be the standard error of estimate. This means that as r gets larger, the rate of error gets smaller. The larger r, the closer the predicted scores will be to the true value.

Finally, notice that when r is 1.00, the standard error of estimate is 0. When there is a perfect correlation between the predicted and predictor variables, there will be absolutely no error of estimate. The predicted score will equal the true score every time, so that the difference between the two will always be 0. Only when there is a perfect correlation will there be perfect prediction.

Coefficients of Determination and Nondetermination

The standard error of estimate is a measure of the amount of error involved in using the regression equation to predict values of Y from values of X. It would also be useful to have a measure of the degree of accuracy in these predictions. The degree of error and the degree of accuracy are inversely related. The greater the accuracy, the lower the rate of error.

If the deviation between the actual and predicted scores is a measure of error, then the deviation between the predicted score and the mean is a measure of accuracy. As we saw at the beginning of this chapter, if we have no information at all, the best we can guess a subject's score is the mean. However, using the regression equation to predict a subject's score improves that guess. Thus, the distance between the mean and the predicted score, $(Y' - \overline{Y})$, is a measure of accuracy.

To obtain a measure of the improvement in accuracy, we need to sum these deviations across all the scores in a distribution. However, this sum is always zero, and so we square each deviation before summing, to obtain $\Sigma(Y' - \overline{Y})^2$, which for the predicted reading levels for the ten children shown in Figure 9-7 is 23.04. This is the deviation in the children's reading levels accounted for by their grade levels. The total variability in the children's actual reading levels is measured by $\Sigma(Y - \overline{Y})^2$, which is 36. The ratio of these two values gives us the proportion of the total variability in children's reading levels that is explained by their grade levels:

$$\text{proportion of explained deviation} = \frac{\text{explained deviation squared}}{\text{total deviation squared}}$$

$$= \frac{\Sigma(Y' - \overline{Y})^2}{\Sigma(Y - \overline{Y})^2} = \frac{23.04}{36} = .64.$$

Thus, 64 percent of the variability in the children's reading levels is explained by the variability in their grade levels. This measure is called the **coefficient of determination**. It is a measure of the proportion of the variability in the predicted variable Y accounted for by the predictor variable X.

The coefficient of determination is always equal to the square of the correlation coefficient, r, between X and Y. Recall that the correlation between grade and reading level among the 10 children listed in Figure 9-7 is .80. The square of .80 is .64, which is the same as the coefficient of determination found above. Thus, if we know the value of r, we can easily determine the value of the coefficient of determination:

$$\text{coefficient of determination} = r^2.$$

If the coefficient of determination is the proportion of variability in Y explained by the variability in X, then the remaining proportion of variability in X is the proportion that is not explained by variability in X. Thus, if 64 percent of the variability in reading levels among the children listed in Figure 9-7

The **coefficient of determination**, which is equal to r^2, is the proportion of variability in the predicted variable Y accounted for by variability in the predictor variable X.

The **coefficient of nondetermination,** which is equal to $1 - r^2$, is the proportion of variability in the predicted variable Y that is not accounted for by variability in the predictor variable X.

is explained by their grade levels, then 100 percent − 64 percent, or 36 percent of the variability in reading levels is *not* accounted for by the children's grade levels and must be due to other factors. This proportion is called the **coefficient of nondetermination** and is found by simply subtracting the coefficient of determination from 1:

$$\text{coefficient of nondetermination} = 1 - r^2.$$

Regression, Correlation, and Causation

In Chapter 8, we examined briefly the relationship between correlation and causation, emphasizing that the existence of a correlation between two variables in no way proves a causal relationship between the two variables. This caution bears repeating. As an example, there is a moderate correlation (somewhere in the range of .40 and .50) between the SAT scores of high school seniors and their grades in their first year of college. In fact, admissions counselors use this correlation to predict from applicants' SAT scores their probable freshman-year GPA. It is important to note first that just because there is a correlation between SAT scores and college GPA does not mean that every student who does well on the SATs will do well in college. A correlation indicates a trend across all the subjects measured but not a guarantee for any single subject.

Even more important is the fact that while a correlation indicates that there is a relationship between two variables, it does not explain why that relationship occurs. In this chapter, we have seen that the variability in children's reading levels can be explained by the variability in their grade levels. This is saying only that there is a tendency for reading and grade levels to vary together. It does not explain why that tendency occurs. We do not have to know why a relationship occurs in order to use information about that relationship to make predictions. We need only be careful that we do not assert more than we actually know.

CHECKING YOUR ANSWERS

1. When determining a regression equation, be careful not to confuse the predicted and predictor variables. The predictor variable (labeled X) is the one whose values you know. The predicted variable (labeled Y) is the one whose values you are trying to predict.

2. Remember that between two variables, there are two separate regression lines. Suppose we have the two variables, IQ and GPA. There will be one regression equation for predicting IQ from GPA (IQ|GPA) and another regression equation for predicting GPA from IQ (GPA|IQ). Be careful to correctly identify which variable is the predictor variable and which is the predicted.

3. When plotting a regression equation, you need only two values. The simplest values of X to use are 0 and the mean. When $X = 0$, then Y' will equal a, the Y-intercept. When X equals the mean of X, then the value of Y' will equal the mean of Y. If you calculate a third value, you can check to make sure that the regression line is a straight line.

4. It is important to differentiate between the standard deviation, s_X or s_Y, and the standard error of estimate, $s_{Y|X}$. The standard deviation is a measure of how far scores lie from the mean. The standard error of estimate is a measure of how far predicted scores may lie from the true score.

$\sum$ S U M M A R Y

▶ A prediction is a guess about which value of a variable an event will have. If we make predictions when we have no relevant information to help us, we are blind guessing.

▶ In blind guessing, if we are paid or rewarded only if we choose the correct value, the best guess is the mode. If we are paid for every guess, but a penalty is deducted for the size of any error, the best guess is the median. And if we are paid for every guess, but a penalty is deducted for the square of the size of any error, the best guess is the mean.

▶ When we are making predictions about which value of a variable an event will have, we can use information from another variable (the predictor variable) if the two variables are correlated. This information can reduce the size of the error in those predictions. The variable about which we are making predictions is the predicted variable.

▶ A regression equation is a mathematical expression giving the predicted value of variable Y in terms of a known value of the predictor variable, X, and the correlation between the two variables.

▶ A linear regression equation has the form $Y' = a + bX$. The value b is the slope of the line and indicates the degree to which the values of the predicted variable increase (or decrease) as the values of the predictor variable increase. The value a is the Y-intercept and is the value predicted for the predicted variable when the value of the predictor variable is zero.

▶ Unless the correlation between predicted and predictor variables is perfect (± 1.00), the predicted scores will tend overall to be closer to the mean than the scores would be if subjects were actually tested. This conservative tendency is known as regression to the mean. The lower the correlation, the closer to the mean the predicted scores will tend to be. If the correlation between predicted and predictor variables is zero, then the predictions will be the mean for every case.

▶ The least-squares criterion defines the accuracy of prediction as the sum of the squared differences between true scores and predicted scores. For this criterion, that sum is lowest with the predicted scores generated by a regression equation.

▶ The standard error of estimate measures the degree to which the true value of scores differs from the predicted values generated by a regression equation and thus is a measure of accuracy. The standard error of estimate is derived from the standard deviation of the predicted variable and the correlation between predicted and predictor variables. When that correlation is perfect (±1.00), the standard error of estimate will be zero, and every prediction will be perfectly accurate. When the correlation is zero, the standard error of estimate will equal the standard deviation of the predicted variable, indicating that the regression equation does not improve the accuracy of predictions at all.

▶ The coefficient of determination, which is equal to r^2, is a measure of the proportion of the variability in the predicted variable, Y, that is accounted for by the variability in the predictor variable, X. The coefficient of nondetermination, which is equal to $1 - r^2$, is a measure of the proportion of variability in the predicted variable, Y, not accounted for by variability in the predictor variable, X.

E X E R C I S E S

Conceptual Exercises

1. Define the following terms:

prediction	regression line
blind guess	regression toward the mean
predictor variable	least-squares criterion
predicted variable	standard error of estimate
slope	coefficient of determination
Y-intercept	coefficient of nondetermination

2. Following are the ages of 10 children. Note that in this group the modal age is 9, the median age is 8, and the mean age is 7.

Ages: 9, 9, 9, 9, 8, 8, 6, 5, 4, 3

Suppose that you do not know any of the children's ages, and you must make blind guesses. Listed below are three different payment systems. For each system, calculate the amount you would be paid if you guessed (i) the mean, (ii) the median, and (iii) the mode. For each of these payment systems, which age would be your best guess?

A. You get paid $1.00 for each guess that is absolutely correct.

B. You get paid 50¢ for every guess, but you lose 10¢ for every year you are off.

C. You get paid 50¢ for every guess, but you lose 1¢ if your guess is off by 1 year, 4¢ if your guess is off by 2 years, 9¢ if your guess is off by 3 years, 16¢ if your guess is off by 4 years, 25¢ if your guess is off by 5 years, and 36¢ if your guess is off by 6 years.

3. Draw graphs of the following straight lines. For each, identify the value of the slope and the Y-intercept.

A. $Y = X$	F. $Y = 2 + X$
B. $Y = 2X$	G. $Y = 4 + X$
C. $Y = .5X$	H. $Y = 2 + .5X$
D. $Y = 4 - X$	I. $Y = 4 + .5X$
E. $Y = 4 - .5X$	J. $Y = 2 - .5X$

4. Listed below are the IQ scores and GPAs for five groups of students:

Group I			Group II			Group III		
Student	IQ	GPA	Student	IQ	GPA	Student	IQ	GPA
1	140	3.9	1	140	3.7	1	140	3.5
2	135	3.7	2	135	3.9	2	135	3.3
3	135	3.7	3	135	3.3	3	135	3.7
4	130	3.5	4	130	3.5	4	130	3.9
5	130	3.5	5	130	3.5	5	130	3.5
6	130	3.5	6	130	3.5	6	130	3.1
7	125	3.3	7	125	3.7	7	125	3.3
8	125	3.3	8	125	3.1	8	125	3.7
9	120	3.1	9	120	3.3	9	120	3.5

Group IV			Group V		
Student	IQ	GPA	Student	IQ	GPA
1	140	3.3	1	140	3.1
2	135	3.1	2	135	3.3
3	135	3.7	3	135	3.3
4	130	3.5	4	130	3.5
5	130	3.5	5	130	3.5
6	130	3.5	6	130	3.5
7	125	3.3	7	125	3.7
8	125	3.9	8	125	3.7
9	120	3.7	9	120	3.9

A. Draw a scatterplot of the scores for each student group.
B. Identify the type of correlation (positive, negative, or null) present between IQ and GPA in each group.
C. Compute the values of Pearson's *r* for each group.
D. Determine the slope and the *Y*-intercept of the regression equation predicting GPA from IQ, write the equation for the regression line, and draw on the graph you constructed in Part A.

5. For each of the regression equations constructed in the Exercise 4, find the GPAs that would be predicted for students with each of the following IQs: (i) 140, (ii) 135, (iii) 130, (iv) 125, (v) 120.
   A. For which of the groups of students are the predicted GPAs exactly the same as their actual GPAs? Why does this occur?
   B. For which of the groups of students are the predicted GPAs different from their actual GPAs? Why does this occur?
   C. For which of the groups of students is the same value predicted for all of the students in the group? Why does this occur?

6. For each of the regression equations constructed in Exercise 4, find the GPAs that would be predicted for students with each of the following IQs: (i) 137, (ii) 131, (iii) 128, (iv) 124.
   A. A person whose IQ is 137 would have a lower predicted GPA in Group II than in Group I, and a person whose IQ is 124 would have a higher predicted GPA in Group IV than in Group V. Why does this occur?

  B. While people whose IQs are 137, 131, 128, and 124 would have different predicted GPAs depending on which group they were in, a person whose IQ is 130 would have the same predicted GPA in all five groups. Why does this occur?

  C. A person whose IQ is 137 would have a higher predicted GPA than a person whose IQ is 124 in Groups I and II but a lower IQ in Groups IV and V. Why does this occur?

7. For each of the five groups of scores shown in Exercise 4, determine the slope and Y-intercept of the regression equation, this time predicting IQ from GPA, and draw the regression line on the graph you constructed.

8. For each of the regression equations constructed in Exercise 7, find the IQ scores that would be predicted for students with each of the following GPAs: (i) 3.9, (ii) 3.7, (iii) 3.5, (iv) 3.3, (v) 3.1.

  A. For which of the groups of students are the predicted IQs exactly the same as their actual IQs? Why does this occur?

  B. For which of the groups of students are the predicted IQs different from their actual IQs? Why does this occur?

  C. For which of the groups of students is the same value predicted for all of the students in the group? Why does this occur?

9. For each of the regression equations constructed in Exercise 7, find the IQ scores that would be predicted for students with each of the following GPAs: (i) 3.8, (ii) 3.6, (iii) 3.4, (iv) 3.2.

  A. A person whose GPA is 3.8 would have a lower predicted IQ in Group II than in Group I, and a person whose GPA is 3.2 would have a higher predicted IQ in Group IV than in Group V. Why does this occur?

  B. While people whose GPAs are 3.8, 3.6, 3.4, and 3.2 would have different predicted IQs, depending on which group they were in, a person whose GPA is 3.5 would have the same predicted IQ in all five groups. Why does this occur?

  C. A person whose GPA is 3.8 would have a higher predicted IQ than a person whose IQ is 3.2 in Groups I and II but a lower GPA in Groups IV and V. Why does this occur?

10. Find the standard error of estimate for each of the five regression equations constructed in Exercise 4, predicting students' GPAs from their IQ scores. Then find the standard error of estimates for each of the five regression equations constructed in Exercise 7, predicting students' IQ scores from their GPAs.

  A. Compare the two standard errors of estimate for each group of students, one for predicting GPAs from IQ scores and the other for predicting IQ scores from GPAs. For which groups of students do these two standard errors of estimate differ? Why does this occur?

  B. For which group of students are these two standard errors of estimate the same? Why does this occur?

11. Recall that the mean of the population of IQ scores theoretically is 100, with a standard deviation of 15, and the mean of the population of SAT verbal scores theoretically is 500, with a standard deviation of 100.

  A. Construct the regression equation predicting SAT verbal scores from IQ scores for each of the following values of *r*: (i) 1.00, (ii) .80, (iii) .60, (iv) .40, (v) .20, and (vi) .00.

  B. Construct one graph, predicting SAT verbal scores from IQ scores. Draw all six regression lines from Part A on the graph. What pattern do you observe in these six lines? What happens to the slope of the lines as *r* goes from 1.00 to .00? Where do the six lines intersect? Why does this pattern occur?

12. For each of the six regression equations from Exercise 11, find the predicted SAT verbal score for each of the following IQ scores: (i) 130, (ii) 115, (iii) 100, (iv) 85, (v) 70.

    A. Compare the predicted SAT verbal scores for the IQ score of 130 across the six values of r. Which value of r generates the highest predicted SAT verbal score? Which value of r generates the lowest predicted SAT verbal score? Why does this occur?

    B. Compare the predicted SAT verbal scores for the IQ score of 70 across the six values of r. Which value of r generates the highest predicted SAT verbal score? Which value of r generates the lowest predicted SAT verbal score? Why does this occur?

    C. Find the distance between the predicted SAT verbal scores for IQs of 130 and 115 by subtracting the predicted SAT verbal score for an IQ of 115 from the predicted SAT verbal score for an IQ of 130. What pattern do you observe in these differences? Which value of r generates the largest difference between predicted SAT verbal scores? Which value of r generates the smallest difference? Why does this occur?

    D. For which IQ score is the predicted SAT verbal score the same value for all the values of r? Why does this occur?

13. Convert the predicted SAT verbal scores for the IQ scores of 115 and 85, found in Exercise 12, to standard scores, using the SAT verbal score mean of 500 and standard deviation of 100.

    A. For the IQ score of 115, how many standard deviations above the mean of 500 is the predicted SAT verbal score for each value of r? Why does this occur?

    B. For the IQ score of 85, how many standard deviations below the mean of 500 is the predicted SAT verbal score for each value of r? Why does this occur?

14. For each value of r shown in Exercise 12, compute the standard error of estimate in predicting SAT verbal scores from IQ scores.

Computational Exercises

15. Recall that the population mean of SAT scores is 500, with a standard deviation of 100, and that the population mean of IQ scores is 100, with a standard deviation of 15. Construct the regression line predicting SAT from IQ scores for each of the following values of r, and then find the predicted SAT score for the listed IQ score:

    A. IQ of 128, $r = .73$
    B. IQ of 93, $r = .47$
    C. IQ of 109, $r = .54$
    D. IQ of 77, $r = .35$
    E. IQ of 100, $r = .82$
    F. IQ of 100, $r = .39$

16. For each of the predicted SAT verbal scores found in Exercise 15, find the standard error of estimate.

17. Jacinda measured the ages of a group of white rats and the speed with which each rat ran a maze:

Rat	Age in Weeks	Time in Seconds
A	3	8
B	8	14
C	6	9
D	5	11
E	1	5
F	4	7

A. Construct the regression equation predicting the rats' maze-running speed from their ages.

B. Use this regression equation to predict maze-running speed for a rat who is two weeks old and a rat who is seven weeks old.

C. Calculate the standard error of estimate.

D. Calculate the coefficient of determination.

18. JoBeth explored the relationship between early motor development and later intellectual level by measuring the age at which infants first began to walk and then their IQs at age six:

Child	Age in Months of Walking	IQ at Six Years
A	10	90
B	13	100
C	11	110
D	9	130
E	12	120

A. Construct the regression equation predicting the child's IQ at age six from the age at which they first started walking.

B. Use this regression equation to predict IQ at 6 years for an infant who first started walking at 10.5 months and an infant who first started walking at 11.5 months.

C. Calculate the standard error of estimate.

D. Calculate the coefficient of determination.

Probability and the Binomial Distribution

10

Basic Concepts in Probability

Probability and Proportion
STEP-BY-STEP PROCEDURE 10-1: Calculating Probabilities

Empirical and Theoretical Distributions
STEP-BY-STEP PROCEDURE 10-2: Calculating Theoretical Probabilities, Assuming All Outcomes Are Equally Likely

The Addition Rule in Probability

The Multiplication Rule of Probability

Using Both the Addition and Multiplication Rules

The Binomial Distribution

The Binomial Equation

The Table of Binomial Probabilities

The Mean and Standard Deviation of a Binomial Distribution
STEP-BY-STEP PROCEDURE 10-3: Calculating the Mean and Standard Deviation of a Binomial Distribution

The Relevance of Theoretical Distributions

CHECKING YOUR ANSWERS

S U M M A R Y

E X E R C I S E S

Conceptual Exercises

Computational Exercises

▶ Many statistical concepts involve the measurement of probability. The statistics that we have examined thus far have been descriptive statistics, which describe a distribution of scores or the relationship between distributions. The concept of probability enables us to move beyond simply describing distributions to making predictions about distributions. In the last chapter, we saw that we can develop regression equations to predict what score a person might receive on one variable from the score that the person actually did receive on another variable. The concepts of probability will extend the types of predictions that we can make.

As we will see in the following chapters, we can use the principles of probability to make predictions about a population from a sample of subjects drawn from that population. No longer will we have to measure every member in order to describe the population. We can describe the population by just measuring a sample of the members. Most political polls are based on this idea. When the *Washington Post* reports that 56 percent of the population will vote for a certain presidential candidate, the *Post* hasn't polled every member of the voting population of the United States. Instead, the *Post* polls a small sample of voters and uses the principles of **probability** to infer from the sample how the entire population would vote.

In this chapter, we will look at the basic mathematical principles of probability so that we can later understand how samples can be used to describe entire populations. We will also examine another theoretical distribution, the binomial distribution. In Chapter 7, we looked at the normal distribution as a theoretical distribution that is very useful in the study of psychology. The binomial distribution is a theoretical distribution that is also useful in making predictions.

Probability is a quantitative expression of the likelihood that an event will occur. An event whose probability is 1 is certain to occur, while an event whose probability is 0 is certain not to occur.

Basic Concepts in Probability

Probability and Proportion

In mathematics, the concept of probability is defined in terms of proportions. In fact, the probability that a given score value will occur is defined as the proportion of times that score value occurs in a distribution of scores.

In my office, I have an M&M dispenser. It holds two bags of M&Ms, and when I push a lever, a handful of M&Ms pour out. Let's consider all of the M&Ms in the container as a population of M&Ms. Table 10-1 shows the

The **probability of score value** *A* occurring, *P(A)*, is defined as the proportion of scores with value A in the distribution of scores:

$$P(A) = \frac{\text{number of occurrences of score value } A}{\text{total number of scores}} = \frac{f(A)}{n}.$$

actual number and proportion of each color M&M in the dispenser. This is a frequency distribution, like the ones that we constructed in Chapter 3. The relative frequency of a score value is the proportion of that score value in the distribution of scores, which is also the probability that that score value will occur.

Suppose we wanted to find the probability that one M&M drawn from the dispenser will be green. All we need to do is find the proportion of green M&Ms in the container. Step-by-Step Procedure 10-1 shows the method for calculating probabilities, based on proportions:

TABLE 10-1 Frequency Distribution of Colors of M&Ms

Color	Frequency	Proportion
Brown	150	.25
Blue	132	.22
Yellow	102	.17
Orange	90	.15
Red	66	.11
Green	60	.10
N	600	1.00

$$P(\text{drawing green M\&M}) = \frac{f(\text{green M\&M})}{n} = \frac{60}{600} = .10.$$

The proportion of green M&Ms in the container is .10, or 10 percent, and so the probability of drawing a green M&M from the dispenser is .10.

We can use this procedure for finding all sorts of probabilities, such as the probability that the next child born will be female, the probability of getting an A in a class, and the probability of being involved in an accident in a given city (count the total number of cars on the road and count the number of cars involved in an accident). As an example, suppose there are 66 men and 84 women in a section of general psychology. We can use Procedure 10-1 to determine the probability that any one student selected from this class is female by simply computing the proportion of female students in the class:

$$P(\text{student is female}) = \frac{f(\text{females})}{n} = \frac{84}{150} = .56.$$

STEP-BY-STEP PROCEDURE 10-1

Calculating Probabilities

$$P(A) = \frac{f(A)}{N}$$

where $P(A)$ = the probability that outcome A will occur
$f(A)$ = the number of occurrences of outcome A
N = the total number of occurrences of all outcomes

1. Count the total number of times that outcome being considered, A, occurs.

2. Count the total number of all occurrences of all outcomes, including outcome A.

3. Divide the result of Step 1 by the result of Step 2 to find the probability of outcome A occurring.

Thus, in this general psychology class, .56 or 56 percent of the students are women, and so the probability that any one student will be a woman is .56. The probability that the student will be a man is 66/150 or .44.

There are several observations we can draw from our examination of probabilities as proportions:

1. Because probabilities are proportions, probabilities will always have values between 0 and 1.00 inclusive. A probability cannot be lower than 0 or greater than 1.00.
2. If the probability of an outcome is 0, that outcome will never occur. On the other hand, if the probability of an outcome is 1.00, that outcome is certain to occur.
3. The sum of the probabilities of all possible outcomes will always be 1.00. Note that in the general psychology class of 150 students, the probability that a student will be female (.56) and the probability that the student will be male (.44) together equal 1.00.

Empirical and Theoretical Distributions

There are two ways to determine probabilities. One way is empirically. The word *empirical* means relying on observation, so empirical probabilities are derived from scores that are actually collected by observing subjects. The probabilities that we have calculated thus far are all **empirical probabilities** because they were determined from actual observations. The frequencies shown in Table 10-1 represent M&Ms that I actually counted. Another term used to describe empirical probabilities is **a posteriori**, which is Latin for "after the fact," referring to probabilities computed after we have made observations and collected scores.

The second way of determining probabilities is theoretically. For example, the normal distribution is a theoretical distribution rather than an empirical distribution. If we assume that IQ scores are normally distributed, we can use the normal distribution table to find that .1587 or 15.87 percent of the population have IQ scores of 115 or greater. We can use that proportion as a measure of probability: the probability that a given person will have an IQ of 115 or greater is .1587. While this probability is based on a proportion, that proportion was not found empirically by actually measuring people's IQs. Rather, the proportion was based on the assumption (or theory) that IQ scores are normally distributed and thence from the normal distribution table. Thus, saying that the probability of having an IQ of 115 or greater is .1587 is a **theoretical probability**, a probability derived from a mathematical theory rather than from scores collected from real live subjects. Theoretical probabilities are also called **a priori** probabilities, from the Latin for "before the fact." Theoretical or a priori probabilities are can be determined before any scores are actually collected.

An **empirical probability** (or **a posteriori probability**) is a probability based on a set of scores drawn from observations that have actually been made in the real world.

A **theoretical probability** (or **a priori probability**) is a probability derived from a theoretical distribution, a distribution based on a mathematical theory rather than on a set of scores drawn from empirical observations.

Suppose that we want to find the probability that students would answer Question 1 on the math test in Joe's study just by guessing. (Researchers use the probability of guessing correctly to determine whether experimental subjects are succeeding by chance alone.) In order to find this probability, we need to know the proportion of students who would select each alternative on Question 1 if they were just guessing. We could find these proportions empirically by giving a group of students a four-alternative multiple-choice question that is beyond their knowledge,

TABLE 10-2 Expected Frequency of Students Selecting Each Alternative on Question 1 of Joe Johnson's Math Test by Guessing

Alternative	Expected Frequency of Students
A (correct answer)	5
B	5
C	5
D	5

one on which they have no clue to the correct answer, and counting the number of students selecting each alternative. However, it would be simpler to find these proportions theoretically. Let's assume that if students are truly guessing on Question 1 of Joe's math test, then each of the alternatives is equally likely to be selected. That is, we're assuming that the students will not have a bias toward selecting any one of the alternatives over the others. Under this assumption, if the twenty students in Joe's study were just guessing on Question 1, we would theoretically expect five students to select each of the four alternatives, as shown in Table 10-2.

We can use Procedure 10-1 to find the probability of a student answering Question 1 correctly just by guessing:

$$P(\text{student guessing correctly on Question 1}) = \frac{f(A)}{n} = \frac{5}{20} = .25.$$

If students are just guessing, the probability of their answering Question 1 correctly is just .25.

Note that the frequencies shown in Table 10-2 were not found empirically but were instead based on assumptions or theories. We first assumed that students were answering just by guessing. We also assumed that if guessing, they were equally likely to select each of the four alternative answers. Thus, the probability of guessing correctly, .25, is a theoretical probability, rather than an empirical probability.

Rather than use Procedure 10-1 to find theoretical probabilities, we can use the simpler method shown in Step-by-Step Procedure 10-2, as long as we make the assumption that all of the score values or outcomes are equally likely to occur.

We can use this procedure to find the probability of guessing correctly on Question 1 of Joe's test. There are a total of four possible outcomes: selecting alternatives *a, b, c,* or *d* for Question 1. A student who is simply guessing is equally likely to choose any of these alternatives. Let's say that alternative *a* is the correct answer to Question 1. Then there is only one outcome that can

---

STEP-BY-STEP PROCEDURE 10-2

Calculating Theoretical Probabilities, Assuming All Outcomes Are Equally Likely

$$P(A) = \frac{\text{number of outcomes classified as A}}{\text{total number of outcomes}}$$

where $P(A)$ = the probability that outcome A will occur

Note: To use this procedure, we must assume that all of the outcomes are equally likely to occur.

1. Count the number of outcomes that can be classified as A, which is the outcome(s) of interest.

2. Count the total number of different outcomes possible.

3. Divide the result of Step 1 by the result of Step 2 to find the probability that A will occur.

---

be classified as A in the formula in Procedure 10-2, and that outcome is choosing alternative *a*. We can put these two values in the formula shown in Procedure 10-2:

$$P(\text{guessing correctly on Question 1}) = \frac{1}{4} = .25.$$

Thus, the probability of guessing correctly on Question 1 is .25.

We could also use Procedure 10-2 to find the probability of guessing incorrectly on Question 1 of Joe's test. In this case, A in the formula in Procedure 10-2 represents an incorrect guess. Since the first alternative on Question 1 is the correct answer, there are three ways of guessing incorrectly: by choosing alternatives *b, c,* or *d*. Thus, there are three outcomes that qualify as A. The total number of different outcomes is still 4. Put these two values in the formula shown in Procedure 10-2:

$$P(\text{guessing incorrectly on Question 1}) = \frac{3}{4} = .75.$$

The probability of guessing incorrectly on Question 1 is .75. Note that we can use this procedure *only if* we assume that the students are equally likely to select each of the four alternative answers when guessing. If we cannot make that assumption, we cannot not use this procedure.

Both types of probability, empirical and theoretical, are useful in the study of statistics. Sometimes we have no way of knowing what proportions would occur without making actual observations. The proportion of males and females born in the United States is based on observation rather than on theory. On the other hand, if we can calculate them, theoretical probabilities are more consistent. If several groups of 20 students were tested on guessing a four-alternative multiple-choice question, it is unlikely that each group would select each alternative 25 percent of the time, or that the proportion of students selecting each alternative in one group would be the same as in another group. However, based on the assumptions we made about guessing, the theoretical probabilities for guessing correctly on a four-alternative question will always be the same. Both empirical and theoretical probabilities have their uses in statistics, and it is important to understand the difference between them.

The Addition Rule in Probability

Thus far, we have looked at determining the simple probability that one score value, outcome, or alternative will occur. We may want to find the probability that a combination of score values or outcomes will occur. For example, suppose we want to find the probability of drawing either a green *or* a red M&M from the dispenser in my office. One way to do this would be to find the proportion of green and red M&Ms in the dispenser:

$$P(\text{drawing green or red M\&M}) = \frac{f(\text{green and red M\&Ms})}{n}$$

$$= \frac{f(\text{green M\&Ms}) + f(\text{red M\&Ms})}{n}$$

$$= \frac{60 + 66}{600} = \frac{126}{600} = .21.$$

Thus, the probability that an M&M drawn from my dispenser will be either green or red is .21.

There is another method of determining this probability. If we know the probability of drawing a green M&M and the probability of drawing a red M&M, we can simply add these two probabilities together to find the probability of drawing either a green or red M&M. Table 10-1 shows that *P*(drawing green M&M) is .10 and *P*(drawing red M&M) is .11. We can combine these two probabilities to find the probability of drawing a green or red M&M:

$$P(\text{green or red}) = P(\text{green}) + P(\text{red}) = .10 + .11 = .21.$$

This example illustrates the **addition rule of probability.**

The addition rule adds several new terms to our statistical vocabulary. First is the term **event**, which is the occurrence of any one outcome under consideration. Drawing one M&M from my dispenser is an event. One student making a choice on Question 1 of Joe Johnson's math test is an event. Each of these events has several possible outcomes. In the event of drawing one M&M, there are six different possible outcomes: red, green, yellow, orange, blue, and brown. In the event of a student answering Question 1, there are four different possible outcomes: alternatives *a, b, c,* and *d.*

The addition rule of probability for two outcomes In one given event, if outcomes A and B are mutually exclusive, the probability that either outcome A or outcome B will occur is the sum of the probability that outcome A will occur and the probability that outcome B will occur: $P(A \text{ or } B) = P(A) + P(B)$.

Outcomes A and B are **mutually exclusive** if when one outcome occurs, the other outcome cannot possibly occur.

To use this addition rule, all of these outcomes must be **mutually exclusive**, which means that if one outcome occurs, then all of the other events are excluded and cannot occur in that event. If we draw a green M&M, then that M&M cannot be red, yellow, orange, blue, or brown. The outcome, "green," excludes all the other outcomes. Similarly, if a student selects alternative *a* for Question 1, the student cannot also select alternatives *b, c,* or *d.* However, if we allowed students to select more than one alternative on Question 1 (as in, "select all that apply"), the outcomes would not be mutually exclusive, and we could not use the addition rule. We can generalize the addition rule for more than two outcomes to form a **general addition rule**.

The general addition rule of probability
In one given event, if outcomes A, B, C, . . . are mutually exclusive, the probability that any one of those outcomes will occur is the sum of the probability that each of the outcomes will occur:
P(A or B or C or . . .) = P(A) + P(B) + P(C) . . .

We can use the addition rule of probability to find the probability of guessing incorrectly on Question 1 of Joe's math test. To guess incorrectly, a student must select alternatives *b, c,* or *d.* These outcomes are mutually exclusive. Selecting one alternative means that the student cannot select either of the other alternatives. As we have seen previously, the probability of a student selecting each of these alternatives is .25, and thus:

P(selecting alternative *b, c,* or *d*) = P(*b*) + P(*c*) + P(*d*) = .25 + .25 + .25 = .75.

This is the same probability that we found previously. Thus, the addition rule of probability gives us a simple way of calculating the probability of one of several possible outcomes occurring on a given event. The rule states that the probability that any one of several possible outcomes will occur is the sum of the probabilities that each of those outcomes will occur.

The Multiplication Rule of Probability

The addition rule deals with the probability of the outcome of a single event. We might want to know the probability of the outcome of more than one event. For example, suppose we wanted to find the probability of a student guessing correctly on both Questions 1 and 2 of Joe's math test. The student's answer on Question 1 would be one event, and the answer on Question 2 would be a second event. Thus, we are asking for the combined probability of the outcome of two separate events. The **multiplication rule of probability** will help us answer this question.

The multiplication rule of probability for two events
If the outcomes of two events are independent, the probability of a given outcome occurring for both events is the product of their individual probabilities:
P(A and B) = P(A)P(B).

The outcomes of two events are **independent** if the outcome of one event has no influence whatsoever on the outcome of the other event.

The multiplication rule introduces a new term, **independent events**, which has a very specific meaning in statistics. To understand this term, let's consider the example of the probability of drawing two green M&Ms from my dispenser. As described before, there are 600 M&Ms in my dispenser, of which 60 are green, so that the probability of drawing one green M&M is .10. Suppose I draw that green M&M from the dispenser and eat it. There are now only 599 M&Ms in the dispenser, with only 59 green ones. The proportion of green M&Ms is now 59/599, or .0985. Thus, after I have eaten one green M&M, the probability of drawing another green M&M has gone down, from .10 to .0985. The outcome of these two events is not independent. The probability of drawing a green M&M on the second draw *depends* on the outcome of the first draw. This method is called *drawing without replacement.* When we do not replace the M&M drawn on the first event before drawing a second M&M, we change the proportion of each color of M&M in the dispenser for the second event, and the outcomes of the two events are not independent.

If we draw one M&M for the first event, note its color, and then replace it in the dispenser before making the second draw, we are *drawing with replacement,* and the outcome of the second event is independent of the outcome of the first event. Suppose again that we draw two M&Ms, one at a time, with replacement. For the first draw, with 60 green M&Ms among 600 M&Ms, the probability of drawing a green M&M is .10. When that green M&M is replaced in the dispenser, there still are 60 green M&Ms and a total of 600 M&Ms in the dispenser, so for the second draw, the probability of drawing a green M&M is still .10. The outcome of the second event is independent of the outcome of the first event.

In order to determine the probability of a student guessing correctly on the first two questions on Joe's math test, we need to first assess whether the outcomes of the two events are independent. If students are simply guessing, their guessing correctly on the first question should have no effect at all on the chances of their guessing correctly on the second question. Thus, the outcomes of these two events are independent, and we can use the multiplication rule to determine the probability of a student guessing correctly on both questions.

To use the multiplication rule, we need to know the probability of guessing correctly on the first question (which we have already determined is .25) and the probability of guessing correctly on the second question. Since each of the questions on Joe's math test has four alternatives, the probability of guessing correctly on any one of the questions is 1 in 4, or .25. This is the information we need to use the multiplication rule:

$$P(\text{Q1 correct and Q2 correct}) = P(\text{Q1 correct}) \times P(\text{Q2 correct})$$

$$= .25 \times .25 = .0625.$$

We can also use the multiplication rule to find the probability of different outcomes occurring on the two events. Suppose we want to find the probability of guessing correctly on Question 1 and incorrectly on Question 2. Again, we need first to find the probability of the outcome of each event individually. The probability of guessing correctly on Question 1 is .25 and the probability of guessing incorrectly on Question 2 is .75.

$$P(\text{Q1 correct and Q2 incorrect}) = P(\text{Q1 correct}) \times P(\text{Q2 incorrect})$$

$$= .25 \times .75 = .1875.$$

We can extend the multiplication rule for the outcomes of two events to cover any number events, to form a **general multiplication rule**.

The general multiplication rule of probability If the outcomes of two or more events are independent, the probability of a given outcome occurring for all events is the product of their individual probabilities:
$$P(\text{A and B and C and} \ldots) = P(A)P(B)P(C) \ldots$$

Suppose we want to find the probability of guessing correctly on the first three questions of Joe's math test. The individual probability of guessing correctly on each question separately is .25, and so the probability of guessing correctly on all three questions is the product of these three separate probabilities:

$$P(\text{Q1 correct and Q2 correct and Q3 correct}) = P(\text{Q1 correct})$$
$$\times\ P(\text{Q2 correct}) \times P(\text{Q3 correct})$$
$$= .25 \times .25 \times .25 = .015625.$$

Thus, the probability of guessing Question 1 correctly is .25; the probability of both guessing Questions 1 and 2 correctly is .0625; and the probability of guessing Questions 1, 2, and 3 all correctly is only .015625. Can you imagine what the probability of correctly guessing all 20 questions on Joe's math test is?

Using Both the Addition and Multiplication Rules

It is rather easy to confuse the times when the addition and multiplication rules are used. The addition rule applies to the *combination of outcomes* for one single event (one draw of an M&M, the answer to one question on the math test). The addition rule says that when we want to find the probability of outcome A *or* B *or* C . . . occurring on one single event, we *add* the individual probabilities. On the other hand, the multiplication rule applies to the probability of the outcomes of a *combination of events* (the outcome of drawing several M&Ms; the answer to several questions on the math test). The multiplication rule says that when we want to find the probability of the outcome of events 1 *and* 2 *and* 3 . . . , we *multiply* the individual probabilities.

Sometimes a question of probability involves using both the addition and the multiplication rules. Suppose we want to find the probability of guessing correctly on just one of the first two questions of Joe's math test. This is a different problem than the one we addressed previously. Previously, we found the probability of guessing Question 1 correctly and Question 2 incorrectly. This is one way of guessing only one of the first two questions correctly. However, there is another way: guessing Question 1 incorrectly and Question 2 correctly. Thus, to find the probability of guessing just one of the first two questions correctly, we need to follow several steps. First, we need to find $P(\text{Q1}$ correct *and* Q2 incorrect), using the multiplication rule as shown below:

$$P(\text{Q1 correct and Q2 incorrect}) = P(\text{Q1 correct}) \times P(\text{Q2 incorrect}) = .25 \times .75 = .1875.$$

Next, we need to find $P(\text{Q1 incorrect and Q2 correct})$:

$$P(\text{Q1 incorrect and Q2 correct}) = P(\text{Q1 incorrect}) \times P(\text{Q2 correct}) = .75 \times .25 = .1875.$$

Since we are trying to find the probability of being correct only on Question 1 *or* Question 2, we combine the above two probabilities, using the addition rule:

$$P(\text{correct only on Q1 or only on Q2}) = P(\text{correct only on Q1}) + P(\text{correct only on Q2})$$
$$= .1875 + .1875 = .3750.$$

Obviously, questions about the combined probability of events can get rather complicated. When working them out, work very methodically and thoroughly think each part through, and you'll find the correct answer.

The Binomial Distribution

In Chapter 8, we examined the concept of dichotomous variables in studying the ϕ coefficient. Recall that dichotomous variables are those that have only two possible values. For example, the variable, sex, is dichotomous, because there are only two values, male and female. The results of a coin toss are dichotomous because the only two values that can occur are heads or tails. These variables are naturally dichotomous because there are only two possible values for each. However, we can reduce any variable to a dichotomous one by separating all the values that could occur into just two categories. For example, at the end of a course, students may have many different final averages, but if the course is graded pass/fail, all of those different averages are reduced to just two final grades, pass or fail. In the previous section, even though each question on Joe Johnson's math test had four alternative answers, we treated the result of a student's answering each question dichotomously when we considered only whether the student was correct or incorrect.

The data that result from measuring subjects on a dichotomous variable are called binomial data. The term "binomial" is from the Latin and means "having two names," which refers to the two values that can occur: correct/incorrect, pass/fail, and heads/tails. Thus, measuring dichotomous variables generates binomial data. A set of scores collected from subjects on a dichotomous variable is called a **binomial distribution.**

We can construct a binomial distribution empirically by measuring a group of subjects on a dichotomous variable. However, more useful is the fact that we can construct a binomial distribution theoretically, without having to test any subjects, as long as we know the probability that each of the two possible outcomes will occur on one event. Let's start with the simplest case, such as the binomial distribution generated by guessing on one true/false question.

Recall from Chapter 7 that we can draw a picture of the normal distribution if we know just two values, the mean and standard deviation of the distribution. Similarly, we can draw a picture of a binomial distribution if we know just two values, the number of events being considered, N, and the probability of the desired outcome of one event, p. First, let's construct the binomial distribution of guessing on one true/false question. In this case, there is only one event (one true/false question), and so N is 1. There are two outcomes to a guess on a true/false question, correct or incorrect, and we need to identify one of them as "the desired outcome." Actually, it's arbitrary which outcome is called the desired one, but since usually we think it's more

The **binomial distribution** is the set of probabilities for X successes in N events, with X taking on values from 0 to N, and where the probability of a success on any one event is known.

TABLE 10-3 Binomial Distribution
of Guessing on One True/False Question

Number of Questions Correct	Proportion
1	.50
0	.50

desirable to be correct than incorrect, we'll say that correct is the desired outcome. If the question is answered simply by guessing, the probability of being correct should be the same as the probability of being incorrect, and so p, the probability of being correct, is .50. Table 10-3 shows the binomial distribution for the outcome of guessing on one true/false question.

This is the simplest case, just to get us started. Now let's construct the binomial distribution generated by guessing on two true/false questions, so that N is 2. Again, the "desired outcome" will be a correct answer, and p, the probability of guessing correctly on one true/false question, is still .50. On two true/false questions, we could have 2 questions correct, 1 correct, or 0 correct. We need to find the probability of each of these possible outcomes.

First, we'll find the probability of two questions correct. There is only one way to get two correct on two questions, so we can simply use the multiplication rule

$$P(2 \text{ correct on 2 questions}) = P(\text{correct on Q1}) \times P(\text{correct on Q2}) = .5 \times .5 = .25.$$

Next, we'll find the probability of getting only one of two questions correct. This is a little more complicated, as there are two ways of getting this outcome. We could get just the first question correct, or we could get just the second question correctly. We need to find each of these probabilities separately, using the multiplication rule, and then combine them, using the addition rule:

$$P(\text{Q1 correct and Q2 incorrect}) = P(\text{Q1 correct}) \times P(\text{Q2 incorrect}) = .5 \times .5 = .25,$$

$$P(\text{Q1 incorrect and Q2 correct}) = P(\text{Q1 incorrect}) \times P(\text{Q2 correct}) = .5 \times .5 = .25,$$

$$P(\text{only Q1 correct or only Q2 correct}) = P(\text{only Q1 correct}) + P(\text{only Q2 correct})$$

$$= .25 + .25 = .50.$$

Finally, we need to find the probability of getting neither of the two questions correct. Like the probability of getting both questions correct, there is only one way of getting neither question correct, by answering both questions incorrectly, and thus we can use the multiplication rule:

$$P(0 \text{ correct on 2 questions}) = P(\text{incorrect on Q1}) \times P(\text{incorrect on Q2}) = .5 \times .5 = .25.$$

All of these results are shown in Table 10-4, the binomial distribution for guessing on two true/false questions.

Note that in Tables 10-3 and 10-4, the proportions add up to 1.00. On one true/false question, we can either answer the question correctly or incorrectly. There are no other possibilities. Therefore, the probability of answering correctly plus the probability of answering incorrectly must add up to 1.00.

Similarly, on two true/false questions, we can get 2 questions correct, 1 correct, or 0 correct. There are no other possibilities, and so the probabilities of those three outcomes must total 1.00. This will be true for all binomial distributions.

Suppose we now wanted to construct the binomial distribution for the results of guessing on three true/false questions. There is only one way to get three of three questions right (RRR, where "R" represents "right") and similarly only one way to get none correct (WWW, where "W" represents "wrong"), and so we could use the multiplication rule for both of these outcomes. However, there are three ways to get two of three questions correct (RRW, RWR, WRR) and similarly three ways to get only one of three questions correct (RWW, WRW, WWR). Therefore, we would need to find the probability of each of these separately to find the probability of getting one of three correct or two of three correct. These computations could get a bit involved. The computations are even more complex when N, the number of events, is even larger. For example, with five true/false questions, there are ten ways of getting three questions correct: RRRWW, RRWRW, RWRRW, WRRRW, RRWWR, RWRWR, WRRWR, RWWRR, WRWRR, and WWRRR. It's cumbersome just trying to identify all the possible combinations that could occur before even doing the computations. There are simpler methods for determining binomial probabilities, which we will explore next.

TABLE 10-4 Binomial Distribution of Guessing on Two True/False Questions

Number of Questions Correct	Proportion
2	.25
1	.50
0	.25

The Binomial Equation

In Chapter 7, we saw that the normal distribution formula can be used to generate the probabilities in the normal distribution. Similarly, the binomial equation can be used to generate the probabilities in a binomial distribution. The binomial equation is used to find the probability of getting X successes in N events, where the probability of success on any one event is p:

$$\text{probability}(X \text{ successes out of } N \text{ events}) = \left(\frac{N!}{X!(N-X)!} \right) p^X (1-p)^{N-X}.$$

There are three variables in the binomial equation: the number of events, N, the probability, p, of the desired outcome occurring on one event, and the number of desired outcomes that occurred, X.

The binomial equation itself can be cumbersome to use, particularly when N is large. Rather than use this formula, most researchers obtain binomial probabilities from tables that have been compiled by statisticians. These tables are comparable to the normal distribution table in Appendix A-1, which we have already examined. Appendix A-2 is a table of binomial probabilities for several values of p and for values of N up to 20. We examine using this table in the next section.

The Table of Binomial Probabilities

The binomial probabilities shown in Appendix A-2 give the probabilities for values of N from 1 through 20 and only for selected values of p. Note also that the highest value of p is .50, so that at first glance it appears that we cannot use the table when p is greater than .50. However, there still is a way to use the table in these cases. Remember that p is the probability of the desired outcome on any one event. If the probability of the desired outcome is greater than .50, the probability of the other outcome will be less than .50. Simply label that outcome the "desired" one, and p will be less than .50.

To check that the table of binomial probabilities gives the same values as we found using the addition and multiplication rules, let's look first at the probabilities listed when N is 2 and p is .50. These were the values of N and p for the binomial distribution of guessing on two true/false questions, as shown in Table 10-4. Note that Appendix A-2 shows the same probabilities, .25, .50, and .25, as in Table 10-3. Thus, the table of binomial probabilities, Appendix A-2, gives us the same values as does the binomial equation. Using Appendix A-2 can save us a lot of computation.

To demonstrate the ease of using Appendix A-2, let's construct the binomial distribution of guessing on Joe Johnson's 20-question math test. Recall again that the questions were multiple choice, with four alternatives per question, so that p, the probability of guessing correctly on one question, is .25. As there were 20 questions on the test, N is 20. We can look up the probabilities of guessing from 0 of 20 correctly to 20 of 20 correctly by looking for N of 20 and p of .25 in Appendix A-2. These results are shown in Table 10-5.

Note that in Table 10-5, the probability of guessing 14 or more questions correctly is listed as .0000. Thus, it appears that there is no chance of guessing 14 or more correctly. This in fact is not the case. There actually is a very small probability of guessing 14 or more correctly, but that probability is so small (less than .00005) that when rounded to 4 decimal places, it rounds to .0000.

We can find the probability of a combination of outcomes by applying the addition rule to the probabilities found in the table of binomial probabilities. For example, suppose we wanted to know

TABLE 10-5 Binomial Distribution of Guessing on Twenty-Question Multiple-Choice Test, with Four Alternatives per Question

Number of Questions Correct	Probability
20	.0000
19	.0000
18	.0000
17	.0000
16	.0000
15	.0000
14	.0000
13	.0002
12	.0008
11	.0030
10	.0099
9	.0271
8	.0609
7	.1124
6	.1686
5	.2023
4	.1897
3	.1339
2	.0669
1	.0211
0	.0032

FIGURE 10-1 Performance Expected if Students Guess on
Twenty-Question Math Test, with Four Alternative Answers per Question

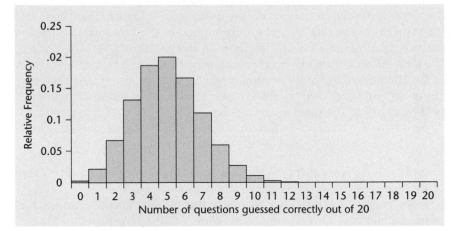

the probability of guessing correctly on fewer than three questions on Joe's
math test. Guessing correctly on fewer than three questions is the same as
guessing correctly on two questions or on one question or on zero questions.
The probabilities of these three outcomes are listed in Table 10-5 and repeated
below:

P(2 of 20 correct)	.0669
P(1 of 20 correct)	.0211
P(0 of 20 correct)	+ .0032
P(fewer than 3 of 20 correct)	.0912.

Thus, the probability of guessing fewer than three questions correctly on the
twenty-question math test is .0912.

In addition to listing the probabilities of a binomial distribution in a
table, we can also show those same probabilities in a graph. For example, a
graph of the binomial distribution generated by guessing on Joe's twenty-
question multiple-choice test is shown in Figure 10-1.

The graph shown in Figure 10-1 appears to be similar in many ways to the
graphs we constructed in Chapter 3. However, there is an important difference. The graphs in Chapter 3 depicted sets of scores that had actually been
empirically collected (presumably). On the other hand, the scores graphed in
Figure 10-1 were not actually collected from students. Instead, Figure 10-1
shows the set of scores predicted by the binomial equation for what would
happen if students guessed on the math test. This is not a distribution that
was actually collected from subjects; it is a theoretical distribution.

The Mean and Standard Deviation of a Binomial Distribution

Step-by-Step Procedure 10-3 shows the method for calculating the mean and standard deviation of a binomial distribution. In the binomial distribution predicting how students would perform on the math test solely by guessing, the total number of events was the number of questions on the test, and so N is 20. The probability of success on any one question, p, was .25. Therefore, the mean number of correct guesses, out of the twenty questions, is Np, which is (20)(.25), or 5. The standard deviation is

$$\sqrt{Np(1-p)} = \sqrt{(20)(.25)(.75)} = \sqrt{3.75} = 1.9.$$

Therefore, if students answered solely by guessing, we would expect a mean of five questions correct, with a standard deviation of 1.9.

The shape of the graph of a binomial distribution depends on the values of two parameters, the total number of events, N, and the probability of a success on any one event, p. Figure 10-2 shows the graphs of binomial distributions when N is 5, 10, and 20 and when p is .25, .50, and .75. Notice that the graphs are symmetrical when p is .50 but are skewed positively when p is less than .50 and skewed negatively when p is greater than .50. This is true for all values of N. Whenever p is .50, the graph of the binomial distribution is symmetrical. Whenever the value of p is less than .50, the graph of the binomial distribution will be skewed positively, and conversely, whenever the value of p is over .50, the graph will be skewed negatively.

STEP-BY-STEP PROCEDURE 10-3

Calculating the Mean and Standard Deviation of a Binomial Distribution

$$\mu = Np$$

$$\sigma = \sqrt{Np(1-p)}$$

where N = the number of events
p = the probability of success on one event

1. To find the mean of a binomial distribution, multiply the number of events, N, by the probability of success on any one event, p.

2. To find the standard deviation of a binomial distribution, first multiply the number of events, N, by the probability of success on any one event, p.

3. Subtract p from 1, and then multiply that result by the result of Step 2.

4. Find the square root of the result of Step 3 to find the standard deviation.

FIGURE 10-2 Effect of Changes in *N* and *p* on Binomial Distributions

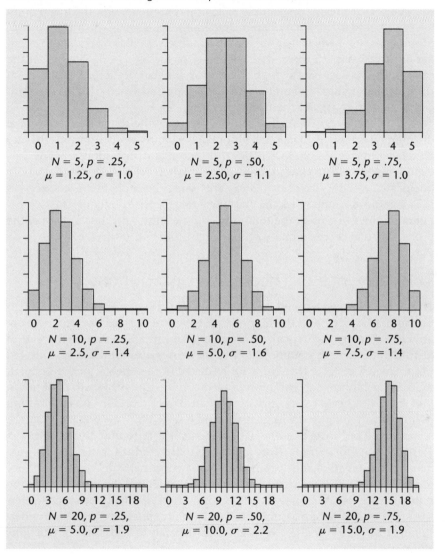

Figure 10-2 shows that the larger *N* is, the greater the value of the mean. For example, with *p* equal to .50, the mean is 2.5 with an *N* of 5, 5.0 with an *N* of 10, and 10.0 with an *N* of 20. The standard deviation also increases as *N* gets larger. This is reasonable, because since *N* is the number of events, the more the total number of events, the more values *X* can be and the more spread out the distribution will be.

We can also see in Figure 10-2 that the larger the value of *p,* the higher the value of the mean. For example, when there are 10 events, the mean number of successes is 2.5 when the probability of success is .25, the mean number of successes is 5.0 when the probability of success is .50, and the mean number of successes is 7.5 when the probability of success is .75. The higher the probability of a success, the higher the mean number of successes will be. On the other hand, the standard deviation is the greatest when *p* is .50. The standard deviation is smaller the farther *p* is from .50.

As we can see in Figure 10-2, there is not just one shape that a binomial distribution can have. In fact, the binomial is a family of distributions that are all related by certain characteristics. All binomial distributions are the predicted number of successes out of *N* events, when each event can have only one of two values, success or failure, and when the probability of success is *p.* The particular shape that the graph will take depends only on the two parameters: the value of *N,* the total number of events, and the value of *p,* the probability of a success on any one event.

The Relevance of Theoretical Distributions

Thus far, we have examined two theoretical distributions, the normal distribution in Chapter 7 and the binomial distribution in this chapter. These are only two of many theoretical distributions. The one thing that all theoretical distributions have in common is that the scores are not actually collected from subjects. Instead, the scores are predicted from a theory. In this chapter, we used the binomial distribution to predict how students would perform on Joe's math test just by guessing. We did not collect scores by actually testing participants, telling them to guess on the test. Rather, we predict what the scores would be, using a mathematical theory, the binomial distribution.

Theoretical distributions are important in the study of statistics. There are many attributes studied in psychology that are normally distributed or binomially distributed. We have already examined at length the usefulness of the normal distribution in analyzing IQ scores. There are many other characteristics and traits that are assumed to be normally distributed, and an understanding of the normal curve enables us to analyze and make predictions about those attributes.

We can also use theoretical distributions to test our hypotheses about subjects' behavior. In this chapter, we used the binomial distribution to predict how students would perform on Joe's math test just by guessing. We could compare those predicted scores to the actual performance of Joe's participants. If those participants' actual performance was significantly better than predicted by the binomial distribution, we could argue that the participants did not succeed on the test just by guessing. In a later chapter, we will look at ways to make this type of comparison.

Thus far, we have examined theoretical distributions of scores. In the next chapter, we examine how theoretical distributions can be used to construct the distribution of sample statistics, such as the distribution of sample means and the distribution of sample proportions. These distributions serve as the basis for testing hypotheses and thus are the foundation for inferential statistics.

CHECKING YOUR ANSWERS

1. Remember that probabilities are defined as proportions, which in turn are relative frequencies. If you were successful in computing relative frequencies in Chapter 3, you can compute probabilities.

2. Remember that probabilities can never be lower than 0 or greater than 1.00. If you find a probability of $-.67$ or $+2.59$, you've definitely made an error.

3. Students sometimes have difficulty differentiating when to use the additive rule or the multiplication rule of probability. The additive rule is used to find the probability of two or more outcomes for one event. The problem will contain the word "or": Find the probability that Outcome 1 *or* 2 will occur in one event. The multiplication rule is used to find the probability of a combination of outcomes over two or more events. The problem will contain the word "and": Find the probability that a given outcome will occur on Event 1 *and* on Event 2. In some cases "and" or "or" will be implied rather than stated explicitly.

4. When working problems involving the binomial distribution, be careful to read exactly what the question asks for. The questions "find the probability of 7 or more . . ." and "find the probability of more than 7 . . ." are not the same.

5. Remember that the binomial formula and the table of binomial probabilities in Appendix A-2 are equivalent. You can use one method to check your work on the other.

6. When working with the binomial distribution, it helps to draw a picture of what the question is asking. Draw a sketch of the distribution, and label all known values. Identify on your sketch the values that you are looking for. Taking the time to draw a picture and use it to help solve the problem can prevent many errors.

7. When you are asked to construct a binomial distribution, remember that the sum of the probabilities for all values of X must total 1.00. Adding up the probabilities to make sure they total 1.00 is a simple way to check your answer.

SUMMARY

▶ Probability is a statement about the proportion of score values in a distribution. The probability that a given score will have value A is the same as the proportion of scores in the distribution that have value A.

▶ Empirical probabilities are based on a set of scores drawn from actual observations that have been made. Theoretical probabilities are based on a set of assumptions (a theory) rather than on empirical observations.

▶   All probabilities will have values between 0 and 1.00, inclusive. If the probability of an outcome is 0, that outcome will never occur. If the probability of an outcome is 1.00, that outcome is certain to occur. The sum of all possible outcomes for an event is always 1.00.

▶   If two or more outcomes are mutually exclusive, then the addition rule states that the combined probability of the occurrence of one of those outcomes is the sum of the individual probabilities that each outcome will occur. Outcomes are mutually exclusive if when one outcome occurs, the other outcomes cannot occur.

▶   If the outcomes of two or more events are independent, then the multiplication rule states that the combined probability of a specified outcome occurring for all of the events is the product of the individual probabilities of that outcome for each individual event. The outcomes of events are independent if the outcome of each event has no influence whatsoever on the outcome of any of the other events.

▶   Dichotomous variables are variables which have only two score values. When dichotomous variables are measured, the resulting data are called binomial.

▶   A binomial distribution is the set of probabilities or proportions for X successes in N events, with the values of X being integers from 0 to N, and with the probability of success on any one event being p.

▶   If we know the value of N, the number of events, and p, the probability of success on one event, we can construct a binomial distribution, using one of several methods: (*a*) using the addition and multiplication rules of probability, (*b*) using the binomial equation, and (*c*) using the table of binomial probabilities.

▶   The binomial equation gives the probability of obtaining X successes in N events, with p as the probability of success on one event. The binomial equation must be computed separately for each value of X.

▶   The table of binomial probabilities (Appendix A-2) gives the results of computing the binomial equation for all values of X for values of N from 1 to 20 and for selected values of p. The binomial table is convenient, as it saves the labor of actually computing the probabilities using the binomial equation.

▶   The mean of a binomial distribution is Np, and the standard deviation is $\sqrt{Np(1 - p)}$. When p is exactly .50, the binomial distribution will be balanced. When p is less than .50, the distribution will be positively skewed, and when p is greater than .50, the distribution will be negatively skewed.

E X E R C I S E S

Conceptual Exercises

1. Define the following terms:

probability	a priori probability
empirical probability	addition rule
a posteriori probability	multiplication rule
theoretical probability	binomial distribution

2. Jeremiah was interested in the probability of guessing correctly on a ten-question true-false quiz.
   A. Using Appendix A-2, determine the probability that students could get 0, 1, 2, . . . , 10 questions correct on the quiz solely by guessing.
   B. If 10,000 students guess on the quiz, find the number of students Jeremiah could expect to get each number of questions correct, if all of the students were guessing.
   C. Using the frequencies you calculated in Part B, calculate the mean and standard deviation, treating the distribution as a population.
   D. Find the mean and standard deviation using Procedure 10-3. Compare the results to those found in Part C.

3. Use the table of probabilities you constructed in Exercise 2, Part A, to find the following:
   A. the probability that a student will guess correctly on 2 or fewer questions.
   B. the probability that a student will guess more than 5 questions correctly.
   C. the probability that a student will guess 9 or 10 questions correctly.
   D. the probability that a student will guess fewer than 3 questions correctly.
   E. the probability that a student will guess either no question correctly or all ten questions correctly.

4. Jeremiah was also interested in the probability of guessing correctly on a ten-question multiple-choice quiz in which each question had four alternative answers.
   A. Using Appendix A-2, determine the probability that students could get 0, 1, 2, . . . , 10 questions correct on the quiz solely by guessing.
   B. If 10,000 students guess on this quiz, find the number of students Jeremiah could expect to get each number of questions correct.
   C. Compare these results to the results of Exercise 2. What is the effect of having four alternatives per question compared to two alternatives?

5. Take five coins and toss all five coins 100 times. Record the number of tosses in which each number of heads, from 0 to 5, came up. Make a table of this frequency distribution.
   A. Divide each frequency by 100 to find the probability of getting from 0 to 5 heads in a coin toss.
   B. Use Appendix A-2 to find the theoretical probability of getting from 0 to 5 heads in a toss of five coins.
   C. Compare the results of the distribution you found by tossing coins to the theoretical distribution you constructed in Part B. How close does the theoretical distribution fit the distribution you found by tossing the coins?
   D. Calculate the mean and standard deviation of the theoretical distribution, using Procedure 10-3.

Computational Exercises

6. Jurgen tested the powers of extrasensory perception by having blindfolded participants guess the suit of a card drawn randomly from a complete deck of cards. (In case you've forgotten, a complete deck has fifty-two cards, with thirteen cards in each of four suits.)
   A. What is the probability that a participant will guess the suit correctly on one card?
   B. If five cards are drawn in succession, with replacement, what is the probability that a participant will guess the suits of all five cards correctly?
   C. If ten cards are drawn in succession, with replacement, what is the probability that a participant will guess the suits of at least five of those cards correctly?

7. Jubal also was interested in parapsychological phenomena. He tested the powers of precognition by having participants predict the value of a die toss. (In case you've forgotten or never knew, a die has six sides, each side marked with dots to represent the values from 1 to 6.) In order to use the binomial table, assume that the probability of guessing correctly on one toss is .15.

   A. What is a probability that a participant will guess the value of the die correctly on one toss?

   B. What is the probability that a participant will guess incorrectly on one toss?

   C. What is the probability that a participant will guess the value of the die correctly on five tosses in a row?

   D. What is the probability that a participant will guess the value of the die correctly on three of five tosses?

8. Suppose that Julia tested rates in a maze with three alternatives: the rats could either turn left, turn right, or go straight. In order to use the binomial table, assume that the probability of choosing any one of the alternatives is .35.

   A. What is the probability that a rat will take the left turn five times out of ten trials?

   B. What is the probability that a rat will take the right turn more than six times out of eight trials?

   C. What is the probability that a rat will take six or fewer right turns out of eight trials?

   D. What is the probability that a rat will go straight ahead less than three times or more than five times out of eight trials?

   E. What is the probability that a rat will either select the left turn or the right turn on every one of seven trials?

9. Suppose that 20 percent of the population in the United States is left-handed.

   A. What is the probability that five people in a group of twenty would be left-handed?

   B. What is the probability that three or fewer people in a group of twenty would be left-handed?

   C. What is the probability that more than twelve people in a group of fifteen would be right-handed?

   D. What is the probability that in a group of five people, all of the people would be left-handed or all of the people would be right-handed?

   E. What is the probability that none of the people in a group of ten would be left-handed?

10. Jerome gave a class a twenty-question multiple-choice test, with four alternatives per question. Using the binomial table in Appendix A-2, construct a table showing the probabilities that students will get from zero correct to twenty correct solely by guessing on this test.

Sampling Distributions

Constructing a Distribution of Sample Proportions

An Example of a Sampling Distribution: A Distribution of Sample Proportions

Criteria for a Sampling Distribution

Methods of Sampling

Theoretical Sampling Distributions

STEP-BY-STEP PROCEDURE 11-1: Constructing a Binomial Sampling Distribution of the Proportion of Successes in n Events

Comparing Empirical and Theoretical Sampling Distributions

Distributions of Sample Means

Constructing an Empirical Distribution of Sample Means

Characteristics of a Distribution of Sample Means

Using the Normal Distribution to Construct Sampling Distributions Theoretically

STEP-BY-STEP PROCEDURE 11-2: Calculating the Mean and Standard Error for a Distribution of Sample Means

STEP-BY-STEP PROCEDURE 11-3: Calculating the Mean and Standard Error of a Distribution of Sample Proportions

Calculating an Unbiased Estimate of the Standard Error when σ Is Not Known

STEP-BY-STEP PROCEDURE 11-4: Calculating an Unbiased Estimate of the Standard Error of the Mean, Using the Sample Standard Deviation, s

The Exactness of Parameter Estimates

Confidence Intervals for Sample Means

STEP-BY-STEP PROCEDURE 11-5: Calculating Confidence Limits (CLs)

Confidence Limits for Sample Proportions and Percentages

Level of Confidence

Factors that Affect the Size of the Confidence Interval

CHECKING YOUR ANSWERS

SUMMARY

EXERCISES

  Conceptual Exercises

  Computational Exercises

ENDNOTE

▶ The statistics that we examined in Chapters 2 to 8 are used to describe a distribution of scores or the relationship between two distributions. In Chapter 9, in which we looked at regression, we moved beyond description. When using a regression equation, we use a subject's score on one variable to predict what that subject's score might be on another variable. Regression equations are used to predict an individual subject's score. We also examined how to use the normal distribution and the binomial distribution to predict the likelihood of certain scores occurring. These predictions all have been of the likelihood of individual subjects' scores. In this chapter, we examine statistical techniques that we can use to make predictions about entire populations of scores.

In Chapter 2, we looked at the difference between populations and samples. Recall that a sample is a subset of scores drawn from a population. The function of a sample statistic is to estimate the value of the corollary population parameter. Joe Johnson, in his study on math anxiety, was not interested just in the performance of the twenty students he tested. Rather, he intended to use their performance as an estimate of the performance of the entire population of math-anxious students.

When we use a sample statistic as an estimate of a population parameter, we are making an inference. Joe used the mean of his sample as an estimate of the population parameter, estimating that the mean of the entire population of math-anxious students on his math test would be 66 percent. He thus made an inference from the value of his sample mean to what the value of the population mean would be. In essence, Joe used a description of a sample of scores to make an inference about the population from which that sample was drawn. The statistical techniques that enable us to make inferences from samples to populations are called **inferential statistics.** Inferential statistics are sometimes referred to as hypothesis-testing statistics because they are the statistical procedures that researchers use to objectively test hypotheses.

In order to understand these statistical techniques, we need first to examine the concept of sampling distributions. We begin by examining a distribution of sample proportions, using a simple example as our first illustration of a sampling distribution. We then turn to distributions of sample means, which are frequently used in psychological research.

Inferential statistics are statistical techniques that use scores from a sample to make inferences about the population from which the sample was drawn.

Constructing a Distribution of Sample Proportions

An Example of a Sampling Distribution: A Distribution of Sample Proportions

In the last chapter, I described the M&M dispenser in my office, and we determined the probability of drawing each color of M&M from the dispenser, as an example of an empirical distribution. The dispenser has a lever on the front, which, when pressed, dispenses a handful of M&Ms. Suppose we consider all of the M&Ms in the container a population of M&Ms and each handful of M&Ms as a sample. Suppose then that we took 100 samples of M&Ms from the jar, one after the other, each time returning the sample to the jar. Recall from the last chapter that this is sampling with replacement. If we did not return the samples to the jar, we would be sampling without replacement. When we return each sample to the jar before drawing another sample, we make sure that the proportion of each color M&M in the population does not change from sample to sample, so that the probability of drawing each color does not change.

In the previous chapter, we drew M&Ms one at a time. This time we are drawing them by the handful. We are drawing a sample of scores rather than just one score. Suppose that every sample that we drew by pressing the lever contained 20 M&Ms. For each sample we draw, we count the number of brown M&Ms and calculate the proportion of brown M&Ms in each sample, dividing the number of brown M&Ms by 20. This proportion of brown M&Ms is a sample statistic.

When we have completed this process for 100 samples of M&Ms, we will have 100 values of the proportion of brown M&Ms in these samples. Table 11-1 shows the results of 100 such samplings, which I actually drew from my M&M dispenser. The first column in Table 11-1 lists the proportion of brown M&Ms per sample. Some of the samples I drew contained no brown M&Ms at all (.00 or 0 percent brown), while other samples were half brown M&Ms (.50 or 50 percent brown). These were the minimum and maximum proportions of brown M&Ms per sample that I drew. The other samples I drew had proportions of brown M&Ms in between these two extremes. Some samples contained nine brown M&Ms (.45 or 45 percent brown), some contained eight brown M&Ms (.40 or 40 percent brown), and so on. The second column in Table 11-1 lists the relative frequency that each of these proportions of brown M&Ms

TABLE 11-1 Empirical Sampling Distribution of the Proportion of Brown M&Ms in 100 Samples of Twenty M&Ms

Proportion of Brown M&Ms per Sample	Relative Frequency
.50	.01
.45	.02
.40	.08
.35	.10
.30	.15
.25	.19
.20	.18
.15	.15
.10	.10
.05	.01
.00	.01

occurred in the samples. Out of the 100 samples drawn, .01 or 1 percent of the samples contained 50 percent brown M&Ms, .02 or 2 percent of the samples contained 45 percent brown M&Ms, and so on.

In previous chapters, we examined many frequency distributions, which listed all of the score values in a sample or population and the frequencies with which those values occurred. The values shown in Table 11-1 also are a distribution but not a frequency distribution of scores. Table 11-1 shows a distribution of sample proportions, also called a **sampling distribution**. There are two important differences between a frequency distribution and a sampling distribution. First, in a frequency distribution of scores, the values come from one sample or one population of subjects, while in a sampling distribution, the values come from many samples. The values shown in Table 11-1 represent 100 samples of M&Ms. The second difference is that the values in a frequency distribution are scores, while the values in a sampling distribution are sample statistics. The statistic listed in Table 11-1 is the proportion of brown M&Ms per sample.

A **sampling distribution** is a distribution of a given statistic, calculated from independently collected samples of size *n,* all drawn from the same population.

A sampling distribution could list statistics other than sample proportions. For example, we could collect 100 samples of children's heights and calculate the mean height of each sample. Listing these 100 mean heights in a table would comprise a distribution of sample means. We could just as easily calculate the standard deviation of heights in those 100 samples, one standard deviation for each sample, which would give us a distribution of sample standard deviations. In general, we could calculate any statistic on a number of samples to give us a distribution of that sample statistic. These distributions are all sampling distributions, distributions of a sample statistic.

Criteria for a Sampling Distribution

There are four important criteria of a sampling distribution. First, a sampling distribution is a distribution of one statistic calculated from many samples. The statistic calculated in the sampling distribution shown in Table 11-1 is the proportion of brown M&Ms.

Second, each sample must contain the same number of scores, designated *n*. All of the 100 samples that I drew from my dispenser contained 20 M&Ms, and so *n* is 20 for this sampling distribution.

A third criterion is that all of the samples must be drawn from the same population. If I had drawn some of the samples from one M&M dispenser, and other samples from another M&M dispenser the result would not be a sampling distribution.

The selection of a sample is **independent** if the selection of any one member of the population for inclusion in the sample does not affect the probability that any other member of the population will be selected.

The final criterion is that the samples used to calculate the statistic must be independently collected. That is the reason that I replaced each sample when I drew 100 samples of M&Ms. If I had drawn the samples without replacement, then the proportion of brown M&Ms in the dispenser would have changed slightly from sample to sample. An **independent** sample is one in which subjects are selected in such a way that selecting one subject for the sample does not affect the probability that any other subject in the population will be selected. The methods of sampling that are used to ensure independence in psychological research are explored briefly in the next section.

Methods of Sampling

One of the four criteria for a sampling distribution is that the samples are independently selected from the population. In the example of samples of M&Ms, independence was ensured by sampling with replacement; that is, by returning each sample of M&Ms to the container before drawing the next sample. Each M&M has an equally likely chance of being picked for a sample, and selecting one particular M&M docs not affect the likelihood that any other M&M will be selected. This is the essence of **random sampling**, which ensures independence.

Random sampling is the process of drawing a sample from a population in such a way that each member of the population has an equal likelihood of being included in the sample.

It is easy to draw a random sample of M&Ms. It is not so easy to do so with human beings. While for some relatively small populations random samples may be feasible, this is not the case for most populations studied in psychology. No researcher has access to the entire population of four-year-old children in the United States or the entire population of white rats. Because of these difficulties, very few researchers in psychology are able to use random sampling to select the subjects who participate in their experiments.

Researchers in psychology often use **random assignment** rather than true random sampling. Most psychological research involves testing subjects under two or more conditions. In these studies, subjects are randomly assigned to the testing conditions. Even if there is bias in sampling, when subjects are randomly assigned to the various testing conditions there is no reason to expect that the subjects in one condition will be any more biased than the subjects in any other condition.

Random assignment is the process of assigning subjects to groups or treatment conditions in an experiment in such a way that a subject has an equal likelihood of being assigned to each of the groups or conditions.

The purpose of random sampling is to ensure that the sample is representative of the population from which it is drawn. As it is often difficult in psychological research to select a truly random sample, it is important for researchers to be aware of possible bias in sampling. There are many research methods that can be used to protect against possible bias in sampling. A discussion of these methods is beyond the scope of this text. These methods are usually studied in courses on research methods and design. It is sufficient here to say that we need to be aware of the possibility of biases in sampling and their effect on the legitimacy of sampling distributions.

Theoretical Sampling Distributions

The sampling distribution of the proportion of brown M&Ms in samples of 20 M&Ms, shown in Table 11-1, is an **empirical sampling distribution**. The proportions were calculated from samples that were actually drawn from a population. I really drew 100 samples of M&Ms and calculated the proportion of brown M&Ms in each sample. As another example, we could construct

An **empirical sampling distribution** is a sampling distribution constructed by drawing actual samples from a population and computing the specified statistic.

an empirical sampling distribution of IQ means by collecting many, many samples of people, testing their IQs, and computing the mean IQ of each sample. In the real world, researchers do not construct sampling distributions empirically. The empirical distribution of the proportion of brown M&Ms is used here just to illustrate exactly what a sampling distribution is.

A **theoretical sampling distribution** is a sampling distribution constructed based on the characteristics of a mathematical theory, such as the binomial distribution or normal distribution.

Rather than construct a sampling distribution empirically, researchers use a **theoretical sampling distribution.** Remember that a theoretical distribution is the set of values and frequency those values would occur, as predicted by a mathematical model or theory. The normal distribution is a theoretical distribution. When we say that IQ scores are normally distributed, we are saying that if we tested the IQs of millions of people, the distribution would be shaped as predicted by the normal distribution. A theoretical sampling distribution is similar, in that we use a mathematical theory to predict how a sample statistic would be distributed if we took millions and millions of samples. For example, we could use the binomial distribution to determine the shape our sampling distribution of the proportion of brown M&Ms in samples of 20 M&Ms, without having to go through the work of drawing 100 samples. This method is described in Step-by-Step Procedure 11-1.

Procedure 11-1 is fairly simple. First, we need to determine the values of n and p. The value of n is the number of events in each sample. In this case an "event" is drawing one M&M from the dispenser. Each of our samples contains 20 M&Ms, so the value of n is 20. The value of p is the proportion of outcomes considered a "success." In this case, a "success" is a brown M&M and the proportion of brown M&Ms in the entire population (i.e., in the entire dispenser) is .25 (25 percent of the M&Ms in the dispenser are brown). Thus, p is .25.

Next, we need to convert all of the values of X, the number of successes, to proportions, by dividing each value of X by n, which in this case is 20. In

---

STEP-BY-STEP PROCEDURE 11-1

Constructing a Binomial Sampling Distribution of the Proportion of Successes in *n* Events

1. Determine the value of n and p. The value of n is the number of events in each sample under consideration. The value of p is the proportion of outcomes considered a "success" in the population of events.

2. Convert all of the values of X, the number of successes, from 0 to n, to proportions by dividing each value of X by n. List these proportions in a column, titled "Sample Proportions."

3. Use the table of binomial probabilities (Appendix A-2) to find the probability of getting X successes in n events, for all values of X, from 0 to n. List these probabilities in a column to the right of the column of proportions, in corresponding order. Title this column "p."

the distribution we are constructing, the value of X could range from 0 to 20 (i.e., we could get from 0 brown M&Ms to 20 brown M&Ms in our samples of 20 M&Ms). So, we divide each integer, from 0 to 20, by 20, to find the possible proportions of brown M&Ms in our samples. These proportions are shown in the left-hand column of Table 11-2.

Next, we need to find the probability of drawing samples with X brown M&Ms per sample. We can use any of the methods for finding binomial probabilities described in Chapter 10. The simplest method is to use the table of binomial probabilities (Appendix A-2). For our distribution, we are looking for the probabilities of X, when n is 20 and p is .25. These probabilities from Appendix A-2 are listed in Table 11-2 in the second column. These two columns in Table 11-2 constitute the theoretical sampling distribution of the proportion of brown M&Ms in samples of 20 M&Ms.

TABLE 11-2 Theoretical Sampling Distribution of the Proportion of Brown M&Ms in Samples of Twenty M&Ms

Proportion of Brown M&Ms per Sample	Relative Frequency
.55	.01
.50	.01
.45	.03
.40	.06
.35	.11
.30	.17
.25	.20
.20	.19
.15	.13
.10	.07
.05	.02
.00	.00

Comparing Empirical and Theoretical Sampling Distributions

Table 11-1 is the empirical sampling distribution of the proportion of brown M&Ms in samples of 20 M&Ms, constructed by actually drawing 100 samples of 20 M&Ms. Table 11-2 is the theoretical sampling distribution. No samples were actually drawn to construct the distribution shown in Table 11-2. Rather, the distribution in Table 11-2 shows the proportions predicted by the mathematical model of the binomial distribution. It represents what we would expect to occur if we drew millions and millions of samples.

Figure 11-1 shows both of these sampling distributions. Comparing the two distributions, first notice that they are not exactly the same. The theoretical distribution predicted that 20 percent of the samples would have 5 brown M&Ms, but only 19 percent of the 100 samples that I actually drew from the container had 5 brown M&Ms. Similarly, the theoretical distribution predicted that only 7 percent of the samples would have 2 brown M&Ms, while 10 percent of the 100 samples that I drew had 2 brown M&Ms. Thus, the theoretical and empirical sampling distributions are not exactly the same. However, looking at Figure 11-1, we can see that even though they are not exactly the same, there is a remarkable degree of similarity between the theoretical and empirical sampling distributions.

You might ask which one is better, the theoretical or the empirical sampling distribution. Which one should we use? Actually, no one ever actually constructs sampling distributions empirically (except authors of statistics texts, trying to make a point). All real-life researchers use theoretical sampling

FIGURE 11-1 Comparing Empirical and Theoretical Distributions of Sample Proportions

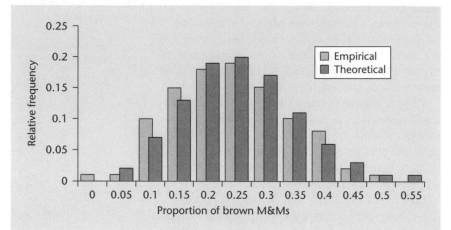

distributions for two reasons. The first reason is that they are much easier to construct. It takes just a few minutes to construct a theoretical sampling distribution (do a few computations and look up probabilities in a table), whereas drawing many samples can be very time consuming. (Can you imagine the amount of time it would take to test the IQs of hundreds of samples of people?)

The second reason that researchers use theoretical sampling distributions is that they are more consistent. If I redid the work of drawing 100 samples to reconstruct the empirical sampling distribution of the proportion of brown M&Ms in samples of 20 M&Ms, I probably would not get exactly the same results that I did the first time. While empirical sampling distributions are not consistent, theoretical sampling distributions are perfectly consistent. We could go through the steps of constructing the theoretical sampling distribution for the proportion of brown M&Ms and would get exactly the same results. Anyone else constructing the same theoretical sampling distribution would get the same results. In fact, a theoretical sampling distribution predicts what an empirical sampling distribution would be if we were able to collect an infinite number of samples. In an empirical sampling distribution, the more samples that we draw, the closer the empirical sampling distribution is likely to come to the theoretical distribution.

If researchers always use theoretical sampling distributions, why did we bother here to look at empirical sampling distributions? To make a point. Students often have difficulty understanding the concept of sampling distributions. It is helpful to see how they can be constructed empirically to understand exactly what they represent. Of course, an obvious question is why would we want to understand what sampling distributions represent?

Admittedly, sampling distributions are rather strange things. Who would want to collect hundreds and hundreds of samples just to draw a graph of how a sample statistic is distributed? The reason is that virtually all of the inferential statistics that we will examine in the remaining chapters of this text are based on the concept of sampling distributions. To understand what those inferential statistics measure, it is absolutely crucial to understand what a sampling distribution is.

The sampling distributions that we have examined thus far have been distributions of sample proportions, which are based on the binomial distribution. We also might want to construct sampling distributions of other statistics, such as the mean or the standard deviation. These sampling distributions are based on the normal distribution, rather than the binomial distribution. To examine how to use the normal distribution to construct a sampling distribution, next we will look at an example of a distribution of sample means.

Distributions of Sample Means

Constructing an Empirical Distribution of Sample Means

In order to understand how to find the mean and standard deviation of a theoretical sampling distribution, we are first going to construct an empirical sampling distribution of means. Again, no real-life researcher would construct a distribution of sample means empirically. We are doing this simply to understand what a sampling distribution of means depicts.

Suppose we consider a group of eight children as a population. The children and their ages are

Ann and Bob	five years old
Carl and Dee	six years old
Eva and Fred	seven years old
Gert and Hal	eight years old

In this population of eight children, there are two children of each age, from five to eight years old. Now suppose that we draw samples of two children from this population. Table 11-3 shows all of the possible samples that we could draw, and the mean age of each sample.[1]

Table 11-4 shows two distributions. On the left is the frequency distribution of the eight children's ages. This is a *distribution of scores*. On the right is the sampling distribution of the means listed in Table 11-3. This is a *distribution of sample means*. These two distributions are closely related because the distribution of sample means was compiled by drawing samples from the distribution of scores. These two distributions are pictured graphically in Figure 11-2. Note that while the distribution of scores is rectangular in shape, the shape of the distribution of sample means is more like the normal distribution.

TABLE 11-3   Samples of Two Children Drawn from a Population
with Equal Numbers of Five- to Eight-Year-Old Children

Sample	$\overline{X}$	Sample	$\overline{X}$	Sample	$\overline{X}$
$Ann_5 + Bob_5$	5.0	$Ann_5 + Carl_6$	5.5	$Ann_5 + Dee_6$	5.5
$Ann_5 + Eva_7$	6.0	$Ann_5 + Fred_7$	6.0	$Ann_5 + Gert_8$	6.5
$Ann_5 + Hal_8$	6.5	$Bob_5 + Carl_6$	5.5	$Bob_5 + Dee_6$	5.5
$Bob_5 + Eva_7$	6.0	$Bob_5 + Fred_7$	6.0	$Bob_5 + Gert_8$	6.5
$Carl_6 + Dee_6$	6.0	$Carl_6 + Eva_7$	6.5	$Carl_6 + Fred_7$	6.5
$Carl_6 + Gert_8$	7.0	$Carl_6 + Hal_8$	7.0	$Dee_6 + Eva_7$	6.5
$Dee_6 + Fred_7$	6.5	$Dee_6 + Gert_8$	7.0	$Dee_6 + Hal_8$	7.0
$Bob_5 + Hal_8$	6.5	$Eva_7 + Fred_7$	7.0	$Eva_7 + Gert_8$	7.5
$Eva_7 + Hal_8$	7.5	$Fred_7 + Gert_8$	7.5	$Fred_7 + Hal_8$	7.5
$Gert_8 + Hal_8$	8.0				

TABLE 11-4   Distribution of Scores and Distribution of Sample Means,
Drawn from a Population of Five- to Eight-Year-Old Children

A. Distribution of Scores				B. Distribution of Sample Means		
Age	Frequency	Relative Frequency		Age	Frequency	Relative Frequency
8	2	.25		8.0	1	.04
7	2	.25		7.5	4	.14
6	2	.25		7.0	5	.18
5	2	.25		6.5	8	.28
				6.0	5	.18
				5.5	4	.14
				5.0	1	.04

We can calculate the mean and standard deviation for both of these distributions. First, let's compute the mean and standard deviation of the distribution of scores:

$$\mu = \frac{2(5) + 2(6) + 2(7) + 2(8)}{8} = \frac{52}{8} = 6.5 \text{ years,}$$

$$\sigma = \sqrt{\frac{2(5 - 6.5)^2 + 2(6 - 6.5)^2 + 2(7 - 6.5)^2 + 2(8 - 6.5)^2}{8}} = 1.12 \text{ years.}$$

In the population of eight children, the mean age is 6.5 years, with a standard deviation of 1.12 years.

FIGURE 11-2 Distribution of Scores and Distribution of Sample Means, Drawn from a Population of Five- to Eight-Year-Old Children

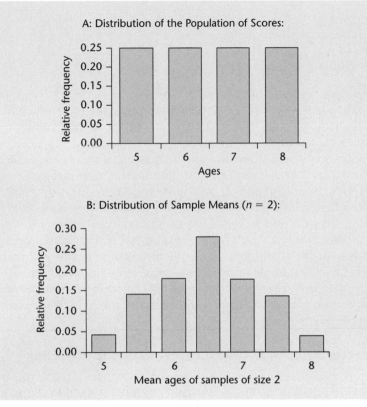

Next, let's compute the mean of the distribution of sample means. To differentiate between the means of the two distributions, we will use the symbol μ to represent the mean of the scores, and the symbol $\mu_{\overline{X}}$ to represent the mean of the sample means. In the computations shown below, remember that the values listed are sample means, not scores:

$$\mu_{\overline{X}} = \frac{1(5.0) + 4(5.5) + 5(6.0) + 8(6.5) + 5(7.0) + 4(7.5) + 1(8.0)}{28} = 6.5 \text{ years.}$$

The mean of the distribution of sample means, $\mu_{\overline{X}}$, is 6.5 years, exactly the same value as the mean of the distribution of scores. Thus, in this example, $\mu_{\overline{X}} = \mu$.

We also can compute the standard deviation of the distribution of sample means, shown in Table 11-4. To differentiate, we use the symbol σ to represent the standard deviation of the scores, and the symbol $\sigma_{\overline{X}}$ to represent the standard deviation of the sample means. Again, in the computations shown below, remember that the values shown are sample means, not scores:

$$\sigma_{\bar{X}} = \sqrt{\frac{(-1.5)^2 + 4(-1.0)^2 + 5(-0.5)^2 + 8(0)^2 + 5(0.5)^2 + 4(1.0)^2 + (1.5)^2}{28}}$$

$$= \sqrt{\frac{15}{28}} = \sqrt{.54} = 0.73 \text{ years.}$$

The standard deviation of the distribution of scores, σ, is 1.12 years, but the standard deviation of the distribution of sample means, $\sigma_{\bar{X}}$ is only 0.73 years. Thus, the sample means cluster closer to the center of the distribution than the scores do.

To summarize, there are three facts to note about these two distributions, the distribution of scores and the distribution of sample means. First, while the graph of the distribution of scores is rectangular in shape, the graph of the distribution of sample means is more normal in shape. The second fact to note is that the distribution of sample means has exactly the same mean, 6.5 years, as the distribution of scores. The third fact is that the standard deviation is less for the distribution of sample means than for the distribution of scores because the sample means are clustered more closely around the mean than the scores are. These three attributes are characteristic of all distributions of sample means, both empirical and theoretical, which we will examine further in the next section.

Characteristics of a Distribution of Sample Means

The shape of a distribution of sample means.   The first characteristic of sampling distributions of the mean is a tendency to be normal in shape, regardless of the shape of the distribution of scores from which the samples were drawn. This can be seen in Figure 11-2. Although the original distribution of scores is rectangular in shape, the distribution of sample means is shaped roughly like the normal distribution.

The distribution of sample means tends to be more normal in shape the larger the sample size. For example, Figure 11-3 compares two distributions of sample means. One distribution is the same distribution shown in Figure 11-2, with a sample size, *n*, of 2. The other distribution is drawn from the same population but has a sample size, *n*, of 4. Notice that the distribution of sample means is more normal in shape with a sample size of 4 than with a sample size of 2. It is not the number of samples that affects the shape of the distribution but the size of the samples. In fact, the larger the size of the samples, the closer the distribution of sample means tends toward the normal distribution. This principle is the basis of the *central limit theorem*.

If the population of scores from which the samples are drawn is itself normally distributed, then the distribution of sample means will also be normally distributed, regardless of the sample size. If the population of scores is not

FIGURE 11-3 Distribution of Sample Means Drawn from a
Population of Five- to Eight-Year-Old Children, with *n* = 2 and *n* = 4

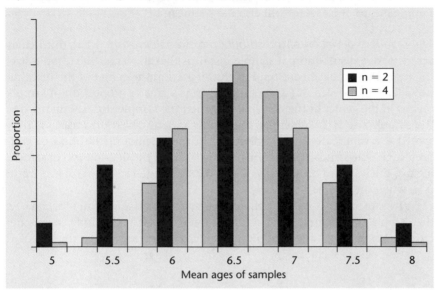

normally distributed, as long as the sample size is at least 20, the distribution
of sample means will be close enough to the normal distribution that we can
use the normal distribution to predict specified proportions of sample means.
This is comparable to the distributions of sample proportions, for which we
can also use the normal distribution when the sample size is at least 20.

The mean of a distribution of sample means. The second characteristic of all
distributions of sample means is that the mean of all the sample means is
equal to the mean of the population from which the samples were drawn:

$$\mu_{\bar{X}} = \mu.$$

Recall that the symbol, μ, represents the mean of a population of scores. The
symbol, $\mu_{\bar{X}}$, represents the mean of a distribution of sample means. For any
theoretical sampling distribution, if we calculate the mean of all of the sample
means shown in Table 11-3, the result will equal the mean of the population
of scores.

Because the mean of a theoretical distribution of sample means is equal
to the mean of the population from which the samples are drawn, we do not
have to select hundreds of samples and calculate their means in order to determine what the mean of the distribution of sample means will be. All we
have to know is the mean of the theoretical distribution of sample means will
be exactly the same as the mean of the population of scores from which the

samples were drawn. For example, since we know that the population of IQ scores has a mean of 100, we also know that every theoretical distribution of sample means of IQ scores will also have a mean of 100.

The standard deviation of a distribution of sample means. The third characteristic of a distribution of sample means is that the larger the sample size, the more the sample means tend to cluster around the center of the distribution. This can be seen in Figure 11-3. There is a greater proportion of sample means in the center of the distribution when the sample size is 4 than when the sample size is 2. Remember that the standard deviation measures how spread out values are in a distribution. In the original distribution of children's ages, the standard deviation, σ, was 1.12. For the distribution of sample means, the standard deviation, $\sigma_{\bar{X}}$, was 0.73 when the sample size was 2 and 0.56 when the sample size was 4.

The same trend occurs in a theoretical sampling distribution of means. As the sample size increases, the standard deviation of the sample means decreases. Using the equation below, we can calculate the value of the standard deviation of sample means:

$$\sigma_{\bar{X}} = \frac{\sigma}{\sqrt{n}}.$$

In a theoretical sampling distribution, the standard deviation of the sample means will equal the standard deviation of the population of scores from which the samples were drawn, divided by the square root of the sample size. The standard deviation of the sample means, $\sigma_{\bar{X}}$, is called the **standard error of the mean.**

> The **standard error** is the standard deviation of a sampling distribution. The standard error of the mean is the standard deviation of a distribution of sample means. The standard error of a proportion is the standard deviation of a distribution of sample proportions.

The standard deviation of a sampling distribution is called the standard error because it measures the exactness of using a sample statistic as an estimate of a population parameter. Remember that the purpose of the sample mean is to estimate the mean of the population from which the sample was drawn. The closer the sample mean is to the value of the population mean, the better the sample mean is as an estimate of the population mean. How do we know how close the sample mean is in value to the population mean? The standard error of the mean tells us.

Using the Normal Distribution to Construct Sampling Distributions Theoretically

Suppose that we want to construct the distribution of sample means for the IQ scores of samples of 25 people drawn from the general population. We can use the formulas in Step-by-Step Procedure 11-2 for the mean and standard error of a distribution of sample means to draw a graph of the distribution, using the three characteristics of sampling distributions. Because the sample size is 25, we know that the graph will be approximately normal in shape. We know that the mean of the sampling distribution will be the same as the mean

---

STEP-BY-STEP PROCEDURE 11-2

Calculating the Mean and Standard Error for a Distribution of Sample Means

$$\mu_{\bar{X}} = \mu$$

$$\sigma_{\bar{X}} = \frac{\sigma}{\sqrt{n}}$$

where μ = the mean of the population of scores from which the samples were drawn

σ = the standard deviation of the population of scores from which the samples were drawn

n = the sample size

1. Calculate the mean of the population of scores. The mean of the sampling distribution equals the mean of the population of scores.

2. Calculate the standard deviation of the population of scores.

3. Find the square root of n, the number of scores in each sample.

4. Divide the standard deviation found in Step 2 by the result of Step 3, to find the standard error of the mean.

---

of the population of scores from which the samples were drawn. The samples were drawn from the population of IQ scores, which has a mean of 100, so we know the mean of the sampling distribution will be 100:

$$\mu_{\bar{X}} = \mu = 100.$$

We also know that the standard error of the mean will equal the standard deviation of the population from which the samples were drawn, divided by the sample size. The population of IQ scores has a standard deviation of 15, which we can use to calculate the standard error of the mean:

$$\sigma_{\bar{X}} = \frac{\sigma}{\sqrt{n}} = \frac{15}{\sqrt{25}} = 3.0.$$

We can use these three characteristics to construct a graph of the distribution of sample means drawn from the population of IQ scores, as shown in Figure 11-4.

The center of the distribution of sample mean IQs is 100. One standard error up from the center is 103; one standard error down from the center is 97. Recall that Appendix A-1 shows that 34.13 percent of the scores in a normal distribution will be between the mean and one standard deviation above the mean. The same is true for sampling distributions. Thus, 34.13 percent of all sample means will be between the mean and one standard error above the mean, or between 100 and 103. Similarly, 34.13 percent of all sample means will be between the mean and one standard error below the mean, or between

FIGURE 11-4 Distribution of Sample Means,
Drawn from the Population of IQ Scores, with $n = 25$

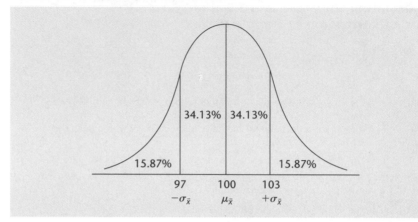

97 and 100. Thus, over two-thirds of the sample means will be between 97
and 103 when the sample size is 25.

We can also use the normal distribution to construct a distribution of
sample proportions. Earlier in this chapter, we looked at the sampling distribution of the proportion of brown M&Ms in samples of 20 M&Ms. We saw
that we can construct a theoretical sampling distribution of sample proportions using the table of binomial probabilities in Appendix A-2. We can also
use the normal distribution, as long as the sample size, n, is at least 20 and if
both np and $n(1 - p)$ are at least 5.

Recall that in the binomial distribution, p is the probability that the desired event will occur. In the M&M example, the desired event is a brown
M&M. The probability, p, that any one M&M drawn from the dispenser would
be brown is .25, equal to the proportion of brown M&Ms in the dispenser. In
this example, we used samples of 20 M&Ms, and so the sample size is large
enough to use the normal distribution. Furthermore, np is 20 × .25, or 5, and
$n(1 - p)$ is 20 × .75, or 15. Since both of these values are at least 5, we can use
the normal distribution to construct the sampling distribution of the proportion of brown M&Ms in samples of 20 M&Ms.

Using the formulas in Step-by-Step Procedure 11-3, we can find the mean
and standard error of a proportion for the distribution of sample proportions
of brown M&Ms:

$$\mu_p = p = .25,$$

$$\sigma_p = \sqrt{\frac{p(1 - p)}{n}} = \sqrt{\frac{.25(.75)}{20}} = \sqrt{\frac{.1875}{20}} = \sqrt{.009} = .09.$$

These calculations show that the mean of the sample proportions of brown
M&Ms in samples of 20 M&Ms is .25. Thus, if we found every possible sample

---

STEP-BY-STEP PROCEDURE 11-3

Calculating the Mean and Standard Error of a Distribution of Sample Proportions

$$\mu_p = p$$

$$\sigma_p = \sqrt{\frac{p(1 - p)}{n}}$$

where n = the number of events in the sample
        p = the probability of the desired outcome occurring on any one event

1. The probability of the desired outcome occurring, p, is the mean of the distribution of sample proportions, μ_p.

2. Subtract p from 1. Multiply the result by p.

3. Divide the result of Step 2 by n. Find the square root of that result to find the standard error of the distribution of sample proportions, σ_p. Note that if we do not know the value of p, the probability of the desired event occurring on any one event in the population, we can compute the sample standard deviation by substituting the sample proportion, P, for the value of p.

FIGURE 11-5   Using the Normal Distribution to Approximate the Sampling Distribution of Proportions of Brown M&Ms in Samples of Twenty M&Ms

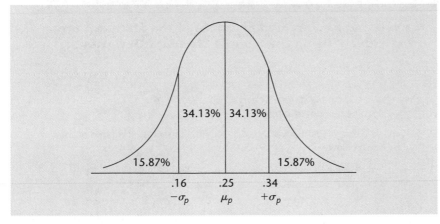

of 20 M&Ms, the average proportion of brown M&Ms in all of those samples would be .25, the same as the proportion of brown M&Ms in the population. The standard error of a proportion is .09. We can use these values to draw a graph of the normal distribution, as shown in Figure 11-5. From this graph, we can see that we can expect 68.26 percent of samples of 20 M&Ms to contain from 16 percent to 34 percent brown M&Ms, which is from 3.2 to 6.8 brown M&Ms.

Calculating an Unbiased Estimate of the Standard Error when σ Is Not Known

There are many cases when a researcher does not know the standard deviation of the population from which a sample is drawn. For example, Joe Johnson measured a sample of 20 math-anxious students' performance on a math test, but he did not know what either the mean or the standard deviation of performance on the math test would be if the entire population of math-anxious students was tested. Similarly, Jane Jeffers measured the incomes of a sample of psychology alumni, but she had no information about the standard deviation of the incomes of the entire population of psychology alumni.

The method for describing a sampling distribution, shown in Procedure 11-2, assumes that we know the value of the population standard deviation, σ. Based on this procedure, if we do not know the value of σ, we cannot describe a sampling distribution for that population. That is the predicament that both Joe and Jane face. To resolve this predicament, we can use the sample standard deviation as an estimate of the population standard deviation. The procedure for calculating this estimate of the standard error of the mean using the sample standard deviation is shown in Step-by-Step Procedure 11-4.

STEP-BY-STEP PROCEDURE 11-4

Calculating an Unbiased Estimate of the Standard Error of the Mean, Using the Sample Standard Deviation, s

$$s_{\overline{X}} = \frac{s}{\sqrt{n}}$$

where s = the sample standard deviation
          n = the number of subjects in the sample

1. Calculate the standard deviation of the sample of scores, using one of the formulas shown below:

definitional formula: computational formula:

$$s = \sqrt{\frac{\Sigma(X - \overline{X})^2}{n - 1}} \qquad\qquad s = \sqrt{\frac{\Sigma X^2 - \frac{(\Sigma X)^2}{n}}{n - 1}}$$

If you need to review how to use these formulas, the definitional formula is described in Procedure 5-2 and the computational formula is described in Procedure 5-3.

2. Find the square root of n, the sample size.

3. Divide the results of Step 1 by the results of Step 2 to find an unbiased estimate of the standard error of the mean.

In Joe's study, the sample consisted of 20 students, who scored a mean of 66.0 on the math test, with a sample standard deviation of 14.7. We can calculate the sample standard error of the mean for Joe's math test, as follows:

$$s_{\bar{x}} = \frac{s}{\sqrt{n}} = \frac{14.7}{\sqrt{20}} = \frac{14.7}{4.5} = 3.3.$$

Thus, the standard error of the mean for the distribution of sample means for Joe's math test is 3.3.

Note that in Procedure 11-4 both formulas for the standard deviation, s, have $n - 1$ in the denominator. Recall from Chapter 5 that if we calculated the sample standard deviation with n in the denominator, the value of the sample standard deviation tends to underestimate the value of the population standard deviation. Thus, dividing by n results in a sample standard deviation that is a *biased estimate* of σ. Calculating the sample standard deviation with $n - 1$ in the denominator gives us an *unbiased estimate* of σ, an estimate that tends to neither underestimate nor overestimate the population standard deviation.

The Exactness of Parameter Estimates

One of the questions that we are addressing in this chapter is how exact are sample statistics as an estimate of the population parameter. Jane Jeffers found that the mean income for her sample of 200 psychology alumni was $52,600. How close is this sample mean to the mean income of the entire population of psychology alumni in the United States, ten years after graduation?

There are two ways that we can measure this exactness. One method is to find the confidence limits for a sample statistic, which we examine in this chapter. The second method is to find the critical values for a population parameter, which we examine in the next chapter. The difference between the two methods is whether we begin with a sample statistic or a population parameter.

Confidence Intervals for Sample Means

Step-by-Step Procedure 11-5 shows the method of finding the confidence limits for a sample mean. Suppose that we select a sample of 25 people from the psychology majors at State University. The mean IQ of the sample was 126. The chair of the Psychology Department wants to estimate the mean IQ of all psychology majors. Rather than test every psychology major, the chair uses the mean of the sample of 25 students as an estimate. How exact is this estimate? How much confidence can we have in this sample mean as an estimate of the mean IQ of the entire population of psychology majors?

Using statistics, there is no way to determine with absolute certainty whether this is a good estimate or not. We are trying to show that the sample

---

STEP-BY-STEP PROCEDURE 11-5

Calculating Confidence Limits (CLs)

For a sample mean: $\overline{X}_{CL} = \overline{X} \pm z\sigma_{\overline{X}}$

or $\overline{X}_{CL} = \overline{X} \pm zs_{\overline{X}}$

where $\overline{X}$ = the sample mean
$\sigma_{\overline{X}}$ = the standard error of estimate when σ is known
$s_{\overline{X}}$ = the standard error of estimate when σ is not known
z = standard scores corresponding to the confidence level

For a sample proportion: $P_{CL} = P \pm zs_p$

where P = the sample proportion
s_p = the standard error for the sample proportion
z = standard scores corresponding to the confidence level

1. Calculate the standard error of the mean, using the appropriate procedure (Procedure 11-2 for a sample mean when σ is known, Procedure 11-4 when σ is not known, and Procedure 11-3 for a sample proportion).

2. For the lower confidence limit, multiply the result of Step 1 by $z = -1.96$ (for the 95 percent level of confidence) or $z = -2.58$ (for the 99 percent level of confidence). Add this result to the sample mean or sample proportion to find the lower confidence limit.

3. For the upper confidence limit, multiply the result of Step 1 by $z = 1.96$ (for the 95 percent level of confidence) or $z = 2.58$ (for the 99 percent level of confidence). Add this result to the sample mean or sample proportion to find the upper confidence limit.

---

with a mean IQ of 126 came from a population with a mean IQ close to 126. While it is certainly possible that our sample came from a population whose mean is close to 126, it is also possible to draw such a sample from a population with a mean far from 126, such as a population with a mean IQ of 50. It isn't very likely, but it is possible. Because it is possible, we cannot say for sure that the sample came from a population with a mean IQ close to 126. While we cannot ask the question absolutely, we can ask how likely is it that the population from which this sample was drawn has a mean of 126? Or, stated another way, how much confidence can we have that the population mean is 126?

To answer this question, we first need to define what we mean by confidence. In statistics, confidence is expressed in terms of a percentage. The two levels of confidence conventionally used in psychology are 95 percent and 99 percent. In fact, we could select any percentage as our level of confidence (say 75 percent or 83 percent), but 95 percent and 99 percent are the two most often used in psychology. For our example of the mean IQ of the population of psychology majors, let's use a confidence level of 95 percent. Thus, our question now is whether we can say that we are 95 percent confident that the population mean IQ is close to 126.

Now we need to define what we mean by "close to 126." Step-by-Step Procedure 11-5 describes a method for finding two values, one below our sample mean of 126 and one above that sample mean, between which we can be 95 percent confident that the true population mean lies.

In Procedure 11-5, our first step is to calculate the standard error of the mean. In this case, we know that the standard deviation of the population of IQ scores, σ, is 15, and so we can use Procedure 11-2:

$$\sigma_{\bar{x}} = \frac{\sigma}{\sqrt{n}} = \frac{15}{\sqrt{25}} = \frac{15}{5} = 3.0.$$

We have already decided to use a confidence level of 95 percent. Our next step is to find the z scores that cut off the center 95 percent of the means in a sampling distribution. If we were using a confidence level of 99 percent, we would find the z scores that cut off the center 99 percent of means. Figure 11-6 shows that z scores of ± 1.96 are the cutoff points for the center 95 percent of the means. We can now convert the z scores of 1.96 to sample means:

$$\bar{X}_{CL} = \mu + z\sigma_{\bar{x}} = 126 + (1.96)3.0 = 126 + 5.9 = 131.9,$$

$$\bar{X}_{CL} = \mu + z\sigma_{\bar{x}} = 126 + (-1.96)3.0 = 126 - 5.9 = 120.1.$$

Thus, if we draw another sample, we can be 95 percent confident that its mean will lie between 120.1 and 131.9, and we can be 95 percent confident

FIGURE 11-6 Confidence Limits for a Mean IQ of 126 from a Sample of 25 People

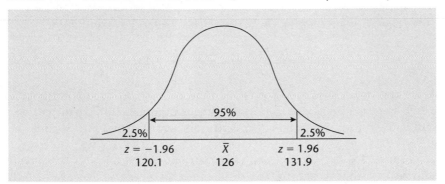

The **confidence limits** are the score values between which a population parameter is expected to lie, with a given probability, as predicted by a sampling distribution. The given probability is called the level of confidence.

The **confidence interval** is the segment of the number line between the lower and upper confidence limits.

The **level of confidence** is the probability that the population parameter will lie within the confidence interval.

that the true mean IQ of the population of psychology majors lies between those two values. These values are called the 95 percent **confidence limits.**

In general, confidence limits are the two values between which we expect, with a given level of confidence, a true population parameter to lie. The **confidence interval** is the distance between the two confidence limits. In this example of the mean IQ of psychology majors, the confidence interval is the distance between mean IQs of 120.1 and 131.9. Finally, the **level of confidence** is the probability that the population parameter (in this case, the mean) will be in the confidence interval; that is, that the population parameter will have a value somewhere between the lower and upper confidence limits. In our example, there is a 95 percent probability that the actual mean IQ of the population of psychology majors is between 120.1 and 131.9.

Confidence Limits for Sample Proportions and Percentages

We can also find confidence limits for sample proportions and percentages. In political polls reported on television and in the newspaper, we often hear that candidate X is predicted to win 59 percent of the vote. We are then told that this prediction is 95 percent accurate within 3 percentage points. In other words, the pollster is telling us how much confidence we can have in this prediction.

When conducting polls, pollsters do not survey all potential voters. Instead, they survey a sample of voters. Thus, the 59 percent in favor of candidate X came from a sample of voters and is being used as an estimate of which candidate the entire population of voters will choose in the election. How exact is this estimate? The pollster tells us that we can be 95 percent sure that in the actual election, the percentage of voters choosing candidate X will be within 3 percent of 59 percent (i.e., between 56 percent and 62 percent).

What the pollster has done is to construct a distribution of sample proportions. Suppose that a sample of 1,000 people were polled. If we assume that the proportion of voters in the population who will vote for candidate X is actually .59, we can calculate the standard error of a proportion for this sampling distribution, using the method described in Procedure 11-3:

$$\sigma_p = \sqrt{\frac{p(1-p)}{n}} = \sqrt{\frac{(.59)(.41)}{1,000}} = .015.$$

As we saw previously, the 95 percent confidence limits are the points that are ± 1.96 standard deviations from the center. As we have just calculated, one standard error for this poll is .015, and thus 1.96 standard errors would be $(1.96 \times .015)$, or .03.

Figure 11-7 depicts this sampling distribution graphically. This graph shows that if the pollster conducted the same poll over and over again, each

FIGURE 11-7 Confidence Limits for Political Poll
of 59 Percent from a Sample of 1,000 People

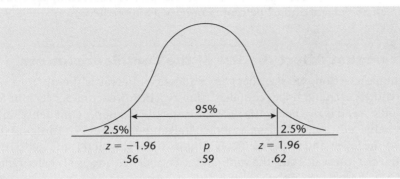

time sampling 1,000 voters, 95 percent of the time the sample percentage would come out between 56 and 62 (i.e., within 3 percent of 59 percent). These are the confidence limits. We could also infer that the true population percentage is in the same range, and thus we could have 95 percent confidence that the actual percentage of voters in the population who will se-lect candidate *X* in the election will be within 3 percent of the 59 percent found in the poll.

Level of Confidence

One question about the level of confidence is why settle for just being 95 per-cent confident? Why not set the confidence level at 100 percent and be ab-solutely sure? The difficulty is that there is always a chance (perhaps very, very small, but still a chance) that the sample percentage is way off from the pop-ulation percentage. The same is true for sample means. Suppose we test the IQs of a sample of 100 people in order to estimate the true mean IQ of the en-tire population of the United States. We try to be very fair in how we select our sample, so that it will truly be representative of the entire U.S. population. Nonetheless, there is always a chance that every one of the 100 people in our sample is a genius. (OK, it's not very likely, but it could happen. That's the point.)

In the same way, even though 59 percent of 1,000 people in the sample polled were supporting candidate *X*, it is always possible that the sample is way off, and in the real election, only 2 percent of the voters choose candi-date *X*. (Again, this is not very likely, but still it could happen.) The only way we could be 100 percent sure would be to say that between 0 percent and 100 percent of the voters will choose candidate *X*, which actually tells us nothing. We don't need a poll to tell us that the vote for candidate *X* will be between 0 percent and 100 percent. What else could it be? In comparison, being 95 percent confident that the vote for candidate X on election day will be between 56 percent and 62 percent is a pretty good prediction.

Factors that Affect the Size of the Confidence Interval

In the last section, we saw that the confidence interval is the distance between the lower and upper confidence limits. The lower confidence limit for a sample mean is $z\sigma_{\overline{X}}$ below the sample mean, and the upper confidence limit is $z\sigma_{\overline{X}}$ above the sample mean, as shown in Figure 11-6. Thus the distance between the lower and upper confidence limits is $2z\sigma_{\overline{X}}$, which is the size of the confidence interval. Thus, the width of the confidence interval is determined by three values: z, σ, and n.

First, the width of the confidence interval is affected by the value of the standard score, z. In turn, the value of z is determined by the level of confidence. When the level of confidence is 95 percent, z is ± 1.96. When the level of confidence is 99 percent, z is ± 2.58. Thus, the higher the level of confidence, the larger will be the value of z, and the wider the confidence interval will be.

In fact, it is desirable to have the confidence interval as narrow as possible. The confidence interval is a measure of the exactness of using the sample mean as an estimate of the population mean. It would be more exact to say that a population mean is between 9 and 10 than between 5 and 15. However, the higher the level of confidence, the wider the confidence interval will be. Thus, there is a trade-off between exactness of prediction and level of confidence. We can increase the level of confidence by selecting a 99 percent level rather than a 95 percent level, but in doing so, we increase the width of the confidence interval, thus reducing the exactness of our estimate.

The second value that influences the width of the confidence interval is the value of σ, the population standard deviation, or the value of s, the sample standard deviation, which is used when the value of σ is not known. The larger the standard deviation, the larger the confidence interval will be. Thus, to improve the exactness of our estimate, we could reduce the value of the standard deviation. The standard deviation is a measure of the amount of spread among the scores in the population or sample. Therefore, anything that we can do to reduce the amount of spread among the scores will reduce the standard deviation, which in turn will reduce the size of the confidence interval, thus increasing the exactness with which the sample mean estimates the population mean.

The last value that affects the size of the confidence interval is n, the number of subjects in the sample. The larger the sample size, the smaller the standard error. Thus, by increasing the size of the sample, we can decrease the size of the confidence interval. This is perhaps the simplest method to use to increase the exactness of estimation. By simply increasing the sample size, we can increase the exactness with which the sample mean estimates the population mean.

CHECKING YOUR ANSWERS

1. The actual computations involved in working with sampling distributions are fairly simple. The difficulty that students usually encounter with this material is understanding the logic of sampling distributions. It is important to differentiate between distributions of scores and distributions of a sample statistic. When you are answering questions about sample means, you must use the distribution of sample means. Similarly, when you are answering questions about sample proportions, you must use the distribution of sample proportions.

2. One frequent error that students make is using the standard deviation instead of the standard error. When calculating the probability of getting a specified sample mean from a population, you must use the standard error of the mean ($\sigma_{\bar{x}}$) and not the standard deviation (σ_x). Remember, the standard deviation measures the distance that scores typically lie from the mean, while the standard error of the mean measures the distance that sample means typically lie from the population mean.

3. In working problems involving sample proportions, be clear whether you are working with the *proportion* of events or the *frequency* of events. Confusing the two can lead to errors.

4. Check your answer to see if it is reasonable. For example, when you are finding confidence limits, be sure that the value of the sample mean is between the lower and upper confidence limits. If your standard error is greater than the standard deviation, you've made an error.

5. Draw a picture of the distribution. Taking the time to sketch the distribution and probabilities you are looking for can help avoid time-consuming errors.

$\sum$ SUMMARY

▶ Inferential statistics are statistical procedures that enable us to make inferences from samples to populations. These are the procedures that researchers use to objectively test hypotheses.

▶ A sampling distribution is the set of values of a sample statistic and the frequencies with which they would occur if many samples of a given size were independently drawn from the same population. A theoretical sampling distribution is the set of values of a sample statistic and their frequencies, as predicted by a mathematical model, such as the normal or binomial distribution.

▶ If a population of scores is normally distributed, then a sampling distribution of a statistic drawn from that population will also be normally distributed. If the samples each consist of twenty or more scores, then the sampling distribution will be sufficiently close to the normal distribution to use the table of normal probabilities, even if the population of scores from which the samples are drawn is not normally distributed.

▶ The mean of a sampling distribution is equal to the mean of the population from which the samples were drawn. The standard deviation of a sampling distribution is equal to the standard deviation of the population of scores from which the samples were drawn, divided by the square root of the sample size.

▶ A sampling distribution of the mean is the distribution of all possible values of the means of samples of size n drawn from a given population of scores and the frequencies of those sample means.

▶ In a sampling distribution of the mean, if the value of the population standard deviation, σ, is not known, then the standard deviation of the sample, s, can be used as an unbiased estimate of σ, as long as the divisor of the formula for s is $n - 1$ and n is 20 or greater.

▶ A biased estimate of a population parameter is a sample statistic that either consistently overestimates or consistently underestimates the value of that parameter. An unbiased estimate is a sample statistic that does not consistently over- or underestimate the parameter's value. To use a sample statistic as an estimator of the population parameter, the estimator should not be biased.

▶ Confidence limits are two values between which we can expect a population parameter to lie, with a given level of confidence. The level of confidence is the probability that the parameter lies between those two values. Conventionally, confidence levels of 95 percent and 99 percent are most commonly used. The confidence interval is the distance between the two confidence limits.

▶ The size of the confidence interval is a measure of the exactness of using the sample statistic as an estimate of the population parameter. The smaller the confidence interval, the more exact the statistic is as an estimate of the population parameter.

▶ The higher the confidence level, the larger the confidence interval will be, and thus the less exact the statistic will be as an estimate of the population parameter. Thus, there is an inverse relationship between confidence level and exactness: the greater the confidence level, the less exact is the estimate, all other things being equal.

▶ In addition to the confidence level, the size of the confidence interval is also affected by the sample size and the standard error. The lower the standard error and the larger the sample size, the smaller the size of the confidence level and thus the more exact the sample statistic will be as an estimate of the population parameter.

E X E R C I S E S

Conceptual Exercises

1. Define the following terms:

   inferential statistics   standard error of a proportion
   sampling distribution   confidence limits
   empirical sampling distribution   confidence interval
   theoretical sampling distribution   level of confidence
   standard error of the mean

2. Explain the difference between a frequency distribution and a sampling distribution.

3. Obtain nine small pieces of paper, all the same size. Write the numbers from 1 to 9 on these pieces of paper, one number per piece of paper. These nine numbers constitute a population.

   A. Draw twenty samples, each sample containing four pieces of paper. For each sample, compute and record the sample mean. Return the pieces of paper to the population and mix them thoroughly before drawing the next sample. Construct a table listing all possible values of the sample means, from 2.5 to 7.5, increasing in units of .25, and the frequency that each value occurred.

   B. Repeat Step A, this time drawing samples, each containing two pieces of paper.

4. For each of the empirical sampling distributions constructed in Exercise 3, find the following:

   A. What is the proportion of samples with means between 4 and 6 inclusive?

   B. What is the proportion of samples with means of 6.5 or more?

   C. What is the proportion of samples with means of 3.5 or less?

   D. For which empirical sampling distribution is the proportion of means greater in the center of the distribution? Why does this occur?

5. Calculate the mean and standard deviation of the population of scores used in Exercise 3. Then calculate the mean and standard deviation separately for the sampling distributions constructed in Steps A and B of Exercise 3.

   A. How close are the means of the sampling distributions to the mean of the distribution of scores? Is the mean of one of the sampling distributions closer than the other? Why does this occur?

   B. Which distribution has the largest standard deviation? Which distribution has the smallest? Why does this occur?

Computational Exercises

6. At State University, the student body is 50 percent male, 50 percent female. In the Psychology Department, seminar classes have a maximum enrollment of twenty students. Construct a sampling distribution of the proportions of males and females in psychology seminar classes, under the assumption that each seminar has exactly twenty students enrolled.

   A. What percentage of seminars can we expect to have exactly 50 percent men and 50 percent women?

   B. What percentage of seminars can we expect to have 75 percent or more men?

   C. What percentage of seminars can we expect to have fewer than five men?

   D. What percentage of seminars can we expect to have either more than 60 percent men or more than 60 percent women?

   E. What percentage of seminars can we expect *not* to have exactly 50 percent men and 50 percent women?

7. Suppose that you have a container filled with poker chips, with the chips marked in equal numbers with the digits "1," "2," "3," "4," and "5." Suppose you drew a sample of two chips from the container.

   A. Write all the possible combinations of digits that that sample of two chips could be. (Hint: there are twenty-five possible combinations.)

   B. Find the mean of each possible sample by adding the 2 digits together and dividing by 2.

C. Construct a frequency distribution of this empirical sampling distribution of the mean. Draw a graph of the distribution.

8. From the frequency table constructed in Exercise 7, find the following:

A. What percentage of samples can we expect to have means of 2.0?

B. What percentage of samples can we expect to have means of 4.0 or greater?

C. What percentage of samples can we expect to have means between 2.0 and 4.0?

9. The original population of poker chips in Exercise 7 contained equal numbers of chips marked "1," "2," "3," "4," and "5."

A. Suppose that there were five of each type of chip in the container, so that a frequency table of the values of the chips would be as follows. Calculate the mean and standard deviation of this distribution of chips.

Chip Value	Frequency
5	5
4	5
3	5
2	5
1	5

B. Calculate the mean and standard error of the frequency distribution of sample means that you constructed in Exercise 7, and compare to the values you found in Parts A and B above. What is the same? What is different? Why?

C. Use Procedure 11-2 to find the mean and standard error for the sampling distribution constructed in Exercise 7, and compare to the mean and standard error calculated in Part B above. Why did this result occur?

10. Recall that the population of IQ scores has a mean of 100 and standard deviation of 15. Suppose that we have IQ scores from a sample of 25 students.

A. What is the probability that the sample will have a mean of 103 or greater?

B. What is the probability that the sample will have a mean less than 100?

C. What is the probability that the sample will have a mean between 95 and 105?

D. What is the probability that the sample will either have a mean of 106 or more or have a mean of 94 or less?

11. The SAT math test has a theoretical mean of 500, with a standard deviation of 100.

A. Compare the standard error of the mean for the following sample sizes: 4, 9, 16, 25, 36, 49, 64, 81, and 100.

B. Find the proportion of sample means that would be either 520 or greater or 480 or lower for each of the sample sizes listed in Part A.

C. Describe the relationship between sample size and the standard error, and the effect that this has on sampling distributions of the mean.

12. Jada has an instructor who routinely fails an average of 30 percent of her students across all of the instructor's classes. Use the normal approximation to the binomial distribution to answer the following:

A. What is the probability that 20 percent or fewer of the students in a class of 25 students will fail?

B. What is the probability that 50 percent of more of the students in a class of 20 students will fail?

C. What is the probability that at least 40 percent of the students in a class of 50 students will pass?

D. In a class of 100 students, what is the probability that 20 or fewer will fail?

13. A pollster conducted a survey of voters' opinions on a local school bond issue.

A. What would the 95 percent confidence limits be if 58 percent of 1,000 people sampled were in favor of the school bond issue?

B. What would the 99 percent confidence limits be for the same sample?

C. What would the 95 percent confidence limits be if 47 percent of another sample of 700 people opposed the school bond issue?

D. What would the 99 percent confidence limits be for the same sample?

E. Explain in regular English what the confidence limits in Part D signify.

14. Recall that the SAT math test has a theoretical mean of 500 and standard deviation of 100.

A. Suppose a sample of 30 mathematically gifted youngsters scored a mean of 575 on the SAT math test. What would the 90 percent confidence limits be?

B. For the same sample, what would the 95 percent confidence limits be?

C. Again for the same sample, what would the 99 percent confidence limits be?

D. In regular English, explain what these confidence limits indicate.

15. Jacqueline tested 2- to 4-year-old children's vocabulary size.

A. She found that a sample of 25 2-year-olds knew a mean of 525 words, with a standard deviation of 50 words. What would the 95 percent confidence limits be?

B. She found that a sample of 30 3-year-old children knew a mean of 960 words, with a standard deviation of 67 words. What would the 95 percent confidence limits be?

C. She found that a sample of 35 4-year-old children knew a mean of 1,850 words, with a standard deviation of 75 words. What would the 95 percent confidence limits be?

D. In regular English, explain what the confidence limits for the sample of 4-year-old children indicate.

E N D N O T E

1. Note that each possible pair of children is listed only once in Table 11-3. Thus, the sample of Ann and Bob is considered the same as the sample of Bob and Ann and therefore is listed only once.

Hypothesis Testing

12

Research Hypotheses

Inferring the Value of the Mean of a Population

The Possible Values of a Population Mean

The Null and Alternate Hypotheses

STEP-BY-STEP PROCEDURE 12-1: Constructing the Null and Alternate Hypotheses for a Parametric Test

The Logic of Hypothesis Testing

The Logic of Testing the Null Hypothesis

The Sampling Distribution Predicted by the Null Hypothesis

The Level of Significance, α

Critical Values

The Decision Rule

The z Test for a Sample Mean

STEP-BY-STEP PROCEDURE 12-2: Calculating the Value of z for a Sample Mean

The Value of p

Unidirectional and Bidirectional Hypothesis Tests

Bidirectional Tests

Unidirectional Tests

The Null and Alternate Hypotheses for Bidirectional and Unidirectional Tests

STEP-BY-STEP PROCEDURE 12-3: Constructing the Distribution of Sample Means Predicted by the Null Hypothesis

The Debate over Unidirectional Tests

Conducting the z Test for a Sample Mean

Conducting a z Test on a Study of Math Anxiety

STEP-BY-STEP PROCEDURE 12-4: Conducting the z Test for a Sample Mean

Verify the Assumptions of the z Test for a Sample Mean

Identify the Null and Alternate Hypotheses

Decide the Level of Significance, α

Find the Critical Value of z

Construct the Sampling Distribution Predicted by the Null Hypothesis

Calculate the Value of z for the Sample Mean

Make a Decision about Rejecting the Null Hypothesis

Decision Making in Statistical Tests

Rejecting the Null Hypothesis When It Is True: Type I Errors

Not Rejecting the Null Hypothesis When It Is False: Type II Errors

Decision Making and Reality

CHECKING YOUR ANSWERS

SUMMARY

EXERCISES

Conceptual Exercises

Computational Exercises

▶ In Chapter 1, we saw that statistics are used for two purposes in scientific research. One is description. We can use statistics to describe the characteristics of a group of scores, scores that are actually collected by researchers or scores predicted by making certain assumptions, such as that the set of scores is normally distributed. We can also use statistics to describe the relationship between groups of scores. The second purpose that statistics serve in scientific research is inferential. Researchers can use statistics to make inferences about a population without having actually to collect scores from every member of the population. In the remaining chapters of this book, we will look at statistical techniques that enable us to make inferences about populations from samples of scores drawn from those populations. These techniques are called inferential statistics. In this chapter, we will look at the basic logic underlying all of these statistical techniques, the logic of hypothesis testing.

In a **parametric statistical test**, the null and alternate hypotheses predict the value of a population parameter.

There are two categories of inferential statistics, parametric and nonparametric. With **parametric statistics**, sample statistics are used to make inferences about the value of the corollary parameter of the population from which the sample was drawn. For example, the mean IQ of a sample of psychology majors can be used to make an inference about the mean IQ of the population of all psychology majors. Similarly, the proportion of voters in a poll sample who say they will vote for candidate X can be used to predict the proportion of voters in the entire population who will select candidate X on election day.

In a **nonparametric statistical test**, the null and alternate hypotheses do not predict the value of a specific population parameter. Generally, nonparametric tests predict the shape of a distribution.

Nonparametric statistics are inferential statistics that do not make inferences about the value of a specific population parameter. Many nonparametric statistics use samples to make inferences about the general shape of a population distribution. For example, with a nonparametric statistic, we can make an inference about the distribution of letter grades given by professors across all of their classes from a small sample of those classes. In this chapter, we begin by examining parametric inferential statistics. We will explore nonparametric statistics in Chapters 15 and 18.

Research Hypotheses

Inferring the Value of the Mean of a Population

Jorge Jiminez was interested in exploring the personality characteristics of students who choose to major in psychology. In particular, he was curious about the degree to which psychology majors believe that people's behavior, attitudes, and opinions can be manipulated through deceit. This belief is characteristic of the Machiavellian personality, named after Nicolò Machiavelli, the sixteenth-century Italian political theorist who wrote *The Prince*.

Jorge obtained a Machiavellian personality test that had been administered to thousands of undergraduate college students. Across all of the students tested, the mean score was 50, with a standard deviation of 12. The scores on this test were normally distributed. Students who scored above the mean were considered to be above average in Machiavellian beliefs.

Jorge believed that psychology majors were not like other college students in their beliefs about the ability to manipulate other people through deceit. So Jorge administered the Machiavellian test to a group of sixteen psychology majors, who scored a mean of 58 on the test. Jorge claimed that this was evidence that the Machiavellian tendencies of psychology majors are not the same as other college students. Is Jorge's claim legitimate?

To decide whether Jorge's claim is legitimate, we should first recognize that the claim is based on an inference about the value of the mean of the population of psychology majors. In claiming that psychology majors are Machiavellian, Jorge is not just speaking about the sixteen students that he tested, but about all psychology majors. Thus, the sixteen students that Jorge tested constitute a sample drawn from the entire population of psychology majors. Because his sample of sixteen psychology majors scored higher than average on the Machiavellian test, Jorge claimed that the entire population of psychology majors is also more Machiavellian than average. Jorge is making an inference that the entire population of psychology majors would perform on the test as his sample performed.

When we make an inference, we are drawing a logical conclusion from factual knowledge. Jorge does not know for a fact what the value of the mean of the population of psychology majors is. Rather, he is drawing a conclusion about the population mean, a conclusion based on the fact that his sample of sixteen psychology majors had a mean of 58 on the Machiavellian test. Jorge is using the mean of his sample to make an inference about the mean of the entire population of psychology majors. When we ask whether Jorge's claim about the mean of the population of psychology majors is legitimate, we are asking whether it is legitimate for Jorge to make an inference about the population mean from the fact that his sample had a mean of 58.

The Possible Values of a Population Mean

We cannot assume that the population of psychology majors would have a mean of exactly 58 on the Machiavellian test just because Jorge's sample did. In our discussion on sampling distributions in the previous chapter, we saw that when we draw samples from a population, the sample means do not always equal the mean of the population from which they were drawn. If we calculate the mean IQ of samples of people drawn from the general population, whose mean IQ is 100, the sample means will not always be exactly 100. In fact, sample means generally will not be the same as the mean of the population from which they were drawn.

Suppose you are shown a brown paper bag full of M&Ms and asked to guess the proportion of different colors of M&Ms that are in the bag. You may draw handfuls of M&Ms from the bag, replacing each handful in the bag before drawing another, to test your guesses, but you may not look in the bag. Suppose you draw a handful that has 30 percent green M&Ms. Does that mean that the population of M&Ms in the bag is necessarily 30 percent green? Of course not. You could have drawn the handful from a bag with 29 or 31 percent green M&Ms. You could have drawn a handful with 30 percent green M&Ms from a bag with a much lower proportion of green M&Ms, such as 20 percent or even 10 percent, and just as likely, the handful could have come from a bag with a much higher proportion of green M&Ms, such as 40 or 50 percent. If your handful contains 30 percent green M&Ms, what proportion of green M&Ms are in the bag? In fact, there are an infinite number of possibilities.

The same is true for Jorge's sample mean of 58. The population from which that sample was drawn does not necessarily have a mean of 58. The population mean could be lower than 58, such as 57 or 55 or even 50. The population mean could be greater than 58, such as 59 or 65 or 90. To simplify things, we can categorize the infinite possible values that the mean of the population of psychology majors might have into three different possibilities. First is the possibility that the population of psychology majors has the same mean on the Machiavellian test as the whole population of college students, which was 50. This is the possibility that as far as being Machiavellian goes, psychology majors are just the same as other college students. Second is the possibility that the mean for the population of psychology majors is greater than 50, which is the possibility that they are more Machiavellian than the average college student, which is what Jorge's sample mean seems to suggest. However, there is a the third possibility, which is that the mean for the population of psychology majors is less than 50, that they are less Machiavellian than the average college student. These three possibilities are shown in Figure 12-1.

It is important to note that together, these three possibilities cover all of the possibilities that exist. The degree of Machiavellianism found in psychology majors is the same as other college students, more than other college

FIGURE 12-1 Three Possibilities for the Mean
Machiavellian Score of the Population of Psychology Majors

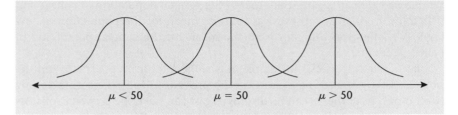

students, or less. The mean Machiavellian score for the population of psychology majors must be equal to 50, more than 50, or less than 50. There are no other possibilities.

We began with the question of whether it is legitimate for Jorge to conclude that the population of psychology majors has different Machiavellian tendencies than the general population of college students, based solely on the fact that his sample had a mean of 58. We can say here that that conclusion is not legitimate. We cannot conclude solely from the fact that Jorge's sample had a mean of 58 that the mean for the population of psychology majors differs from the mean for the general population of college students because it is possible that Jorge's sample came from a population with a mean of 50, the same as the general population of college students. Of course, it is also possible that Jorge's sample came from a population with a mean less than 50 or a mean greater than 50. At this point, it is not legitimate for Jorge to draw any conclusion about what mean Machiavellian score the population of psychology majors might have.

The Null and Alternate Hypotheses

Jorge's belief that psychology majors' Machiavellian tendencies are not the same as those of other college students is a **hypothesis**, which is a testable assertion about the relationship between variables. In this case, there are two variables: the type of college major and the Machiavellian test scores. Jorge's assertion is that there is a relationship between the type of college major and scores on the Machiavellian test, that the mean of those test scores is different for psychology majors than for students with other majors.

Because we know that Jorge's sample of sixteen psychology majors scored a mean of 58 on the Machiavellian test, we might ask why Jorge's hypothesis was not just that the mean for the population of psychology majors is greater than 50. Recall that Jorge held his beliefs about psychology majors' Machiavellian tendencies *before* he ever tested his sample. In fact, he measured his participants' Machiavellian tendencies in order to find evidence to support

A **hypothesis** is a testable assertion about the relation between variables in a population of scores.

his beliefs. Researchers first formulate hypotheses and then collect scores from a sample of subjects to test those hypotheses. Even though Jorge's sample had a mean greater than that of the general population of college students, his original hypothesis was that the mean for the population of psychology majors was different from the mean for the general population of college students.

Because a hypothesis is testable, it is subject to disproof. This is not the same as saying that a hypothesis can be proved. In the sciences, including psychology, hypotheses can be disproved but can never be proved. Consider again drawing samples of M&Ms from a brown paper bag, with replacement, in order to guess the proportion of green M&Ms in the bag. Suppose you guess that the bag contains absolutely no green M&Ms. If a handful of M&Ms contains even one green M&M, your guess is disproved. On the other hand, does drawing a handful of M&Ms that contains no green ones prove that the bag contains no green M&Ms? No, it doesn't. There could be green M&Ms in the bag and you just didn't grab them in your handful. You could draw millions of handfuls of M&Ms with no green M&Ms and that still would not prove that the bag contains no green M&Ms, because it is always possible there is at least one green M&M lurking in the bag.

Jorge's hypothesis is that there is a relationship between the type of major in college (psychology vs. other majors) and scores on the Machiavellian test. The opposite assertion, that there is no such relationship, is also a hypothesis. This hypothesis asserts that the mean on the Machiavellian test for psychology majors is the same as the mean for the general college student population. Thus, we have two hypotheses, one asserting that there is a difference between psychology majors and other college students on the Machiavellian test and the other asserting that there is no difference.

These two hypotheses are mutually exclusive. Recall that for mutually exclusive events, if one event occurs, the other event cannot occur. Thus, the mean for psychology majors cannot be both 50 and not 50. In addition to being mutually exclusive, these two hypotheses are also exhaustive. A set of events is exhaustive if it contains all possibilities. In this case, the two hypotheses are exhaustive because the mean for psychology majors must be either 50 or not 50. There are no other possibilities. Because these two hypotheses are both mutually exclusive and exhaustive, one and only one of these hypotheses must be true.

The hypothesis that on the Machiavellian test there is no difference between the mean for the population of psychology majors and the mean for the general population of college students is called the **null hypothesis.** The word "null" means "amounting to nothing." The null hypothesis for Jorge's study is that there is no relationship between the type of major in college and performance on the Machiavellian test. In effect, the null hypothesis asserts that the results of Jorge's study happened just by chance, that the true mean for the population of psychology majors is 50, the same as the mean for the

The **null hypothesis** (symbolized by H_0) is the assertion that there is no relationship in a population of scores between the variables being studied, that the sample results were due solely to chance sampling.

general population of college students and that Jorge's sample had a mean of 58 only because of chance sampling. The null hypothesis in an experiment is always the hypothesis that asserts that there really is no relationship in the population between the variables being studied, that the results of the study were simply due to chance sampling.

The other hypothesis, that on the Machiavellian test the mean for the population of psychology majors is different from the mean of the general population of college students, is called the **alternate hypothesis.** It is the alternate to the null hypothesis. The alternate hypothesis is the one that expresses the researcher's beliefs, the assertion that there is a relationship between the variables under study. In Jorge's study, the alternate hypothesis asserts that there really is a relationship between the type of college major and performance on the Machiavellian test, that overall, the scores of psychology majors are different from the scores of other college students.

The **alternate hypothesis** (symbolized by H_1) is the assertion that there is a relationship in a population of scores between the variables being studied, that the sample results were caused by that relationship.

The fundamental difference between the null and alternate hypotheses is the prediction of whether there is a relationship between the variables being studied. As seen below, in Jorge's study, the fundamental difference between the hypotheses is whether or not there is a relationship between type of college major and performance on the Machiavellian test. The symbol H_0 represents the null hypothesis, while the symbol H_1 represents the alternate hypothesis:

H_0: The mean Machiavellian score of the population of psychology majors is the same as the mean of the general population of college students.

H_1: The mean Machiavellian score of the population of psychology majors is different from the mean of the general population of college students.

The null and alternate hypotheses of every statistical test have this fundamental difference. The alternate hypothesis always argues that there is a relationship between the variables being studied. The null hypothesis always argues that there is no relationship between the variables being studied, and the results of the study were due solely to chance.

The null and alternate hypotheses of Jorge's study involve inferences about a specific population parameter, the mean of the population of psychology majors on the Machiavellian test. The null hypothesis predicts that the population mean is 50. The alternate hypothesis predicts that the population mean is not 50. We can thus restate the null and alternate hypotheses:

$$H_0: \mu_{\text{psychology majors}} = 50,$$
$$H_1: \mu_{\text{psychology majors}} \neq 50.$$

Remember that the null and alternate hypotheses are mutually exclusive. One of these hypotheses must be true, but only one can be true. In Jorge's study, either the mean Machiavellian score of the population of psychology

---

STEP-BY-STEP PROCEDURE 12-1

Constructing the Null and Alternate Hypotheses for a Parametric Test

1. On two separate lines, write the symbols H_0 and H_1 to symbolize the null hypothesis and alternate hypothesis, respectively.

2. Identify the sample statistic to be tested, then identify the population parameter that statistic estimates. Write the symbol for that parameter after the symbols H_0 and H_1.

3. Identify the population from which the sample was drawn. Be specific. As a subscript below the parameter symbol from Step 2, write a brief description of this population, enough to be able to identify it.

4. Identify the population to which you will compare the sample statistic. What value does the parameter identified in Step 2 have in that population? Write that value on both lines after the symbol for the population parameter, leaving a space in between.

5. Determine whether you are predicting that the parameter of the population from which the sample was drawn is less than ($<$), more than ($>$), or different than ($\neq$) the value identified in Step 4. On the line for the alternate hypothesis, H_1, write the appropriate sign in between the parameter symbol, from Step 2, and the value from Step 4.

6. Write the opposite sign in the same space on the line for the null hypothesis, H_0:
  A. If H_1 predicts the population parameter will be less than the value ($<$), then use the sign $\geq$ for H_0.
  B. If H_1 predicts the population parameter will be greater than the value ($>$), then use the sign $\leq$ for H_0.
  C. If H_1 predicts the population parameter will be different from the value ($\neq$), then use the sign $=$ for H_0.

7. Try writing the hypotheses in English to make sure that you understand them.

---

majors is 50 (H_0) or the mean is not 50 (H_1). Step-by-Step Procedure 12-1 describes a method for constructing the alternate and null hypotheses for a parametric test.

The Logic of Hypothesis Testing

The Logic of Testing the Null Hypothesis

The null and alternate hypotheses express two mutually exclusive and exhaustive possibilities, one of which must be true and only one of which can be true. If we could eliminate one of the possibilities, then, by default, we could conclude that the other possibility must be the one that is true. If we could eliminate the null hypothesis by somehow showing that it is not true, then it would be legitimate to conclude that the alternate hypothesis is true.

Thus, rather than confirm the alternate hypothesis directly, we will do so indirectly by finding evidence to justify eliminating the null hypothesis. The logic of testing the null hypothesis is thus:

> ▶ Because the null and alternate hypotheses are mutually exclusive and exhaustive, either the null hypothesis is true or the alternate hypothesis is true.
> ▶ We cannot directly show that the alternate hypothesis is true.
> ▶ However, if we can show that the null hypothesis is false, we can eliminate it from consideration and, by default, demonstrate that the alternate hypothesis must be true.

Our goal now is to find a way to test the null hypothesis to determine whether we can show that it is false. The method for achieving this goal involves the concept of a sampling distribution, which we explore in the next section.

The Sampling Distribution Predicted by the Null Hypothesis

In order to find evidence to eliminate the null hypothesis, we need to construct the sampling distribution predicted by the null hypothesis. As we saw in the last chapter, we can construct a distribution of sample means if we know the mean and standard deviation of the population of scores from which the samples are drawn. The null hypothesis for Jorge's study predicts that the mean for the population of psychology majors is 50, the same as the mean for the general population of students. If there is no difference between these two populations, as asserted by the null hypothesis, then the standard deviation of Machiavellian scores for the population of psychology majors would be the same as the standard deviation for the general population of college students, which we saw previously was 12. We can use this value to find the standard error of the mean for the sampling distribution predicted by the null hypothesis, using a sample size of 16, which is the number of psychology majors in Jorge's study:

$$\sigma_{\bar{X}} = \frac{\sigma}{\sqrt{n}} = \frac{12}{\sqrt{16}} = 3.0.$$

Figure 12-2 shows the sampling distribution predicted by the null hypothesis of Jorge's study, with 95 percent confidence limits. Note that in conducting a statistical test on the results of Jorge's research, we will not actually use these confidence limits. We are using them here solely to illustrate the concept of the sampling distribution predicted by the null hypothesis. Figure 12-2 shows that if we took a sample of 16 students from the general population of college students, who have a mean Machiavellian score of 50, there is a 95 percent chance that the sample would have a mean between 44.12 and

FIGURE 12-2   95 Percent Confidence Limits for Sampling
Distribution Predicted by the Null Hypothesis in Jorge's Study

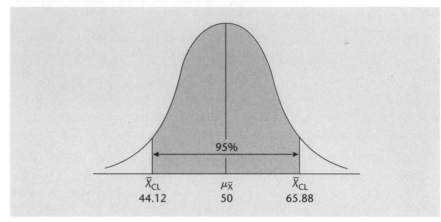

55.88, a 2.5 percent chance that the sample mean would be 44.12 or less, and a 2.5 percent chance that the sample mean would be 55.88 or greater.

Remember that our objective is to show that the null hypothesis of Jorge's study is false. To do this, we need to show that Jorge's sample of 16 psychology majors, with a mean, $\overline{X}$, of 58, did not come from the sampling distribution depicted in Figure 12-2, which has a mean, $\mu_{\overline{X}}$, of 50. However, as Figure 12-2 demonstrates, there is a chance that a sample drawn from this distribution might have a mean of 58. In fact, we can expect 2.5 percent of samples drawn from this distribution to have means of 55.88 or greater.

To eliminate the null hypothesis conclusively, beyond a shadow of a doubt, we would need to show that there is absolutely no chance that Jorge's sample came from the sampling distribution shown in Figure 12-2. There is a difficulty in trying to do this, a difficulty that stems from the characteristics of a normal distribution. In the example of predicting the color of M&Ms in a brown paper bag, we saw that drawing a sample with just one green M&M would conclusively disprove the hypothesis that the bag contained no green M&Ms. The chance of drawing a sample containing a green M&M from a bag containing no green M&Ms is absolutely zero.

However, with a sampling distribution, which is based on the normal distribution, we can never say that there is an absolute zero chance of drawing any given value. Remember that the tails of a normal distribution never actually reach the X-axis. The sampling distribution shown in Figure 12-2 is a normal distribution. No matter how far we go from the mean of 50, there is a chance that we could get a sample with a mean that far from 50. The probability may be extremely small, but there will still be some chance, no matter how small. Since there is a chance of drawing a sample with a mean of 58 from the sampling distribution shown in Figure 12-2, we will not be able to conclude that, without a shadow of a doubt, there is a zero percent chance that the null hypothesis is true.

If we cannot eliminate the null hypothesis with absolute certainty, then we need to set some other standard. This brings us to the concept of levels of significance, which we explore in the next section.

The Level of Significance, α

Since there is always some probability that a sample mean came from the sampling distribution predicted by the null hypothesis, we need to set a standard to use to eliminate the null hypothesis. To understand this crucial idea, let's consider an example of flipping a coin 100 times. If the coin came up heads 50 percent of the time, we'd probably assume that the coin was fair. What if the coin came up heads 60 percent of the time? 70 percent of the time? 80 percent of the time? What if the coin came up heads every time? How large does the percent of heads have to be before we'll decide that the coin is definitely not fair?

If we tossed a penny 100 times and it came up heads 100 times, we'd certainly suspect that the coin wasn't fair. Of course, it actually is possible for a fair coin to come up heads 100 times. However, the possibility is so infinitesimally small that we would decide that the coin is not fair. In fact, we probably would decide that the coin wasn't fair if it came up heads 90 times out of 100, or even 80 times out of 100. Even though there is some chance that a fair coin will come up heads 80 percent of the time, the probability is so small that we would decide that the coin isn't fair. Thus, at some cutoff point, some boundary, the probability that the coin is fair will be so small, we'll decide that the coin isn't fair.

In hypothesis testing, we set the same sort of cutoff point. While we can't show that there is a zero percent chance that a sample came from a particular distribution, we can show that the chance is very small, say only 1 or 2 or 5 percent. The question now is, how small is small enough? Are we willing to decide that the null hypothesis is true if the chances of it being true are 10 percent? Or do we want to set a more stringent standard and eliminate the null only if the chances of it being true are 5 percent? We could even set the cutoff point at 1 percent or one-tenth of a percent (0.1 percent). The probability that we select is called the **level of significance**, symbolized by α (alpha). It is the cutoff point for deciding whether or not to eliminate the null hypothesis.

The level of significance that we select is the chance that we are willing to be wrong. Suppose we set the level of significance of Jorge's study at 5 percent. If the chance of Jorge's sample coming from a population with a mean of 50 is 5 percent or less, then we will decide that the null hypothesis is false. But, even if we decide that the null hypothesis isn't true, there still is a 5 percent

The **level of significance** (symbolized α) is the probability criterion selected as a basis for rejecting the null hypothesis. If the probability that the null hypothesis is true is equal to or less than α, we will reject the null hypothesis. If the probability that the null hypothesis is true is more than α, we will not reject the null hypothesis

(or less) chance that the sample did in fact come from a population with a mean of 50. Thus, if we set the level of significance at 5 percent, there is a 5 percent chance that we will be wrong in deciding that the null hypothesis is false. If we set the level of significance at 1 percent, there is a 1 percent chance that we will be wrong in eliminating the null hypothesis.

Since we have a choice in selecting the level of significance, how do we decide which level of significance to select? The level of significance selected depends on the consequences of making an error in eliminating the null hypothesis. Suppose we are conducting medical research where the consequences of making an error when eliminating the null hypothesis could have life-threatening consequences for patients. In that case, we would want a very stringent level of significance, such as 0.1 percent (1 chance in 1,000 of being wrong) or even 0.01 percent (1 chance in 10,000 of being wrong).

In other disciplines, the consequences of being wrong in eliminating the null hypothesis generally are not as devastating as in medical research, and so the level of significance does not need to be as stringent. In the discipline of sociology, researchers may use a level of significance of 10 percent. In psychology, the convention is to use a 5 percent level of significance. A convention is a generally accepted practice. Thus, most researchers in psychology use 5 percent as an acceptable level of significance.

Critical Values

As we have seen, the level of significance, α, is the criterion selected as a basis for deciding that the null hypothesis is false. Suppose that we select a level of significance of 5 percent (.05), conforming to the conventions in psychology. If there is 5 percent or less chance that Jorge's sample came from a population with a mean of 50, we will be able to eliminate the null hypothesis. We now need to determine whether the chance of Jorge's sample coming from a population with a mean of 50 is 5 percent or less.

To do this, we use the sampling distribution predicted by the null hypothesis, which we have already determined has a mean, $\mu_{\overline{X}}$, of 50, and a standard error of the mean, $\sigma_{\overline{X}}$, of 3.0. We need to find the values of z in this sampling distribution that cut off the most extreme 5 percent of the samples. These values of z are called the **critical values of z**.

The **critical value of z** is the standard score in a sampling distribution that falls at the boundary between rejecting and not rejecting the null hypothesis. The critical value of z has α beyond it in the relevant tail(s) of the sampling distribution.

The null hypothesis for Jorge's study is that the mean of the population of psychology majors is 50. This hypothesis could be false if the mean were far below 50 or if the mean were far above 50. Thus, we need to consider both tails of the sampling distribution. Of course, in this example we know that Jorge's sample had a mean of 58, which is above the mean of 50 predicted by the null hypothesis. However, the null and alternate hypotheses are actually constructed at the inception of the study, before any subjects are tested. When Jorge began, he hypothesized that the mean for psychology majors would be different from that of other college students, and so we need to consider both the lower and upper tails of the sampling distribution. Figure 12-3

FIGURE 12-3 Rejection Regions in Sampling Distribution
Predicted by the Null Hypothesis in Jorge's Study, with $\alpha = .05$

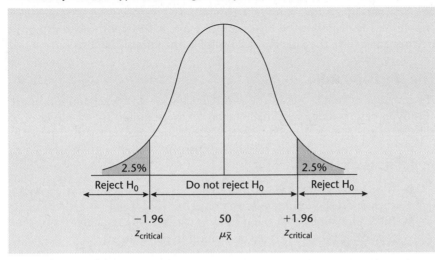

shows the sampling distribution predicted by the null hypothesis in Jorge's study, with both tails marked.

We have selected a level of significance of 5 percent (.05), which we need to divide between the two tails. If we put 5 percent in each tail, we would have a combined probability of 10 percent of rejecting the null hypothesis rather than the 5 percent level that we have selected. To have an overall probability of 5 percent for the level of significance, we need to put 2.5 percent in each tail, for a total of 5 percent. These percents are shown in Figure 12-3.

For Jorge's study, the critical values of z are the values of z that cut off 2.5 percent of the samples in each tail. The normal distribution table in Appendix A-1 shows that a z of ±1.96 cut off 2.5 percent of the cases in each tail. Thus, the critical values of z for Jorge's study are ±1.96, which are shown in Figure 12-3.

The segment of the X-axis that falls beyond each critical value of z is called the **rejection region.** If the sample statistic falls on the boundary or in the rejection region, then we can reject the null hypothesis. If the sample statistic does not fall on the boundary or in the rejection region, then we cannot reject the null hypothesis.

Note that Figures 12-2 and 12-3 are very similar but not identical. Both represent the sampling distribution predicted by the null hypothesis of Jorge's study, with a mean, $\mu_{\bar{X}}$, of 50. However, Figure 12-2 shows the 95 percent confidence limits for that distribution, while Figure 12-3 shows the critical values of z for a 5 percent confidence level. These points are the same. The 95 percent confidence limits are the points that cut off the center 95 percent of a sampling distribution, while the critical values of z for an α of .05 are

The **rejection region** is the segment of the number line in the tail(s) of the sampling distribution beyond the critical value of z. If the sample statistic falls in the rejection region, then the probability of drawing that sample from the sampling distribution is less than α, and we can reject the null hypothesis.

the points that cut off a total of 5 percent in the tails of a sampling distribution. For both of these, the values of z are ± 1.96. The difference between Figures 12-2 and 12-3 is that confidence limits are concerned with the portion of samples in the center of the distribution, while with hypothesis testing, we are concerned with the portion of samples in the tails of the distribution.

The Decision Rule

The previous sections contain the word *decide* several times. Eliminating the null hypothesis is a decision made based on the standard set by the level of significance, α. The decision is whether or not to eliminate the null hypothesis. For Jorge's study, we have selected a 5 percent level of significance. Thus, for this study, the decision rule is

▶ If the probability that the null hypothesis is true is 5 percent or less, then reject the null hypothesis.
▶ If the probability that the null hypothesis is true is greater than 5 percent, then do not reject the null hypothesis.

It is important to remember that this is a decision. When we make a decision to reject a null hypothesis, we have not proved beyond a shadow of a doubt that the null hypothesis is false. We cannot claim that it is a fact that Jorge's sample did not come from the general population of college students. Rather, rejecting the null hypothesis is a decision that we made. We did not make this decision arbitrarily. We do have evidence supporting this decision, evidence that there is very little probability that the null hypothesis is true. Because the probability of the null hypothesis being true is so small (5 percent or less), we have decided that the null hypothesis is false. Nonetheless, this is a decision and not absolute fact.

Of course, it could turn out that a study does not provide enough evidence to be able to reject the null hypothesis. If the probability that the null hypothesis is true is greater than α, that is, if the chance of Jorge's sample coming from a population with a mean of 50 is greater than α, then we cannot reject the null hypothesis. Failing to reject the null hypothesis does not mean that we therefore accept the null hypothesis, that we have proved that it is true. On the contrary! Remember that we can never prove directly that a hypothesis is true. Failing to reject the null hypothesis does not mean that we accept it. If we do not reject the null hypothesis, then there still are two possibilities. The mean of the population of psychology majors still either is 50 or is not 50. Failing to reject the null hypothesis does not prove that the mean is 50. If we do not reject the null hypothesis, all we can conclude is that we have not found enough evidence to support the researcher's hypothesis.

The z Test for a Sample Mean

To determine whether Jorge's sample mean of 58 falls in either of the rejection regions shown in Figure 12-3, we need to convert the sample mean to a

---

STEP-BY-STEP PROCEDURE 12-2

Calculating the Value of *z* for a Sample Mean

$$z_{\overline{X}} = \frac{\overline{X} - \mu_{\overline{X}}}{\sigma_{\overline{X}}} = \frac{\overline{X} - \mu}{\dfrac{\sigma}{\sqrt{n}}}$$

1. Calculate the mean of the sample of scores.

2. Subtract the population mean predicted by the null hypothesis from the sample mean found in Step 1.

3. Find the square root of the sample size, *n*.

4. Divide the standard deviation of the population predicted by the null hypothesis by the square root of the sample size found in Step 3.

5. Divide the results of Step 2 by the results of Step 4 to find the value of $z_{\overline{X}}$, the *z* representing the sample mean.

---

value of *z*, using the population mean, 50, and standard error of the mean, 3.0, for the sampling distribution predicted by the null hypothesis: Step-by-Step Procedure 12-2 shows the method for converting the sample mean to *z*. We can use the formula shown in Procedure 12-2 to find the value of $z_{\overline{X}}$ for Jorge's sample mean of 58:

$$z_{\overline{X}} = \frac{\overline{X} - \mu_{\overline{X}}}{\sigma_{\overline{X}}} = \frac{58 - 50}{3.0} = \frac{8}{3.0} = 2.67.$$

Jorge's sample mean of 58 has a $z_{\overline{X}}$ of 2.67, which is in the rejection region located in the upper tail of the sampling distribution shown in Figure 12-3. Thus, according to the decision rule, we can reject the null hypothesis and conclude that Jorge's sample does provide evidence that the population of psychology majors does have different Machiavellian tendencies than the general population of college students.

Frequently in the psychological literature, the phrase **significant difference** is used when the null hypothesis is rejected. In writing the results of Jorge's study, we might say that "there was a significant difference on the Machiavellian test between the sample mean for psychology majors ($\overline{X} = 58$) and the mean for the general population of college students ($\mu = 50$)." The term "significant" indicates that the null hypothesis was rejected. Thus, it indicates that we have concluded that the results of the study were not simply due to chance variation but that there is evidence that there is a relationship between the variables under study.

If we fail to reject the null hypothesis, the term **insignificant difference** is used. For example, suppose that Jorge did another study comparing the Machiavellian tendencies of business majors to that of other college students and found a sample mean of 51 for the business majors. With a sample size

In an inferential statistical test, the difference between a sample statistic and the value predicted by the null hypothesis is **significant** if that difference is large enough to reject the null hypothesis. If the difference is not large enough to reject the null hypothesis, then the difference is **insignificant**.

again of 16, the value of $z_{\bar{X}}$ would be 0.33, which is not in either of the rejection regions shown in Figure 12-4. We would report this as an **insignificant difference.** There is a difference between the sample mean of 51 for the business majors and the mean of the general population of college students, 50, but because we were not able to reject the null hypothesis, this difference is not significant.

The Value of *p*

Another symbol used in the psychological research to report the results of a statistical test is the symbol *p*, which represents the probability of obtaining the sample mean from the sampling distribution predicted by the null hypothesis. The normal distribution table in Appendix A-1 shows that the actual probability of obtaining Jorge's sample mean of 58 coming from a sampling distribution with a mean of 50 is .0076 (the probability of obtaining a value of *z* of ±2.67 or greater). Thus, for Jorge's sample, the value of *p* is .0076, which certainly is less than our level of significance, .05. Since the value of *p* is less than .05, we can make the decision to reject the null hypothesis. In reporting the results of this study, we might write, "The mean of the sample of psychology majors was significantly different from the mean of the general population of college students, *z* = 2.67, *p* < .05."

The value, *p*, is the probability of obtaining a sample statistic from the sampling distribution predicted by the null hypothesis.

We do not actually need to know the precise value of *p*. If the value of *z* calculated from our sample mean equals the critical value of *z*, then we know that the probability of obtaining that *z* is equal to the level of significance, α. For the upper rejection region, if the value of the *z* calculated from the sample mean is greater than the critical value of *z*, then we know that the probability of obtaining that *z* is less than the level of significance, α. The third possibility is that the value of *z* for the sample mean is less than the critical value of *z*, in which case the probability of obtaining the *z* is greater than α:

$$\text{If } z_{\bar{X}} = z_{\text{critical}} \text{ then } p = \alpha.$$

$$\text{If } z_{\bar{X}} > z_{\text{critical}} \text{ then } p < \alpha.$$

$$\text{If } z_{\bar{X}} < z_{\text{critical}} \text{ then } p > \alpha.$$

Thus, as long as we know the critical value of *z*, we can determine whether the value of *z* calculated from the sample mean is large enough to reject the null hypothesis.

What decision do we make if the value of *z* calculated from the sample statistic exactly equals the critical value of *z*? In this case, we are allowed to reject the null hypothesis. Thus, if the value of *z* for Jorge's sample was exactly 1.96, we could reject the null hypothesis. However, the value of *z* must be exactly equal to the critical value of *z*, and not rounded up to that value. If the value of *z* for Jorge's sample was 1.959, it would not be legitimate to reject the null hypothesis, despite the fact that we could round 1.959 to 1.96. In order to reject the null hypothesis, the value of *z* calculated from the sample mean must be greater than or exactly equal to the critical value of *z*.

We can restate our decision rule for Jorge's study, using the critical values of z:

If $z_{\bar{X}} \geq z_{\text{critical}}$ then reject the null hypothesis.

If $z_{\bar{X}} < z_{\text{critical}}$ then do not reject the null hypothesis.

This decision rule expresses the same thing as the decision rule that we examined previously. If the value of z calculated from the sample mean is equal to or greater than the critical value of z, then the probability, p, of obtaining that sample mean from the distribution predicted by the null hypothesis will be equal to or less than the level of significance, α, and it is legitimate to reject the null hypothesis.

Unidirectional and Bidirectional Hypothesis Tests

We have examined in considerable detail the concepts on which the z test for a sample mean are based. In the next section, we examine another example of how to use that inferential test. Before doing so, we need first to understand one additional concept, that of the distinction between unidirectional and bidirectional tests.

Bidirectional Tests

In Jorge's study, the alternate hypothesis was that the mean Machiavellian score for psychology majors was not 50, the mean for the general population of college students. Consequently, there were rejection regions in both the lower and upper tails of the sampling distribution predicted by the null hypothesis. In testing the null hypothesis, we would reject the null hypothesis if the sample mean were far enough above 50 that the value of $z_{\bar{X}}$ fell in the upper rejection region or if the sample mean were far enough below 50 that $z_{\bar{X}}$ fell in the lower rejection region.

Tests such as Jorge's, in which the alternate hypothesis asserts that the population mean under study is not equal to a specified value, are called **bidirectional tests**, because there are two possible directions in which the population mean might lie. For Jorge's study, the alternate hypothesis asserts that the population mean for psychology majors could lie in the direction above 50 or it might lie in the direction below 50. Bidirectional tests are often called *nondirectional tests* because the alternate hypothesis does not indicate a specific direction in which the population mean is expected to lie. Bidirectional tests are also called **two-tailed tests** because rejection regions occur in both tails of the sampling distribution predicted by the null hypothesis.

For a parametric test, a **bidirectional test** is one in which the alternate hypothesis predicts that a parameter of one population will be different from the same parameter in another population but does not specify in which direction that difference will occur. Bidirectional tests are also called **two-tailed tests** because rejection regions lie in both tails of the sampling distribution predicted by the null hypothesis.

Unidirectional Tests

It is also possible to conduct an inferential test in which the alternate hypothesis specifies the direction in which the population mean is expected to

TABLE 12-1   Unidirectional and Bidirectional Hypotheses
Predicting the Mean Machiavellian Score for Three Populations

	Null Hypothesis	Alternate Hypothesis
Unidirectional:	$\mu_{\text{business majors}} \leq 50$	$\mu_{\text{business majors}} > 50$
	$\mu_{\text{religion majors}} \geq 50$	$\mu_{\text{religion majors}} < 50$
Nondirectional:	$\mu_{\text{psychology majors}} = 50$	$\mu_{\text{psychology majors}} \neq 50$

For a parametric test, a **unidirectional test** is one in which the alternate hypothesis predicts that a parameter of one population will be either less than or greater than the same parameter in another population. Unidirectional tests are also called **one-tailed tests** because the rejection region lies in only one tail of the sampling distribution predicted by the null hypothesis.

lie. For example, suppose that Jorge is testing a theory that the career goals of students, and thus the majors they select, depend in part upon their level of Machiavellianism, that students low in Machiavellianism tend to select careers that are altruistic in nature, such as the ministry, while students high in Machiavellianism tend to select careers that are less altruistic, such as business. Thus, Jorge could hypothesize that the population of business majors has a mean Machiavellian score greater than the 50 of the general population of college students. He could also hypothesize that the population of religion majors has a mean Machiavellian score less than 50. These hypotheses predict the specific direction in which the population mean under consideration lies.

Inferential tests in which the alternate hypothesis asserts a specific direction are called **unidirectional tests.** We shall see that the rejection region for unidirectional tests lies entirely in only one tail of the sampling distribution predicted by the null hypothesis, and so these tests are also called **one-tailed tests.** Finally, unidirectional tests are often called simply *directional tests* because the alternate hypothesis predicts that the population mean under consideration lies in a specific direction.

The Null and Alternate Hypotheses for Bidirectional and Unidirectional Tests

There are only three possible assertions that the alternate hypothesis of a *z* test for a sample mean can make: that the mean of the population under consideration is less than, greater than, or different from some value. Thus, Jorge predicted that the mean for religion majors is less than 50, the mean for business majors is greater than 50, and the mean for psychology majors is different from 50 (i.e., not equal to 50). Table 12-1 shows these three forms of the alternate hypothesis, together with the corresponding null hypothesis.

Note that the assertion made by the null hypothesis is the negation of the assertion made by the alternate hypothesis. In Table 12-1, when the alternate hypothesis asserts that the mean of the experimental population will be larger than 50, the null hypothesis asserts that the mean will not be larger than 50. When the alternate hypothesis asserts that the experimental population's mean will be less than 50, the null hypothesis asserts that the mean will not be less than 50. When the alternate hypothesis asserts that the experimental

FIGURE 12-4 Alternate Hypotheses and Rejection Regions
for Unidirectional and Bidirectional Hypotheses Shown in Table 12-1

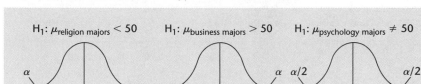

population's mean will be different from 50, the null hypothesis asserts that the experimental population's mean will be equal to 50. In general, an alternate hypothesis will contain one of the three signs: $<$, $>$, or $\neq$. The null hypothesis will contain the opposite sign: $\geq$, $\leq$, or $=$.

Figure 12-4 shows the rejection regions for the three sets of hypotheses listed in Table 12-1. As can be seen in Figure 12-4, for unidirectional hypotheses, the sign ($<$ or $>$) contained in the alternate hypothesis points in the direction of the rejection region. When the alternate hypothesis is that the population mean under consideration is less than a given value, the rejection region is in the lower tail of the sampling distribution. When the alternate hypothesis is that the population mean is greater than a given value, the rejection region is in the upper tail. Finally, as we have seen with Jorge's study of psychology majors, when the alternate hypothesis is that the population mean is not equal to a given value, there are rejection regions in both tails of the sampling distribution.

As we saw with the example of Jorge's study of psychology majors, if we want the probability of rejecting the null to equal α, then with a bidirectional hypothesis, we need to divide α between the two tails of the distribution, so that the overall probability of rejecting the null hypothesis is α. However, for a unidirectional hypothesis, the rejection region is in only one tail, and so the size of that rejection region is α. As a consequence, for a given value of α, there are different critical values of z, depending on whether the test is unidirectional or bidirectional. For example, as we saw with Jorge's study, with an α of 5 percent, the critical values of z were ± 1.96 because 5 percent of the cases in a sampling distribution lie beyond the values of z of $+1.96$. However, for a unidirectional test with a rejection region in the upper tail, the critical value of z is $+1.65$ because 5 percent of the cases lie beyond that value of z in the upper tail. Thus, to determine the critical value of z, we need to know whether the test is unidirectional or bidirectional. Table 12-2 lists the critical values of z for unidirectional and bidirectional tests for several values of α. The general procedure for constructing the sampling distribution predicted by the null hypothesis for both unidirectional and bidirectional tests is described in Step-by-Step Procedure 12-3.

TABLE 12-2   Critical Values of z for Unidirectional and Bidirectional Tests for Selected Values of α

Significance Level (α)	Bidirectional Test (two-tailed test)	Unidirectional Test (one-tailed test)
.10	1.65	1.28
.05	1.96	1.65
.025	2.24	1.96
.01	2.58	2.33
.005	2.81	2.58
.001	3.30	3.08

STEP-BY-STEP PROCEDURE 12-3

Constructing the Distribution of Sample Means Predicted by the Null Hypothesis

1. Draw a graph of the normal distribution. Draw a line vertically down the center of the graph to indicate the mean. Label the mean with the value predicted by the null hypothesis.

2. Draw a line in the appropriate tail(s) of the graph to indicate the rejection region.
   A. If the alternate hypothesis predicts that the population mean will be less than the mean predicted by the null hypothesis, draw the line in the lower tail.
   B. If the alternate hypothesis predicts that the population mean will be greater than the mean predicted by the null hypothesis, draw the line in the upper tail.
   C. If the alternate hypothesis predicts that the population mean will be different than the mean predicted by the null hypothesis, draw lines in both tails.

3. Find the appropriate value(s) of z in Table 12-2. If the rejection region is in only one tail of the distribution, use the column for one-tailed tests to find the value of α. If the rejection region is in both tails of the distribution, use the column for two-tailed tests to find the value of α. Find the value of z that corresponds to α. Write that value of z under the line(s) indicating the boundary of the rejection region. Remember that values of z in the lower half of the graph are negative.

The Debate over Unidirectional Tests

In recent years, there has been considerable debate among researchers in psychology as to whether it is ever legitimate to use a unidirectional inferential test. On the one hand, some statisticians argue that even if a researcher predicts that the sample mean will lie in one direction relative to the mean asserted by the null hypothesis, given the nature of the normal distribution, there is a possibility, no matter how small, that the sample mean could have a value in the opposite direction. Since this possibility exists, these statisticians argue that all inferential tests should be bidirectional, unless it is literally impossible for the results to happen in the direction opposite to that predicted.

On the other hand, other statisticians argue that inferential tests are used as a part of the scientific method, in which experiments are conducted in order to test scientific theories, including psychological theories. If a psychological theory predicts that the results of an experiment will occur in a given direction, then a result in the opposite direction would not provide support for the theory. In fact, such a result may be an indication that the theory requires revision.

It is not the purpose here to attempt to resolve this debate, which is ongoing and vigorous. It also is not the purpose here to indicate a preference for one position or the other. However, because unidirectional tests are reported in the psychological literature, it is important for you to understand how they are conducted and what inferences can be drawn from them. Therefore, in this and subsequent chapters, we will examine both bidirectional and unidirectional inferential tests. As an example of a unidirectional *z* test of a sample mean, in the next section, we return to Joe Johnson's study of math-anxious students.

Conducting the *z* Test for a Sample Mean

Conducting a *z* Test on a Study of Math Anxiety

Suppose that the math test Joe administered to his sample of 20 students was a standardized test (albeit a very brief one) that had been used with thousands of students. Among all of the students who had ever taken the test, the mean score was 14.3 questions correct, with a standard deviation of 4 questions. Previously, these math test scores were reported as the percent correct, but to prevent confusion here, we will conduct this analysis on the number correct. All of the thousands of students who have taken the math test constitute a population. Joe's sample of math-anxious students had a mean of 13.2 questions correct. Joe believes that there is a relationship between math anxiety and math test performance, such that students with math anxiety perform poorly on math tests compared to students without math anxiety. We can conduct a *z* test of the results of Joe's study. Step-by-Step Procedure 12-4 summarizes the steps involved in conducting the *z* test for a sample mean.

Verify the Assumptions of the *z* Test for a Sample Mean

The assumptions of a statistical test are the conditions that must be met in order to legitimately use that test. The assumptions that must be met for the *z* test for a sample mean are listed in Procedure 12-4. If we use the *z* test, readers of our research report will assume that we met these conditions.

STEP-BY-STEP PROCEDURE 12-4

Conducting the *z* Test for a Sample Mean

1. Verify that the following assumptions have been met:
   A. The subjects in the sample were randomly and independently selected from the population in question.
   B. Either the population in question is normally distributed or the sample size is at least 20. If either of these conditions is met, then the sampling distribution of the mean will be normally distributed, so that we can use the normal distribution table to find the critical value.
   C. The value of σ is known. The value of σ is needed to calculate the value of *z*.
   D. The scores are measured with an interval or ratio scale. It is valid to calculate the mean of a distribution only if the scores are from an interval or ratio scale.

2. Write the null and alternate hypotheses. For the *z* test for a sample mean, the hypotheses will have one of the following three forms:

Nondirectional	Unidirectional	
$H_0: \mu = \mu_0$	$H_0: \mu \geq \mu_0$	$H_0: \mu \leq \mu_0$
$H_1: \mu \neq \mu_0$	$H_1: \mu < \mu_0$	$H_1: \mu > \mu_0$

where μ_0 is the value of the population mean predicted by the null hypothesis.

3. Decide the level of significance, α.

4. Find the critical value of *z* in Table 12-2.

5. Draw a graph of the sampling distribution predicted by the null hypothesis, indicating the rejection region.
   A. For a bidirectional test, the rejection region is in both tails of the distribution.
   B. For a unidirectional test, the rejection region is in one tail of the distribution. If the alternate hypothesis predicts that the proportion mean is less than some value, the rejection region is in the lower tail. If the alternate hypothesis predicts that the proportion mean is more than some value, the rejection region is in the upper tail.

6. Convert the sample mean to a standard score, using Procedure 12-2:

7. Make a decision on whether or not to reject the null hypothesis:
   A. If $z_{\bar{x}}$ is in the rejection region bounded by z_{critical}, so that $p \leq \alpha$, then reject the null hypothesis.
   B. If $z_{\bar{x}}$ is not in the rejection region bounded by z_{critical}, so that $p > \alpha$, then do not reject the null hypothesis.

The first assumption is that the subjects were selected randomly and independently from the population in question. We will assume that Joe met this condition when he selected students to participate in his study. The second assumption is that the population in question is normally distributed or the sample size is at least 20. We do not know whether scores on the math test that Joe used are normally distributed. However, the size of his sample is 20, so this condition is met. The next assumption is that the value of σ, the population standard deviation, is known. This condition is met, as we know that the population standard deviation on Joe's math test is 4.0. Finally, in order to use the z test, the scores must have been measured on either an interval or ratio scale. The number of questions correct is a ratio scale of measurement, and thus we have met all of the assumptions for the z test.

Identify the Null and Alternate Hypotheses

Procedure 12-1, which we have already examined, describes a method for constructing the null and alternate hypotheses. Recall that the alternate hypothesis always asserts that there is a relationship between the variables under consideration, which in this case are the degree of math anxiety and math test performance. Joe hypothesized that math-anxious students do worse on math tests than do students without math anxiety. Expressed more formally, this hypothesis is that the mean math test score for the population of math-anxious students is less than 14.3, the mean math test score obtained by the general population of students who took the test. This is the basis of the alternate hypothesis, which in this case is unidirectional. We can express this alternate hypothesis in mathematical notation:

$$H_1: \mu_{\text{math-anxious students}} < 14.3.$$

The null hypothesis asserts that there is no relationship between the variables under consideration. Since the alternate hypothesis predicts the direction of the relationship between math anxiety and math test performance, the null hypothesis predicts that the mean math test score for the population of math-anxious students is either equal to or less than the mean math test score for the general population of students who took the test:

$$H_0: \mu_{\text{math-anxious students}} \geq 14.3.$$

Decide the Level of Significance, α

As discussed previously, in psychology, the convention is to use a 5 percent level of significance. We will select 5 percent as our level of significance for Joe's test, which will enable us to compare these results with the results of Jorge's study, examined previously.

Find the Critical Value of z

We can use Table 12-2 to determine the critical value of z for this z test for a sample mean. We could also find the critical value of z in the normal distribution table shown in Appendix A-1. For a unidirectional test, with an α of 5 percent (.05), the critical value of z is 1.65. A word of caution is needed here! Because the alternate hypothesis asserts that the mean math test score for the population of math-anxious students will be less than 14.3, the rejection region is in the lower tail of the sampling distribution. Therefore, the value of *z* must be negative. Consequently, for this *z* test, the critical value of *z* is −1.65.

Construct the Sampling Distribution Predicted by the Null Hypothesis

Procedure 12-3, which we examined previously, describes the method for constructing a graph of the sampling distribution predicted by the null hypothesis. For this *z* test, the mean of this sampling distribution is 14.3. The rejection region is in the lower tail, beyond a value of $z = -1.65$. The sampling distribution predicted by the null hypothesis for this *z* test of Joe's study is shown in Figure 12-5.

Calculate the Value of *z* for the Sample Mean

The next step in conducting a *z* test of the sample mean from Joe's study is to convert the sample mean to a value of *z*. The method is shown in Procedure 12-2. Joe's sample had a mean of 13.2, while the mean predicted by the null hypothesis is 14.3 and the population standard deviation, *s*, as we have seen, is 4.0. These are the values that we need to convert the sample mean to a value of *z*:

$$z_{\bar{X}} = \frac{\bar{X} - \mu_{\bar{X}}}{\sigma_{\bar{X}}} = \frac{\bar{X} - \mu}{\dfrac{\sigma}{\sqrt{n}}} = \frac{13.2 - 14.3}{\dfrac{4}{\sqrt{20}}} = -1.23.$$

When conducting the *z* test on the results of Jorge's study, we first calculated the value of the standard error of the mean and then later calculated the value

FIGURE 12-5 Rejection Region in Sampling Distribution Predicted by Null Hypothesis in Joe's Study, with $\alpha = .05$

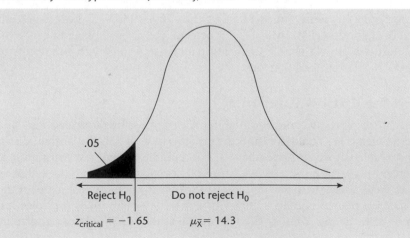

.05

Reject H_0 Do not reject H_0

$z_{\text{critical}} = -1.65$ $\mu_{\bar{X}} = 14.3$

of *z* using this standard error. In this case, the value of *z* was calculated using the values of the standard deviation, σ, and the sample size directly. Both methods can be used and will give the same value of *z*. For the sample mean in Joe's study, the value of *z* is -1.23.

Make a Decision about Rejecting the Null Hypothesis

The final step in conducting the *z* test of a sample mean is to make a decision about whether or not to reject the null hypothesis. For the *z* test of the sample mean from Joe's study, the critical value of *z* is negative, so that the decision rule is

If $z_{\bar{X}} < z_{\text{critical}}$ then reject the null hypothesis.

If $z_{\bar{X}} \geq z_{\text{critical}}$ then do not reject the null hypothesis.

If the value of *z* calculated from the sample mean is less than the critical value of *z*, -1.65, then the *z* for the sample mean falls in the rejection region shown in Figure 12-5 and we can reject the null hypothesis. In this case, however, the value of *z* we calculated from the sample mean is -1.23, which is greater than the critical value of *z* and does not fall in the rejection region. Therefore, the evidence provided by Joe's sample mean of 13.2 does not provide enough evidence to enable us to reject the null hypothesis. Thus, Joe's study does not provide enough evidence to conclude that the population of math-anxious students scores lower on the standardized math test than the general population of students does.

In reporting the result of this research, Joe might write that "there was an insignificant difference between the math test scores of the math-anxious students in this study, $\bar{X} = 13.2$, and the standardized mean of the math test, 14.3, $z = -1.23, p > .05$." The term, "insignificant difference," refers to the fact that while the two means did differ, that difference was not great enough to reject the null hypothesis. Consequently, this study cannot be used as evidence that math-anxious students perform more poorly on math tests than do students without math anxiety. This doesn't mean that there is no relationship between math anxiety and math test performance, just that this particular study failed to provide any significance evidence of such a relationship.

It is important to remember that because we failed to reject the null hypothesis, we cannot conclude that the null hypothesis is true and that the population of math-anxious students performs exactly the same on the math test as the general population of students. In fact, legitimately, we can conclude nothing. Before conducting the *z* test, there were two possibilities, expressed by the null and alternate hypotheses. Either the mean math test score for the population of math-anxious students is less than 14.3 or that mean is equal to or greater than 14.3. Because we failed to reject the null hypothesis, both the null hypothesis and alternate hypothesis still may be true. We still have two possibilities. After failing to reject the null hypothesis, we have no more information about the mean math test score of the population of math-anxious students than we did before we conducted the *z* test.

Decision Making in Statistical Tests

We hope that the results of our statistical tests always conform to the reality in the world. If there in fact is no relationship between two variables in the real world, as predicted by the null hypothesis, we hope that our statistical test will confirm this and we will not reject the null hypothesis. Also, if there really is a relationship between two variables in the real world, as predicted by the alternate hypothesis, we hope that our statistical test will also confirm this and we will reject the null hypothesis. However, statistical tests are not perfect.

The essence of a statistical test is the decision we make about the null hypothesis. When we reject the null hypothesis, we decide that it is not true. This is a decision, not a fact. Even though we decide that the null hypothesis is false, there still is some possibility that it may be true. Thus, the decision that we make about the null hypothesis may not correspond to what is really true in the world. Table 12-3 shows the four possible outcomes associated with our decision about the null hypothesis. Two of these outcomes are correct decisions, in which the decision made about the null hypothesis accurately reflects reality. Two of the outcomes shown in Table 12-3, however, are errors, in which the decision made about the null hypothesis contradicts the actual state of reality. We will examine these two types of errors, in turn.

Rejecting the Null Hypothesis When It Is True: Type I Errors

First, let's consider the case that there really is no relationship between two variables in a given population. For example, in Joe Johnson's study, let's suppose that in reality there actually is no relationship between math anxiety

TABLE 12-3   Possible Outcomes in Decision Making in Inferential Tests

Decision made	Reality	
	H_0 **is actually true**	H_0 **is actually false**
Do not reject H_0	*Correct decision:* Probability of not rejecting H_0 when it is true is $1 - \alpha$	*Type II error:* Probability of not rejecting H_0 when it is false is β
Reject H_0	*Type I error:* Probability of rejecting H_0 when it is true is α	*Correct decision:* Probability of rejecting H_0 when it is false is $1 - \beta$

FIGURE 12-6   Probability of Type I and Type II Errors

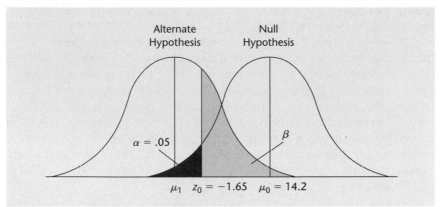

and math test performance. If this is the case, then the mean math test score for the population of math-anxious students is 14.3, the same as the mean for the general population of students taking the test. If we conduct a statistical test and do not reject the null hypothesis, then the results of the statistical test are correct. We would be saying that there is not enough evidence to decide that the sample did not come from a population with a mean of 14.3, which would be a correct decision.

However, what if we do reject the null hypothesis? According to the hypotheses of Joe's study, we would decide that the sample came from a population with a mean less than 14.3, when in reality the sample came from a population with a mean of 14.3. Thus, our decision would be wrong. This is called a **Type I error**—rejecting the null hypothesis when the null hypothesis is actually true.

What is the chance of a Type I error happening in a statistical test? In Figure 12-6, the graph on the right shows the distribution of sample means that could be drawn from a population with a mean of 14.3. Remember that we set the level of significance for testing Joe's hypothesis at $\alpha = .05$, so that the critical value of z was -1.65. We can convert this value of z to a sample mean value:

A **Type I error** occurs if the null hypothesis is rejected when in fact there is no relationship in the population between the variables being studied. The probability of a Type I error occurring is α, the level of significance.

$$\overline{X} = z\sigma_{\overline{X}} + \mu_{\overline{X}} = (-1.65)(0.89) + 14.3 = 12.8.$$

Thus, if Joe's sample mean was 12.8 or less, we could reject the null hypothesis.

However, it is possible to get a sample with a mean of 12.8 or less from a population with a mean of 14.3. In fact, in any normal distribution, 5 percent of the values will have values of z lower than -1.65. Thus, in a population with a mean of 14.3, 5 percent of the samples will have means of 12.8 or less. In Joe's study, if the null hypothesis is true and the mean math score for the population of math-anxious students is really 14.3, then there is a 5 percent chance that the sample mean will be 12.8 or less and we will reject the null hypothesis, making a Type I error.

The probability of a Type I error is set by α, the level of significance we select. If there is no relationship between the variables being studied, when α is set at .05, 5 percent of the sample means will be beyond the critical value of z and we will reject the null hypothesis. Thus, α is the probability of a Type I error, rejecting the null hypothesis when the null hypothesis is really true. If we want to reduce the chance of making a Type I error, deciding that there is a relationship between the variables being studied when there really isn't, we can use a smaller value of α. If we select an α of .01, then there will be only 1 percent chance of making a Type I error. If we select an α of .001, then there will be only 0.1 percent chance of making a Type I error.

So why don't we just use the smallest value of α possible to reduce the chances of claiming that there is a relationship when there really isn't? The difficulty is that if we use a smaller value of α to lower the chances of rejecting the null hypothesis when it is really true, at the same time we increase the chances of failing to reject the null hypothesis when it is really false. This is the second type of statistical testing error: There really is a relationship between the variables in the real world but our statistical test isn't powerful enough to measure it, so that we end up not rejecting the null hypothesis.

Not Rejecting the Null Hypothesis When It Is False: Type II Errors

In considering Type I errors, we supposed that there really wasn't a relationship between the variables being studied. Now suppose that there really is a relationship. If we reject the null hypothesis, we would decide that there is a relationship between the variables that really exists, which is a correct decision. However, we could also fail to reject the null hypothesis and not decide that there is a relationship when there really is. This is a **Type II error.** The probability of making a Type II error is labeled β ("beta"). In Figure 12-6, β is shown in the upper tail of the distribution on the right.

The probability of making a Type II error is inversely related to the probability of making a Type I error. Thus, there is a trade-off between Type I and Type II errors. If we reduce the probability of making a Type I error by selecting a more stringent value of α, we increase the probability of making a Type II error. In consequence, when we take steps to ensure that we do not reject the null hypothesis when it is really true, we increase the likelihood that we will fail to reject the null hypothesis when it is really true.

Scientific research tends to be conservative, as the probability of Type II errors, β, generally is greater than the probability of Type I errors, α. There is good reason for scientific research to be conservative, to be more concerned with not claiming that a difference exists when it really doesn't than with failing to identify differences that really do exist.

A **Type II error** occurs if the null hypothesis is not rejected when in fact there is a relationship in the population between the variables being studied. The probability of a Type II error is β.

For example, in the 1950s, obstetricians were concerned with finding a drug that would prevent miscarriages. They believed that they had evidence that diethylstilbestrol (DES) was effective in preventing miscarriages and prescribed it for women whose pregnancies appeared threatened. Eventually, it was shown that DES has no effect whatsoever on stopping miscarriages and obstetricians stopped prescribing it. Thus, these medical researchers committed a Type I error. They claimed that there was a relationship between the drug DES and preventing miscarriages, when in fact no such relationship existed. This error led to severe consequences, because until the error was caught, DES was prescribed for pregnant women and the children who were born from those pregnancies later developed serious medical anomalies related to the presence of the DES while they were developing *in utero*. To prevent inadvertent consequences such as this is the reason that researchers are more concerned with preventing Type I than Type II errors.

Of course, researchers want to be able to find evidence of a real relationship between variables and thus they want the **power** of a statistical test to be as great as possible. The power of a test, which is $1 - \beta$, is inversely related to the probability of making a Type II error. The power of a test is the probability of legitimately identifying a relationship between variables that actually exists. We will examine the concept of power in more depth in the next chapter.

The **power of a statistical test** is the probability of rejecting the null hypothesis when in fact there is a relationship in the population between the variables being studied. The power of a statistical test is $1 - \beta$.

Decision Making and Reality

Type I and Type II errors are mistakes in decision making. In hypothesis testing, we are making a decision about whether our sample provides enough evidence to demonstrate a relationship between the variables being studied, and that decision may be wrong. We may decide that there is a relationship when there really isn't (a Type I error) or we may decide that we don't have enough evidence to conclude that there is a relationship, when there really is (a Type II error).

The terms "error" and "mistake" suggest that we should be able to recognize when our decision is wrong and correct the fault. In fact, when conducting a hypothesis test, we never actually know if we are making a Type I or Type II error. Jorge concluded that there is a relationship between Machiavellianism and the type of college major, but there is a chance that Jorge's conclusion is wrong, that no such relationship actually exists. How do we know whether Jorge's decision is wrong? How do we know whether there really is a relationship between Machiavellianism and college major? We can't know, independent of the results of research such as Jorge's study and similar experiments on the relationship between these variables.

To be able to tell whether Jorge is making a Type I error, we would have to have some other means of determining whether there really is a relationship between Machiavellianism and college major. If we gave every college student in the entire population the Machiavellian test, we would know exactly what the mean Machiavellian score for each type of major is. We cannot test every college student in the world, and so we rely on samples. However, sample means can vary. The sample mean generally will not be the exact value of the population mean, and in fact, may differ considerably. There is always a possibility that the sample came from the population predicted by the null hypothesis. We use statistical tests to determine whether that possibility is small enough to decide that the null hypothesis is false, that there really is a relationship between the variables under study.

Because statistical tests are not perfect, there always is the possibility of error. If we could show that there is a zero percent chance that the null hypothesis is true, then statistical tests would be perfect. We would know for certain whether there really is a relationship between the variables being studied. However, statistical tests are not that powerful. Statistical tests can tell us that the chances that the null hypothesis is true are less than 5 percent, or less than 1 percent, but they can never tell us that the chances are zero percent. Thus, there is always the possibility of error.

While we cannot know whether we are making a Type I or II error, we can be aware that the possibility of making an error exists. Thus, when Jorge rejected the null hypothesis in his study, there is a small possibility that his decision was wrong. Therefore, Jorge is cautious in the claims he makes from his study. He does not say that he has proved that there is a relationship between Machiavellianism and college major, because there still is a chance, albeit a very small chance (5 percent), that there actually is no such relationship. Instead, Jorge says that his study provides evidence that a relationship between Machiavellianism and college major exists, which is a more cautious statement than claiming to have proved the relationship.

Of course, researchers want to avoid making both Type I and Type II errors. No researcher wants to claim that there is a relationship between the variables being studied when in reality there isn't (a Type I error). Researchers also do not want to go through all the effort of conducting a study, only to fail to find enough evidence to identify a relationship between variables that really exists (a Type II error). While we cannot eliminate the possibility of Type I and Type II errors entirely, we can reduce the possibility of their occurring. To do this relates to the power of a statistical test, which we will examine in greater depth in the next chapter.

CHECKING YOUR ANSWERS

1. In this chapter on hypothesis testing, there actually are no new statistical computations to learn. The chapter concentrates on the logic of hypothesis testing rather than new computations. Not surprisingly, the errors that students often make initially when learning about hypothesis testing are logical errors rather than computational. Many students have difficulty understanding the logic of hypothesis testing when first introduced to it. Reread each section as many times as you need to understand the concepts. It will eventually click.

2. Some students have difficulty identifying the population the statistical test concerns. In both of the tests described in this chapter, we have one sample of subjects. That sample came from a population. It is that population that the statistical test concerns.

3. In deciding whether a test is unidirectional or bidirectional, read the problem carefully. If the problem contains directional terms such as "more," "longer," or "higher," then the test is unidirectional and the rejection region will be in the upper tail. If the problem contains directional terms such as "less," "shorter," or "lower," then the test is also unidirectional but the rejection region will be in the lower tail. The directional words give an indication of the location of the rejection region. If the problem does not contain directional words but instead contains words such as "not the same as" or "different than," then the test is bidirectional and the rejection region will be located in both the upper and lower tails.

4. When calculating the value of z, be careful with negative signs. If the rejection region is in the upper tail and the value of z is negative, you cannot reject the null hypothesis, no matter how large the value of z. Similarly, you cannot reject the null hypothesis if the rejection region is in the lower tail and the value of z is positive.

5. Some students have difficulty with the concept of α. In statistical tests, there is generally no way that we can prove absolutely which population a sample came from. All we can do is prove that there is a very low probability that the sample came from a certain population. That very low probability is α. In psychology, α is set at .05 by convention. If we can show that there is 5 percent or less chance that a sample came from a certain population, we will say that it didn't. When you conduct a statistical test, use an α of .05 unless directed otherwise.

6. Be careful in the way you state your decision about the statistical test. If the statistic you calculate falls in the rejection region, then you can say that the study supports the alternate hypothesis, the researcher's hypothesis. However, it is cautious not to claim that the study *proved* the researcher's hypothesis because, with an α of .05, there still is a 5 percent chance that the researcher is wrong. On the other hand, if the statistic you calculate does not fall in the rejection region, there is very little that you can say. One thing that you *cannot* say is that you have evidence to support the null hypothesis or that you have proven the null hypothesis is true. If the statistic does not fall in the rejection region, then you still have two hypotheses left, both the null hypothesis and the alternate hypothesis. All you have done is failed to reject the null hypothesis.

7. Some students have difficulty understanding the concepts of Type I and Type II errors. Remember that we are trying to make a decision about what is happening in the world. That decision could be wrong, could be an error. Suppose you are trying to decide whether a certain person, X, loves you. If you decide that X really loves you when in fact X does not, that is a Type I error. If you decide that X really doesn't love you when in fact X does, that is a Type II error.

Σ SUMMARY

▶ Inferential statistical tests are used to assess the legitimacy of using samples to make statements about the population from which the samples were drawn.

▶ In parametric tests, sample statistics are used to make inferences about the value of the corollary parameter in the population. Nonparametric tests do not make inferences about specific population parameters but often use samples to make inferences about the general shape of the population from which they were drawn.

▶ A hypothesis is a testable assertion about the relationship between variables. In an inferential test, there are two mutually exclusive and exhaustive hypotheses: the null hypothesis, which asserts that no relationship exists between the variables under consideration, and the alternate hypothesis, which asserts that there is a relationship between those variables.

▶ An inferential test is a test of the null hypothesis. In statistics, there is no way to directly test the alternate hypothesis, which asserts that there is a relationship between the variables being studied. Therefore, to find evidence to support the alternate hypothesis, it is necessary to do so indirectly by determining whether there is evidence to reject the null hypothesis, which asserts that no such relationship exists.

▶ An inferential test is a logical decision based on evidence provided by one or more samples of scores. If there is sufficient evidence, we decide to reject the null hypothesis, thus deciding that the null hypothesis is false and that by default the alternate hypothesis is true. If there is not sufficient evidence, then we do not decide to reject the null hypothesis.

▶ In statistics, because we cannot prove that the null hypothesis is false with absolute certainty, we set a criterion, called the level of significance (α). If the probability that the null hypothesis is true is α or less, then we decide to reject the null hypothesis. Otherwise, we do not.

▶ In a bidirectional test, the alternate hypothesis predicts that the mean of the population under consideration is not equal to a specified value. In a unidirectional test, the alternate hypothesis predicts that the mean of the population under consideration either is greater than a specified value or is less than a specified value. Bidirectional tests are also called nondirectional tests and two-tailed tests. Unidirectional tests are also called directional tests and one-tailed tests.

▶ The z test for a sample mean uses a sample mean as evidence to determine whether the mean of the population under consideration is not a specified value.

▶ The critical value of z is the value of z that cuts off α of the cases in the relevant tail of the sampling distribution predicted by the null hypothesis. For a bidirectional test, the value of α is divided between the two tails of the sampling distribution. Thus there are two critical values of z, one positive and one negative. For a unidirectional test, the value of α is located entirely in one tail of the sampling distribution, the upper tail if the alternate hypothesis predicts that the mean of the population under study will be greater than a specified value and the lower tail if the alternate hypothesis predicts that that mean will be less than a specified value.

▶ The rejection region is the area of the sampling distribution in the tail(s) corresponding to values of z that are equal to the critical value of z or are farther from the mean than the critical value of z. If the value of z calculated from the sample mean falls in the rejection region, then it is legitimate to reject the null hypothesis.

▶ The sample mean is significantly different from the specified value tested if the null hypothesis is rejected. Otherwise, that difference is insignificant.

▶ A Type I error occurs if the null hypothesis is rejected when in fact there is no relationship between the variables under study. The probability of a Type I error occurring is α, the level of significance.

▶ A Type II error occurs if we fail to reject the null hypothesis when there actually is a relationship between the variables under study. The probability of a Type II error occurring is β.

▶ The power of a statistical test is the probability, equal to $1 - \beta$, of rejecting the null hypothesis when in fact a relationship between the variables under study exists.

E X E R C I S E S

Conceptual Exercises

1. Define the following terms:

   parametric statistical test   insignificant difference

   nonparametric statistical test   unidirectional hypothesis

   hypothesis   one-tailed test

   null hypothesis   nondirectional hypothesis

   alternate hypothesis   two-tailed test

   level of significance   Type I error

   critical value   Type II error

   rejection region   power of a statistical test

   significant difference

2. Suppose that you have a container filled with 50 percent red candies, 30 percent yellow candies, 15 percent orange candies, and 5 percent green candies. Indicate whether it would be possible or impossible to draw each of the following samples from this container:

   A. A sample of 6 candies, in which there are no red candies.

   B. A sample of 3 candies, in which all the candies are green.

   C. A sample of 12 candies, 50 percent of which are blue.

   D. A sample of 10 candies, 6 of which are orange.

   E. A sample of 15 candies, 20 percent of which are black.

3. Use the binomial table in Appendix A-2 to determine the probability of drawing each of the samples listed in the previous exercise.

   A. Based on these probabilities, are there any samples that you can with absolute certainty decide did not come from the container?

   B. Based on these probabilities, are there any samples that you cannot decide with absolute certainty did not come from the container?

   C. For the samples you identified in Part B above, can you with absolute certainty decide that those samples did come from the container described in the previous exercise?

4. Jeff believes that eating a diet high in sugar and highly refined carbohydrates lowers intelligence in children. He tested several samples of children raised on such a diet. Jeff's

null hypothesis states that eating this diet does not lower IQ, that the children in his samples came from the normal population. Find the probability of drawing a sample with each of the means below, or lower, from the normal population, which has a mean of 100 and standard deviation of 15.

A. A sample of 16 children with a mean IQ of 96.0.

B. A sample of 10 children with a mean IQ of 94.0.

C. A sample of 25 children with a mean IQ of 95.0.

D. A sample of 30 children with a mean IQ of 91.0.

5. Consider the following about the samples that Jeff tested in the previous exercise:

A. Of the four samples described, which samples, if any, can you decide with absolute certainty did not come from the normal population with a mean of 100? Why?

B. Of the four samples described, which samples, if any, can you decide with absolute certainty did come from the normal population with a mean of 100? Why?

C. Of the four samples described, which samples, if any, can you decide with a absolute certainty did not come from a population with lower than normal intelligence? Why?

D. Of the four samples described, which samples, if any, can you decide with absolute certainty did come from a population with lower than normal intelligence? Why?

E. Based on the above, explain whether it is possible to identify with absolute certainty from which population any of these samples was drawn.

6. Write in regular English the null and alternate hypotheses for Jeff's study described in Exercise 4. Then write both hypotheses in statistical notation.

7. Explain the difference between unidirectional and bidirectional hypotheses.

8. If what researchers want is to show that the alternate hypothesis is true, explain why it is necessary to consider the null hypothesis.

9. Explain the difference between the null and the alternate hypotheses.

10. Explain the difference between one-tailed and two-tailed tests.

11. What does it mean to say that the null hypothesis predicts that the results of the study were due solely to chance? What does it mean if when we reject the null hypothesis, we say that the results were not solely due to chance?

Computational Exercises

12. Write, first in regular English and then in statistical notation, the null and alternate hypotheses for each of the following studies:

A. The mean score of the population of fifth-grade children on a standardized reading test was 89, with a standard deviation of 10. A researcher instituted a program encouraging a sample of 20 sets of parents to read to their children to show that this would help improve the children's reading scores.

B. The mean score on a standardized depression inventory was 37, with a standard deviation of 8.5. On this inventory, a higher score indicates a greater degree of depression. A researcher instituted a program giving pets to a sample of 25 elderly depressed people to show that this would help lower their level of depression.

C. The mean birth weight of infants born at a large metropolitan hospital is 7.8 pounds, with a standard deviation of 1.3 pounds. A researcher measured the weight of a sample of 15 babies born to alcoholic mothers to show that alcoholism caused low birth weight in infants.

D. A manufacturer of computer disks installed a new system to produce 3.5-inch disks, with a guaranteed standard deviation of only .05 inch. The manufacturer believed the new system was producing disks that were defective in size and to verify his suspicions hired a consultant to test a sample of 50 disks.

E. A researcher tested the hypothesis that college students do not get the eight hours' sleep a night that they need (standard deviation = 1.5 hours) by having a sample of ten students record the number of hours each slept per night for a period of one month.

13. Identify whether the alternate hypothesis in each study described in the previous exercise is a unidirectional or a bidirectional hypothesis.

14. Find the critical value of *z* at the 95 and 99 percent levels of significance for each of the studies described in Exercise 12.

15. Using the values of *z* for the 95 and 99 percent levels of significance found in the previous exercise, draw a graph of a rejection region(s) for each of the studies described in Exercise 12.

16. For each of the critical values of *z* listed in Table 12-2, draw a graph for each of the following. On each graph, indicate the critical value(s) of *z* and the proportion of cases that would be found in each rejection region.

A. A one-tailed test with the rejection region in the lower tail.

B. A one-tailed test with the rejection region in the upper tail.

C. A two-tailed test.

17. Conduct a *z* test for a sample mean for each of the studies described in Exercise 11, following the steps described in Procedure 12-4. Listed below is the information you need to conduct these tests, in addition to the information given in Exercise 11. After completing the tests, write in regular English what each test showed.

A. Sample mean = 95. Test with α = .05.

B. Sample mean = 33.5. Test with α = .05.

C. Sample mean = 8.4 pounds. Test with α = .05.

D. Sample mean = 3.48 inches. Test with α = .01.

E. Sample mean = 7.1 hours. Test with α = .05.

18. For each of the studies described in Exercise 11, explain in regular English what a Type I error and a Type II error would be.

19. Julian found several studies in the psychological literature that reported that children in elementary school commit an average of eight aggressive acts at recess during a typical week, with a standard deviation of 2.3. Assume that these values represent population parameters. Julian hypothesizes that the aggressiveness of firstborn boys is different from the level shown by other children. Julian tested a sample of twenty-one firstborn boys and found that they committed a mean of six aggressive acts per week. Test Julian's hypothesis, with an α of .05.

20. Jolene obtained information from the State University Bookstore that indicated that for the previous term, students spent a mean of $243.00 on textbooks, with a standard deviation of $44.00. Jolene suspected that psychology textbooks cost more than average. She randomly sampled twenty-five psychology majors and found that in the previous semester they had spent a mean of $254.50 on textbooks. Test Jolene's hypothesis, with an α of .05.

Parametric Tests for One Sample

13

Student's *t* Test for a Sample Mean

How the *t* Test Differs from the *z* Test

The Concept of Degrees of Freedom

Conducting the *t* Test for a Sample Mean

STEP-BY-STEP PROCEDURE 13-1:
Conducting the t Test for a Sample Mean

The *z* Test for a Sample Proportion

STEP-BY-STEP PROCEDURE 13-2: Conducting
the z Test for a Sample Proportion

Conducting the *z* Test for a Sample
Proportion

A Look Back at Parametric Tests
for One Sample

The Power of a Statistical Test

The Relationship between α and β

The Relationship between α, β, and
the Power of a Statistical Test

The Relationship between Standard
Deviation and Power

The Relationship between
Sample Size and Power

The Relationship between
Effect Size and Power

Significant Differences and
Meaningful Differences

Testing Hypotheses about a Population

CHECKING YOUR ANSWERS

S U M M A R Y

E X E R C I S E S

Conceptual Exercises

Computational Exercises

E N D N O T E

▶ In the last chapter, we explored one example of a parametric test, the *z* test for a sample mean, which is designed to test whether the mean of a population differs significantly from a specified value. For example, we used the *z* test for a sample mean to determine that Jorge Jiminez had enough evidence to decide that the mean Machiavellian score for the population of psychology majors is not the same as the mean for the general population of college students. The *z* test for a sample mean is designed to be used with one sample of scores to make an inference about the mean of the population from which that sample was drawn.

There are other cases in which we might wish to make an inference about a population parameter from a single sample of scores, cases for which the *z* test for a sample mean is not appropriate. For example, we may want to assess whether the proportion of psychology majors graduating with honors is different from the overall proportion of students graduating with honors at State University. In this case, we are making an inference about a population proportion rather than a population mean, an inference for which the *z* test for a sample mean is not appropriate.

There also may be situations in which we wish to make an inference about a population mean but cannot use the *z* test for a sample mean because we have not met all of the assumptions required for that test. For instance, in order to use the *z* test for a sample mean, we must know the value of the population standard deviation, σ, because that value is used in the formula converting the sample mean to a value of *z*. There are many occasions in which we do not know the value of the population standard deviation and hence cannot use the *z* test for a sample mean.

In this chapter, we examine two tests designed for situations such as these. The first is the *t* test for a sample mean, which can be used to test hypotheses about the mean of the population from which a single sample is drawn when the population standard deviation is not known or when other assumptions of the *z* test have not been met. The second test we examine is the *z* test for a sample proportion, which is used to make an inference about a population proportion. Both of these tests, like the *z* test for a sample mean, are parametric hypothesis tests in that they are used to make an inference about the value of a population parameter. All three of these tests are also used to make inferences from a single sample of scores. In the ensuing chapters, we examine hypothesis tests that can be used to make inferences from two or more samples of scores.

In addition to examining the *t* test for a sample mean and the *z* test for a sample proportion, in this chapter we explore the concept of power, which is related to the concepts of Type I and Type II errors that we examined in the previous chapter. We also explore the concept of effect size, which is related to the concept of power. Effect size and power both affect our chances of correctly identifying real population differences.

Student's *t* Test for a Sample Mean

In order to use the *z* test for a sample mean, we must meet several conditions, one of which was that we know the value of the population standard deviation, σ. When conducting research, there are of course occasions when we do know the value of σ. For example, we would know σ if we were measuring IQ, GRE, or SAT scores. However, for most variables measured in research, the value of the population standard deviation, σ, is not known. For instance, suppose we are measuring the speed in which rats learn to run a maze. It is highly unlikely that we will know the standard deviation of the maze-running speed for the population of all rats in the entire universe. In the cases in which we do not know the population standard deviation, we cannot use the *z* test for a sample mean.

Statistician William Gosset, working at the turn of the nineteenth century, developed a statistical test to use in situations where the value of the population standard deviation is not known. In Gosset's test, the sample standard deviation, *s*, is used to estimate the value of the population standard deviation, σ. Gosset published his test under the pseudonym of Student. The test is called the Student's *t* test for a sample mean.

How the *t* Test Differs from the *z* Test

The *t* test actually differs from the *z* test, which we have already examined, in only two ways. As we saw in Chapter 12, the formula for converting a sample mean to a value of *z* is

$$z_{\bar{X}} = \frac{\bar{X} - \mu}{\sigma_{\bar{X}}} = \frac{\bar{X} - \mu}{\frac{\sigma}{\sqrt{n}}}.$$

In the *t* test, the formula for converting a sample mean to a value of *t* is very similar:

$$t = \frac{\bar{X} - \mu}{s_{\bar{X}}} = \frac{\bar{X} - \mu}{\frac{s}{\sqrt{n}}}.$$

The only difference between the two formulas is the source of the standard deviation. The formula for *z* uses the population standard deviation, σ, while

FIGURE 13-1   Comparing the *z* and *t* Distributions

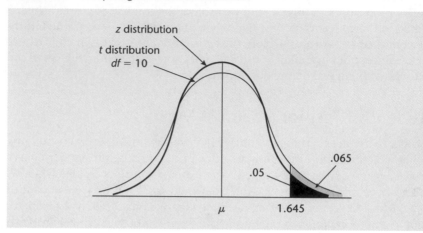

the formula for *t* uses the sample standard deviation, *s*, as an estimate of *σ*. Thus, one difference between the *z* and *t* tests is whether the population or sample standard deviation, *σ* or *s*, is used in the formula.

The other difference between the *z* and *t* tests is the statistical table we use to find the critical value. Recall that when conducting the *z* test for a sample mean, as long as we meet the assumptions of the test, we can assume that the sampling distribution of *z* will be normally distributed and we can use the normal distribution table to find the critical value of *z*. On the other hand, because the sampling distribution of *t* is not normally distributed, we cannot use the normal distribution table to find critical values of *t*. Figure 13-1 shows examples of graphs of the *z* and *t* distributions. As can be seen, the *t* distribution is flatter and more spread out than the *z* distribution. In the normal distribution, 5 percent of the scores lie above a *z* of 1.645. (Thus, when *α* is .05, the critical *z*, to three decimal places, is 1.645.) Because the *t* distribution is more spread out than the *z* distribution, more than 5 percent of the scores lie above a *t* of 1.645. Consequently, the critical value of *t* for an *α* of .05 cannot be 1.645.

How spread out the *t* distribution is depends upon the number of scores in the sample. The smaller the sample size, the flatter and more spread out the *t* distribution is. As a consequence, the critical value of *t* changes with the sample size. Recall that the critical value is the point in a distribution that cuts off *α* percent of the values. With an *α* of 5 percent in an unidirectional test, the critical *t* is the point in the *t* distribution that has 5 percent of the values above it. The more spread out the *t* distribution is, the higher that point will be. Thus, the smaller the sample size, the greater will be the critical *t* for each value of *α*.

This can be seen in Table 13-1, which shows several values for the critical *t*. (These critical values are all for a unidirectional test with an α of .05.) Table 13-1 shows that as the number of scores in the sample increases, the critical value of *t* decreases. When there are only two scores in the sample, the critical value of *t* is 6.314, but when there are six scores, the critical *t* is lowered to 2.015. With 21 scores per sample, the critical *t* is 1.725 and with 121 scores, the critical *t* is only 1.658. Note that as the sample size increases, the critical value of *t* approaches 1.645, which is the critical value of *z* for a unidirectional test with an α of .05. Thus, as the sample size increases, the *t* distribution comes closer and closer to the *z* distribution. In fact, with an infinitely large sample size ($n = \infty$), the *t* distribution is exactly the same as the *z* distribution, and the critical value of *t* is the same as the critical value of *z*.

In summary, the *t* test differs from the *z* test only in which measure of variability (s or σ) is used in the formula and in which table is used to find the critical value. Thus, the *t* test is basically like the *z* test, with an adjustment for the fact that the population standard deviation is not known.

TABLE 13-1 Critical Values of *t* for a Unidirectional Test, with α = .05

Number of Scores in Sample	Critical Value of *t*
2	6.314
3	2.920
4	2.353
5	2.132
6	2.015
11	1.812
16	1.753
21	1.725
26	1.706
31	1.697
41	1.684
61	1.671
121	1.658
∞	1.645

The Concept of Degrees of Freedom

In Table 13-1, you may have noticed that the many of sample sizes listed were a bit peculiar (e.g., 21, 41, and 61 rather than 20, 40, and 60). The critical values of *t* listed in Table 13-1 were taken from the table of critical values for *t*, shown in Appendix A-3, in which the critical values of *t* are listed by degrees of freedom (*df*), rather than by sample size. Degrees of freedom for the *t* test are derived from the number of scores per sample.

All of the statistical tests that we will examine in the remainder of this text will have degrees of freedom. The **degrees of freedom** for a statistical test are the number of values that are free to vary, given certain restrictions. For example, suppose you have to guess the values of the scores in a set, and all you know is that there are five scores and their total sum is 20:

The **degrees of freedom** (*df*) for a statistical test are the number of values that are free to vary, given certain restrictions. For the *t* test for a sample mean, the degrees of freedom are $n - 1$.

Score 1	?
Score 2	?
Score 3	?
Score 4	?
Score 5	?
Total	20

What value would you guess for each of the five scores? In fact, you could guess any value at all for each of the first four scores. Suppose we made the guesses shown below:

Score 1	3
Score 2	5
Score 3	6
Score 4	2
Score 5	?
Total	20

subtotal = 16 (for Scores 1–4)

These four scores have a subtotal of 16, and so, to make the total of all five scores equal to 20, Score 5 must have a value of 4. In this example, the first four scores are free to vary over the whole range of possible numeric values. However, once we know the values of the first four scores, there is one and only one value that the fifth and final score can have if the sum of all five scores is to equal 20.

Recall that the degrees of freedom are the number of values that are free to vary, given certain restrictions. In this example, there are two given facts, or restrictions: the number of scores in the set (5) and the sum of the scores (20). How many scores are free to vary, given that there are 5 scores in the set that total 20? In this example, 4 of the scores are free to vary, and so the degrees of freedom are 4. When there are 11 scores in a set, 10 of them are free to vary and the degrees of freedom are 10. When there are 21 scores in a set, 20 of them are free to vary and the degrees of freedom are 20. Thus, for one set of scores, the degrees of freedom are always one less than the sample size: $df = n - 1$.

Conducting the *t* Test for a Sample Mean

The *t* test for a sample mean is conducted in the same manner as the *z* test for a sample mean, with these two differences: the sample standard deviation is used for the *t* test, rather than the population standard deviation, and the critical values are found in the table shown in Appendix A-3, rather than the normal distribution table, shown in Appendix A-1. Step-by-Step Procedure 13-1 describes the method for conducting the *t* test for a sample mean.

In order to demonstrate how to conduct the *t* test for a sample mean, let's use an example drawn from the life of William Gosset. In 1899, Gosset was employed as a chemist in the Guinness Brewery in Dublin, Ireland, where he was responsible for developing procedures to use in quality control. At that time, the mathematical field of statistics was in its infancy, and statistical procedures were often developed to solve pragmatic problems in business and industry. Gosset actually developed the *t* test to handle small samples in testing the quality of Guinness ales.

Conducting the *t* Test for a Sample Mean

1. Verify that the following assumptions have been met:
   A. The subjects in the sample were randomly and independently selected from the population in question.
   B. The distribution in question is approximately normally distributed. The *t* test is not appropriate if the distribution is greatly skewed.
   C. The scores are measured with an interval or ratio scale. It is valid to calculate the mean of a distribution only if the scores are from an interval or ratio scale.

2. Write the null and alternate hypotheses. For the *t* test for a sample mean, the hypotheses will have one of the following three forms:

Bidirectional	Unidirectional
$H_0: \mu = \mu_0$	$H_0: \mu \geq \mu_0$ $H_0: \mu \leq \mu_0$
$H_1: \mu \neq \mu_0$	$H_1: \mu < \mu_0$ $H_1: \mu > \mu_0$

where μ_0 is the population mean predicted by the null hypothesis.

3. Decide the level of significance, α.

4. Find the critical value of *t* in Appendix A-3. The degrees of freedom are the number of subjects, minus 1.

5. Draw a graph of the sampling distribution predicted by the null hypothesis, indicating the rejection region.
   A. For a bidirectional test, the rejection region is in both tails of the distribution.
   B. For a unidirectional test, the rejection region is in one tail of the distribution. If the alternate hypothesis predicts that the proportion mean is less than some value, the rejection region is in the lower tail. If the alternate hypothesis predicts that the proportion mean is more than some value, the rejection region is in the upper tail.

6. Convert the sample mean to a standard score, using the formula below:

$$t_{\bar{X}} = \frac{\bar{X} - \mu}{\dfrac{s}{\sqrt{n}}},$$

where $\mu = \mu_0$, the population mean predicted by the null hypothesis.

7. Make a decision on whether or not to reject the null hypothesis:

   A. If $t_{\bar{X}}$ is in the rejection region bounded by t_{critical}, then $p \leq \alpha$, and therefore decide that sample did not come from a population with the mean predicted by the null hypothesis (reject the null hypothesis).
   B. If $t_{\bar{X}}$ is not in the rejection region bounded by t_{critical}, then $p > \alpha$, and therefore do not decide that sample did not come from a population with the mean predicted by the null hypothesis (do not reject the null hypothesis).

TABLE 13-2 Alcoholic Content by Volume
in Sample of Ten Bottles of Guinness Extra Stout

5.87	5.93	5.98	6.03	6.09
6.12	6.15	6.21	6.24	6.28

Suppose that Jill Jones decides to undertake a quality control project of her own, testing the alcohol content of bottled Guinness Extra Stout, which according to the bottle label, has an alcohol content of 6 percent, by volume. Jill, who of course is of legal age, purchased a bottle of Guinness Extra Stout at each of the ten pubs in the vicinity of State University. She then measured the alcoholic content of the ale in each bottle. The results are shown in Table 13-2.

Step 1: Verify that the assumptions of the test are met. The assumptions of the *t* test for a sample mean are shown in Procedure 13-1. The first assumption is that the subjects in the sample were randomly and independently selected. The subjects in this case are bottles of Guinness Extra Stout, purchased from ten different pubs. We can assume that the chances of any one bottle being included were not affected by the other bottles selected, and so the bottles were independently selected. If we can assume that the bartenders were not biased in which bottle they selected to sell to Jill, we can also assume that the bottles were randomly selected. The second assumption is that the population distribution is approximately normally distributed. The distribution we are evaluating is the alcoholic content of bottles of Guinness Extra Stout. There is no obvious skew in the sample, and we could expect that the variation in the bottles' alcoholic content would be the same above and below the true percent of alcohol in Guinness Extra Stout. The third assumption is that the scores are measured on either an interval or ratio scale. The percent of alcohol by volume is a ratio scale of measurement.

Step 2: Write the null and alternate hypotheses. Jill is conducting a quality control study to see whether the alcoholic content of the Guinness Extra Stout available in her locale differs significantly from the 6 percent level that is the standard set by the Guinness Brewery. Thus, the null hypothesis is that the mean alcoholic content of Guinness Extra Stout is 6 percent. The alternate hypothesis is that the mean alcoholic content of Guinness Extra Stout is not 6 percent. This is a bidirectional test. The standard set by Guinness would be violated if the alcoholic content is significantly less than 6 percent. It would also be violated if the alcoholic content is significantly greater than 6 percent. This is the essence of a bidirectional test. The hypotheses for this study are

$$H_0: \mu_{\bar{x}} = 6 \text{ percent,}$$

$$H_1: \mu_{\bar{x}} \neq 6 \text{ percent.}$$

Step 3: Decide the level of significance, α. We will use the conventional level of significance, $\alpha = .05$.

FIGURE 13-2 Sampling Distribution Predicted by the Null Hypothesis for the Mean Alcoholic Content of Guinness Extra Stout, with $\alpha = .05$

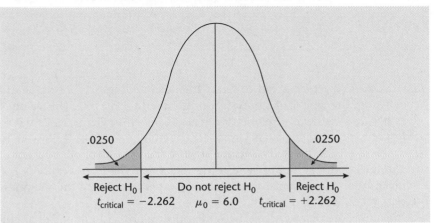

Step 4: Identify the critical value(s) of the statistic. Appendix A-3 shows the critical values of *t* for selected values of α. For the *t* test for one sample, the degrees of freedom are the number of subjects, minus 1: $df = n - 1 = 10 - 1 = 9$. For $\alpha = .05$ and 9 degrees of freedom, Appendix A-3 shows that the critical value of *t* is ± 2.262.

Step 5: Indicate the rejection region on a graph of the sampling distribution. The sampling distribution predicted by the null hypothesis is shown in Figure 13-2. Because the hypotheses are bidirectional, the rejection region lies in both tails of the distribution. If the value of *t* for the sample is in either rejection region, we can reject the null hypothesis.

Step 6: Calculate the statistic from the sample of scores. In order to calculate the value of *t*, we need to first calculate the mean and standard deviation of the samples of scores shown in Table 13-2. The mean alcoholic content, by volume, of the 10 bottles is 6.09 percent, with a standard deviation of .136 percent:

$$\bar{X} = \frac{\Sigma X}{n} = \frac{60.9}{10} = 6.09,$$

$$s = \sqrt{\frac{\Sigma(X - \bar{X})^2}{n - 1}} = \sqrt{\frac{0.1672}{10 - 1}} = \sqrt{.0186} = .136.$$

Note that the value of the sample standard deviation, *s*, is calculated with $n - 1$ in the denominator, so that *s* will be an unbiased estimate of the population standard deviation, σ. With the values of the mean and standard deviation of the sample, we can now calculate the value of t:

$$t_{\bar{X}} = \frac{\bar{X} - \mu}{s_{\bar{X}}} = \frac{\bar{X} - \mu}{\dfrac{s}{\sqrt{n}}} = \frac{6.09 - 6.00}{\dfrac{.136}{\sqrt{10}}} = 2.091.$$

Step 7: Decide whether or not to reject the null hypothesis.   The value of t calculated for the sample of scores shown in Table 13-2 is 2.091. This value of t does not lie in either of the rejection regions shown in Figure 13-2, and so we do not have enough evidence to reject the null hypothesis. If Jill were to report the results of this study, she might write that "the alcoholic content of the Guinness Extra Stout available in the pubs near State University is not significantly different from the standard of 6 percent set by the Guinness Brewery ($t = 2.088$, $p > .05$)."

We must note that we are *not* accepting the null hypothesis and claiming that Jill's study proves that the null hypothesis is true, that the Guinness Extra Stout in Jill's locale has a 6 percent alcoholic content. Jill's sample of ten bottles had a mean alcoholic content of 6.09 percent, and that certainly does not show that the alcoholic content of all the Guinness Extra Stout in her area is exactly 6 percent. In fact, the results of Jill's study are inconclusive. While we cannot claim that the Guinness Extra Stout available in Jill's locale has a 6 percent alcoholic content, her study did not provide enough evidence to show that the alcoholic content differs significantly from 6 percent. Thus, in this study we cannot reject the null hypothesis, and we are never able to accept the null hypothesis. In short, we can draw no conclusion at all from Jill's study.

The *z* Test for a Sample Proportion

Both the z and t tests for a sample mean are used to measure whether a population mean differs significantly from a specified value. There are situations in which we are concerned with the proportion of some event in a population rather than the mean of the population. The z test for a sample proportion can be used in these cases.

In order to use the z test for a sample proportion, the events in the population must be mutually exclusive dichotomies. As we saw in our examination of probabilities in Chapter 10, the events in a population are dichotomous when two and only two values can occur. The two possible outcomes for a toss of a coin are heads or tails, and thus these events are dichotomous. These two possible outcomes are also mutually exclusive. If a tossed coin turns up heads, it cannot also at the same time turn up tails. The occurrence of heads on any one toss excludes the possibility of tails.

While the *z* test for a sample proportion can be used for variables whose values are naturally occurring dichotomies, it is also possible to reduce the values of many other variables to a dichotomy. For example, we could reduce the percent correct that students receive on a general psychology test to a dichotomy by recording the scores simply as "pass" or "fail." Because many variables can similarly be reduced to mutually exclusive dichotomies, the *z* test for a sample proportion is very useful.

The *z* test for a sample proportion is the same as the *z* test for a sample mean, except that we use proportions rather than means. Consider, as an example, the proportion of men and women in psychology. In psychology graduate programs across the United States, there are approximately 50 percent women and 50 percent men. In comparison, in many psychology departments the proportions of men and women faculty are not so evenly distributed. Suppose the Psychology Department at State University has 30 faculty, of whom eight are women and twenty-two are men. Let's consider the State University Psychology Department to be a sample selected from the population of psychology faculty to see if the proportion of women faculty is less than the proportion of women graduate students in the United States. The general method for using the *z* test for a sample proportion is shown in Step-by-Step Procedure 13-2.

Conducting the *z* Test for a Sample Proportion

Step 1: Verify that the assumptions of the test are met.   The assumptions of the *z* test for a sample proportion are shown in Procedure 13-2. We will assume that we selected State University at random from all of the colleges and universities in the United States. The sample size is 30. The value of p_0 is the proportion of the desired event, women, in the population predicted by the null distribution, which we will see is .50. (Remember that "desired event" does not mean that female faculty are more desirable than male faculty, but simply that female is the outcome whose proportion we are testing.) Therefore, both np_0 and $n(1 - p_0)$ are 15, meeting the second assumption. The scale of measurement has only two values, male and female, which are dichotomous and mutually exclusive, meeting the third assumption. Thus, we have verified that the assumptions of the test have been met.

Step 2: Write the null and alternate hypotheses.   We are asserting that the proportion of women in the population of psychology faculty in the United States is less than the proportion of women in the population of psychology graduate students in the United States. This assertion is the alternate hypothesis:

$$H_1: p_{\text{women psych faculty}} < .50.$$

STEP-BY-STEP PROCEDURE 13-2

Conducting the *z* Test for a Sample Proportion

1. Verify that the following assumptions have been met:
   A. The subjects in the sample were randomly and independently selected from the population in question.
   B. The sample size is at least 20 and both np and $n(1 - p)$ are at least 5. If both of these conditions are met, then the distribution of sample proportions will be normally distributed, so that we can use the normal distribution table to find the critical value.
   C. The scores are measured on a dichotomous scale, in which there are only two possible mutually exclusive values.

2. Write the null and alternate hypotheses. For the *z* test for a sample proportion, the hypotheses will have one of the following three forms:

Bidirectional	Unidirectional	
$H_0: p = p_0$	$H_0: p \geq p_0$	$H_0: p \leq p_0$
$H_1: p \neq p_0$	$H_1: p < p_0$	$H_1: p > p_0$

where p_0 is the population proportion predicted by the null hypothesis.

3. Decide the level of significance, α.

4. Find the critical value of *z* in Table 12-2.

5. Draw a graph of the sampling distribution predicted by the null hypothesis, indicating the rejection region.
   A. For a bidirectional test, the rejection region is in both tails of the distribution.
   B. For a unidirectional test, the rejection region is in one tail of the distribution. If the alternate hypothesis predicts that the population proportion is less than some value, the rejection region is in the lower tail. If the alternate hypothesis predicts that the population proportion is more than some value, the rejection region is in the upper tail.

6. Convert the sample proportion to a standard score, using the formula below:

$$z_P = \frac{P - p_0}{\sqrt{\dfrac{p_0(1 - p_0)}{n}}},$$

where p_0 is the population proportion predicted by the null hypothesis, P is the sample proportion, and n is the sample size.

7. Make a decision on whether or not to reject the null hypothesis:
   A. If z_P is in the rejection region bounded by z_{critical}, then $p \leq \alpha$, and therefore decide that sample did not come from a population with the proportion predicted by the null hypothesis (reject the null hypothesis).
   B. If z_P is not in the rejection region bounded by z_{critical}, then $p > \alpha$, and therefore do not reject the null hypothesis.

The null hypothesis is the opposite assertion, that the proportion of female faculty in psychology is not less than the proportion of female graduate students in psychology, .50:

$$H_0: p_{\text{women psych faculty}} \geq .50.$$

Step 3: Decide the level of significance, α. For the tests we have examined thus far, we used $\alpha = .05$. To show how to use other values of α, let's use an α of .01 for this example. Thus, there will have to be a 1 percent or less chance that the sample came from a population with 50 percent psychology female faculty in order to reject the null hypothesis.

Step 4: Identify the critical value(s) of the statistic. We are going to convert the sample proportion to a standard score so that we can use the normal approximation to the binomial distribution. The appropriate table is the normal distribution table. We can use the critical values shown in Table 12-2. The hypotheses are unidirectional, so we are doing a one-tailed test. For a one-tailed test, with $\alpha = .01$, the critical value of z is -2.33.

Step 5: Indicate the rejection region on a graph of the sampling distribution. The sampling distribution to test the null hypothesis is shown in Figure 13-3. Because the alternate hypothesis predicts that the proportion of women in the population of psychology faculty will be less than .50, the rejection region is in the lower tail.

FIGURE 13-3 Sampling Distribution Predicted by the Null Hypothesis for the Analysis of the Proportion of Women Faculty, with $\alpha = .01$

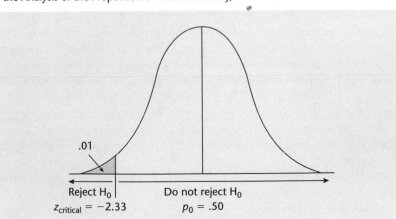

Step 6: Calculate the statistic from the sample of scores.   In order to calculate the value of z_P, first we need to find the proportion, P, of women in the sample. There are 30 psychology faculty at State University, of whom 8 are women. Thus, 8/30 or .27 of the psychology faculty are women. Next, we need to convert this proportion to a standard score. The proportion predicted by the null hypothesis is p_0. The null hypothesis predicts that 50 percent of the population of psychology faculty in the United States will be women, and so p_0 is .50. There were 30 faculty in the sample, and so n is 30. These are the values we need to convert the sample proportion to a standard score:

$$z_P = \frac{P - p_0}{\sqrt{\dfrac{p_0(1 - p_0)}{n}}} = \frac{.27 - .50}{\sqrt{\dfrac{.50(.50)}{30}}} = \frac{-.23}{\sqrt{\dfrac{.25}{30}}} = \frac{-.23}{.09} = -2.56.$$

Step 7: Decide whether or not to reject the null hypothesis.   We can now make a decision about the null hypothesis, based on this value of z. A z of -2.56 is in the rejection region of the distribution shown in Figure 13-3. Therefore, there is less than a 1 percent chance of drawing a sample with 27 percent women from a population with 50 percent women. Thus, we can reject the null hypothesis and conclude that the population of psychology faculty has less than 50 percent women. We might report the results of this study as "the proportion of women in the psychology faculty at State University, .27, is significantly less than the proportion of women typically found in psychology graduate programs, $z = -2.56$, $p < .05$."

A Look Back at Parametric Tests for One Sample

All three of the tests we have examined thus far—the z and t tests for a sample mean and the z test for a sample proportion—measure whether a population parameter differs significantly from a specified value. For the z and t tests for a sample mean, the population parameter was the population mean: the mean Machiavellian test score of the population of students majoring in psychology and the mean alcoholic content of the "population" of Guinness Extra Stout in the vicinity of State University. For the z test for a sample proportion, the parameter was a proportion: the proportion of women in the population of Psychology Department faculty. In all three examples, we are testing whether the population parameter differs significantly from a specified value: 50 for the Machiavellian test, 6 percent for the alcoholic content of Guinness Extra Stout, and .50 for the proportion of female psychology faculty members.

Note that in all of these examples, we are trying to show that the parameter is *not* the specified value. This is the nature of statistical tests of differences. Inferential tests cannot confirm that a parameter *is* a certain value; they can only tell us the likelihood that a parameter *is not* a certain value. It would be much simpler to do research (and understand statistics) if inferential tests could directly show us the exact value of a parameter, but that is beyond their capabilities. Nonetheless, these inferential tests can give us an indication of the value of a parameter, by a process of elimination. For instance, the *z* test for a proportion showed us that the proportion of women in the population of psychology faculty was *not* .50 or above by a process of elimination allowing us to infer that the true proportion is significantly less than .50.

The Power of a Statistical Test

In the last chapter, we examined the concepts of Type I and Type II errors, both of which are mistakes that can occur in making a decision on whether to reject the null hypothesis of a statistical test. The null hypothesis always asserts that there is no relationship between the variables under consideration. If, as a result of a statistical test, we decide that the null hypothesis is false when there actually is no relationship between the variables, we commit a Type I error. On the other hand, if we conclude that we do not have enough evidence to reject the null hypothesis when a relationship between the variables really does exist, we commit a Type II error.

The Relationship between α and β

The probability of making a Type I error is set by the level of significance, α. If we select a .05 level of significance, then there is a 5 percent chance that we will decide that our sample did not come from the distribution predicted by the null hypothesis when in fact it did, a Type I error. If we select a .01 level of significance, then the chance of rejecting the null hypothesis in error is only 1 percent. We can decrease the probability of making a Type I error simply by selecting a more stringent level of significance.

The dilemma is that when we reduce the probability of making a Type I error, we automatically increase the probability of making a Type II error (assuming that all other factors remain the same). The complementary relationship between the probability of Type I and Type II errors is shown in Figure 13-4, which shows examples of sampling distributions for two levels of significance, $\alpha = .05$ and $\alpha = .025$.

The examples in Figure 13-4 represent a one-tailed statistical test, with the rejection region in the upper tail. In both examples, the distribution on the left represents the distribution predicted by the null hypothesis and the distribution on the right represents the distribution predicted by the alternate hypothesis. Using a one-tailed test with the rejection region in the upper tail in these examples is arbitrary. We could just as well have selected a two-tailed test or a one-tailed test with the rejection region in the lower tail. The

FIGURE 13-4   Example of the Relationship between Type I and Type II Errors

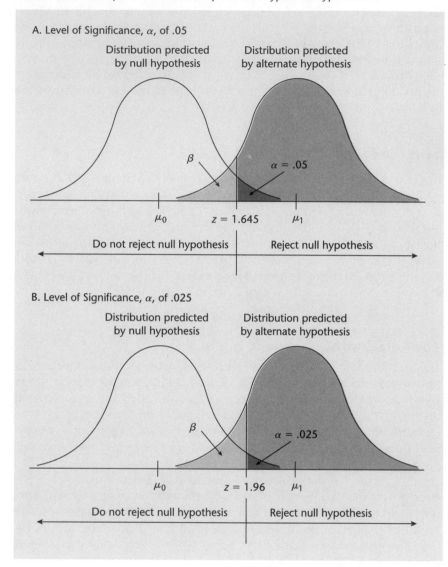

A. Level of Significance, α, of .05

Distribution predicted by null hypothesis

Distribution predicted by alternate hypothesis

β

$\alpha = .05$

μ_0 $z = 1.645$ μ_1

Do not reject null hypothesis   Reject null hypothesis

B. Level of Significance, α, of .025

Distribution predicted by null hypothesis

Distribution predicted by alternate hypothesis

β

$\alpha = .025$

μ_0 $z = 1.96$ μ_1

Do not reject null hypothesis   Reject null hypothesis

location of the distribution predicted by the alternate hypothesis is also arbitrary. The location shown in Figure 13-4 represents only one of many possible locations. While these choices were arbitrary, what is important is that the two examples are exactly the same, except for the level of significance, α, so that we will be able to see the effect of changes in α on the probability of a Type II error, β.

In example A of Figure 13-4, the level of significance, α, is .05, and thus there is a 5 percent chance of making a Type I error. In example B, the level of significance has been reduced by half, to .025, thereby also reducing the chance of a Type I error to 2.5 percent. Thus, simply by selecting a more stringent level of significance, we have reduced the probability of a Type I error.

However, when we reduce the size of α, the size of β automatically increases. In each example, the distribution on the right represents the distribution predicted by the alternate hypothesis, which asserts that there actually is a relationship between the variables being studied. As can be see in Figure 13-4, even if the alternate hypothesis is true, it is still possible that our sample might give us a value of z less than the critical value of z, so that we do not have enough evidence to reject the null hypothesis. This is a Type II error, failing to reject the null hypothesis when there really is a relationship between the variables being studied.

The area in the lower tail of the distribution on the right, the distribution predicted by the alternate hypothesis, represents β, the probability of a Type II error occurring. Compare the size of the area representing β in the two examples. The size of α is smaller in example A than in example B, but the size of β is larger. If we selected an even more stringent level of significance, such as an α of .01, the probability of a Type I error would decrease, but the probability of a Type II error, β, would increase.

In a perfect world, researchers would like the probability of both Type I and Type II errors occurring to be zero. However, statistical tests are not perfect, and in any statistical test, there is always a probability that either a Type I or a Type II error will occur. In addition, decreasing the probability of one type of error automatically increases the probability of the other type occurring. Fortunately, there are other factors that affect the probability of a Type II error, which we will examine shortly. But first, we need to examine the relationship between Type I and Type II errors and the power of a statistical test.

The Relationship between α, β, and the Power of a Statistical Test

As we saw in the last chapter, the power of a statistical test is the probability that we will decide that the null hypothesis is false when it actually is false. This is the same as saying that power is the probability that we will decide that the alternate hypothesis is true when it really is true. If a relationship actually exists between the variables being studied, power is the probability that the statistical test will allow us to decide that our research provides evidence of that relationship.

Both power and Type II errors relate to the decision made in a statistical test in the case where a relationship actually does exist between the variables under study. Power is the probability of making a correct decision, of deciding that there is a relationship when a relationship actually exists. If there

FIGURE 13-5   Example of the Relationship between Type II Errors and Power

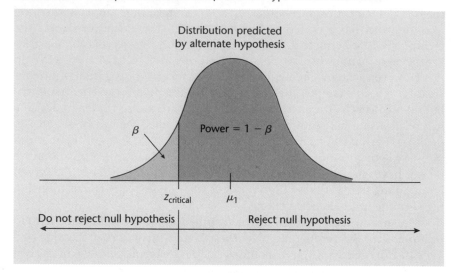

Distribution predicted
by alternate hypothesis

β

Power = $1 - \beta$

z_{critical} μ_1

Do not reject null hypothesis

Reject null hypothesis

actually is a relationship between the variables, the probability of an incorrect decision (of making a Type II error) is β, and consequently the probability of a correct decision (the power of the test) is $1 - \beta$.

This relationship between the probability of a Type II error and the power of a statistical test is shown in Figure 13-5. Even if there truly is a relationship between the variables being studied, it is always possible that our sample will not differ enough from the value predicted by the null hypothesis to reject it, which is a Type II error. If the probability of this occurring is 10 percent, then the probability that the sample will differ enough to reject the null hypothesis is 90 percent. Similarly, if the probability of not deciding a relationship exists when it really does (a Type II error) is 20 percent, then the probability of successfully deciding a relationship exists when it really does is 80 percent. Thus, the greater the probability of a Type II error, the smaller the power of the statistical test. Inversely, the lower the probability of a Type II error, the greater the power of the statistical test.

As we saw in the previous section, the probabilities of a Type I error, α, and Type II error, β, are complements. If we decrease α by selecting a more stringent level of significance, the size of β automatically increases. As we have just seen, there is also a complementary relationship between the probability of a Type II error, β, and the power of a statistical test. If the size of β increases, the power of the test decreases. Thus, selecting a more stringent level of significance, α, has the effect of both increasing the probability of a Type II error, β, and decreasing the power of the statistical test, $1 - \beta$.

Fortunately, there are other factors, in addition to the level of significance, α, that affect both the probability of a Type II error, β, and the power of the statistical test, $1 - \beta$. These factors are the size of the standard deviation in the sample being tested, the size of the sample, and the effect size. We will examine each of these factors in turn.

The Relationship between Standard Deviation and Power

The standard deviation of a distribution of scores is a measure of the variability among those scores. When students take a test in school, the students will not all receive exactly the same score. In an experiment, rats will not all run a maze in exactly the same amount of time. There will be some variability in the values of the scores in a distribution, some degree to which the scores will differ from each other and from the mean. The standard deviation measures this spread among the scores in a distribution. The larger the degree of spread among the scores, the larger the value of the standard deviation will be.

The statistical tests that we have examined thus far have all used the standard error as a measure of the spread in the sampling distributions predicted by the null and alternate hypotheses. The standard error of a sampling distribution is derived from the standard deviation of the distribution of scores. If all other things are equal, the larger the standard deviation, the larger the standard error will be. For example, assume we take samples of 25 scores from two distributions of scores, such that distribution A has a standard deviation of 20 and distribution B, a standard deviation of 10, half the size of the standard deviation of distribution A. When we calculate the standard error of the mean for both of these samples, we can see that the standard error of the sampling distribution drawn from distribution A is twice as large as the standard error of the sampling distribution drawn from distribution B:

$$s_{\bar{X}_A} = \frac{s_A}{\sqrt{n}} = \frac{20}{\sqrt{25}} = 4.0,$$

$$s_{\bar{X}_B} = \frac{s_B}{\sqrt{n}} = \frac{10}{\sqrt{25}} = 2.0.$$

Hence, the larger the spread among the scores in a distribution, the larger the spread in the sampling distribution drawn from that distribution of scores. Furthermore, the larger the spread in the sampling distribution, the greater will be the overlap between the distributions predicted by the null and alternate hypotheses in a statistical test. This can be seen in the two examples shown in Figure 13-6. The standard error of the distributions in example A is approximately twice the size of the standard error of the distributions in example B. As a consequence, there is much greater overlap between the two distributions in example A than between the two distributions in example B.

Note that except for the amount of spread in the distributions, all other factors are exactly the same between examples A and B. Because there is greater overlap between the distributions in example A than in example B, the

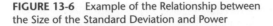

FIGURE 13-6 Example of the Relationship between the Size of the Standard Deviation and Power

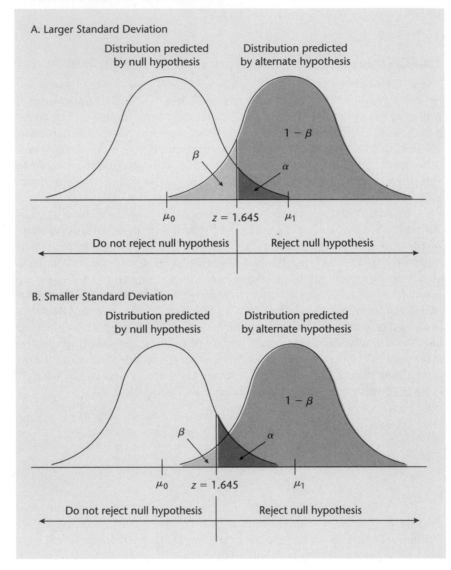

size of β, the probability of a Type II error, is larger in A than in B. Conversely, the power, $1 - \beta$, is smaller in A than in B. Thus, given that all other things are equal, the smaller the standard deviation, the lower the probability of a Type II error and the greater the power of the statistical test. Consequently, we can reduce the probability of a Type II error and increase the power of the statistical test we use simply by reducing the variability among the scores, thus reducing the standard deviation.

The Relationship between Sample Size and Power

The size of the standard error of a sampling distribution is determined in part by the size of the standard deviation of the distribution of scores from which the sample was drawn. In addition, the size of the standard error is determined by the sample size, the number of subjects in the sample. For any given standard deviation, the larger the sample size, the smaller the standard error.

The relationship between sample size and the size of the standard error can be seen in Table 13-3, which lists the standard error of the mean for samples drawn from the population of SAT scores. To keep the computations simple, all of the sample sizes selected in Table 13-3 have integer square roots. Recall that theoretically SAT scores have a mean, μ, of 500 and a standard deviation, σ, of 100.

Table 13-3 shows that as the sample size increases, the standard error decreases. Compared to the original standard deviation of 100, there is a 75 percent reduction in the variability measured by the standard error with a sample size of 16 and a 90 percent reduction with a sample size of 100. The reduction in variability is larger when a small sample size is increased than when a large sample size is increased. We achieve an 80 percent reduction in variability compared to the original standard deviation, with a sample size of 25. However, if we increase that sample size fourfold, to 100, we achieve only an additional 10 percent reduction in variability.

TABLE 13-3   Effect of Sample Size on the Standard Error of the Mean of Samples Drawn from the Population of SAT Scores, $\sigma = 100$

Sample Size	$\sigma_{\bar{x}}$	Percent Reduction in Variability
1	100.0	0
4	50.0	50
9	33.0	67
16	25.0	75
25	20.0	80
36	16.7	83.3
49	14.3	85.7
64	12.5	87.5
81	11.1	88.8
100	10.0	90.0

Of course, any reduction in the variability measured by the standard error has the effect of reducing the overlap between the distributions predicted by the null and alternate hypotheses of a statistical test. Thus the probability of a Type II error is reduced, and the power of the test is increased. As we have seen, we can reduce the size of the standard error both by reducing the variability in the original distribution of scores, thus reducing the size of the standard deviation, and by increasing the sample size.

The Relationship between Effect Size and Power

The final factor that affects the power of a statistical test is the distance between the parameter predicted by the null hypothesis and the true value of that parameter in the population under study. In the last chapter, we examined Jorge Jiminez's research on the Machiavellian tendencies of psychology majors. Recall that for the general population of college students, the mean Machiavellian score was 50. The null hypothesis of Jorge's study asserted that the mean for the population of psychology majors was no different from the mean for the general population of college students. We do not know what the true mean for the population of psychology majors actually is, but assuming that the alternate hypothesis is really true, the farther that true mean is from 50, the more powerful the statistical test is.

Effect size is a measure of the effect that one variable has on another variable. In a statistical test, given that the alternate hypothesis is true, that there is a relationship between two variables, the greater effect of one of those variables on the other, the more powerful the statistical test is.

For the parameter under consideration (i.e., either the population mean or population proportion), the difference between the value predicted by the null hypothesis and the true value of that parameter is called the **effect size**. In Jorge's study, this difference would be larger if the true mean Machiavellian score for psychology majors were 60 than if it were 55. The farther the true mean Machiavellian score is from 50, the value predicted by the null hypothesis, the greater the effect size. In essence, the effect size is a measure of the effect that the type of college major has on the students' Machiavellian score.

The relationship between effect size and power can be seen in the hypothetical examples shown in Figure 13-7. The difference between the true value of the population mean and the value predicted by the null hypothesis is greater in example B than in example A. The true value of the population mean in example A is fairly close to the value predicted by the null hypothesis compared to example B. As a consequence, there is a great deal of overlap between the two distributions in example A. The probability of a Type II error, β, is well over 50 percent, and consequently, the power of the statistical test, $1 - \beta$, is less than 50 percent in example A.

There is a comparatively greater distance between the true value of the population mean and the value predicted by the null hypothesis in example B. Thus, the effect size is greater in example B than in example A. Because the effect size is greater in example B, there is considerably less overlap between the two distributions in example B than example A. Notice that

FIGURE 13-7 Example of the Relationship between the Effect Size and Power

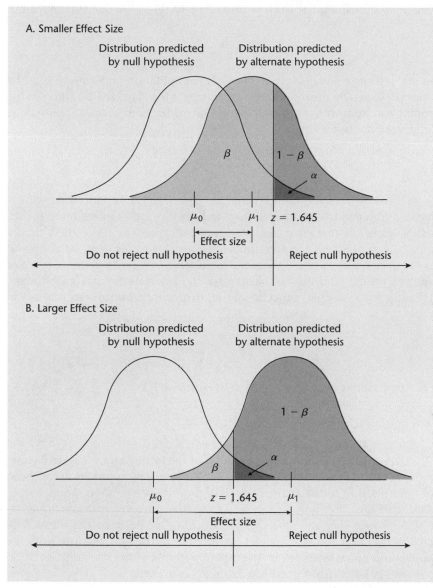

the probability of a Type II error is much less in example B than in example A and also that the power of the test is much greater in B than in A. Thus, given that all other things are equal, the greater the effect size, the smaller the probability of a Type II error and the greater the power of the statistical test.

Jacob Cohen[1] has devised a statistic to measure effect size. For a one-sample bidirectional test of the value of a population mean, this statistic is

$$d = \frac{|\mu_1 - \mu_0|}{\sigma},$$

where μ_1 is the true value of the mean of the population under study, μ_0 is the value predicted by the null hypothesis, and σ is the standard deviation of the population from which the sample was drawn. The formula for a one-sample unidirectional test is similar:

$$d = \frac{\mu_1 - \mu_0}{\sigma}.$$

Of course, in hypothesis testing, we do not know the true value of the mean of the population under study, and thus we cannot determine the actual value of the true effect size. However, we can estimate the effect size by using the sample mean as an estimate of the value of the mean of the population under study. If the value of the population standard deviation, σ, is not known, we can also use the sample standard deviation, s, as an estimate. Thus, for a one-sample bidirectional test, the formula for this estimate of the effect size is

$$\text{est. } d = \frac{|\overline{X} - \mu_0|}{s}.$$

For a one-sample unidirectional test, the formula is

$$\text{est. } d = \frac{\overline{X} - \mu_0}{s}.$$

This measure of effect size is a variant of the formula for a standard score, z. Recall that a standard score compares the distance of a score from the mean of a distribution to the standard deviation of the distribution. Thus, a standard score measures how far a score is from the mean to a measure of the average distance that the scores in the distribution lie from the mean. The measure of effect size, d, compares the distance of the sample mean from the population mean predicted by the null hypothesis to the standard deviation of the population from which the sample was drawn.

We can calculate the effect size for the mean Machiavellian score of the population of psychology measures, using the mean of the sample tested by Jorge Jiminez. Recall that Jorge's sample of psychology majors had a mean Machiavellian score of 58, that the null hypothesis predicted that the population mean for psychology majors was 50, the same as the mean for the general population of college students, and that the standard deviation of the distribution of Machiavellian test scores for that general population was 12. These are the values we need to calculate an estimate of the effect size:

$$\text{est. } d = \frac{\overline{X} - \mu_0}{s} = \frac{58 - 50}{12} = 0.67.$$

Thus, we can estimate that the effect size for Jorge's study is 0.67, assuming that the alternate hypothesis is true and there actually is a relationship between the type of college major and Machiavellianism. This means that the difference between the sample mean in Jorge's study and the mean predicted by the null hypothesis is two-thirds the average distance of scores from the mean in the distribution of Machiavellian test scores.

How large an effect size is 0.67? According to Cohen, a large effect size is in the range of 0.8. A difference of this size is easily recognized, such as the mean difference in the IQs of college freshmen and college faculty. A medium effect size is in the range of 0.5. According to Cohen, an example of a medium effect size is the difference in mean height of fourteen- and eighteen-year-old girls. Finally, a small effect size is in the range of 0.2, a difference that is not readily apparent to most people. On most standardized math tests, the effect size for difference between the mean score achieved by males and females is in the range of 0.1. Thus, on the SAT math test, with a theoretical standard deviation of 100, the mean difference between boys' and girls' scores are in the range of 10 points. This difference is certainly small, if not almost trivial.

Before leaving this topic, one caveat needs emphasis. In order to determine the exact value of β, the probability of a Type II error, and $1 - \beta$, the power of a statistical test, we need to know the exact value of the mean of the population under consideration, assuming that the alternate hypothesis is true. However, unless we can measure every member of a population, we can never know the exact value of a population mean. Because we seldom can measure all of the members of a population, rarely will we know the exact value of the power of a statistical test.

Even if we do not exactly know the power of a test, we do know that power will be greater with decreases in the standard deviation, increases in the sample size, and increases in the effect size. Remember that power is the probability that as a result of a statistical test, we will decide that there is a relationship between the variables being studied when that relationship really exists. Even if an effect size is very small, a statistical test may be powerful enough to indicate a significant relationship. This brings us to the issue of whether a significant difference is always meaningful.

Significant Differences and Meaningful Differences

As we have seen, the term *significant difference* means that the difference between the sample statistic and the value predicted by the null hypothesis was large enough that the probability of that difference occurring is less than α, the level of significance selected. Thus, *significant* simply indicates that the null hypothesis was rejected. A powerful statistical test is one for which there is a high probability of finding a significant result (i.e., of rejecting the null hypothesis) when there actually is a relationship between the variables under study. Stated in other terms, a powerful statistical test is one that gives us a high probability of deciding that there is a relationship between the variables under study when that relationship actually exists.

However, saying that a difference is significant is not the same thing as saying that the difference is meaningful. We can obtain a significant result from a statistical test when the relationship is very weak or even trivial. As we have seen, we can increase the power of a statistical test by reducing the variability among the scores and by simply increasing the sample size. If we increase the sample size enough, we can increase the power of a statistical test so that even a trivial relationship between variables will generate a significant test result. Thus, a significant result indicates only that there is evidence that the relationship between variables actually exists. However, the fact that the result is significant says nothing about how strong or weak that relationship is.

As we saw, the mean standardized math test scores of males and females differs by only approximately one-tenth of a standard deviation. We could give samples of students a standardized math test and if the sample size was large enough, we might conduct a statistical test that would allow us to conclude that this difference is significant. While a difference of 0.1 standard deviations may be significant (i.e., may result in rejecting the null hypothesis), is that difference meaningful? Or is the difference trivial, of little value?

Whether a significant difference is also meaningful is not a question that can be answered with statistics. It is a question of interpretation, a value judgment. Certainly some researchers have seen the difference between male and female standardized math scores as very meaningful, while other researchers see that difference as trivial and unimportant. Cohen's measure of effect size, *d,* gives us a means of evaluating the strength of the relationship between the variables being studied, of differentiating between small and large effects, which is one method of judging the meaningfulness of a relationship between variables. The important thing to remember here is that a significant result of a statistical test is only an indication that there is some degree of relationship between the variables being studied, but that significance by itself tells us nothing about how strong or meaningful that relationship is.

Testing Hypotheses about a Population

In this and the previous chapter, we have examined ways to test hypotheses using a single sample. All one-sample parametric tests are designed to measure whether there is a relationship between two variables by determining whether a sample statistic differs significantly from some known value. For example, Jorge Jiminez was trying to measure whether there is a relationship between the type of college major and Machiavellianism by testing whether the mean Machiavellian score of his sample of psychology majors differed significantly from 50, the mean score of the general population of college students. In effect, Jorge is using the sample mean as an estimate of the mean Machiavellian score of the entire population of psychology majors to assess whether there is evidence to claim that the population mean of psychology majors differs significantly from the mean of the general population of college students.

One question is why we need to use a sample as an estimate of the population mean. If what Jorge wants to know is the mean Machiavellian score of the population of psychology majors, why not just find that value? The difficulty is that it is seldom feasible or even possible to measure every member of a population. Because we generally cannot test the entire population, we must rely on samples to obtain an estimate of the population parameter in which we are interested.

Another question is since the mean of the sample is an estimate of the population mean, why do we have to conduct a statistical test? Why can't we just assume that the population mean will be the same as the sample mean? Why can't we assume that the mean Machiavellian score for the population of psychology majors is 58, the same as the mean for Jorge's sample? Why can't we assume that the mean alcoholic content of Guinness Extra Stout available in the pubs near State University is 6.09 percent, the same as Jill's sample? The reason is that when we draw samples from a population, the samples will not all have the same mean. Because the scores in a population vary, the means of samples of those scores will also vary. Generally, the mean of a sample will not have exactly the same value as the mean of the population from which the sample was drawn.

Certainly, it is possible that the mean Machiavellian score for the entire population of psychology majors is 58. It is entirely possible to draw a sample with a mean of 58 from a population whose mean is 58. However, it is also possible that Jorge's sample came from a population with a mean of 57, or 56, or even 50. That is the difficulty. The mean Machiavellian score of the general population of college students is 50, and Jorge wants to find evidence that the mean of the population of psychology majors is not the same value. Since it is possible to draw a sample with a mean of 58 from a population with a mean of 50, Jorge cannot simply claim that his sample shows that the mean for the population of psychology majors is not 50, the same as the mean for the general population of college students. He must conduct a statistical test to show that the probability of his sample coming from a population with a mean of 50 is so small that it is legitimate to conclude that the mean score for the population of psychology majors is not 50, that his sample provides evidence that there really is a relationship between the type of college major and Machiavellianism.

In all of these one-sample parametric tests, we have compared a sample statistic (a sample mean or a sample proportion) to a known value. Jorge knew that the mean Machiavellian score of the general population of psychology majors was 50. Jill Jones knew that the standard set by the Guinness brewery for the alcoholic content of Guinness Extra Stout was 6 percent. There are many circumstances in conducting research in which we do not have a known value against which to compare a sample statistic. For instance, Jorge might want to compare the Machiavellianism of psychology majors and business majors but not know the mean score of either population. There are parametric tests that enable us to compare two samples, drawn from different populations. These two-sample parametric tests are the subject of the next chapter.

CHECKING YOUR ANSWERS

1. Some students have difficulty trying to decide when to use the *z* test and when to use the *t* test. In order to use *z*, you must know the value of the population standard deviation, σ. If you don't know that value, you must use the *t* test. In addition, in order to use the *z* test, either the population from which the sample of scores was drawn must be normally distributed or the sample size must be at least 20. If neither of these conditions is met, then you must use the *t* test.

2. When calculating the standard deviation for a *t* test, remember that it is a sample statistic and that you must divide by $n - 1$ in the denominator, rather than just by *n*. However, when converting the standard deviation to the standard error, you divide the standard deviation by the square root of *n*.

3. One of the greatest difficulties that students have in solving problems with the *z* and *t* tests is in constructing the null and alternate hypotheses. Look in the problem for the sentence(s) that give the researcher's hypothesis. If the researcher's hypothesis contains words like "greater," "larger," "higher," "bigger," the alternate hypothesis is that the population parameter (μ or *p*) will be more than the specified value and the alternate hypothesis will contain the symbol ">." On the other hand, if the researcher's hypothesis contains words like "smaller," "lower," "shorter," the alternate hypothesis is that the population parameter (μ or *p*) will be less than the specified value, and the alternate hypothesis will contain the symbol "<." Finally, if the researcher's hypothesis does not contain any unidirectional terms, then the alternate hypothesis is simply that the population parameter (μ or *p*) will not be equal to the specified value and the alternate hypothesis will contain the symbol "$\neq$."

4. Be careful which table you use in Appendix A. For the *z* test, use Appendix A-1. For the *t* test, use Appendix A-3.

5. Students sometimes have difficulty understanding why the value of *p* must be equal to or less than the value of α in order to reject the null hypothesis. In a statistical test, *p* is the probability that the sample statistic under consideration came from the population predicted by the null hypothesis. In order to reject the null hypothesis, the logic of hypothesis testing requires that that probability be α or less, where α is the selected level of significance. If *p* is greater than α, then the probability that the null hypothesis is true is too great to reject the null hypothesis.

$\sum$ S U M M A R Y

▶ Statistical tests for one sample are used to test hypotheses about whether a population parameter, such as the mean or a proportion, differs significantly from a specified value.

▶ One-sample parametric tests use a sample to test an inference about a population parameter. The inference can be unidirectional (testing whether a population parameter is greater than a specified value or testing whether a parameter is less than a specified value) or bidirectional (testing whether a population parameter is simply not a specified value).

▶ The *t* test for a sample mean is designed to test whether a population mean is significantly different from a specified value. The *z* and *t* tests for a sample mean are equivalent, the *z* test being used when the population standard deviation, σ, is known and the *t* test, when σ is not known. In the *t* test for a sample mean, the sample standard deviation, *s*, is used as an estimate of the population standard deviation, σ.

▶ The distribution of the *t* statistic is flatter and more spread out than the normal distribution, used in the *z* test for a sample mean. Consequently, there are a greater number of cases in the tail(s) of the *t* distribution, above a given value of *t*, than there are above the corresponding value of *z* in the normal distribution, so that the critical value of *t* for a given significance level is larger than the equivalent critical value of *z*.

▶ As sample size increases, the *t* distribution becomes increasingly normal in shape, and thus the critical value of *t* for a given significance level approaches the corollary critical value of *z* .

▶ In the table of critical values of *t*, the critical values are listed by degrees of freedom. The degrees of freedom are the number of scores in a sample that are free to vary within certain restrictions. For the *t* test of a sample mean, the degrees of freedom are the sample size, *n*, minus 1.

▶ The *z* test for a sample proportion is designed to test whether a population proportion is significantly different from a specified value.

▶ The steps for conducting either the *t* test for a sample mean or the *z* test for a sample proportion are the same as the steps for conducting the *z* test for a sample mean: (i) Verify that the assumptions of the test are met. (ii) Write the null and alternate hypotheses. (iii) Decide the level of significance, α. (iv) Identify the critical value(s) of the statistic. (v) Indicate the rejection region on a graph of the sampling distribution predicted by the null hypothesis. (vi) Calculate the value of the statistic from the sample of scores. (vii) On the basis of the value of that statistic, decide whether or not to reject the null hypothesis.

▶ The power of a statistical test is the probability that the result of a statistical test will be to decide that there is a relationship between the variables under study when that relationship actually exists. Power is expressed as $1 - \beta$, and is the complement of the probability of a Type II error, β.

▶ The power of a statistical test can be increased by selecting a less stringent level of significance, α, by reducing the variability among the population of scores from which the sample is drawn and by increasing the sample size. The power of a statistical test is also directly related to the effect size.

▶ Effect size is the difference between the true value of the population parameter under consideration and the value of that parameter predicted by the null hypothesis, relative to the standard deviation of the population from which the sample being tested was drawn. Effect size is a measure of the strength of the relationship between the variables under study.

EXERCISES

Conceptual Exercises

1. Explain what is meant by the following terms:

   degrees of freedom

   effect size

2. Identify the assumptions of a *t* test for a sample mean. For what types of data may the test be used? What are the consequences if any of the assumptions are violated?

3. Identify the assumptions of a *z* test for a sample proportion. For what types of data may the test be used? What are the consequences if any of the assumptions are violated?

4. Compare the *z* test for a sample mean and the *t* test for a sample mean. How are they the same? How are they different?

5. Explain what is meant by the power of a statistical test. Why is power the complement of the probability of a Type II error?

6. Explain why selecting a less stringent significance level increases the power of a statistical test, assuming that all other things are equal.

7. Explain why decreasing the variability in the population from which the sample being tested is drawn increases the power of a statistical test, assuming that all other things are equal.

8. Explain why increasing the sample size increases the power of a statistical test, assuming that all other things are equal.

9. Explain why the power of a statistical test is related to the effect size of the relationship between the variables under study.

Computational Exercises

10. Identify the critical values of *t* for the following tests:
    A. A study with $H_1: t \neq 0$, $\alpha = .05$, and $n = 15$.
    B. A study with $H_1: t < 0$, $\alpha = .01$, and $n = 10$.
    C. A study with $H_1: t > 0$, $\alpha = .05$, and $n = 23$.
    D. A study with $H_1: t \neq 0$, $\alpha = .01$, and $n = 40$.

11. Identify the critical values of z_p for the following tests:
    A. A study with $H_1: z_p \neq 0.50$ and $\alpha = .05$.
    B. A study with $H_1: z_p < 0.50$ and $\alpha = .01$.

   C. A study with H_1: $z_P > 0.50$ and $\alpha = .05$.

   D. A study with H_1: $z_P \neq 0.50$ and $\alpha = .01$.

12. The Psychology Department at State University gives a standardized exam to their students in general psychology at the end of the term. Across all faculty, the mean score was 71 percent correct. Julius was serving as a teaching assistant for a section of general psychology and thought that his section would score higher on the test than students in all the other sections. His section of general psychology, consisting of 30 students, scored a mean of 79 percent, with a standard deviation of 12 percent.

   A. Using the *t* test for a sample mean, test Julius's hypothesis that his section of general psychology students will perform better on the standardized test than the other professors' students, with $\alpha = .05$.

   B. What does the result of this statistical test show about Julius's belief?

13. Among the normal population, 80 percent are right-eye dominant. Jebediah tested 30 people with IQs over 130 for eye dominance and found that 40 percent of the sample were left-eye dominant.

   A. Using the *z* test for a sample proportion, test Jebediah's hypothesis that intellectually gifted people are more likely to be left-eye dominant, with $\alpha = .05$.

   B. What does the result of this statistical test show about the proportion of left-eye dominant people in the gifted population?

14. Jerry tested toddlers' preferences for a playmate by allowing one child to roam freely in a room in which there were already two other children, one boy and one girl. Jerry recorded only the amount of time that the test child played with just one of the other children, recording whether the chosen playmate was the same sex or the opposite sex as the test child. If toddlers had no preference, then they should choose the same-sex playmate 50 percent of the time and the opposite sex playmate 50 percent of the time. Jerry observed 20 children and found that they played with the same-sex playmate 60 percent of the time. Test Jerry's hypothesis that toddlers will exhibit a sex bias in their choice of playmates.

   A. What is the appropriate statistical test to conduct for this study? Why?

   B. Conduct that statistical test on the results above, with $\alpha = .05$.

   C. What does the result of this test show about the possible sex bias in toddlers' playmate preferences?

15. The Office of Admissions at State University developed a study skills program as part of the freshman orientation. At the end of the first semester, the mean GPA of incoming freshman without the study skills program was 2.83. Listed below are the first-term GPAs of twenty new freshmen who completed the study skills course. Test the hypothesis that the course improved freshmen's first-term GPAs.

| 2.41 | 2.70 | 2.74 | 2.77 | 2.79 | 2.80 | 2.83 | 2.87 | 2.89 | 2.90 |
| 2.92 | 2.95 | 2.99 | 3.01 | 3.06 | 3.10 | 3.14 | 3.22 | 3.29 | 3.56 |

   A. What is the appropriate statistical test to conduct for this study? Why?

   B. Conduct that statistical test on the results above, with $\alpha = .01$.

   C. What does the result of this test show about the effect of the study skills program on freshmen's GPAs at State University?

16. The mean GPA of all students at State University is 2.94. Janice tested a sample of 15 students who were all firstborn in their families and found that their mean GPA was

3.12, with a standard deviation of 0.25. Test the hypothesis that firstborn children have a mean GPA higher than the mean for the general population of students at State University.

A. What is the appropriate statistical test to conduct for this study? Why?

B. Conduct that statistical test on the results above, with $\alpha = .05$.

C. What does the result of this test show about the relationship between birth order and GPA among the students at State University?

17. At State University, 20 percent of students graduate with honors. Jasmine found that among a sample of 25 students who were last born children in their families, 15 percent graduated with honors. Test the hypothesis that lastborn children are less likely to graduate with honors than the general population of students graduating at State University.

A. What is the appropriate statistical test to conduct for this study? Why?

B. Conduct that statistical test on the results above, with $\alpha = .05$.

C. What does the result of this test show about the relationship between birth order and graduating with honors among the students at State University?

_E N D N O T E_

1. Jacob Cohen was the first to use the term *effect size* to identify this difference. Cohen's work on the relationship between effect size and power is extensive. See, for example, Jacob Cohen, *Statistical power analysis for the behavioral sciences*, (2d ed.; Hillsdale, NJ: Lawrence Erlbaum Associates, 1988).

Parametric Tests for Two Samples

14

Between-Subjects and Within-Subjects Tests

The *t* Test for a Difference between Means: A Between-Subjects Test

The Distribution of Differences between Two Sample Means when σ Is Known

A Pooled Estimate of the Standard Deviation of a Population when σ Is Not Known

STEP-BY-STEP PROCEDURE 14-1: Calculating the Pooled Standard Deviation of Two Samples

Conducting the *t* Test for a Difference between Means

STEP-BY-STEP PROCEDURE 14-2: Conducting the t Test for a Difference between Means

The *t* Test for a Mean Difference: A Within-Subjects Test

The Distribution of a Mean Difference

Conducting the *t* Test for a Mean Difference

STEP-BY-STEP PROCEDURE 14-3: Conducting the t Test for a Mean Difference

A Parametric Test of the Strength of a Relationship: Pearson's Product-Moment Correlation

The Sampling Distribution of *r*

Testing the Significance of Pearson's Product-Moment Correlation

STEP-BY-STEP PROCEDURE 14-4: Conducting a Test of the Strength of Pearson's Product-Moment Correlation

A Word on Significant Correlations and Meaningful Correlations

Parametric Tests Revisited

CHECKING YOUR ANSWERS

SUMMARY

EXERCISES

Conceptual Exercises

Computational Exercises

▶ In Chapter 13, we examined statistical tests that can be used on samples drawn from one population. In all of these tests, a characteristic of population is estimated, based on a single statistic calculated on a sample drawn from that population. However, there are research questions that these tests cannot answer. For example, consider the special courses and books that claim to improve students' Graduate Record Exam (GRE) scores. The GRE is a standardized test that is required for application to many graduate programs in the Arts and Sciences. There are many special courses and books on the market that students take to help improve their GRE scores. We could conduct a study to test whether these courses and books actually do help improve GRE scores.

Suppose that a sample of 25 students from State University took a course to improve their GRE math scores and, after the course, received a mean GRE math score of 575. Theoretically, the population mean of GRE math scores is 500, with a standard deviation of 100. Using the *z* test for a sample mean, the sample's mean is significantly greater than the population mean of 500, $p < .05$. Does this show that the course improved the students' GRE scores? No, it doesn't. It is possible that the 25 students in the sample would have scored higher than average on the GRE math test, even without the special course. It is possible that students at State University generally do better than average on the GRE math test. By using the *z* test for a sample mean, we have no way of knowing whether these 25 students did better than average because of the special course or simply because they come from a population of students who do very well on the GRE.

Rather than compare one sample mean to the mean of the general population, we could compare two samples of students from State University, one sample who took the special course and one sample who did not. To ensure that there is no bias in the way that the samples are selected, we would randomly assign the students to one of these two samples. Then, if there is a significant difference between these two samples, it could not be due to the college the students attended, because they all were students at the same school. In order to test this difference, we need a statistical test that will compare two sample means. The *z* test for a sample mean cannot help us because that test compares one sample mean to a known population mean, and we have two sample means. Thus, we need a test that will allow us to compare two samples, which is the subject of this chapter and the next.

In this chapter, we examine three parametric tests that can be used with two samples of scores. All of these tests are parametric tests, because they are used to make inferences about the parameters of the populations from which the samples are drawn. We begin by examining two parametric tests that compare the means of two samples, the *t* test for the difference between sample means, and the *t* test for a mean difference. To understand the distinction between these tests, we need first to examine the concepts of between-subjects and within-subjects tests.

Between-Subjects and Within-Subjects Tests

The first two parametric tests we examine in this chapter assess whether a given characteristic (or parameter) differs between two populations, based on the difference between two samples, one drawn from each population. There are two major categories of these statistical tests. One category is **between-subjects tests**, in which the subjects in one sample are unrelated to the subjects in the other sample. If one sample consists of ten people and the other sample consists of ten different, unrelated people, the statistical test will be between-subjects. In a between-subjects test, each subject gives one score. In some statistics books, between-subjects samples are also called independent samples.

The other category is **within-subjects tests**, in which there is one group of subjects, each of whom is tested twice. In a within-subjects test in which one group of subjects is tested, each subject contributes two scores, one for each sample. "Before and after" tests are an example of within-subjects tests. Another example is when each subject is tested in two different conditions, such as taking a test with time limits and then without time limits. A special type of within-subjects test is a test in which two different samples of subjects are tested, but the subjects in the two samples are related in some way. For example, if one group consisted of husbands and the other group, their wives, we could consider these subjects one group of related pairs. Other examples are testing pairs of twins and testing college dorm roommates. Within-subjects tests are also called repeated measures tests, paired scores tests, dependent samples tests, and correlated samples tests. Basically, if you can pair the scores, one from each sample, in some meaningful way, the scores are within subjects, and if you cannot, the scores are between subjects.

Using a within-subjects experimental design has some advantages over a between-subjects design. The principal statistical advantage in using a within-subjects design is that the variability among the scores may be reduced. Recall that a reduction in the standard deviation can increase the power of the statistical test, so that we are more likely to find a significant difference when there truly is a relationship between the variables under study. By using the same (or related) subjects in the two samples, we reduce the individual

In a **between-subjects test,** two different, unrelated samples of subjects are tested, each subject contributing one score. The result is two sets of scores from two different samples of subjects.

In a **within-subjects test,** one sample of subjects is tested, each subject contributing two scores. A special case of within-subjects test is when one sample of pairs of subjects is tested, where the pairs are related in some fashion. Each person in the pair contributes one score, and the scores are analyzed as a pair in the statistical test. The result is two sets of scores from one sample of subjects or pairs of subjects.

variation attributable to using different subjects in the two samples. This can be an advantage in increasing the probability of finding a significant difference when one truly exists.

While a within-subjects test has advantages, there are disadvantages as well. For instance, there are difficulties in designing an experiment using a within-subjects sample. For instance, suppose we test the same sample of students twice, first with a timed test and then with an untimed test. If the students performed better on the untimed test, we might conclude that the improvement was due to the lack of time pressure. However, the improvement could simply be due to the fact that the students took the untimed test second, after they had gained practice and experience when they first took the test timed. There are ways to control for these confounding effects, which are examined at length in courses on research design. These techniques, however, add to the complexity of the experiment.

In the sections that follow, we first examine a between-subjects parametric test, the *t* test, for a difference between sample means. We then examine a within-subjects parametric test, the *t* test for a mean difference.

The *t* Test for a Difference between Means: A Between-Subjects Test

The Distribution of Differences between Two Sample Means when σ Is Known

In Chapter 11, we examined the concept of a distribution of sample means. If we drew a large number of samples, all the same size, from a population of scores, the result would be a distribution of sample means. Now, we are considering a distribution of differences between two sample means. In order to understand this concept, let's suppose we have a population of scores that consists of equal numbers of the values, 1, 2, and 3. Now suppose that we draw samples of two scores from this distribution. Table 14-1 shows the distribution of sample means that we could draw from this population. This sampling distribution is similar to the ones we constructed in Chapter 11.

Now suppose that instead of drawing one sample at a time, we draw two samples at a time. The first sample mean we draw will be labeled $\overline{X}_1$, and the second sample mean drawn will be $\overline{X}_2$. For each pair of samples that we draw, we will find the difference between the two means, $(\overline{X}_1 - \overline{X}_2)$. Suppose that we repeat this process 1,000 times. Sometimes the two means will have the same value, and so the difference between them, $(\overline{X}_1 - \overline{X}_2)$,

TABLE 14-1 Distribution of Sample Means, with $n = 2$, Drawn from a Population with Three Score Values, 1, 2, and 3

$\overline{X}$	Frequency
3.0	.11
2.5	.22
2.0	.34
1.5	.22
1.0	.11

will be 0. Some pairs will have a difference of 0.5; other pairs will have a difference of −0.5. Some pairs will have a difference of ±1; some, a difference of ±1.5. The largest difference between two means will be ±2.0, the difference between the highest score value, 3, and the lowest score value, 1.

If we repeat the process of drawing two samples and finding the difference between them 1,000 times, we will have a set of 1,000 differences between two sample means. These 1,000 values are a distribution of differences between two sample means. This distribution is shown in Table 14-2 and pictured graphically in Figure 14-1. Notice that the center of the distribution of differences between means shown in Figure 14-1 is at 0 and that the distribution is balanced. Notice also that the distribution is roughly normal in shape. If we used a sample size larger than 2, the distribution would be even closer to normal in shape.

We can use the information in Table 14-2 to find the probability of drawing two samples with a given difference between their means. For example, there is a 2 percent chance of drawing two sample means with a difference of ±2.0. There is a 10 percent chance of drawing two sample means with a difference of ±1.5.

The sampling distribution shown in Figure 14-1 is an empirical sampling distribution, that is, the distribution was constructed by actually drawing

TABLE 14-2 Distribution of Differences between Two Sample Means Drawn from a Population

$\bar{X}_1 - \bar{X}_2$	Relative Frequency
2.0	.01
1.5	.05
1.0	.12
0.5	.20
0.0	.24
−0.5	.20
−1.0	.12
−1.5	.05
−2.0	.01

FIGURE 14-1 Distribution of Differences between Two Sample Means Drawn from a Population

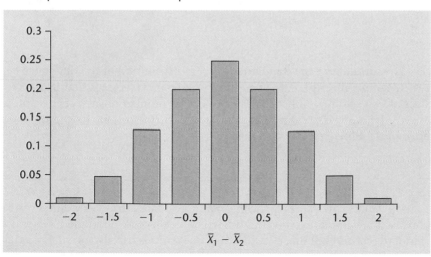

samples. However, constructing distributions of differences between means empirically for most populations would take thousands of hours because most populations in the real world contain more than three values and most samples that we draw will have more than two scores per sample.

The alternative to constructing a sampling distribution empirically is to construct it theoretically. We can do this if we know three things. First, we need to know the shape of the distribution so that we know which probability table is appropriate. If the assumptions of the test are met, distributions of differences between means are normally distributed. So, we can use the normal distribution table, Appendix A-1, if we know the population standard deviation. If that value is not known, then we use the *t* table in Appendix A-3. The other two things that we need to know are the mean and standard deviation of the distribution of differences between means.

If the two samples are drawn from the same population, then the mean of a distribution of differences between those sample means is always 0. Consider the possible differences that could occur between two sample means from the same population. Sometimes the sample means will have the same value, and so the difference is 0. Sometimes the first sample mean will be larger, and the difference will be positive. An equal number of times, the second sample mean will be larger, and the difference will be negative. Figure 14-1 shows that the positive differences balance out the negative differences, and so the balance point of the distribution of differences will be 0:

$$\mu_{\bar{X}_1 - \bar{X}_2} = 0.$$

Recall that the standard error of a distribution of sample means is based on the standard deviation of the population from which the samples were drawn. When the population standard deviation, σ, is known, we can write the formula for the standard error of the mean in two ways, as shown below:

$$\sigma_{\bar{X}} = \frac{\sigma}{\sqrt{n}} = \sigma\sqrt{\frac{1}{n}}.$$

The formula for the standard error of a distribution of the difference between sample means is similar to the formula above, except that it uses the sizes of two samples, rather than just one. The number of subjects in sample 1 is n_1; the number of subjects in sample 2 is n_2. The formula for the standard error of the difference between means is shown below:

$$\sigma_{\bar{X}_1 - \bar{X}_2} = \sigma\sqrt{\frac{1}{n_1} + \frac{1}{n_2}}.$$

We can use the values of the mean and standard error of the difference to construct a formula to convert a difference between two sample means to a standard score. Recall that a standard score measures the distance that a value lies from the center of a distribution. In this case, the value is the difference between two sample means, $(\overline{X}_1 - \overline{X}_2)$. The center of the distribution is the difference between the means of the two populations from which the samples were drawn, $(\mu_1 - \mu_2)$:

$$z_{\overline{X}_1 - \overline{X}_2} = \frac{(\overline{X}_1 - \overline{X}_2) - (\mu_1 - \mu_2)}{\sigma_{\overline{X}_1 - \overline{X}_2}}.$$

The null hypothesis predicts that there is no difference between the populations from which the samples are drawn. If the two population means are the same, then the difference between them will be zero: $(\mu_1 - \mu_2) = 0$. We can use this fact to simplify the formula:

$$z_{\overline{X}_1 - \overline{X}_2} = \frac{(\overline{X}_1 - \overline{X}_2) - 0}{\sigma_{\overline{X}_1 - \overline{X}_2}} = \frac{\overline{X}_1 - \overline{X}_2}{\sigma_{\overline{X}_1 - \overline{X}_2}}.$$

Finally, we can insert the formula for the standard error of the difference between means:

$$z_{\overline{X}_1 - \overline{X}_2} = \frac{\overline{X}_1 - \overline{X}_2}{\sigma_{\overline{X}_1 - \overline{X}_2}} = \frac{\overline{X}_1 - \overline{X}_2}{\sigma\sqrt{\dfrac{1}{n_1} + \dfrac{1}{n_2}}}.$$

This formula is based on the assumption that the value of the population standard deviation, σ, is known. If we know the value of σ, we can use this formula to conduct the z test for a difference between sample means. However, when conducting psychological research, we generally do not know the value of σ. In these cases, we need to use an estimate of σ, which we examine in the next section.

A Pooled Estimate of the Standard Deviation of a Population when σ Is Not Known

The t test for a difference between means is used when the value of the population standard deviation is not known. In order to conduct the t test for a difference between means, we need to convert the formula for the comparable z test to include the sample standard deviation, rather than the population standard deviation. As seen in the previous section, the formula for the z test for a difference between means is

$$z_{X_1 - \overline{X}_2} = \frac{\overline{X}_1 - \overline{X}_2}{\sigma\sqrt{\dfrac{1}{n_1} + \dfrac{1}{n_2}}}.$$

The null hypothesis for both the z and t tests assumes that both samples are drawn from the same population. There is only one population standard deviation, σ, and so the formula for z includes only one value for σ. However, in the *t* test, we are using the sample standard deviation, *s*, as an estimate for σ. As we have two samples, we will have two sample standard deviations, s_1 and s_2.

Both sample standard deviations, s_1 and s_2, are estimates of the standard deviation of the population. Rather than just use one of these sample standard deviations as the estimate of σ, we can obtain a more stable estimate by combining the two sample standard deviations into one measure, which is called the **pooled standard deviation.**

We cannot simply add the values of the two sample standard deviations together to obtain a pooled value because the result would not actually be an estimate of the standard deviation of the population. To understand why adding the sample standard deviations together does not work, consider a population of five scores: 1, 2, 3, 4, and 5. The standard deviation of this population is 1.4. Now suppose that we draw two samples from the population, each with three scores. The first sample consists of the scores 1, 2, and 4 and has a standard deviation of 1.53. The second sample consists of the scores 3, 4, and 5 and has a standard deviation of 1.00:

A **pooled standard deviation** is a combination of the standard deviations from two or more samples, hypothetically all drawn from the population, in order to provide a more stable estimate of the standard deviation of that population.

$$s_1 = \sqrt{\frac{\Sigma(X_1 - \bar{X}_1)^2}{n_1 - 1}} = \sqrt{\frac{4.7}{3 - 1}} = \sqrt{\frac{4.7}{2}} = \sqrt{2.35} = 1.53,$$

$$s_2 = \sqrt{\frac{\Sigma(X_2 - \bar{X}_2)^2}{n_2 - 1}} = \sqrt{\frac{2.0}{3 - 1}} = \sqrt{\frac{2.0}{2}} = \sqrt{1.00} = 1.00.$$

Both of these sample standard deviations, 1.53 and 1.00, are estimates of the value of the standard deviation of the population, 1.4. If we add the two sample standard deviations together, the sum is 2.53, which certainly is not a very good estimate of the population standard deviation of 1.4.

There are three different methods that we can use to pool the standard deviations of two samples. As we will see, all three methods give us the exact same value.

Method 1: Using the squared deviations from the mean.   As can be seen in the definitional formula for the sample standard deviation, used in the computations above, the squared deviations from the mean are divided by $n - 1$. To pool the standard deviations of two samples, we first pool together the squared deviations of each sample, then pool together ($n_1 - 1$) and ($n_2 - 1$) and finally divide:

$$s_{\bar{X}_1 - \bar{X}_2} = \sqrt{\frac{\Sigma(X_1 - \bar{X}_1)^2 + \Sigma(X_2 - \bar{X}_2)^2}{(n_1 - 1) + (n_2 - 1)}} = \sqrt{\frac{4.7 + 2.0}{2 + 2}} = \sqrt{\frac{6.7}{4}} = \sqrt{1.675} = 1.29.$$

Thus, the pooled standard deviation of Samples 1 and 2 is 1.29.

Method 2: Using the values of the sample standard deviations.   If the sample standard deviations for both samples have already been calculated, we can use those values to find the pooled standard deviation rather than recalculating the sum of the squared deviations for each sample. As shown below, for one sample, the sum of the squared deviations is equal to $(n - 1)s^2$:

$$s = \sqrt{\frac{\Sigma(X - \bar{X})^2}{n - 1}},$$

$$s^2 = \frac{\Sigma(X - \bar{X})^2}{n - 1},$$

$$(n - 1)s^2 = \Sigma(X - \bar{X})^2.$$

We can substitute this value in the formula for the pooled standard deviation:

$$s_{\bar{X}_1 - \bar{X}_2} = \sqrt{\frac{(n_1 - 1)s_1^2 + (n_2 - 1)s_2^2}{(n_1 - 1) + (n_2 - 1)}}.$$

This formula will give us the same value as the formula based on combining the squared deviations from the mean:

$$s_{\bar{X}_1 - \bar{X}_2} = \sqrt{\frac{(n_1 - 1)s_1^2 + (n_2 - 1)s_2^2}{(n_1 - 1) + (n_2 - 1)}} = \sqrt{\frac{(3 - 1)1.53^2 + (3 - 1)1.0^2}{(3 - 1) + (3 - 1)}}$$

$$= \sqrt{\frac{4.7 + 2.0}{4}} = \sqrt{\frac{6.7}{4}} = \sqrt{1.675} = 1.29.$$

Method 3: Used when the size of the two samples is equal. If the two samples have exactly the same number of scores, so that $n_1 = n_2$, there is a very simple method that we can use to pool the two sample standard deviations:

$$s_{\bar{X}_1 - \bar{X}_2} = \sqrt{\frac{s_1^2 + s_2^2}{2}} = \sqrt{\frac{2.35 + 1.00}{2}} = \sqrt{\frac{3.35}{2}} = \sqrt{1.675} = 1.29.$$

Note that this formula can be used *only* if the two samples contain exactly the same number of scores. If the sample sizes differ by even one score, either the first or second method must be used. The steps used in these three methods of pooling two sample standard deviations are described in Step-by-Step Procedure 14-1.

Remember that the pooled standard deviation is just an estimate of σ and rarely is exactly the same value as σ. Note that the value of the pooled standard deviation lies between the values of the two sample standard deviations. In this example, the standard deviation of Sample 1 is 1.53 and the standard deviation of Sample 2 is 1.00. The pooled standard deviation, 1.29, is between these two values. This will always be true.

STEP-BY-STEP PROCEDURE 14-1

Calculating the Pooled Standard Deviation of Two Samples

Method 1: Using the Sum of the Squared Deviations

$$s_{\bar{X}_1 - \bar{X}_2} = \sqrt{\frac{\Sigma(X_1 - \bar{X}_1)^2 + \Sigma(X_2 - \bar{X}_2)^2}{(n_1 - 1) + (n_2 - 1)}}$$

where X_1 = the scores in Sample 1
$\bar{X}_1$ = the mean of Sample 1
n_1 = the number of scores in Sample 1
X_2 = the scores in Sample 2
$\bar{X}_2$ = the mean of Sample 2
n_2 = the number of scores in Sample 2

1. For each sample, compute the following:
  A. Calculate the sample mean.
  B. For each score, subtract the sample mean from the score, and then square that result.
  C. Sum the results of Step 1B for all of the scores in the sample.

2. Add the results of Step 1C for Sample 1 to the results of Step 1C for Sample 2.

3. Subtract 1 from n_1, the number of scores in Sample 1. Subtract 1 from n_2, the number of scores in Sample 2. Add these two results together.

4. Divide the result of Step 2 by the result of Step 3.

5. To find the pooled standard deviation, find the square root of the result of Step 4.

Method 2: Using the Standard Deviations of the Two Samples

$$s_{\bar{X}_1 - \bar{X}_2} = \sqrt{\frac{(n_1 - 1)s_1^2 + (n_2 - 1)s_2^2}{(n_1 - 1) + (n_2 - 1)}}$$

where s_1 = the standard deviation of Sample 1
  n_1 = the number of scores in Sample 1
  s_2 = the standard deviation of Sample 2
  n_2 = the number of scores in Sample 2

1. For each sample, compute the following:
  A. Square the value of the standard deviation.
  B. Subtract 1 from n, the number of scores in the sample.
  C. Multiply the result of Step 1A by the result of Step 1B.

2. Add the results of Step 1C for Sample 1 to the results of Step 1C for Sample 2.

3. Subtract 1 from n_1, the number of scores in Sample 1. Subtract 1 from n_2, the number of scores in Sample 2. Add these two results together.

4. Divide the result of Step 2 by the result of Step 3.

5. To find the pooled standard deviation, find the square root of the result of Step 4.

Method 3: Use When the Sample Sizes are Equal

Note that this method may be used only when the two samples have exactly the same number of scores.

$$s_{\bar{X}_1 - \bar{X}_2} = \sqrt{\frac{s_1^2 + s_2^2}{2}}$$

where s_1 = the standard deviation of Sample 1
  s_2 = the standard deviation of Sample 2

1. Square the value of the standard deviation for each sample. Add these squares together.

2. Divide the result of Step 1 by 2 to find the pooled standard deviation.

To convert the formula for the z test for a difference between means to a t test, we simply substitute the pooled sample standard deviation for the population standard deviation in the formula for the z test:

$$z_{\bar{X}_1 - \bar{X}_2} = \frac{\bar{X}_1 - \bar{X}_2}{\sigma \sqrt{\dfrac{1}{n_1} + \dfrac{1}{n_2}}}, \qquad t_{\bar{X}_1 - \bar{X}_2} = \frac{\bar{X}_1 - \bar{X}_2}{s_{\bar{X}_1 - \bar{X}_2} \sqrt{\dfrac{1}{n_1} + \dfrac{1}{n_2}}}.$$

The method for using this formula to calculate the value of t for a difference between means is shown in Step-by-Step Procedure 14-2.

STEP-BY-STEP PROCEDURE 14-2

Conducting the *t* Test for a Difference between Means

1. Verify that the following assumptions have been met:
   A. The subjects in each sample were randomly and independently selected. Each subject is a member of only one sample.
   B. The distribution in question is approximately normally distributed. The t test is not appropriate if the distribution is greatly skewed.
   C. The sample variances are approximately equal.
   D. The scores are measured with an interval or ratio scale.

2. Write the null and alternate hypotheses. For the t test for a difference between means, the hypotheses will have one of the following three forms:

Bidirectional

$H_0: \mu_{\bar{X}_1} = \mu_{\bar{X}_2}$ or $\mu_{\bar{X}_1 - \bar{X}_2} = 0$

$H_1: \mu_{\bar{X}_1} \neq \mu_{\bar{X}_2}$ or $\mu_{\bar{X}_1 - \bar{X}_2} \neq 0$

Unidirectional

$H_0: \mu_{\bar{X}_1} \leq \mu_{\bar{X}_2}$ or $\mu_{\bar{X}_1 - \bar{X}_2} \leq 0$

$H_1: \mu_{\bar{X}_1} > \mu_{\bar{X}_2}$ or $\mu_{\bar{X}_1 - \bar{X}_2} > 0$

$H_0: \mu_{\bar{X}_1} \geq \mu_{\bar{X}_2}$ or $\mu_{\bar{X}_1 - \bar{X}_2} \geq 0$

$H_1: \mu_{\bar{X}_1} < \mu_{\bar{X}_2}$ or $\mu_{\bar{X}_1 - \bar{X}_2} < 0$

3. Decide the level of significance, α.

4. Find the critical value of t in Appendix A-3, with $df = (n_1 - 1) + (n_2 - 1)$.

5. Draw a graph of the sampling distribution predicted by the null hypothesis, indicating the rejection region.
   A. For a bidirectional test, the rejection region is in both tails of the distribution.

   B. For a unidirectional test, the rejection region is in one tail of the distribution. If H_1 predicts that the difference is less than 0, the rejection region is in the lower tail. If H_1 predicts that the difference is greater than 0, the rejection region is in the upper tail. The convention is to designate the sample with the larger mean as Sample 1, so that the value of t will be positive.

6. Convert the difference between the sample means to a value of t, using the formula below. Step-by-Step Procedure 14-1 describes three methods for calculating the pooled sample standard deviation, $s_{\bar{X}_1 - \bar{X}_2}$.

$$t_{\bar{X}_1 - \bar{X}_2} = \frac{\bar{X}_1 - \bar{X}_2}{s_{\bar{X}_1 - \bar{X}_2} \sqrt{\dfrac{1}{n_1} + \dfrac{1}{n_2}}}$$

where $\bar{X}_1$ is the mean of Sample 1, $\bar{X}_2$ is the mean of Sample 2, n_1 is the number of subjects in Sample 1, n_2 is the number of subjects in Sample 2, and $s_{\bar{X}_1 - \bar{X}_2}$ is the standard error of the difference between the means.

7. Make a decision on whether or not to reject the null hypothesis:
   A. If $t_{\bar{X}_1 - \bar{X}_2}$ is in the rejection region bounded by t_{critical}, then $p \leq \alpha$, and therefore decide that there is a significant difference between the means of the populations from which the samples were drawn (reject the null hypothesis).
   B. If $t_{\bar{X}_1 - \bar{X}_2}$ is not in the rejection region bounded by t_{critical}, then $p > \alpha$, and therefore do not make any decision about the difference between the means of the populations from which the samples were drawn (do not reject the null hypothesis).

Conducting the *t* Test for a Difference between Means

We can use the *t* test of a difference between means to assess Joe Johnson's hypothesis that anxiety lowers math performance in math-anxious students. Recall that Joe tested a sample of twenty math-anxious students on a twenty-question math test, whose scores are shown in Table 14-3. Suppose that at the same time, Joe also tested another sample of sixteen students who did not have math anxiety. Suppose also that Joe matched the students in the two samples on overall intelligence and prior math ability, so that those variables wouldn't affect the results of his study. The scores of both samples are shown in Table 14-3. The means and standard deviations of both these samples are given at the bottom of Table 14-3.

The sixteen students without math anxiety scored a mean of 76.6 percent correct on Joe's math test, while the twenty students with math anxiety scored a mean of 66.0 percent correct. Thus, the students without math anxiety scored 10.6 percent more correct on the test than students with math anxiety did. Does this prove that the mean score of the entire population of math-anxious students is lower than the mean score of the population of

TABLE 14-3   Scores on Twenty-Question Math Test from Samples of Students with and without Math Anxiety

Students without Math Anxiety (%)				Students with Math Anxiety (%)			
100	95	95	90	95	90	90	80
85	80	80	75	75	75	70	70
75	70	70	70	70	60	60	60
65	65	60	50	60	60	55	55
				55	50	50	40

$$\overline{X}_{wo/MA} = 76.6\% \qquad\qquad\qquad \overline{X}_{w/MA} = 66.0\%$$

$$s_{wo/MA} = 13.9\% \qquad\qquad\qquad s_{w/MA} = 14.7\%$$

$$s_{\overline{X}_1 - \overline{X}_2} = \sqrt{\left[\frac{(n_1 - 1)s_1^2 + (n_2 - 1)s_2^2}{(n_1 - 1) + (n_2 - 1)}\right]} = \sqrt{\frac{(16 - 1)13.9^2 + (20 - 1)14.7^2}{(16 - 1) + (20 - 1)}} = \sqrt{\frac{(15)193.21 + (19)216.09}{34}}$$

$$= \sqrt{\frac{2898.15 + 4105.71}{34}} = \sqrt{\frac{7003.86}{34}} = \sqrt{206.00} = 14.35.$$

$$t_{\overline{X}_1 - \overline{X}_2} = \frac{\overline{X}_1 - \overline{X}_2}{s_{\overline{X}_1 - \overline{X}_2}\sqrt{\dfrac{1}{n_1} + \dfrac{1}{n_2}}} = \frac{76.6\% - 66.0\%}{14.35\sqrt{\dfrac{1}{20} + \dfrac{1}{16}}} = \frac{10.6\%}{14.35\sqrt{.05 + .0625}} = \frac{10.6\%}{14.35\sqrt{.1125}}$$

$$= \frac{10.6\%}{14.35(.335)} = \frac{10.6\%}{4.8\%} = 2.21.$$

students without math anxiety? No, it doesn't. There is a possibility, however small, that both samples were drawn from the same population. We can test that possibility with the t test for a difference between means.

The method for conducting the t test for difference between means is shown in Step-by-Step Procedure 14-2, which we can use to test the hypothesis that the mean math score of the population of math-anxious students is less than the mean math score of the population of students without math anxiety.

Step 1: Verify that the assumptions of the test are met. The first assumption is that the subjects were randomly and independently selected. There is no individual who is a member of both samples, and the members of one sample have no relationship to the members of the other sample. Thus, the t test for a difference between means is a between-subjects test. The second assumption is that the populations from which the samples were drawn are approximately normally distributed. The third assumption is that the sample variances are approximately equal. For Joe's study, the two samples' standard deviations were 14.7 percent and 13.9 percent, which is approximately equal. The fourth assumption is that the scores are measured on an interval or ratio scale. The scores in Joe's study, the percent of problems correct on a math test, are measured on a ratio scale.

Step 2: Write the null and alternate hypotheses. There are two ways that we can write the hypotheses for a t test for a difference between means. The first way is to compare the two population means. For Joe's study, we are predicting that the mean math score of the population of students without math anxiety is greater than the mean math score of the population of math-anxious students. This is the alternate hypothesis, and the null hypothesis is the opposite:

$$H_0: \mu_{\text{without anxiety}} \leq \mu_{\text{with anxiety}},$$

$$H_1: \mu_{\text{without anxiety}} > \mu_{\text{with anxiety}}.$$

The second way to write the hypotheses is to compare the difference between the populations to the value, 0. Since we are predicting that the population mean of students without math anxiety will be greater than the population mean of math-anxious students, the difference between the two will be greater than 0:

$$H_0: \mu_{\text{without anxiety}} \quad \mu_{\text{with anxiety}} \leq 0,$$

$$H_1: \mu_{\text{without anxiety}} - \mu_{\text{with anxiety}} > 0.$$

Note that both ways of writing the hypotheses say the same thing. Also note that it is conventional to label the sample with the larger mean as Sample 1, so that the value of t calculated from the two sample means will be a positive value.

Step 3: Decide the level of significance, α.   We will use the conventional level of significance, $\alpha = .05$.

Step 4: Identify the critical value(s) of the statistic.   Since we are predicting that the difference between the population means will be greater than 0, this is a unidirectional t test. The degrees of freedom are $(n_1 - 1) + (n_2 - 1)$, which is $(20 - 1) + (16 - 1)$, or 34. We encounter a problem in attempting to find the critical value of t in Appendix A-3, because the table does not list the critical values of t for $df = 34$.

To keep the size of the tables usable, tables of critical values do not list all possible values of the degrees of freedom. Thus, the table of critical values for the t test lists critical values for 30 and 40 df but not the values in between. In these cases, when the specific degrees of freedom of a statistical test are not listed, we must always use the critical value for the next smaller degrees of freedom. In this example, because the table does not list critical values of t for $df = 34$, we must use the critical value for the next smaller value, $df = 30$. If we were to use the critical value of t for the next larger df, we would be exceeding the level of significance that we have selected.

For 30 df and $\alpha = .05$, the critical value of t is 1.697. If the value of t that we calculate is 1.697 or greater, we will be able to reject the null hypothesis. Notice that Appendix A-3 lists only positive values of t. If the rejection region is in the lower tail, we need to remember to make the value of t negative.

Step 5: Indicate the rejection region on a graph of the sampling distribution. Figure 14-2 shows the sampling distribution of t for the difference between

FIGURE 14-2 Sampling Distribution for the t Test
for a Difference between Means, $\alpha = .05$ and $df = 34$

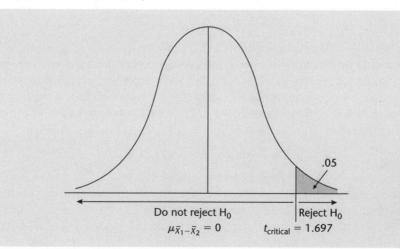

.05

Do not reject H$_0$

$\mu_{\bar{x}_1 - \bar{x}_2} = 0$

Reject H$_0$

$t_{critical} = 1.697$

two sample means. Because the alternate hypothesis predicts that the difference between the population means will be greater than zero, the rejection region is in the upper tail. If the value of t that we calculate falls in the rejection region, we can reject the null hypothesis.

Step 6: Calculate the statistic from the sample of scores.   Table 14-3 shows the calculations needed to find the value of t. Note that we need to compute the means and standard deviations for each sample separately and then use those values in the formula for t. The formula for the t measuring the difference between means is shown in Procedure 14-2. Remember that this formula requires the value of the pooled standard deviation of the two samples and that Procedure 14-1 gives three different methods for finding that value. Table 14-3 shows that the value of t for the difference between Joe's two samples is 2.21.

Step 7: Decide whether or not to reject the null hypothesis.   The value of t is in the rejection region, and so we can reject the null hypothesis. Thus, there is a significant difference between the mean math scores of students with and without math anxiety. We can conclude that students with math anxiety score lower on math tests than do students without math anxiety. Joe might report the results of this study in the following way: "On the math test, the mean for the math-anxious students was 10.6 percent lower than the mean of the students without math anxiety, which was a significant difference, $t_{34} = 2.21$, $p < .05$." The subscript for t here refers to the 34 df in the statistical test.

The t Test for a Mean Difference: A Within-Subjects Test

The Distribution of a Mean Difference

We have just examined the t test for a difference between means, which we can use when we have scores from two independent groups of subjects. Joe Johnson tested two independent samples of subjects, one sample of students with math anxiety and another sample of students without math anxiety. To test Joe's hypothesis, we compared the means of these two samples, using the between-subjects t test for a difference between means.

Another way that Joe could test his hypothesis would be to select one sample of math-anxious students and train them how to relax to reduce anxiety. Suppose that Joe gave a math test to math-anxious students before and after the relaxation-training program to see if reducing anxiety improves their math performance. This is a within-subjects design, in which there is one sample of subjects, each contributing two scores. Because each subject contributes two scores (one before training and one after), the scores are paired

TABLE 14-4   Difference in Procedure of Between-Subjects and Within-Subjects *t* Tests

Test	Basic Procedure
Between-subjects: *t* test for a difference between means	1. Calculate each sample mean separately.
	2. Find difference between sample means.
Within-subjects: *t* test for a mean difference	1. Find difference between each pair of scores.
	2. Calculate mean of those differences.

meaningfully. We can subtract the "before" score from the "after" score for each student, to find the difference. If we then calculate the mean of all these differences, we would have the mean difference between the students' scores before and after training.

For the *t* test for a difference between means (the between-subjects *t* test), we calculated the mean for each sample separately and then found the difference between the means. In the *t* test for a mean difference (the within-subjects *t* test), we first calculate the difference between each subject's two scores and then calculate the mean of those differences. The difference in the procedure of these two tests is summarized in Table 14-4.

The sampling distributions for these two *t* tests are different. We have already explored the sampling distribution of a difference between two sample means. Now let's examine how the sampling distribution of a mean difference is constructed.

Suppose we have a population of scores, containing equal numbers of the values, 1, 2, 3, 4, and 5. Now suppose we draw samples from the population, each sample consisting of *pairs* of scores. For each pair of scores, we find the difference by subtracting score 2 from score 1. The sample thus consists of differences between pairs of scores. We can then calculate the mean of these differences, or more concisely, the *mean difference*. Since we are drawing both scores of each pair from the same population, we can expect that sometimes the difference between the two scores will be zero. Sometimes score 1 will be larger and the difference will be positive. Sometimes score 2 will be larger and the difference will be negative. But over all the differences, there will be a tendency for the positive and negative differences to balance out and the mean difference to be zero.

If we repeated this process over and over again, drawing samples of pairs of scores, finding the difference between them, and then calculating the mean difference, we would have a distribution of mean differences from these samples. These sample mean differences will be normally distributed around a center of zero. Not all of our samples will have a mean difference of exactly zero. Some of the samples will have more positive differences than negative differences, so that the mean difference will be positive. Other samples will have more negative differences than positive, so that the mean difference will be negative. However, if we draw enough samples, across all of them, the positive and negative mean differences will balance out, and center around zero.

This then is a distribution of mean differences. Recall that the formula for the value of t for a distribution of sample means is

$$t = \frac{\bar{X} - \mu}{s_{\bar{X}}} = \frac{\bar{X} - \mu}{\frac{s}{\sqrt{n}}}.$$

For the distribution of mean differences, the values in the distribution are the means of differences between scores rather than the means of samples of scores. To reflect this change, we can convert the formula thus:

$$t = \frac{\bar{X}_D - \mu_D}{s_{\bar{X}_D}} = \frac{\bar{X}_D - \mu_D}{\frac{s_D}{\sqrt{n}}},$$

where $\bar{X}_D$ represents the mean difference of the sample and μ_D represents the mean of the population of differences.

This formula can be further simplified. Across all samples, the mean of the population of differences should be zero, if the null hypothesis is true. Therefore, we can replace μ_D with 0, and so the formula for the value of t for a mean difference is

$$t = \frac{\bar{X}_D}{s_{\bar{X}_D}} = \frac{\bar{X}_D}{\frac{s_D}{\sqrt{n}}}.$$

Conducting the *t* Test for a Mean Difference

As a demonstration of how to conduct the *t* test for a mean difference, we will analyze the results of Joe Johnson's study in which he gave math-anxious students a math test before and after relaxation training. Table 14-5 shows the results of this study. Step-by-Step Procedure 14-3 shows the method for conducting the *t* test for a mean difference.

The hypotheses for the *t* test for a mean difference predict whether the population difference between the before and after scores is 0. If there is no difference between the before and after scores, then the population mean difference would be 0. If there is a difference in the population between before and after scores, then the population mean difference will not be 0. These hypotheses are very similar to the hypotheses for the *t* test for a difference between means.

TABLE 14-5 Math Test Scores for a Sample of Math-Anxious
Students before and after Relaxation Training

Student	Before	After	After − Before
1	95	90	−5
2	90	100	10
3	90	95	5
4	80	85	5
5	75	70	−5
6	75	85	10
7	70	90	20
8	70	80	10
9	70	70	0
10	60	75	15
11	60	70	10
12	60	65	5
13	60	60	0
14	60	55	−5
15	55	65	10
16	55	60	5
17	55	55	0
18	50	65	15
19	50	40	−10
20	40	45	5
	$\bar{X}_{\text{before}} = 66.0$	$\bar{X}_{\text{after}} = 71.0$	$\bar{X}_{\text{difference}} = 5.0$

Step 1: Verify that the assumptions of the test are met.   Using the *t* test assumes that the subjects are randomly and independently selected. In order to use the *t* test for a mean difference, the scores must be logically paired in some way. In this example, each student is tested before and after the relaxation training, which is a logical basis for pairing the scores. The *t* test also assumes that the distribution is approximately normally distributed and that the scores are measured on an interval or ratio scale of measurement.

Step 2: Write the null and alternate hypotheses.   We are predicting that the math-anxious students' math test scores will be higher after relaxation training than before. When calculating the differences between scores, it is conventional to subtract the score we expect to be smaller from the score we expect to be larger, so that over all the pairs of scores, the expected difference

STEP-BY-STEP PROCEDURE 14-3

Conducting the *t* Test for a Mean Difference

1. Verify that the following assumptions have been met:
   A. The subjects in the sample were randomly and independently selected from the population in question. The scores of the two samples are logically paired.
   B. The distribution in question is approximately normally distributed. The *t* test is not appropriate if the distribution is greatly skewed.
   C. The scores are measured with an interval or ratio scale. It is valid to calculate the mean of a distribution only if the scores are from an interval or ratio scale.

2. Write the null and alternate hypotheses. For the *t* test for a sample mean, the hypotheses will have one of the following three forms:

   Bidirectional   Unidirectional

   $H_0: \mu_D = 0$ $H_0: \mu_D \geq 0$ $H_0: \mu_D \leq 0$

   $H_1: \mu_D \neq 0$ $H_1: \mu_D < 0$ $H_1: \mu_D > 0$

3. Decide the level of significance, α.

4. Find the critical value of *t* in Appendix A-3. The degrees of freedom are the number of pairs of scores, minus 1.

5. Draw a graph of the sampling distribution predicted by the null hypothesis, indicating the rejection region.
   A. For a bidirectional test, the rejection region is in both tails of the distribution.
   B. For a unidirectional test, the rejection region is in one tail of the distribution. If the alternate hypothesis predicts that the mean difference is less than 0, the rejection region is in the lower tail. If the alternate hypothesis predicts that the mean difference is more than 0, the rejection region is in the upper tail.

6. Convert the sample mean to a standard score, using the formula below:

$$t_D = \frac{\bar{X}_D}{s_{\bar{X}_D}} = \frac{\bar{X}_D}{\dfrac{s_D}{\sqrt{n}}}$$

   where $\bar{X}_D$ is the mean difference between scores 1 and 2 for each subject, $s_{\bar{X}_D}$ is the standard error of the mean difference, and *n* is the number of pairs of scores.

7. Make a decision on whether or not to reject the null hypothesis:
   A. If the value of *t* found in Step 6 is in the rejection region bounded by t_{critical}, then $p \leq \alpha$, and therefore decide that sample did not come from a population with the mean predicted by the null hypothesis (reject the null hypothesis).
   B. If the value of *t* found in Step 6 is not in the rejection region bounded by t_{critical}, then $p > \alpha$, and therefore do not decide that sample did not come from a population with the mean predicted by the null hypothesis (do not reject the null hypothesis).

will be positive, yielding a positive value of *t*. In this case, we expect the "after" scores to be higher than the "before" scores, and so we will subtract the before score from the after score: (after − before). We are predicting that the mean difference will be positive; that is, larger than 0:

$$H_0: \mu_{\text{after−before}} \le 0,$$

$$H_1: \mu_{\text{after−before}} > 0.$$

Step 3: Decide the level of significance, α. We will use the conventional level, $\alpha = .05$.

Step 4: Identify the critical value(s) of the statistic. There are twenty students in the sample in Table 14-5, each student giving one pair of scores. The degrees of freedom are the number of pairs of scores, minus 1, or 19. Appendix A-3 shows that the critical value of *t*, with $\alpha = .05$ and 19 degrees of freedom, is 1.729.

Step 5: Indicate the rejection region on a graph of the sampling distribution. Figure 14-3 shows the rejection region for testing the mean difference, with $\alpha = .05$ and 19 degrees of freedom.

Step 6: Calculate the statistic from the sample of scores. The mean of the differences between before and after scores shown in Table 14-5 is 5.0 percent, and the standard deviation is 7.8 percent. With these values, we can convert

FIGURE 14-3 Sampling Distribution for $t_{\text{after−before}}$ with $\alpha = .05$ and *df* = 19

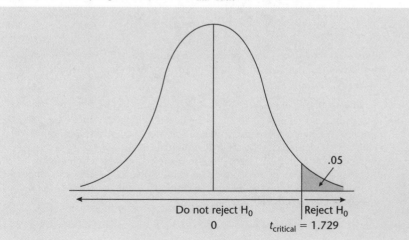

the mean of the differences to a value of t:

$$t_{\bar{X}_D} = \frac{\bar{X}_D}{s_{\bar{X}_D}} = \frac{\bar{X}_D}{\frac{s_D}{\sqrt{n}}} = \frac{5.0\%}{\frac{7.8\%}{\sqrt{20}}} = 2.87.$$

Step 7: Decide whether or not to reject the null hypothesis.   The value of t calculated in Step 6, 2.87, is in the rejection region shown in Figure 14-3. Therefore, we can reject the null hypothesis and conclude that the math-anxious students scored higher on the math test after relaxation training than before the training. It appears that relaxation training helps alleviate anxiety, to improve math performance. We could report these results by saying that "the mean math test scores for the math-anxious students were 5 percent higher after the relaxation training than before, $t_{19} = 2.87$, $p < .05$." The fact that the value of p was reported as less than .05 indicates that this result was significant.

A Parametric Test of the Strength of a Relationship: Pearson's Product-Moment Correlation

The statistical tests we have examined thus far represent one category of inferential tests. These tests assess whether there is a relationship between two variables by determining whether there is a significant difference in the scores on one variable between two levels of the other variable. The other category is inferential statistics that assess the strength of the relationship between two variables. All of these tests are based on measures of correlation. We have already examined how to compute correlational measures in Chapter 8. In this section, we examine how to conduct an inferential test on Pearson's product-moment correlation coefficient, r.

A test of Pearson's r is a parametric test. Recall that in parametric tests, sample statistics are used to make an inference about the corollary parameter of a population. Pearson's product-moment correlation coefficient, r, is a sample statistic, measuring the correlation between two samples of scores, representing two interval or ratio variables. The corollary parameter is the correlation between two populations of scores representing the same variables. The population correlation coefficient is symbolized ρ (rho).

The Sampling Distribution of r

Recall that a sampling distribution is the distribution of a statistic calculated on a very large number of samples, all the same size and all drawn from the same population. Suppose that we measure each member of a population of subjects on two variables so that we have two populations of scores. If both variables are either interval or ratio, we could calculate the value of Pearson's product-moment correlation coefficient, ρ, to measure the strength of the relationship between the two variables in this population of subjects. Suppose also that there is absolutely no relationship between the two variables, so that ρ is 0.

Now suppose that we drew a sample from the population of subjects, noted the scores that these subjects received when tested on the two variables, and then found the value of Pearson's product-moment correlation coefficient, r, for this sample. If we repeated this process many times, each time drawing a sample of the same size and calculating the value of Pearson's r for each sample, the result would be a distribution of sample correlation coefficients; that is, a sampling distribution of r.

If we measured the correlation between two variables in samples of subjects drawn from the same population and the correlation between those variables was actually zero in that population, what values of r could we expect? Just as we cannot expect that the mean of a sample will be exactly equal to the mean of the population from which the sample was drawn, we cannot expect all of our samples to have a correlation, r, of exactly 0. Occasionally, we might actually draw a sample in which the value of r is exactly 0. However, sometimes, just by the luck of the draw, a sample might have a value of r greater than 0; sometimes the sample r will be less than 0. Thus, we can expect variation among the values of r in samples drawn from the same population.

While we cannot expect all samples to have an r of 0, if the samples are drawn from a population in which ρ is 0, we can expect that the average value of r across a large number of samples will be 0. Recall that the average of the means of a large number of samples drawn from the same population will equal the mean of that population: $\mu_{\bar{X}} = \mu$. In the same way, the average of the values of Pearson's r calculated on a large number of samples drawn from a population with a correlation, ρ, of 0 will also be 0: $\mu_r = \rho = 0$. While some of the samples will have a positive value of r and some will have a negative r, there is no reason to expect more positive r's or more negative r's. In fact, over a large number of samples, the positive and negative values of r will balance out, so that the average value of r will be 0.

Thus, if we are constructing a sampling distribution of r from samples drawn from a population in which there is absolutely no correlation between the variables under study, so that ρ is 0, the mean value of r, μ_r, will be 0. As we will see, this is the sampling distribution predicted by the null hypothesis of a statistical test of the strength of the value of Pearson's r. We turn next to examining how to conduct this statistical test.

Testing the Significance of Pearson's Product-Moment Correlation

In Chapter 8, we examined the relationship between math test scores and systolic blood pressure in a sample of ten of Joe Johnson's math-anxious students.

Recall that using Pearson's formula, we found a correlation coefficient, *r*, of −.93 between math performance and blood pressure in these scores. We can use this sample statistic to test the hypothesis that there is a relationship between math test scores and blood pressure in the entire population of math-anxious students.

Remember, we know that the sample has a correlation of −.91. We are not testing whether the two variables are correlated in the sample. We are testing whether we can use this sample correlation as evidence that there is a similar correlation in the population from which the sample was drawn. The logic of testing the significance of a correlation is very similar to the logic on which the *z* and *t* tests are based. We have a sample in which math test scores and blood pressure have a correlation of −.91. The question is whether math test scores and blood pressure are correlated in the population from which the sample was drawn. There are two possibilities:

▶ *Possibility 1.* There is a correlation between math test scores and blood pressure in the entire population of math-anxious students, which is reflected in the correlation found in the sample.
▶ *Possibility 2.* There is not a correlation between math test scores and blood pressure in the population of math-anxious students, and the correlation in the sample was only a fluke of random sampling.

According to his hypothesis, Joe Johnson asserts the first possibility to be true, that there actually is a relationship between math test scores and blood pressure in the population of math-anxious students. To show that the first possibility is true, we need to eliminate the second possibility, that the correlation in the sample was only a fluke. We need to show that there is very little likelihood that we would get a sample with a correlation of −.91 from a population in which there is no relationship between math test scores and blood pressure. We do this by conducting a statistical test on the correlation in the sample. Step-by-Step Procedure 14-4 describes the method of conducting this statistical test, using Pearson's product-moment correlation.

Step 1: Verify that the assumptions of the test are met. Procedure 14-4 lists several assumptions on which the statistical test of Pearson's *r* is based. The two most important assumptions are that the subjects are randomly and independently sampled and that both variables are measured on either an interval or ratio scale. Violations of the remaining assumptions do not threaten the validity of the statistical test if the sample size is sufficiently large (i.e., 25 or greater).

Step 2: Write the null and alternate hypotheses. In this statistical test, we are trying to determine the value of the population correlation between math test scores and blood pressure in math-anxious students. If there is no correlation in the population, then ρ would be 0. Remember that a correlation of 0 indicates that there is no relationship between the variables being tested.

STEP-BY-STEP PROCEDURE 14-4

Conducting a Test of the Strength of Pearson's Product-Moment Correlation

1. Verify that the following assumptions have been met:
   A. The subjects are randomly and independently sampled.
   B. The variables X and Y are related linearly.
   C. The population distributions of both variables X and Y are normal in form.
   D. For each value of variable X, the values of variable Y are normal in form, and for each value of variable Y, the values of variable X are normal in form. Distributions for which this is true are said to exhibit bivariate normality.
   E. The variability of values of variable X associated with each value of variable Y are the same, and the variability of values of variable Y associated with each value of variable X are also the same. (This assumption is called homoscedasticity.)
   F. Both variable X and variable Y are measured in an interval or ratio scale.

2. Write the null and alternate hypotheses.

Bidirectional	Unidirectional	
$H_0: \rho_{XY} = 0$	$H_0: \rho_{XY} \geq 0$	$H_0: \rho_{XY} \leq 0$
$H_1: \rho_{XY} \neq 0$	$H_1: \rho_{XY} < 0$	$H_1: \rho_{XY} > 0$

3. Decide the level of significance, α.

4. Compute the degrees of freedom. For testing r, the degrees of freedom are $(n - 2)$, where n is the number of pairs of scores. Find the critical value of r in Appendix A-5.

5. Draw a graph of the sampling distribution, indicating the rejection region. For a bidirectional test, the rejection region will be in both tails. For a unidirectional test, the region will be in the lower tail when the alternate hypothesis predicts that ρ is less than 0 and will be in the upper tail when the alternate hypothesis predicts that ρ is greater than 0.

6. Calculate the statistic from the scores of the subjects in the sample, using the formula below. Step-by-Step Procedure 8-1 describes how to use this formula:

$$r_{XY} = \frac{\sum XY - \dfrac{\sum X \sum Y}{n}}{\sqrt{\left(\sum X^2 - \dfrac{(\sum X)^2}{n}\right)\left(\sum Y^2 - \dfrac{(\sum Y)^2}{n}\right)}}.$$

7. Decide whether or not to reject the null hypothesis:
   A. If the value of r calculated in Step 6 is in the rejection region, then $p \leq \alpha$, and therefore decide that there is a significant relationship between the variables under study (reject the null hypothesis).
   B. If the value of r calculated in Step 6 is not in the rejection region, then $p > \alpha$, and therefore make no decision about the relationship between the variables under study (do not reject the null hypothesis).

Joe is predicting that the higher the student's blood pressure, the lower that student's math test score, which would be a negative correlation. Thus, the alternate hypothesis is predicting that there will be a negative correlation in the population, that ρ will be less than 0. The null hypothesis predicts the opposite, that there will not be a negative correlation in the population, that ρ will not be less than 0. This is a unidirectional test:

$$H_0: \rho_{\text{math scores} \times \text{blood pressure}} \geq 0,$$

$$H_1: \rho_{\text{math scores} \times \text{blood pressure}} < 0.$$

Step 3: Decide the level of significance, α.   The third step is to choose the level of significance. To gain experience in using levels of significance other than .05, let's select an α of .01 for this study.

Step 4: Identify the critical value(s) of the statistic.   The next step is to identify the critical values. For a unidirectional test, there will be one critical value. A bidirectional test would have two critical values. Appendix A-5 shows the critical values of r for selected values of α. In this table, the critical values of r are listed by degrees of freedom.

For inferential tests using Pearson's product-moment correlation, the degrees of freedom are $(n - 2)$, the number of *pairs* of scores, minus 2. (For these degrees of freedom, two scores are subtracted from n, one score for each of the samples.) Note that n here represents the number of pairs of scores, not the total number of scores or the number of subjects. For Joe's study, there are 10 pairs of scores, and so the degrees of freedom are $(10 - 2)$, or 8.

The values shown in Appendix A-5 are the critical values of r needed to reject the null hypothesis. Appendix A-5 shows that with $\alpha = .01$ and $df = 8$, for a one-tailed test, the critical value of r is $-.7155$. (Note that since the alternate hypothesis predicts that ρ will be less than 0, we need to remember to add the negative sign to the value of r given in Appendix A-5.) In order to reject the null hypothesis, the sample must have a value of r that is $-.7155$ or lower.

Step 5: Indicate the rejection region on a graph of the sampling distribution.
We can draw a graph of the sampling distribution predicted by the null hypothesis, as shown in Figure 14-4. This graph tells us that in order to reject the null hypothesis, the sample value of r must be $-.7155$ or lower.

Step 6: Calculate the statistic from the sample of scores.   In Chapter 8, we have already calculated the value of Pearson's r for the scores from Joe's sample of 10 students and found that the value of r was $-.91$. If we had not already calculated the value of Pearson's r, we would do so now. The steps in calculating the value of Pearson's r are described in Step-by-Step Procedure 8-1 of Chapter 8.

FIGURE 14-4   Sampling Distribution for Pearson's *r*, with $\alpha = .05$ and $df = 18$

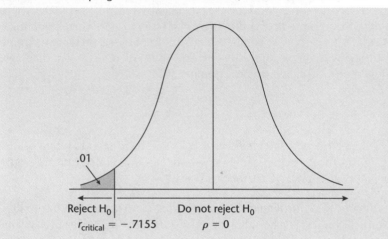

Step 7: Decide whether or not to reject the null hypothesis.   The value of *r* for Joe's sample, $-.91$, is very clearly in the rejection region shown in Figure 14-4, and so we can reject the null hypothesis. The null hypothesis was that Joe's sample came from a population with no correlation between math test scores and systolic blood pressure. We can use the result of Joe's study as evidence that there is a negative correlation between math test scores and systolic blood pressure in the population of math-anxious students, that students with higher blood pressure tend to have lower math scores. In scientific journals, the results of this statistical test would be reported with the following terminology: "There was a significant negative correlation between math test scores and systolic blood pressure, $r = -.91, p < .01$."

A Word on Significant Correlations and Meaningful Correlations

An examination of the critical values of *r* shown in Table 4 of Appendix A shows that it is possible to achieve a significant result in a statistical test with comparatively small values of *r*, particularly if the sample size is large. For example, with $df = 100$, a bidirectional test of *r* will yield a significant result with an *r* as low as .1946, for a 5 percent significance level. An *r* of .1946 has a coefficient of determination, r^2, of .038, which indicates that less than 4 percent of the variability in one variable is accounted for by the other variable. While a correlation of .1946 may be a significant result, we might well argue that it is difficult to meaningfully interpret a relationship between variables that accounts for only 4 percent of the variation between the two variables.

Not all significant results are equally meaningful. Remember that the term *significance* means only that the null hypothesis was rejected, that the study provides enough evidence to show that there is a relationship between the variables in the population of subjects being studied. However, the fact that a correlation is significant tells us nothing about how large or meaningful that correlation is. We need to use other measures, such as the coefficient of determination, to interpret the meaningfulness of the results of a statistical test.

Parametric Tests Revisited

In the last three chapters, we have examined several parametric inferential tests. The basis of all of these tests is to use samples to make an inference about the value of a population parameter. Both the *z* and *t* tests for a sample mean use one sample to make an inference about the value of the mean of a population. The *t* test for a difference between means and the *t* test for a mean difference use two samples to make an inference about the difference between the means of the populations from which those samples were drawn. Finally, the inferential test of Pearson's product-moment correlation uses the correlation between two samples of scores to make an inference about the value of the correlation between two variables in a population.

Some students find that it is not easy at first to understand the logic on which these parametric tests are based. It is important to remember that these tests are tools that we can use to describe populations when we have little or no opportunity to measure all of the members of the population. Without these tests, Joe Johnson would have to test every math-anxious student in the world before he could make any statements about them. Jane Jeffers would have to poll every psychology alumnus in the world before she could make any statements about their incomes. These parametric tests allow us to make statements about population parameters by measuring only a small group of subjects sampled from the population.

It is also important to remember that a sample alone, even with the help of an inferential test, cannot tell us the exact value of a population parameter. Inferential tests tell us what the population parameter *is not*. The *z* and *t* tests for a sample mean can tell us that it is highly unlikely that the mean of a population is a specified value. The *z* and *t* tests comparing two means can tell us that it is likely the means of the two populations differ but not what the exact values of those population means are nor exactly how large the difference between the population means is. The test of Pearson's *r* can tell us that it is likely that there is a correlation in the population but cannot tell us exactly how strong that correlation is.

All of the tests that we have examined thus far are parametric tests, used to estimate the value of a parameter in the population under study. While these tests do not give us the exact value of that parameter, they do give us enough information to test psychological theories. What is important here is to not read more into the results of a statistical test than is legitimate. A statistical test can tell us that the evidence of a study indicates a relationship exists between two variables, but it cannot tell us how strong that relationship is or what causes the relationship to occur.

CHECKING YOUR ANSWERS

1. At this point in the study of statistics, one difficulty that students encounter is trying to determine which statistical test to use. The answer depends upon (*a*) the scale of measurement, (*b*) whether you are trying to show a relationship between two variables in a population or a difference between two populations, (*c*) the number of samples of scores that you have, and (*d*) if there are two samples, whether the scores come from two groups of unrelated subjects or either from one group of subjects or two groups of related subjects.

2. Calculating the value of *t* for a difference between means can be complicated. Do the process one step at a time. First calculate the pooled standard deviation, following Procedure 14-1, and then calculate the value of *t*.

3. Remember that we may calculate the pooled standard deviation by finding the average of the squares of the standard deviations of the two samples only if the number of subjects in those samples are equal.

4. One difficulty in conducting tests of a difference between means is in deciding whether a unidirectional test is significant. To avoid problems, identify one sample as Sample 1 and the other as Sample 2. Carefully examine the researcher's hypothesis to determine whether Sample 1 is expected to be greater than Sample 2 (rejection region in upper tail) or Sample 2 is expected to be greater than Sample 1 (rejection region in lower tail). Next, make sure that you subtract the mean for Sample 2 from the mean for Sample 1. Following these steps carefully should help you avoid confusion.

5. Follow the same procedure when conducting a *t* test for a mean difference, except that when you find the difference between each pair of scores, be sure you subtract the score labeled "2" from the score labeled "1" for each subject.

6. Some students have difficulty deciding when to use the *t* test for a difference between means and when to use the *t* test for a mean difference. When there are two different groups of subjects and there is no natural relationship between the members of the two groups, use the *t* test for a difference between means. When there is one group of subjects or when there is a natural relationship between the members of two groups, so that they can be paired, use the *t* test for a mean difference.

7. The most frequent error that students make in testing the significance of Pearson's *r* is in computing the degrees of freedom. Remember that the degrees of freedom for Pearson's *r* is $n - 2$, and *n* is the number of subjects in the sample, *not* the total number of scores. Also remember that in using the table in Appendix A-5 that you use the appropriate column for the type of test you are conducting, unidirectional or bidirectional. Finally, remember that if the alternate hypothesis predicts a negative correlation, you need to add a negative sign in front of the critical value that you find in the table.

8. Some students have difficulty formulating the null and alternate hypotheses in inferential tests of the strength of a correlation using Pearson's *r.* Hypotheses asserting whether or not a correlation exists in the population always use the value of 0. To test whether there is a positive correlation, the alternate hypothesis predicts that the population correlation will be greater than zero. To test whether there is a negative correlation, the alternate hypothesis predicts that the population correlation will be less than zero. Finally, to test simply whether there is a correlation (either positive or negative), the alternate hypothesis predicts that the population correlation will not equal zero.

SUMMARY

▶ Parametric inferential tests use samples to make inferences about the value of a parameter in a population. Parametric tests can be used only when scores are measured on a scale for which it is meaningful to compute the parameter (generally either interval or ratio scales). In addition, most parametric tests make an assumption that the population distribution is at least approximately normally distributed.

▶ For between-subjects inferential tests, two unrelated samples of subjects are measured, each subject providing one score. For within-subjects inferential tests, either one sample of subjects is measured, each subject providing two scores, or two samples are measured, in which the subjects in the two samples are meaningfully paired in some way.

▶ Parametric tests of the difference between two sample means test whether there is a relationship between two variables by demonstrating whether the scores on one variable differ significantly between two levels of the other variable.

▶ The *t* test for a difference between means measures whether there is a significant difference between the means of two populations and is a between-subjects test. The *t* test is used when the population standard deviation is not known and in other conditions in which the assumptions of the *z* test are violated.

▶ The *t* test for a mean difference measures whether there is a significant difference between the means of two populations that are related in some way. It is a within-subjects test. The two populations may consist of the same members, tested under two different conditions, or may consist of different members who are related in some way.

▶ Statistical tests of the strength of a relationship use a sample to test an inference about the correlation present in the population from which the sample was drawn. The inference can be unidirectional (that there is a positive correlation in the population or that there is a negative correlation in the population) or bidirectional (that there simply is a correlation in the population).

▶ A test of the significance of the strength of Pearson's product-moment correlation coefficient measures whether there is a significant correlation between two variables in a population. The variables may be either both interval, both ratio, or a combination of interval and ratio.

▶ Remember that a significant result of a statistical test only means that the evidence of the study indicates that there is a relationship between two variables in the populations being studied. A significant result does not tell us how strong that relationship is or why it occurs.

E X E R C I S E S

Conceptual Exercises

1. Explain the difference between a between-subjects statistical test and a within-subjects statistical test.

2. Construct two populations of scores as follows: In one container, labeled "A," put 24 slips of paper, 8 slips each marked "5," "6," and "7." In the other container, labeled "B," put another 24 slips of paper, 8 slips each marked "6," "7," and "8." Calculate the mean and standard deviation of the scores in each container. Note that both sets of scores have the same standard deviation, but that the mean of set A is less than the mean of Set B.

   A. From container A, draw fifty samples of two slips of paper, each time recording the mean of the two digits and replacing the slips in the container. Construct a frequency distribution of the sample means, and calculate the mean and standard error.

   B. Repeat Step A for the scores in container B. Compare the means and standard errors of the two distributions of sample means.

   C. From container A, draw one sample of two slips, labeled Sample 1, find the mean and replace the sample in the container. Draw a second sample of two slips from container A, labeled Sample 2, find the mean of that sample and replace the slips in the container. Then subtract the mean of Sample 2 from the mean of Sample 1 and record the difference between the sample means. Repeat this process fifty times. Construct a table of the distribution of differences between means, and calculate the mean of that distribution and standard error.

   D. Repeat Step C, except draw Sample 1 from container A and Sample 2 from container B.

   E. The distribution constructed in Part C consists of differences between means drawn from the same population, while the distribution constructed in Part D consists of differences between means drawn from two different populations. Compare these two distributions. How are they the same? How are they different?

   F. Suppose you drew two samples, and found that the difference between their means is -2.0. Is there any way to determine whether the two samples came from the same container or whether they came from different containers?

3. Recall that IQ scores are normally distributed, with a mean of 100 and standard deviation of 15. Suppose that you draw two samples from this population and find the difference between their means. Determine the probability of drawing two samples from the same population with differences between the means at least as large as the following:

   A. $\overline{X}_1 = 103.6$, $n_1 = 10$; $\overline{X}_2 = 107.2$, $n_2 = 10$.
   B. $\overline{X}_1 = 97.3$, $n_1 = 20$; $\overline{X}_2 = 104.6$, $n_2 = 15$.
   C. $\overline{X}_1 = 110.4$, $n_1 = 18$; $\overline{X}_2 = 101.2$, $n_2 = 20$.
   D. $\overline{X}_1 = 106.7$, $n_1 = 25$; $\overline{X}_2 = 95.1$, $n_2 = 40$.

4. Identify the assumptions of the z test for a difference between means. For what types of data may this test be used?

5. Identify the assumptions of the t test for a difference between means. For what types of data may this test be used?

6. Identify the assumptions of the t test for a mean difference. For what types of data may this test be used?

7. Identify the assumptions of a test of Pearson's product-moment correlation. For what types of data may the test be used? What are the consequences if any of the assumptions are violated?

8. Explain why each of the tests described in this chapter is considered a parametric inferential test.

Computational Exercises

9. Determine the critical value of z for each of the following hypotheses:
   A. A study with $H_1: z_1 \neq z_2$ and $\alpha = .05$.
   B. A study with $H_1: z_1 < z_2$ and $\alpha = .01$.
   C. A study with $H_1: z_1 > z_2$ and $\alpha = .05$.
   D. A study with $H_1: z_1 \neq z_2$ and $\alpha = .01$.

10. Janet compared two commercially promoted methods for improving SAT scores. She had two groups of students enroll in the courses and afterward take the SAT. The students' SAT verbal scores are shown below. Note that the theoretical standard deviation of the SAT verbal test is 100.

Method 1	Method 2
413	429
453	444
479	473
513	487
528	492
537	507
582	515
590	524
628	545
655	570

   A. Test Janet's hypothesis, using the z test for a difference between means, with $\alpha = .05$.
   B. What does the result of this statistical test indicate about Janet's hypothesis?

11. Calculate the value of t for the difference between the following sample means:
   A. $\overline{X}_1 = 406$, $s_1 = 53$, $n_1 = 10$; $\overline{X}_2 = 365$, $s_2 = 51$, $n_2 = 10$.
   B. $\overline{X}_1 = 48.3$, $s_1 = 7.1$, $n_1 = 13$; $\overline{X}_2 = 46.1$, $s_2 = 6.9$, $n_2 = 15$.
   C. $\overline{X}_1 = 1.29$, $s_1 = 0.34$, $n_1 = 20$; $\overline{X}_2 = 1.01$, $s_2 = 0.37$, $n_2 = 18$.
   D. $\overline{X}_1 = 76.8$, $s_1 = 12.7$, $n_1 = 30$; $\overline{X}_2 = 91.9$, $s_2 = 13.4$, $n_2 = 25$.

12. Determine the critical value of t for each of the following hypotheses:
    A. A study with H_1: $t_1 \neq t_2$, $n_1 = 10$, $n_2 = 8$, and $\alpha = .05$.
    B. A study with H_1: $t_1 < t_2$, $n_1 = 15$, $n_2 = 18$, and $\alpha = .01$.
    C. A study with H_1: $t_1 > t_2$, $n_1 = 8$, $n_2 = 7$, and $\alpha = .05$.
    D. A study with H_1: $t_1 \neq t_2$, $n_1 = 13$, $n_2 = 12$, and $\alpha = .01$.

13. Jemima conducted study groups for two sections of general psychology for which she served as a teaching assistant. In one study group, she lectured only. In the other study group, she used a combination of lecture and small-group discussions. Jemima believed that students would do better on the final exam in the discussion-group section than in the lecture-only section. Statistics from the final exam scores for both sections are shown below. Assume that the students' scores are approximately normally distributed.

Study Group	Mean	Standard Deviation	n
Lecture only	72.3	12.4	25
Lecture and discussion	77.2	11.5	27

    A. Test Jemima's hypothesis, using the t test for a difference between means, with $\alpha = .05$.
    B. What does the result of this statistical test indicate about Jemima's hypothesis?

14. Listed below are two sets of scores:

X_1	X_2
6	3
8	3
7	4
6	5
9	6
7	7
11	8
10	8

    A. Assume first that the two sets of scores were collected from different groups of subjects. Calculate the value of t for a difference between means. Find the critical value of t for this test, with $\alpha = .05$ and assuming a unidirectional hypothesis.
    B. Next, assume that the two sets of scores were collected from one group of subjects. Calculate the value of t for a mean difference. Find the critical value of t for this test, again with $\alpha = .05$ and assuming a unidirectional hypothesis.
    C. Compare the two values of t calculated for these data. Why do these values differ?
    D. Which test appears to be more powerful? Why do you think this occurs?

15. Jessica compared the effects of standard reinforcements versus chocolate-coated reinforcements on the rate at which rats learned to run a maze. She believed that rats would learn the maze in fewer trials with chocolate-coated reinforcements than with standard reinforcements. In a within-subjects design, she tested one group of rats. For half the rats, she first used the standard reinforcer in the maze-learning task, and for the remaining rats, she used the chocolate-coated reinforcers first. After that task was completed, she then trained each rat with the reinforcer not used in the first task. The

rats were trained in two different mazes to prevent prior exposure from affecting the results. The number of trials to criterion for each rat is shown below:

	Type of Reinforcer	
Rat	Standard	Chocolate
1	15	12
2	19	14
3	21	17
4	23	23
5	26	19
6	30	21
7	32	25
8	35	24
9	40	40

A. Test Jessica's hypothesis, using the t test for a mean difference, with $\alpha = .05$.

B. What does the result of this statistical test indicate about Jessica's hypothesis?

16. Identify the critical values of Pearson's r for the following tests:

A. A study with $H_1: r \neq 0$, $\alpha = .05$, and $n = 10$.

B. A study with $H_1: r < 0$, $\alpha = .01$, and $n = 20$.

C. A study with $H_1: r > 0$, $\alpha = .05$, and $n = 15$.

D. A study with $H_1: r \neq 0$, $\alpha = .01$, and $n = 25$.

17. Juliet studied the relationship between college grades and SAT scores by recording high school seniors' SAT scores and then, one year later, their first-year college grade point average, predicting a positive relationship between SAT and GPA. The results are shown below.

Student	SAT Score	GPA
1	1,160	2.52
2	1,250	3.14
3	1,470	3.52
4	1,020	2.31
5	1,220	3.15
6	1,390	3.76
7	1,140	2.93
8	1,280	2.76
9	1,070	2.68
10	1,190	3.39

A. Conduct a test of Pearson's product-moment correlation, with $\alpha = .05$.

B. What does the result of this statistical test show about the relationship between SAT scores and GPA?

18. Juanita compared two methods of helping dyslexic children read. She trained two groups of dyslexic children under one of the methods and then gave both groups a

reading test. For normal children, the mean score on the test was 59.2 ($\sigma = 13.6$). Assume that these scores were normally distributed. The 10 children given method A scored a mean of 37.8 on the test, while the 12 children given method B scored a mean of 45.8.

A. What is the appropriate statistical test to conduct for this study? Why?

B. Conduct that statistical test on the results above, with $\alpha = .05$.

C. What does the result of this test show about Juanita's hypothesis?

19. Judd conducted a study testing the superiority of chocolate-covered rat reinforcers. The study was similar to that described in Problem 15, except that Judd used two different groups of rats, testing each group with one type of reinforcer. The trials to criterion are shown below:

Reinforcer	Mean	Standard Deviation	n
Standard	14.2	2.7	14
Chocolate	11.7	2.4	15

A. What is the appropriate statistical test to conduct for this study? Why?

B. Conduct that statistical test on the results above, with $\alpha = .05$.

C. What does the result of this statistical test indicate about Judd's hypothesis?

20. Joab conducted another study on hyperaggressive children. He first had observers count the number of aggressive acts each of twelve children made in one week. He then put the children on an additive-free diet for one month, after which the observers reevaluated the children. Joab believed that the diet would reduce the children's level of aggression. The results were

Child	Before	After
1	30	24
2	32	23
3	35	27
4	35	29
5	38	27
6	39	38
7	40	40
8	42	32
9	42	37
10	45	45
11	46	38
12	48	40

A. What is the appropriate statistical test to conduct for this study? Why?

B. Conduct that statistical test on the results above, with $\alpha = .05$.

C. What does the result of this test show about Joab's hypothesis?

21. Jessamyn studied the relationship between time spent studying and test scores among students in her statistics class by recording the number of problems that the students turned in as homework and their test scores. The results are shown below.

Student	Number of Problems	Test score (%)
1	17	85
2	23	93
3	15	81
4	24	90
5	10	75
6	18	89
7	13	78
8	21	94
9	12	70
10	19	87
11	15	80
12	20	96

A. What is the appropriate statistical test to conduct for this study? Why?

B. Conduct that statistical test on the results above, with $\alpha = .05$.

C. What does the result of this test show about the relationship between the number of problems students work and their test scores?

Nonparametric Tests for Two Samples

15

A Sampling Distribution of Ranks

A Distribution of Rank Sums

The Total, Minimum, and Maximum Rank Sums

The Sampling Distribution of *U*

The Mann-Whitney *U* Test: A Between-Subjects Nonparametric Test

Conducting the Mann-Whitney *U* Test for Sample Sizes of 20 or Less

STEP-BY-STEP PROCEDURE 15-1: Conducting the Mann-Whitney U Test

STEP-BY-STEP PROCEDURE 15-2: Calculating the Value of Mann-Whitney's U

Alternate Method for Calculating *U*

Conducting the Mann-Whitney *U* Test for Sample Sizes Greater than 20

STEP-BY-STEP PROCEDURE 15-3: Converting U to a Standard Score

The Wilcoxon Signed-Ranks Test: A Within-Subjects Nonparametric Test

The Sampling Distribution of *W*

STEP-BY-STEP PROCEDURE 15-4: Conducting the Wilcoxon Signed-Ranks Test

STEP-BY-STEP PROCEDURE 15-5: Calculating the Value of W for the Wilcoxon Signed-Ranks Test

Conducting Wilcoxon's Test when *n* Is 50 or Less

Conducting Wilcoxon's Test when *n* Is Greater than 50

STEP-BY-STEP PROCEDURE 15-6: Converting the Value of W to a Standard Score

A Nonparametric Test of the Strength of a Relationship: Spearman's Rank-Order Correlation

STEP-BY-STEP PROCEDURE 15-7: Conducting a Test of Spearman's Rank-Order Correlation

Hypothesis Testing Revisited

CHECKING YOUR ANSWERS

SUMMARY

EXERCISES

Conceptual Exercises

Computational Exercises

▶ Thus far, we have examined several parametric tests that make inferences about the value of a population parameter, such as the mean of a population, a population proportion, or the correlation between two variables in a population. These tests are very useful when the scores being analyzed are measured on an interval or ratio scale, for which those parameters are meaningful. However, parametric tests are not appropriate for scores measured on an ordinal or nominal scale.

For both interval and ratio scales, the size of the interval remains the same across the entire range of possible scores. Measurement scales measuring the heights of objects have equal intervals. For instance, 1 inch is the same distance between 1 and 2 inches as between 1,000 and 1,001 inches. Similarly, temperature is measured on an interval scale. One degree Fahrenheit is the same amount of heat, whether it is the difference between 1 and 2 degrees Fahrenheit or between 101 and 102 degrees Fahrenheit. Parametric tests are designed for use with scores that are measured on scales with equal intervals.

However, for scores measured on either an ordinal or nominal scale, which do not have equal intervals, other inferential tests are available. In a later chapter, we will examine the chi-square test, which is very useful for scores measured on a nominal scale. In this chapter, we will examine three inferential tests that can be used with scores measured on an ordinal scale.

A **nonparametric inferential test** uses a sample of scores to make inferences about the general distribution of the population from which the sample was drawn. These tests are called "nonparametric" because they do not make inferences about the parameters of populations. Nonparametric tests suitable for data measured on an ordinal scale of measurement are based on a sampling distribution of ranks.

In an ordinal scale of measurement, the scores can be meaningfully placed in order by size. Thus, the larger the score, the more of the thing being measured. This is not true for scores measured on a nominal scale. Suppose we measured the nominal variable "sex" with the value of 1 representing males and the value of 2 representing females. The fact that the greater number, "2," represents females does not mean that females have more sex than males do or that females are in any way superior to males. When using nominal scales, different values are used merely to assign subjects to different categories. The order of the categories is not meaningful in any way, and thus the size of the numbers representing the categories carries no meaning. On the other hand, for ordinal scales, the size (or magnitude) of the scores does carry meaning. For example, in the study of development, numbers are frequently assigned to indicate children's stage or level of development. A child in stage 3 is at a higher level of development than a child in stage 2. Here, the order of the numbers is meaningful.

When the scores can be placed in meaningful order, it is possible to rank the scores from highest to lowest. These rankings are the basis for the three nonparametric tests that we will examine in this chapter. The first test we examine, the Mann-Whitney U test, uses ranks to compare two samples of scores received by two separate, independent groups of subjects. We next examine the Wilcoxon signed-ranks test, which similarly uses ranks to compare two groups of scores, but for the Wilcoxon, the scores come from one sample of subjects or from two related samples of subjects. Finally, we explore an inferential test of Spearman's rank-order correlation coefficient, r_S. The method for calculating the value of r_S, which we examined in Chapter 8, is also based on ranking scores.

These three nonparametric tests may be used with scores measured on any scale for which order is meaningfully ranked. Ordinal, interval, and ratio scales all have meaningful order, and thus these tests may be used for scores measured on all scales except a nominal scale of measurement. However, since parametric tests may be used with scores measured on interval and ratio scales, and since parametric tests tend to be more powerful than nonparametric tests, the three nonparametric tests we examine in this chapter are primarily used with ordinal data. To understand what the values of these nonparametric statistics, U, W, and r_S, measure, we will first look at a sampling distribution based on ranks.

A Sampling Distribution of Ranks

A Distribution of Rank Sums

In previous chapters, we have looked at several sampling distributions, such as the distribution of sample means, the distribution of sample proportions, the distribution of the difference between sample means, and the distribution of a mean difference. All of these sampling distributions are based on the notion of what would happen if we drew hundreds and hundreds of samples from a population.

For example, the t test for a difference between means is based on the idea of drawing hundreds of pairs of samples from a population and finding the difference between the means of the two samples in each pair. We found that the differences between the means of hundreds of pairs of samples would be approximately normally distributed. Some of the differences would be negative, with the mean of Sample 1 being larger than the mean of Sample 2. An equal number of differences would be positive, with the mean of Sample 2 being larger than the mean of Sample 1. Across the difference between the means of hundreds and hundreds of pairs of samples, all drawn from the same population, these differences would center around 0. Thus, without ever actually having to draw hundreds and hundreds of pairs of samples, we can figure out what the sampling distribution would be like if we did.

Now, let's suppose that rather than calculating the means of pairs of samples we instead rank the scores in the two samples. Suppose that we have a population of scores measured on an ordinal scale, so that we can meaningfully rank the scores. Now suppose that we draw two samples from that population, one sample with two scores and the second sample with three scores. We mark the scores clearly, so that we know which sample each score came from. Then we put all the scores into one group and rank them, from a rank of 1 for the score with the lowest value to a rank of 5 for the score with the highest value. Then we separate the scores into the two samples again.

As an illustration, suppose that the two populations consisted of the class standings of 100 students, and thus that those standings ranged from 1 (student with the highest GPA) to 100 (student with the lowest GPA). We draw a sample of 2 students from one population, whose class standings are 19 and 42. From the other population, we draw a sample of 3 students, with class standings of 3, 56, and 82. We combine these two samples into one group and assign ranks, from lowest to highest, as follows:

Class Standing	From Sample	Rank
3	2	1
19	1	2
42	1	3
56	2	4
82	2	5

The ranks assigned to the class standings in Sample 1 are ranks 2 and 3, while the ranks assigned to the class standings in Sample 2 are ranks, 1, 4, and 5. This is one possible outcome of the ranks for two samples containing 2 and 3 scores, respectively.

Table 15-1 shows that there are ten possible combinations that could occur. One possibility is that the two lowest scores are in Sample 1 and the three highest scores in Sample 2. Another possibility is that Sample 1 contains the two highest scores, in which case Sample 2 would contain the three lowest scores. Table 15-1 lists every combination possible, for two samples, with two and three scores, respectively. (Check out Table 15-1, and see if you can think of some combination that's not listed.)

The **rank sum** of a sample of scores is the sum of the ranks assigned to the scores in the sample when those scores are rank-ordered.

Now suppose that we find the sum of the ranks, or **rank sum**, for each of the pair of samples listed in Table 15-1. These rank sums are shown in Table 15-1. We can see that for Sample 1, with 2 scores, the rank sum varies from 3 to 9, and that for Sample 2, with 3 scores, the rank sum varies from 6 to 12. There is only one combination of ranks that yields a rank sum of 3 or 12, but there are several combinations that yield a rank sum of 6, 7, or 8.

From the information provided in Table 15-1, we can construct a distribution of these rank sums, showing each possible value of rank sum that can occur for two samples, with sample sizes of 2 and 3, and the number of times each of those values occurs. This distribution is shown in Table 15-2. Note that while the rank sums are listed separately for the two samples in Table 15-1, they

TABLE 15-1 Possible Combinations of Ranks and Resultant Rank Sums for Two Samples, with Sample Sizes of 2 and 3

Combination	Sample 1	Sum of Ranks	Sample 2	Sum of Ranks	Total Sum of Ranks
1	1, 2	3	3, 4, 5	12	15
2	1, 3	4	2, 4, 5	11	15
3	1, 4	5	2, 3, 5	10	15
4	1, 5	6	2, 3, 4	9	15
5	2, 3	5	1, 4, 5	10	15
6	2, 4	6	1, 3, 5	9	15
7	2, 5	7	1, 3, 4	8	15
8	3, 4	7	1, 2, 5	8	15
9	3, 5	8	1, 2, 4	7	15
10	4, 5	9	1, 2, 3	6	15

are listed together in one column in Table 15-2. We can see that out of 20 possible outcomes (10 for Sample 1 and 10 for Sample 2), the lowest rank sum is 3 and the highest rank sum is 12, both of which occurred once.

The information in Table 15-2 is a sampling distribution of rank sums for the sample sizes of 2 and 3. This is comparable to a sampling distribution of the difference between means, as Table 15-2 gives the values of all of the possible rank sums that could occur if two samples (with sizes of 2 and 3) were drawn from the same population, along with the frequency of their occurrences. The sampling distribution of rank sums is not a parametric distribution because the rank sums are not a population parameter. Thus, any statistical test based on the sampling distribution of rank sums will not be a parametric test.

TABLE 15-2 Sampling Distribution of Rank Sums, with Sample Sizes of 2 and 3

Rank Sum	Number of Occurrences
12	1
11	1
10	2
9	3
8	3
7	3
6	3
5	2
4	1
3	1

The Total, Minimum, and Maximum Rank Sums

There are several noteworthy characteristics of the distribution of rank sums, shown in Tables 15-1 and 15-2. First, note that the total sum of the ranks for both samples in this example is always 15. Whenever we have 2 samples, one with 2 scores and the other with 3 scores, the ranks given to those scores will be the ranks of 1, 2, 3, 4, and 5, which totals 15. If there were a total of 6 scores in the two samples (for example, 2 samples of 3 scores each or 1 sample of 2 scores and the other of 4 scores), the scores will be given the ranks of 1, 2, 3, 4, 5, and 6, which totals 21. Thus, whenever the two samples have a total of 6 scores, the total sum of ranks will always be 21.

The **total rank sum** for two samples, one with size n_1 and the other with size n_2, is

$$\frac{(n_1 + n_2)(n_1 + n_2 + 1)}{2}.$$

The **total rank sum** depends entirely upon the number of scores in the two samples, one with size n_1 and the other with size n_2:

$$\text{total rank sum} = \frac{(n_1 + n_2)(n_1 + n_2 + 1)}{2}.$$

As a check, we will use this formula to find the total sum of ranks for our two samples, one with two scores and the other with three scores:

$$\frac{(n_1 + n_2)(n_1 + n_2 + 1)}{2} = \frac{(2 + 3)(2 + 3 + 1)}{2} = \frac{5 \times 6}{2} = \frac{30}{2} = 15.$$

Next, let's look at the sum of the ranks for each sample individually. In this example, the lowest sum for Sample 1 occurs when it contains the two lowest ranks (Ranks 1 and 2), so that the lowest possible sum is 3. The highest sum for Sample 1 occurs when it contains the two highest ranks (Ranks 4 and 5), so that the highest possible sum for Sample 1 is 9. Similarly, the lowest for Sample 2, which has three scores, occurs when it contains the three lowest ranks (Ranks 1, 2, and 3, for a sum of 6). Sample 2 has its highest sum when it contains the three highest ranks (Ranks 3, 4, and 5, for a sum of 12).

The **minimum rank sum** for two samples, with sizes n_1 and n_2, where n_1 is less than n_2, is

$$\text{minimum sum of ranks} = \frac{n_1(n_1 + 1)}{2},$$

and the **maximum rank sum** is:

$$\text{maximum sum of ranks} = \frac{n_2(n_2 + 1)}{2} + n_1 n_2.$$

Across both samples, the **minimum rank sum** occurs when the smaller of the two samples contains the lowest ranks. In this example, the smaller sample is Sample 1, with two scores, which has a minimum sum of ranks of 3. Thus, for these two samples, the minimum sum of ranks is 3. In general, the minimum sum of ranks can only occur for the smaller sized sample. Let Sample 1 be the smaller sized sample. Then, the minimum sum of ranks is

$$\text{minimum rank sum} = \frac{n_1(n_1 + 1)}{2}.$$

For our example, Sample 1, with two scores, is the smaller sized sample. We can see that this formula indicates that the minimum sum of ranks that can occur is 3, which is the same value that we found by listing all of the possible samples:

$$\frac{n_1(n_1 + 1)}{2} = \frac{2(2 + 1)}{2} = \frac{6}{2} = 3.$$

Just as the minimum sum of ranks can only occur for the smaller sized sample, the **maximum rank sum** can occur only for the sample with the larger sample size. Table 15-1 shows that the maximum sum of ranks occurs for the larger sized sample only when the minimum sum of ranks occurs for the smaller sized sample. Thus, if the sum of ranks is at the minimum for one sample, it will be at the maximum for the other sample. Because the sum of ranks for the two samples always adds up to the same value, we can use this information to construct a formula for the maximum sum of ranks, still assuming that n_1 is smaller than n_2:

$$\text{maximum sum of ranks} = \frac{(n_1 + n_2)(n_1 + n_2 + 1)}{2} - \frac{n_1(n_1 + 1)}{2}.$$

This equation can be rearranged algebraically to simplify it:

$$\text{maximum sum of ranks} = n_1 n_2 + \frac{n_2(n_2 + 1)}{2}.$$

Checking this formula for our two samples, with two and three scores, respectively, we find:

$$n_1 n_2 + \frac{n_2(n_2 + 1)}{2} = 2(3) + \frac{3(3 + 1)}{2} = 6 + \frac{12}{2} = 6 + 6 = 12.$$

Thus, with sample sizes of 2 and 3, the maximum sum of ranks is 12, which is the same value we found in Table 15-1 by listing all of the possible combinations of ranks.

The Sampling Distribution of *U*

The sampling distribution of rank sums that we have considered thus far is for the sample sizes of 2 and 3. We could construct the sampling distribution of rank sums for any combination of sample sizes. However, this could quickly become quite laborious because the number of possible combinations increases rapidly as the sample size increases. With sample sizes of 2 and 3, we found 10 different possible combinations of ranks. With sample sizes of 3 and 4, there are 35 different combinations of ranks for the two samples. When the sample sizes are 8 and 9, there are a total of 24,310 different combinations! It would take a considerable length of time to list all of those combinations, to construct the sampling distribution of rank sums for sample sizes of 8 and 9.

As we can see, the total number of different combinations in a sampling distribution of rank sums depends upon the sizes of the two samples. In addition, the total rank sum, minimum rank sum, and maximum rank sum all vary with the size of the two samples. For example, we saw that for two samples, with the smaller sample having two scores, the lowest rank sum was 3. When the smaller sample size is 5, the lowest rank sum will be 15, and when the smaller sample size is 10, the lowest rank sum will be 55. Thus, the larger the sample size, the greater the minimum value of the sum of the ranks. The fact that the minimum rank sum can vary makes it difficult to interpret the results. Suppose we found that one of two samples had a rank sum of 30? Is this high? Is it low? We can't really tell without knowing the sizes of both samples and then calculating the minimum and maximum rank sums. This is one difficulty in using the rank sum directly as the basis of a statistical test.

Another problem with using rank sums is that unless the two samples are equal in size, the minimum and maximum rank sums will differ for the two samples. We saw that with sample sizes of 2 and 3, the rank sum for the smaller-sized sample ranged from 3 to 9, while the rank sum for the larger sized sample ranged from 6 to 12. This will also cause difficulties in interpreting the results of a statistical test based directly on these rank sums.

These problems are solved in part by converting the rank sums of the two samples to a value called U. For any two samples, there are two values of U, one for each sample, labeled U_1 and U_2. The minimum value for both U_1 and U_2 is zero, no matter what the sample size is. In addition, the maximum value for both U_1 and U_2 will be the same, and thus for any two samples, the range of values that U can have will be the same for both samples.

The formula for converting the rank sum for Sample 1 (with a sample size of n_1) is

$$U_1 = n_1 n_2 + \frac{n_1(n_1 + 1)}{2} - \Sigma\text{ranks}_1.$$

The formula for converting the rank sum for Sample 2 (with a sample size of n_2) is

$$U_2 = n_1 n_2 + \frac{n_2(n_2 + 1)}{2} - \Sigma\text{ranks}_2.$$

Table 15-3 shows the value of U for each of the rank sums we found for sample sizes of 2 and 3, shown in Table 15-1. Note that while the minimum and maximum rank sums for Samples 1 and 2 are different, the value of U for both samples ranges from a minimum of 0 to a maximum of 6. Note also that for each sample, the lowest rank sum has the highest value of U and the highest

TABLE 15-3 Possible Rank Sums and Values of U for Two Samples, with Sample Sizes of 2 and 3

Sample 1		Sample 2		
Sum of Ranks	U_1	**Sum of Ranks**	U_2	$U_1 + U_2$
3	6	12	0	6
4	5	11	1	6
5	4	10	2	6
6	3	9	3	6
7	2	8	4	6
8	1	7	5	6
9	0	6	6	6

rank sum has the lowest value of U. Thus, a *higher* value of U indicates that the sample had a *lower* rank sum, and vice versa.

Table 15-3 also shows that, for sample sizes 2 and 3, the values of U_1 and U_2 always total 6, which is the value of $n_1 n_2$:

$$U_1 + U_2 = n_1 n_2.$$

This means that if we know the value of U_1, we can find the value of U_2 by subtracting the value of U_1 from $n_1 n_2$:

$$U_2 = n_1 n_2 - U_1.$$

The values of U for two samples form the basis of the Mann-Whitney U test, which is a between-subjects nonparametric test and which we examine next.

The Mann-Whitney *U* Test: A Between-Subjects Nonparametric Test

Conducting the Mann-Whitney *U* Test for Sample Sizes of 20 or Less

The method for conducting the Mann-Whitney U test when both samples contain 20 or fewer scores is shown in Step-by-Step Procedure 15-1. Note that the Mann-Whitney U test makes only two assumptions, that the subjects are randomly and independently sampled and that the scores are measured on at least an ordinal scale. The Mann-Whitney U test makes no assumption about the shape of the distributions, so we can use the test for a distribution of scores that is skewed.

Suppose that for the psychology statistics class at State University, laboratory sections are taught by graduate students and that grad students June and Joan each teach several lab sections. The undergraduate students majoring in psychology firmly believe that Joan is a harder grader than June. The students want to conduct a scientific test to validate their belief. However, the registrar's office has legitimately refused to allow the psychology majors access to the official grade records. Suppose we draw two samples of students, one from June's sections and one from Joan's sections, and ask them for their final grades. At State University grades are recorded on the plus/minus system. The grades received by the students in the two samples are shown in Table 15-4.

TABLE 15-4 Grades Received by Students in Samples Selected from Two Statistics Classes

June's Class		Joan's Class	
Grade	**Rank**	**Grade**	**Rank**
A	13	B+	11
A−	12	B−	7
B	9.5	C	3.5
B	9.5	C	3.5
B−	7	C−	2
B−	7	D	1
C+	5		
	$T_1 = 63$		$T_2 = 28$

Conducting the Mann-Whitney *U* Test

1. Verify that the following assumptions have been met:
   A. The subjects are randomly and independently sampled. Each subject is tested in only one sample.
   B. The scores are measured on at least an ordinal scale of measurement.

2. Write the null and alternate hypotheses. The hypotheses of the Mann-Whitney *U* test have the following form:

Bidirectional H_0: The distribution of Population 1 is the same as the distribution of Population 2.
   H_1: The distribution of Population 1 is different from the distribution of Population 2.

Unidirectional H_0: The distribution of Population 1 is not less than the distribution of Population 2.
   H_1: The distribution of Population 1 is less than the distribution of Population 2.

   H_0: The distribution of Population 1 is not greater than the distribution of Population 2.
   H_1: The distribution of Population 1 is greater than the distribution of Population 2.

3. Decide the level of significance, α.

4. If both sample sizes are 20 or less, find the critical values of *U* in Appendix A-9. If the sample sizes are more than 20, find the critical value of *z* in Appendix A-1.

5. Draw a number line, indicating the rejection region for U_1.
   A. If the hypotheses are bidirectional, the rejection region will be in both ends of the number line.
   B. If the alternate hypothesis predicts that Sample 1 will be larger than Sample 2, then Sample 1 should have the smaller value of *U*, and the rejection region will be in the lower segment of the number line.
   C. If the alternate hypothesis predicts that Sample 1 will be smaller than Sample 2, then Sample 1 should have the larger value of *U*, and the rejection region will be in the upper segment of the number line.

6. Calculate the value of *U* for Sample 1, following the method described in Procedure 15-2. If the sample sizes are greater than 20, convert the value of *U* for Sample 1 to a standard score, following the method described in Step-by-Step Procedure 15-3.

7. Decide whether or not to reject the null hypothesis:
   A. If the value of *U* or z_U calculated in Step 6 is in the rejection region, then $p \leq \alpha$, and reject the null hypothesis.
   B. If the value of *U* or z_U calculated in Step 6 is not in the rejection region, then $p > \alpha$, and do not reject the null hypothesis.

Step 1: Verify that the assumptions of the test are met.   The first assumption is that the subjects are randomly and independently selected and that no subject is a member of both samples. The samples were selected from two separate classes, and so this assumption is met. The only other assumption is that the scores are measured on at least an ordinal scale of measurement. This ensures that the scores can legitimately be ranked. We can rank letter grades, and so this assumption is met.

Step 2: Write the null and alternate hypotheses.   The null and alternate hypotheses for the Mann-Whitney U test make predictions about the relative frequency distributions of the two populations of scores being compared. The null hypothesis predicts that there is no difference between the two populations—that their frequency distributions are identical. For example, Graph A in Figure 15-1 shows two populations with identical frequency distributions.

FIGURE 15-1   Examples of Frequency Distributions that Do and Do Not Differ

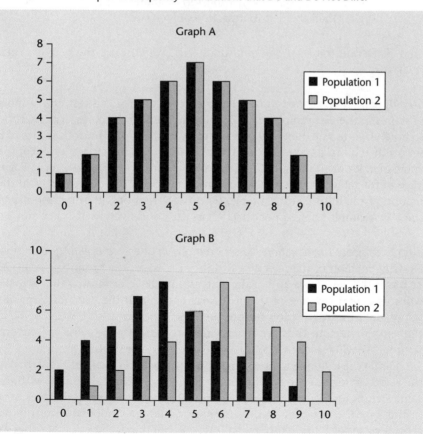

If we drew a sample from each of these populations, we would predict no significant difference between the rank sums for the two samples.

In Figure 15-1, Graph B shows two populations with different frequency distributions. Population 1 has more scores with lower values than does Population 2. If we drew samples from these two populations, we would expect the sample from Population 1 to have lower scores overall than does the sample from Population 2. Consequently, the sample from Population 1 would likely have a lower rank sum than would the sample from Population 2. Therefore, in essence, comparing the value of U for two samples is a way of comparing whether those samples come from populations with the same or different frequency distributions.

In our example, we are trying to show that June gives higher grades than Joan; thus, this is a unidirectional test:

H_0: The relative frequency distribution of grades in June's classes is not higher than the distribution in Joan's classes.

H_1: The relative frequency distribution of grades in June's classes is higher than the distribution in Joan's classes.

Step 3: Decide the level of significance, α.   We will use the conventional level, $\alpha = .05$.

Step 4: Identify the critical value(s) of the statistic.   For this test, the number of scores in the first sample, n_1, is 7, and the number of scores in the second sample, n_2, is 6. Appendix A-9 lists the critical values of U for four values of α for unidirectional and bidirectional tests. First, select the correct table for the value of α. We are doing a unidirectional test, with $\alpha = .05$, so we use the first page of the table. Find n_1 in the margin at the top of the table, and n_2 in the margin at the left side of the table. Find the values of U that correspond to these two sample sizes. Appendix A-9 lists the critical values of U as 8 and 34.

Step 5: Indicate the rejection region on a graph of the sampling distribution. Drawing a graph of the rejection region for U when the sample sizes are 20 or less is different from any of the statistics we have examined thus far. We will calculate two values of U, one for each sample. If the value of U for one sample falls in the rejection region, then the other value of U will also be in the rejection region. Thus, we actually need to test only the value of U for one sample. We will test the value of U for Sample 1, June's class.

While the example we are using is a unidirectional test, let's look first at the rejection regions for a bidirectional test. For a bidirectional test, with the same significance level of .05, Appendix A-9 gives us two critical values of U, in this case the values of 8 and 34. These values are comparable to the two critical values of z for a bidirectional z test. Recall that if the value of z that we calculate falls between the two critical values of z, we do not reject the null

FIGURE 15-2 Example of Rejection Regions for a Bidirectional Mann-Whitney U Test

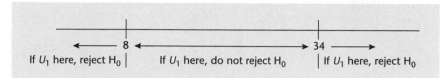

hypothesis. Similarly, if the value of U that we calculate falls between the two critical values of U that we obtained in Appendix A-9, we do not reject the null hypothesis. For the bidirectional z test, we can reject the null hypothesis if the value of z that we calculate is less than or equal to the lower critical z or if it is greater than or equal to the higher critical z. Similarly, for the bidirectional U test, we can reject the null hypothesis if the value of U that we calculate is less than or equal to the lower critical U from Appendix A-9 or if it is greater than or equal to the higher critical U. An example of the rejection region for a bidirectional test is shown in Figure 15-2.

In a unidirectional z test, we can reject the null hypothesis only if the value of z we calculate falls in one tail of the distribution. If we are predicting that the value of z that we calculate will fall in the upper tail, but instead it falls in the lower tail, we cannot reject the null. The situation for the unidirectional test of U is a bit more complicated because there will be two values of U. Whenever one of the values of U falls in the lower rejection region, the other value of U will automatically fall in the upper rejection region. As a consequence, whether the null is rejected depends upon which value of U, U_1 or U_2, falls in which rejection region.

If the alternate hypothesis predicts that the frequency distribution for Population 1 is higher than the distribution for Population 2, then U_1 must be in the *lower* rejection region and U_2 in the *upper* rejection region in order to reject the null. If the alternate hypothesis predicts that the frequency distribution for Population 1 is lower than the distribution for Population 2, the U_1 must be in the *upper* rejection region and U_2 in the *lower* rejection region in order to reject the null. The value of U for the sample representing the population predicted to have the higher distribution must be in the lower rejection region.

Common sense would lead us to think that if we are predicting Population 1 to have the higher frequency distribution, then U_1 should be in the upper rejection region in order to reject the null. However, recall that the sample that has the higher frequency distribution will likely have the higher rank sum and that the sample with the higher rank sum will have the *lower* value of U. In our example, we are predicting that the distribution of grades in June's classes will be higher than the distribution of grades in Joan's classes. Since we are predicting that the sample from June's class will have the higher rank sum, we are predicting that June's sample will have the *lower* value of U.

FIGURE 15-3   Rejection Region for Unidirectional Mann-Whitney U Test, $n_1 = 6$ and $n_2 = 7$

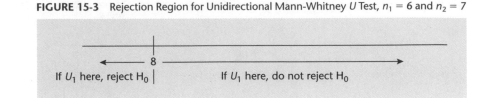

Figure 15-3 shows the rejection region for testing U_1 in our comparison of June's and Joan's grades.

Step 6: Calculate the statistic from the sample of scores.   Table 15-4 lists the ranks assigned to the grades. We examined how to assign ranks in Chapter 8, when we calculated Spearman's rank-order correlation. If you don't remember how to assign ranks, go back and review the process described in Step-by-Step Procedure 8-2. In assigning ranks for the Mann-Whitney U test, we combine the scores from the two samples and rank both samples together. The lowest grade in both samples is a D, which receives a rank of 1. The next lowest grade is a C−, which receives a rank of 2. There are two grades of C, which occupy the places of ranks 3 and 4, and so we give them the average of these ranks, or 3.5. We continue this way, until the highest grade receives a rank of 13. The highest rank will equal the number of scores in both samples combined, $n_1 + n_2$.

The sum of the ranks for Sample 1, T_1, is 63, and the sum of the ranks for Sample 2, T_2, is 28. We use these rank sums to calculate the value of U_1 and U_2, following the method described in Step-by-Step Procedure 15-2, which shows that the value of U_1 is 7 and the value of U_2 is 35:

$$U_1 = n_1 n_2 + \frac{n_1(n_1 + 1)}{2} - T_1 = (7)(6) + \frac{7(7 + 1)}{2} - 63 = 42 + \frac{56}{2} - 63$$

$$= 42 + 28 - 63 = 7,$$

$$U_2 = n_1 n_2 - U_1 = 42 - 7 = 35.$$

Step 7: Decide whether or not to reject the null hypothesis.   The value of U_1 for June's sample, is 7. This value lies in the rejection region shown in Figure 15-3. Therefore, we can reject the null hypothesis and conclude that the grades received by students in June's classes are significantly higher than the grades received by students in Joan's classes.

Alternate Method for Calculating U

In Procedure 15-2, the value of U is calculated with the use of a formula. There is an algorithm that can be used to find the value of U, which is not based on

---

Calculating the Value of Mann-Whitney's *U*

$$U_1 = n_1 n_2 + \frac{n_1(n_1 + 1)}{2} - T_1$$

$$U_2 = n_1 n_2 + \frac{n_2(n_2 + 1)}{2} - T_2 = n_1 n_2 - U_1$$

where n_1 = the number of subjects in Sample 1
n_2 = the number of subjects in Sample 2
T_1 = the sum of the ranks assigned to Sample 1
T_2 = the sum of the ranks assigned to Sample 2

1. Combine the scores from both samples into one group and assign ranks, giving the score with the lowest value the rank of 1 and the score with the highest value the rank of $(n_1 + n_2)$.

2. Sum the ranks assigned to the scores in Sample 1.

3. Multiply the number of scores in Sample 1 by the number of scores in Sample 2.

4. Add 1 to the number of scores in Sample 1. Multiply this result by the number of scores in Sample 1. Divide this result by 2.

5. Add the results of Steps 3 and 4, then subtract the result of Step 2 to find the value of U_1.

6. Subtract the result of Step 5 from the result of Step 3 to find the value of U_2.

---

using a formula and does not involve ranking the scores. To determine the value of *U* for one of two samples, for each score in the sample selected count 1 point for each score in the other sample that is greater in value and half a point for each score in the other sample that is equal in value. For example, there are seven scores in June's sample in Table 15-4. The number of scores in Joan's sample that are higher than each of these seven scores are shown below:

Grade in June's Class	Number of Higher or Equal Grades in Joan's Class
A	0
A−	0
B	1
B	1
B−	1.5
B−	1.5
C+	2
	$U = 7$

Follow the same procedure to find the value of U for the other sample:

Grade in June's Class	Number of Higher or Equal Grades in June's Class
B+	2
B−	5
C	7
C	7
C−	7
D	7
	$U = 35$

As a check, $U_1 + U_2$ will equal $n_1 n_2$, the product of the number of scores in each sample.

Conducting the Mann-Whitney *U* Test for Sample Sizes Greater than 20

Appendix A-9 lists the critical values of U only for sample sizes up to 20. If the sample size is larger than 20, we cannot use Appendix A-9. However, for sample sizes greater than 20, the sampling distribution of U is approximately normal in shape. Therefore, we can use the probabilities of the normal distribution, found in Appendix A-1, to test hypotheses about the value of U. All we need to do is to convert the value of U to z, as shown in Step-by-Step Procedure 15-3.

The method for testing U using the normal distribution is the same as the method for testing z. Remember, though, that for a unidirectional test, if the alternate hypothesis predicts that Population 1 is greater than Population 2, the value of U_1 is expected to be in the *lower* tail of the sampling distribution, and if the alternate hypothesis predicts that Population 1 is less than Population 2, then the value of U_1 is expected to be in the *upper* tail of the sampling distribution.

Suppose that Jane Jeffers wanted to compare the incomes received by psychology majors according to the specialties in which they were interested as undergraduates. In Jane's original survey, twenty clinical psychology majors and twenty-five experimental psychology majors responded. Their incomes are listed in Table 15-5. Jane believed that the students interested in clinical psychology would end up earning higher incomes than would the students interested in experimental psychology. Because distributions of income frequently are skewed, it would be appropriate to analyze these data using a nonparametric test, such as the Mann-Whitney U test. However, since there were over twenty incomes in the experimental psychology group, we cannot use Appendix A-9 and must convert U to a value of z in order to conduct the test. We will still follow the same steps listed in Procedure 15-1 to conduct the Mann-Whitney test.

STEP-BY-STEP PROCEDURE 15-3

Converting *U* to a Standard Score

$$\mu_U = \frac{n_1 n_2}{2}$$

$$\sigma_U = \sqrt{\frac{n_1 n_2 (n_1 + n_2 + 1)}{12}}$$

$$z_U = \frac{U - \mu_U}{\sigma_U}$$

where n_1 = the number of subjects in Sample 1
n_2 = the number of subjects in Sample 2

1. Multiply the number of scores in Sample 1 by the number of scores in Sample 2.

2. Divide the result of Step 1 by 2 to find the mean of the sampling distribution of *U*.

3. Add the number of scores in Sample 1 to the number of scores in Sample 2. Add 1 to the result. Then multiply that result by the result of Step 2 and divide by 12.

4. To find the standard error of the sampling distribution of *U*, find the square root of the result of Step 3.

5. Find the value of *U* for Sample 1, following the method described in Procedure 15-2.

6. To convert the value of *U* to a standard score, z_U, subtract the result of Step 1 from the result of Step 5, then divide that result by the result of Step 4.

Step 1: Verify that the assumptions of the test are met. The first assumption of the Mann-Whitney test is that the subjects are randomly and independently sampled. We will assume that this assumption has been met. The other assumption is that the scores are measured on at least an ordinal scale of measurement. As income levels can be ordered, this assumption is met.

Step 2: Write the null and alternate hypotheses. As described before, the hypotheses of the Mann-Whitney concern whether the frequency distributions of the populations from which the samples came are the same or different. Jane is trying to show that the clinical psychology alumni have higher incomes than do the experimental psychology alumni, which is a unidirectional test.

> H_0: The relative frequency distribution of incomes for clinical psychology alumni is not higher than the distribution for experimental psychology alumni.

TABLE 15-5 Incomes Received by Alumni Who Majored in Clinical and Experimental Psychology

Clinical Psychology Alumni		Experimental Psychology Alumni	
Incomes	**Ranks**	**Incomes**	**Ranks**
$114,000	45	96,000	40
$111,000	44	86,000	37
$107,000	43	80,000	34
$104,000	42	78,000	32
$97,000	41	73,000	30
$91,000	39	69,000	29
$89,000	38	68,000	28
$85,000	36	65,000	26
$82,000	35	63,000	25
$79,000	33	62,000	24
$75,000	31	57,000	21
$66,000	27	52,000	19
$61,000	23	47,000	17
$59,000	22	45,000	16
$55,000	20	42,000	14
$49,000	18	40,000	13
$44,000	15	35,000	10
$39,000	12	32,000	9
$37,000	11	30,000	8
$24,000	5	29,000	7
		27,000	6
		21,000	4
		18,000	3
		15,000	2
		9,000	1
$\Sigma_{\text{ranks}_1} = 580$		$\Sigma_{\text{ranks}_2} = 455$	

H_1: The relative frequency distribution of incomes for clinical psychology alumni is higher than the distribution for experimental psychology alumni.

Step 3: Decide the level of significance, α. We will use the conventional significance level of .05.

Step 4: Find the critical value of z. For a unidirectional test, with $\alpha = .05$, the critical value of z is either $+1.65$ or -1.65. In this example, we will find the value of U for the clinical psychology alumni. As we are predicting that the clinical alumni's incomes will be greater than the experimental alumni, we are predicting that the U for the clinical alumni will be *lower* than the U for the experimental alumni. Therefore, we are predicting a negative value of z, and so the critical z is -1.65.

Step 5: Determine the rejection region. For this test, if the value of z that we calculate is -1.65 or less, we will reject the null hypothesis.

Step 6: Calculate the value of U and convert to a value of z. We can follow Procedure 15-2 to calculate the value of U for the clinical psychology alumni. We will call the clinical alumni "Population 1" and the experimental alumni "Population 2." Table 15-5 shows that the sum of ranks for the clinical alumni is 580. In this example, n_1 is 20 and n_2 is 25. These are the values that we need to calculate the value of U:

$$U_1 = n_1 n_2 + \frac{n_1(n_1 + 1)}{2} - T_1 = (20 \times 25) + \frac{20(21)}{2} - 580 = 500 + 210 - 580 = 130.$$

Next, we need to convert this value of U, 130, to a value of z. To do this, we must first find the value of μ_U and σ_U, following the method described in Procedure 15-3:

$$\mu_U - \frac{n_1 n_2}{2} = \frac{20 \times 25}{2} = \frac{500}{2} = 250,$$

$$\sigma_U = \sqrt{\frac{n_1 n_2 (n_1 + n_2 + 1)}{12}} = \sqrt{\frac{(20)(25)(20 + 25 + 1)}{12}}$$

$$= \sqrt{\frac{(20)(25)(46)}{12}} = \sqrt{\frac{23,000}{12}} = \sqrt{1,916.67} = 43.8.$$

We now have the values we need to convert U to z:

$$z_U = \frac{U - \mu_U}{\sigma_U} = \frac{130 - 250}{43.8} = \frac{-120}{43.8} = -2.74.$$

Step 7: Decide whether or not to reject the null hypothesis. In Step 5, we determined that if the value of z that we calculate is -1.65 or less, then we would reject the null hypothesis. In fact, the value of z_U, -2.74, is in this rejection region, and thus we can reject the null hypothesis. This study provides evidence that clinical psychology alumni do have higher incomes than do experimental psychology alumni.

The Wilcoxon Signed-Ranks Test:
A Within-Subjects Nonparametric Test

The Sampling Distribution of *W*

Where the Mann-Whitney *U* test is a between-subjects test, the Wilcoxon signed-ranks test is a within-subjects test and can be used when two sets of scores are obtained from one sample of subjects or when the sets of scores come from two separate samples of subjects, who can be logically related in some meaningful way. We will examine an example in this section in which the scores are provided by husband-wife pairs, which certainly is a meaningful relationship.

The Wilcoxon signed-ranks test combines the techniques used in the Mann-Whitney *U* test and the *t* test for a mean difference. Like the Mann-Whitney *U* test, the Wilcoxon signed-ranks test can be used with any scores that can be ranked. And similar to the *t* test for a mean difference, the Wilcoxon test is based on finding the difference between the scores for each pair of subjects.

Suppose we want to compare the marital satisfaction of husbands and wives. We select a sample of twelve husband-wife pairs and give them each a survey to assess marital satisfaction. Possible scores on the survey range from 0 to 50, with the higher score indicating greater marital satisfaction. Table 15-6 shows the marital satisfaction scores for each husband-wife pair in the sample. The fourth column in Table 15-6 shows the difference between

TABLE 15-6   Marital Satisfaction Scores for Twelve Husband-Wife Pairs

Pair	Husband	Wife	(H − W)	Rank	+ Ranks*	− Ranks*
1	49	26	23	10	10	
2	32	12	20	9	9	
3	41	23	18	8	8	
4	37	22	15	7	7	
5	44	31	13	6	6	
6	28	39	−11	5		5
7	27	18	9	4	4	
8	43	36	7	3	3	
9	29	34	−5	2		2
10	33	35	−2	1		1
11	44	44	0			
12	33	33	0			

*Σ(+ ranks) = 47, Σ(− ranks) = 8.

the scores for the spouses in each pair, found by subtracting the wife's score from the husband's score. The method for finding these differences is similar to the method we used in calculating the *t* test for a mean difference.

The method of ranking these differences for the Wilcoxon signed-ranks test involves two steps. First, the differences are assigned ranks irrespective of the sign (positive or negative) of the difference. Pairs of scores that are equal, thus for which the difference is zero, are not assigned ranks, but rather are eliminated from the analysis. Only pairs of scores with nonzero differences are assigned ranks. The pair of scores with the smallest difference (either positive or negative) is assigned the rank of 1. In Table 15-6, husband-wife pair 10 has the smallest difference, −2, and is ranked 1. The pair of scores with the next smallest difference is assigned the rank of 2, and so on, until the pair of scores with the greatest difference is assigned the highest rank, which is equal to the number of pairs of scores with a nonzero difference. In Table 15-6, 10 pairs of scores have a nonzero difference, and therefore the highest rank assigned is 10.

The ranks assigned in this fashion are a measure of the degree of similarity between the pairs of scores. When a husband and wife give marital satisfaction ratings that are very similar, such as pair 10, with ratings of 33 and 35, the difference between those ratings is small and the pair is assigned a comparatively low rank. When the marital satisfaction ratings of a husband-wife pair are very dissimilar, such as pair 1 in Table 15-6, the difference between the ratings is large and the pair is assigned a comparatively high rank. Thus, the more dissimilar the husband-wife ratings, the higher the rank that is assigned, so that these ranks are an indication of the degree to which husbands and wives gave similar ratings. The ranks for the ten husband-wife pairs who had nonzero differences between their marital satisfaction ratings are shown in the fifth column in Table 15-6.

As noted previously, when we assign these ranks, we ignore the sign (positive or negative) of the difference. The sign of a difference indicates which score of the pair was greater in value. In the example shown in Table 15-6, if the husband gave a higher satisfaction rating than the wife did, the difference was positive. However, if the wife gave the higher satisfaction rating, the difference was negative. Because the signs are ignored in assigning the ranks, these ranks indicate the degree to which the ratings given by each husband-wife pair were similar, regardless of whether it was the husband or the wife who gave the higher satisfaction rating.

The next step in ranking the difference between pairs of scores for the Wilcoxon ranked-sums test involves separating the ranks for positive differences from the ranks for negative differences. We make one list of the ranks representing all of the differences that were positive. These ranks are shown in the sixth column of Table 15-6 and represent the ranks for the differences for all of the husband-wife pairs in which the husband gave the higher marital satisfaction rating. Husband-wife pairs 1, 2, 3, 4, 5, 7, and 8 had positive differences in column 4, which indicated that the husband's score was higher than the wife's score. The sum of these positive ranks is 47. Then we make another list of the ranks representing all of the differences that were negative. These ranks are shown in the seventh column of Table 15-6 and represent the ranks for the differences for all of the husband-wife pairs in which the wife gave the higher marital satisfaction rating. Husband-wife pairs 6, 9, and 10 had negative differences in column 4, which indicated that the wife's score was higher than the husband's. The sum of these negative ranks is 8.

The Wilcoxon signed-ranks test measures the probability of getting a particular value of these signed ranks. Suppose that there is no overall difference between husbands' and wives' marital satisfaction. If that were the case, the husbands' and wives' marital satisfaction scores wouldn't always match exactly. However, we could expect that approximately half the time the husband's score would be larger, and the other half of the time the wife's would be larger. We could also expect that large differences would favor the wife as frequently as the husband, and similarly for small differences. Thus, we would expect that the sum of the positive ranks would be approximately the same as the sum of the negative ranks. If the sum of the positive ranks is very different from the sum of the negative ranks, it would suggest that there is a difference between the marital satisfaction of husbands and wives. The Wilcoxon signed-ranks test measures the chance of the sums of the positive and negative ranks being as different as those observed in the sample. The smaller of the two signed rank sums is labeled W. The method for conducting the Wilcoxon signed-ranks test is shown in Step-by-Step Procedure 15-4. Step-by-Step Procedure 15-5 describes the method for calculating the value of W.

Conducting Wilcoxon's Test when *n* Is 50 or Less

Step 1: Verify that the assumptions of the test are met.   The Wilcoxon signed-ranks test assumes that the subjects are randomly and independently selected. It also assumes that the scores can be logically paired. Each subject contributing two scores is one way that scores can be logically paired. A second way is illustrated in our example of a marital satisfaction survey. Pairing husband-and-wife scores together is a logical pairing. The second assumption of the Wilcoxon signed-ranks test is that the scores are measured on at least an ordinal scale, so that they can meaningfully be ranked.

Step 2: Write the null and alternate hypotheses.   In setting up this study, we made no prediction about whether the husbands' or wives' scores were greater. We are testing only to see if marital satisfaction differs between husbands and wives, which is a bidirectional test. Thus, the null hypothesis is that the distributions of husbands' and wives' marital satisfaction scores are identical. The alternate hypothesis is that the distributions of husbands' and wives' marital satisfaction scores are different.

STEP-BY-STEP PROCEDURE 15-4

Conducting the Wilcoxon Signed-Ranks Test

1. Verify that the following assumptions have been met:
  A. The subjects are randomly and independently sampled. Either each subject contributes two scores or the two samples of subjects are logically related.
  B. The scores are measured on at least an ordinal scale of measurement.

2. Write the null and alternate hypotheses. The hypotheses of the Wilcoxon signed-ranks test have the following form:

Bidirectional H_0: The distribution of Population 1 is the same as the distribution of Population 2.
        H_1: The distribution of Population 1 is different from the distribution of Population 2.

Unidirectional H_0: The distribution of Population 1 is not less than the distribution of Population 2.
        H_1: The distribution of Population 1 is less than the distribution of Population 2.

        H_0: The distribution of Population 1 is not greater than the distribution of Population 2.
        H_1: The distribution of Population 1 is greater than the distribution of Population 2.

3. Decide the level of significance, α.

4. If the sample size is 50 or less, find the critical value of W in Appendix A-8. If the sample size is more than 50, find the critical value of z in Appendix A-1.

5. Draw a number line, indicating the rejection region for W.

6. Calculate the value of W, following the method described in Procedure 15-5. If the sample size is greater than 50, convert the value of W for sample 1 to a standard score, following the method described in Procedure 15-6.

7. Decide whether or not to reject the null hypothesis:
  A. For a bidirectional test, if W is no greater than the critical value of W, reject the null hypothesis.
  B. For a unidirectional test, if H_1 predicts that Population 1 will be larger than Population 2, then W must be the sum of the negative ranks and W must be no greater than the critical value of W, to reject the null hypothesis.
  C. For a unidirectional test, if H_1 predicts that Population 1 will be smaller than Population 2, then to reject the null hypothesis, W must be the sum of the positive ranks and W must be no greater than the critical value of W.

Step 3: Decide the level of significance, α.   We will again use the conventional level of significance, $\alpha = .05$.

Step 4: Identify the critical value(s) of the statistic.   There originally were 12 pairs of spouses in the sample. However, 2 of those pairs had differences of zero, and those pairs are not counted in the analysis. Therefore, the number

---

STEP-BY-STEP PROCEDURE 15-5

Calculating the Value of *W* for the Wilcoxon Signed-Ranks Test

1. List the scores in pairs. The first column of scores represents Population 1. The second column of scores represents Population 2.

2. Find the difference between each pair of scores: Score 1 − Score 2. Cross out any differences of 0.

3. Ignoring the signs, rank the differences, from lowest to highest. If there are tied differences, assign them the average of the ranks they would occupy. The highest rank will equal the number of pairs of scores, minus the number of pairs with zero differences.

4. Sum the ranks for the positive differences. Separately, sum the ranks for the negative differences. The smaller of these two values is *W*.

FIGURE 15-4   Rejection Region for Wilcoxon Signed-Ranks Test, $\alpha = .05$ and $n = 10$

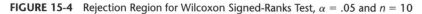
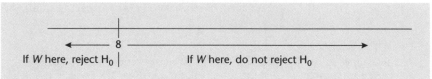

of pairs that contributed to the value of *W* is 10. With an *n* of 10, $\alpha = .05$, and a bidirectional test, Appendix A-8 shows that the critical value of *W* is 8.

Step 5: Indicate the rejection region on a graph of the sampling distribution. Figure 15-4 shows a number line representing the rejection region for this Wilcoxon signed-ranks test. As this is a bidirectional test, it does not matter whether the sum of positive ranks or the sum of negative ranks is *W*. However, if this were a unidirectional test, it would be of consequence. For example, suppose that we were predicting that wives would have greater marital satisfaction. We subtracted each wife's score from her husband's (H − W). If the wives have greater satisfaction, then these differences should be negative. Thus, we would expect the sum of the negative ranks to be larger and the sum of the positive ranks to be smaller. *W* is the smaller sum. In order to support the hypothesis that wives have greater satisfaction, *W* must be the sum of the positive ranks. Be very careful with unidirectional tests to identify the correct rank sum to support the hypothesis.

Step 6: Calculate the statistic from the sample of scores.   We have already calculated the sum of the positive and negative ranks. The sum of the positive ranks was 47, and the sum of the negative ranks was 8. Since 8 is the smaller sum, the value of W is 8.

Step 7: Decide whether or not to reject the null hypothesis. Since this is a bidirectional test, either the sum of the positive ranks or the sum of the negative ranks can be W. The value of W, 8, is equal to the critical value shown in Figure 15-4. Therefore, we can reject the null hypothesis. The scores in Table 15-6 are evidence that there is a significant difference between husbands' and wives' marital satisfaction.

Conducting Wilcoxon's Test when *n* Is Greater than 50

Appendix A-8 lists critical values of W for samples in which n is 50 or less. If n is over 50, we cannot use Appendix A-8, but we can use the normal distribution to test the significance of W by converting W to a value of z. In fact, even though Appendix A-8 lists critical values of W for values of n up to 50, the normal approximation to W is close enough when n is at least 10 that we can use the normal distribution when n is 10 or greater. Step-by-Step Procedure 15-6 shows the method for converting the value of W to a standard score. Remember that for unidirectional tests, the same cautions apply about which rank sum is W.

Since we can use the normal approximation with an n as small as 10, as an example, we will convert the value of W that we just calculated for the

---

STEP-BY-STEP PROCEDURE 15-6

Converting the Value of *W* to a Standard Score

$$\mu_W = \frac{n(n + 1)}{4}$$

$$\sigma_W = \sqrt{\frac{n(n + 1)(2n + 1)}{24}}$$

$$z_W = \frac{W - \mu_W}{\sigma_W}$$

where n = the number of nonzero differences

1. Add 1 to n. Multiply the result by n.

2. Divide the result of Step 1 by 4 to find the mean of the sampling distribution of W.

3. Multiply n by 2, then add 1. Multiply that result by the result of Step 1.

4. Divide the result of Step 3 by 24. Find the square root of that result to find the standard error of the sampling distribution of W.

5. Subtract the result of Step 2 from the value of W found using Procedure 15-4. To convert W to a standard score, divide that result by the result of Step 4.

husband-wife pairs to a z. To do so, we first need to find the values of the mean and standard deviation of the sampling distribution of W for an n of 10, μ_W and σ_W:

$$\mu_W = \frac{n(n+1)}{4} = \frac{10(10+1)}{4} = \frac{10(11)}{4} = \frac{110}{4} = 27.5,$$

$$\sigma_W = \sqrt{\frac{n(n+1)(2n+1)}{24}} = \sqrt{\frac{10(10+1)(20+1)}{24}}$$

$$= \sqrt{\frac{10(11)(21)}{24}} = \sqrt{\frac{2,310}{24}} = \sqrt{96.25} = 9.8.$$

Recall that the value of W that we calculated for the husband-wife pairs was 8. We can put these values in the formula to convert W to a value of z:

$$z_W = \frac{W - \mu_W}{\sigma_W} = \frac{8 - 27.5}{9.8} = \frac{-19.5}{9.8} = -1.99.$$

Recall that the hypothesis we are testing is bidirectional. The alternate hypothesis asserted only that the level of satisfaction of husbands and wives differed but did not predict which spouse would have the higher satisfaction level. This is a bidirectional test. With the conventional α of .05, the critical values of z for a bidirectional test are ± 1.96. If the value of z_W that we calculate either is $+1.96$ or greater or is -1.96 or less, we can reject the null hypothesis. The value of z_W that we calculated was -1.99, which falls in the lower rejection region. Therefore, we can reject the null hypothesis. These data provide evidence that the satisfaction levels of husbands and wives do differ.

A Nonparametric Test of the Strength of a Relationship: Spearman's Rank-Order Correlation

As we have seen in this and the previous chapters on hypothesis testing, all inferential tests are conducted to determine whether one or more samples provide evidence of a relationship between variables in the population(s) from which the sample(s) were drawn. We saw in Chapter 14 that there are two ways of demonstrating this relationship. One method is to determine whether there is a significant difference in the scores on one variable between two levels of the other variable. The other method is to assess the strength of the relationship. In this chapter, both the Mann-Whitney and Wilcoxon tests are nonparametric examples of the first method. For example, we used the Mann-Whitney test to assess whether there was a significant difference in grade distributions (one variable) between two graduate student instructors (the second variable). Using Spearman's rank-order correlation coefficient in an inferential test is an example of the second method for demonstrating a relationship between variables.

Just as we can conduct an inferential test on Pearson's product-moment correlation, so we can test the significance of Spearman's rank-order correlation. In Chapter 8, we calculated the correlation in Joe's sample of math-anxious students between math scores and self-ratings on anxiety, using Spearman's rank-order correlation. Recall that Spearman's rank-order correlation can be used for ordinal scores as well as for interval and ratio scores. A statistical test of Spearman's rank-order correlation gives us a way to test hypotheses about relationships between variables in cases in which one or both variables are measured on an ordinal scale of measurement. The procedure for testing a sample value of Spearman's rank-order correlation, r_S, is nearly identical to the procedure for testing Pearson's r. The only differences lie in the assumptions of the test and the table used to find the critical value of r_S.

Recall that in Chapter 8, we saw that Joe Johnson gave ten of the students in his sample a math test and a questionnaire in which the students made self-ratings on their anxiety levels. Joe believed that there was a relationship between math scores and students' self-perceptions of anxiety in the population of math-anxious students. He believed that the more anxious students saw themselves, the less well they did on the math test. We can test Joe's hypothesis, using Spearman's rank-order correlation. Step-by-Step Procedure 15-7 describes the method for testing Spearman's rank-order correlation.

Step 1: Verify that the assumptions of the test are met. The assumptions for Spearman's r_S are shown in Procedure 15-7. There are only two assumptions. The first is that the subjects are randomly and independently sampled. This is an assumption of many statistical tests. The second assumption is that both variables are measured on at least an ordinal scale of measurement. Notice that the test for Spearman's rank-order correlation makes no assumptions about the shape of the distribution of scores, as the test for Pearson's product-moment correlation did.

Step 2: Write the null and alternate hypotheses. Joe predicts that in the population of math-anxious students, the higher the students' self-ratings of anxiety, the lower will be their math scores. This is a negative correlation. Thus, Joe's alternate hypothesis is that the population correlation between math scores and self-ratings on anxiety will be negative. The null hypothesis is that the population correlation will not be negative. Note that the population correlation is symbolized ρ_S. The null and alternate hypotheses are

$$H_0: \rho_S \geq 0,$$

$$H_1: \rho_S < 0.$$

As the alternate hypothesis predicts that the correlation will be negative, this is a one-tailed test.

Step 3: Decide the level of significance, α. We will use a significance level, $\alpha = .05$.

Conducting a Test of Spearman's Rank-Order Correlation

1. Verify that the following assumptions have been met:
   A. The subjects are randomly and independently sampled.
   B. Variables X and Y are both measured on at least an ordinal scale.

2. Write the null and alternate hypotheses.

Bidirectional	Unidirectional	
$H_0: \rho_S = 0$	$H_0: \rho_S \geq 0$	$H_0: \rho_S \leq 0$
$H_1: \rho_S \neq 0$	$H_1: \rho_S < 0$	$H_1: \rho_S > 0$

3. Decide the level of significance, α.

4. Find the critical value of r_S in Appendix A-6.

5. Draw a graph of the sampling distribution, indicating the rejection region. The rejection region is in both tails for a bidirectional test. For a unidirectional test, the rejection region is in the lower tail when the alternate hypothesis predicts that ρ_S is less than 0 and in the upper tail when the alternate hypothesis predicts that ρ_S is greater than 0.

6. Calculate the value of r_S from the scores of the subjects in the sample, using the formula below. Step-by-Step Procedure 8-2 describes how to use this formula. Remember that you must first rank the scores in each sample before you use the formula:

$$r_S = 1 - \frac{6 \Sigma D^2}{n(n^2 - 1)}.$$

7. Decide whether or not to reject the null hypothesis:
   A. If the value of r_S calculated in Step 6 is in the rejection region, then $p \leq \alpha$, and reject the null hypothesis.
   B. If the value of r_S calculated in Step 6 is not in the rejection region, then $p > \alpha$, and do not reject the null hypothesis.

Step 4: Identify the critical value(s) of the statistic.   Appendix A-6 lists the critical values of r_S, for selected values of α and n. Joe's alternate hypothesis predicts that the correlation will be negative, and therefore this is a one-tailed test. With $\alpha = .05$ and $n = 10$, we can find that the critical value of r_S shown in Appendix A-6 is $-.564$. Note that Appendix A-6 lists only positive values of r_S. If the alternate hypothesis predicts a negative correlation, we need to remember to insert a negative sign before the critical value of r_S found in Appendix A-6. In order to reject the null hypothesis, the sample must have a value of r_S of $-.564$ or lower.

Step 5: Indicate the rejection region on a graph of the sampling distribution.
Figure 15-5 shows a graph of the sampling distribution for Spearman's r_S for a one-tailed test, with $\alpha = .05$ and $n = 10$. Because Joe's hypothesis predicts that the correlation will be negative, the rejection region is in the lower tail of the distribution.

FIGURE 15-5 Sampling Distribution for Spearman's r_S, with $\alpha = .05$ and $n = 10$

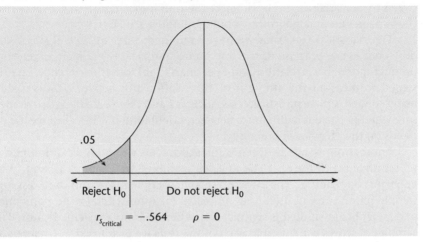

Step 6: Calculate the statistic from the sample of scores. In Chapter 8, we calculated the value of Spearman's rank-order correlation between math scores and self-ratings on anxiety for Joe's sample of twenty students and found that r_S was $-.74$. If you have forgotten how to compute the value of Spearman's r_S, the steps are described in Step-by-Step Procedure 8-2 in Chapter 8.

Step 7: Decide whether or not to reject the null hypothesis. The value of $r_S = -.74$ is clearly in the rejection region shown in Figure 15-5, and so we can reject the null hypothesis. We can use the results of Joe's study as evidence that there is a significant negative correlation between math test scores and self-ratings on anxiety in the population of math-anxious students, that the higher the students' self-ratings on anxiety, the lower were their math scores. In a scientific report, we would use the terminology, "$r_S = -.74$, $p < .05$," which tells us that the probability of drawing a sample with a correlation of $-.93$ from a population with a correlation of 0 is less than $\alpha = .05$, and thus the null hypothesis was rejected.

Hypothesis Testing Revisited

In the last five chapters, we have examined the concepts involved in hypothesis testing. The purpose of hypothesis testing is to be able to use samples to make statements about the populations from which the samples were drawn. All of the statistical tests that we have examined are based on the distribution of a sample statistic. z, t, r, r_S, U, and W are all sample statistics. Each statistical test measures the probability of the sample statistic occurring if the null hypothesis is true. The null hypothesis always asserts that there is no relationship between the variables being studied. If there is very little probability that the sample statistic would occur if there actually is no relationship between those variables, then we reject the null hypothesis and conclude that the variables are related in the population under study.

The statistical tests that we have examined differ in several ways. One difference is the purpose of the test. Some statistical tests, such as Pearson's product-moment correlation and Spearman's rank-order correlation, are designed to measure the strength of the relationship between the variables being studied. Other statistical tests, such as z and t tests, are designed to measure whether there is a difference between populations. Which test we use depends on the purpose of our study.

Another difference between statistical tests is the number of samples of scores involved in the test. The tests we examined in Chapters 12 and 13 involve just one sample. The z and t tests for a sample mean and the z test for a sample proportion all used one sample to measure whether the population parameter being studied is significantly different from a specified value. Two samples of scores were used in each of the tests we examined in Chapters 14 and 15. The z and t tests for a difference between means, the z test for a mean difference, the Mann-Whitney U test, and the Wilcoxon signed-ranks test all measure whether there is a significant difference between the populations from which two samples were drawn. Tests of Pearson's product-moment correlation and Spearman's rank-order correlation test the significance of the correlation between two variables, represented by two samples of scores obtained from the same or related subjects. In the next two chapters, we will examine statistical tests that can test the differences between three or more samples of scores.

A third difference exists between statistical tests that compare two populations. For some of these tests, the between-subjects tests, the two samples consist of scores from different groups of unrelated subjects. In between-subjects tests, each subject contributes one score. For the other two-population tests, the within-subjects tests, the two samples consist of scores from one group of subjects. In these tests, each subject contributes two scores, one to each sample. A special type of within-subjects test is when the two groups of subjects are used, but the subjects are related in some logical way, so that the scores of the two groups can be paired.

A final difference between statistical tests is whether they are parametric or nonparametric. Parametric tests measure the value of a population parameter, such as the population mean or the population correlation. Parametric tests assume that the population is either normally or binomially distributed, and interval or ratio scores are required in order to use parametric tests. On the other hand, nonparametric tests generally measure whether the shape or location on the number line of an entire distribution is identical to another distribution. Nonparametric tests are not limited to normal or binomial distributions. All nonparametric tests can be used with ordinal scores, and the χ^2 test, which we examine in Chapter 18, can be used with nominal scores.

CHECKING YOUR ANSWERS

1. At this point in the study of statistics, one difficulty that students encounter is trying to determine which statistical test to use. The answer depends upon (a) the scale of measurement, (b) whether you are trying to show a relationship between two variables in a population, or a difference between two populations, (c) the number of samples you have, and (d) if there are two samples, whether they are from the same or different subjects. Determine each of these, and you will know which test to use.

2. When calculating the value of U for the Mann-Whitney test, be sure that you combine the two samples together to rank the scores. Do not rank the scores in the samples separately.

3. The most common difficulty in the Mann-Whitney test is determining whether a unidirectional test is significant. Remember that if you predict that Sample 1 is greater than Sample 2, then the value of U for Sample 1 must be the smaller of the two to be significant. If you predict that Sample 1 is smaller than Sample 2, then the value of U for Sample 1 must be the greater of the two to be significant.

4. When conducting the Wilcoxon test, remember that the degrees of freedom are based on the number of pairs of scores in which the ranks were *not* equal. In effect, if a pair of scores have the same rank, they are eliminated from the sample and do not count toward the degrees of freedom.

5. For a unidirectional test of Wilcoxon's W, remember that if you predict that Population 1 is greater than Population 2, the sum of the negative ranks must be larger than the sum of the positive ranks for W to be significant. If you predict that Population 1 is less than Population 2, then the sum of the positive ranks must be larger than the sum of the negative ranks for W to be significant.

6. If you conduct a test of U or W by converting the statistic to a z, first follow the appropriate procedure to calculate the value of z, and then simply follow the procedure for a z test of a sample mean to complete the test.

7. Just as with Pearson's r, some students have difficulty formulating the null and alternate hypotheses in inferential tests of the strength of a correlation using Spearman's r_S. Hypotheses asserting whether or not a correlation exists in the population always use the value of 0. To test whether there is a positive correlation, the alternate hypothesis predicts that the population correlation will be greater than zero. To test whether there is a negative correlation, the alternate hypothesis predicts that the population correlation will be less than zero. Finally, to test simply whether there is a correlation (either positive or negative), the alternate hypothesis predicts that the population correlation will not equal zero.

Σ

SUMMARY

▶ Nonparametric inferential tests are used to test hypotheses either when the scores are measured on a nominal or ordinal scale of measurement or when the distribution of scores in the population cannot be assumed to be at least approximately normally distributed.

▶ The Mann-Whitney U test is a nonparametric test that measures whether or not the frequency distributions of scores from two populations are significantly different. The Mann-Whitney is based on the sum of ranks and thus can be used for scores that are at least ordinal. It is a between-subjects test and therefore is used when the two samples consist of different, unrelated subjects.

▶ The Wilcoxon signed-ranks test is a nonparametric test that also measures whether or not the frequency distributions of scores from two populations are significantly different. The Wilcoxon test is used when the two sets of scores either come from one sample of subjects or from two samples of subjects who are related in some meaningful way. The Wilcoxon test is based on finding the difference between each pair of scores and then ranking these differences.

▶ When using Spearman's rank-order correlation coefficient in an inferential test, the inference can be unidirectional (that there is a positive correlation in the population or that there is a negative correlation in the population) or bidirectional (that there simply is a correlation in the population). A test of the significance of Spearman's rank-order correlation coefficient measures whether there is a significant correlation between two variables in a population, both of which are at least ordinal variables.

E X E R C I S E S

Conceptual Exercises

1. Suppose that you have two sets of scores, one with three scores and the other with four scores, so that together there are seven scores. Assume that there are no duplicate values. Assume also that the scores are rankable. List all of the possible ways that these seven rankable scores could be divided into the two sets.

   A. Verify that for each combination of ranks the total sum of the ranks for Set 1, T_1, and the total sum of the ranks for Set 2, T_2, equals $n(n + 1)/2$.

   B. What is the lowest possible total sum of ranks for Set 1? What is the lowest possible total sum of ranks for Set 2? Explain why this occurs.

   C. What is the highest possible total sum of ranks for Set 1? What is the highest possible total sum of ranks for Set 2? Explain why this occurs.

   D. Identify the value of T_1 that corresponds to each value of T_2. Can there be more than one value of T_2 that corresponds to any one of the values of T_1? Explain why.

   E. Convert each value of T_1 to a value of U_1 and each value of T_2 to a value of U_2. Verify that each value of U_1 and its corresponding value of U_2 add up to $n_1 n_2$.

   F. For these two sets, with three and four scores, what is the lowest value U can have? What is the highest value? If U_1 is the highest possible value, what value will U_2 have?

   G. Construct a relative frequency distribution. First list all possible values of U_1 when the two sets have three and four scores. Next, list the corresponding values of U_2. In a third column, list the number of times these values of U occur in the list of all possible combinations of ranks. Finally, convert each of these frequencies to a relative frequency by dividing by the total number of possible combinations of ranks.

2. From the relative frequency table constructed in the previous exercise, representing two sets of scores, with three and four scores, respectively, determine the following:

   A. the probability of drawing a sample with a U of 0

   B. the probability of drawing a sample with a U of 12

C. the probability of drawing a sample with a U of 2 or less

D. the probability of drawing a sample with a U of 10 or more

3. Suppose that you have "before" and "after" scores from a group of five subjects, and suppose also that the differences between those scores are rankable. Assume that there are no tied ranks. Also assume that in finding the differences, we subtract the "before" scores from the "after" scores, so that a negative difference indicates that the "before" score was larger and a positive difference indicates that the "after" score was larger.

A. List all possible combinations of positive and negative ranks for these five scores, from all five ranks being negative to all five ranks being positive.

B. Construct a relative frequency table listing all possible sums of negative ranks when $n = 5$, the corresponding sums of positive ranks, and the frequencies and relative frequencies that these sums will occur.

4. From the table of relative frequencies for sums of ranks constructed in the previous exercise, determine the following probabilities:

A. the probability of getting a sum of negative ranks of 0

B. the probability of getting a sum of positive ranks of 0

C. the probability of getting a sum of negative ranks of 15

D. the probability of the sum of negative ranks being 3 or less

5. Identify the assumptions of the Mann-Whitney U test. For what types of data may the test be used?

6. Identify the assumptions of the Wilcoxon signed-ranks test. For what types of data may the test be used?

7. Identify the assumptions of a test of Spearman's rank-order correlation. For what types of data may the test be used?

Computational Exercises

8. Determine the critical value of U for each of the following:

A. $n_1 = 7, n_2 = 10$, H_1: Distribution 1 is not the same as Distribution 2, with $\alpha = .05$.

B. $n_1 = 15, n_2 = 15$, H_1: Distribution 1 is less than Distribution 2, with $\alpha = .01$.

C. $n_1 = 10, n_2 = 12$, H_1: Distribution 1 is greater than Distribution 2, with $\alpha = .05$.

D. $n_1 = 15, n_2 = 20$, H_1: Distribution 1 is not the same as Distribution 2, with $\alpha = .01$.

9. Jamal, a left-hander, believes in the natural superiority of left-handed people. To test this belief, he compared the class rank of randomly selected left- and right-handed high school seniors. The results are shown below:

Left-handers	Right-handers
3d	2d
8th	10th
13th	15th
19th	18th
26th	23d
33d	35th
40th	44th
48th	50th
55th	53d

A. Test Jamal's hypothesis, using the Mann-Whitney U test, with $\alpha = .05$.

B. What does the result of this statistical test indicate about Jamal's hypothesis?

10. There is research that suggests that listening to music by Mozart helps improve performance on intellectual tasks. Jonathan decided to compare the effect of Mozart's music with that of the more modern music by the Beach Boys. He exposed two groups of students to a 15-minute session of music-listening and then tested both groups on an analogies task. He had the students rate the perceived difficulty of each analogy and their scores consisted of the sum of these difficulty ratings. (The higher the rating, the more difficult.) The students' scores are shown below:

Mozart: 39, 43, 45, 47, 50, 50, 56, 59, 59, 60, 61,
63, 64, 66, 69, 70, 72, 72, 74, 75, 78, 80

Beach Boys: 27, 32, 35, 39, 42, 43, 43, 45, 48, 49, 51,
53, 55, 58, 62, 62, 63, 65, 67, 67, 68, 68

A. Test Jonathan's hypothesis, using the Mann-Whitney U test, with $\alpha = .05$.

B. What does the result of this statistical test indicate about Jonathan's hypothesis?

11. Determine the critical value of W for each of the following:

A. $n = 10$, H_1: Distribution 1 is not the same as Distribution 2, with $\alpha = .05$.

B. $n = 24$, H_1: Distribution 1 is less than Distribution 2, with $\alpha = .01$.

C. $n = 26$, H_1: Distribution 1 is greater than Distribution 2, with $\alpha = .05$.

D. $n = 45$, H_1: Distribution 1 is not the same as Distribution 2, with $\alpha = .01$.

12. Jamila was interested in studying the effectiveness of a new golf club designed specifically for women, called the Big Bart. She first recorded ten women golfers' rank standings at the local golf course and then provided Big Barts for their use for one month, after which she noted the women's latest rankings. The results are shown below.

Golfer	Before	After
1	8	6
2	11	8
3	15	18
4	21	14
5	27	21
6	32	38
7	35	25
8	37	28
9	40	32
10	45	27

A. Test Jamila's hypothesis, using the Wilcoxon test, with $\alpha = .05$.

B. What does the result of this statistical test indicate about Jamila's hypothesis?

13. Identify the critical values of Spearman's r_s for the following tests:

A. A study with H_1: $r_s \neq 0$, $\alpha = .05$, and $n = 15$.

B. A study with H_1: $r_s < 0$, $\alpha = .05$, and $n = 19$.

C. A study with H_1: $r_s > 0$, $\alpha = .05$, and $n = 23$.

D. A study with H_1: $r_s \neq 0$, $\alpha = .01$, and $n = 10$.

14. Jacob studied the relationship between the amount of exercise and perceived difficulty of exercise by having 10 men record the number of hours they exercised in one week and then having them rate the difficulty of that exercise on a scale of 1 (very easy) to 10 (very difficult), with the following results.

Man	Hours Exercise	Perceived Difficulty
1	2.0	4
2	3.5	3
3	1.0	8
4	5.0	3
5	2.0	6
6	3.0	5
7	4.5	4
8	7.0	2
9	4.0	6
10	5.0	4

A. Conduct a test of Spearman's rank-order correlation, with $\alpha = .05$.

B. What does the result of this statistical test show about the relationship between the amount of exercise and its perceived difficulty?

15. Joelle studied the effect of two methods to reduce aggression in hyperaggressive children. She trained one group using a token economy for four weeks and for the same length of time put the other group on a low-sugar diet. She then had three trained observers rate the children's levels of aggressiveness. The observers did not know which group the children were in. The sum of the observers' ratings are shown below:

Token Economy	Special Diet
24	15
27	18
29	19
31	23
35	27
38	28

A. What is the appropriate statistical test to conduct for this study? Why?

B. Conduct that statistical test on the results above, with $\alpha = .01$.

C. What does the result of this test show about Joelle's hypothesis?

16. Juliana conducted a study comparing husbands' and wives' perceptions of their mates' involvement in the rearing of their children. Each spouse was asked to rate their mate's involvement in child rearing as a percentage, from 0 percent (completely uninvolved) to 100 percent (completely involved). The ratings that each person gave his/her spouse are shown below:

Couple	Husband (%)	Wife (%)
1	75	50
2	90	90
3	84	45
4	33	50
5	99	75
6	60	70
7	80	40
8	95	70
9	90	50
10	60	25

A. What is the appropriate statistical test to conduct for this study? Why?

B. Conduct that statistical test on the results above, with $\alpha = .05$.

C. What does the result of this test show about Juliana's hypothesis?

17. Some people believe that children do better in kindergarten if they start later. Joy studied this belief by recording 16 kindergarten children's age at the end of the school year and then compiling their grades into a class rank, with the child receiving the highest marks ranked as 1 and the child receiving the lowest marks ranked as 16. The results are shown below.

Child	Age	Rank on Grades
1	6.8	2
2	6.6	10
3	6.0	14
4	6.9	3
5	5.8	13
6	6.4	9
7	5.9	6
8	6.6	5
9	6.1	15
10	6.5	8
11	6.8	7
12	6.2	16
13	6.6	1
14	6.4	11
15	6.0	12
16	6.7	4

A. What is the appropriate statistical test to conduct for this study? Why?

B. Conduct that statistical test on the results above, with $\alpha = .05$.

C. What does the result of this test show about the relationship between kindergarteners' age and grades?

A Statistical Test for More than Two Samples: The One-Factor Analysis of Variance

16

Analyzing the Variance among Scores

Partitioning the Sum of Squares

Partitioning the Degrees of Freedom

Analyzing the Variance in a Set of Scores

The Analysis of Variance for a Between-Subjects Factor

The General Procedure for a One-Factor ANOVA

STEP-BY-STEP PROCEDURE 16-1: Conducting the ANOVA for One Factor

STEP-BY-STEP PROCEDURE 16-2: Calculating the Value of F for a One-Factor Between-Subjects ANOVA

Calculating the Sum of Squares

Calculating the Degrees of Freedom

Constructing the Summary Table and Calculating the Value of F

Finding the Critical Value of F

Making a Decision about the Null Hypothesis

Posttests for the Analysis of Variance

STEP-BY-STEP PROCEDURE 16-3: Calculating the Value of t to Compare the Means of Two Treatment Conditions

The Analysis of Variance for a Within-Subjects Factor

STEP-BY-STEP PROCEDURE 16-4: Calculating the Value of F for a One-Factor Within-Subjects ANOVA

Calculating the Sums of Squares

Calculating the Degrees of Freedom

Constructing the Summary Table and Calculating the Value of F

Conducting Posttests

Comparing Between- and Within-Subjects Tests

CHECKING YOUR ANSWERS

SUMMARY

EXERCISES

Conceptual Exercises

Computational Exercises

ENDNOTES

▶ The tests that we examined in the last two chapters are used to compare two samples of scores. For example, using the *t* test for a difference between sample means, we can determine whether the mean of one population is different from the mean of another population. There are often situations in which it would be useful to be able to compare more than two populations at a time. For example, a researcher studying the effects of a new drug on depression might want to know whether the effect of the drug varies with differences in the amount of the drug given to find the optimum dose. Suppose this researcher wants to test five different levels of the drug. The researcher could compare these levels two at a time. However, this would involve conducting ten separate *t* tests, which could be very time consuming.

Even more important is the fact that when we conduct more than one *t* test on a group of scores, we increase the probability of making a Type I error in at least one of those tests. Recall that a Type I error is deciding that the null hypothesis is wrong when it is in fact true and that the probability of making a Type I error is set by the level of significance, α. If we select a significance level of .05, then we have a 5 percent chance of rejecting the null hypothesis when it is true. Of course, we would have a 95 percent chance of not rejecting a true null hypothesis.

Suppose we conduct two *t* tests on a group of scores. The probability of not rejecting a true null hypothesis on both of these tests would be $.95^2$ or .90. Thus, the overall probability of making a Type I error, rejecting a true null hypothesis, on at least one of these two *t* tests would be $1 - .90$, or .10. If we conduct 10 *t* tests on a group of scores, as the drug researcher proposes, the probability of not rejecting a true null hypothesis on all 10 tests would be $.95^{10}$ or .60, and the probability of a Type I error on at least one of the 10 tests would be $1 - .60$, or .40.

It would be useful to have a technique with which we could compare the effect of all five levels of drug dosage in one statistical test, so that the overall probability of a Type I error is no more than the level of significance selected. The analysis of variance is a statistical test that is designed to accomplish the task of comparing more than two samples of scores. In this and the next chapter we explore the analysis of variance, a very powerful statistical test.

Analyzing the Variance among Scores

In Chapter 5, we looked at statistics that measure how spread out a group of scores is. The standard deviation, which is one such statistic, measures how far scores vary from the center of the distribution. The *t* test for a difference between sample means in essence compares the deviation between two groups of scores to the deviation within each group of scores. The numerator of the formula for *t* measures how far one sample mean deviates from the other sample mean, which is a measure of how far the scores in one sample deviate from the scores in the other sample. The denominator of the *t* formula contains the standard deviations of the two samples, which are measures of the deviation of scores within each sample:

$$t = \frac{\text{deviation between two samples}}{\text{deviation within each sample}}.$$

To illustrate this idea, Table 16-1 contains three sets of samples. In Set I, the two samples contain the same five scores. The scores are spread out from the mean within each group, but there is no deviation between the sample means. Thus, the scores deviate *within* each group, but the scores do not deviate *between* the two groups. The value of *t* for these two samples reflects these deviations. The numerator is zero, which shows that there is no deviation between the two samples. The denominator is not zero, which shows that the scores do deviate within each of the two samples.

TABLE 16-1   Comparing the Deviation of Scores within Samples and between Samples

Set I: Deviation within Groups

						$\overline{X}$	s
Sample 1:	2	3	4	5	6	4.0	1.6
Sample 2:	2	3	4	5	6	4.0	1.6

$$t_{\overline{X}_2 - \overline{X}_1} = \frac{0}{1.6\sqrt{2/5}} = 0$$

Set II: Deviation between Groups

						$\overline{X}$	s
Sample 1:	3	3	3	3	3	3.0	0.0
Sample 2:	5	5	5	5	5	5.0	0.0

$$t_{\overline{X}_2 - \overline{X}_1} = \frac{5 - 3}{0\sqrt{2/5}} = \infty$$

Set III: Deviation between and within Groups

						$\overline{X}$	s
Sample 1:	1	2	3	4	5	3.0	1.6
Sample 2:	3	4	5	6	7	5.0	1.6

$$t_{\overline{X}_2 - \overline{X}_1} = \frac{5 - 3}{1.6\sqrt{2/5}} = 2.00$$

In Set II, the five scores in Sample 1 all have the value of 3, and the five scores in Sample 2 all have the value of 5. Thus, there is no deviation *within* each group, but there is deviation *between* the groups. This is reflected in the value of *t*. The denominator is zero, which shows that there is no deviation among the scores within each sample. The numerator is not zero, which shows that there is a difference, or deviation, between the two sample means.

Of course, the samples in Sets I and II are not very realistic. In the real world, it would be very unlikely to find two samples in which there is absolutely no deviation within groups or in which there is no deviation between groups. The samples in Set III are more realistic, in that the scores deviate both within each group and also between the two groups. Note that the scores in Set III have the same deviation within each group as the scores in Set I and the same deviation between the two groups as the scores in Set II do.

Partitioning the Sum of Squares

In Chapter 5, we examined the concept of the variance, which is the square of the standard deviation:

$$s^2 = \frac{\Sigma(X - \overline{X})^2}{n - 1}.$$

The **sum of squares** is the sum of the squared deviations of scores from the center of a set of scores. The sum of squares is the numerator in the formula for the variance and standard deviation, which are measures of the distance between scores in a set.

The numerator of the formula for the variance, $\Sigma(X - \overline{X})^2$, is the sum of the squared deviation of each score from the mean. In an analysis of variance, the sum of the squared deviations is called the **sum of squares** (abbreviated *SS*). The numerator of the variance, $\Sigma(X - \overline{X})^2$, is the total sum of squares for all of the scores, or SS_T, and is a measure of how much the scores deviate from the mean.

For each of the three sets of samples shown in Table 16-1, we can combine the two samples into one group and calculate the sum of squares. These calculations are shown in Table 16-2. Note that for all three sets, the mean of all ten scores in both samples combined is 4.0. We need symbols to differentiate between the mean of the scores in both samples combined and the means of the samples separately. We will represent the mean of each sample as $\overline{X}_i$, where *i* represents the sample number. Thus, the mean of Sample 1 is $\overline{X}_1$ and the mean of Sample 2 is $\overline{X}_2$. The mean of all the scores in both samples combined is symbolized by $\overline{X}_T$, representing the total mean of all of the scores. This value is also called the **grand mean.**[1]

The **grand mean** is the mean of all of the scores in an analysis of variance.

Table 16-2 shows that for Set I, the total sum of squares is 20. Because there is absolutely no deviation between the two samples, the total sum of squares of 20 must reflect the squared deviations of scores from each sample mean. This is the squared deviation *within* each group. For Set II, the total sum of squares is 10. In Set II, there is no deviation among the scores within each group, and so the total sum of squares of 10 must reflect the degree that scores

TABLE 16-2 Analyzing the Squared Deviations from the Grand Mean in the Three Sets of Scores Shown in Table 16-1

		Set I: Deviation within Groups		Set II: Deviation between Groups		Set III: Deviation within and between Groups
	X	$(X - \bar{X}_T)^2$	X	$(X - \bar{X}_T)^2$	X	$(X - \bar{X}_T)^2$
Sample 1:	2	$(2 - 4)^2 = 4$	3	$(3 - 4)^2 = 1$	1	$(1 - 4)^2 = 9$
	3	$(3 - 4)^2 = 1$	3	$(3 - 4)^2 = 1$	2	$(2 - 4)^2 = 4$
	4	$(4 - 4)^2 = 0$	3	$(3 - 4)^2 = 1$	3	$(3 - 4)^2 = 1$
	5	$(5 - 4)^2 = 1$	3	$(3 - 4)^2 = 1$	4	$(4 - 4)^2 = 0$
	6	$(6 - 4)^2 = 4$	3	$(3 - 4)^2 = 1$	5	$(5 - 4)^2 = 1$
Sample 2:	2	$(2 - 4)^2 = 4$	5	$(5 - 4)^2 = 1$	3	$(3 - 4)^2 = 1$
	3	$(3 - 4)^2 = 1$	5	$(5 - 4)^2 = 1$	4	$(4 - 4)^2 = 0$
	4	$(4 - 4)^2 = 0$	5	$(5 - 4)^2 = 1$	5	$(5 - 4)^2 = 1$
	5	$(5 - 4)^2 = 1$	5	$(5 - 4)^2 = 1$	6	$(6 - 4)^2 = 4$
	6	$(6 - 4)^2 = 4$	5	$(5 - 4)^2 = 1$	7	$(7 - 4)^2 = 9$
SS_{total}:		$\Sigma(X - \bar{X}_T)^2 = 20$		$\Sigma(X - \bar{X}_T)^2 = 10$		$\Sigma(X - \bar{X}_T)^2 = 30$

in Sample 1 deviate from scores in Sample 2, the squared deviations *between* the two groups.

For Set III, the total sum of squares is 30. Remember that in Set III, the scores deviate both within each group and between the groups. The within-groups deviation in Set III is the same as the within-groups deviation in Set I. As we saw, there is no between-groups deviation in Set I, and so the total sum of squares, 20, for Set I is a measure of the within-groups deviation. Because Set III has the same within-groups deviation as Set I, 20 of the 30 points in the total sum of squares for Set III must reflect the squared deviations *within* the groups in Set III. In Set II, there is no within-groups deviation, so that the total sum of squares, 10, for Set II must be a measure of the between-groups deviation. Set III has the same between-groups deviation as Set II, and so 10 of the 30 points in the total sum of squares for Set III must reflect the squared deviations *between* the groups in Set III. Thus, we can divide the total sum of squares for Set III into two parts, the squared deviation of scores within each group and the squared deviation of scores between the two groups:

$$SS_{total} = SS_{within} + SS_{between}.$$

We can show this relationship directly in the scores in Set III. We can divide the deviation of each score from the grand mean into two parts, the deviation of the score from the sample mean, $(X - \bar{X})$, and the deviation of the sample mean from the grand mean, $(\bar{X} - \bar{X}_T)$. For example, in Sample 2 of Set

FIGURE 16-1   Partitioning the Deviation of a Score

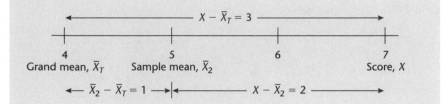

III, the deviation of the score of 7 from the sample mean, 5, is 2. The deviation of the sample mean, 5, from the grand mean, 4, is 1. The sum of these deviations is equal to the deviation of the score, 7, from the grand mean, 4:

$$(X - \bar{X}_T) = (X - \bar{X}_i) + (\bar{X}_i - \bar{X}_T),$$
$$(7 - 4) = (7 - 5) + (5 - 4),$$
$$3 = 2 + 1.$$

In essence, we are dividing the distance between a score and the grand mean into two parts: the distance between the score and the sample mean and the distance between the sample mean and the grand mean. This is shown graphically in Figure 16-1.

Dividing the deviation of a score into parts is called partitioning the deviation. The deviation of the score from the sample mean is the within-groups deviation, which is the value we find in calculating the numerator of the formula for the sample standard deviation. The deviation of the sample mean from the grand mean is the between-groups deviation. It is a measure of how far the sample mean lies from the grand mean. In dividing the deviation into two parts, we are partitioning the deviation into the within-groups deviation and the between-groups deviation.

Table 16-3 shows the partitioning of the deviation of each score in Set III from the grand mean. The sums of the squared deviations for each of these partitions are shown below:

$$SS_{between} = \Sigma(\bar{X}_i - \bar{X}_T)^2 = 10,$$
$$SS_{within} = \Sigma(X - \bar{X}_i)^2 = 20,$$
$$SS_{total} = \Sigma(X - \bar{X}_T)^2 = 30.$$

Compare these values to the sums of squares we calculated in Table 16-2. The within-groups sum of squares for Set III is exactly the same value as the

TABLE 16-3 Partitioning the Sum of Squares in a Set of Scores

Sample 1:	X	Within-Groups Deviation $(X - \bar{X}_1)^2$	Between-Groups Deviation $(\bar{X}_1 - \bar{X}_T)^2$	Total Deviation $(X - \bar{X}_T)^2$
	1	$(1 - 3)^2 = 4$	$(3 - 4)^2 = 1$	$(1 - 4)^2 = 9$
	2	$(2 - 3)^2 = 1$	$(3 - 4)^2 = 1$	$(2 - 4)^2 = 4$
	3	$(3 - 3)^2 = 0$	$(3 - 4)^2 = 1$	$(3 - 4)^2 = 1$
	4	$(4 - 3)^2 = 1$	$(3 - 4)^2 = 1$	$(4 - 4)^2 = 0$
	5	$(5 - 3)^2 = 4$	$(3 - 4)^2 = 1$	$(5 - 4)^2 = 1$
Sample 1 subtotals:		$\Sigma(X - \bar{X}_1)^2 = 10$	$\Sigma(\bar{X}_1 - \bar{X}_T)^2 = 5$	$\Sigma(X - \bar{X}_T)^2 = 15$

Sample 2:	X	Within-Groups Deviation $(X - \bar{X}_2)^2$	Between-Groups Deviation $(\bar{X}_2 - \bar{X}_T)^2$	Total Deviation $(X - \bar{X}_T)^2$
	3	$(3 - 5)^2 = 4$	$(5 - 4)^2 = 1$	$(3 - 4)^2 = 1$
	4	$(4 - 5)^2 = 1$	$(5 - 4)^2 = 1$	$(4 - 4)^2 = 0$
	5	$(5 - 5)^2 = 0$	$(5 - 4)^2 = 1$	$(5 - 4)^2 = 1$
	6	$(6 - 5)^2 = 1$	$(5 - 4)^2 = 1$	$(6 - 4)^2 = 4$
	7	$(7 - 5)^2 = 4$	$(5 - 4)^2 = 1$	$(7 - 4)^2 = 9$
Sample 2 subtotals:		$\Sigma(X - \bar{X}_2)^2 = 10$	$\Sigma(\bar{X}_2 - \bar{X}_T)^2 = 5$	$\Sigma(X - \bar{X}_T)^2 = 15$
Totals for both samples:		$\Sigma(X - \bar{X}_i)^2 = 20$	$\Sigma(\bar{X}_i - \bar{X}_T)^2 = 10$	$\Sigma(X - \bar{X}_T)^2 = 30$
		SS_{within}	$SS_{between}$	SS_{total}

total sum of squares for Set I in Table 16-2. Remember that in Set I, there is no between-groups deviation. Both samples in Set I have exactly the same scores. Thus, the **within-groups sum of squares**, $\Sigma(X - \bar{X}_i)^2$, measures how spread out the scores are within each sample.

The between-groups sum of squares for Set III, calculated in Table 16-3, is 10, which is the same as the total sum of squares for Set II in Table 16-2. Remember that in Set II, there is no within-groups deviation. All of the scores in Sample 1 have the value of 3, and all of the scores in Sample 2 have the value of 5. Thus, in Set II, the only deviation is between the groups. The sum of squares in Set II is entirely due to the deviation between the two samples. Thus, the **between-groups sum of squares**, $\Sigma(\bar{X}_i - \bar{X}_T)^2$, measures the between-groups deviation, the distance between two samples of scores.

In summary, the numerator of the formula for the variance, which is the square of the standard deviation, is the sum of the squared deviations of scores from the grand mean. We can partition that sum of squares into two parts, the squared deviations of scores within the samples and the squared

The **within-groups sum of squares** is the sum of the squared deviations of each score from the mean of the sample containing that score. It is a measure of the variation of the scores within the samples, which is assumed to be attributable to random variation.

The **between-groups sum of squares** is the sum of the squared deviations of each sample mean from the grand mean in an analysis of variance. It is a measure of the variation between the sample means, which is assumed to be attributable to the factor being studied.

FIGURE 16-2 Partitioning the Sum of the Squared Deviations

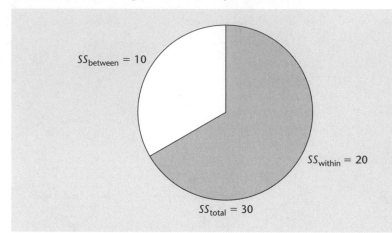

To **partition the sum of squares** is to divide the total sum of squares into parts, each part attributable to a different source of variability.

deviations between the two samples. Figure 16-2 shows the partitioning of the sum of scores graphically.

Partitioning the Degrees of Freedom

We have encountered the concept of degrees of freedom when examining other statistical tests. Recall from Chapter 13 that the degrees of freedom for a statistical test are the number of scores that are free to vary, given certain constraints. For example, with the *t* test for a difference between sample means, the degrees of freedom are $(n_1 - 1) + (n_2 - 1)$, the sum of the number of scores in each sample, less one score per sample.

For the variance, the denominator gives the degrees of freedom:

$$s_T^2 = \frac{\Sigma(X - \bar{X}_T)^2}{n_T - 1}.$$

For the variance of the total group of scores, the degrees of freedom are the total number of scores, minus 1: $n_T - 1$. In Table 16-3, the total number of scores is 10, and so the degrees of freedom are $10 - 1$, or 9. Just as we partitioned the total sum of squares into two parts, the between-groups sum of squares and the within-groups sum of squares, we can partition the total degrees of freedom into two parts, the between-groups degrees of freedom and the within-groups degrees of freedom.

The between-groups degrees of freedom are simple to calculate. It is the number of samples, minus 1. In Table 16-3, there are two samples, and so the between-groups degrees of freedom are $2 - 1$, or 1.

If we calculate the variance of the scores shown in Table 16-3 for Sample 1 and 2 separately, we would use the following formulas:

$$s_1^2 = \frac{\Sigma(X - \bar{X}_1)^2}{n_1 - 1}, \quad s_2^2 = \frac{\Sigma(X - \bar{X}_2)^2}{n_2 - 1}.$$

The degrees of freedom for the variance of Sample 1 are $(n_1 - 1)$. There are 5 scores in Sample 1, and so the degrees of freedom for Sample 1 are $(5 - 1)$, or 4. The degrees of freedom for the variance of Sample 2 are $(n_2 - 1)$. There are 5 scores in Sample 2, and so the degrees of freedom for Sample 2 are also 4. The within-groups degrees of freedom are the sum of the degrees of freedom for each sample, which is $4 + 4$, or 8.

We have now calculated the between-groups degrees of freedom and the within-groups degrees of freedom. Notice that the two values add up to the total degrees of freedom. Thus, we have partitioned the total degrees of freedom into two parts:

$$df_{between} = 1,$$

$$df_{within} = 8,$$

$$df_{total} = 9.$$

Analyzing the Variance in a Set of Scores

The formula for the total variance in a group of scores is the sum of squares divided by the degrees of freedom:

$$s_T^2 = \frac{\Sigma(X - \bar{X}_T)^2}{n_T - 1} = \frac{\text{total sum of squares}}{\text{total degrees of freedom}} = \frac{30}{9} = 3.3.$$

Recall that the standard deviation is the square root of the variance, which for Set III is 1.8.

We can use a similar formula to measure the variance within the samples. The within-groups variance is also called the **within-groups mean square**, MS_{within}:

$$MS_{within} = \frac{\Sigma(X - \bar{X}_1)^2 + \Sigma(X - \bar{X}_2)^2}{(n_1 - 1) + (n_2 - 1)}$$

$$= \frac{\text{within-groups sum of squares}}{\text{within-groups degrees of freedom}}$$

$$= \frac{20}{8} = 2.5.$$

The square root of the value of MS_{within} is 1.58. As seen in Table 16-1, the standard deviation of Sample 1 in Set III is 1.58, as is the standard deviation of Sample 2. The within-groups mean square is equivalent to the average variance within the samples. We can also use a similar formula for the between-groups deviations. This is the **between-groups mean square**, $MS_{between}$:

$$MS_{between} = \frac{\Sigma(\overline{X}_1 - \overline{X}_T)^2 + \Sigma(\overline{X}_2 - \overline{X}_T)^2}{2 - 1}$$

$$= \frac{\text{between-groups sum of squares}}{\text{between-groups degrees of freedom}}$$

$$= \frac{10}{1} = 10.0.$$

At the beginning of this section, we looked at the t test as a comparison of the between-groups deviation to the within-groups deviation:

$$t = \frac{\text{deviation between two groups}}{\text{deviation within each group}}.$$

We can use the between-groups mean square as a measure of the deviation between two groups and the within-groups mean square as a measure of the deviation within the groups. This value is symbolized F:

$$F = \frac{MS_{between}}{MS_{within}} = \frac{10}{2.5} = 4.0.$$

The total variance of a distribution of scores is a measure of the degree to which the scores vary from the grand mean of the distribution.

The between-groups variance of a distribution of scores consisting of two or more samples is a measure of the degree to which the sample means vary from the grand mean of the distribution. The between-groups variance is assumed to be attributable to the factor being studied.

The within-groups variance of a distribution of scores consisting of two or more samples is a measure of the degree to which the scores of each sample vary from the mean of the sample. The within-groups variance is assumed to reflect random variation.

The F statistic compares the between-groups variance to the within-groups variance. As we saw before, the t statistic compares the between-groups deviation to the within-groups deviation. Recall that the variance is the square of the standard deviation. This relationship is also seen between F and t. The value of F is based on measuring the variance among scores, while the value of t is based on the standard deviation. When comparing two samples, the F statistic is always the square of the t statistic:

$$F = t^2.$$

In Table 16-1, we can see that the value of t comparing the two samples in Set III is 2.00. The value of F comparing the same two samples is 4.00, which is the square of t. Thus, the t and the F statistics effectively measure the same thing. The statistics are just calculated in different ways. The numerator of the t statistic measures the distance between two sample means, $\overline{X}_1 - \overline{X}_2$. The numerator of the F statistic measures the square distance of each sample mean from the grand mean: $(\overline{X}_1 - \overline{X}_T)^2 + (\overline{X}_2 - \overline{X}_T)^2$. For the two samples we have been analyzing, the difference between the two means, 3 and 5, is 2. The grand mean is 4, and so the mean of Sample 1, 3, is 1 point below the grand mean and the mean of Sample 2, 5, is 1 point above the grand mean. Both the t and the F statistics are measuring the distance between the sample means, just in slightly different ways.

Because the *t* statistic is based on subtracting one sample mean from the other, we can use the *t* test to compare only two samples at a time. There is no way to directly find the distance between three or more means using *t*. On the other hand, the *F* statistic is based on the distance between each sample mean and the grand mean. By subtracting the grand mean from each, we can use this statistic to compare the distance between more than two sample means. One of the advantages of the *F* statistic is that we can use it to compare more than two samples at a time.

The *F* statistic analyzes the total variance in a set of scores by comparing the variance between the samples to the variance of the scores within each sample. This technique is called the analysis of variance, abbreviated ANOVA.

The Analysis of Variance for a Between-Subjects Factor

We have been with Joe Johnson through his efforts to study the effect that math anxiety has on math performance. Suppose now that Joe wants to compare two methods for alleviating math anxiety. One method is to give math-anxious students relaxation training; the other is to train students in confidence building to help them believe that they can succeed in math courses. Joe wants to compare the math performance of students who have gone through each type of training with the performance of students who have had no training to alleviate math anxiety. To conduct this study, Joe selected three samples of ten math-anxious students, all of whom had previously failed a statistics class. At the beginning of the next term, these thirty students enrolled in another statistics class. One sample of students enrolled in a confidence-building program, while the second sample of students enrolled in a program to learn relaxation techniques. The third sample of students was given no special training to alleviate math anxiety. At the end of the term, Joe gave all three samples a twenty-question math test. The number correct for each student is shown in Table 16-4.

The General Procedure for a One-Factor ANOVA

Step-by-Step Procedure 16-1 describes the method for using ANOVA to conduct a statistical test. Note that these are the same basic steps that we have used in conducting all of the statistical tests that we have examined. However, the null and alternate hypotheses for the ANOVA are a little different than the hypotheses for the previous tests. In the last two chapters, the null and alternate hypotheses all compared two populations. The ANOVA, on the other hand, can be used to compare more than two populations. The null hypothesis for the ANOVA asserts that the means of the populations are all the same.

TABLE 16-4 Math Test Scores of Students with Confidence Training, Relaxation Training, and No Training (between-subjects design)

A_1: Confidence Training	A_2: Relaxation Training	A_3: No Training
16	19	16
15	17	10
14	17	11
14	16	12
13	14	9
19	15	11
19	14	12
18	13	8
17	13	12
15	12	9

The alternate hypothesis asserts that the null hypothesis is not true, that the means of the populations are not all the same.

Note that Procedure 16-1 is the method for conducting an ANOVA for one factor. In the next chapter, we will examine how to use an ANOVA for studies in which there are two factors. A **factor** is a variable on which subjects are divided into groups. In Joe's study, the participants are divided into groups on the variable, type of anxiety-alleviating training. Thus, the type of training is the factor being studied.

A **factor** is a variable whose values are used to divide the subjects into groups.

If the factor being studied is a variable that measures a characteristic of the subjects, each value of that factor being studied is called a **level.** When the factor being studied is sex of subject, then the values, male and female, are the levels. When the factor being studied is age of subjects, then the age groups into which subjects are divided are the levels. If the factor being studied consists of different ways subjects are treated in an experiment, then each value of that factor is called a **treatment.** In Joe's study, the factor is type of training, and there are three treatments: confidence training, relaxation training, and no training. The levels or treatments of the factor being studied are assigned identifying numbers. We will identify the sample given confidence training as Sample 1, the sample given relaxation training as Sample 2, and the sample given no training as Sample 3.

If the factor is a variable that measures a characteristic of the subjects, the values that divide the subjects into groups are called **levels.**

If the subjects are divided into groups according to the way they are treated in the experiment, the values of the factor are called **treatments.**

The number of levels or types of treatment in a factor is labeled n_A. In Joe's study, n_A is 3, indicating there are three types of training. In an ANOVA, the minimum number of levels or types of treatment is two. There have to be at least two groups to compare. There is no maximum number of levels or types of treatment. We can test as many different levels or treatments of a factor as logically makes sense.

STEP-BY-STEP PROCEDURE 16-1

Conducting the ANOVA for One Factor

1. Verify that the following assumptions have been met:
   A. The subjects in each sample were randomly and independently selected.
   B. The distributions are approximately normally distributed.
   C. The population variances are equal.
   D. The scores are measured with an interval or ratio scale.

2. Write the null and alternate hypotheses. For the ANOVA for one factor, where the number of groups of subjects is n_A, the hypotheses will have the following form:

$$H_0: \mu_1 = \mu_2 = \mu_3 = \cdots = \mu_A$$

$$H_1: H_0 \text{ is not true.}$$

3. Decide the level of significance, α.

4. Calculate the between-groups degrees of freedom and the within-groups degrees of freedom, following the method described in Procedure 16-2 or 16-4. Find the critical value of F in Appendix A-4 for those degrees of freedom.

5. Draw a graph of the sampling distribution predicted by the null hypothesis, indicating the rejection region. For F, the rejection region is in the upper tail.

6. Calculate the value of F, following the method described in Procedure 16-2.

7. Make a decision on whether or not to reject the null hypothesis:
   A. If F is in the rejection region bounded by $F_{critical}$, then $p \leq \alpha$, and therefore decide that there is enough evidence to conclude that the means of the populations are not all the same (reject the null hypothesis).
   B. If F is not in the rejection region bounded by $F_{critical}$, then $p > \alpha$, and therefore do not decide that there is enough evidence to conclude that the means of the populations are not all the same (do not reject the null hypothesis).

The factor being studied can be either between-subjects or within-subjects. For a **between-subjects factor**, different, unrelated subjects are tested under each value of the factor being studied. Each subject contributes one score. In Joe's study, different participants were tested under each type of anxiety-alleviating training, and so we would use the ANOVA for a between-subjects factor to test the results of this study. For a **within-subjects factor**, the same or related subjects are tested under all of the values of the factor being studied. When the same subjects are tested in all conditions, each subject contributes n_A scores. We will examine how to calculate an ANOVA for a within-subjects factor later in this chapter.

Step-by-Step Procedure 16-2 describes the method for calculating a between-subjects one-factor ANOVA. The result of this ANOVA will be a value of F. As we have seen, in calculating F, the total variance is partitioned into two segments, the between-groups variance and the within-groups variance. The between-groups variance is the variance among the groups tested under

A **between-subjects factor** is a factor in which different subjects are tested under each level or treatment. Each subject is tested in only one group for that factor.

A **within-subjects factor** is a factor in which the same subjects are tested under each level or treatment. Each subject is tested in all of the groups for that factor.

STEP-BY-STEP PROCEDURE 16-2

Calculating the Value of *F* for a One-Factor Between-Subjects ANOVA

1. Calculate the sums of squares

The following symbols are used in this procedure:

n_S = the number of subjects per sample
n_A = the number of samples
$\overline{X}_T$ = the grand mean, the mean of all of the scores
$\overline{X}_i$ = the mean of sample *i*, where *i* can be from 1 to n_A
X = a score. The symbol X_i represents the scores in sample *i*.

A. Between-groups sum of squares

$$SS_{between} = n_S \Sigma(\overline{X}_i - \overline{X}_T)^2$$

(1) Calculate the grand mean of all of the scores in all of the samples, $\overline{X}_T$.
(2) Calculate the mean of each sample of scores, $\overline{X}_i$.
(3) Subtract the grand mean from each sample mean, and then square each deviation. There are n_A samples, and so there should be n_A squared deviations.
(4) Add up the squared deviations found in Step 3 for all of the samples, and then multiply that sum by n_S, the number of scores per sample, to find the value of $SS_{between}$.

B. Within-groups sum of squares

$$SS_{within} = \Sigma(X_i - \overline{X}_i)^2$$

(1) Find the deviation of each score from the mean of the sample containing that score, and then square the deviation. There are a total of $n_A n_S$ scores, and so there should be $n_A n_S$ squared deviations.
(2) Sum all of the squared deviations from Step 1 to find the value of SS_{within}.

C. Total sum of squares

$$SS_{total} = \Sigma(X - \overline{X}_T)^2$$

(1) Subtract the grand mean, $\overline{X}_T$, from each score, and then square this deviation. There are a total of $n_A n_S$ scores, and so there should be $n_A n_S$ squared deviations.
(2) Sum all of the squared deviations from Step 1 to find the value of SS_{total}.
(3) As a check: $SS_{total} = SS_{between} + SS_{within}$.

2. Calculate the degrees of freedom
A. $df_{between} = n_A - 1$, where n_A is the number of samples.
B. $df_{within} = n_A(n_S - 1)$, where n_S is the number of scores per sample.
C. $df_{total} = n_A n_S - 1$.
D. As a check, $df_{total} = df_{between} + df_{within}$.

3. Construct the summary table and calculate *F*
A. Construct a table with five columns. Label the columns: "Sources of Variance," "SS," "df," "MS," and "F." Label the first row with the name of the factor being studied. Label the second row "Within." Label the third row "Total."
B. Write the values for the sums of squares and degrees of freedom calculated above into the appropriate columns in the summary table.
C. For the first two rows, divide the value of the sum of squares by the value of the degrees of freedom, to find the values of the mean square, *MS*:

$$MS_{between} = \frac{SS_{between}}{df_{between}}, \quad MS_{within} = \frac{SS_{within}}{df_{within}}.$$

D. Divide the value of $MS_{between}$ by the value of $MS_{within\ groups}$ to find the value of *F*:

$$F = \frac{MS_{between}}{MS_{within}}.$$

different types of treatment of the factor being studied. In Joe's study, the between-groups variance is the variance among the three types of anxiety-alleviating training: confidence training, relaxation training, and no training. Thus, the between-groups variance is due to the type of training. The within-groups variance is the variance of scores within each level or treatment condition, which is assumed to be due to random variation.

Calculating the Sum of Squares

We can use Procedure 16-2 to analyze the variance in the scores from Joe's study. The first step is to calculate the values of the sums of squares for each source of variance.

The between-groups sum of squares.   First, we calculate the between-groups sum of squares. The computations are shown in Figure 16-3. Note that the number of squared deviations in the second step is equal to the number of levels or treatments in the factor being studied, n_A. In Joe's study, there are three treatment conditions and so there are three squared deviations, one for each treatment condition. Figure 16-3 shows that the between-groups sum of squares is 140.

The within-group sum of squares.   Next, we calculate the within-groups sum of squares. The computations for this value are shown in Figure 16-4. Note that Step 1 is computed separately for each treatment condition, subtracting the mean of that treatment condition from each score in the group, and then squaring each deviation. There are n_S scores in each treatment condition and so there will be n_S squared deviations for each group. In Joe's study, each treatment condition contains ten scores and so there are ten squared deviations for each of the three treatment conditions, or a total of thirty squared deviations across all three treatment conditions. The final step is to add up these squared deviations across all the treatment conditions. Figure 16-4 shows that the within-groups sum of squares for Joe's study is 132.

FIGURE 16-3   Calculating the Between-Groups Sum of Squares for a Test of Joe's Math Study

1. Calculate grand mean: $\bar{X}_T = \dfrac{\Sigma X}{n_T} = \dfrac{210}{30} = 14.0$.

2. Calculate sample means, subtract the grand mean from each sample mean, and square the deviations:

$$\bar{X}_1 = \frac{\Sigma X_1}{n} = \frac{160}{10} = 16.0, \quad (\bar{X}_1 - \bar{X}_T)^2 = (16 - 14)^2 = 2^2 = 4;$$

$$\bar{X}_2 = \frac{\Sigma X_2}{n} = \frac{150}{10} = 15.0, \quad (\bar{X}_2 - \bar{X}_T)^2 = (15 - 14)^2 = 1^2 = 1;$$

$$\bar{X}_3 = \frac{\Sigma X_3}{n} = \frac{110}{10} = 11.0, \quad (\bar{X}_3 - \bar{X}_T)^2 = (11 - 14)^2 = (-3)^2 = 9.$$

3. Add up the squared deviations and multiply by n_S, the number of scores per sample:

$$SS_{between} = n\Sigma(\bar{X}_i - \bar{X}_T)^2$$
$$= 10(4 + 1 + 9) = 10(14) = 140.$$

FIGURE 16-4   Calculating the Within-Groups Sum of Squares for a Test of Joe's Math Study

1. For each sample separately, subtract the sample mean from each score and then square the deviation. Add up all of the squared deviations for each sample.

Sample 1: Confidence Training $(X - \bar{X}_1)^2$	Sample 2: Relaxation Training $(X - \bar{X}_2)^2$	Sample 3: No Training $(X - \bar{X}_3)^2$
$(16 - 16)^2 = 0$	$(19 - 15)^2 = 16$	$(16 - 11)^2 = 25$
$(15 - 16)^2 = 1$	$(17 - 15)^2 = 4$	$(10 - 11)^2 = 1$
$(14 - 16)^2 = 4$	$(17 - 15)^2 = 4$	$(11 - 11)^2 = 0$
$(14 - 16)^2 = 4$	$(16 - 15)^2 = 1$	$(12 - 11)^2 = 1$
$(13 - 16)^2 = 9$	$(14 - 15)^2 = 1$	$(9 - 11)^2 = 4$
$(19 - 16)^2 = 9$	$(15 - 15)^2 = 0$	$(11 - 11)^2 = 0$
$(19 - 16)^2 = 9$	$(14 - 15)^2 = 1$	$(12 - 11)^2 = 1$
$(18 - 16)^2 = 4$	$(13 - 15)^2 = 4$	$(8 - 11)^2 = 9$
$(17 - 16)^2 = 1$	$(13 - 15)^2 = 4$	$(12 - 11)^2 = 1$
$(15 - 16)^2 = 1$	$(12 - 15)^2 = 9$	$(9 - 11)^2 = 4$
$\Sigma(X - \bar{X}_1)^2 = 42$	$\Sigma(X - \bar{X}_2)^2 = 44$	$\Sigma(X - \bar{X}_3)^2 = 46$

2. Add up these sums of squared deviations:

$$SS_{within} = \Sigma(X - \bar{X}_i)^2 = 42 + 44 + 46 = 132.$$

The total sum of squares.   Finally, we calculate the total sum of squares. The procedure for the total sum of squares is the same as the procedure for the within-groups sum of squares, except that the grand mean is subtracted from each score rather than the mean of each treatment condition. Again, there will be n_S squared deviations for each treatment condition, or a total of $n_A n_S$ squared deviations across all of the treatment conditions. For Joe's study, there are 10 scores per treatment condition and 3 treatment conditions, for a total of (3)(10) or 30 scores, and thus there are 30 squared deviations in the total sum of squares. The computations for the total sum of squares are shown in Figure 16-5, which shows that the total sum of squares for Joe's study is 272. As a check, the total sum of squares should equal the sum of the between-groups and within-groups sums of squares.

$$SS_{total} = SS_{between} + SS_{within} = 140 + 132 = 272.$$

Alternate methods of calculating the sums of squares.   The method for calculating the sums of squares described in Procedure 16-2 is structurally similar to the definitional formula of the standard deviation, which is based on

FIGURE 16-5   Calculating the Total Sum of Squares for a Test of Joe's Math Study

1. Subtract the grand mean from each score and then square the deviation.

Sample 1: Confidence Training $(X_1 - \bar{X}_T)^2$	Sample 2: Relaxation Training $(X_2 - \bar{X}_T)^2$	Sample 3: No Training $(X_3 - \bar{X}_T)^2$
$(16 - 14)^2 = \ 4$	$(19 - 14)^2 = 25$	$(16 - 14)^2 = \ 4$
$(15 - 14)^2 = \ 1$	$(17 - 14)^2 = \ 9$	$(10 - 14)^2 = 16$
$(14 - 14)^2 = \ 0$	$(17 - 14)^2 = \ 9$	$(11 - 14)^2 = \ 9$
$(14 - 14)^2 = \ 0$	$(16 - 14)^2 = \ 4$	$(12 - 14)^2 = \ 4$
$(13 - 14)^2 = \ 1$	$(14 - 14)^2 = \ 0$	$(9 - 14)^2 = 25$
$(19 - 14)^2 = 25$	$(15 - 14)^2 = \ 1$	$(11 - 14)^2 = \ 9$
$(19 - 14)^2 = 25$	$(14 - 14)^2 = \ 0$	$(12 - 14)^2 = \ 4$
$(18 - 14)^2 = 16$	$(13 - 14)^2 = \ 1$	$(8 - 14)^2 = 36$
$(17 - 14)^2 = \ 9$	$(13 - 14)^2 = \ 1$	$(12 - 14)^2 = \ 4$
$(15 - 14)^2 = \ 1$	$(12 - 14)^2 = \ 4$	$(9 - 14)^2 = 25$
$\Sigma(X_1 - \bar{X}_T)^2 = 82$	$\Sigma(X_2 - \bar{X}_T)^2 = 54$	$\Sigma(X_3 - \bar{X}_T)^2 = 136$

2. Add up these sums of squared deviations:

$$SS_{total} = \Sigma(X - \bar{X}_T)^2 = 82 + 54 + 136 = 272.$$

As a check, $SS_{total} = SS_{between} + SS_{within} = 140 + 132 = 272.$

actually calculating the deviation of each score from the mean. Each of the sums of squares in Procedure 16-2 is derived in a similar fashion, calculating the deviation of the scores from the sample means, the deviation of those sample means from the grand mean, and the deviation of the scores from the grand mean. This method is used so that you could see exactly what each sum of squares measures.

However, just as there are alternate ways of finding the standard deviation, such as the computational formula described in Chapter 5, there are alternate, more computationally friendly ways of calculating the sums of squares in an analysis of variance. While these methods may be easier to calculate, it is not as easy to see what the sums of squares measure. If you are interested in finding out more about other methods for calculating the sums of squares in an analysis of variance, advanced statistics books described these methods, as do books devoted entirely to the analysis of variance.[2]

Calculating the Degrees of Freedom

Next, we calculate the degrees of freedom for each of the three sources of variance. The two values we need to calculate the degrees of freedom are n_A, the

TABLE 16-5 Summary Table for the Between-Subjects
ANOVA of Joe Johnson's Math Anxiety Study

Sources of Variance	SS	df	MS	F
Type of Training	140.00	2	70.00	14.31
Within	132.00	27	4.89	
Total	272.00	29		

number of levels or treatment conditions in the factor being studied, and n_S, the number of scores per level or treatment condition. For the scores in Table 16-4, n_A is 3 and n_S is 10:

$$df_{between} = n_A - 1 = 3 - 1 = 2,$$

$$df_{within} = n_A(n_S - 1) = 3(10 - 1) = 3(9) = 27,$$

$$df_{total} = n_A n_S - 1 = (3)(10) - 1 = 30 - 1 = 29.$$

As a check, the total degrees of freedom will always equal the sum of the other degrees of freedom:

$$df_{total} = df_{between} + df_{within} = 2 + 27 = 29.$$

Constructing the Summary Table and Calculating the Value of F

The next step is to construct the summary table. Table 16-5 shows the summary table for the analysis of variance of the scores in Joe's study. To find the mean squares, we divide the sum of squares by the degrees of freedom for that source of variance:

$$MS_{between} = \frac{SS_{between}}{df_{between}} = \frac{140}{2} = 70.00,$$

$$MS_{within} = \frac{SS_{within}}{df_{within}} = \frac{132}{27} = 4.89.$$

Note that we do not calculate a value of the mean square for the total. To find the value of F, we divide the between-groups mean square by the within-groups mean square:

$$F = \frac{MS_{between}}{MS_{within}} = \frac{70}{4.89} = 14.31.$$

Finding the Critical Value of F

The value of F for the type of training in Joe's study is 14.31. In order to determine whether this is a significant F and we can reject the null hypothesis,

FIGURE 16-6 Finding the Critical Value of *F*

TABLE A-4
Critical Values of *F*, $\alpha = .05$

df_{within}	$df_{between}$ 1	2	3	4	5	6	
1	161	200	216	225	230	234	⋯
2	18.51	19.00	19.16	19.25	19.30	19.33	⋯
3	10.13	9.55	9.28	9.12	9.01	8.94	⋯
4	7.71	6.94	6.59	6.39	6.26	6.16	⋯
5	6.61	5.79	5.41	5.19	5.05	4.95	⋯
⋮	⋮	⋮	⋮	⋮	⋮	⋮	⋯
26	4.22	3.37	2.98	2.74	2.59	2.47	⋯
27	4.21	**3.35**	2.96	2.73	2.57	2.46	⋯
28	4.20	3.34	2.95	2.71	2.56	2.44	⋯
29	4.18	3.33	2.93	2.70	2.54	2.43	⋯
30	4.17	3.32	2.92	2.69	2.53	2.42	⋯

we find the critical value of *F* in Appendix A-4. The critical values of *F* are listed according to the value of α and the degrees of freedom for the two mean squares in the *F* ratio. A portion of the table from Appendix A-4 is shown in Figure 16-6. As can be seen, this portion of the table is for a .05 significance level. Appendix A-4 also lists critical values for a .01 significance level.

The between-groups degrees of freedom are listed in the columns across the top of the table. In Figure 16-6, between-groups degrees of freedom from 1 to 6 are listed, but Appendix A-4 has additional values. For Joe's study comparing three instructional methods, the between-groups degrees of freedom are 2. Note that that column is highlighted in Figure 16-6.

The within-groups degrees of freedom are listed to the left of the rows of the table. To keep this example simple, only selected values are listed. However, the complete table in Appendix A-4 lists within-groups degrees of freedom from 1 to over 100. For Joe's study, the within-groups degrees of freedom are 27. The row for $df = 27$ is also highlighted in Figure 16-6.

The critical value at the intersection of $df_{between} = 2$ and $df_{within} = 27$ is 3.35, which for a significance level of .05 is the critical value for the *F* ratio in this test of Joe's study. If the value of *F* that we calculated for the scores in Table 16-4 is 3.35 or larger, then we can reject the null hypothesis. The value of *F* that we calculated is 14.31, which is larger than the critical value of 3.35, and so we can reject the null hypothesis.

Making a Decision about the Null Hypothesis

The null hypothesis for this study is that the means of the populations for the three types of anxiety-alleviating training are the same. The null hypothesis asserts that if all math-anxious students were given either relaxation training or confidence training, their mean math score would be no different than if they were given no training at all. When we reject the null hypothesis, we can say that this is not true, that not all of the means are equal. However, we cannot conclude that all of the means are different. We can get a significant value of F if just one of the means is significantly different from the others. Because F is a measure of the deviation of sample means from the grand mean, it is even possible (albeit rare) to obtain a significant value of F when none of the sample means differ significantly from each other. In order to determine which means, if any, are different, we have to do further analysis.

Posttests for the Analysis of Variance

If the value of F were significant for a factor that has only two treatments, then we would know that the means for those two treatments are significantly different. If there are only two treatment conditions, then the significance of the F ratio of necessity indicates that there is a significant difference between the means of those two groups, in which case no further analysis is necessary. However, if the value of F is significant for a factor that has more than two treatments, then we do not know which means are significantly different. Because the value of F is significant, we know that in all probability there is a significant difference between at least one pair of means, but we do not know which pair and we do not know whether more than one pair of means is significantly different. In order to find out, we need to do further tests. These tests are called **posttests.**

One way to find out which means are significantly different is to use the t test for a difference between sample means.[3] This test is an a priori posttest, meaning that it was planned before the analysis began. A posteriori posttests are not planned beforehand but are conducted when a significant F occurs that the researcher did not anticipate. In using the t test for a difference between sample means as a posttest, we can use the within-groups mean square, MS_{within}, as a measure of the variance for the denominator of the t test. Step-by-Step Procedure 16-3 describes the method for calculating this value of t.

We can use Procedure 16-3 to test the three means from Joe's study. The confidence-training group scored a mean of 16 correct on the math test, the relaxation-training group scored a mean of 15 correct, and the no-training group scored a mean of 11 correct. The value of MS_{within} as shown in

---

STEP-BY-STEP PROCEDURE 16-3

Calculating the Value of t to Compare the Means of Two Treatment Conditions

For a between-subjects ANOVA   For a within-subjects ANOVA

$$t = \frac{\bar{X}_j - \bar{X}_k}{\sqrt{\dfrac{2MS_{within}}{n_S}}}$$ $$t = \frac{\bar{X}_j - \bar{X}_k}{\sqrt{\dfrac{2MS_{treatment \times subjects}}{n_S}}}$$

where
$\bar{X}_j$ = the mean of one sample
$\bar{X}_k$ = the mean of another sample
MS_{within} = the within-groups mean square for a between-subjects ANOVA
$MS_{treatment \times subjects}$ = the treatment $\times$ subject mean square for a within-subjects ANOVA
n_S = the number of scores in each sample

1. The means for each sample were calculated when conducting the analysis of variance. Subtract the sample mean for treatment condition k from the sample mean for treatment condition j.

2. The value of MS_{within} or $MS_{treatment \times subjects}$ was calculated when conducting the analysis of variance. Multiply this value by 2, and then divide that result by n_S, the number of scores per sample. Find the square root of this result.

3. Divide the result of Step 1 by the result of Step 2 to find the value of t.

4. The method for testing this value of t is the same as Step-by-Step Procedure 14-2, which describes the method for conducting the t test for a difference between sample means. The degrees of freedom for this t test are $2(n_S - 1)$.

Table 16-5 is 132.00. These are the values we need to use the formula in Procedure 16-3:

$$t_{confidence\ vs.\ no\ training} = \frac{\bar{X}_1 - \bar{X}_3}{\sqrt{\dfrac{2MS_{within}}{n_S}}} = \frac{16 - 11}{\sqrt{\dfrac{2(4.89)}{10}}} = \frac{5}{\sqrt{.978}} = \frac{5}{.99} = 5.051,$$

$$t_{relaxation\ vs.\ no\ training} = \frac{\bar{X}_2 - \bar{X}_3}{\sqrt{\dfrac{2MS_{within}}{n_S}}} = \frac{15 - 11}{\sqrt{\dfrac{2(4.89)}{10}}} = \frac{4}{\sqrt{.978}} = \frac{4}{.99} = 4.040,$$

$$t_{confidence\ vs.\ relaxation} = \frac{\bar{X}_1 - \bar{X}_2}{\sqrt{\dfrac{2MS_{within}}{n_S}}} = \frac{16 - 15}{\sqrt{\dfrac{2(4.89)}{10}}} = \frac{1}{\sqrt{.978}} = \frac{1}{.99} = 1.010.$$

Joe predicted that math-anxious students would perform better on the math test after both confidence training and relaxation training than they did with no training at all. These are unidirectional hypotheses, or one-tailed tests. Recall that the degrees of freedom for a t test of a difference between sample means are $(n_1 - 1) + (n_2 - 1)$. In these posttests, the number of scores is the same for the two samples, and so the degrees of freedom are $2(n_s - 1)$, which for these comparisons is $2(10 - 1)$ or 18. The critical value of t, for a one-tailed test with 18 df and $\alpha = .05$, is 1.734. The t comparing the mean of the confidence-training group to the mean of the no-training group is 5.051, which is greater than the critical value of t. Thus, the math-anxious students scored significantly higher on the math test after confidence training than after no training. The t comparing the mean of the relaxation-training group to the mean of the no-training group is 4.040, which is also greater than the critical value of t. Therefore, the math-anxious students also scored significantly higher on the math test after relaxation training than after no training at all.

Joe made no specific predictions on which of the experimental training methods—confidence training or relaxation training—would result in higher math performance. Therefore, to compare these means would be a two-tailed test. The critical value of t, for a two-tailed test with 18 df and $\alpha = .05$, is 2.101. The t comparing the mean of the confidence-training group to the mean of the relaxation-training group is 1.010, which is not greater than the critical value of t. This is not enough evidence to conclude that there is a significant difference in performance on the math test between the confidence-training and relaxation-training groups.

The Analysis of Variance for a Within-Subjects Factor

In a within-subjects design, each subject is tested under all of the treatments of factor being studied. As we have previously seen, a special case of within-subjects design is when different but logically related subjects are tested under each treatment. In the last section, we analyzed the variance of the scores in Joe's study, assuming that different subjects were tested in each treatment condition. Let's assume that the same participants were tested in all three of the treatment conditions, which would be a within-subjects design.

Of course, in real life we would never analyze the same set of scores as both a between-subjects design and a within-subjects design. If this were a real study, we would use only the analysis that is appropriate for the way the participants were actually tested. There are also serious flaws in using Joe's study as a within-subjects design. Nonetheless, our purpose here is to compare the analysis of variance for a between-subjects design and a within-subjects design, using the same set of scores. As we will see, the total variance remains the same in analyzing the scores from Joe's study, but the partition of that total variance is different in a within-subjects analysis than in a between-subjects analysis.

In analyzing the results of Joe's study as a within-subjects design, we will assume that Joe selected one group of ten participants and gave them the math test before any training. He then gave half the participants relaxation training and half confidence training and then gave them another math test. Finally, he gave the participants the type of training they had not yet received and afterward, administered a third math test. All of the math tests were equivalent. We will analyze the same scores shown in Table 16-4.

The method for testing hypotheses with the one-factor within-subjects ANOVA is exactly same as the method for the one-factor between-subjects ANOVA, shown in Procedure 16-1. The method for calculating the value of F for a one-factor within-subjects ANOVA is shown in Step-by-Step Procedure 16-4. This procedure is very similar to Procedure 16-2, the method for calculating the value of F for a one-factor between-subjects ANOVA.

The most important difference between a between-subjects and within-subjects ANOVA is that in the within-subjects ANOVA there is one additional source of variance, the variance due to differences between the subjects. In Joe's study, there well could be differences among the participants that affect their math test scores, in addition to what type of anxiety-alleviating training they received before testing. One likely difference between participants is their math ability. Some math-anxious students have higher math ability than other math-anxious students. In the between-subjects design, there is no way to identify this variance due to differences between the subjects. In the within-subjects design, because subjects are tested in all types of treatment, there is a method to identify this variance and partition it out so that it will not affect the results of the analysis. We want the analysis to measure the effect of the type of treatment, not the effect of individual differences between the participants, such as their math ability. Thus, if we are able to partition out the variance due to the participants' individual differences, our analysis will be a more accurate assessment of the effect of the type of treatment on the participants' scores.

Calculating the Sums of Squares

We will use Procedure 16-4 to analyze the variance in the scores from Joe's study, assuming this time that the study is a within-subjects design. The first step in Procedure 16-4 is to calculate the value of the sum of squares for each source of variance.

The between-groups sum of squares.　　The first source we will consider is the between-groups variance. The procedure for calculating the between-groups sum of squares for a within-subjects ANOVA is identical to the procedure for a between-subjects ANOVA. The between-groups sum of squares is that portion of the total sum of squares that is attributable to the differences in

Calculating the Value of *F* for a One-Factor Within-Subjects ANOVA

1. Calculate the sums of squares.
The following symbols are used in this procedure:

n_S = the number of subjects per sample

n_A = the number of samples

$\bar{X}_T$ = the grand mean, the mean of all of the scores

$\bar{X}_i$ = the mean of sample *i*, where *i* can be from 1 to n_A

$\bar{X}_k$ = the mean score for subject *k*, where *k* can be from 1 to n_S

X = a score

X_i = the scores in sample *i*

X_k = the scores for subject *k*

A. Between-Groups Sum of Squares

$$SS_{between} = n_S \Sigma (\bar{X}_i - \bar{X}_T)^2$$

The procedure for calculating the between-groups sum of squares for a within-subjects ANOVA is exactly the same as the procedure for a between-subjects ANOVA, which is described in Procedure 16-2, Step 1A.

B. Subject's Sum of Squares

$$SS_{subjects} = n_A \Sigma (\bar{X}_k - \bar{X}_T)^2$$

(1) For each subject separately, calculate the mean of that subject's scores. In a within-subjects analysis, each subject will have n_A scores, one for each sample.

(2) Subtract the grand mean from each subject's mean score, and then square that deviation. There are n_S subjects, and so there should be n_S squared deviations.

(3) Sum the squared deviations found in Step 2 above, and then multiply that sum by n_A, the number of samples, to find the value of $SS_{subjects}$.

C. Treatment × Subjects Sum of Squares

$$SS_{treatment \times subjects} = \Sigma (X - \bar{X}_i)(X - \bar{X}_k)$$

(1) Calculate the following for each score separately:

(a) Calculate the deviation of the score from the mean of the sample containing that score.

(b) Calculate the deviation of the score from the mean score of the subject contributing that score.

(c) Multiply the deviation from Step 1*a* by the deviation from Step 1*b*.

(2) Sum all of the deviation cross products for all of the scores. There are $n_A n_S$ scores and so there will be $n_A n_S$ deviation cross products. This sum is the value of $SS_{treatment \times subjects}$.

D. Total Sum of Squares

$$SS_{total} = \Sigma (X - \bar{X}_T)^2$$

The procedure for calculating the total sum of squares for a within-subjects ANOVA is exactly the same as the procedure for a between-subjects ANOVA, which is described in Procedure 16-2, Step 1C. As a check:

$$SS_{total} = SS_{between} + SS_{subjects} + SS_{treatment \times subjects}.$$

2. Calculate the degrees of freedom.

A. $df_{between} = n_A - 1$, where n_A is the number of samples.

B. $df_{subjects} = n_S - 1$, where n_S is the number of scores per sample.

C. $df_{treatment \times subjects} = (n_A - 1)(n_S - 1)$.

D. $df_{total} = n_A n_S - 1$.

E. As a check, $df_{total} = df_{between} + df_{subjects} + df_{treatment \times subjects}$.

3. Construct the summary table and calculate *F*.

A. Construct a table with five columns. Label the columns: "Sources of Variance," "*SS*," "*df*," "*MS*," and "*F*." Label the first row with the name of the factor being studied. Label the second row, "Subjects"; the third row, "Treatment × Subjects," and the fourth row, "Total."

B. Write the values for the sums of squares and degrees of freedom calculated above into the appropriate columns in the summary table.

C. For the first three rows, divide the value of the sum of squares by the value of the degrees of freedom to find the values of the mean square, *MS*:

$$MS_{between} = \frac{SS_{between}}{df_{between}}, \quad MS_{subjects} = \frac{SS_{subjects}}{df_{subjects}},$$

$$MS_{treatment \times subjects} = \frac{SS_{treatment \times subjects}}{df_{treatment \times subjects}}$$

D. Divide the value of $MS_{between}$ by the value of $MS_{treatment \times subjects}$ to find the value of *F*:

$$F = \frac{MS_{between}}{MS_{treatment \times subjects}}$$

treatments that the subjects received. In Joe's study, the between-groups sum of squares is the portion of the total sum of squares attributable to the effects of the three anxiety-alleviating methods that Joe studied. Since we are analyzing the same scores in this within-subjects analysis as we previously tested in the between-subjects analysis, the effect of the three treatments remains the same. As we saw previously, the between-groups sum of squares for Joe's study is 140.

The subjects sum of squares. The next source of variance in a within-subjects ANOVA is subjects, a source we have not encountered before. Where the between-groups sum of squares measures the differences in the scores attributable to the difference between the treatments, the subjects sum of squares measures the differences in the scores attributable to differences between the subjects themselves. As we considered previously, some of the variation in the scores is due to differences among the participants, such as differences in math ability. In a within-subjects design, each subject is tested under each of the treatment conditions, and so we can measure the variance that is attributable to these differences among the subjects.

Figure 16-7 shows the steps in calculating the subjects sum of squares. The procedure for calculating the subjects sum of squares is similar to the procedure for calculating the between-groups sum of squares. Recall that to find the value of the between-groups sum of squares, we subtracted the grand mean from each sample mean and then squared each of those deviations. For the subjects sum of squares, we first find the mean score for each subject by adding up each subject's scores and then dividing by the number of scores contributed by each subject. For example, participant 1 in Joe's study contributed three scores, 16, 19, and 16, one for each treatment condition. The mean of these three scores is 17 correct.

Next, we subtract the grand mean from each subject's mean score and then square that deviation. We can see in Figure 16-7 that the deviation of the first participant's mean score from the grand mean is 3, and the square of that deviation is 9. The subjects sum of squares is found by summing these squared deviations for all of the subjects and then multiplying that sum by the number of scores contributed per subject, which is the same as the number of treatment conditions. Figure 16-7 shows that the subjects sum of squares for Joe's study is 60.00.

The treatment $\times$ subjects sum of squares. The next source, treatment $\times$ subjects, is another source that we have not yet encountered and is equivalent to the within-groups source of variance in a between-subjects analysis. Recall that in a between-subjects ANOVA, each score contributes to the mean of one treatment condition and that the within-groups sum of squares is calculated by finding the deviation of each score from the mean of the treatment condition containing that score and then squaring those deviations. In

FIGURE 16-7   Calculating the Subject Sum of Squares for a Test of Joe's Math Study

1. For each subject separately, calculate the mean of the subject's three scores.
2. Subtract the grand mean from the mean score for each subject, then square this deviation.

Subject	Sample 1: Confidence Training	Sample 2: Relaxation Training	Sample 3: No Training	Mean Score for Each Subject	$(\bar{X}_k - \bar{X}_T)^2$
1	16	19	16	17.0	$(17 - 14)^2 = 9$
2	15	17	10	14.0	$(14 - 14)^2 = 0$
3	14	17	11	14.0	$(14 - 14)^2 = 0$
4	14	16	12	14.0	$(14 - 14)^2 = 0$
5	13	14	9	12.0	$(12 - 14)^2 = 4$
6	19	15	11	15.0	$(15 - 14)^2 = 1$
7	19	14	12	15.0	$(15 - 14)^2 = 1$
8	18	13	8	13.0	$(13 - 14)^2 = 1$
9	17	13	12	14.0	$(14 - 14)^2 = 0$
10	15	12	9	12.0	$(12 - 14)^2 = 4$

$$\Sigma(\bar{X}_k - \bar{X}_T)^2 = 20$$

3. Add up these squared deviations, then multiply that sum by the number of samples, n_A, to find the value of the subjects sum of squares:

$$SS_{subjects} = n_A\Sigma(\bar{X}_k - \bar{X}_T)^2 = 3(20) = 60.$$

a within-subjects ANOVA, each score contributes both to the mean of one treatment condition and to the mean score of one subject. For example, in the scores from Joe's study, shown in Table 16-4, the first score listed, 16, contributes to the sample mean of the confidence training group and to the mean score for participant 1.

In the treatment × subjects sum of squares, we find the deviation of each score from the mean of the treatment condition containing that score and the deviation of that score from the mean score of the subject contributing the score. For each score, we then multiply these two deviations together to find the deviations cross product. The value of the treatment × subjects sum of squares is the sum of these deviation cross products. Figure 16-8 shows the steps in calculating the treatment × subjects sum of squares for the scores in Joe's study, which is 72.00.

The subjects sum of squares and the treatment × subjects sum of squares in a within-subjects ANOVA are equal to the within-groups sum of squares for a between-subjects ANOVA when calculated on the same set of scores. In this within-subjects analysis of Joe's study, the subjects sum of squares is 60 and the treatment × subjects sum of squares is 72. These two sums of squares

FIGURE 16-8 Calculating the Treatment × Subjects Sum of Squares for a Test of Joe's Math Study

1. For each of the three samples, subtract the sample mean from each score in the sample. The sample means were calculated previously for the between-subjects sum of squares.

2. For each of the subjects, subtract the subject's mean score from each of that subject's scores. These subjects' mean scores were already calculated for the subjects sum of squares.

3. For each score separately, multiply the deviation from the sample mean by the deviation from the subject's mean score.

Subject	Sample 1: Confidence Training $(X - \bar{X}_{l=1})(X - \bar{X}_k)$	Sample 2: Relaxation Training $(X - \bar{X}_{l=2})(X - \bar{X}_k)$	Sample 3: No Training $(X - \bar{X}_{l=3})(X - \bar{X}_k)$
1	$(16 - 16)(16 - 17) = 0$	$(19 - 15)(19 - 17) = 8$	$(16 - 11)(16 - 17) = -5$
2	$(15 - 16)(15 - 14) = -1$	$(17 - 15)(17 - 14) = 6$	$(10 - 11)(10 - 14) = 4$
3	$(14 - 16)(14 - 14) = 0$	$(17 - 15)(17 - 14) = 6$	$(11 - 11)(11 - 14) = 0$
4	$(14 - 16)(14 - 14) = 0$	$(16 - 15)(16 - 14) = 2$	$(12 - 11)(12 - 14) = -2$
5	$(13 - 16)(13 - 12) = -3$	$(14 - 15)(14 - 12) = -2$	$(9 - 11)(9 - 12) = 6$
6	$(19 - 16)(19 - 15) = 12$	$(15 - 15)(15 - 15) = 0$	$(11 - 11)(11 - 15) = 0$
7	$(19 - 16)(19 - 15) = 12$	$(14 - 15)(14 - 15) = 1$	$(12 - 11)(12 - 15) = -3$
8	$(18 - 16)(18 - 13) = 10$	$(13 - 15)(13 - 13) = 0$	$(8 - 11)(8 - 13) = 15$
9	$(17 - 16)(17 - 14) = 3$	$(13 - 15)(13 - 14) = 2$	$(12 - 11)(12 - 14) = -2$
10	$(15 - 16)(15 - 12) = -3$	$(12 - 15)(12 - 12) = 0$	$(9 - 11)(9 - 12) = 6$
Subtotals:	30	23	19

4. Add up these deviation cross products. In this example, the deviation cross products are subtotaled for each sample (the sums are shown above) and then these subtotals are added up:

$$SS_{\text{treatment} \times \text{subjects}} = \Sigma(X - \bar{X}_i)(X - \bar{X}_k) = 30 + 23 + 19 = 72.$$

together equal 132, which is the value of the within-groups sum of squares in the between-subjects ANOVA.

In a between-subjects ANOVA, the within-groups variance is attributed to random variation among the scores, variation that is not due to the different treatment conditions. In a within-subjects ANOVA, this variance is partitioned into two sources. One source is individual differences among the participants, differences such as math ability. The other source, labeled treatment × subjects, is the remaining random variation among the scores, variation that cannot be attributed to either differences in the treatments or differences among the subjects.

Recall that the *F* ratio compares the variation attributable to the different treatments to the random variation among the scores. In a within-subjects ANOVA, the variance attributable to differences among the subjects is removed from the measure of the random variation among the scores, generally resulting in a smaller value in the denominator of the *F* ratio. This in turn results in a larger value of F, increasing the probability of achieving significance. Thus, removing the variance attributable to differences among the subjects from the within-groups variance in a within-subjects ANOVA may have the net effect of increasing the power of the statistical test.

The total sum of squares.   The final sum of squares to calculate is the total sum of squares. The procedure for calculating this value in a within-subjects ANOVA is identical to the procedure for a between-subjects ANOVA. As we already saw, the value of the total sum of squares for the scores from Joe's study is 272. As a check, the sums of squares for the between-groups, subjects, and treatment $\times$ subjects sources of variance should add up to the total sum of squares:

$$SS_{total} = SS_{between} + SS_{subjects} + SS_{treatment \times subjects} = 140 + 60 + 72 = 272.$$

Calculating the Degrees of Freedom

The next step in calculating a within-subjects analysis of variance is to determine the values of the degrees of freedom for each source of variance. The two values that we need to calculate the degrees of freedom are n_A, the number of levels or treatment conditions, and n_S, the number of scores per level or treatment condition. For the scores from Joe's study, there are three treatment conditions and ten scores per treatment condition:

$$df_{between} = n_A - 1 = 3 - 1 = 2,$$

$$df_{subjects} = n_S - 1 = 10 - 1 = 9,$$

$$df_{treatment \times subjects} = (n_A - 1)(n_S - 1) = (3 - 1)(10 - 1) = (2)(9) = 18,$$

$$df_{total} = n_A n_S - 1 = (3)(10) - 1 = 30 - 1 = 29.$$

As a check, $df_{total} = df_{between} + df_{subjects} + df_{treatment \times subjects} = 2 + 9 + 18 = 29$.

Constructing the Summary Table and Calculating the Value of *F*

The next step is to construct the summary table. Table 16-6 shows the summary table for the within-subjects analysis of variance of the scores in Joe's

TABLE 16-6   Summary Table for the Within-Subjects ANOVA of Joe Johnson's Math Anxiety Study

Sources of Variance	SS	df	MS	F
Type of Training	140.00	2	70.00	17.50
Subjects	60.00	9	6.67	
Training $\times$ Subjects	72.00	18	4.00	
Total	272.00	29		

study. To find the mean squares, we divide the sum of squares by the degrees of freedom for that source of variance:

$$MS_{between} = \frac{SS_{between}}{df_{between}} = \frac{140}{2} = 70.00,$$

$$MS_{subjects} = \frac{SS_{subjects}}{df_{subjects}} = \frac{60}{9} = 6.67,$$

$$MS_{treatment \times subjects} = \frac{SS_{treatment \times subjects}}{df_{treatment \times subjects}} = \frac{72}{18} = 4.00.$$

To find the value of F, we divide the between-subjects mean square by the treatment × subjects mean square:

$$F = \frac{MS_{between}}{MS_{treatment \times subjects}} = \frac{70.00}{4.00} = 17.50.$$

The value of F for the type of training in Joe's study, using the within-subjects ANOVA, is 17.50. There are 2 and 18 df. The critical value of F from Appendix A-4, with $\alpha = .05$, is 3.55. The value of F that we calculated is larger than the critical value of 3.55, and so we can reject the null hypothesis. Again, rejecting the null hypothesis tells us that the means of the treatment conditions are not all the same value. To determine which means are significantly different, we need to conduct posttests.

Conducting Posttests

The procedure for conducting posttests on the results of a within-subjects analysis of variance is nearly the same as the procedure for a between-subjects analysis of variance. The only difference is that the treatment × subjects mean square is used in the denominator in calculating the value of t. The steps in conducting these posttests are described in Procedure 16-3. The calculations for the posttests comparing the means from Joe's study are shown below:

$$t_{confidence\ vs.\ no\ training} = \frac{\bar{X}_1 - \bar{X}_3}{\sqrt{\dfrac{2MS_{treatment \times subjects}}{n_S}}} = \frac{16 - 11}{\sqrt{\dfrac{2(4.00)}{10}}} = \frac{5}{\sqrt{.80}} = \frac{5}{.89} = 5.618,$$

$$t_{relaxation\ vs.\ no\ training} = \frac{\bar{X}_2 - \bar{X}_3}{\sqrt{\dfrac{2MS_{treatment \times subjects}}{n_S}}} = \frac{15 - 11}{\sqrt{\dfrac{2(4.00)}{10}}} = \frac{4}{\sqrt{.80}} = \frac{4}{.89} = 4.494,$$

$$t_{confidence\ vs.\ relaxation} = \frac{\bar{X}_1 - \bar{X}_2}{\sqrt{\dfrac{2MS_{treatment \times subjects}}{n_S}}} = \frac{16 - 15}{\sqrt{\dfrac{2(4.00)}{10}}} = \frac{1}{\sqrt{.80}} = \frac{1}{.89} = 1.124.$$

Recall that Joe predicted that math-anxious students would perform better on the math test after both confidence training and relaxation training than they did with no training at all. Again, these are unidirectional hypotheses, or one-tailed tests. The degrees of freedom for these posttests are $2(n_S - 1)$, which for this comparison is $2(10 - 1)$ or 18. The critical value of t, for a one-tailed test with 18 df and $\alpha = .05$, is 1.734. For the difference between the means of the confidence-training group and the no-training group, the value of t is 5.618, which is greater than this critical value of t. For the difference between the means of the relaxation-training group and the no-training group, the value of t is 4.494, which is also greater than the critical value of t. Therefore, the math-anxious students scored significantly higher on the math test after relaxation training and after confidence training than after no training at all.

Recall that Joe made no specific predictions on which of the experimental training methods, confidence training or relaxation training, would result in higher math performance. Therefore, to compare these means would be a bidirectional or two-tailed test. The critical value of t, for a two-tailed test with 18 df and $\alpha = .05$, is 2.101. The t comparing the mean of the confidence-training group to the mean of the relaxation-training group is 1.124, which is not greater than the critical value of t. This is not enough evidence to conclude that there is a significant difference in performance on the math test between the confidence-training and relaxation-training groups.

Comparing Between- and Within-Subjects Tests

In this chapter, we have analyzed the same set of scores twice, once using the between-subjects ANOVA and then using the within-subjects ANOVA. In real life, we would not analyze one set of scores with both tests. Only one test would be appropriate, and we would use only that appropriate test. However, in a textbook, we can do things that we would not ordinarily do. We analyzed the results of Joe's study twice in order to compare the results of the analysis of variance for a between-subjects design and a within-subjects design. Because in the within-subjects ANOVA, we can partition out the variance due to individual differences among subjects, the within-subjects ANOVA is potentially more powerful.

TABLE 16-7 Comparison of Results of Between-Subjects and Within-Subjects ANOVAs

Source	Between-Subjects	Within-Subjects
$MS_{between}$	70.00	70.00
MS_{within}	4.89	4.00
$F_{observed}$	14.31	17.50
df_{within}	27	18
$F_{critical}$	3.35	3.55

Table 16-7 lists several values calculated in the between-subjects and within-subjects analyses of the scores from Joe's study. First, notice that the between-groups mean square, the variation attributable to the type of training the students received, is the same for both analyses. Thus, the difference in the value of F is not due to any difference in the variation due to the treatment the students received. For the within-groups variation, remember that the variation due to individual differences among the subjects is removed in a within-subjects ANOVA. As a consequence, the mean square used in the denominator of F, MS_{within}, is smaller for the within-subjects ANOVA, 4.00, than for the between-subjects ANOVA, 4.89. This in turn affects the size of F, so that the value of F is larger for the within-subjects ANOVA, 17.50, than for the between-subjects ANOVA, 14.31

There is, however, a trade-off. While in these analyses, the value of F is larger for the within-subjects ANOVA than for the between-subjects ANOVA, the degrees of freedom are smaller for the within-subjects analysis than for the between-subjects analysis. In the within-subjects analysis, not only is the sum of squares attributable to individual subject differences removed from the within-groups sum of squares, the degrees of freedom attributable to those individual subject differences are also removed from the within-groups degrees of freedom. Thus, MS_{within} is smaller, but so is df_{within}. As can be seen in Table 16-7, for the between-subjects ANOVA, there are 27 within-groups degrees of freedom but only 18 for the within-subjects ANOVA.

One consequence of this reduction in the degrees of freedom is that the critical value of F is greater for the within-subjects ANOVA than for the between-subjects ANOVA. In order to reject the null hypothesis, the observed value of F must be at least 3.35 for the between-subjects ANOVA but must be 3.55 or greater for the within-subjects ANOVA. Thus for this within-subjects analysis of the scores from Joe's study, not only is the observed value of F greater but so is the critical value of F that must be met in order to reject the null hypothesis.

While there is a trade-off, generally the trade-off favors the results of within-subjects test. Generally, the increase in the observed value of F is greater than the increase in the critical value of F required to reject the null hypothesis. For example, in this analysis, compared to the between-subjects ANOVA, for the within-subjects ANOVA the observed value of F increased 3.19 points while the critical value of F increased only 0.20 points. This does not hold true for every analysis, but it is generally true and accounts for why the within-subjects analysis is considered a more powerful test than the between-subjects analysis.

Of course, we do not decide after a study has been conducted and scores have been collected to do a within-subjects analysis. We conduct the appropriate test, a between-subjects test when different, unrelated subjects are tested in each sample and a within-subjects test when the same or related subjects are tested in each sample. The decision about which test to use is actually made when designing the study. If it is possible to design an experiment as a within-subjects study, it is generally desirable to do so because the appropriate statistical test, a within-subjects test, usually is more powerful.

In this chapter, we have seen that the one-factor ANOVA is a powerful statistical test that enables us to compare more than two samples of scores in a single analysis. This is not the only advantage of the analysis of variance. An additional advantage is that it is possible to compare more than one factor at a time in an analysis of variance. In the next chapter, we examine the method for conducting an analysis of variance on two factors simultaneously.

CHECKING YOUR ANSWERS

1. Calculating an ANOVA is a long process, involving many steps, but each step is fairly straightforward. If you take each step one at a time, working carefully, you can avoid most errors.

2. The calculations for each of the sums of squares involves finding deviations and then squaring those deviations. For each source, the sum of these deviations before squaring is always zero. Use this as a check to make sure that you have calculated the deviations accurately.

3. In calculating the sums of squares (*SS*), the sum of all the component sums of squares should equal the total sums of squares. Similarly, the sum of all the component degrees of freedom should equal the total degrees of freedom. Remember that the total degrees of freedom are always the total number of scores, minus 1.

4. Calculating the mean squares is straightforward: divide the sum of squares for each component by its degrees of freedom. Note that the sum of component mean squares will *not* equal the total mean square. In fact, a total mean square is not even calculated.

5. The most common error that occurs in calculating the value of *F* is using the wrong error term in the denominator. For the between-subjects analysis, there is only one within-groups mean square, which is the error term. For the within-subjects analysis, the error term is the treatment × subjects mean square.

6. The most common error that occurs in determining whether the value of *F* is significant is mixing up the degrees of freedom for the numerator (between mean square) and denominator (within mean square). The degrees of freedom for the within mean square nearly always are larger than the degrees of freedom for the between mean square. Consequently, nearly always you'll look for the smaller degrees of freedom in the column headings and the larger degrees of freedom in the row headings.

7. The best way to make sense of posttests is to graph the results. Determine which sample means you are comparing, and draw a graph. The graph should help you understand why the result of a posttest is either significant or insignificant, as well as spotting any errors you may have made.

 ## SUMMARY

▶ The analysis of variance is a statistical test that can be used to compare samples of scores drawn from more than two populations in one statistical test.

▶ The analysis of variance generates a statistic, labeled *F*, that compares the degree to which the sample means differ from each other to the degree to which the scores within each sample differ from each other.

▶ In previous chapters, we used the formula for the standard deviation to measure how far scores in a group differ from each other. The standard deviation is the square root of a statistic, called the variance. Both the standard deviation and the variance are statistics measuring the deviation among the scores in a group.

▶ In the formula for the variance, the numerator represents the sum of squares, which is the squared deviation of each score in the group from the mean. The denominator represents the degrees of freedom, which is based on the number of deviations represented in the numerator.

▶ In the analysis of variance, the total variance is partitioned into the variance due to differences between the samples of scores and the variance due to differences within the samples of scores.

▶ If the analysis of variance is used to compare two samples of scores, the resulting value of F will be equal to the square of the value of t computed for the same two samples of scores.

▶ The analysis of variance can be used when each sample of scores comes from a different group of subjects (a between-subjects ANOVA) or when each sample of scores comes from the same group or related groups of subjects (a within-subjects ANOVA).

E X E R C I S E S

Conceptual Exercises

1. Define the following terms:

sum of squares	factor
between-groups sum of squares	levels
within-groups sum of squares	treatments
partitioning the sum of squares	between-subjects factor
total variance	within-subjects factor
between-groups variance	within-groups variance

2. Listed below are three sets of scores, each consisting of scores from two samples of subjects:

Set I		Set II		Set III	
Sample 1	Sample 2	Sample 1	Sample 2	Sample 1	Sample 2
10	10	4	8	8	12
8	8	4	8	6	10
6	6	4	8	4	8
4	4	4	8	2	6
2	2	4	8	0	4

A. Compute the standard deviation for the scores in each sample. Which samples have the same standard deviation?

B. Using the formula for a *t* test for the difference between sample means, compute the value of *t* for each set of samples. Explain what these values of *t* indicate.

3. For each of the sets of scores in Exercise 2, find the grand mean for all of the scores in samples 1 and 2 combined. Then, for each of the scores, find the total deviation (i.e., the difference between the score and the grand mean), the within-groups deviation (i.e., the difference between the score and the sample mean), and the between-groups deviation (i.e., the difference between the sample mean and the grand mean). For each score, verify that the total deviation equals the sum of the within-groups and between-groups deviations.

4. Square each of the deviations from the previous exercise and then for each set of scores, find the within-groups sum of squares, the between-groups sum of squares, and the total sum of squares.
    A. Explain why the between-groups sum of squares is zero in Set I.
    B. Explain why the within-groups sum of squares is zero in Set II.
    C. Explain why the within-groups sum of squares is the same for Sets I and III.
    D. Explain why the between-groups sum of squares is the same for Sets II and III.

5. Only for the scores in Set III of Exercise 2, determine the following:
    A. Find the within-groups degrees of freedom, the between-groups degrees of freedom, and the total degrees of freedom. Verify that the total degrees of freedom are equal to the sum of the within-groups and between-groups degrees of freedom.
    B. Describe how the total degrees of freedom are related to the number of scores in the set.
    C. Describe how the between-groups degrees of freedom are related to the number of samples in the set.
    D. Describe how the within-groups degrees of freedom are related to the number of subjects per sample and the number of samples.

6. Only for the scores in Set III of Exercise 2, determine the following:
    A. Calculate the variance for all ten scores in Set III, using the formula for the sample variance (Step-by-Step Procedure 5-2 or 5-3). Divide the total sum of squares by the total degrees of freedom to confirm that the ANOVA analyzes the total variance in a set of scores.
    B. Find the within-groups mean square and the between-groups mean square.
    C. Find the value of *F*, using the between-groups and within-groups mean squares.
    D. Find the square root of the value of *F* and compare to the value of *t* for Set III calculated in Exercise 2. Describe the relationship between *F* and *t*.

7. Follow Step-by-Step Procedure 16-2 to calculate the value of *F* for the two samples of scores in Set III of Exercise 2 to confirm that this procedure calculates the same value as found in Exercise 6.

8. Describe the difference between the term "between-groups" and the term "between-subjects." Similarly, describe the difference between the term "within-groups" and the term "within-subjects."

9. Describe the difference between a level of a factor and a treatment.

10. Explain why the subjects sum of squares and the treatment $\times$ subjects sum of squares for a within-subjects analysis of variance together are equivalent to the within-groups sum of squares for a between-subjects analysis of variance.

11. Listed below are two small samples of scores:

Sample 1	Sample 2
1	5
3	6
4	8
5	10
7	11

A. Conduct a between-subjects analysis of variance on these scores.

B. Add 2 to each score in both samples. Conduct a between-subjects analysis of variance on these scores. Compare the results of this analysis to the analysis conducted in part A and explain any similarities or differences that occur.

C. In the original set of scores, add 5 to the last score in each sample. Conduct a between-subjects analysis of variance on these scores. Compare the results of this analysis to the analysis conducted in part A, and explain any similarities or differences that occur.

D. In the original set of scores, subtract 2 from each score in Sample 2. Conduct a between-subjects analysis of variance on these scores. Compare the results of this analysis to the analysis conducted in part A, and explain any similarities or differences that occur.

Computational Exercises

12. Jezebel investigated the effect of the type of breakfast students ate on their academic performance. One group ate a breakfast high in protein. A second group ate a breakfast high in carbohydrates. The third group ate a breakfast balanced between protein and carbohydrates, and a fourth group ate no breakfast. That morning, Jezebel gave all the students a test of general knowledge with a thirty-minute time limit to increase the pressure, with the results below:

High Protein	High Carbohydrates	Balanced	No Breakfast
32	17	26	9
31	16	24	7
29	15	23	7
27	11	22	6
24	10	19	4
19	9	18	3

A. Conduct a between-subjects analysis of variance, using Procedures 16 1 and 16 2.

B. Conduct the appropriate posttests on the results.

C. In regular English, describe what the ANOVA and posttests demonstrate.

13. Juanita studied the effect of various cold medications on people's reaction times to determine whether the medications are safe to use while operating heavy equipment.

Five groups were tested, each under the influence of one of the following: nasal decongestant, cough suppressant, expectorant, pain reliever, and no medication. The scores below are the average number of seconds each participant took to respond over ten trials:

Decongestant	Suppressant	Expectorant	Pain Reliever	No Medication
10	8	6	4	4
11	7	4	1	4
9	9	5	2	3
9	6	3	2	2
6	5	2	1	2

A. Conduct a between-subjects analysis of variance, using Procedures 16-1 and 16-2.

B. Conduct the appropriate posttests on the results.

C. In regular English, describe what the ANOVA and posttests demonstrate.

14. Assume that in the previous exercise, Juanita tested one group of five participants under all five types of medication. On five consecutive days, each participant was given one of the types of medication and then tested after one hour. To control the effects of practice, the order in which the medications were given over the five days was different for each participant.

A. Conduct a within-subjects analysis of variance, using Procedure 16-4.

B. Conduct the appropriate posttests on the results.

C. In regular English, describe what the ANOVA and posttests demonstrate.

D. Compare the summary table for the ANOVA conducted in this problem to the summary table constructed in the previous exercise. What remains the same? What differs?

E. Compare the advantages and disadvantages of using the between-subjects ANOVA and the within-subjects ANOVA.

15. Jafar studied the effect of different types of music on academic performance. On three different days, he tested the same group of participants on equivalent forms of an academic achievement test after listening to one of the types of music listed below. The participants' scores on the test were

Participant	Mozart	Frank Sinatra	Rolling Stones
1	21	11	16
2	18	15	18
3	22	9	17
4	16	7	13
5	19	11	15
6	21	7	14
7	17	10	18
8	19	9	17
9	18	11	16

A. Conduct a within-subjects analysis of variance, using Procedure 16-4.

B. Conduct the appropriate posttests on the results.

C. In regular English, describe what the ANOVA and posttests demonstrate.

E N D N O T E S

1. The symbol $\overline{X}_T$ is used, rather than $\overline{X}_G$ for grand mean, to be consistent with the symbols used in the analysis of variance, in which the total sum of squares for all of the scores is symbolized SS_{total} or SS_T.

2. One book that describes a very user-friendly method for conducting the analysis of variance is Geoffrey Keppel's *Design and Analysis: A Researcher's Handbook* (2d ed., Englewood Cliffs, NJ: Prentice-Hall, 1982).

3. This test is recommended if the researcher predicts that the means will be significantly different before conducting the analysis of variance. Other tests are recommended if the researcher does not decide to compare the means until after conducting the analysis of variance. These other tests are beyond the scope of this book. For further information, you can consult advanced books on statistical tests, such as *Design and Analysis: A Researcher's Handbook*.

A Statistical Test Comparing More than Two Samples: The Two-Factor Analysis of Variance

17

The Interaction between Factors

The Analysis of Variance for Two Between-Subjects Factors

Assumptions of the Analysis of Variance

STEP-BY-STEP PROCEDURE 17-1: Conducting the ANOVA for Two Factors

Identifying the Sources of Variance

Notation System Used in a Two-Factor ANOVA

Constructing the Null and Alternate Hypotheses for the Main Effects of A and B

Constructing the Null and Alternate Hypotheses for the Interaction of A and B

Computing the Values of F

Calculating the Sums of Squares

STEP-BY-STEP PROCEDURE 17-2: Calculating the Value of F for a Two-Factor Between-Subjects ANOVA

Computing the Degrees of Freedom

Computing the Mean Squares

Computing the Value of F

Determining the Significance of F

Posttests for a Two-Factor Analysis of Variance

Posttests for the Main Effects

STEP-BY-STEP PROCEDURE 17-3: Calculating the Value of t to Compare the Means of Two Levels of Factor A in a Two-Factor ANOVA

STEP-BY-STEP PROCEDURE 17-4: Calculating the Value of t to Compare the Means of Two Levels of Factor B in a Two-Factor ANOVA

Posttests for the Interaction of A and B

STEP-BY-STEP PROCEDURE 17-5: Calculating the Value of t to Compare the Means of Two Levels of a Factor A at One Level of Factor B

STEP-BY-STEP PROCEDURE 17-6: Calculating the Value of t to Compare the Means of Two Treatment Groups of a Factor B at One Level of Factor A

Other Analyses of Variance

CHECKING YOUR ANSWERS

SUMMARY

EXERCISES

Conceptual Exercises

Computational Exercises

ENDNOTE

▶ In the last chapter, we saw that one of the strengths of the analysis of variance is that we can test more than two levels of a factor at one time, such as the three types of anxiety-alleviating training that Joe Johnson used in his study. Another strength of the analysis of variance is that it can be used to analyze more than one factor at one time. In this chapter, we will look at using the ANOVA to analyze two factors at the same time. In fact, the ANOVA can be used to examine any number of factors, so that it can be used to analyze the results from very complex experimental designs.

As an example, suppose we were investigating factors that influence the suicide rates among adults in the United States. One factor might be age, in that we might expect higher rates of suicide for some age groups than for others. Another factor might be sex. There is evidence that men more frequently commit suicide (although women more frequently attempt suicide, unsuccessfully). We could conduct two separate studies, one to analyze the effect that age has on suicide rates and the other, the effect of sex. We would then have to analyze the results of these two studies separately, using the one-factor ANOVA that we studied in the last chapter. On the other hand, using the power of the two-factor ANOVA, we could conduct just one study, collecting data from both men and women in several age groups, and analyze the data representing these two factors simultaneously, in one ANOVA. Thus, one advantage of the ANOVA is that we do not have to conduct a separate study for each factor of interest.

The Interaction between Factors

An **interaction** between two factors occurs when the effect of one factor on the scores differs between levels of the other factor.

Another advantage of the two-factor ANOVA is that we can examine the interaction between the two factors. An **interaction** between two variables occurs when the effect of one factor on the scores depends on the value of the other factor. In an interaction, the combination of two factors has an effect on the scores that cannot be accounted for by either factor alone.

For instance, Figure 17-1 shows four examples of the effect that sex and age might have on suicide rates. In graph A, the effect of age on suicide rates is the exact opposite for males and females. Among males, the suicide rate declines with age, with 20-year-olds having the highest suicide rate and 60-year-olds having the lowest. Among females, the effect of age on suicide rates is the opposite, in that the suicide rate increases with age, so that 60-year-olds have

FIGURE 17-1   Examples of Possible Interactions
between Sex and Age on the Rate of Suicide

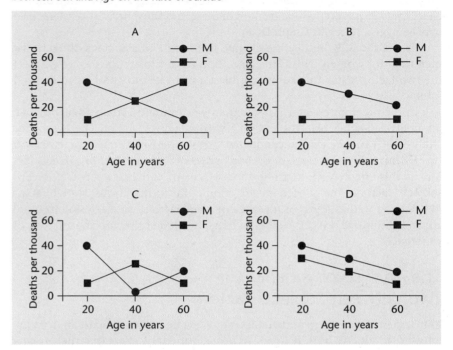

the highest suicide rate among women. This is an interaction. The effect of
the factor age on suicide rates is different for each level of the other factor, sex.

Graph B in Figure 17-1 shows another possible interaction between sex
and age. In Graph B, the suicide rates decline with age for men, from 40 per
1,000 for 20-year-olds down to 20 per 1,000 for 60-year-olds. However, for
women, the suicide rate remains constant across age, with every age group
having a rate of 10 suicides per 1,000. This also is an interaction, albeit a different interaction from the one shown in Graph A.

Graph C in Figure 17-1 shows a third possible interaction in the effect
of sex and age on suicide rates. For the males, suicide rates decline from 20 to
40 years old and then rise again for the 60-year-olds. For the females, suicide
rates rise from 20 to 40 years old and then decline again for the 60-year-olds.
Because the effect of age on suicide rates differs for the two levels, male and
female, this also is an interaction.

In Graph D of Figure 17-1, there is no interaction in the effect of sex and
age on suicide rates. The suicide rates for men decline with age for men, from
a high for the 20-year-olds to a low for the 60-year-olds. The suicide rates for
women also decline with age to exactly the same degree as they do for men.

It is true that, overall, women have a lower suicide rate than men. However, the effect that age has on the suicide rates of women is no different from the effect that age has on the suicide rates of men, and thus there is no interaction between age and sex in Graph D.

In Graphs A, B, and C, the change in the rate of suicide is different for men than for women. This is the definition of an interaction. As we will see, the two-factor ANOVA makes it possible for us to identify and examine such interactions.

In the previous chapter, we saw that we can use the analysis of variance on a between-subjects factor and on a within-subjects factor. The two-factor analysis of variance can be conducted on two between-subjects factors, on two within-subjects factors, or on one between- and one within-subjects factor. In this chapter, we examine the analysis of variance for two between-subjects factors. The procedure for conducting other forms of two-factor ANOVAs, as well as ANOVAs for three or more factors, can be found in more advanced statistic texts, as well as in texts devoted entirely to the analysis of variance.[1]

The Analysis of Variance for Two Between-Subjects Factors

In his unending quest to find methods to alleviate students' math anxiety, Joe Johnson conducted a study in which he examined the effect that the amount of time students spend preparing has on their math test performance. The participants in this study were students who had not yet taken a statistics course. In the experiment, Joe first gave all participants a brief but comprehensive lecture on how to compute measures of central tendency. Following this lecture, one group of students was given two hours in which to study the material and practice working problems. A second group was given one hour, and the third group was given no study time. Each group of students was then given a twenty-question test on measures of central tendency. The conditions for taking this test were the same for all three groups of students. Thus, in this study one factor is amount of preparation time, with three levels (0, 1, and 2 hours). In addition, in this study, Joe tested both students with high math anxiety and students with little or no math anxiety. This constitutes a second factor, degree of math anxiety, with two levels (high and low). The scores that the students received in this study are shown in Table 17-1.

In the ANOVAs that we examined in the last chapter, there was only one factor, and so the between-groups variance was the variance attributable to that factor. In a two-factor ANOVA, we will calculate the between-groups variance for each of the two factors, and so we need a way to differentiate these two factors. The solution is simply to label the factors A and B. Thus, the notation SS_A represents the between-groups sum of squares for factor A, and SS_B represents the between-groups sum of squares for factor B.

TABLE 17-1   Math Scores of Students Tested under Three Levels of Preparation Time and Two Levels of Degree of Anxiety

Degree of Anxiety	Preparation Time		
	A_1: 0 Hours	A_2: 1 Hour	A_3: 2 Hours
High: B_1	10	11	19
	9	8	17
	5	9	13
	7	5	15
	4	7	11
Low: B_2	18	19	20
	16	16	19
	14	17	18
	16	13	16
	11	15	12

Step-by-Step Procedure 17-1 shows the steps involved in testing hypotheses using the two-factor ANOVA. These steps are very similar to the ones that we have followed previously in testing hypotheses. We need to check to make sure that we have met the assumptions of the test, construct the null and alternate hypotheses, determine the value of α, and find the critical values of F that determine the region in which we can reject the null hypothesis.

Assumptions of the Analysis of Variance

The analysis of variance is based on the assumption that the subjects in each sample are randomly and independently selected. If this assumption is violated, we cannot assume that the samples are representative of the populations from which they were drawn. The analysis of variance is also based on the assumption that those populations are normally distributed. If it appears from the samples drawn that there may be serious violations of this assumption, it may be wise to select a nonparametric statistical method rather than the analysis of variance. A third assumption is that the variances of the populations are equal. We can use the sample variances as an estimate of the population variances to see if this assumption is seriously violated. Finally, the analysis of variance, like other parametric tests, is designed for use with scores that are measured on an interval or ratio scale.

Identifying the Sources of Variance

There is one notable difference in the steps of testing hypotheses with the two-factor ANOVA. In previous chapters, for each statistical test, we had one null hypothesis and one alternate hypothesis. For example, in the one-factor

STEP-BY-STEP PROCEDURE 17-1

Conducting the ANOVA for Two Factors

1. Verify that the following assumptions have been met:
  A. The subjects in each sample were randomly and independently selected.
  B. The distributions are approximately normally distributed.
  C. The population variances are equal.
  D. The scores are measured with an interval or ratio scale.

2. Write the null and alternate hypotheses for each between-groups source of variance. For the ANOVA for two factors, there will be three between-groups sources of variance: factor A, factor B, and the interaction between A and B.
  A. For factor A, where the number of levels is n_A, the hypotheses will have the following form:

$$H_0: \mu_{A_1} = \mu_{A_2} = \mu_{A_3} = \cdots = \mu_{A_i},$$

  H_1: H_0 is not true.

  B. For factor B, where the number of levels is n_B, the hypotheses will have the following form:

$$H_0: \mu_{B_1} = \mu_{B_2} = \mu_{B_3} = \cdots = \mu_{B_j},$$

  H_1: H_0 is not true.

  C. For the interaction between factors A and B, the hypotheses will have the following form:

$$H_0: (\mu_{A_1 B_j} - \mu_{A_1}) = (\mu_{A_2 B_j} - \mu_{A_2}) = \cdots = (\mu_{A_i B_j} - \mu_{A_i}) \text{ for all levels } j \text{ of}$$
  factor B and $(\mu_{A_i B_1} - \mu_{B_1}) = (\mu_{A_i B_2} - \mu_{B_2}) = \cdots = (\mu_{A_i B_j} - \mu_{B_j})$ for all levels i of factor A,

  H_1: H_0 is not true.

3. Decide the level of significance, α.

4. For each between-groups source of variance, calculate the between-groups degrees of freedom and the within-groups degrees of freedom, following the method described in Procedure 17-2. Find the critical value of F in Appendix A-4 for those degrees of freedom.

5. For each between-groups source of variance, draw a graph of the sampling distribution predicted by the null hypothesis, indicating the rejection region. For F, the rejection region is in the upper tail.

6. For each between-groups source of variance, calculate the value of F, following the method described in Procedure 17-2 for two between-subjects factors.

7. For each between-groups source of variance, make a decision on whether or not to reject the null hypothesis:
  A. If F is in the rejection region bounded by F_{critical}, then $p \leq \alpha$, and therefore decide that there is enough evidence to conclude that the means of the populations are not all the same (reject the null hypothesis).
  B. If F is not in the rejection region bounded by F_{critical}, then $p > \alpha$, and therefore do not decide that there is enough evidence to conclude that the means of the populations are not all the same (do not reject the null hypothesis).

analysis of variance, the null and alternate hypotheses were assertions about the between-groups source of variance, the factor under study. For the two-factor ANOVA, there are three between-groups sources of variance, each requiring its own set of hypotheses. In order to construct these hypotheses, we need to identify the sources of variance.

Recall that in the one-factor ANOVA, we partition the total variance in the scores into two parts. One part is the variance due to the difference in scores *between* the groups tested, which we assume is due to the effects of the factor being tested. In the example of Joe Johnson's study that we used in Chapter 16, this factor was the type of training the students received. The second part into which we divide the variance is the difference in scores *within* each of the groups tested, the error variance. Thus, we divide the total variance into two parts: the between-groups variance and the within-groups variance. Stated in other words, there are two **sources of variance**: the between-groups differences due to factor being tested and the within-group differences. The null and alternate hypotheses pertain to the between-group source of variance, the type of anxiety-alleviating treatment that the students received.

In the example we are using in this chapter, there are two factors, preparation time and degree of anxiety, rather than just one. In addition, there is the possibility of an interaction between these two factors. All of these are between-group sources of variance. Thus, in a two-factor ANOVA, the between-group variance is partitioned between three different sources: the variance attributable to factor A, to factor B, and to the interaction between A and B. In addition to these three between-group sources of variance, there is the within-groups variance, assumed to be attributable to random variation.

In summary, for the two-factor between-subjects ANOVA, we will divide the total variance into the variance due to four difference sources: three between-group sources of variance (A, B, and the interaction between A and B) and one within-groups source. We need to construct null and alternate hypotheses separately for each of the between-groups sources of variance.

> A **source of variance** is a variable that causes the scores in a distribution to vary in value from each other. A **within-groups source of variance**, also called the error variance, is caused by random variation in scores among the subjects within each group. A **between-groups source of variance** is a factor or interaction of factors that causes the scores to differ between the groups tested.

Notation System Used in a Two-Factor ANOVA

In an analysis of variance, we need to assign codes to each of these main effects and their levels, as well as to the interaction. In analyzing the scores from Joe's study, we will call preparation time factor A. (Which factor is labeled A and which is labeled B is completely arbitrary. However, once you decide, be consistent.) Table 17-2 shows the codes assigned to the levels of each factor and to the six groups formed by the interaction of the two factors in Joe's study.

The notation A_i represents the levels of factor A, preparation time. A_1 is the zero-hour condition, A_2 is the one-hour condition, and A_3 is the two-hour condition. The notation B_j represents the levels of factor B, degree of anxiety.

TABLE 17-2   Groups Formed by Interaction between
Preparation Time (*A*) and Degree of Anxiety (*B*)

Preparation Time (*A*)	Degree of Anxiety (*B*)	
	High Anxiety (*B*$_1$)	**Low Anxiety (*B*$_2$)**
0 Hours (*A*$_1$)	High-anxiety students given no preparation time (*A*$_1$*B*$_1$)	Low-anxiety students given no preparation time (*A*$_1$*B*$_2$)
1 Hour (*A*$_2$)	High-anxiety students given 1 hour preparation time (*A*$_2$*B*$_1$)	Low-anxiety students given 1 hour preparation time (*A*$_2$*B*$_2$)
2 Hours (*A*$_3$)	High-anxiety students given 2 hours preparation time (*A*$_3$*B*$_1$)	Low-anxiety students given 2 hours preparation time (*A*$_3$*B*$_2$)

B_1 represents the high-anxiety students, and B_2 represents the low-anxiety students. In an analysis of variance, the overall influence of each of the factors is called a **main effect** to differentiate between the effect of each factor alone and the effect of the interaction between the factors. Thus, in Joe's study, we have the main effect of factor *A*, preparation time, and the main effect of factor *B*, degree of anxiety.

> A **main effect** is the overall influence on the scores of one of the factors in an analysis of variance.

Table 17-2 shows that the interaction of factors *A* and *B* forms six groups, designated A_iB_j. These groups are called **cells.** For example, cell A_1B_1 consists of the scores of the high-anxiety students given no preparation time, and cell A_3B_2 contains the scores of the low-anxiety students given two hours' preparation time. To determine the number of cells, simply multiply the number of levels in factor *A* by the number of levels in factor *B*.

> In an analysis of variance, a **cell** is a group of scores tested under one combination of levels of all the factors in the analysis.

Finally, in many texts and journals, the within-groups variance is designated by $S|AB$, which stands for "subjects within each *AB* cell." Some texts and journals identify the within-groups variance as the error variance, as this variance is assumed to be attributable to random error. For the two-factor ANOVA, we will continue to use the term "within-groups" to refer to this source of variance.

Constructing the Null and Alternate Hypotheses for the Main Effects of *A* and *B*

Joe is testing the theory that increasing the amount of time spent studying will improve math test performance. Thus, he hypothesized that there will be differences in the students' math scores under the three amounts of time that the students were given to prepare for the test. This is the alternate hypothesis for factor *A*. The opposite hypothesis is that there will be no significant differences in the students' math scores for the three different preparation time periods, which is the null hypothesis. These hypotheses can be represented symbolically:

$$H_0: \mu_{2\ hours} = \mu_{1\ hour} = \mu_{0\ hours},$$

$$H_1: H_0 \text{ is not true.}$$

Note that the null and alternate hypotheses for an ANOVA are bidirectional. In a unidirectional t test, the critical value of t is either a positive or negative number, depending upon the direction of the difference predicted in the alternate hypothesis. However, for F, the critical value is always positive. Because F is based on square deviations, negative values of F cannot occur. Consequently, the hypotheses for an ANOVA are always bidirectional. Unidirectional hypotheses can be tested in the posttests for an ANOVA, as the posttest we are using is a form of t test for a difference between means.

In our two-factor ANOVA, the second factor, degree of anxiety, is labeled factor B. In Table 17-2, there are two levels of degree of anxiety: low and high. Joe hypothesizes that overall the students with low math anxiety will score higher on the math test than the highly anxious students do. This is the alternate hypothesis for factor B. The null hypothesis is that there will be no significant difference between the math scores of students with high and low math anxiety:

$$H_0: \mu_{non\text{-}anxious} = \mu_{math\text{-}anxious},$$

$$H_1: \mu_{non\text{-}anxious} \neq \mu_{math\text{-}anxious}.$$

Constructing the Null and Alternate Hypotheses for the Interaction of *A* and *B*

The third source of variance for which we need to construct hypotheses is the interaction between preparation time and degree of anxiety. Recall that in an interaction, the effect of one factor varies between levels of the other factor. Figure 17-2 contains two graphs, one illustrating an interaction between two factors and the other illustrating the absence of an interaction. These graphs continue the example of the interaction of age and sex on suicide rates. In the graphs in Figure 17-2, there are four levels of age (20, 40, 60, and 80 years old) and two levels of sex (men and women).

Graph 1 in Figure 17-2 illustrates the presence of an interaction between age and sex. For women, the mean suicide rate is the same for all four age groups, but for men, the mean suicide rate declines with age. Thus, the effect of age (factor A) on suicide rate depends in part on the sex of the person committing suicide (factor B). Note that the size of the deviation between the cell means and the main effect means of age differ between the four age groups. The deviation is greatest for 20-year-olds and smallest for 80-year-olds. The deviations are shown for the men, but the same size deviations occur for the women.

FIGURE 17-2 Distance between Cell Means and
Main Effect Means for an Interaction and No Interaction

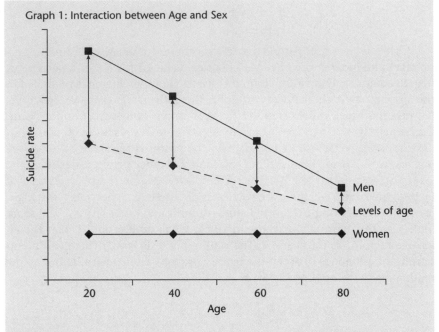

Graph 1: Interaction between Age and Sex

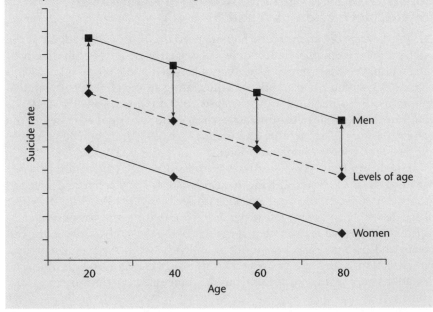

Graph 2: No Interaction between Age and Sex

In Graph 2, in which there is no interaction, the deviations between the cell means and the main effect means of age are the same size for all four age groups. In Graph 2, there are evident differences in suicide rate between the four levels of age; 20-year-olds have the highest suicide rate and 80-year-olds the lowest. There are also evident differences in suicide rate between the two sexes, with men committing suicide more frequently than women do. Thus, there are differences among the cell means; the cells representing men have higher suicide rates than do the cells representing women. Likewise, the cells representing younger people have higher suicide rates than do the cells representing older people. However, these differences among the cell means are entirely attributable to the mean effects of age and sex. The effect of age on suicide rates is exactly the same for men as for women in Graph 2, and the effect of sex on suicide rates is exactly the same for each age group. Thus, there is no interaction between age and sex in Graph 2.

When there is an interaction between factors, the size of the deviations of the cell means from the main effect means differs between levels of each factor; when there is no interaction, there is no difference in the size of these deviations. This relationship forms the basis of the null and alternate hypotheses for the interaction between factors *A* and *B*:

$H_0: (\mu_{A_1 B_j} - \mu_{A_1}) = (\mu_{A_2 B_j} - \mu_{A_2}) = \cdots = (\mu_{A_i B_j} - \mu_{A_i})$ for all levels of *j* of factor *B* and

$\quad (\mu_{A_i B_1} - \mu_{B_1}) = (\mu_{A_i B_2} - \mu_{B_2}) = \cdots = (\mu_{A_i B_j} - \mu_{B_j})$ for all levels of *i* of factor *A*;

$H_1: H_0$ is not true.

Computing the Values of *F*

Calculating the Sums of Squares

For the one-factor between-subjects ANOVA, we computed three different sums of squares, one for each of the three sources of variance: (1) the between-groups variance, attributable to the factor being studied; (2) the within-groups variance; and (3) the total variance. For the two-factor between-subjects ANOVA, we will compute five different sums of squares, one for each of the five sources of variance: (1) variance due to factor *A* (preparation time); (2) variance due to factor *B* (degree of anxiety); (3) variance due to interaction between *A* and *B*; (4) the within-groups variance; and (5) the total variance. Procedure 17-2 shows the method for finding these sums of squares.

The sum of squares for factor A.   First, we will calculate the sum of squares for factor *A*, preparation time. The procedure for finding this sum of squares is the same as the procedure for computing the between-groups sum of squares in a one-factor ANOVA. We calculate the grand mean of all of the scores and then the mean of the scores in each level of factor *A*. There are n_A

STEP-BY-STEP PROCEDURE 17-2

Calculating the Value of *F* for a Two-Factor Between-Subjects ANOVA

1. Calculate the sums of squares

The following symbols are used in this procedure:

n_S = the number of subjects in each A_iB_j combination
n_A = the number of levels in factor A
n_B = the number of levels in factor B
$\overline{X}_T$ = the grand mean, the mean of all of the scores
$\overline{X}_{A_i}$ = the mean of level i for factor A, where i can be from 1 to n_A
$\overline{X}_{B_j}$ = the mean of level j for factor B, where j can be from 1 to n_B
$\overline{X}_{A_iB_j}$ = the mean of cell A_iB_j for the interaction $A \times B$
X = a score

A. Sum of squares for factor *A*

$$SS_A = n_B n_S \Sigma(\overline{X}_{A_i} - \overline{X}_T)^2$$

(1) Calculate the grand mean of all of the scores in all of the samples, $\overline{X}_T$.
(2) Calculate the mean of the scores in each level of factor A, $\overline{X}_{A_i}$. There are n_A levels in factor A and $n_B n_S$ scores in each level.
(3) Subtract the grand mean from the mean of each level and then square each deviation. There are n_A levels in factor A and so there should be n_A squared deviations.
(4) Add up the squared deviations found in Step 3 for all of the levels of factor A, and then multiply that sum by $n_B n_S$, the number of scores in each level of factor A, to find the value of SS_A.

B. Sum of squares for factor *B*

$$SS_B = n_A n_S \Sigma(\overline{X}_{B_j} - \overline{X}_T)^2$$

(1) Calculate the mean of the scores in each level of factor B, $\overline{X}_{B_j}$. There are n_B levels in factor B and $n_A n_S$ scores in each level.
(2) Subtract the grand mean from the mean of each level, and then square each deviation. There are n_B levels in factor B, and so there should be n_B squared deviations.
(3) Add up the squared deviations found in Step 2 for all of the levels of factor B, and then multiply that sum by $n_A n_S$, the number of scores in each level of factor B to find the value of SS_B.

C. Sum of squares for the *A* × *B* interaction

$$SS_{A \times B} = n_S \Sigma(\overline{X}_{A_iB_j} - \overline{X}_{A_i})(\overline{X}_{A_iB_j} - \overline{X}_{B_j})$$

(1) Calculate the following for each cell separately:
(a) Calculate the mean of the scores in the cell. There will be $n_A n_B$ cells, with n_S scores in each cell.
(b) Calculate the deviation of the cell mean from the mean of the level of factor A containing that cell.
(c) Calculate the deviation of the cell mean from the mean of the level of factor B containing that cell.
(d) Multiply the deviation from Step 1*b* by the deviation from Step 1*c*.

STEP-BY-STEP PROCEDURE 17-2

(continued)

(2) Sum all of the deviation cross products for all of the scores. There are $n_A n_B$ cells, and so there will be $n_A n_B$ deviation cross products. Multiply this sum by the number of scores per cell, n_S. This result is the value of $SS_{A \times B}$.

D. Within-groups sum of squares

$$SS_{within} = \Sigma(X_{A_i B_j} - \bar{X}_{A_i B_j})^2$$

(1) Find the deviation of each score from the mean of the cell containing that score, and then square the deviation. There are a total of $n_A n_B n_S$ scores and so there should be $n_A n_B n_S$ squared deviations.
(2) Sum all of the squared deviations from Step 1 to find the value of SS_{within}.

E. Total sum of squares

$$SS_{total} = \Sigma(X - \bar{X}_T)^2$$

(1) Subtract the grand mean, $\bar{X}_T$, from each score, and then square this deviation. There are a total of $n_A n_B n_S$ scores and so there should be $n_A n_B n_S$ squared deviations.
(2) Sum all of the squared deviations from Step 1 to find the value of SS_{total}.
(3) As a check: $SS_{total} = SS_A + SS_B + SS_{A \times B} + SS_{within}$.

2. Calculate the degrees of freedom
   A. $df_A = n_A - 1$, where n_A is the number of levels in factor A.
   B. $df_B = n_B - 1$, where n_B is the number of levels in factor B.
   C. $df_{A \times B} = (n_A - 1)(n_B - 1)$.
   D. $df_{within} = n_A n_B(n_S - 1)$, where n_S is the number of scores per cell.
   E. $df_{total} = n_A n_B n_S - 1$.
   F. As a check, $df_{total} = df_A + df_B + df_{A \times B} + df_{within}$.

3. Construct the summary table and calculate F
   A. Construct a table with five columns. Label the columns: "Sources of Variance," "SS," "df," "MS," and "F." Label the first row with the name of factor A; the second row with the name of factor B; the third row with the names of both factors, with a "$\times$" in between; the fourth row, "within," and the final row, "*Total.*"
   B. Write the values for the sums of squares and degrees of freedom calculated above into the appropriate columns in the summary table.
   C. For all rows except the Total, divide the value of the sum of squares by the value of the degrees of freedom to find the values of the mean square, MS:

   $$MS_A = \frac{SS_A}{df_A}, \quad MS_B = \frac{SS_B}{df_B}, \quad MS_{A \times B} = \frac{SS_{A \times B}}{df_{A \times B}}, \quad MS_{within} = \frac{SS_{within}}{df_{within}}.$$

   D. Divide the value of MS for each between-groups source of variance (A, B, and $A \times B$) by the value of MS_{within} to find the value of F:

   $$F = \frac{MS_A}{MS_{within}}, \qquad F = \frac{MS_B}{MS_{within}}, \qquad F = \frac{MS_{A \times B}}{MS_{within}}.$$

levels in factor A, with $n_B n_S$ scores per level. For the scores in Joe's study, there are three levels in factor A, preparation time, and so there are three means, with 2×5 or 10 scores contributing to each mean.

The next step is to subtract the grand mean from the mean of each of the levels and then square that deviation. There will be n_A squared deviations. Again, for Joe's study, as there are three levels of factor A, there are three squared deviations. As a check, if we sum the deviations before squaring them, the result should be zero. If it is not zero, there is an error somewhere.

The final step is to sum the squared deviations and then multiply that sum by $n_B n_S$, the number of levels in factor B times the number of scores per cell. For Joe's study, there are two levels in factor B, degree of anxiety, and five students tested per cell, and so $n_B n_S$ is 2×5 or 10. As a check, this is the same as the number of scores contributing to each of the levels of factor A.

The result obtained is the sum of squares for factor A. Figure 17-3 shows these calculations for the scores in Joe's study. As seen in Figure 17-3, the sum of squares for factor A, SS_A, is 140.

The sum of squares for factor B. The next sum of squares to compute is for factor B, degree of anxiety. The procedure for calculating SS_B is the same as the procedure for calculating SS_A. We do not need to calculate the grand mean, as that value was already computed in finding SS_A. First, calculate the mean of the scores in each level of factor B. There will be n_B means, with $n_A n_S$ scores per mean. Next, subtract the grand mean from the mean of each level of factor B

FIGURE 17-3 Calculating the Sum of Squares for Factor A in a Test of Joe's Math Study

1. Calculate grand mean:

$$\bar{X}_T = \frac{\Sigma X}{n_T} = \frac{390}{30} = 13.$$

2. Calculate the mean of the scores in each level of factor A, subtract the grand mean from each of these means, and square the deviations:

$$\bar{X}_{A_1} = \frac{\Sigma X_{A_1}}{n_B n_S} = \frac{110}{10} = 11, (\bar{X}_{A_1} - \bar{X}_T)^2 = (11 - 13)^2 = -2^2 = 4;$$

$$\bar{X}_{A_2} = \frac{\Sigma X_{A_2}}{n_B n_S} = \frac{120}{10} = 12, (\bar{X}_{A_2} - \bar{X}_T)^2 = (12 - 13)^2 = -1^2 = 1;$$

$$\bar{X}_{A_3} = \frac{\Sigma X_{A_3}}{n_B n_S} = \frac{160}{10} = 16, (\bar{X}_{A_3} - \bar{X}_T)^2 = (16 - 13)^2 = 3^2 = 9.$$

3. Add up the squared deviations and multiply by n_S, the number of scores per AB cell, and then by n_B, the number of levels in factor B:

$$SS_A = n_B n_S \Sigma (\bar{X}_{A_i} - \bar{X}_T)^2$$

$$= (2)(5)(4 + 1 + 9) = 10(14) = 140.$$

FIGURE 17-4 Calculating the Sum of Squares for Factor *B* in a Test of Joe's Math Study

1. Calculate the mean of the scores in each level of factor *B*, subtract the grand mean from each of these means, and square the deviations:

$$\overline{X}_{B_1} = \frac{\Sigma X_{B_1}}{n_A n_S} = \frac{150}{15} = 10, \ (\overline{X}_{B_1} - \overline{X}_T)^2 = (10 - 13)^2 = -3^2 = 9;$$

$$\overline{X}_{B_2} = \frac{\Sigma X_{B_2}}{n_A n_S} = \frac{240}{15} = 16, \ (\overline{X}_{B_2} - \overline{X}_T)^2 = (16 - 13)^2 = 3^2 = 9.$$

3. Add up the squared deviations and multiply by n_S, the number of scores per *AB* cell, and then by n_A, the number of levels in factor *A*:

$$SS_B = n_A n_S \Sigma(\overline{X}_{B_1} - \overline{X}_T)^2$$

$$= (3)(5)(9 + 9) = 15(18) = 270.$$

and square that deviation. In Joe's study, there are two levels in factor *B*, degree of anxiety, and so there are two level means in the computations, with 3×5 or 15 scores contributing to each mean. Again, as a check, before squaring, the sum of the deviations should be zero. This is true for all of the sums of squares. Finally, sum all of the squared deviations and multiply the sum by $n_A n_S$, the numbers of levels in factor *A* times the number of subjects per cell, to find the value of the sum of squares for factor *B*, SS_B. Figure 17-4 shows the computations for SS_B for the scores in Joe's study, which equals 270.

Sum of squares for the interaction between A and B. The procedure for calculating the sum of squares for the $A \times B$ interaction is comparable to the procedure for calculating the treatment × subjects sum of squares in a within-subjects one-factor analysis of variance, which we examined in the previous chapter. For these sums of squares, rather than calculating squared deviations, we find deviation cross products. In a two-factor ANOVA, the scores in each cell contribute both to the mean of one level of factor *A* and to the mean of one level of factor *B*. For example, cell A_1B_1, which contains the scores for the high-anxiety students given no preparation time, contributes both to the mean of the no preparation time condition of factor *A*, preparation time, and to the mean for the high-anxiety students of factor *B*, degree of anxiety.

In calculating the sum of squares for the interaction, we find the deviation of each cell mean from the means of the levels of factors *A* and *B* to which that cell contributes and then find the cross product of these deviations. Thus, for cell A_1B_1, we first subtract the mean for level A_1 from the mean for cell A_1B_1, then separately subtract the mean for level B_1 from the mean for cell A_1B_1, and finally multiply these two deviations together.

Recall that we can determine the number of cells in an analysis by multiplying the number of levels in factor *A* by the number of levels in factor *B*, $n_A n_B$. As there are $n_A n_B$ cells, there will be $n_A n_B$ cell means and $n_A n_B$ deviation

FIGURE 17-5   Calculating the Sum of Squares for the $A \times B$ Interaction in a Test of Joe's Math Study

1. For each AB cell, calculate the following: (*a*) Find the mean of the scores in the cell. (*b*) Find the deviation of the cell mean from the mean of the level of factor A containing the cell. (*c*) Find the deviation of the cell mean from the mean of the level of factor B containing the cell. (*d*) Multiply these two deviations together to find the cross product.

$$\overline{X}_{A_1B_1} = \frac{\Sigma X_{A_1B_1}}{n_S} = \frac{35}{5} = 7, (\overline{X}_{A_1B_1} - \overline{X}_{A_1})(\overline{X}_{A_1B_1} - \overline{X}_{B_1}) = (7 - 11)(7 - 10) = 12;$$

$$\overline{X}_{A_2B_1} = \frac{\Sigma X_{A_2B_1}}{n_S} = \frac{40}{5} = 8, (\overline{X}_{A_2B_1} - \overline{X}_{A_2})(\overline{X}_{A_2B_1} - \overline{X}_{B_1}) = (8 - 12)(8 - 10) = 8;$$

$$\overline{X}_{A_3B_1} = \frac{\Sigma X_{A_3B_1}}{n_S} = \frac{75}{5} = 15, (\overline{X}_{A_3B_1} - \overline{X}_{A_3})(\overline{X}_{A_3B_1} - \overline{X}_{B_1}) = (15 - 16)(15 - 10) = -5;$$

$$\overline{X}_{A_1B_2} = \frac{\Sigma X_{A_1B_2}}{n_S} = \frac{75}{5} = 15, (\overline{X}_{A_1B_2} - \overline{X}_{A_1})(\overline{X}_{A_1B_2} - \overline{X}_{B_2}) = (15 - 11)(15 - 16) = -4;$$

$$\overline{X}_{A_2B_2} = \frac{\Sigma X_{A_2B_2}}{n_S} = \frac{80}{5} = 16, (\overline{X}_{A_2B_2} - \overline{X}_{A_2})(\overline{X}_{A_2B_2} - \overline{X}_{B_2}) = (16 - 12)(16 - 16) = 0;$$

$$\overline{X}_{A_3B_2} = \frac{\Sigma X_{A_3B_2}}{n_S} = \frac{85}{5} = 17, (\overline{X}_{A_3B_2} - \overline{X}_{A_3})(\overline{X}_{A_3B_2} - \overline{X}_{B_2}) = (17 - 16)(17 - 16) = 1.$$

2. Add up the deviation cross products and multiply by n_S, the number of scores per AB cell:

$$SS_{A \times B} = n_S \Sigma(\overline{X}_{A_iB_j} - \overline{X}_{A_i})(\overline{X}_{A_iB_j} - \overline{X}_{B_j})$$

$$= 5(12 + 8 + (-5) + (-4) + 0 + 1) = 5(12) = 60.$$

cross products in the final sum. For Joe's study, there are 3 levels of factor A, preparation time, and 2 levels of factor B, degree of anxiety, and so there are 3×2 or 6 cells, and thus 6 cell means and 6 deviation cross products in the final sum.

The last step is to sum the deviation cross products, and then multiply by n_S, the number of scores per cell. The result is the sum of squares for the interaction, $SS_{A \times B}$. Figure 17-5 shows the computations involved in finding the value of $SS_{A \times B}$, which equals 60 for the scores in Joe's study.

Within-groups sum of squares.   The next sum of squares reflects the variance within each cell, which is assumed to be attributable to random variation. The steps in computing this sum of squares are simple. First, subtract the cell mean from each score in that cell. The number of deviations will equal to the total number of scores, which is $n_A n_B n_S$, the number of levels in factor A times the number of levels in factor B times the number of scores per cell. Next, square each of these deviations. Finally, sum up all of the squared deviations to find the value of the within-groups sum of squares, SS_{within}. As with all sums

FIGURE 17-6 Calculating the Within-Groups
Sum of Squares for a Test of Joe's Math Study

1. For each cell separately, subtract the cell mean from each score in the cell and then square the deviation. Add up all of the squared deviations for each cell.

Cell A_1B_1 $(X - \bar{X}_{A_1B_1})^2$	Cell A_2B_1 $(X - \bar{X}_{A_2B_1})^2$	Cell A_3B_1 $(X - \bar{X}_{A_3B_1})^2$
$(10 - 7)^2 = 9$	$(11 - 8)^2 = 9$	$(19 - 15)^2 = 16$
$(9 - 7)^2 = 4$	$(8 - 8)^2 = 0$	$(17 - 15)^2 = 4$
$(5 - 7)^2 = 4$	$(9 - 8)^2 = 1$	$(13 - 15)^2 = 4$
$(7 - 7)^2 = 0$	$(5 - 8)^2 = 9$	$(15 - 15)^2 = 0$
$(4 - 7)^2 = 9$	$(7 - 8)^2 = 1$	$(11 - 15)^2 = 16$
$\Sigma(X - \bar{X}_{A_1B_1})^2 = 26$	$\Sigma(X - \bar{X}_{A_2B_1})^2 = 20$	$\Sigma(X - \bar{X}_{A_3B_1})^2 = 40$

Cell A_1B_2 $(X - \bar{X}_{A_1B_2})^2$	Cell A_2B_2 $(X - \bar{X}_{A_2B_2})^2$	Cell A_3B_2 $(X - \bar{X}_{A_3B_2})^2$
$(18 - 15)^2 = 9$	$(19 - 16)^2 = 9$	$(20 - 17)^2 = 9$
$(16 - 15)^2 = 1$	$(16 - 16)^2 = 0$	$(19 - 17)^2 = 4$
$(14 - 15)^2 = 1$	$(17 - 16)^2 = 1$	$(18 - 17)^2 = 1$
$(16 - 15)^2 = 1$	$(13 - 16)^2 = 9$	$(16 - 17)^2 = 1$
$(11 - 15)^2 = 16$	$(15 - 16)^2 = 1$	$(12 - 17)^2 = 25$
$\Sigma(X - \bar{X}_{A_1B_2})^2 = 28$	$\Sigma(X - \bar{X}_{A_2B_2})^2 = 20$	$\Sigma(X - \bar{X}_{A_3B_2})^2 = 40$

2. Add up these sums of squared deviations:

$$SS_{within} = \Sigma(X - \bar{X}_{A_iB_j})^2$$

$$= 26 + 20 + 40 + 28 + 20 + 40 = 174.$$

of squares, the sum of the deviations before squaring should equal zero. If the sum is not zero, you can locate the error by summing the deviations before squaring separately for each of the cells, which also should equal zero. Figure 17-6, which shows the computations for the math scores in Joe's study, indicates that the value of SS_{within} is 174.

Total sum of squares.   The last sum of squares to compute is the total sum of squares. The procedure for computing this value is exactly like the procedure for the within-groups sum of squares, except that the grand mean is subtracting from each score rather than the cell mean. The steps are simply to subtract the grand mean from each score, square each of these deviations, and then sum the squared deviations. The number of deviations will be $n_A n_B n_S$, the number of levels in factor A times the number of levels in factor B times the number of scores per cell. Again, the sum of the deviations before squaring should equal zero. Figure 17-7 shows the computations for the math test scores. The total sum of squares for these scores is 644.

FIGURE 17-7   Calculating the Total Sum of Squares for a Test of Joe's Math Study

1. For each score, subtract the grand mean from the score and then square the deviation.

Level A_1 $(X - \bar{X}_T)^2$	Level A_2 $(X - \bar{X}_T)^2$	Level A_3 $(X - \bar{X}_T)^2$
$(10 - 13)^2 = 9$	$(11 - 13)^2 = 4$	$(19 - 13)^2 = 36$
$(9 - 13)^2 = 16$	$(8 - 13)^2 = 25$	$(17 - 13)^2 = 16$
$(5 - 13)^2 = 64$	$(9 - 13)^2 = 16$	$(13 - 13)^2 = 0$
$(7 - 13)^2 = 36$	$(5 - 13)^2 = 64$	$(15 - 13)^2 = 4$
$(4 - 13)^2 = 81$	$(7 - 13)^2 = 36$	$(11 - 13)^2 = 4$
$(18 - 13)^2 = 25$	$(19 - 13)^2 = 36$	$(20 - 13)^2 = 49$
$(16 - 13)^2 = 9$	$(16 - 13)^2 = 9$	$(19 - 13)^2 = 36$
$(14 - 13)^2 = 1$	$(17 - 13)^2 = 16$	$(18 - 13)^2 = 25$
$(16 - 13)^2 = 9$	$(13 - 13)^2 = 0$	$(16 - 13)^2 = 9$
$(11 - 13)^2 = 4$	$(15 - 13)^2 = 4$	$(12 - 13)^2 = 1$
$\Sigma(X - \bar{X}_T)^2 = 254$	$\Sigma(X - \bar{X}_T)^2 = 210$	$\Sigma(X - \bar{X}_T)^2 = 180$

2. Add up these sums of squared deviations:

$$SS_{Total} = \Sigma(X - \bar{X}_T)^2$$

$$= 254 + 210 + 180 = 644.$$

As a final check, the sum of the component sums of squares should equal the total sum of squares:

$$SS_{total} = SS_A + SS_B + SS_{A \times B} + SS_{within}$$

$$= 140 + 270 + 60 + 174 = 644.$$

If the sum of the four component sums of squares do not equal the total sum of squares, there is an error somewhere in your computations.

At times, computing the sums of squares may seem like a lot of work. In fact, it can take quite a bit of work to do all the computations involved in an ANOVA. But, remember! Doing just one ANOVA on the results of Joe's study saves us all the work involved in computing 35 separate *t* tests.

Computing the Degrees of Freedom

In order to compute the degrees of freedom, we need the values of n_A, n_B, and n_S. We already used these values in computing the sums of squares. The value of n_A is the number of levels in factor A, preparation time. Joe gave students three different amounts of time to prepare for the test (0, 1, and 2 hours), and so the value of n_A is 3. The value of n_B is the number of levels in factor B, degree of anxiety. Joe used two different levels for degree of anxiety, high anxiety and low anxiety, and so the value of n_B is 2. The value of n_S is the number of scores per cell. There were five scores in each cell in Joe's study, and so the value of n_S is 5.

These are the three values we need to compute the degrees of freedom for each source of variance. The formulas are given in Procedure 17-2:

$$df_A = n_A - 1 = 3 - 1 = 2,$$
$$df_B = n_B - 1 = 2 - 1 = 1,$$
$$df_{A \times B} = (n_A - 1)(n_B - 1) = (3 - 1)(2 - 1) = (2)(1) = 2,$$
$$df_{within} = n_A n_B (n_S - 1) = (3)(2)(5 - 1) = 6(4) = 24,$$
$$df_{total} = n_A n_B n_S - 1 = (3)(2)(5) - 1 = 30 - 1 = 29.$$

Just as with the sums of squares, the degrees of freedom for the four component sources of variance should add up to equal the total degrees of freedom:

$$df_{total} = df_A + df_B + df_{A \times B} + df_{within} = 2 + 1 + 2 + 24 = 29.$$

Computing the Mean Squares

Computing the mean square for each source of variance is a simple matter of dividing the sum of squares by the degrees of freedom for each source:

$$MS_A = \frac{SS_A}{df_A} = \frac{140}{2} = 70,$$

$$MS_B = \frac{SS_B}{df_B} = \frac{270}{1} = 270,$$

$$MS_{A \times B} = \frac{SS_{A \times B}}{df_{A \times B}} = \frac{60}{2} = 30,$$

$$MS_{within} = \frac{SS_{within}}{df_{within}} = \frac{174}{24} = 7.25.$$

Remember that a mean square for the total is never computed.

Computing the Value of *F*

The final set of computations in the analysis of variance is to use the mean squares to find the values of F. We compute F only for the between-groups sources of variance, factor A, factor B, and the interaction between A and B. To find F, we divide the mean square for each of these between-group sources of variance by the mean square for the within-groups mean square:

$$F = \frac{MS_A}{MS_{within}} = \frac{70}{7.25} = 9.66,$$

$$F = \frac{MS_B}{MS_{within}} = \frac{270}{7.25} = 37.24,$$

$$F = \frac{MS_{A \times B}}{MS_{within}} = \frac{30}{7.25} = 4.14.$$

TABLE 17-3 Summary Table for the Analysis of Variance of Scores in Table 17-1

Sources of Variance	SS	df	MS	F
Preparation time	140.00	2	70.00	9.66*
Degree of anxiety	270.00	1	270.00	37.24*
Time × anxiety	60.00	2	30.00	4.14*
Within	174.00	24	7.25	
Total	644.00	29		

*$p < .05$.

It is customary to list the results of an analysis of variance, including the sums of squares, degrees of freedom, mean squares, and the values of F in a table. The results of the ANOVA for Joe's study are shown in Table 17-3.

Determining the Significance of F

The last step in conducting the analysis of variance is to determine the significance of each value of F. Table A-4 in Appendix A lists critical values of F, for $\alpha = .05$ and .01. We will use the conventional α of .05. Recall that the critical values of F in Table A-4 are listed by the degrees of freedom of the numerator and denominator of each mean square.

Let's begin by finding the critical value for the value of F, 9.66, that we found for factor A, preparation time. This value of F was calculated by dividing the mean square for factor A (the numerator) by the within-groups mean square (the denominator). The numerator, factor A, had 2 df, while the denominator, the within-groups source, had 24 df. In Table A-4, we find that with 2 df in the numerator and 24 df in the denominator, the critical value of F is 3.40. Because the value of F that we found for factor A in Joe's study, 9.66, is greater than the critical value of 3.40, we can reject the null hypothesis that there are no significant differences in math test scores between the students given the three different preparation times.

At this point, we need to be very careful in interpreting the results of this analysis. The null hypothesis stated that there were no significant differences between the three testing conditions. Rejecting the null hypothesis does *not* indicate that the mean score of each preparation time group was significantly different from the other two. They may be, but a significant F does not guarantee it. To find out exactly where the significant differences are, we need to conduct a posttest.

The next source of variance, factor B, degree of anxiety, had 1 df in the numerator and 24 df for the denominator. (For a two-factor between-groups ANOVA, the denominators will all have the same degrees of freedom.) Table A-4 indicates that the critical value of F, for 1 df in the numerator and 24 df in the denominator, is 4.26. In our analysis of Joe's study, factor B, degree of anxiety, had an *F* of 37.24, which certainly is greater than the critical *F* of 4.26. Therefore, we can also reject the null hypothesis for degree of anxiety.

Because factor *B* has only two levels, the significant value of *F* found in the analysis of variance for factor *B* indicates that there is a significant difference between the mean math scores in these two levels. Whenever there are only two levels of a factor tested, if the value of *F* is significant, we automatically know that the scores for those two levels are significantly different, and there is no need to conduct a posttest. The students with high math anxiety scored a mean of ten questions correct on Joe's math test, while the students with low math anxiety scored a mean of sixteen questions correct. Thus, the students will little or no math anxiety performed significantly better, across all preparation times, than the students with high math anxiety did. Figure 17-8 shows this result graphically.

Finally, we need to determine the significance of the interaction between preparation time and degree of anxiety. The *F* for this interaction had 2 *df* in the numerator and 24 *df* in the denominator, the same as for factor *A*, preparation time. Recall that Table A-4 showed that the critical value of *F* for 2 and 24 *df* is 3.40. The value of *F* for the interaction in Joe's study is 4.14, which is greater than the critical value of 3.40. Thus, there is a significant difference in the interaction between preparation time and degree of anxiety in

FIGURE 17-8   Mean Math Test Scores of High-Anxiety and Low-Anxiety Students

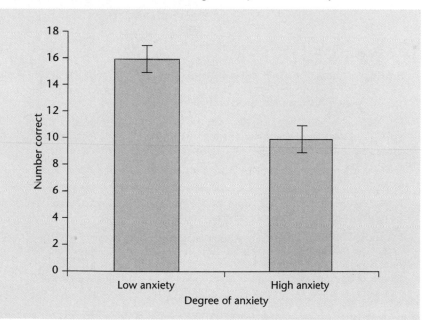

Joe's study. Finding exactly where that significant difference lies requires a posttest, the subject we will examine in the next section.

Posttests for a Two-Factor Analysis of Variance

Posttests for the Main Effects

Step-by-Step Procedure 17-3 describes a method for conducting a posttest on factor A in a two-factor ANOVA. This procedure is very similar to that of conducting a posttest for a one-factor ANOVA, in which we computed a value of *t* using the within-groups mean square in the denominator. For the two-factor ANOVA, we will use the within-groups mean square, MS_{within}, in the denominator.

Figure 17-9 shows the mean scores received by students in Joe's study in each of the three preparation time periods. Students given no time to prepare received the lowest mean score, 11 correct, while students given two hours to prepare received the highest mean score, 16 correct. The mean score of the students given one hour to prepare was in between, 12 correct. To find out

---

STEP·BY·STEP PROCEDURE 17-3

Calculating the Value of *t* to Compare the Means of Two Levels of Factor *A* in a Two-Factor ANOVA

$$t = \frac{\overline{X}_{A_j} - \overline{X}_{A_k}}{\sqrt{\dfrac{2MS_{within}}{n_B n_S}}}$$

where $\overline{X}_{A_j}$ = the mean of one treatment group of factor *A*
  $\overline{X}_{A_k}$ = the mean of another treatment group of factor *A*
  MS_{within} = the within-groups mean squares
  n_B = the number of levels of factor *B*
  n_S = the number of scores in each *AB* cell

1. The mean for each level of factor *A* was calculated in the procedure for the ANOVA. Subtract the mean for treatment group *k* from the mean for treatment group *j*.

2. Multiply the number of levels of factor *B*, n_B, by the number of scores in each *AB* cell, n_S.

3. Multiply the value for MS_{within} from the ANOVA by 2, then divide that result by the result of Step 2. Find the square root of this result.

4. Divide the result of Step 1 by the result of Step 3 to find the value of *t*. The method for testing this value of *t* is the same as Procedure 14-2, which describes the method for conducting the *t* test for a difference between sample means. The degrees of freedom are the number of scores in the comparison, minus 2, which is $df = 2(n_B n_S - 1)$.

FIGURE 17-9   Mean Math Test Scores for the Two Levels of Factor *A*, Preparation Time

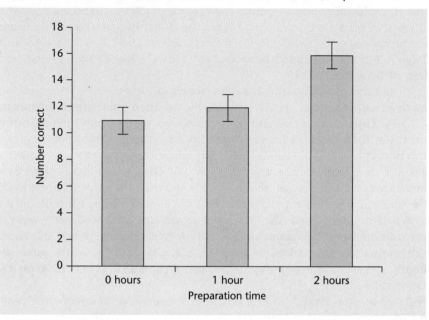

FIGURE 17-10   Posttest Computations for Factor *A*, Preparation Time

Two hours vs. one hour:

$$t = \frac{\overline{X}_{A_3} - \overline{X}_{A_2}}{\sqrt{\dfrac{2MS_{\text{within}}}{n_B n_S}}} = \frac{16 - 12}{\sqrt{\dfrac{2(7.25)}{(2)(5)}}} = \frac{4}{\sqrt{\dfrac{14.50}{10}}} = \frac{4}{\sqrt{1.45}} = \frac{4}{1.20} = 3.33$$

Two hours vs. zero hours:

$$t = \frac{\overline{X}_{A_3} - \overline{X}_{A_1}}{\sqrt{\dfrac{2MS_{\text{within}}}{n_B n_S}}} = \frac{16 - 11}{\sqrt{\dfrac{2(7.25)}{(2)(5)}}} = \frac{5}{\sqrt{\dfrac{14.50}{10}}} = \frac{5}{\sqrt{1.45}} = \frac{5}{1.20} = 4.17$$

One hour vs. zero hours:

$$t = \frac{\overline{X}_{A_2} - \overline{X}_{A_1}}{\sqrt{\dfrac{2MS_{\text{within}}}{n_B n_S}}} = \frac{12 - 11}{\sqrt{\dfrac{2(7.25)}{(2)(5)}}} = \frac{1}{\sqrt{\dfrac{14.50}{10}}} = \frac{1}{\sqrt{1.45}} = \frac{1}{1.20} = 0.83$$

exactly whether the differences between these means are significant, we can use the method described in Procedure 17-3.

Figure 17-10 shows the computations involved in the posttests on the levels of factor *A*, preparation time. There are three comparisons, comparing all possible combinations of the three levels of preparation time. These are all values of t. Note that in these comparisons, the larger mean is listed first, so that the value of t will be positive. Because Joe predicted that the greater the amount of preparation time, the higher the students' math scores, these are unidirectional tests. The degrees of freedom are $2(n_A n_S - 1) = 2(9) = 18$, and Table A-3 in the Appendix shows that the critical value of t for a one-tailed test, with 18 df, is 1.734.

The value of t comparing the mean scores of students given two and one hours preparation time is 3.32, which is greater than the significant value of t, 1.734. Thus, students given two hours scored significantly higher on the math test than did students given one hour to prepare. The students given two hours preparation time also scored significantly higher than did students given no preparation time, $t = 4.15$, $p < .05$. Thus, the students given two hours study time performed significantly better than the students in either of the other preparation time conditions. The value of t comparing the mean scores of students given one hour preparation time and students given no preparation time, 0.83, is not greater than the critical value of t, 1.734. Thus, this study does not provide evidence that, across all of these students, one hour preparation time improved performance compared to having no preparation time at all.

Step-by-Step Procedure 17-4 describes the method for conducting posttests for levels of factor B in a two-factor ANOVA. This procedure is exactly like the procedure for factor A, except that the notations for A and B are reversed. As discussed above, because factor B, degree of anxiety, contained only two levels, we do not need to conduct posttests on factor B. However, should you need to conduct posttests on factor B in analyzing the results of another study, just remember that the procedure is exactly like that for factor A.

Posttests for the Interaction of *A* and *B*

Recall that in a significant interaction, the effect of one factor is different for one level of the second factor than for the other level of the second factor. In the analysis of variance, we found that there was a significant interaction between the two factors, preparation time and degree of anxiety, in Joe's study. This suggests that the various amounts of preparation time had a different effect on math scores for the math-anxious students than for the nonanxious students. However, the ANOVA itself does not tell us exactly what the difference in effect was. In order to find out, we again need to conduct posttests.

There are two possible sets of posttests that we can conduct. First, we can compare the levels of factor A at each level of factor B. For Joe's study, this would mean comparing the three levels of preparation time at each level of degree of anxiety (i.e., separately for the math-anxious students and the nonanxious students). The other type of posttest is to compare the levels of factor B at each level of factor A. For Joe's study, this would mean comparing

STEP-BY-STEP PROCEDURE 17-4

Calculating the Value of *t* to Compare the Means of Two Levels of Factor *B* in a Two-Factor ANOVA

$$t = \frac{\overline{X}_{B_j} - \overline{X}_{B_k}}{\sqrt{\dfrac{2MS_{within}}{n_A n_S}}}$$

where $\overline{X}_{B_j}$ = the mean of one treatment group of factor *B*
  $\overline{X}_{B_k}$ = the mean of another treatment group of factor *B*
 MS_{within} = the within-groups mean squares
   n_A = the number of levels of factor *A*
   n_S = the number of scores in each *AB* cell

1. The mean for each level in factor *B* was calculated in the procedure for the ANOVA. Subtract the mean for treatment group *k* from the mean for treatment group *j*.

2. Multiply the number of levels of factor *A*, n_A, by the number of scores in each *AB* cell, n_S.

3. Multiply the value for MS_{within} from the ANOVA by 2, then divide that result by the result of Step 2. Find the square root of this result.

4. Divide the result of Step 1 by the result of Step 3, to find the value of *t*. The method for testing this value of *t* is the same as Procedure 14-2, which describes the method for conducting the *t* test for a difference between sample means. The degrees of freedom are the number of scores in the comparison, minus 2, which is $df = 2(n_A n_S - 1)$.

the math-anxious and nonanxious students' performance separately for each level of preparation time. We will examine both types of posttests for significant interactions, using the results from Joe's study as an example.

Comparisons of levels of factor A at each level of factor B.   First, we will examine posttests in which we compare levels of factor *A*, preparation time, separately for math-anxious and nonanxious students. Figure 17-11 shows a graph of the students' mean math scores under each testing condition, separately for the math-anxious students and the nonanxious students. Step-by-Step Procedure 17-5 describes the method of computing *t* for these posttests.

Compare the formula shown in Procedure 17-5, testing levels of factor *A* at each level of *B*, to the formula in Procedure 17-3, which compares levels of factor *A* across both levels of *B*. The main difference in the formulas lies in the denominator. When we test the main effects of factor *A*, the denominator of the within-groups mean square is $n_B n_S$, which, for Joe's study, is 2×5, or 10. This reflects the fact that there were ten students in each level of preparation time (math-anxious and nonanxious students combined). In Procedure 17-5,

FIGURE 17-11   Mean Math Test Scores for the
Three Levels of Preparation Time, by Degree of Anxiety

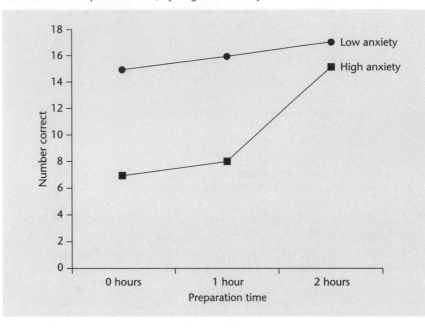

when we test the effect of factor *A* at each level of *B* separately, the denominator of the within-groups mean square is simply n_S, which, for Joe's study, is 5. This indicates that there were five math-anxious students in each testing condition and, separately, five nonanxious students in each testing condition. Other than this difference, the method described in Procedure 17-5 is exactly like that in Procedure 17-3.

Figure 17-12 shows the computations for all of the comparisons of the levels of preparation time at each level of degree of anxiety. There may seem to be quite a bit of computation involved, but it actually goes fairly quickly, as the denominator is the same for all of the comparisons. In addition, the critical value of *t* is the same for all of the comparisons. Recall that for the main effects of factor *A*, there were 18 *df* of freedom in each posttest comparison. In the interaction posttests, we are testing only one level of *B* at a time and thus are using only half the number of subjects. Therefore, for the interaction posttests, the degrees of freedom are $2(n_S - 1)$, which is $2(5 - 1)$ or 8. Table A-3 in the Appendix shows that for an α of .05, the critical value of *t* for 8 *df* is 1.860.

The first set of three comparisons concerns the students with high math anxiety. The highly anxious students given two hours to prepare scored a mean of 15 correct on the math test, which was significantly greater than the

---

STEP-BY-STEP PROCEDURE 17-5

Calculating the Value of *t* to Compare the Means of Two Levels of a Factor *A* at One Level of Factor *B*

$$t = \frac{\overline{X}_{A_j B_i} - \overline{X}_{A_k B_i}}{\sqrt{\dfrac{2MS_{within}}{n_S}}}$$

where $\overline{X}_{A_j B_i}$ = the mean of one group of factor *A* tested at level *i* for factor *B*

$\overline{X}_{A_k B_i}$ = the mean of another group of factor *A* tested at level *i* for factor *B*

MS_{within} = the within-groups mean squares

n_S = the number of scores in each *AB* cell

1. Identify the two *AB* cells being compared. The two cells should represent different levels of factor *A*, but the same level of factor *B*. The means for these cells were calculated in the procedure for the ANOVA. Subtract the mean for cell $A_k B_i$ from the mean for cell $A_j B_i$.

2. Multiply the value for MS_{within} from the ANOVA by 2, then divide that result by n_S. Find the square root of this result.

3. Divide the result of Step 1 by the result of Step 2 to find the value of *t*. The method for testing this value of *t* is the same as Procedure 14-2, which describes the method for conducting the *t* test for a difference between sample means. The degrees of freedom are the number of scores in the comparison, minus 2, which is $df = 2(n_S - 1)$.

---

mean score, 8 correct, of students given only one hour to prepare, $t = 4.12$, and also significantly greater than the mean score, 7 correct, of students given no preparation time, $t = 4.71$. Both of these values of *t* are greater than the critical value of *t*, 1.860. However, the difference between highly anxious students given one hour to prepare and those given no preparation time was not significant, $t = 0.59$. From this evidence, we cannot conclude that one hour preparation time helps these students improve their math test performance compared to having no time to prepare at all.

The second set of three comparisons are of the performance of students with low math anxiety. Figure 17-12 shows that for none of the comparisons did the value of *t* exceed the critical value. Thus, none of these comparisons was significant for the low-anxiety students. The greatest difference in performance for the low-anxiety students was between those given two hours preparation time, who scored a mean of 17 correct, and those given no preparation time, who scored a mean of 15 correct. The value of *t* for this comparison is 1.18, which is not greater than the critical value of *t*. Thus, we can conclude that the amount of preparation time had a significant effect on the performance of the high-anxiety students but did not have a significant effect on the performance of the low-anxiety students.

FIGURE 17-12 Posttest Computations Comparing Levels of
Preparation Time Separately for High-Anxiety and Low-Anxiety Students

High-Anxiety Students

Two vs. one hour:
$$t = \frac{\overline{X}_{A_3B_1} - \overline{X}_{A_2B_1}}{\sqrt{\dfrac{2MS_{within}}{n_S}}} = \frac{15 - 8}{\sqrt{\dfrac{2(7.25)}{5}}} = \frac{7}{\sqrt{\dfrac{14.50}{5}}} = \frac{7}{1.70} = 4.12$$

Two vs. zero hours:
$$t = \frac{\overline{X}_{A_3B_1} - \overline{X}_{A_1B_1}}{\sqrt{\dfrac{2MS_{within}}{n_S}}} = \frac{15 - 7}{\sqrt{\dfrac{2(7.25)}{5}}} = \frac{8}{\sqrt{\dfrac{14.50}{5}}} = \frac{8}{1.70} = 4.71$$

One vs. zero hours:
$$t = \frac{\overline{X}_{A_2B_1} - \overline{X}_{A_1B_1}}{\sqrt{\dfrac{2MS_{within}}{n_S}}} = \frac{8 - 7}{\sqrt{\dfrac{2(7.25)}{5}}} = \frac{1}{\sqrt{\dfrac{14.50}{5}}} = \frac{1}{1.70} = 0.59$$

Non-Anxious Students

Two vs. one hour:
$$t = \frac{\overline{X}_{A_3B_2} - \overline{X}_{A_2B_2}}{\sqrt{\dfrac{2MS_{within}}{n_S}}} = \frac{17 - 16}{\sqrt{\dfrac{2(7.25)}{5}}} = \frac{1}{\sqrt{\dfrac{14.50}{5}}} = \frac{1}{1.70} = 0.59$$

Two vs. zero hours:
$$t = \frac{\overline{X}_{A_3B_2} - \overline{X}_{A_1B_2}}{\sqrt{\dfrac{2MS_{within}}{n_S}}} = \frac{17 - 15}{\sqrt{\dfrac{2(7.25)}{5}}} = \frac{2}{\sqrt{\dfrac{14.50}{5}}} = \frac{2}{1.70} = 1.18$$

One vs. zero hours:
$$t = \frac{\overline{X}_{A_2B_2} - \overline{X}_{A_1B_2}}{\sqrt{\dfrac{2MS_{within}}{n_S}}} = \frac{16 - 15}{\sqrt{\dfrac{2(7.25)}{5}}} = \frac{1}{\sqrt{\dfrac{14.50}{5}}} = \frac{1}{1.70} = 0.59$$

Comparisons of levels of factor B at each level of factor A. The second
method of conducting posttests on a significant interaction, comparing levels of factor *B* at each level of *A,* is described in Step-by-Step Procedure 17-6.
Normally, we would do either the comparisons in Procedure 17-5 or those in
Procedure 17-6, whichever is more meaningful. However, to illustrate all of
these posttests, we will do both types of comparisons on the results of Joe's
study.

Figure 17-13 shows the mean math test scores of the high-anxiety and
low-anxiety students, for each of the three levels of preparation time. This
graph visually demonstrates that the students with low math anxiety scored
higher under each level of preparation time than the highly anxious students
did. However, we do not know if any or all of these differences are significant
until we conduct the posttests. Figure 17-14 shows the computations for the
posttest comparisons of the high-anxiety and low-anxiety students' performance under each level of preparation time. The degrees of freedom are the

---

STEP-BY-STEP PROCEDURE 17-6

Calculating the Value of t to Compare the Means of Two Treatment Groups of a Factor B at One Level of Factor A

$$t = \frac{\overline{X}_{A_iB_j} - \overline{X}_{A_iB_k}}{\sqrt{\dfrac{2MS_{within}}{n_S}}}$$

where $\overline{X}_{A_iB_j}$ = the mean of one group of factor B tested at level i for factor A
$\overline{X}_{A_iB_k}$ = the mean of another group of factor B tested at level i for factor A
MS_{within} = the within-groups mean squares
n_S = the number of scores in each AB cell

1. Identify the two AB cells being compared. The two cells should represent different levels of factor B, but the same level of factor A. The means for these cells were calculated in the procedure for the ANOVA. Subtract the mean for cell A_iB_k from the mean for cell A_iB_j.

2. Multiply the value for MS_{within} from the ANOVA by 2, then divide that result by n_S. Find the square root of this result.

3. Divide the result of Step 1 by the result of Step 2, to find the value of t. The method for testing this value of t is the same as Procedure 14-2, which describes the method for conducting the t test for a difference between sample means. The degrees of freedom are the number of scores in the comparison, minus 2, which is $df = 2(n_S - 1)$.

---

number of scores involved in the comparison, which is $2(n_S - 1)$, or 8. As Joe predicted that low-anxiety students would do better on the math test than high-anxiety students did, these comparisons are unidirectional. The critical value of t for a one-tailed test, with 8 df, is 1.860.

When given no preparation time, the low-anxiety students scored a mean of 15 correct on the math test, while the high-anxiety students scored a mean of 7 correct, which is a significant difference, $t = 4.71$, $p < .05$. Similarly, the students with low anxiety had a mean score of 16 correct when given one hour preparation time, while the mean for the high-anxiety students was 7, again a significant difference, $t = 4.71$, $p < .05$. However, there was no significant difference when the students were given two hours preparation time. In this condition, low-anxiety students scored a mean of 17 correct, while high-anxiety students scored a mean of 15 correct.

From these posttest analyses, we might conclude that differences in preparation time had no significant effect on the math test performance of students low in math anxiety but did have a significant effect for students with high math anxiety. However, this significant improvement was seen only when the highly anxious students were given two hours preparation time. One hour's preparation time was not sufficient to lead to a significant improvement

FIGURE 17-13 Mean Math Test Scores for Math-Anxious Students and Non-Anxious Students in Each Level of Preparation Time

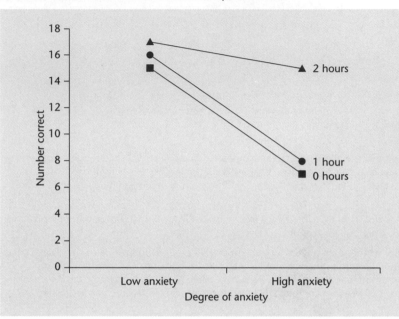

FIGURE 17-14 Posttest Computations Comparing Mean Score for High-Anxiety and Low-Anxiety Students Separately for Each Preparation Time

Zero hours preparation time:

$$t = \frac{\overline{X}_{A_1B_2} - \overline{X}_{A_1B_1}}{\sqrt{\dfrac{2MS_{\text{within}}}{n_S}}} = \frac{15 - 7}{\sqrt{\dfrac{2(7.25)}{5}}} = \frac{8}{\sqrt{\dfrac{14.50}{5}}} = \frac{8}{\sqrt{2.90}} = \frac{8}{1.70} = 4.71$$

One hour preparation time:

$$t = \frac{\overline{X}_{A_2B_2} - \overline{X}_{A_2B_1}}{\sqrt{\dfrac{2MS_{\text{within}}}{n_S}}} = \frac{16 - 8}{\sqrt{\dfrac{2(7.25)}{5}}} = \frac{8}{\sqrt{\dfrac{14.50}{5}}} = \frac{8}{\sqrt{2.90}} = \frac{8}{1.70} = 4.71$$

Two hours preparation time:

$$t = \frac{\overline{X}_{A_3B_2} - \overline{X}_{A_3B_1}}{\sqrt{\dfrac{2MS_{\text{within}}}{n_S}}} = \frac{17 - 16}{\sqrt{\dfrac{2(7.25)}{5}}} = \frac{1}{\sqrt{\dfrac{14.50}{5}}} = \frac{1}{\sqrt{2.90}} = \frac{1}{1.70} = 0.59$$

over no preparation time at all. Furthermore, the posttests reveal that while the high-anxiety students scored significantly lower than the low-anxiety students when given one hour preparation time or no preparation time, the difference was insignificant when the students were given two hours preparation time. Thus, it appears that given sufficient preparation time, the math test scores of high-anxiety students do not differ significantly from that of low-anxiety students.

Note that all of these conclusions are drawn from the posttests conducted on the interaction between preparation time and degree of anxiety. From the analysis of the main effects, we were able to conclude only that overall, low-anxiety students did significantly better on the math test than high-anxiety students and that students given either two hours or one hour preparation time did significantly better than those given no preparation time. The analysis of the interaction allowed us to explore the relationship between preparation time and degree of anxiety in much greater depth, to discover that the differences due to preparation time were significant for high-anxiety students but not for low-anxiety students and that the difference in test performance between the high-anxiety and low-anxiety students was not significant when given sufficient preparation time.

The two-factor ANOVA allows us a far greater depth of analysis than any of the other statistical tests that we have examined thus far. It is the analysis of the interaction between factors that makes this depth possible. This is one of the great strengths of the analysis of variance that makes all of the computations worthwhile.

Other Analyses of Variance

The analysis of variance that we have examined in this chapter is used when there are two between-subjects factors. Recall that in the previous chapters, there were slightly different procedures for a one-factor between-subjects ANOVA and a one-factor within-subjects ANOVA. This is also the case when the ANOVA examines two factors. The procedure is slightly different for within-subjects factors than the procedure described here for between-subjects factors. Describing the steps in conducting other two-factor ANOVAs would be lengthy and thus is beyond the scope of this text. However, you should know that ANOVAs do exist for two within-subject factors, as well as for one between- and one within-subjects factor.

Thus far, we have examined how to conduct an ANOVA on one and two factors at a time. It is also possible to conduct an ANOVA on three and four factors at a time. In fact, the number of factors analyzed is limited only by the logic of the experimental design and the patience of the person doing the computations. The strength of ANOVA lies in the fact that it enables researchers to design complex experiments that investigate the interaction between several factors. This greatly increases the quality of psychological research. If you are interested in learning more about the possibilities provided by the analysis of variance, more information is available in advanced statistics books.

CHECKING YOUR ANSWERS

1. Calculating an ANOVA is a long process, involving many steps, but each step is fairly straightforward. If you take each step one at a time, working carefully, you can avoid most errors.

2. The formula for the sum of squares for every source involves squared deviations. As a check, the sum of these deviations *before squaring* should equal zero. If the sum of the deviations does not equal zero, you've made an error in calculations somewhere.

3. For the three between-groups sources (*A, B,* and the interaction between *A* and *B*), the sum of the squared deviations is multiplied by a value of *n* to find the sum of squares. For factor *A*, the sum of squared deviations is multiplied by $n_B n_S$; for factor *B*, by $n_A n_S$; and for the interaction $A \times B$, by n_S. A general rule is that the sum of the squared deviations is multiplied by all of the values of *n* in the analysis *except* the values of *n* for the factors involved in the sources which that sum of squared deviations represents.

4. Another check to make sure that you have the right values of *n* with which to multiply the sum of the squared deviations is that that number is equal to the number of scores in one level of the factor involved. Thus, for factor *A*, the sum of the squared deviations is multiplied by $n_B n_S$ and there are $n_B n_S$ scores in each level of *A*.

5. In calculating the sums of squares (*SS*), the sum of all the component sums of squares should equal the total sum of squares. Similarly, the sum of all the component degrees of freedom should equal the total degrees of freedom. Remember that the total degrees of freedom is always the total number of scores, minus 1.

6. Calculating the mean squares is straightforward: divide the sum of squares for each component by its degrees of freedom. Note that the sum of component mean squares will *not* equal the total mean square. In fact, a total mean square is not even calculated.

7. The most common error that occurs in calculating the value of *F* is using the wrong error term in the denominator. Follow the instructions in the appropriate Procedure to make sure you are using the correct error term.

8. The most common error that occurs in determining whether the value of *F* is significant is mixing up the degrees of freedom for the numerator ($MS_{between}$) and denominator (MS_{within}). The degrees of freedom for the within mean square nearly always is larger than the degrees of freedom for the between mean square. Consequently, nearly always you'll look for the smaller degrees of freedom in the column headings and the larger degrees of freedom in the row headings.

9. The best way to make sense of posttests is to graph the results. Determine which sample means you are comparing, and draw a graph. The graph should help you understand why the results of a posttest were either significant or insignificant, as well as spotting any errors you may have made.

∑ *S U M M A R Y*

▶ A two-factor analysis of variance tests hypotheses about the effect of two variables and their interaction on subjects' performance. Each variable can have two or more levels.

▶ An interaction between two variables occurs when the effect on subjects' performance of one variable depends on the value of the other variable. There is no interaction if the effect of one variable is the same for all of the levels of the other variable.

▶ In a two-factor ANOVA, the total variance is partitioned into four parts: the variance due to the effect of factor A, the variance due to the effect of factor B, the variance due to the effect of the interaction between A and B, and the variance due to random variation in the subjects' performance within each group (i.e., the error variance).

▶ A source of variance is a variable that possibly contributes to the variation in a group of scores. In a two-factor ANOVA, A and B and the interaction between A and B are all between-group sources of variance.

▶ The procedure for conducting a two-factor ANOVA is exactly like that of a one-factor ANOVA, except that the researcher formulates null and alternate hypotheses for each of the between-group sources of variance.

▶ The computations for a two-factor ANOVA are like those for a one-factor ANOVA, except that in the two-factor ANOVA, the sums of squares, degrees of freedom, and mean square are computed for all four sources of variance (A, B, A × B, and within groups), and values of F are computed for all three between-groups sources of variance.

▶ If a factor has only two levels, then a significant value of F indicates that there is a significant difference in performance between those two levels. If a factor has more than two levels, then a significant value of F indicates that there is a significant difference in performance between at least two levels and possibly more. To determine exactly which levels have significant differences in performance, posttests are necessary. If the value of F is not significant, then there are no significant differences between any of the levels of that factor.

E X E R C I S E S

Conceptual Exercises

1. Define the following terms:

   interaction   source of variance

   main effect   between-groups source of variance

   cell   within-groups source of variance

2. The following are sample means representing two factors, each with two levels. One of the cell means is not listed.

	A_1	A_2
B_1	200	100
B_2	300	

A. What value must the missing cell be so that it is impossible to have a significant F for factor A?

B. What value must the missing cell be so that it is impossible to have a significant F for factor B?

C. What value must the missing cell be so that it is impossible to have a significant F for the interaction between A and B?

3. Suppose you have a set of data representing two factors, with two levels on each factor. Construct sample means for this set of data such that it is possible to have a significant value of F only for the sources of variance listed below:

A. for factor A only

B. for factor B only

C. for factors A and B

D. for the interaction only

E. for factor A and the interaction

F. for factor B and the interaction

G. for all three sources of variance

4. Each of the groups of sample means below represent a study on the relationship between fear of failure and sex on grade point average (GPA):

I.

	Fear of Failure		
	High	Medium	Low
Men	3.25	3.50	3.75
Women	3.25	3.00	2.75

IV.

	Fear of Failure		
	High	Medium	Low
Men	3.00	3.00	3.75
Women	3.00	3.50	3.25

II.

	Fear of Failure		
	High	Medium	Low
Men	3.25	3.25	3.25
Women	3.75	3.75	3.75

V.

	Fear of Failure		
	High	Medium	Low
Men	3.00	3.25	3.50
Women	3.00	3.25	3.50

III.

	Fear of Failure		
	High	Medium	Low
Men	2.75	3.00	3.25
Women	3.25	3.50	3.75

VI.

	Fear of Failure		
	High	Medium	Low
Men	3.25	3.50	3.75
Women	3.75	3.50	3.25

A. For which group is it possible to have a significant F only for the factor Fear of Failure? Why?

B. For which group is it possible to have a significant F only for the factor Sex? Why?

C. For which group is it possible to have a significant F only for the interaction? Why?

D. For which group is it possible to have significant values of F both for the factor Sex and for the factor Fear of Failure but not for the interaction? Why?

E. For which group is it possible to have significant value of F both for the factor Fear of Failure and for the interaction but not for the factor Sex? Why?

F. For which group is it possible to have significant values of F both for the factor Sex and for the interaction but not for the factor Fear of Failure? Why?

5. A summary table from an analysis of variance is shown below. Many of the values are missing. Use the values provided to fill in the remainder of the table.

Sources of Variance	SS	df	MS	F
A		2		4.00
B		3		
A × B	60			
Within			5.00	
Total	1,330	239		

6. Listed below is a set of scores representing two factors, each with two levels:

	A_1	A_2
B_1	3	7
	4	8
	5	9
	6	10
	7	11
B_2	1	5
	2	6
	3	7
	4	8
	5	9

A. Conduct a two-factor analysis of variance on these scores.

B. Add 2 to every score in every cell. Conduct a two-factor analysis of variance on these scores. Compare the results of this analysis to the analysis conducted in part A, and explain any similarities or differences that occur.

C. In the original set of scores, add 4 to every score in the last cell (A_2B_2). Conduct a two-factor analysis of variance on these scores. Compare the results of this analysis to the analysis conducted in part A, and explain any similarities or differences that occur.

D. In the original set of scores, add 5 to the last score in each sample. Conduct a two-factor analysis of variance on these scores. Compare the results of this analysis to the analysis conducted in part A, and explain any similarities or differences that occur.

Computational Exercises

7. The cell means for four studies, each with two factors, are listed below. Calculate the sums of squares for each of the between-groups factors: factor A, factor B, and the interaction between A and B. There are ten subjects in each cell.

Set I

	A_1	A_2
B_1	9	3
B_2	3	1

Set II

	A_1	A_2	A_3
B_1	4	7	10
B_2	6	3	6

Set III

	A_1	A_2
B_1	8	4
B_2	6	8
B_3	4	0

Set IV

	A_1	A_2	A_3
B_1	13	8	6
B_2	14	10	3
B_3	16	9	5
B_4	17	13	6

8. The number of levels in each of two factors, *A* and *B,* and the number of subjects tested per cell for four studies are listed below. Calculate the degrees of freedom for each set of scores.

Set	n_A	n_B	n_S
I	2	4	7
II	5	3	4
III	3	6	10
IV	2	3	14

9. Find the critical value of *F* for the .05 and .01 significance levels for each of the three sources of variance in each of the sets of scores in the previous exercise.

10. Jaime compared the effects of high- and low-sugar breakfast cereals on children's activity levels. She tested two groups each of boys and girls by first giving them either high- or low-sugar cereals, and then, one-half hour later, measuring their activity level, using a pedometer that measured the number of tenths of miles the children moved. The results are shown below:

Group	High-Sugar Cereal	Low-Sugar Cereal
Boys	10	5
	7	4
	9	7
	6	4
	8	5
Girls	5	3
	4	4
	6	5
	3	1
	2	2

A. Using Procedure 17-2, conduct a two-factor analysis of variance.

B. Conduct the appropriate posttests on the results.

C. In regular English, describe what the ANOVA and posttests demonstrate.

11. Jordan studied the effect of different types of music on academic performance between traditional-age and nontraditional age students. He tested different participants in each group. He gave the participants an academic achievement test after listening to one of the types of music listed below. The participants' scores on the test were

Student Age	Mozart	Frank Sinatra	Rolling Stones
Traditional	21	9	29
	24	12	26
	22	10	30
	18	5	24
	20	9	26

Nontraditional	22	14	15
	20	18	18
	25	11	20
	18	9	13
	20	13	19

A. Conduct a two-factor analysis of variance, using Procedure 17-2.

B. Conduct the appropriate posttests on the results.

C. In regular English, describe what the ANOVA and posttests demonstrate.

12. Jake tested the effects of the amount of exercise that participants got per week on their weight loss. He had participants keep a journal of the number of hours they exercised and used that information to divide the participants into the low-exercise, moderate-exercise, and high-exercise groups. He then recorded the amount of weight each participant lost in one month, with the results shown below:

Group	Low Exercise	Moderate Exercise	High Exercise
Men	4	7	10
	2	5	7
	3	7	9
	4	5	8
	2	6	11
Women	7	8	10
	4	10	9
	3	7	12
	6	7	11
	5	8	13

A. Conduct a two-factor analysis of variance using Procedure 17-2.

B. Conduct the appropriate posttests on the results.

C. In regular English, describe what the ANOVA and posttests demonstrate.

E N D N O T E

1. One book that is particularly recommended is Geoffrey Keppel's *Design and Analysis: A Researcher's Handbook* (2d ed., Englewood Cliffs, NJ: Prentice-Hall, 1982).

Chi Square

18

Calculating χ^2

Contingency Tables

Observed and Expected Frequencies

Computing χ^2

STEP-BY-STEP PROCEDURE 18-1: Calculating the Value of χ^2

Using χ^2 to Measure the Correlation between Two Variables

The ϕ' Coefficient (Cramer's Statistic)

STEP-BY-STEP PROCEDURE 18-2: Calculating the Value of ϕ' (Cramer's Statistic)

χ^2 and ϕ' as Measures of the Strength of a Relationship

Collapsing a Contingency Table

Measuring the Significance of χ^2

The χ^2 Test of Association

Testing the Association between Variables

STEP-BY-STEP PROCEDURE 18-3: Testing Hypotheses with χ^2

Tests of Association as Tests of Independence

The χ^2 Test for Goodness of Fit

Testing the Goodness of Fit

Comparing the Two Types of χ^2 Tests

CHECKING YOUR ANSWERS

SUMMARY

EXERCISES

Conceptual Exercises

Computational Exercises

▶ In the past six chapters, we have examined quite a few statistical tests that can be used to test hypotheses about variables measured on ordinal, interval, and ratio scales of measurement. In this chapter, we examine a statistical test that can be used on scores that represent a nominal scale of measurement. The statistic on which this test is based is **chi square,** χ^2 (*chi* is pronounced "ki," rhyming with "eye").

Chi square is a very versatile statistic. It can be used to measure the correlation between two nominal variables or the correlation between one nominal variable and another variable, measured on any of the other scales of measurement. Chi square can also be used to conduct statistical tests for nominal variables. Before we examine these various uses for χ^2, we first need to understand how it is calculated.

Chi square (χ^2) is a measure of the degree of relationship between two variables that yield data that can be listed in a contingency table with *r* rows (representing one variable) and *c* columns (representing the other variable).

Calculating χ^2 : Chi Square

Contingency Tables

Table 18-1 shows the results of asking 250 people about their favorite type of television program. This table represents two variables, sex and type of television program. Chi square can be used to measure the relationship between these two variables. Table 18-1 is a **contingency table**, showing the relationship between two variables. We examined contingency tables before when we looked at the ϕ coefficient in Chapter 8. The contingency tables for the ϕ coefficient each contained two rows and two columns. Contingency tables for χ^2 are not limited to two rows and columns.

A **contingency table** is a table that shows the frequency of subjects in each combination of levels of two variables.

In a contingency table for χ^2, the row headings list levels of variable X and the column headings list levels of variable Y. Thus, the contingency table contains *r* levels of variable X (*r* for "rows") and *c* levels of variable Y (*c* for "columns"). Either *r* or *c* must be at least 2 and can possibly be any integer

TABLE 18-1 Observed Frequencies of Men and Women Who Watch Four Types of Television Programs

Sex	Television Show Category			
	News	**Sports**	**Talk Shows**	**Comedies**
Men	37	22	43	48
Women	23	24	31	22

greater than 2. These contingency tables are called "$r \times c$ contingency tables." For example, a 3×4 contingency table would have 3 rows and 4 columns, indicating that there are 3 levels of variable X and 4 levels of variable Y represented. Table 18-1 is a 2×4 contingency table, indicating that there are 2 levels of variable X, sex, and 4 levels of variable Y, type of television program, represented.

A contingency table is different from the frequency tables we used in previous chapters. In frequency tables, the levels of each variable are listed in columns, as are the number of subjects in each level. Table 18-2 gives the same information as shown in Table 18-1, except that Table 18-2 lists the information in a frequency table. The first column shows the levels of the variable, sex (either "men" or "women"). The second column shows the levels of the second variable, type of television program ("news," "sports," "talk shows," and "comedies"). The last column indicates the number of participants who scored in each of the eight combinations of these levels.

In a contingency table, the levels of the two variables are listed as column and row headings. In Table 18-1, the column headings, such as "news" and "sports," are levels of the variable, favorite type of program. The row headings, "men" and "women," are the levels of the variable, sex. The numbers listed in the table are the numbers of participants in each combination of levels of the two variables. Each combination of levels in a contingency table is called a **cell**. For example, Table 18-1 shows that the cell frequency for men who selected news as their favorite program is 37. That tells us that 37 participants scored "male" on the variable, sex, and "news" on the variable, favorite program.

Note that the number in a cell represents the number of subjects in that combination of categories and not the scores of any subjects. All of the previous analyses that we have explored have involved scores, such as math test scores or psychology alumni's incomes. For χ^2, we count the number of subjects, not their scores. In the contingency table, each subject is counted once, in one combination of categories.

TABLE 18-2 Frequency Table of Relationship between Sex and Type of Television Program, from Table 18-1

Sex	TV Program	Frequency
Men:	News	37
	Sports	22
	Talk shows	43
	Comedies	48
Women:	News	23
	Sports	24
	Talk shows	31
	Comedies	22

A **cell** in a contingency table is the frequency of subjects in one combination of the levels of two variables.

Observed frequency is the number of subjects actually observed in a study to have a given score value or combination of score values.

Expected frequency is the number of subjects expected to have a given score value or combination of score values if there is no relationship between the variable(s) under study or as predicted theoretically.

Observed and Expected Frequencies

The numbers shown in Table 18-1 are called **observed frequencies**, which, as the term suggests, are the frequencies that we actually observed in the experiment. After tabulating these observed frequencies in a contingency table, the next step in calculating the value of χ^2 is to construct a table of the **expected frequencies**, the frequencies we would expect if there is absolutely no relationship between the two variables, sex and favorite type of program. To measure the strength of the relationship between these two variables, the formula for χ^2 measures how far each observed frequency deviates from the frequency that would be expected if there were no relationship. To measure this deviation, we need to determine what those expected frequencies are.

Figure 18-1 shows the process of constructing a table of the expected frequencies for the contingency table shown in Table 18-1. To construct a table of expected frequencies, the first step is to find the row totals and column totals for the table of observed frequencies. These sums are called the **marginal values.** In the last column of Figure 18-1, the marginal values indicate the total number of men (150) and women (100) in the study. The marginal values in the last row of Step 1 in Figure 18-1 indicate the total number of participants who preferred each type of television program.

The second step is to draw another table to be used for the expected frequencies, with the same number of rows and columns as the observed frequencies table. Then copy the row totals and column totals from the observed frequencies table onto the expected frequencies table. This is shown in Step 2 of Figure 18-1. Note that the individual cells of the expected frequencies are still blank.

The third step is to calculate the expected frequency for each cell by multiplying the row total for that cell by the column total for that cell and then dividing by the total number of subjects, n. For example, to find the expected frequency of men whose favorite type of program is news, we multiply the total number of men (150) by the total number of people, both men and women, in the survey who preferred news (60) and then divide by the total number of participants, 250, as follows:

$$\text{expected frequency} = \frac{(\text{row total})(\text{column total})}{n} = \frac{(60)(150)}{250} = 36.0.$$

The computations to find the expected frequencies for all of the cells are shown in Step 3 of Figure 18-1.

The final expected frequencies table is shown at the bottom of Figure 18-1. Note that the observed frequencies table and the expected frequencies table have the same row and column totals. However, the observed frequencies table and the expected frequencies table have different frequencies listed in the individual cells of the tables.

These expected frequencies, shown again in Table 18-3, are what would occur if there was absolutely no relationship between sex and television preferences. Of the 250 people represented in the table, 60 percent are men and 40 percent are women. In Table 18-3, notice that there is absolutely no difference between the sexes in their favorite types of programs. For each type of program, 60 percent of the participants are men and 40 percent are women.

Remember from our examination of regression that when there is no correlation between two variables, knowing a subject's score on one variable gives us no information at all about the value of that subject's score on the other

A **marginal value** in a contingency table is the number of subjects in a given level of one variable across all of the levels of the other variable represented in the table.

FIGURE 18-1   Constructing a Table of Expected Frequencies

Step 1: Find the row totals and column totals for the table of observed frequencies

	Television Show Category				
Sex	**News**	**Sports**	**Talk Shows**	**Comedies**	**Total**
Men	37	22	43	48	150
Women	23	24	31	22	100
Total	60	46	74	70	250

Step 2: Write row and column totals on table of expected frequencies

	Television Show Category				
Sex	**News**	**Sports**	**Talk Shows**	**Comedies**	**Total**
Men					150
Women					100
Total	60	46	74	70	250

Step 3: Calculate expected frequency for each cell

	Television Show Category				
Sex	**News**	**Sports**	**Talk Shows**	**Comedies**	**Total**
Men	$\dfrac{(60)(150)}{250}$	$\dfrac{(46)(150)}{250}$	$\dfrac{(74)(150)}{250}$	$\dfrac{(70)(150)}{250}$	150
Women	$\dfrac{(60)(100)}{250}$	$\dfrac{(46)(100)}{250}$	$\dfrac{(74)(100)}{250}$	$\dfrac{(70)(100)}{250}$	100
Total	60	46	74	70	250

Completed table of expected frequencies:

	Television Show Category				
Sex	**News**	**Sports**	**Talk Shows**	**Comedies**	**Total**
Men	36.0	27.6	44.4	42.0	150
Women	24.0	18.4	29.6	28.0	100
Total	60	46	74	70	250

variable. The same is true for a table of expected values. Knowing what sex a person is doesn't help us predict what type of program that person would prefer and knowing the person's TV program preference gives us no indication of what sex the person is. The expected frequencies are the values that would occur if there is absolutely no correlation between the two variables.

TABLE 18-3   Expected Frequencies for Data Shown in Table 18-1

Sex	Television Show Category				Total
	News	Sports	Talk Shows	Comedies	
Men	36.0	27.6	44.4	42.0	150
	(60% of 60)	(60% of 46)	(60% of 74)	(60% of 70)	(60% of 250)
Women	24.0	18.4	29.6	28.0	100
	(40% of 60)	(40% of 46)	(40% of 74)	(40% of 70)	(40% of 250)
Total	60	46	74	70	250

There is one important qualification. In order to use χ^2, the expected frequency of all of the cells must be at least five. If any of the expected frequencies is less than 5, χ^2 cannot be used. There is a test that can be used in this situation, Fisher's test of exact probabilities, which is described in more advanced statistics texts. Another option is to combine cells, a technique we will examine later in this chapter.

Computing χ^2

Step-by-Step Procedure 18-1 describes the steps in calculating χ^2. The first step in Procedure 18-1 is to construct a contingency table of the observed frequencies, which we have already done for this example. The second step is to construct a table of the expected frequencies, which we have also already completed. In the remaining steps, these observed and expected frequencies are used to calculate the value of χ^2. The computations for these remaining steps are shown in Figure 18-2. The first column of Figure 18-2 lists the observed frequencies from Table 18-1, and the second column lists the expected frequencies from Table 18-3.

The next step in calculating the value of χ^2 is to subtract the expected frequency from the observed frequency for each cell. Chi square is designed to measure how far each observed frequency is from the expected frequency. The larger the relationship between sex and preferred program—that is, the more men prefer some types of programs and women prefer other types— then the farther the observed frequencies will be from the expected frequency. If there is absolutely no relationship, then the observed frequencies will be the same as the frequencies expected if there is no relationship, and so χ^2 will be 0. The larger the relationship, the farther the observed frequencies will be from the expected frequencies, and the larger χ^2 will be.

The sum of the deviations of the observed frequencies from the expected frequencies is always zero. This fact can serve as a check to make sure that we have computed the deviations correctly. However, because the sum of the

---

STEP-BY-STEP PROCEDURE 18-1

Calculating the Value of χ^2

$$\chi^2 = \sum \frac{(O - E)^2}{E}$$

where O = the frequencies observed in the experiment
E = the frequencies expected if there is no relationship between the two variables being studied

1. List the observed frequencies in a contingency table. Calculate the row totals and the column totals.

2. Construct a table of the expected frequencies, as follows:
  A. Draw an empty table with the same number of rows and columns as the observed frequencies contingency table, and list the row totals and column totals found for the observed frequencies.
  B. For each cell in the table, multiply the row total for that cell by the column total for that cell, then divide by n, the total number of subjects, to find the expected frequency to be listed in that cell:

$$\text{expected frequency} = \frac{(\text{row total})(\text{column total})}{n}.$$

3. For each cell in the observed frequencies table, complete the following:
  A. Subtract the expected frequency from the observed frequency.
  B. Square the deviation found in Step 3A.
  C. Divide the result of Step 3B by the expected frequency used in Step 3A.

4. Sum the results of Step 3 for all cells to find the value of χ^2.

FIGURE 18-2   Calculating χ^2 for the Observed Frequencies in Table 18-1

Observed (O)	Expected (E)	$O - E$	$(O - E)^2$	$\dfrac{(O - E)^2}{E}$
37	36.0	1.0	1.00	0.03
22	27.6	−5.6	31.36	1.14
43	44.4	−1.4	1.96	0.04
48	42.0	6.0	36.00	0.86
23	24.0	−1.0	1.00	0.04
24	18.4	5.6	31.36	1.70
31	29.6	1.4	1.96	0.07
+ 22	+ 28.0	−6.0	36.00	+ 1.29
250	250.0			$\chi^2 = 5.17$

deviations is always zero, it does not serve us as a measure of the relationship between the variables. To circumvent this problem, each of these deviations is squared. This is the next step in calculating the value of χ^2. In Figure 18-2, the values of these squared deviations are listed in the fourth column.

Next, each squared deviation is divided by its expected frequency. For example, in the first row, when the squared deviation of 1.00 is divided by its expected frequency, 36.0, the result is 0.03. The final step is to sum these values. The result is the value of χ^2, which for the frequencies shown in Figure 18-2 is 5.17.

The value of χ^2 can range anywhere from 0 to $n(L-1)$, where n is the total number of subjects and L is the smaller of either the number of columns or the number of rows in the contingency table. Thus, the maximum value of χ^2 depends on the size of the contingency table and the total number of subjects represented in that table. If the observed frequencies are identical to the expected frequencies, then χ^2 will be 0, which indicates that there is absolutely no relationship between variables X and Y. The more that the observed values vary from the expected values, the larger χ^2 will be and the stronger the relationship between variables X and Y.

Using χ^2 to Measure the Correlation between Two Variables

In Chapter 8, we examined three measures of correlation: Pearson's r, Spearman's r_S, and the ϕ coefficient. All three of these measures yield correlation coefficients that can have values from -1.00 to $+1.00$. Because χ^2 can have values greater than $+1.00$, it is not a correlation coefficient. Thus, we cannot interpret the value of χ^2 in the same way that we interpreted the correlation coefficients we examined in Chapter 8. However, there is a technique we can use to convert a value of χ^2 to a correlation coefficient, which is called the ϕ' coefficient.

The ϕ' Coefficient (Cramer's Statistic)

The *phi'* (ϕ') **coefficient** is a measure of the correlation, or degree of relationship, between two dichotomous nominal variables.

Step-by-Step Procedure 18-2 shows the method for converting χ^2 to ϕ' (Greek *phi'*, pronounced "fie prime"; "fie" rhymes with pie). The ϕ' statistic is also called Cramer's statistic. We can use Procedure 18-2 to convert the value of χ^2, 5.17, which we found for the relationship between sex and preferred television program, to a correlation coefficient. The first step is to determine the value of L, which is the smaller of either the number of columns or the number of rows in the contingency table. In Table 18-1, the number of columns, c, is 4, and the number of rows, r, is 2. The smaller of these is 2, and so the

---

STEP-BY-STEP PROCEDURE 18-2

Calculating the Value of ϕ' (Cramer's Statistic)

$$\phi' = \sqrt{\frac{\chi^2}{n(L - 1)}}$$

where χ^2 = the value of χ^2 calculated from a contingency table
   n = the total number of subjects
   L = the smaller of c (the number of columns) or r (the number of rows)

1. Count the number of columns and the number of rows in the contingency table. Whichever is smaller is L. Subtract 1 from L.

2. Multiply the result of Step 1 by n, the number of subjects in the contingency table.

3. Divide the value of χ^2 by the results of Step 2.

4. Find the square root of Step 3 to find ϕ'.

---

value of L is 2. The number of participants shown in Table 18-1, n, is 250. These are the values we need to convert χ^2 to ϕ' as follows:

$$\phi' = \sqrt{\frac{\chi^2}{n(L - 1)}} = \sqrt{\frac{5.17}{250(2 - 1)}} = \sqrt{\frac{5.17}{250(1)}} = \sqrt{\frac{5.17}{250}} = \sqrt{.021} = .15.$$

Thus, the correlation between sex and type of favorite television program in the data shown in Table 18-1 is .15. This indicates that there is some relationship between the two variables but not a very strong relationship.

The value of ϕ' can range from 0 to +1.00. Note that because χ^2 is always a positive number, ϕ' will also be positive. Thus, we can never have negative correlations with ϕ'. If there is no relationship between the two variables being tested, then ϕ' will be 0. When there is a perfect relationship, ϕ' equals 1.00. Note that ϕ' can reach 1.00 only when the number of columns equals the number of rows. To understand why this is true, we need first to understand what a perfect correlation between nominal variables is.

χ^2 and ϕ' as Measures of the Strength of a Relationship

Figure 18-3 shows five contingency tables representing the results of studies looking at the relationship between reading an assigned text chapter and passing a quiz in five hypothetical classes. Each class consists of 100 students. Figure 18-3 shows the values of ϕ' and χ^2 for each class.

The data in Class A represent a perfect positive relationship, with $\phi' = +1.00$. For Class A, χ^2 is 100, which is the same as the number of participants, n. Note that all of the students who read the chapter passed the quiz and that

FIGURE 18-3 Examples of the Strength of the Relationship between Reading Chapter and Passing Quiz, as Measured by χ^2 and ϕ'

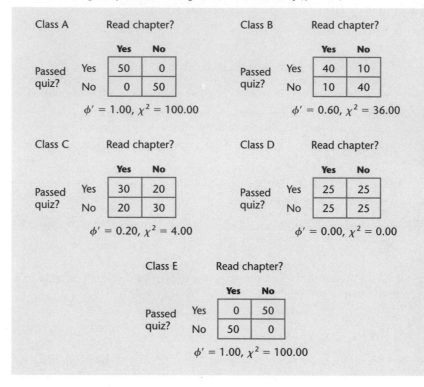

all of the students who did not read the chapter failed. If we know whether or not a student read the chapter, we can predict perfectly whether or not that student passed the quiz. This is the nature of a perfect relationship.

When the relationship is not perfect, the value of χ^2 is less than *n*. For example, in Class B, most but not all of the students who read the chapter passed the quiz and most but not all of the students who failed did not read the chapter. We would be correct 80 percent of the time in predicting that students who read the chapter would pass the quiz. There is a correlation present, but it is not perfect. In Class B, the value of ϕ' is .60 and χ^2 is 36.

The relationship between reading and passing is even weaker in Class C. There are slightly more passing students who read the chapter than who did not. There also are slightly more failing students who did not read the chapter than who did. If we predicted that passing students had read the chapter and failing students had not, we would be correct only 60 percent of the time, which is just 10 percent better than chance. The value of ϕ' is .20 and χ^2 is only 4 in Class C.

In Class D, there is no relationship at all between reading and passing. Among the students who read the chapter, just as many passed as failed. The same is true for the students who did not read the chapter. If we were to predict that passing students had read the chapter and failing students had not, we would be correct only 50 percent of the time, which is no better than chance. In Class D, the value of both ϕ' and χ^2 is 0.

Finally, note that Class E has a perfect relationship, but in the opposite direction from the relationship found in Class A. In Class E, all of the passing students did not read the chapter, while all of the failing students did. If we call the relationship between reading and passing in Class A a positive correlation, then the relationship in Class E is a negative relationship. However, for Class E the value of ϕ' is 1.00 and χ^2 is 100, the same values as for Class A. Neither χ^2 nor ϕ' differentiate between positive and negative relationships.

We can see from these examples that in general, the stronger the relationship, the larger the value of χ^2. The lowest possible value of both χ^2 and ϕ' is 0, which occurs when there is absolutely no relationship present. In these 2×2 tables, the largest possible value of χ^2 is n, the total number of subjects, and the largest possible value of ϕ' for a 2×2 contingency table is 1.00. These values occur when there is a perfect correlation, either positive or negative.

As mentioned previously, a perfect correlation as measured by χ^2 or ϕ' can occur only when the number of columns and rows are the same. Consider the relationship between type of television program and sex shown in Table 18-1. The only way that our predictions could be perfect is if all of the men prefer one type of TV program and all the women prefer another type. The relationship in Table 18-1 is not perfect because we cannot predict exactly which TV program either men or women prefer.

In general, to make perfect predictions, for each row and column, all of the cases must be in one cell with the remaining cells having frequencies of zero, which can occur only if the number of columns and rows are equal. Figure 18-4 shows examples of perfect relationships for several sizes of contingency tables. For each contingency table, the number of subjects, n, is 120. The value of χ^2 for the 2×2 table in Figure 18-4 is 120, which is equal to n. The frequencies in the 3×3 table have a χ^2 of 240, which is $2n$. For the 4×4 table, χ^2 is

FIGURE 18-4 Examples of Perfect Relationships as Measured by χ^2 and ϕ'

Grade Level	Pass	Fail
Senior	60	0
Junior	0	60

$$\chi^2 = 120, \phi' = 1.00$$

Grade Level	Honors	Pass	Fail
Senior	40	0	0
Junior	0	40	0
Sophomore	0	0	40

$$\chi^2 = 240, \phi' = 1.00$$

Grade Level	A	B	C	D
Senior	30	0	0	0
Junior	0	30	0	0
Sophomore	0	0	30	0
Freshman	0	0	0	30

$$\chi^2 = 360, \phi' = 1.00$$

TABLE 18-4 Collapsing a Table of Observed Frequencies

Sex	Television Show Category		Total
	Comedies	**Other**	
Men	48	102	150
Women	22	78	100
Total	70	180	250

360, which is $3n$. Thus, the maximum value of χ^2 depends on the number of subjects, n, and the size of the contingency table. As can be seen here, the maximum value is $n(L - 1)$, where L is the smaller of either the number of rows or columns. Although the value of χ^2 varies with the size of the contingency table, the value of ϕ' is 1.00 for all three tables shown in Figure 18-4. Thus ϕ' is not dependent on the size of the contingency table.

Collapsing a Contingency Table

If the number of rows is not equal to the number of columns, then the value of ϕ' cannot reach 1.00. If we do want to measure the correlation between two nominal variables with a coefficient that can take on values from 0 to 1.00, to be comparable to other correlation coefficients, we can combine cells so that the number of rows and columns are equal. Combining cells is also a method for handling tables in which some of the expected values are less than 5.

As an example of the process of collapsing a contingency table, Table 18-4 shows a 2×2 table constructed by combining columns from Table 18-1. In Table 18-4, the frequencies for three types of TV programs (news, sports, and talk shows) are combined into one category, "Other." For this 2×2 table, the value of χ^2 is 2.98, and ϕ' is .11, which indicates that there is a very weak correlation in this data between sex and the person's preference for comedies or other programming. We could repeat this process to isolate each of the other types of programs.

Measuring the Significance of χ^2

In addition to converting χ^2 to a measure of correlation, we can also find the significance level of the relationship between variables X and Y, as measured by χ^2. This process is comparable to testing the significance of Pearson's r or Spearman's r_S. In the sections that follow, we will test the significance of χ^2 in a variety of statistical tests. It would be useful here to first examine how to determine the significance level of χ^2.

First, let's assume that the frequencies shown in Table 18-1 represent an entire population of 250 people. In that case, we know that there is a relationship between sex and type of television program in this population. The value of 5.17 for χ^2 and .15 for ϕ' are direct measures of that relationship. If Table 18-1 represents an entire population, then there is a correlation between sex and type of television program in this population (albeit a rather low correlation and a very small population).

Now suppose that Table 18-1 does not represent an entire population but rather represents a sample of participants drawn from a much larger population. While we know that the correlation in the sample is .15, as measured by

ϕ', is there a correlation between sex and type of television program in the entire population? In essence, we are here testing a hypothesis about the relationship between the two variables in the population. The null hypothesis is that there is no relationship between the two variables in the population. The alternate hypothesis is that there is such a relationship. Stated in other terms, the null and alternate hypotheses are:

H_0: For each value of X, the relative frequency distributions of Y are identical.

H_1: For each value of X, the relative frequency distributions of Y are different.

Appendix A-7 shows the critical values of χ^2 for several values of α. The degrees of freedom for χ^2 are the number of rows, minus one, times the number of columns, minus one. For the variables, sex and type of television program, shown in Table 18-1, there are two rows and four columns, and thus the degrees of freedom are

$$df = (\text{number of rows} - 1)(\text{number of columns} - 1) = (2 - 1)(4 - 1) = 3.$$

Appendix A-7 shows that the critical value of χ^2 with $\alpha = .05$ and 3 df is 7.82.

In general, if the value of χ^2 calculated on the data in a contingency table is equal to or greater than the critical value, we can reject the null hypothesis and conclude that there is a relationship between the two variables tested in the population from which the sample of subjects was drawn. On the other hand, if the value of χ^2 calculated for a contingency table is less than the critical value of χ^2, obtained from Table A-7, then we cannot reject the null hypothesis. We do not have enough evidence to conclude that there is a relationship between the two variables in the population in question.

The value of χ^2 calculated for the contingency table shown in Table 18-1 was 5.17. From Table A-7, we found that the critical value of χ^2, with an α of .05, is 7.82. The value of χ^2 that we obtained from the contingency table in Table 18-1 is less than the critical value, and thus we could not reject the null hypothesis in this case. There would be insufficient evidence to conclude that there is a relationship between sex and type of television program in the population from which the sample shown in Table 18-1 was drawn.

The χ^2 Test of Association

Testing the Association between Variables

The example that we have just examined—the relationship between sex and type of television program—is a test of the strength of the association between the two variables. Strength of association is another way of saying strength of the relationship between the two variables. In previous chapters,

---

STEP-BY-STEP PROCEDURE 18-3

Testing Hypotheses with χ^2

1. Verify that the following assumptions have been met:
- A. The subjects are randomly and independently sampled.
- B. Each subject is counted in one and only one category.
- C. The expected frequency of each cell in the contingency table is at least 5. If there are only two rows and two columns in the contingency table, then the expected frequency of each cell is at least 10.

2. Write the null and alternate hypotheses. For the χ^2 test, there is only one form for the null and alternate hypotheses:

H_0: For each value of X, the relative frequency distributions of Y are identical.
H_1: For each value of X, the relative frequency distributions of Y are different.

3. Decide the level of significance, α.

4. Compute the degrees of freedom. For testing χ^2, the degrees of freedom are the number of rows, minus 1, times the number of columns, minus 1:

$$df = (\text{number of rows} - 1) \times (\text{number of columns} - 1).$$

Find the critical value of r in Appendix A-7.

5. Draw a graph of the sampling distribution, indicating the rejection region. For χ^2, the rejection region is always in the upper tail.

6. Calculate the statistic from the scores of the subjects in the sample, using the formula below. Procedure 18-1 describes how to use this formula:

$$\chi^2 = \sum \frac{(O - E)^2}{E}.$$

7. Decide whether or not to reject the null hypothesis:
- A. If the value of χ^2 calculated in Step 6 is in the rejection region, then $p \leq \alpha$, and reject the null hypothesis.
- B. If the value of χ^2 calculated in Step 6 is not in the rejection region, then $p > \alpha$, and do not reject the null hypothesis.

---

we examined procedures for testing the strength of the relationship between two interval or ratio variables, using Pearson's product-moment correlation, as well as procedures testing the strength of the relationship between two ordinal variables, using Spearman's rank-order correlation. These were both tests of the strength of association between two variables. Using χ^2, we can conduct a similar test of association for the relationship between two nominal variables. The general method for testing hypotheses with χ^2 is described in Step-by-Step Procedure 18-3.

Figure 18-5 shows the frequency of men and women enrolled as majors in five different academic programs, business, science, social science, education, and humanities. In many colleges, men are more likely to major in some

FIGURE 18-5 Calculating χ^2 for the Frequency of Men and Women Majoring in Five Academic Programs

A. Observed Frequencies

Sex	Business	Sciences	Social Sciences	Education	Humanities
Men	64	40	34	32	30
Women	32	24	46	56	42

B. Steps in Calculating the Value of χ^2

Observed (O)	Expected (E)	O − E	(O − E)²	$\dfrac{(O - E)^2}{E}$
64	48	16	256	5.33
40	32	8	64	2.00
34	40	−6	36	0.90
32	44	−12	144	3.27
30	36	−6	36	1.00
32	48	−16	256	5.33
24	32	−8	64	2.00
46	40	6	36	0.90
56	44	12	144	3.27
+ 42	+ 36	6	36	+ 1.00
400	400			$\chi^2 = 25.00$

programs and women, in others. Let's test the hypothesis that there is a relationship between sex and type of major, using the data in Figure 18-5.

Step 1: Verify that the assumptions of the test are met. The assumptions for the χ^2 test of association are shown in Procedure 18-3. The first assumption is that the subjects in the sample were randomly and independently selected. This means that each member of the population had a equal chance of being selected and that the selection of one member did not affect the probability that any other member of the population would be selected.

The second assumption is that no subject is counted more than once. If a subject is counted in one category, that subject is not counted in any other categories. This is true for the data shown in Figure 18-5. Each participant in the table is either a man or a woman and is enrolled in only one program. As a check to ensure that each participant is counted only once, the sum of the observed frequencies should equal n, the total number of participants.

FIGURE 18-6   Observed Relative Frequency Distribution for Academic Major, by Sex

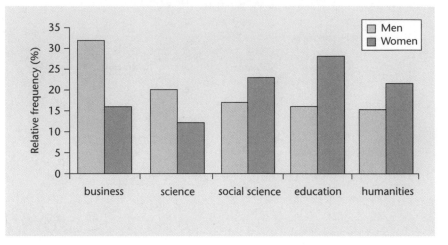

The third assumption is that the expected frequencies for all of the cells are at least 5. The lowest expected frequency for the frequencies in Figure 18-5 is 32, and so this assumption is met.

Step 2: Write the null and alternate hypotheses.   In Chapter 12, we saw that a statistical hypothesis is an assertion that there is a relationship between variables in the population being studied. The hypothesis here is that there is a relationship between sex and academic major in the population of college students. The null hypothesis would be that there is no relationship between these two variables in the population of college students.

We could construct a relative frequency graph of the academic majors of men and women, as shown in Figure 18-6. These are the actual relative frequencies observed in the sample of college students. Notice that the shape of the distribution is different for men than for women. A greater percentage of the men major in business and science, while a greater percentage of the women major in social sciences, education, or humanities. Determining whether these differences are significant is the purpose of this statistical test.

In the previous section, we saw that the expected frequencies used to calculate χ^2 are the frequencies expected if there is no relationship between the two variables. Thus, these are the frequencies that would be expected if the null hypothesis were true. If there were no relationship between sex and academic major, then the shape of the relative frequency distribution for men would be the same as the shape of the women's distribution.

The null hypothesis for this study predicts that the relative frequency distribution of academic majors is the same for both values of sex, male and female. The alternate hypothesis predicts that the relative frequency distribution of academic majors is different for males than for females:

H_0: The relative frequency distribution of academic majors for men and women are the same.

H_1: The relative frequency distribution of academic majors for men and women are different.

The hypotheses make assertions about relative frequency, rather than just frequency, so that the test is not affected by differences in the total number of men and women. What is relevant is not whether the *number* of men and women in each major differs but whether the *proportion* (i.e., relative frequency) differs.

Step 3: Decide the level of significance, α.   We will use a significance level of $\alpha = .05$. As we will see, a χ^2 test is always one-tailed.

Step 4: Identify the critical value(s) of the statistic.   Appendix A-7 shows the critical values of χ^2 for several values of α. Recall that the degrees of freedom for χ^2 are the number of rows, r, minus one, times the number of columns, c, minus one. For this study, there are two rows and five columns, and thus the degrees of freedom are

$$df = (r - 1)(c - 1) = (2 - 1)(5 - 1) = 4.$$

Appendix A-7 shows that the critical value of χ^2 with $\alpha = .05$ and 4 *df* is 9.49. In order to reject the null hypothesis, the sample must have a value of χ^2 of 9.49 or greater.

Step 5: Indicate the rejection region on a graph of the sampling distribution. We can now construct a graph of the sampling distribution, as shown in Figure 18-7. The shape of a χ^2 distribution is different than the shape of the normal distribution, in that the shape of the χ^2 distribution is skewed positively. Since χ^2 does not generate negative values, the rejection region is always in the upper tail.

If the value of χ^2 that we calculate for the sample of data is 9.49 or larger, we can reject the null hypothesis. The computations for the value of χ^2 are shown in Figure 18-5. These computations show that the value of χ^2 is 25.00. This value of χ^2 is in the rejection region, and therefore we can reject the null hypothesis, which stated that there is no relationship between sex and academic major. Thus, this evidence provides support for the claim that there is a significant association between sex and the academic majors of college students and that men tend to enroll in different majors than women do.

FIGURE 18-7   Sampling Distribution for χ^2 with $\alpha = .05$ and $df = 3$

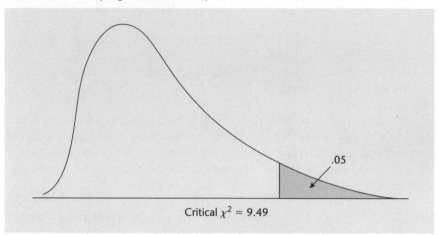

Critical $\chi^2 = 9.49$

Tests of Association as Tests of Independence

In some statistics books, the χ^2 test of association is called a test of independence. If there is an association between two variables, then the value a subject has on one variable depends on the value of that subject's score on the other variable. In this case, the variables are dependent. However, if there is no association between two variables, then those variables are independent. Thus, a test of the association between two variables is also a test of whether the variables are independent or dependent.

As an example, suppose you suspect that Jethro, a graduate student and lab instructor, gives higher grades to female students than to male students. We select two samples of students, one male and one female, from Jethro's lab section and find the distribution of grades as shown in Figure 18-8. Our assertion is that the two variables, sex and grades, are not independent in Jethro's sections. If the two variables are independent, then the distribution of grades for male students would be exactly like the distribution for female students. If the two distributions differ, then sex and grades are not independent. We can follow the general method for testing hypotheses with χ^2 described in Procedure 18-3 to test the independence of sex and grades in Jethro's lab sections.

Step 1: Verify that the assumptions of the test are met.   Using the χ^2 test assumes that the subjects are randomly and independently selected and that each subject is counted in only one category. The χ^2 test also assumes that no cell has an expected frequency less than 5. For the samples of males and females selected from Jethro's lab sections, these assumptions are met.

FIGURE 18-8 Calculating χ^2 for the Distribution of Grades for Male and Female Students

A. Observed Frequencies

Sex	Letter Grade				
	A	**B**	**C**	**D**	**F**
Male	10	20	40	20	10
Female	20	40	30	10	0

B. Steps in Calculating the Value of χ^2

Observed (O)	Expected (E)	O − E	$(O - E)^2$	$\dfrac{(O - E)^2}{E}$
10	15	−5	25	1.67
20	30	−10	100	3.33
40	35	5	25	0.71
20	15	5	25	1.67
10	5	5	25	5.00
20	15	5	25	1.67
40	30	10	100	3.33
30	35	−5	25	0.71
10	15	−5	25	1.67
+ 0	+ 5	−5	25	+ 5.00
200	200			$\chi^2 = 24.76$

Step 2: Write the null and alternate hypotheses.   The null hypothesis is that the relative frequency distribution of grades from Jethro's lab sections are the same for males and females. The alternative hypothesis is that the distributions are different for males and females.

Step 3: Decide the level of significance, α.   We will use the conventional level of significance, $\alpha = .05$.

Step 4: Identify the critical value(s) of the statistic.   The degrees of freedom for the χ^2 test are $(c - 1)(r - 1)$, where c is the number of columns and r is the number of rows in the contingency table. The contingency table shown in Figure 18-8 has five columns and two rows, and thus the degrees of freedom are $(5 - 1)(2 - 1) = 4$. Again, Appendix A-7 shows that the critical value of χ^2 with 4 df and $\alpha = .05$ is 9.49.

Step 5: Indicate the rejection region on a graph of the sampling distribution.   Figure 18-7 shows the sampling distribution for χ^2 with 4 df and $\alpha = .05$.

FIGURE 18-9   Observed Relative Frequency Distribution
for Final Grades in Jethro's Lab Section, by Sex

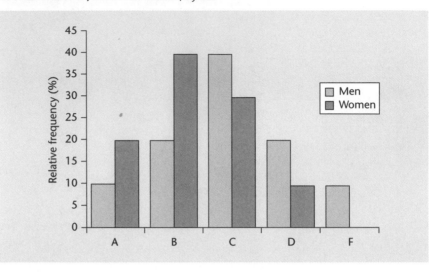

Step 6: Calculate the statistic from the sample of scores.   Procedure 8-2 de-scribes the method for calculating χ^2, and the steps in calculating its value are shown in Figure 18-8. The value of χ^2 for the observed frequencies in Fig-ure 18-8 is 24.76.

Step 7: Decide whether or not to reject the null hypothesis.   The value of χ^2, 24.76, is in the rejection region shown in Figure 18-7. Therefore, we can con-clude that the relative frequency distribution of grades for males in Jethro's lab sections is significantly different than the distribution of grades for fe-males. The distribution of grades for men and women in Jethro's lab is shown in Figure 18-9, in which we can see that Jethro tends to give higher grades to female students than to male students, and thus that the grade distribution for females is higher than the grade distribution for males. For Jethro, grades and sex are not independent.

   In this example, we were able to reject the null hypothesis and conclude that sex and grades were not independent in Jethro's class. Note that while this χ^2 test is sometimes called a test of independence, it is actually a test of the association between variables, in which we are actually trying to show is that the two variables are *not* independent. The null hypothesis is that the variables are independent, while the alternate hypothesis is that they are de-pendent. In hypothesis testing, we are always trying to eliminate or reject the null hypothesis to provide support for the alternate hypothesis.

   If the value of χ^2 were not great enough to reject the null hypothesis, it would not mean that we had proved that the two variables were independent.

This often is a difficult concept to grasp and bears repeating. When we fail to reject the null hypothesis, we have in fact proved nothing. We are still left with two possible hypotheses, the null and the alternate, and if we fail to reject the null, we have no evidence to decide which hypothesis is true. The most we can say is that we do not have enough evidence to decide that the two variables are in fact dependent.

One of the great conundrums in statistics is that while many statistical tests make assumptions of independence, it is impossible to prove the independence of two variables. Researchers may use the χ^2 test if they have any doubts about whether their data meet the assumptions of independence. If in conducting the χ^2 test, the researchers find a significant value of χ^2, they would not then use the statistical test that requires independence. However, if they do not find a significant value of χ^2, they will conclude properly that there is not sufficient evidence that the variables are dependent. The researchers then decide, on the basis of this lack of evidence, to assume that the variables are independent, so that they can proceed with the statistical test requiring independence. The researchers have not proved that the variables are independent; they have simply failed to prove that the variables are dependent and then merely assumed that they are independent.

The χ^2 Test for Goodness of Fit

Testing the Goodness of Fit

Another way that we can use χ^2 is to test whether a frequency distribution varies significantly from a set of theoretical predictions. In statistical parlance, this is testing the **goodness of fit** between the observed and predicted frequencies. For example, at State University, 10 percent of the student body is African-American, 5 percent is Asian-American, 8 percent is Native American, 7 percent is Hispanic, 60 percent are of Northern European origin, and the remaining 10 percent represent other ethnic groups. Johanna believes that the proportion of minority students (i.e., non–Northern European) majoring in the social sciences is greater than the proportion found in the university at large. To test this hypothesis, Johanna recorded the number of minority and nonminority students majoring in the social sciences. These frequencies are shown in Figure 18-10.

Goodness of fit is the degree to which the observed frequencies in a contingency table conform to frequencies predicted theoretically.

We can use the χ^2 goodness-of-fit test to test Johanna's hypothesis. The method for deriving the expected values for the goodness-of-fit test is different from the method used in the test of association, in which the expected values are the frequencies we would expect if there is no relation between the variables under study. In Johanna's test for goodness of fit, the expected values are the frequencies of minority and nonminority social science majors we would expect if the proportions are the same as the university-wide proportions. In the university as a whole, 40 percent of the students are minority

FIGURE 18-10 Calculating χ^2 for the Proportion of Minority and Nonminority Social Science Majors

	Minority Status		
	Minority	**Nonminority**	**Total**
Observed frequency	216	264	480
Expected percentage	40%	60%	100%

Steps in Calculating the Value of χ^2

Observed (O)	**Expected (E)**	**O − E**	**(O − E)²**	**$\dfrac{(O-E)^2}{E}$**
216	192	24	576	3.00
+ 264	+ 288	−24	576	+ 2.00
480	480			$\chi^2 = 5.00$

and 60 percent are nonminority. There are 280 students majoring in one of the social sciences. If the proportions of minorities and nonminorities in the social sciences is the same as the university-wide proportions, we would expect 40 percent of 480, or 192, social science majors to be minorities and 60 percent of 480, or 288 social science majors to be nonminorities. These are the expected values we will use in this test of goodness of fit.

Step 1: Verify that the assumptions of the test are met.   Using the χ^2 test assumes that the subjects are randomly and independently selected, that each subject is counted in only one category, and that no cell has an expected frequency less than 5. For a test of Johanna's theory, these assumptions are met.

Step 2: Write the null and alternate hypotheses.   The null hypothesis is that the relative frequency distribution of minority and nonminority social science majors is the same as the distribution for the university as a whole. The alternative hypothesis is that the distribution for social science majors is not the same as the distribution of the university as a whole.

Step 3: Decide the level of significance, α.   We will use the conventional level of significance, $\alpha = .05$.

Step 4: Identify the critical value(s) of the statistic.   While the contingency table in Figure 18-10 has two rows, it actually contains only one row of observed frequencies, the number of minority and nonminority social science majors. The second row gives the university-wide percentages, which are the basis for the expected values. Thus, the table of observed frequencies has one row and two columns. When there is only one row, the degrees of freedom for χ^2 test are $c - 1$, where c is the number of columns. For the contingency table in Figure 18-8, the degrees of freedom are $2 - 1$ or 1. Appendix A-7 shows that the critical value of χ^2 for with 1 *df* and $\alpha = .05$ is 3.84.

Step 5: Indicate the rejection region on a graph of the sampling distribution. The sampling distribution for χ^2 with 1 *df* is like the distribution shown in Figure 18-7, except that the critical value is 3.84.

Step 6: Calculate the statistic from the sample of scores. Procedure 8-2 describes the method for calculating χ^2. The steps in calculating the value of χ^2 are shown in Figure 18-10. The value of χ^2 for the observed frequencies in Figure 18-10 is 5.00.

Step 7: Decide whether or not to reject the null hypothesis. The value of χ^2, 5.00, is in the rejection region shown in Figure 18-7. Therefore, we can conclude that the proportion of minorities majoring in the social sciences is significantly greater than the proportion found in the university as a whole.

Comparing the Two Types of χ^2 Tests

We have examined two types of hypothesis tests that use χ^2: the χ^2 test of association (sometimes called the test of independence) and the χ^2 test of goodness of fit. These two tests are closely related. We use the same general procedure to conduct both tests, as well as the same formula for χ^2. In these ways the two tests are similar.

There are differences between a test of association and a test of goodness of fit. One difference is that the test of association measures the relationship between two variables while the goodness of fit involves only one variable, as seen in our example of the proportion of minority and nonminority social science majors. Another difference between the two tests is that the test of association measures the deviation of the observed frequencies from what would be expected if there were no relationship between the two variables under study while the test of goodness of fit measures the deviation of the observed frequencies from a set of theoretical or a priori predictions.

Both χ^2 tests are tests of the strength of relationship. In the test of association, researchers are hoping to show that there is an association, or relationship, between the two variables tested. In the test of goodness of fit, researchers are trying to demonstrate a relationship between an empirical distribution and what that distribution would be, as predicted by some theory. Thus, the fundamental difference lies in how the researcher questions are posed, rather than in how the hypothesis tests are conducted.

1. Students sometimes have difficulties determining the expected frequencies when calculating χ^2. Follow the example shown in Figure 18-1 carefully. Remember that the row and column totals for the expected frequencies table must be the same as the row and column totals for the observed frequencies table.

2. The formula for χ^2 is different than the other formulas we have calculated thus far, in that the summation sign represents the final step in calculations. Thus, all calculations are done *before* that final summation.

3. When computing χ^2, remember to divide the squared difference found in the numerator by each observed frequency's own expected frequency. Do not use the same expected frequency in the divisor for all of the squared differences unless the expected frequencies are in fact all the same.

4. The value of χ^2 can vary from 0 to n. If you get a value greater than n or a negative value, there is an error somewhere in your calculations.

5. Remember that the degrees of freedom for χ^2 are not based on the number of subjects, as with other statistical tests, but rather are based on the number of cells in the contingency table. The degrees of freedom are equal to the number of columns, minus one, times the number of rows, minus one.

SUMMARY

▶ The statistic, χ^2, is a measure of the relationship between two nominal variables. It can also be used for ordinal, interval, or ratio variables by reducing those variables to a nominal scale of measurement.

▶ The data from which χ^2 is computed are generally displayed in contingency tables in which the values of one variable are listed in the row headings and the values of the other variable are listed in the column headings. The cells of the contingency table list the frequency of subjects with each combination of values of the two variables.

▶ The formula for χ^2 is based on finding the difference between the observed frequency and expected frequency for each combination of values of the two variables being tested. The observed frequency is the number of subjects who were observed to have that combination of values. The expected frequency is the number of subjects who would be expected to have that combination of values if there were no relationship between the two variables.

▶ χ^2 can be converted to a correlation coefficient, the ϕ' coefficient, through Cramer's equation. The ϕ' coefficient can have values from 0, indicating no correlation, to 1.00, indicating a perfect correlation.

▶ The χ^2 test of association measures the significance of the association, or correlation, between two variables.

▶ The test of association is also sometimes called a test of independence, in that it assesses whether there is an independent or dependent relationship between the variables under study.

▶ The χ^2 test of goodness of fit measures the degree to which a frequency distribution fits or matches the distribution predicted by some theory.

E X E R C I S E S

Conceptual Exercises

1. Define the following terms:

chi square (χ^2) marginal value

contingency table   *phi'* (ϕ') coefficient

cell   test of association

observed frequency   test of goodness of fit

expected frequency

2. The psychology majors at State University decided to measure whether their professors were biased in grading according to the sex of their students. They surveyed their fellow students and recorded the letter grades given to men and women in five professors' classes, with the following results. Examine the data in these tables without yet calculating the correlation.

Professor I	A	B	C	D	F
Women	16	20	14	0	0
Men	0	0	14	20	16

Professor II	A	B	C	D	F
Women	12	15	14	5	4
Men	4	5	14	15	12

Professor III	A	B	C	D	F
Women	8	10	14	10	8
Men	8	10	14	10	8

Professor IV	A	B	C	D	F
Women	4	5	14	15	12
Men	12	15	14	5	4

Professor V	A	B	C	D	F
Women	0	0	14	20	16
Men	16	20	14	0	0

A. In which of the groups does there appear to be a grading bias favoring women? Why?

B. In which of the groups does there appear to be a grading bias favoring men? Why?

C. In which of the groups does there appear to be no grading bias? Why?

D. Which of the groups appears to exhibit the strongest grading bias? Why?

3. Use χ^2 to analyze each of the sets of data shown in Exercise 2. Convert each value of χ^2 to a ϕ' coefficient.

A. Which of the groups has the lowest value of x^2? What does this indicate about the strength of the relationship in the group(s)?

B. Which of the groups has the highest value of x^2? What does this indicate about the strength of the relationship in the group(s)?

4. Suppose you have a group of 90 men and 60 women, for a total of 150 people. In the whole group, 50 people are registered as Democrats and 100 people are registered as Republicans.

A. Construct a 2 × 2 table with the cell frequencies of Democrat men, Democrat women, Republican men, and Republican women such that there is absolutely no relationship between sex and party affiliation.

B. Construct a 2 × 2 table with the cell frequencies of Democrat men, Democrat women, Republican men, and Republican women such that there is the strongest possible relationship between sex and party affiliation.

C. Calculate the value of x^2 and the ϕ' coefficient for each 2 × 2 table you constructed. Do these values confirm the strength of the relationships you predicted?

5. Identify the assumptions of a test of Pearson's x^2 test for association. For what types of data may the test be used? What are the consequences if any of the assumptions are violated?

Computational Exercises

6. Identify the critical values of x^2 for the following tests:

A. A study with a contingency table with three rows and four columns, $\alpha = .05$.

B. A study with a contingency table with one row and two columns, $\alpha = .01$.

C. A study with a contingency table with five rows and two columns, $\alpha = .05$.

D. A study with a contingency table with six rows and three columns, $\alpha = .01$.

7. There is a common belief that children who watch violence on TV are more aggressive than children who do not. Jackson tested this belief by observing a group of children and noting whether or not they watched violent TV programs and whether or not they were aggressive on the playground, with the results below. Conduct a x^2 test of association on the results of these observations, with a .05 significance level.

	Aggressive?	
Watch TV Violence?	Yes	No
Yes	41	9
No	17	33

8. Professors often have the suspicion that those who are regarded as easy graders receive higher student evaluations than those who are regarded as hard graders. Jay tested this suspicion by asking students to rate eighty professors as either easy or hard graders. He then verified whether those professors were above or below average on student evaluations, with the results below. Conduct a x^2 test of association on the results of these observations, with a .05 significance level.

	Type of Grader	
Student Evaluations	Easy	Hard
Above average	20	20
Below average	15	25

9. Jeanne compared the socio-economic level of Democrats and Republicans by surveying a random sample of registered voters. She believed that the results would show a difference in socio-economic level by political affiliation. She classified the voters into socio-economic levels according to type of job and income, with the results below. Conduct a χ^2 test of association on the results of these observations, with a .05 significance level.

Political Party	Lower	Low-Mid	High-Mid	Upper
Democrats	41	45	38	26
Republicans	9	15	42	34

10. Jan studied various ethnic groups' support for a proposed change in the immigration laws by asking 700 people if they were in favor of, opposed to, or neutral to the legislation, with the results below. Conduct a χ^2 test of association on the results of these observations, with a .05 significance level.

Ethnic Group	In Favor	Neutral	Opposed
Irish-American	20	30	50
African-American	90	70	40
Asian-American	20	10	20
Scandinavian-American	10	20	20
Hispanic-American	60	20	20

11. The psychology majors at State University decided to measure whether graduate student Julio was biased in grading according to the sex of his students. They surveyed their fellow students and recorded the letter grades given to men and women in five of graduate student Julio's lab sections, with the results below. Conduct a χ^2 test of association on the results of these observations, with a .05 significance level.

Sex	A	B	C	D	F
Women	12	15	14	5	4
Men	4	5	14	15	12

12. At State University over the past five years, 750 women and 1,250 men have applied for admission to the graduate program in psychology. Of those applicants, 25 women and 55 men were accepted into the program. Use the χ^2 test of goodness of fit to test whether the frequencies of men and women accepted into the graduate program differ significantly from the proportions who apply for admission, using a significance level of .05.

13. Jessica suspected that one of the psychology instructors at State University was more rigid in grading than the other instructors. For all of the courses in psychology the previous term, the faculty gave 15 percent A's, 25 percent B's, 30 percent C's, 20 percent D's, and 10 percent F's. Jessica surveyed 60 students who had received a grade from the suspected instructor the previous term, with the results below. Use the χ^2 test of goodness of fit to test whether the frequencies of grades given by this instructor differ from the percentages given by the psychology faculty as a whole, using a significance level of .05.

A, 6; B, 8; C, 18; D, 19; F, 9

14. Shown below is an observed distribution of 220 IQ scores, as well as the frequencies expected if this distribution is normal. Use the χ^2 test for goodness of fit to test whether the distribution is in fact normal in shape, with $\alpha = .05$.

IQ	Observed Frequency	Expected Frequency
135–139	5	3
130–134	7	4
125–129	9	9
120–124	13	13
115–119	15	21
110–114	22	27
105–109	27	30
100–104	30	31
95–99	28	28
90–94	25	22
85–89	20	15
80–84	14	9
75–79	5	8

Deciding Which Statistic to Use

19

Consider the Characteristics of the Distribution

    The Scale of Measurement

    The Shape of the Distribution

Consider the Purpose the Statistic Serves

    Describing a Distribution of Scores

Describing the Relationship between Variables and Making Predictions

Testing Hypotheses about the Relationship between Variables

▶ We have traveled far in exploring the wide variety of statistics that can be used to describe and to make inferences from scores collected in experimental research. This exploration is only the beginning, as the statistics that we examined are the most basic ones, the statistics that you are most likely to encounter in your professional career. Of course, when trying to decide which statistic to use, even the number of statistics that we have examined can be confusing. In this text, we have examined these statistics one at a time to understand what each measures and what information it can provide. In order to understand how to determine which statistic to use for a particular set of data, it would be helpful to examine the major categories of statistics and the purpose they serve.

Statistics fundamentally are tools that we can use to describe sets of scores and the relationship between them, as well as to validate using samples of scores as examples of the performance of entire populations. Remember that researchers collect scores in testing subjects in order to find evidence to support their arguments and test their theories. Without this evidence from research, we would have no way to judge the legitimacy of those arguments and theories. Statistics give us a way to talk about the results obtained from research, to describe those results, and to evaluate exactly what evidence the research provides.

Consider the Characteristics of the Distribution

The Scale of Measurement

When deciding which statistic to use, the first criterion to consider is the scale of measurement. In Chapter 2, we saw that a measurement scale is a system of numbers that we use to measure and record subjects' characteristics and performance. There are four measurement scales, each providing different information:

▶ In a **nominal scale of measurement**, numbers are used to name or categorize the values of a variable. Assigning code numbers to different ethnic groups is a nominal scale. Because there is no natural order in nominal variables (e.g.., one ethnic group is not higher or lower than another), the size or magnitude of the numbers in a nominal scale is meaningless. Nominal scales are qualitative, not quantitative.

▶ In an **ordinal scale of measurement**, numbers are used to represent the order of the values of a variable. Class ranks represent an ordinal scale, as do numbers assigned to letter grades. There is a natural order in ordinal variables (e.g.., a grade of A is higher than a grade of B), thus ordinal scales have magnitude and are quantitative. However, the size of the measurement unit is either unknown or is not equal across the entire scale, so that a larger number indicates more of the thing being measured but not precisely how much more.

▶ In an **interval scale of measurement**, the size of the unit of measurement is known and is equal across the entire scale. The Fahrenheit and Celsius temperature scales are interval scales, as are calendar years (ignoring the fact of leap years). For these scales, a precise unit of measurement is used throughout the scale, so that the difference between numbers tells us precisely how much more of the thing being measured the larger number represents.

▶ In a **ratio scale of measurement**, the value zero represents the absence of the thing being measured. The Kelvin temperature scale is a ratio scale, as 0°K represents the complete absence of heat. Many physical dimensions, such as height, weight, and speed, are measured on ratio scales, as are frequency counts, such as the number of questions correct. The number of trials to criterion, however, is an interval scale, as it is impossible for a subject to receive a score of zero.

In addition to distinguishing between these four measurement scales, we need to differentiate between continuous and discrete variables. For a **discrete variable**, the dimension being measured occurs in natural, indivisible units, such as the number of children or trials to criterion. For a **continuous variable**, such as time and speed, there are no natural units in the dimension being measured. In ordinary language, we generally think of discrete variables as being counted and continuous variables as being measured.

The Shape of the Distribution

In deciding which statistic to use, the second criterion to consider is the shape of the distribution. In particular, we need to distinguish between two different characteristics:

▶ **Symmetrical vs. unsymmetrical.** Symmetrical distributions are balanced around the center, so that the lower half is a mirror image of the upper half. Unsymmetrical distributions are skewed, so that the

scores in one half of the distribution are spread out farther from the
mean than they are in the other half.

▶ **Unimodal vs. multimodal.** The graph of a unimodal distribution
has only one peak, while the graph of a multimodal distribution has
two or more peaks. Multimodal distributions can occur when scores
from two distinct populations are combined, such as the heights of
adult men and women.

Consider the Purpose the Statistic Serves

In this text, we have seen that we can use statistics to serve many purposes.
Which statistic we use depends on the purpose we want it to serve: to describe

FIGURE 19-1   Describing a Distribution of Scores

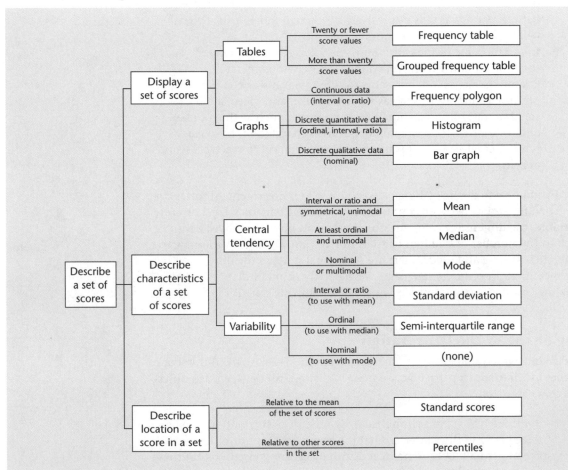

FIGURE 19-2 Describing the Correlation between Variables and Making Predictions

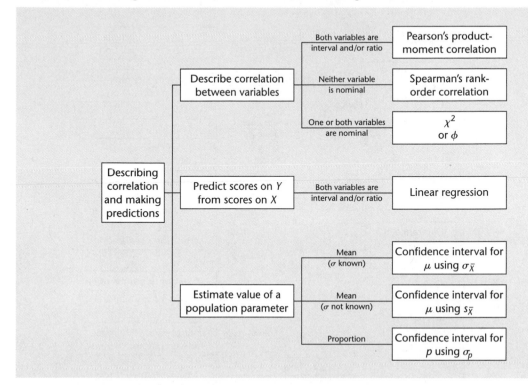

a set of scores, to describe the relationships between scores and make predictions, or to test hypotheses about the relationship between variables.

Describing a Distribution of Scores

We have explored a variety of ways to describe a distribution of scores. We can summarize the distribution by constructing a frequency table or graph. We can describe the center point of the distribution, using measures of central tendency, and the spread in the distribution, using measures of variability. We can also describe the location of individual scores in the distribution, using measures of relative standing. The criteria to use in deciding which of these descriptive statistics to use are summarized in Figure 19-1.

Describing the Relationship between Variables and Making Predictions

Descriptive statistics include the procedures we use to measure the correlation between two variables, as represented by two different distributions of scores.

FIGURE 19-3   Testing Hypotheses about the Relationship between Two Variables

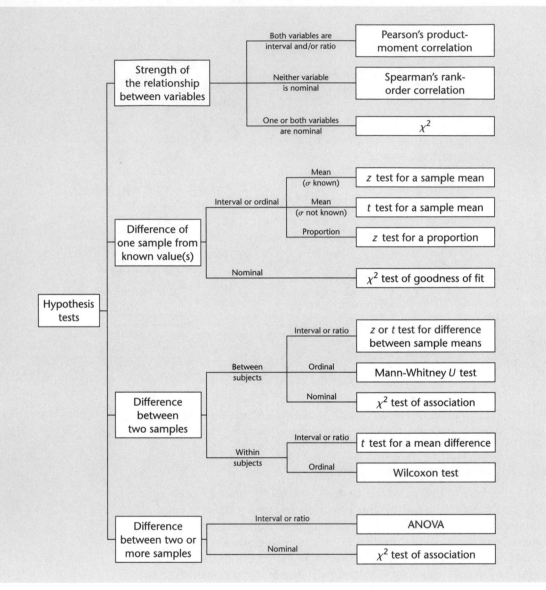

We can then use that correlation to predict the value of a subject's score on one of those variables from information about the subject's score on the other variable. Based on the concept of sampling distributions, we can also predict the value of a population parameter. The concept of sampling distributions is the link between descriptive and inferential statistics. Figure 19-2 shows the criteria to use in measuring correlation and in prediction.

Testing Hypotheses about the Relationship between Variables

All hypothesis tests use samples to make inferences about the relationship between variables in a population. Because scores and consequently samples of scores vary, samples are not exact replicas of the populations from which they were drawn. Hypothesis tests evaluate whether it is legitimate to infer from a relationship between variables in a sample that that relationship exists in the population.

There are two fundamental ways in which we can test the relationship between two variables. One is to test whether the correlation between the variables in a sample can be used to infer that there is a similar correlation in the population. The other method is to test whether a characteristic of a sample differs from known value(s) or between two or more samples. This method is based on the fact that if there is a relationship between two variables, then scores measured on one variable will differ between values of the other variable. Figure 19-3 summarizes the criteria to use in selecting a hypothesis test.

Appendix A:
Statistical Tables

Table A-1   Proportions of Area under the Normal Curve

Table A-2   Binomial Probabilities

Table A-3   Critical Values of t

Table A-4   Critical Values of F

Table A-5   Critical Values for Pearson's Product-Moment Correlation (r)

Table A-6   Critical Values for Spearman's Rank-Order Correlation (r_S)

Table A-7   Critical Values of χ^2

Table A-8   Critical Values of W for the Wilcoxon Test

Table A-9   Critical Values of the Mann-Whitney U

TABLE A-1 Proportions of Area under the Normal Curve

z			z			z		
0.00	.0000	.5000	0.45	.1736	.3264	0.90	.3159	.1841
0.01	.0040	.4960	0.46	.1772	.3228	0.91	.3186	.1814
0.02	.0080	.4920	0.47	.1808	.3192	0.92	.3212	.1788
0.03	.0120	.4880	0.48	.1844	.3156	0.93	.3238	.1762
0.04	.0160	.4840	0.49	.1879	.3121	0.94	.3264	.1736
0.05	.0199	.4801	0.50	.1915	.3085	0.95	.3289	.1711
0.06	.0239	.4761	0.51	.1950	.3050	0.96	.3315	.1685
0.07	.0279	.4721	0.52	.1985	.3015	0.97	.3340	.1660
0.08	.0319	.4681	0.53	.2019	.2981	0.98	.3365	.1635
0.09	.0359	.4641	0.54	.2054	.2946	0.99	.3389	.1611
0.10	.0398	.4602	0.55	.2088	.2912	1.00	.3413	.1587
0.11	.0438	.4562	0.56	.2123	.2877	1.01	.3438	.1562
0.12	.0478	.4522	0.57	.2157	.2843	1.02	.3461	.1539
0.13	.0517	.4483	0.58	.2190	.2810	1.03	.3485	.1515
0.14	.0557	.4443	0.59	.2224	.2776	1.04	.3508	.1492
0.15	.0596	.4404	0.60	.2257	.2743	1.05	.3531	.1469
0.16	.0636	.4364	0.61	.2291	.2709	1.06	.3554	.1446
0.17	.0675	.4325	0.62	.2324	.2676	1.07	.3577	.1423
0.18	.0714	.4286	0.63	.2357	.2643	1.08	.3599	.1401
0.19	.0753	.4247	0.64	.2389	.2611	1.09	.3621	.1379
0.20	.0793	.4207	0.65	.2422	.2578	1.10	.3643	.1357
0.21	.0832	.4168	0.66	.2454	.2546	1.11	.3665	.1335
0.22	.0871	.4129	0.67	.2486	.2514	1.12	.3686	.1314
0.23	.0910	.4090	0.68	.2517	.2483	1.13	.3708	.1292
0.24	.0948	.4052	0.69	.2549	.2451	1.14	.3729	.1271
0.25	.0987	.4013	0.70	.2580	.2420	1.15	.3749	.1251
0.26	.1026	.3974	0.71	.2611	.2389	1.16	.3770	.1230
0.27	.1064	.3936	0.72	.2642	.2358	1.17	.3790	.1210
0.28	.1103	.3897	0.73	.2673	.2327	1.18	.3810	.1190
0.29	.1141	.3859	0.74	.2704	.2296	1.19	.3830	.1170
0.30	.1179	.3821	0.75	.2734	.2266	1.20	.3849	.1151
0.31	.1217	.3783	0.76	.2764	.2236	1.21	.3869	.1131
0.32	.1255	.3745	0.77	.2794	.2206	1.22	.3888	.1112
0.33	.1293	.3707	0.78	.2823	.2177	1.23	.3907	.1093
0.34	.1331	.3669	0.79	.2852	.2148	1.24	.3925	.1075
0.35	.1368	.3632	0.80	.2881	.2119	1.25	.3944	.1056
0.36	.1406	.3594	0.81	.2910	.2090	1.26	.3962	.1038
0.37	.1443	.3557	0.82	.2939	.2061	1.27	.3980	.1020
0.38	.1480	.3520	0.83	.2967	.2033	1.28	.3997	.1003
0.39	.1517	.3483	0.84	.2995	.2005	1.29	.4015	.0985
0.40	.1554	.3446	0.85	.3023	.1977	1.30	.4032	.0968
0.41	.1591	.3409	0.86	.3051	.1949	1.31	.4049	.0951
0.42	.1628	.3372	0.87	.3078	.1922	1.32	.4066	.0934
0.43	.1664	.3336	0.88	.3106	.1894	1.33	.4082	.0918
0.44	.1700	.3300	0.89	.3133	.1867	1.34	.4099	.0901

Note: In each section, the first column lists the absolute value of z, the second column lists the proportion expected between that value of z and the mean, and the third column lists the proportion expected beyond that value of z, in the tail of the distribution.

TABLE A-1 *continued*

z			z			z		
1.35	.4115	.0885	1.80	.4641	.0359	2.25	.4878	.0122
1.36	.4131	.0869	1.81	.4649	.0351	2.26	.4881	.0119
1.37	.4147	.0853	1.82	.4656	.0344	2.27	.4884	.0116
1.38	.4162	.0838	1.83	.4664	.0336	2.28	.4887	.0113
1.39	.4177	.0823	1.84	.4671	.0329	2.29	.4890	.0110
1.40	.4192	.0808	1.85	.4678	.0322	2.30	.4893	.0107
1.41	.4207	.0793	1.86	.4686	.0314	2.31	.4896	.0104
1.42	.4222	.0778	1.87	.4693	.0307	2.32	.4898	.0102
1.43	.4236	.0764	1.88	.4699	.0301	2.33	.4901	.0099
1.44	.4251	.0749	1.89	.4706	.0294	2.34	.4904	.0096
1.45	.4265	.0735	1.90	.4713	.0287	2.35	.4906	.0094
1.46	.4279	.0721	1.91	.4719	.0281	2.36	.4909	.0091
1.47	.4292	.0708	1.92	.4726	.0274	2.37	.4911	.0089
1.48	.4306	.0694	1.93	.4732	.0268	2.38	.4913	.0087
1.49	.4319	.0681	1.94	.4738	.0262	2.39	.4916	.0084
1.50	.4332	.0668	1.95	.4744	.0256	2.40	.4918	.0082
1.51	.4345	.0655	1.96	.4750	.0250	2.41	.4920	.0080
1.52	.4357	.0643	1.97	.4756	.0244	2.42	.4922	.0078
1.53	.4370	.0630	1.98	.4761	.0239	2.43	.4925	.0075
1.54	.4382	.0618	1.99	.4767	.0233	2.44	.4927	.0073
1.55	.4394	.0606	2.00	.4772	.0228	2.45	.4929	.0071
1.56	.4406	.0594	2.01	.4778	.0222	2.46	.4931	.0069
1.57	.4418	.0582	2.02	.4783	.0217	2.47	.4932	.0068
1.58	.4429	.0571	2.03	.4788	.0212	2.48	.4934	.0066
1.59	.4441	.0559	2.04	.4793	.0207	2.49	.4936	.0064
1.60	.4452	.0548	2.05	.4798	.0202	2.50	.4938	.0062
1.61	.4463	.0537	2.06	.4803	.0197	2.51	.4940	.0060
1.62	.4474	.0526	2.07	.4808	.0192	2.52	.4941	.0059
1.63	.4484	.0516	2.08	.4812	.0188	2.53	.4943	.0057
1.64	.4495	.0505	2.09	.4817	.0183	2.54	.4945	.0055
1.65	.4505	.0495	2.10	.4821	.0179	2.55	.4946	.0054
1.66	.4515	.0485	2.11	.4826	.0174	2.56	.4948	.0052
1.67	.4525	.0475	2.12	.4830	.0170	2.57	.4949	.0051
1.68	.4535	.0465	2.13	.4834	.0166	2.58	.4951	.0049
1.69	.4545	.0455	2.14	.4838	.0162	2.59	.4952	.0048
1.70	.4554	.0446	2.15	.4842	.0158	2.60	.4953	.0047
1.71	.4564	.0436	2.16	.4846	.0154	2.61	.4955	.0045
1.72	.4573	.0427	2.17	.4850	.0150	2.62	.4956	.0044
1.73	.4582	.0418	2.18	.4854	.0146	2.63	.4957	.0043
1.74	.4591	.0409	2.19	.4857	.0143	2.64	.4959	.0041
1.75	.4599	.0401	2.20	.4861	.0139	2.65	.4960	.0040
1.76	.4608	.0392	2.21	.4864	.0136	2.66	.4961	.0039
1.77	.4616	.0384	2.22	.4868	.0132	2.67	.4962	.0038
1.78	.4625	.0375	2.23	.4871	.0129	2.68	.4963	.0037
1.79	.4633	.0367	2.24	.4875	.0125	2.69	.4964	.0036

(continues)

TABLE A-1   *continued*

z			z			z		
2.70	.4965	.0035	2.90	.4981	.0019	3.10	.4990	.0010
2.71	.4966	.0034	2.91	.4982	.0018	3.11	.4991	.0009
2.72	.4967	.0033	2.92	.4982	.0018	3.12	.4991	.0009
2.73	.4968	.0032	2.93	.4983	.0017	3.13	.4991	.0009
2.74	.4969	.0031	2.94	.4984	.0016	3.14	.4992	.0008
2.75	.4970	.0030	2.95	.4984	.0016	3.15	.4992	.0008
2.76	.4971	.0029	2.96	.4985	.0015	3.20	.4993	.0007
2.77	.4972	.0028	2.97	.4985	.0015	3.25	.4994	.0006
2.78	.4973	.0027	2.98	.4986	.0014	3.30	.4995	.0005
2.79	.4974	.0026	2.99	.4986	.0014	3.35	.4996	.0004
2.80	.4974	.0026	3.00	.4987	.0013	3.40	.4997	.0003
2.81	.4975	.0025	3.01	.4987	.0013	3.45	.4997	.0003
2.82	.4976	.0024	3.02	.4987	.0013	3.50	.4998	.0002
2.83	.4977	.0023	3.03	.4988	.0012	3.60	.4998	.0002
2.84	.4977	.0023	3.04	.4988	.0012	3.70	.4999	.0001
2.85	.4978	.0022	3.05	.4989	.0011	3.80	.4999	.0001
2.86	.4979	.0021	3.06	.4989	.0011	3.90	.49995	.00005
2.87	.4979	.0021	3.07	.4989	.0011	4.00	.49997	.00003
2.88	.4980	.0020	3.08	.4990	.0010	∞	.50000	.00000
2.89	.4981	.0019	3.09	.4990	.0010			

TABLE A-2 Binomial Probabilities

N	X	.05	.10	.15	.20	.25	.30	.35	.40	.45	.50
							p				
1	0	.9500	.9000	.8500	.8000	.7500	.7000	.6500	.6000	.5500	.5000
	1	.0500	.1000	.1500	.2000	.2500	.3000	.3500	.4000	.4500	.5000
2	0	.9025	.8100	.7225	.6400	.5625	.4900	.4225	.3600	.3025	.2500
	1	.0950	.1800	.2550	.3200	.3750	.4200	.4550	.4800	.4950	.5000
	2	.0025	.0100	.0225	.0400	.0625	.0900	.1225	.1600	.2025	.2500
3	0	.8574	.7290	.6141	.5120	.4219	.3430	.2746	.2160	.1664	.1250
	1	.1354	.2430	.3251	.3840	.4219	.4410	.4436	.4320	.4084	.3750
	2	.0071	.0270	.0574	.0960	.1406	.1890	.2389	.2880	.3341	.3750
	3	.0001	.0010	.0034	.0080	.0156	.0270	.0429	.0640	.0911	.1250
4	0	.8145	.6561	.5220	.4096	.3164	.2401	.1785	.1296	.0915	.0625
	1	.1715	.2916	.3685	.4096	.4219	.4116	.3845	.3456	.2995	.2500
	2	.0135	.0486	.0975	.1536	.2109	.2646	.3105	.3456	.3675	.3750
	3	.0005	.0036	.0115	.0256	.0469	.0756	.1115	.1536	.2005	.2500
	4	.0000	.0001	.0005	.0016	.0039	.0081	.0150	.0256	.0410	.0625
5	0	.7738	.5905	.4437	.3277	.2373	.1681	.1160	.0778	.0503	.0312
	1	.2036	.3280	.3915	.4096	.3955	.3602	.3124	.2592	.2059	.1562
	2	.0214	.0729	.1382	.2048	.2637	.3087	.3364	.3456	.3369	.3125
	3	.0011	.0081	.0244	.0512	.0879	.1323	.1811	.2304	.2757	.3125
	4	.0000	.0004	.0022	.0064	.0146	.0284	.0488	.0768	.1128	.1562
	5	.0000	.0000	.0001	.0003	.0010	.0024	.0053	.0102	.0185	.0312
6	0	.7351	.5314	.3771	.2621	.1780	.1176	.0754	.0467	.0277	.0156
	1	.2321	.3543	.3993	.3932	.3560	.3025	.2437	.1866	.1359	.0938
	2	.0305	.0984	.1762	.2458	.2966	.3241	.3280	.3110	.2780	.2344
	3	.0021	.0146	.0415	.0819	.1318	.1852	.2355	.2765	.3032	.3125
	4	.0001	.0012	.0055	.0154	.0330	.0595	.0951	.1382	.1861	.2344
	5	.0000	.0001	.0004	.0015	.0044	.0102	.0205	.0369	.0609	.0938
	6	.0000	.0000	.0000	.0001	.0002	.0007	.0018	.0041	.0083	.0156
7	0	.6983	.4783	.3206	.2097	.1335	.0824	.0490	.0280	.0152	.0078
	1	.2573	.3720	.3960	.3670	.3115	.2471	.1848	.1306	.0872	.0547
	2	.0406	.1240	.2097	.2753	.3115	.3177	.2985	.2613	.2140	.1641
	3	.0036	.0230	.0617	.1147	.1730	.2269	.2679	.2903	.2918	.2734
	4	.0002	.0026	.0109	.0287	.0577	.0972	.1442	.1935	.2388	.2734
	5	.0000	.0002	.0012	.0043	.0115	.0250	.0466	.0774	.1172	.1641
	6	.0000	.0000	.0001	.0004	.0013	.0036	.0084	.0172	.0320	.0547
	7	.0000	.0000	.0000	.0000	.0001	.0002	.0006	.0016	.0037	.0078
8	0	.6634	.4305	.2725	.1678	.1001	.0576	.0319	.0168	.0084	.0039
	1	.2793	.3826	.3847	.3355	.2670	.1977	.1373	.0896	.0548	.0312
	2	.0515	.1488	.2376	.2936	.3115	.2965	.2587	.2090	.1569	.1094
	3	.0054	.0331	.0839	.1468	.2076	.2541	.2786	.2787	.2568	.2188
	4	.0004	.0046	.0185	.0459	.0865	.1341	.1875	.2322	.2627	.2734
	5	.0000	.0004	.0026	.0092	.0231	.0467	.0808	.1239	.1719	.2188
	6	.0000	.0000	.0002	.0011	.0038	.0100	.0217	.0413	.0703	.1094
	7	.0000	.0000	.0000	.0001	.0004	.0012	.0033	.0079	.0164	.0312
	8	.0000	.0000	.0000	.0000	.0000	.0001	.0002	.0007	.0017	.0039

(continues)

TABLE A-2 *continued*

N	X	.05	.10	.15	.20	.25	.30	.35	.40	.45	.50
						p					
9	0	.6302	.3874	.2316	.1342	.0751	.0404	.0207	.0101	.0046	.0020
	1	.2985	.3874	.3679	.3020	.2253	.1556	.1004	.0605	.0339	.0176
	2	.0629	.1722	.2597	.3020	.3003	.2668	.2162	.1612	.1110	.0703
	3	.0077	.0446	.1069	.1762	.2336	.2668	.2716	.2508	.2119	.1641
	4	.0006	.0074	.0283	.0661	.1168	.1715	.2194	.2508	.2600	.2461
	5	.0000	.0008	.0050	.0165	.0389	.0735	.1181	.1672	.2128	.2461
	6	.0000	.0001	.0006	.0028	.0087	.0210	.0424	.0743	.1160	.1641
	7	.0000	.0000	.0000	.0003	.0012	.0039	.0098	.0212	.0407	.0703
	8	.0000	.0000	.0000	.0000	.0001	.0004	.0013	.0035	.0083	.0176
	9	.0000	.0000	.0000	.0000	.0000	.0000	.0001	.0003	.0008	.0020
10	0	.5987	.3487	.1969	.1074	.0563	.0282	.0135	.0060	.0025	.0010
	1	.3151	.3874	.3474	.2684	.1877	.1211	.0725	.0403	.0207	.0098
	2	.0746	.1937	.2759	.3020	.2816	.2335	.1757	.1209	.0763	.0439
	3	.0105	.0574	.1298	.2013	.2503	.2668	.2522	.2150	.1665	.1172
	4	.0010	.0112	.0401	.0881	.1460	.2001	.2377	.2508	.2384	.2051
	5	.0001	.0015	.0085	.0264	.0584	.1029	.1536	.2007	.2340	.2461
	6	.0000	.0001	.0012	.0055	.0162	.0368	.0689	.1115	.1596	.2051
	7	.0000	.0000	.0001	.0008	.0031	.0090	.0212	.0425	.0746	.1172
	8	.0000	.0000	.0000	.0001	.0004	.0014	.0043	.0106	.0229	.0439
	9	.0000	.0000	.0000	.0000	.0000	.0001	.0005	.0016	.0042	.0098
	10	.0000	.0000	.0000	.0000	.0000	.0000	.0000	.0001	.0003	.0010
11	0	.5688	.3138	.1673	.0859	.0422	.0198	.0088	.0036	.0014	.0005
	1	.3293	.3835	.3248	.2362	.1549	.0932	.0518	.0266	.0125	.0054
	2	.0867	.2131	.2866	.2953	.2581	.1998	.1395	.0887	.0513	.0269
	3	.0137	.0710	.1517	.2215	.2581	.2568	.2254	.1774	.1259	.0806
	4	.0014	.0158	.0536	.1107	.1721	.2201	.2428	.2365	.2060	.1611
	5	.0001	.0025	.0132	.0388	.0803	.1321	.1830	.2207	.2360	.2256
	6	.0000	.0003	.0023	.0097	.0268	.0566	.0985	.1471	.1931	.2256
	7	.0000	.0000	.0003	.0017	.0064	.0173	.0379	.0701	.1128	.1611
	8	.0000	.0000	.0000	.0002	.0011	.0037	.0102	.0234	.0462	.0806
	9	.0000	.0000	.0000	.0000	.0001	.0005	.0018	.0052	.0126	.0269
	10	.0000	.0000	.0000	.0000	.0000	.0000	.0002	.0007	.0021	.0054
	11	.0000	.0000	.0000	.0000	.0000	.0000	.0000	.0000	.0002	.0005
12	0	.5404	.2824	.1422	.0687	.0317	.0138	.0057	.0022	.0008	.0002
	1	.3413	.3766	.3012	.2062	.1267	.0712	.0368	.0174	.0075	.0029
	2	.0988	.2301	.2924	.2835	.2323	.1678	.1088	.0639	.0339	.0161
	3	.0173	.0852	.1720	.2362	.2581	.2397	.1954	.1419	.0923	.0537
	4	.0021	.0213	.0683	.1329	.1936	.2311	.2367	.2128	.1700	.1208
	5	.0002	.0038	.0193	.0532	.1032	.1585	.2039	.2270	.2225	.1934
	6	.0000	.0005	.0040	.0155	.0401	.0792	.1281	.1766	.2124	.2256
	7	.0000	.0000	.0006	.0033	.0115	.0291	.0591	.1009	.1489	.1934
	8	.0000	.0000	.0001	.0005	.0024	.0078	.0199	.0420	.0762	.1208
	9	.0000	.0000	.0000	.0001	.0004	.0015	.0048	.0125	.0277	.0537
	10	.0000	.0000	.0000	.0000	.0000	.0002	.0008	.0025	.0068	.0161
	11	.0000	.0000	.0000	.0000	.0000	.0000	.0001	.0003	.0010	.0029
	12	.0000	.0000	.0000	.0000	.0000	.0000	.0000	.0000	.0001	.0002

TABLE A-2 *continued*

N	X	.05	.10	.15	.20	.25	.30	.35	.40	.45	.50
13	0	.5133	.2542	.1209	.0550	.0238	.0097	.0037	.0013	.0004	.0001
	1	.3512	.3672	.2774	.1787	.1029	.0540	.0259	.0113	.0045	.0016
	2	.1109	.2448	.2937	.2680	.2059	.1388	.0836	.0453	.0220	.0095
	3	.0214	.0997	.1900	.2457	.2517	.2181	.1651	.1107	.0660	.0349
	4	.0028	.0277	.0838	.1535	.2097	.2337	.2222	.1845	.1350	.0873
	5	.0003	.0055	.0266	.0691	.1258	.1803	.2154	.2214	.1989	.1571
	6	.0000	.0008	.0063	.0230	.0559	.1030	.1546	.1968	.2169	.2095
	7	.0000	.0001	.0011	.0058	.0186	.0442	.0833	.1312	.1775	.2095
	8	.0000	.0000	.0001	.0011	.0047	.0142	.0336	.0656	.1089	.1571
	9	.0000	.0000	.0000	.0001	.0009	.0034	.0101	.0243	.0495	.0873
	10	.0000	.0000	.0000	.0000	.0001	.0006	.0022	.0065	.0162	.0349
	11	.0000	.0000	.0000	.0000	.0000	.0001	.0003	.0012	.0036	.0095
	12	.0000	.0000	.0000	.0000	.0000	.0000	.0000	.0001	.0005	.0016
	13	.0000	.0000	.0000	.0000	.0000	.0000	.0000	.0000	.0000	.0001
14	0	.4877	.2288	.1028	.0440	.0178	.0068	.0024	.0008	.0002	.0001
	1	.3593	.3559	.2539	.1539	.0832	.0407	.0181	.0073	.0027	.0009
	2	.1229	.2570	.2912	.2501	.1802	.1134	.0634	.0317	.0141	.0056
	3	.0259	.1142	.2056	.2501	.2402	.1943	.1366	.0845	.0462	.0222
	4	.0037	.0349	.0998	.1720	.2202	.2290	.2022	.1549	.1040	.0611
	5	.0004	.0078	.0352	.0860	.1468	.1963	.2178	.2066	.1701	.1222
	6	.0000	.0013	.0093	.0322	.0734	.1262	.1759	.2066	.2088	.1833
	7	.0000	.0002	.0019	.0092	.0280	.0618	.1082	.1574	.1952	.2095
	8	.0000	.0000	.0003	.0020	.0082	.0232	.0510	.0918	.1398	.1833
	9	.0000	.0000	.0000	.0003	.0018	.0066	.0183	.0408	.0762	.1222
	10	.0000	.0000	.0000	.0000	.0003	.0014	.0049	.0136	.0312	.0611
	11	.0000	.0000	.0000	.0000	.0000	.0002	.0010	.0033	.0093	.0222
	12	.0000	.0000	.0000	.0000	.0000	.0000	.0001	.0005	.0019	.0056
	13	.0000	.0000	.0000	.0000	.0000	.0000	.0000	.0001	.0002	.0009
	14	.0000	.0000	.0000	.0000	.0000	.0000	.0000	.0000	.0000	.0001
15	0	.4633	.2059	.0874	.0352	.0134	.0047	.0016	.0005	.0001	.0000
	1	.3658	.3432	.2312	.1319	.0668	.0305	.0126	.0047	.0016	.0005
	2	.1348	.2669	.2856	.2309	.1559	.0916	.0476	.0219	.0090	.0032
	3	.0307	.1285	.2184	.2501	.2252	.1700	.1110	.0634	.0318	.0139
	4	.0049	.0428	.1156	.1876	.2252	.2186	.1792	.1268	.0780	.0417
	5	.0006	.0105	.0449	.1032	.1651	.2061	.2123	.1859	.1404	.0916
	6	.0000	.0019	.0132	.0430	.0917	.1472	.1906	.2066	.1914	.1527
	7	.0000	.0003	.0030	.0138	.0393	.0811	.1319	.1771	.2013	.1964
	8	.0000	.0000	.0005	.0035	.0131	.0348	.0710	.1181	.1647	.1964
	9	.0000	.0000	.0001	.0007	.0034	.0116	.0298	.0612	.1048	.1527
	10	.0000	.0000	.0000	.0001	.0007	.0030	.0096	.0245	.0515	.0916
	11	.0000	.0000	.0000	.0000	.0001	.0006	.0024	.0074	.0191	.0417
	12	.0000	.0000	.0000	.0000	.0000	.0001	.0004	.0016	.0052	.0139
	13	.0000	.0000	.0000	.0000	.0000	.0000	.0001	.0003	.0010	.0032
	14	.0000	.0000	.0000	.0000	.0000	.0000	.0000	.0000	.0001	.0005
	15	.0000	.0000	.0000	.0000	.0000	.0000	.0000	.0000	.0000	.0000
16	0	.4401	.1853	.0743	.0281	.0100	.0033	.0010	.0003	.0001	.0000
	1	.3706	.3294	.2097	.1126	.0535	.0228	.0087	.0030	.0009	.0002

(continues)

TABLE A-2   *continued*

N	X	.05	.10	.15	.20	.25	.30	.35	.40	.45	.50
16	2	.1463	.2745	.2775	.2111	.1336	.0732	.0353	.0150	.0056	.0018
	3	.0359	.1423	.2285	.2463	.2079	.1465	.0888	.0468	.0215	.0085
	4	.0061	.0514	.1311	.2001	.2252	.2040	.1553	.1014	.0572	.0278
	5	.0008	.0137	.0555	.1201	.1802	.2099	.2008	.1623	.1123	.0667
	6	.0001	.0028	.0180	.0550	.1101	.1649	.1982	.1983	.1684	.1222
	7	.0000	.0004	.0045	.0197	.0524	.1010	.1524	.1889	.1969	.1746
	8	.0000	.0001	.0009	.0055	.0197	.0487	.0923	.1417	.1812	.1964
	9	.0000	.0000	.0001	.0012	.0058	.0185	.0442	.0840	.1318	.1746
	10	.0000	.0000	.0000	.0002	.0014	.0056	.0167	.0392	.0755	.1222
	11	.0000	.0000	.0000	.0000	.0002	.0013	.0049	.0142	.0337	.0667
	12	.0000	.0000	.0000	.0000	.0000	.0002	.0011	.0040	.0115	.0278
	13	.0000	.0000	.0000	.0000	.0000	.0000	.0002	.0008	.0029	.0085
	14	.0000	.0000	.0000	.0000	.0000	.0000	.0000	.0001	.0005	.0018
	15	.0000	.0000	.0000	.0000	.0000	.0000	.0000	.0000	.0001	.0002
	16	.0000	.0000	.0000	.0000	.0000	.0000	.0000	.0000	.0000	.0000
17	0	.4181	.1668	.0631	.0225	.0075	.0023	.0007	.0002	.0000	.0000
	1	.3741	.3150	.1893	.0957	.0426	.0169	.0060	.0019	.0005	.0001
	2	.1575	.2800	.2673	.1914	.1136	.0581	.0260	.0102	.0035	.0010
	3	.0415	.1556	.2359	.2393	.1893	.1245	.0701	.0341	.0144	.0052
	4	.0076	.0605	.1457	.2093	.2209	.1868	.1320	.0796	.0411	.0182
	5	.0010	.0175	.0668	.1361	.1914	.2081	.1849	.1379	.0875	.0472
	6	.0001	.0039	.0236	.0680	.1276	.1784	.1991	.1839	.1432	.0944
	7	.0000	.0007	.0065	.0267	.0668	.1201	.1685	.1927	.1841	.1484
	8	.0000	.0001	.0014	.0084	.0279	.0644	.1143	.1606	.1883	.1855
	9	.0000	.0000	.0003	.0021	.0093	.0276	.0611	.1070	.1540	.1855
	10	.0000	.0000	.0000	.0004	.0025	.0095	.0263	.0571	.1008	.1484
	11	.0000	.0000	.0000	.0001	.0005	.0026	.0090	.0242	.0525	.0944
	12	.0000	.0000	.0000	.0000	.0001	.0006	.0024	.0081	.0215	.0472
	13	.0000	.0000	.0000	.0000	.0000	.0001	.0005	.0021	.0068	.0182
	14	.0000	.0000	.0000	.0000	.0000	.0000	.0001	.0004	.0016	.0052
	15	.0000	.0000	.0000	.0000	.0000	.0000	.0000	.0001	.0003	.0010
	16	.0000	.0000	.0000	.0000	.0000	.0000	.0000	.0000	.0000	.0001
	17	.0000	.0000	.0000	.0000	.0000	.0000	.0000	.0000	.0000	.0000
18	0	.3972	.1501	.0536	.0180	.0056	.0016	.0004	.0001	.0000	.0000
	1	.3763	.3002	.1704	.0811	.0338	.0126	.0042	.0012	.0003	.0001
	2	.1683	.2835	.2556	.1723	.0958	.0458	.0190	.0069	.0022	.0006
	3	.0473	.1680	.2406	.2297	.1704	.1046	.0547	.0246	.0095	.0031
	4	.0093	.0700	.1592	.2153	.2130	.1681	.1104	.0614	.0291	.0117
	5	.0014	.0218	.0787	.1507	.1988	.2017	.1664	.1146	.0666	.0327
	6	.0002	.0052	.0301	.0816	.1436	.1873	.1941	.1655	.1181	.0708
	7	.0000	.0010	.0091	.0350	.0820	.1376	.1792	.1892	.1657	.1214
	8	.0000	.0002	.0022	.0120	.0376	.0811	.1327	.1734	.1864	.1669
	9	.0000	.0000	.0004	.0033	.0139	.0386	.0794	.1284	.1694	.1855
	10	.0000	.0000	.0001	.0008	.0042	.0149	.0385	.0771	.1248	.1669
	11	.0000	.0000	.0000	.0001	.0010	.0046	.0151	.0374	.0742	.1214
	12	.0000	.0000	.0000	.0000	.0002	.0012	.0047	.0145	.0354	.0708
	13	.0000	.0000	.0000	.0000	.0000	.0002	.0012	.0045	.0134	.0327
	14	.0000	.0000	.0000	.0000	.0000	.0000	.0002	.0011	.0039	.0117

TABLE A-2 *continued*

N	X					p					
		.05	.10	.15	.20	.25	.30	.35	.40	.45	.50
18	15	.0000	.0000	.0000	.0000	.0000	.0000	.0000	.0002	.0009	.0031
	16	.0000	.0000	.0000	.0000	.0000	.0000	.0000	.0000	.0001	.0006
	17	.0000	.0000	.0000	.0000	.0000	.0000	.0000	.0000	.0000	.0001
	18	.0000	.0000	.0000	.0000	.0000	.0000	.0000	.0000	.0000	.0000
19	0	.3774	.1351	.0456	.0144	.0042	.0011	.0003	.0001	.0000	.0000
	1	.3774	.2852	.1529	.0685	.0268	.0093	.0029	.0008	.0002	.0000
	2	.1787	.2852	.2428	.1540	.0803	.0358	.0138	.0046	.0013	.0003
	3	.0533	.1796	.2428	.2182	.1517	.0869	.0422	.0175	.0062	.0018
	4	.0112	.0798	.1714	.2182	.2023	.1491	.0909	.0467	.0203	.0074
	5	.0018	.0266	.0907	.1636	.2023	.1916	.1468	.0933	.0497	.0222
	6	.0002	.0069	.0374	.0955	.1574	.1916	.1844	.1451	.0949	.0518
	7	.0000	.0014	.0122	.0443	.0974	.1525	.1844	.1797	.1443	.0961
	8	.0000	.0002	.0032	.0166	.0487	.0981	.1489	.1797	.1771	.1442
	9	.0000	.0000	.0007	.0051	.0198	.0514	.0980	.1464	.1771	.1762
	10	.0000	.0000	.0001	.0013	.0066	.0220	.0528	.0976	.1449	.1762
	11	.0000	.0000	.0000	.0003	.0018	.0077	.0233	.0532	.0970	.1442
	12	.0000	.0000	.0000	.0000	.0004	.0022	.0083	.0237	.0529	.0961
	13	.0000	.0000	.0000	.0000	.0001	.0005	.0024	.0085	.0233	.0518
	14	.0000	.0000	.0000	.0000	.0000	.0001	.0006	.0024	.0082	.0222
	15	.0000	.0000	.0000	.0000	.0000	.0000	.0001	.0005	.0022	.0074
	16	.0000	.0000	.0000	.0000	.0000	.0000	.0000	.0001	.0005	.0018
	17	.0000	.0000	.0000	.0000	.0000	.0000	.0000	.0000	.0001	.0003
	18	.0000	.0000	.0000	.0000	.0000	.0000	.0000	.0000	.0000	.0000
	19	.0000	.0000	.0000	.0000	.0000	.0000	.0000	.0000	.0000	.0000
20	0	.3585	.1216	.0388	.0115	.0032	.0008	.0002	.0000	.0000	.0000
	1	.3774	.2702	.1368	.0576	.0211	.0068	.0020	.0005	.0001	.0000
	2	.1887	.2852	.2293	.1369	.0669	.0278	.0100	.0031	.0008	.0002
	3	.0596	.1901	.2428	.2054	.1339	.0716	.0323	.0123	.0040	.0011
	4	.0133	.0898	.1821	.2182	.1897	.1304	.0738	.0350	.0139	.0046
	5	.0022	.0319	.1028	.1746	.2023	.1789	.1272	.0746	.0365	.0148
	6	.0003	.0089	.0454	.1091	.1686	.1916	.1712	.1244	.0746	.0370
	7	.0000	.0020	.0160	.0545	.1124	.1643	.1844	.1659	.1221	.0739
	8	.0000	.0004	.0046	.0222	.0609	.1144	.1614	.1797	.1623	.1201
	9	.0000	.0001	.0011	.0074	.0271	.0654	.1158	.1597	.1771	.1602
	10	.0000	.0000	.0002	.0020	.0099	.0308	.0686	.1171	.1593	.1762
	11	.0000	.0000	.0000	.0005	.0030	.0120	.0336	.0710	.1185	.1602
	12	.0000	.0000	.0000	.0001	.0008	.0039	.0136	.0355	.0727	.1201
	13	.0000	.0000	.0000	.0000	.0002	.0010	.0045	.0146	.0366	.0739
	14	.0000	.0000	.0000	.0000	.0000	.0002	.0012	.0049	.0150	.0370
	15	.0000	.0000	.0000	.0000	.0000	.0000	.0003	.0013	.0049	.0148
	16	.0000	.0000	.0000	.0000	.0000	.0000	.0000	.0003	.0013	.0046
	17	.0000	.0000	.0000	.0000	.0000	.0000	.0000	.0000	.0002	.0011
	18	.0000	.0000	.0000	.0000	.0000	.0000	.0000	.0000	.0000	.0002
	19	.0000	.0000	.0000	.0000	.0000	.0000	.0000	.0000	.0000	.0000
	20	.0000	.0000	.0000	.0000	.0000	.0000	.0000	.0000	.0000	.0000

TABLE A-3 Critical Values of *t*

	Level of Significance for a Unidirectional (One-Tailed) Test					
	.10	.05	.025	.01	.005	.0005
	Level of Significance for a Bidirectional (Two-Tailed) Test					
df	.20	.10	.05	.02	.01	.001
1	3.078	6.314	12.706	31.821	63.657	636.619
2	1.886	2.920	4.303	6.965	9.925	31.598
3	1.638	2.353	3.182	4.541	5.8411	2.941
4	1.533	2.132	2.776	3.747	4.604	8.610
5	1.476	2.015	2.571	3.365	4.032	6.859
6	1.440	1.943	2.447	3.143	3.707	5.959
7	1.415	1.895	2.365	2.998	3.499	5.405
8	1.397	1.860	2.306	2.896	3.355	5.041
9	1.383	1.833	2.262	2.821	3.250	4.781
10	1.372	1.812	2.228	2.764	3.169	4.587
11	1.363	1.796	2.201	2.718	3.106	4.437
12	1.356	1.782	2.179	2.681	3.055	4.318
13	1.350	1.771	2.160	2.650	3.012	4.221
14	1.345	1.761	2.145	2.624	2.977	4.140
15	1.341	1.753	2.131	2.602	2.947	4.073
16	1.337	1.746	2.120	2.583	2.921	4.015
17	1.333	1.740	2.110	2.567	2.898	3.965
18	1.330	1.734	2.101	2.552	2.878	3.922
19	1.328	1.729	2.093	2.539	2.861	3.883
20	1.325	1.725	2.086	2.528	2.845	3.850
21	1.323	1.721	2.080	2.518	2.831	3.819
22	1.321	1.717	2.074	2.508	2.819	3.792
23	1.319	1.714	2.069	2.500	2.807	3.767
24	1.318	1.711	2.064	2.492	2.797	3.745
25	1.316	1.708	2.060	2.485	2.787	3.725
26	1.315	1.706	2.056	2.479	2.779	3.707
27	1.314	1.703	2.052	2.473	2.771	3.690
28	1.313	1.701	2.048	2.467	2.763	3.674
29	1.311	1.699	2.045	2.462	2.756	3.659
30	1.310	1.697	2.042	2.457	2.750	3.646
40	1.303	1.684	2.021	2.423	2.704	3.551
60	1.296	1.671	2.000	2.390	2.660	3.460
120	1.289	1.658	1.980	2.358	2.617	3.373
∞	1.282	1.645	1.960	2.326	2.576	3.291

Note: If the observed value of *t* is equal to or greater than the critical value listed for the appropriate degrees of freedom and level of significance, then reject H_0. Use the upper set of column headings for a unidirectional test and the lower set of column headings for a bidirectional test.

TABLE A-4 A. Critical Values of *F*, $\alpha = .05$

df_{within}	$df_{between}$											
	1	**2**	**3**	**4**	**5**	**6**	**7**	**8**	**9**	**10**	**11**	**12**
1	161	200	216	225	230	234	237	239	241	242	243	244
2	18.51	19.00	19.16	19.25	19.30	19.33	19.36	19.37	19.38	19.39	19.40	19.41
3	10.13	9.55	9.28	9.12	9.01	8.94	8.88	8.84	8.81	8.78	8.76	8.74
4	7.71	6.94	6.59	6.39	6.26	6.16	6.09	6.04	6.00	5.96	5.93	5.91
5	6.61	5.79	5.41	5.19	5.05	4.95	4.88	4.82	4.78	4.74	4.70	4.68
6	5.99	5.14	4.76	4.53	4.39	4.28	4.21	4.15	4.10	4.06	4.03	4.00
7	5.59	4.74	4.35	4.12	3.97	3.87	3.79	3.73	3.68	3.63	3.60	3.57
8	5.32	4.46	4.07	3.84	3.69	3.58	3.50	3.44	3.39	3.34	3.31	3.28
9	5.12	4.26	3.86	3.63	3.48	3.37	3.29	3.23	3.18	3.13	3.10	3.07
10	4.96	4.10	3.71	3.48	3.33	3.22	3.14	3.07	3.02	2.97	2.94	2.91
11	4.84	3.98	3.59	3.36	3.20	3.09	3.01	2.95	2.90	2.86	2.82	2.79
12	4.75	3.88	3.49	3.26	3.11	3.00	2.92	2.85	2.80	2.76	2.72	2.69
13	4.67	3.80	3.41	3.18	3.02	2.92	2.84	2.77	2.72	2.67	2.63	2.60
14	4.60	3.74	3.34	3.11	2.96	2.85	2.77	2.70	2.65	2.60	2.56	2.53
15	4.54	3.68	3.29	3.06	2.90	2.79	2.70	2.64	2.59	2.55	2.51	2.48
16	4.49	3.63	3.24	3.01	2.85	2.74	2.66	2.59	2.54	2.49	2.45	2.42
17	4.45	3.59	3.20	2.96	2.81	2.70	2.62	2.55	2.50	2.45	2.41	2.38
18	4.41	3.55	3.16	2.93	2.77	2.66	2.58	2.51	2.46	2.41	2.37	2.34
19	4.38	3.52	3.13	2.90	2.74	2.63	2.55	2.48	2.43	2.38	2.34	2.31
20	4.35	3.49	3.10	2.87	2.71	2.60	2.52	2.45	2.40	2.35	2.31	2.28
21	4.32	3.47	3.07	2.84	2.68	2.57	2.49	2.42	2.37	2.32	2.28	2.25
22	4.30	3.44	3.05	2.82	2.66	2.55	2.47	2.40	2.35	2.30	2.26	2.23
23	4.28	3.42	3.03	2.80	2.64	2.53	2.45	2.38	2.32	2.28	2.24	2.20
24	4.26	3.40	3.01	2.78	2.62	2.51	2.43	2.36	2.30	2.26	2.22	2.18
25	4.24	3.38	2.99	2.76	2.60	2.49	2.41	2.34	2.28	2.24	2.20	2.16
26	4.22	3.37	2.98	2.74	2.59	2.47	2.39	2.32	2.27	2.22	2.18	2.15
27	4.21	3.35	2.96	2.73	2.57	2.46	2.37	2.30	2.25	2.20	2.16	2.13
28	4.20	3.34	2.95	2.71	2.56	2.44	2.36	2.29	2.24	2.19	2.15	2.12
29	4.18	3.33	2.93	2.70	2.54	2.43	2.35	2.28	2.22	2.18	2.14	2.10
30	4.17	3.32	2.92	2.69	2.53	2.42	2.34	2.27	2.21	2.16	2.12	2.09
40	4.08	3.23	2.84	2.61	2.45	2.34	2.25	2.18	2.12	2.07	2.04	2.00
50	4.03	3.18	2.79	2.56	2.40	2.29	2.20	2.13	2.07	2.02	1.98	1.95
60	4.00	3.15	2.76	2.52	2.37	2.25	2.17	2.10	2.04	1.99	1.95	1.92
70	3.98	3.13	2.74	2.50	2.35	2.23	2.14	2.07	2.01	1.97	1.93	1.89
80	3.96	3.11	2.72	2.48	2.33	2.21	2.12	2.05	1.99	1.95	1.91	1.88
100	3.94	3.09	2.70	2.46	2.30	2.19	2.10	2.03	1.97	1.92	1.88	1.85
125	3.92	3.07	2.68	2.44	2.29	2.17	2.08	2.01	1.95	1.90	1.86	1.83
200	3.89	3.04	2.65	2.41	2.26	2.14	2.05	1.98	1.92	1.87	1.83	1.80
1,000	3.85	3.00	2.61	2.38	2.22	2.10	2.02	1.95	1.89	1.84	1.80	1.76
∞	3.84	2.99	2.60	2.37	2.21	2.09	2.01	1.94	1.88	1.83	1.79	1.75

(continues)

Note: If the observed value of *F* is equal to or greater than the critical value listed for the appropriate degrees of freedom and level of significance, then reject H_0. The $df_{between}$ is the degrees of freedom for the numerator of *F*. The df_{within} is the degrees of freedom for the denominator of *F*.

TABLE A-4   *continued*

df_{within}	14	16	20	24	30	40	50	75	100	200	500	∞
1	245	246	248	249	250	251	252	253	253	254	254	254
2	19.42	19.43	19.43	19.44	19.46	19.47	19.47	19.48	19.49	19.49	19.50	19.50
3	8.71	8.69	8.69	8.64	8.62	8.60	8.58	8.47	8.56	8.54	8.54	8.53
4	5.87	5.84	5.84	5.77	5.74	5.71	5.70	5.68	5.66	5.65	5.64	5.63
5	4.64	4.60	4.60	4.53	4.50	4.46	4.44	4.42	4.40	4.38	4.37	4.36
6	3.96	3.92	3.92	3.84	3.81	3.77	3.75	3.72	3.71	3.69	3.68	3.67
7	3.52	3.49	3.49	3.41	3.38	3.34	3.32	3.29	3.28	3.25	3.24	3.23
8	3.23	3.20	3.20	3.12	3.08	3.05	3.03	3.00	2.98	2.96	2.94	2.93
9	3.02	2.98	2.98	2.90	2.86	2.82	2.80	2.77	2.76	2.73	2.72	2.71
10	2.86	2.82	2.82	2.74	2.70	2.67	2.64	2.61	2.59	2.56	2.55	2.54
11	2.74	2.70	2.70	2.61	2.57	2.53	2.50	2.47	2.45	2.42	2.41	2.40
12	2.64	2.60	2.60	2.50	2.46	2.42	2.40	2.36	2.35	2.32	2.31	2.30
13	2.55	2.51	2.51	2.42	2.38	2.34	2.32	2.28	2.26	2.24	2.22	2.21
14	2.48	2.44	2.39	2.35	2.31	2.27	2.24	2.21	2.19	2.16	2.14	2.13
15	2.43	2.39	2.33	2.29	2.25	2.21	2.18	2.15	2.12	2.10	2.08	2.07
16	2.37	2.33	2.28	2.24	2.20	2.16	2.13	2.09	2.07	2.04	2.02	2.01
17	2.33	2.29	2.23	2.19	2.15	2.11	2.08	2.04	2.02	1.99	1.97	1.96
18	2.29	2.25	2.19	2.15	2.11	2.07	2.04	2.00	1.98	1.95	1.93	1.92
19	2.26	2.21	2.15	2.11	2.07	2.02	2.00	1.96	1.94	1.91	1.90	1.88
20	2.23	2.18	2.12	2.08	2.04	1.99	1.96	1.92	1.90	1.87	1.85	1.84
21	2.20	2.15	2.09	2.05	2.00	1.96	1.93	1.89	1.87	1.84	1.82	1.81
22	2.18	2.13	2.07	2.03	1.98	1.93	1.91	1.87	1.84	1.81	1.80	1.78
23	2.14	2.10	2.04	2.00	1.96	1.91	1.88	1.84	1.82	1.79	1.77	1.76
24	2.13	2.09	2.02	1.98	1.94	1.89	1.86	1.82	1.80	1.76	1.74	1.73
25	2.11	2.06	2.00	1.96	1.92	1.87	1.84	1.80	1.77	1.74	1.72	1.71
26	2.10	2.05	1.99	1.95	1.90	1.85	1.82	1.78	1.76	1.72	1.70	1.69
27	2.08	2.03	1.97	1.93	1.88	1.84	1.80	1.76	1.74	1.71	1.68	1.67
28	2.06	2.02	1.96	1.91	1.87	1.81	1.78	1.75	1.72	1.69	1.67	1.65
29	2.05	2.00	1.94	1.90	1.85	1.80	1.77	1.73	1.71	1.68	1.65	1.64
30	2.04	1.99	1.93	1.89	1.84	1.79	1.76	1.72	1.69	1.66	1.64	1.62
40	1.95	1.90	1.84	1.79	1.74	1.69	1.66	1.61	1.59	1.55	1.53	1.51
50	1.90	1.85	1.78	1.74	1.69	1.63	1.60	1.55	1.52	1.48	1.46	1.44
60	1.86	1.81	1.75	1.70	1.65	1.59	1.56	1.50	1.48	1.44	1.41	1.39
70	1.84	1.79	1.72	1.67	1.62	1.56	1.53	1.47	1.45	1.40	1.37	1.35
80	1.82	1.77	1.70	1.65	1.60	1.54	1.51	1.45	1.42	1.38	1.35	1.32
100	1.79	1.75	1.68	1.63	1.57	1.51	1.48	1.42	1.39	1.34	1.30	1.28
125	1.77	1.72	1.65	1.60	1.55	1.49	1.45	1.39	1.36	1.31	1.27	1.25
200	1.74	1.69	1.62	1.57	1.52	1.45	1.42	1.35	1.32	1.26	1.22	1.19
1,000	1.70	1.65	1.58	1.53	1.47	1.41	1.36	1.30	1.26	1.19	1.13	1.08
∞	1.69	1.64	1.57	1.52	1.46	1.40	1.35	1.28	1.24	1.17	1.11	1.00

$df_{between}$

TABLE A-4 *continued* B. Critical Values of F, $\alpha = .01$

df_{within}	$df_{between}$											
	1	2	3	4	5	6	7	8	9	10	11	12
1	4,052	4,999	5,403	5,625	5,764	5,859	5,928	5,981	6,022	6,056	6,082	6,106
2	98.49	99.00	99.17	99.25	99.30	99.33	99.36	99.37	99.39	99.40	99.41	99.42
3	34.12	30.82	29.46	28.71	28.24	27.91	27.67	27.49	27.34	27.23	27.13	27.05
4	21.20	18.00	16.69	15.98	15.52	15.21	14.98	14.80	14.66	14.54	14.45	14.37
5	16.26	13.27	12.06	11.39	10.97	10.67	10.45	10.29	10.15	10.05	9.96	9.89
6	13.74	10.92	9.78	9.15	8.75	8.47	8.26	8.10	7.98	7.87	7.79	7.72
7	12.25	9.55	8.45	7.85	7.46	7.19	7.00	6.84	6.71	6.62	6.54	6.47
8	11.26	8.66	7.59	7.01	6.63	6.37	6.19	6.03	5.91	5.82	5.74	5.67
9	10.56	8.02	6.99	6.42	6.06	5.80	5.62	5.47	5.35	5.26	5.18	5.11
10	10.04	7.56	6.55	5.99	5.64	5.39	5.21	5.06	4.95	4.85	4.78	4.71
11	9.65	7.20	6.22	5.67	5.32	5.07	4.88	4.74	4.63	4.54	4.46	4.29
12	9.33	6.93	5.95	5.41	5.06	4.82	4.65	4.50	4.39	4.30	4.22	4.05
13	9.07	6.70	5.74	5.20	4.86	4.62	4.44	4.30	4.19	4.10	4.02	3.85
14	8.86	6.51	5.56	5.03	4.69	4.46	4.28	4.14	4.03	3.94	3.86	3.80
15	8.68	6.36	5.42	4.89	4.56	4.32	4.14	4.00	3.89	3.80	3.72	3.67
16	8.53	6.23	5.29	4.77	4.44	4.20	4.03	3.89	3.78	3.69	3.61	3.55
17	8.40	6.11	5.18	4.67	4.34	4.10	.93	3.79	3.68	3.59	3.52	3.45
18	8.28	6.01	5.09	4.58	4.25	4.01	3.85	3.71	3.60	3.51	3.44	3.37
19	8.18	5.93	5.01	4.50	4.17	3.94	3.77	3.63	3.52	3.43	3.36	3.30
20	8.10	5.85	4.94	4.43	4.10	3.87	3.71	3.56	3.45	3.37	3.30	3.23
21	8.02	5.78	4.87	4.37	4.04	3.81	3.65	3.51	3.40	3.31	3.24	3.17
22	7.94	5.72	4.82	4.31	3.99	3.76	3.59	3.45	3.35	3.26	3.18	3.12
23	7.88	5.66	4.76	4.26	3.94	3.71	3.54	3.41	3.30	3.21	3.14	3.07
24	7.82	5.61	4.72	4.22	3.90	3.67	3.50	3.36	3.25	3.17	3.09	3.03
25	7.77	5.57	4.68	4.18	3.86	3.63	3.46	3.32	3.21	3.13	3.05	2.99
26	7.72	5.53	4.64	4.14	3.82	3.59	3.42	3.29	3.17	3.09	3.02	2.96
27	7.68	5.49	4.60	4.11	3.79	3.56	3.39	3.26	3.14	3.06	2.98	2.93
28	7.64	5.45	4.57	4.07	3.76	3.53	3.36	3.23	3.11	3.03	2.95	2.90
29	7.60	5.42	4.54	4.04	3.73	3.50	3.33	3.20	3.08	3.00	2.92	2.87
30	7.56	5.39	4.51	4.02	3.70	3.47	3.30	3.17	3.06	2.98	2.90	2.84
40	7.31	5.18	4.31	3.83	3.51	3.29	3.12	2.99	2.88	2.80	2.73	2.66
50	7.17	5.06	4.20	3.72	3.41	3.18	3.02	2.88	2.78	2.70	2.62	2.56
60	7.08	4.09	4.13	3.65	3.34	3.12	2.95	2.82	2.72	2.63	2.56	2.50
70	7.01	4.92	4.08	3.60	3.29	3.07	2.91	2.77	2.67	2.59	2.51	2.45
80	6.96	4.88	4.04	3.56	3.25	3.04	2.87	2.74	2.64	2.55	2.48	2.41
100	6.90	4.82	3.98	3.51	3.20	2.99	2.82	2.69	2.59	2.51	2.43	2.36
125	6.84	4.78	3.94	3.47	3.17	2.95	2.79	2.65	2.56	2.47	2.40	2.33
200	6.76	4.71	3.88	3.41	3.11	2.90	2.73	2.60	2.50	2.41	2.34	2.28
1,000	6.66	4.62	3.80	3.34	3.04	2.82	2.66	2.53	2.43	2.34	2.26	2.20
∞	6.64	4.60	3.78	3.32	3.02	2.80	2.64	2.51	2.41	2.32	2.24	2.18

(*continues*)

TABLE A-4　*continued*

df_{within}	14	16	20	24	30	40	50	75	100	200	500	∞
1	6,142	6,169	6,208	6,234	6,261	6,286	6,302	6,323	6,334	6,352	6,361	6,366
2	99.43	99.44	99.45	99.46	99.47	99.48	99.48	99.49	99.49	99.49	99.50	99.50
3	26.92	26.83	26.69	26.60	26.50	26.41	26.35	26.27	26.23	26.18	26.14	26.12
4	14.24	14.15	14.02	13.93	13.83	13.74	13.69	13.61	13.57	13.52	13.48	13.46
5	9.77	9.68	9.55	9.47	9.38	9.29	9.24	9.17	9.13	9.07	9.04	9.02
6	7.60	7.52	7.39	7.31	7.23	7.14	7.09	7.02	6.99	6.94	6.90	6.88
7	6.35	6.27	6.15	6.07	5.98	5.90	5.85	5.78	5.75	5.70	5.67	5.65
8	5.56	5.48	5.36	5.28	5.20	5.11	5.06	5.00	4.96	4.91	4.88	4.86
9	5.00	4.92	4.80	4.73	4.64	4.56	4.51	4.45	4.41	4.36	4.33	4.31
10	4.60	4.52	4.41	4.33	4.25	4.17	4.12	4.05	4.01	3.96	3.93	3.91
11	4.29	4.21	4.10	4.02	3.94	3.86	3.80	3.74	3.70	3.66	3.62	3.60
12	4.05	3.98	3.86	3.78	3.70	3.61	3.56	3.49	3.46	3.41	3.38	3.36
13	3.85	3.78	3.67	3.59	3.51	3.42	3.37	3.30	3.27	3.21	3.18	3.16
14	3.70	3.62	3.51	3.43	3.34	3.26	3.21	3.14	3.11	3.06	3.02	3.00
15	3.56	3.48	3.36	3.29	3.20	3.12	3.07	3.00	2.97	2.92	2.89	2.87
16	3.45	3.37	3.25	3.18	3.10	3.01	2.96	2.98	2.86	2.80	2.77	2.75
17	3.35	3.27	3.16	3.08	3.00	2.92	2.86	2.79	2.76	2.70	2.67	2.65
18	3.27	3.19	3.07	3.00	2.91	2.83	2.78	2.71	2.68	2.62	2.59	2.57
19	3.19	3.12	3.00	2.92	2.84	2.76	2.70	2.63	2.60	2.54	2.51	2.49
20	3.13	3.05	2.94	2.86	2.77	2.69	2.63	2.56	2.53	2.47	2.44	2.42
21	3.07	2.99	2.88	2.80	2.72	2.63	2.58	2.51	2.47	2.42	2.38	2.36
22	3.02	2.94	2.83	2.75	2.67	2.58	2.53	2.46	2.42	2.37	2.33	2.31
23	2.97	2.89	2.78	2.70	2.62	2.53	2.48	2.41	2.37	2.32	2.28	2.26
24	2.93	2.85	2.74	2.66	2.58	2.49	2.44	2.36	2.33	2.27	2.23	2.21
25	2.89	2.81	2.70	2.62	2.54	2.45	2.40	2.32	2.29	2.23	2.19	2.17
26	2.86	2.77	2.66	2.58	2.50	2.41	2.36	2.28	2.25	2.19	2.15	2.13
27	2.83	2.74	2.63	2.55	2.47	2.38	2.33	2.25	2.21	2.16	2.12	2.10
28	2.80	2.71	2.60	2.52	2.44	2.35	2.30	2.22	2.18	2.13	2.09	2.06
29	2.77	2.68	2.57	2.49	2.41	2.32	2.27	2.19	2.15	2.10	2.06	2.03
30	2.74	2.66	2.55	2.47	2.38	2.29	2.24	2.16	2.13	2.07	2.03	2.01
40	2.56	2.49	2.37	2.29	2.20	2.11	2.05	1.97	1.94	1.88	1.84	1.81
50	2.46	2.39	2.26	2.18	2.10	2.00	1.94	1.86	1.82	1.76	1.71	1.68
60	2.40	2.32	2.20	2.12	2.03	1.93	1.87	1.79	1.74	1.68	1.63	1.60
70	2.35	2.28	2.15	2.07	1.98	1.88	1.82	1.74	1.69	1.62	1.56	1.53
80	2.32	2.24	2.11	2.03	1.94	1.84	1.78	1.70	1.65	1.57	1.52	1.49
100	2.26	2.19	2.06	1.98	1.89	1.79	1.73	1.64	1.59	1.51	1.46	1.43
125	2.23	2.15	2.03	1.94	1.85	1.75	1.68	1.59	1.54	1.46	1.40	1.37
200	2.17	2.09	1.97	1.88	1.79	1.69	1.62	1.53	1.48	1.39	1.33	1.28
1,000	2.09	2.01	1.89	1.81	1.71	1.51	1.54	1.44	1.38	1.28	1.19	1.11
∞	2.07	1.99	1.87	1.79	1.69	1.59	1.52	1.41	1.36	1.25	1.15	1.00

TABLE A-5 Critical Values for Pearson's Product-Moment Correlation (*r*)

	Level of Significance for a Unidirectional (One-Tailed) Test				
	.05	.025	.01	.005	.0005
	Level of Significance of a Bidirectional (Two-Tailed) Test				
df = *n* − 2	.10	.05	.02	.01	.001
1	.9877	.9969	.9995	.9999	1.0000
2	.9000	.9500	.9800	.9900	.9990
3	.8054	.8783	.9343	.9587	.9912
4	.7293	.8114	.8822	.9172	.9741
5	.6694	.7545	.8329	.8745	.9507
6	.6215	.7067	.7887	.8343	.9249
7	.5822	.6664	.7498	.7977	.8982
8	.5494	.6319	.7155	.7646	.8721
9	.5214	.6021	.6851	.7348	.8471
10	.4973	.5760	.6581	.7079	.8233
11	.4762	.5529	.6339	.6835	.8010
12	.4575	.5324	.6120	.6614	.7800
13	.4409	.5139	.5923	.6411	.7603
14	.4259	.4973	.5742	.6226	.7420
15	.4124	.4821	.5577	.6055	.7246
16	.4000	.4683	.5425	.5897	.7084
17	.3887	.4555	.5285	.5751	.6932
18	.3783	.4438	.5155	.5614	.6787
19	.3687	.4329	.5034	.5487	.6652
20	.3598	.4227	.4921	.5368	.6524
25	.3233	.3809	.4451	.4869	.5974
30	.2960	.3494	.4093	.4487	.5541
35	.2746	.3246	.3810	.4182	.5189
40	.2573	.3044	.3578	.3932	.4896
45	.2428	.2875	.3384	.3721	.4648
50	.2306	.2732	.3218	.3541	.4433
60	.2108	.2500	.2948	.3248	.4078
70	.1954	.2319	.2737	.3017	.3799
80	.1829	.2172	.2565	.2830	.3568
90	.1726	.2050	.2422	.2673	.3375
100	.1638	.1946	.2301	.2540	.3211

Note: If the observed value of *r* is equal to or greater than the critical value listed for the appropriate degrees of freedom and level of significance, then reject H_0. Use the upper set of column headings for a unidirectional test and the lower set of column headings for a bidirectional test.

TABLE A-6   Critical Values for Spearman's Rank-Order Correlation (r_S)

	Level of Significance for a Unidirectional (One-Tailed) Test			
	.05	**.025**	**.005**	**.001**
	Level of Significance of a Bidirectional (Two-Tailed) Test			
n	**.10**	**.05**	**.01**	**.002**
5	.900	1.000		
6	.829	.886	1.000	
7	.715	.786	.929	1.000
8	.620	.715	.881	.953
9	.600	.700	.834	.917
10	.564	.649	.794	.879
11	.537	.619	.764	.855
12	.504	.588	.735	.826
13	.484	.561	.704	.797
14	.464	.539	.680	.772
15	.447	.522	.658	.750
16	.430	.503	.636	.730
17	.415	.488	.618	.711
18	.402	.474	.600	.693
19	.392	.460	.585	.676
20	.381	.447	.570	.661
21	.371	.437	.556	.647
22	.361	.426	.544	.633
23	.353	.417	.532	.620
24	.345	.407	.521	.608
25	.337	.399	.511	.597
26	.331	.391	.501	.587
27	.325	.383	.493	.577
28	.319	.376	.484	.567
29	.312	.369	.475	.558
30	.307	.363	.467	.549

Note: If the observed value of r_S is equal to or greater than the critical value listed for the number of pairs of scores, *n,* and the selected level of significance, then reject H_0. Use the upper set of column headings for a unidirectional test and the lower set of column headings for a bidirectional test.

TABLE A-7   Critical Values of χ^2

			Level of Significance		
df	.10	.05	.02	.01	.001
1	2.71	3.84	5.41	6.64	10.83
2	4.60	5.99	7.82	9.21	13.82
3	6.25	7.82	9.84	11.34	16.27
4	7.78	9.49	11.67	13.28	18.46
5	9.24	11.07	13.39	15.09	20.52
6	10.64	12.59	15.03	16.81	22.46
7	12.02	14.07	16.62	18.48	24.32
8	13.36	15.51	18.17	20.09	26.12
9	14.68	16.92	19.68	21.67	27.88
10	15.99	18.31	21.16	23.21	29.59
11	17.28	19.68	22.62	24.72	31.26
12	18.55	21.03	24.05	26.22	32.91
13	19.81	22.36	25.47	27.69	34.53
14	21.06	23.68	26.87	29.14	36.12
15	22.31	25.00	28.26	30.58	37.70
16	23.54	26.30	29.63	32.00	39.29
17	24.77	27.59	31.00	33.41	40.75
18	25.99	28.87	32.35	34.80	42.31
19	27.20	30.14	33.69	36.19	43.82
20	28.41	31.41	35.02	37.57	45.32
21	29.62	32.67	36.34	38.93	46.80
22	30.81	33.92	37.66	40.29	48.27
23	32.01	35.17	38.97	41.64	49.73
24	33.20	36.42	40.27	42.98	51.18
25	34.38	37.65	41.57	44.31	52.62
26	35.56	38.88	42.86	45.64	54.05
27	36.74	40.11	44.14	46.96	55.48
28	37.92	41.34	45.42	48.28	56.89
29	39.09	42.69	46.69	49.59	58.30
30	40.26	43.77	47.96	50.89	59.70
32	42.59	46.19	50.49	53.49	62.49
34	44.90	48.60	53.00	56.06	65.25
36	47.21	51.00	55.49	58.62	67.99
38	49.51	53.38	57.97	61.16	70.70
40	51.81	55.76	60.44	63.69	73.40
44	56.37	60.48	65.34	68.71	78.75
48	60.91	65.17	70.20	73.68	84.04
52	65.42	69.83	75.02	78.62	89.27
56	69.92	74.47	79.82	83.51	94.46
60	74.40	79.08	84.58	88.38	99.61

Note: If the observed value of χ^2 is equal to or greater than the critical value listed for the appropriate degrees of freedom and level of significance, then reject H_0. If both *r* and *c* are at least 2, then $df = (r - 1)(c - 1)$, where *r* is the number of rows and *c* is the number of columns. If *r* is 1, then $df = (c - 1)$. If *c* is 1, then $df = (r - 1)$.

TABLE A-8 Critical Values of *W* for the Wilcoxon Test

	Level of Significance for a One-Tailed Test					Level of Significance for a One-Tailed Test			
	.05	.025	.01	.005		.05	.025	.01	.005
	Level of Significance for a Two-Tailed Test					Level of Significance for a Two-Tailed Test			
n	.10	.05	.02	.01	*n*	.10	.05	.02	.01
5	0	—	—	—	28	130	116	101	91
6	2	0	—	—	29	140	126	110	100
7	3	2	0	—	30	151	137	120	109
8	5	3	1	0	31	163	147	130	118
9	8	5	3	1	32	175	159	140	128
10	10	8	5	3	33	187	170	151	138
11	13	10	7	5	34	200	182	162	148
12	17	13	9	7	35	213	195	173	159
13	21	17	12	9	36	227	208	185	171
14	25	21	15	12	37	241	221	198	182
15	30	25	19	15	38	256	235	211	194
16	35	29	23	19	39	271	249	224	207
17	41	34	27	23	40	286	264	238	220
18	47	40	32	27	41	302	279	252	233
19	53	46	37	32	42	319	294	266	247
20	60	52	43	37	43	336	310	281	261
21	67	58	49	42	44	353	327	296	276
22	75	65	55	48	45	371	343	312	291
23	83	73	62	54	46	389	361	328	307
24	91	81	69	61	47	407	378	345	322
25	100	89	76	68	48	426	396	362	339
26	110	98	84	75	49	446	415	379	355
27	119	107	92	83	50	466	434	397	373

Note: For a given *n* (the number of pairs of scores, minus the pairs having zero differences), if the observed value is less than or equal to the value in the table for the selected level of significance, reject H_0. Use the upper set of column headings for a unidirectional test and the lower set of column headings for a bidirectional test.

TABLE A-9 A. Critical Values of the Mann-Whitney U for a Unidirectional Test at $\alpha = .05$ or a Bidirectional Test at $\alpha = .10$

n_2	\multicolumn{20}{c}{n_1}

n_2	1	2	3	4	5	6	7	8	9	10	11	12	13	14	15	16	17	18	19	20
1	—	—	—	—	—	—	—	—	—	—	—	—	—	—	—	—	—	—	0	0
	—	—	—	—	—	—	—	—	—	—	—	—	—	—	—	—	—	—	19	20
2	—	—	—	—	0	0	0	1	1	1	1	2	2	2	3	3	3	4	4	4
	—	—	—	—	10	12	14	15	17	19	21	22	24	26	27	29	31	32	34	36
3	—	—	0	0	1	2	2	3	3	4	5	5	6	7	7	8	9	9	10	11
	—	—	9	12	14	16	19	21	24	26	28	31	33	35	38	40	42	45	47	49
4	—	—	0	1	2	3	4	5	6	7	8	9	10	11	12	14	15	16	17	18
	—	—	12	15	18	21	24	27	30	33	36	39	42	45	48	50	53	56	59	62
5	—	0	1	2	4	5	6	8	9	11	12	13	15	16	18	19	20	22	23	25
	—	10	14	18	21	25	29	32	36	39	43	47	50	54	57	61	65	68	72	75
6	—	0	2	3	5	7	8	10	12	14	16	17	19	21	23	25	26	28	30	32
	—	12	16	21	25	29	34	38	42	46	50	55	59	63	67	71	76	80	84	88
7	—	0	2	4	6	8	11	13	15	17	19	21	24	26	28	30	33	35	37	39
	—	14	19	24	29	34	38	43	48	53	58	63	67	72	77	82	86	91	96	101
8	—	1	3	5	8	10	13	15	18	20	23	26	28	31	33	36	39	41	44	47
	—	15	21	27	32	38	43	49	54	60	65	70	76	81	87	92	97	103	108	113
9	—	1	3	6	9	12	15	18	21	24	27	30	33	36	39	42	45	48	51	54
	—	17	24	30	36	42	48	54	60	66	72	78	84	90	96	102	108	114	120	126
10	—	1	4	7	11	14	17	20	24	27	31	34	37	41	44	48	51	55	58	62
	—	19	26	33	39	46	53	60	66	73	79	86	93	99	106	112	119	125	132	138
11	—	1	5	8	12	16	19	23	27	31	34	38	42	46	50	54	57	61	65	69
	—	21	28	36	43	50	58	65	72	79	87	94	101	108	115	122	130	137	144	151
12	—	2	5	9	13	17	21	26	30	34	38	42	47	51	55	60	64	68	72	77
	—	22	31	39	47	55	63	70	78	86	94	102	109	117	125	132	140	148	156	163
13	—	2	6	10	15	19	24	28	33	37	42	47	51	56	61	65	70	75	80	84
	—	24	33	42	50	59	67	76	84	93	101	109	118	126	134	143	151	159	167	176
14	—	2	7	11	16	21	26	31	36	41	46	51	56	61	66	71	77	82	87	92
	—	26	35	45	54	63	72	81	90	99	108	117	126	135	144	153	161	170	179	188
15	—	3	7	12	18	23	28	33	39	44	50	55	61	66	72	77	83	88	94	100
	—	27	38	48	57	67	77	87	96	106	115	125	134	144	153	163	172	182	191	200
16	—	3	8	14	19	25	30	36	42	48	54	60	65	71	77	83	89	95	101	107
	—	29	40	50	61	71	82	92	102	112	122	132	143	153	163	173	183	193	203	213
17	—	3	9	15	20	26	33	39	45	51	57	64	70	77	83	89	96	102	109	115
	—	31	42	53	65	76	86	97	108	119	130	140	151	161	172	183	193	204	214	225
18	—	4	9	16	22	28	35	41	48	54	61	68	75	82	88	95	102	109	116	123
	—	32	45	56	68	80	91	103	114	123	137	148	159	170	182	193	204	215	226	237
19	0	4	10	17	23	30	37	44	51	58	65	72	80	87	94	101	109	116	123	130
	19	34	47	59	72	84	96	108	120	132	144	156	167	179	191	203	214	226	238	250
20	0	4	11	18	25	32	39	47	54	62	69	77	84	92	100	107	115	123	130	138
	20	36	49	62	75	88	101	113	126	138	151	163	176	188	200	213	225	237	250	262

(continues)

Note: For a bidirectional test, if the observed value of U falls between the two values listed in the table for n_1 and n_2, do not reject H_0. Otherwise, reject H_0. For a unidirectional test, where H_1 predicts Distribution 1 > Distribution 2, then the observed value of U for Sample 1 must be equal to or less than the smaller critical value of U to reject H_0.

TABLE A-9 *continued*   B. Critical Values of the Mann-Whitney *U* for a Unidirectional Test at $\alpha = .025$ or a Bidirectional Test at $\alpha = .05$

n_2	\(n_1\) 1	2	3	4	5	6	7	8	9	10	11	12	13	14	15	16	17	18	19	20
1	—	—	—	—	—	—	—	—	—	—	—	—	—	—	—	—	—	—	—	—
								0	0	0	0	1	1	1	1	1	2	2	2	2
2	—	—	—	—	—	—	—	16	18	20	22	23	25	27	29	31	32	34	36	38
					0	1	1	2	2	3	3	4	4	5	5	6	6	7	7	8
3	—	—	—	—	15	17	20	22	25	27	30	32	35	37	40	42	45	47	50	52
				0	1	2	3	4	4	5	6	7	8	9	10	11	11	12	13	13
4	—	—	—	16	19	22	25	28	32	35	38	41	44	47	50	53	57	60	63	67
			0	1	2	3	5	6	7	8	9	11	12	13	14	15	17	18	19	20
5	—	—	15	19	23	27	30	34	38	42	46	49	53	57	61	65	68	72	76	80
			1	2	3	5	6	8	10	11	13	14	16	17	19	21	22	24	35	27
6	—	—	17	22	27	21	36	40	44	49	53	58	62	67	71	75	80	84	89	93
			1	3	5	6	8	10	12	14	16	18	20	22	24	26	28	30	32	34
7	—	—	20	25	30	36	41	46	51	56	61	66	71	76	81	86	91	96	101	106
		0	2	4	6	8	10	13	15	17	19	22	24	26	29	31	34	36	38	41
8	—	16	22	28	34	40	46	51	57	63	69	74	80	86	91	97	102	108	111	119
		0	2	4	7	10	12	15	17	20	23	26	28	31	34	37	39	42	45	48
9	—	18	25	32	38	44	51	57	64	70	76	82	89	95	101	107	114	120	126	132
		0	3	5	8	11	14	17	20	23	26	29	33	36	39	42	45	48	52	55
10	—	20	27	35	42	49	56	63	70	77	84	91	97	104	111	118	125	132	138	145
		0	3	6	9	13	16	19	23	26	30	33	37	40	44	47	51	55	58	62
11	—	22	30	38	46	53	61	69	76	84	91	99	106	114	121	129	136	143	151	158
		1	4	7	11	14	18	22	26	29	33	37	41	45	49	53	57	61	65	69
12	—	23	32	41	49	58	66	74	82	91	99	107	115	123	131	139	147	155	163	171
		1	4	8	12	16	20	24	28	33	37	41	45	50	54	59	63	67	72	76
13	—	25	35	44	53	62	71	80	89	97	106	115	124	132	141	149	158	167	175	184
		1	5	9	13	17	22	26	31	36	40	45	50	55	59	64	67	74	78	83
14	—	27	37	47	57	67	76	86	95	104	114	123	132	141	151	160	171	178	188	197
		1	5	10	14	19	24	29	34	39	44	49	54	59	64	70	75	80	85	90
15	—	29	40	50	61	71	81	91	101	111	121	131	141	151	161	170	180	190	200	210
		1	6	11	15	21	26	31	37	42	47	53	59	64	70	75	81	86	92	98
16	—	31	42	53	65	75	86	97	107	118	129	139	149	160	170	181	191	202	212	222
		2	6	11	17	22	28	34	39	45	51	57	63	67	75	81	87	93	99	105
17	—	32	45	57	68	80	91	102	114	125	136	147	158	171	180	191	202	213	224	235
		2	7	12	18	24	30	36	42	48	55	61	67	74	80	86	93	99	106	112
18	—	34	47	60	72	84	96	108	120	132	143	155	167	178	190	202	213	225	236	248
		2	7	13	19	25	32	38	45	52	58	65	72	78	85	92	99	106	113	119
19	—	36	50	63	76	89	101	114	126	138	151	163	175	188	200	212	224	236	248	261
		2	8	13	20	27	34	41	48	55	62	69	76	83	90	98	105	112	119	127
20	—	38	52	67	80	93	106	119	132	145	158	171	184	197	210	222	235	248	261	273

TABLE A-9   *continued*   C. Critical Values of the Mann-Whitney *U* for a Unidirectional Test at $\alpha = .01$ or a Bidirectional Test at $\alpha = .02$

											n_1									
n_2	1	2	3	4	5	6	7	8	9	10	11	12	13	14	15	16	17	18	19	20
1	—	—	—	—	—	—	—	—	—	—	—	—	—	—	—	—	—	—	—	—
2	—	—	—	—	—	—	—	—	—	—	—	—	0	0	0	0	0	0	1	1
													26	28	30	32	34	36	37	39
3	—	—	—	—	—	—	0	0	1	1	1	2	2	2	3	3	4	4	4	5
							21	24	26	29	32	34	37	40	42	45	47	50	52	55
4	—	—	—	—	0	1	1	2	3	3	4	5	5	6	7	7	8	9	9	10
					20	23	27	30	33	37	40	43	47	50	53	57	60	63	67	70
5	—	—	—	0	1	2	3	4	5	6	7	8	9	10	11	12	13	14	15	16
				20	24	28	32	36	40	44	58	52	56	60	64	68	72	76	80	84
6	—	—	—	1	2	3	4	6	7	8	9	11	12	13	15	16	18	19	20	22
				23	28	33	38	42	47	52	57	61	66	71	75	80	84	89	94	98
7	—	—	0	1	3	4	6	7	9	11	12	14	16	17	19	21	23	24	26	28
			21	27	32	38	43	49	54	59	65	70	75	81	86	91	96	102	107	112
8	—	—	0	2	4	6	7	9	11	13	15	17	20	22	24	26	28	30	32	34
			24	30	36	42	49	55	61	67	73	79	84	90	96	102	108	114	120	126
9	—	—	1	3	5	7	9	11	14	16	18	21	23	26	28	31	33	36	38	40
			26	33	40	47	54	61	67	74	81	87	94	100	107	113	120	126	133	140
10	—	—	1	3	6	8	11	13	16	19	22	24	27	30	33	36	38	41	44	47
			29	37	44	52	59	67	74	81	88	96	103	110	117	124	132	139	146	153
11	—	—	1	4	7	9	12	15	18	22	25	28	31	34	37	41	44	47	50	53
			32	40	48	57	65	73	81	88	96	104	112	120	128	135	143	151	159	167
12	—	2	5	8	11	14	17	21	24	28	31	35	38	42	46	49	53	56	60
	—		34	43	52	61	70	79	87	96	104	113	121	130	138	146	155	163	172	180
13	—	0	2	5	9	12	16	20	23	27	31	35	39	43	47	51	55	59	63	67
		26	37	47	56	66	75	84	94	103	112	121	130	139	148	157	166	175	184	193
14	—	0	2	6	10	13	17	22	26	30	34	38	43	47	51	56	60	65	69	73
		28	40	50	60	71	81	90	100	110	120	130	139	149	159	168	178	187	197	207
15	—	0	3	7	11	15	19	24	28	33	37	42	47	51	56	61	66	70	75	80
		30	42	53	64	75	86	96	107	117	128	138	148	159	169	179	189	200	210	220
16	—	0	3	7	12	16	21	26	31	36	41	46	51	56	61	66	71	76	82	87
		32	45	57	68	80	91	102	113	124	135	146	157	168	179	190	201	212	222	233
17	—	0	4	8	13	18	23	28	33	38	44	49	55	60	66	71	77	82	88	93
		34	47	60	72	84	96	108	120	132	143	155	166	178	189	201	212	224	234	247
18	—	0	4	9	14	19	24	30	36	41	47	53	59	65	70	76	82	88	95	100
		36	50	63	76	89	102	111	126	139	151	163	175	187	200	212	224	236	248	260
19	—	1	4	9	15	20	26	32	38	44	50	56	63	69	75	82	88	94	101	107
		37	53	67	80	94	107	120	133	146	159	172	184	197	210	222	235	248	260	273
20	—	1	5	10	16	22	28	34	40	47	53	60	67	73	80	83	93	100	107	114
		39	55	70	84	98	112	126	140	153	167	180	193	207	220	233	247	260	273	286

(continues)

TABLE A-9 *continued* D. Critical Values of the Mann-Whitney U for a Unidirectional Test at $\alpha = .005$ or a Bidirectional Test at $\alpha = .01$

n_2	1	2	3	4	5	6	7	8	9	10	11	12	13	14	15	16	17	18	19	20
1	—	—	—	—	—	—	—	—	—	—	—	—	—	—	—	—	—	—	—	—
2	—	—	—	—	—	—	—	—	—	—	—	—	—	—	—	—	—	—	0 38	0 40
3	—	—	—	—	—	—	—	—	0 27	0 30	0 33	1 35	1 38	1 41	2 43	2 46	2 49	2 52	3 54	3 57
4	—	—	—	—	—	0 24	0 28	1 31	1 35	2 38	2 42	3 45	3 49	4 52	5 55	5 59	6 62	6 66	7 69	8 72
5	—	—	—	—	0 25	1 29	1 34	2 38	3 42	4 46	5 50	6 54	7 58	7 63	8 67	9 71	10 75	11 79	12 83	13 87
6	—	—	—	0 24	1 29	2 34	3 39	4 44	5 49	6 54	7 59	9 63	10 68	11 73	12 78	13 83	15 87	16 92	17 97	18 102
7	—	—	—	0 28	1 34	3 39	4 45	6 50	7 56	9 61	10 67	12 72	13 78	15 83	16 89	18 94	19 100	21 105	22 111	24 116
8	—	—	—	1 31	2 38	4 44	6 50	7 57	9 63	11 69	13 75	15 81	17 87	18 94	20 100	22 106	24 112	26 118	28 124	30 130
9	—	—	0 27	1 35	3 42	5 49	7 56	9 63	11 70	13 77	16 83	18 90	20 97	22 104	24 111	27 117	29 124	31 131	33 138	36 144
10	—	—	0 30	2 38	4 46	6 54	9 61	11 69	13 77	16 84	18 92	21 99	24 106	26 114	29 121	31 129	34 136	37 143	39 151	42 158
11	—	—	0 33	2 42	5 50	7 59	10 67	13 75	16 83	18 92	21 100	24 108	27 116	30 124	33 132	36 140	39 148	42 156	45 164	48 172
12	—	—	1 35	3 45	6 54	9 63	12 72	15 81	18 90	21 99	24 108	27 117	31 125	34 134	37 143	41 151	44 160	47 169	51 177	54 186
13	—	—	1 38	3 49	7 58	10 68	13 78	17 87	20 97	24 106	27 116	31 125	34 135	38 144	42 153	45 163	49 172	53 181	56 191	60 200
14	—	—	1 41	4 52	7 63	11 73	15 83	18 94	22 104	26 114	30 124	34 134	38 144	42 154	46 164	50 174	54 184	58 194	63 203	67 213
15	—	—	2 43	5 55	8 67	12 78	16 89	20 100	24 111	29 121	33 132	37 143	42 153	46 164	51 174	55 185	60 195	64 206	69 216	73 227
16	—	—	2 46	5 59	9 71	13 83	18 94	22 106	27 117	31 129	36 140	41 151	45 163	50 174	55 185	60 196	65 207	70 218	74 230	79 241
17	—	—	2 49	6 62	10 75	15 87	19 100	24 112	29 124	34 148	39 148	44 160	49 172	54 184	60 195	65 207	70 219	75 231	81 242	86 254
18	—	—	2 52	6 66	11 79	16 92	21 109	26 118	31 131	37 149	42 156	47 169	53 181	58 194	64 206	70 218	75 231	81 243	87 255	92 268
19	—	0 38	3 54	7 69	12 83	17 97	22 111	28 124	33 138	39 151	45 164	51 177	56 191	63 203	69 216	74 230	81 242	87 255	93 268	99 281
20	—	0 40	3 57	8 72	13 87	18 102	24 116	30 130	36 144	42 158	48 172	54 186	60 200	67 213	73 227	79 241	86 254	92 268	99 281	105 295

Appendix B:
Answers to Exercises

Chapter 2

3. (A) sample (B) population (C) population (D) sample (E) population (F) sample

6. (A) variable (B) constant (C) variable (D) variable (E) constant (F) variable

8. Sex is a variable.

9. (A) variable (B) value (C) value (D) variable (E) value (F) value (G) variable (H) variable

10. (A) nominal (B) ratio (C) nominal (D) ratio (E) ratio (F) ordinal (G) interval (H) ordinal (I) nominal

11. (A) ordinal (B) nominal (C) interval (D) ratio (E) ratio (F) nominal (G) ratio

14. (A) Set I: 1, Set II: 100, Set III: .01 (B) $X = 241$, $LRL = 240.5$, $URL = 241.5$; $X = 250$, $LRL = 249.5$, $URL = 250.5$ (C) $X = 3,400$, $LRL = 3,350$, $URL = 3,450$; $X = 4,000$, $LRL = 3,950$, $URL = 4,050$ (D) $X = 3.30$, $LRL = 3.295$, $URL = 3.305$; $X = 3.37$, $LRL = 3.365$, $URL = 3.375$

15. (A) $LRL = 46.5$, $URL = 47.5$ (B) $LRL = 585$, $URL = 595$ (C) $LRL = 6,450$, $URL = 6,550$ (D) $LRL = 9,950$, $URL = 10,050$ (E) $LRL = 3.55$, $URL = 3.65$ (F) $LRL = 14.95$, $URL = 15.05$ (G) $LRL = 0.185$, $URL = 0.195$ (H) $LRL = 0.995$, $URL = 1.005$

Chapter 3

10.

Number of Patients	f	Relative Frequency	Cumulative Frequency	Relative Cumulative Frequency
32	1	.03	30	1.00
31	1	.03	29	.97
30	3	.10	28	.93
29	1	.03	25	.83
28	0	.00	24	.80
27	3	.10	24	.80
26	5	.17	21	.70
25	5	.17	16	.53

Number of Patients	f	Relative Frequency	Cumulative Frequency	Relative Cumulative Frequency
24	2	.07	11	.37
23	4	.13	9	.30
22	0	.00	5	.17
21	2	.07	5	.17
20	3	.10	3	.10

11.

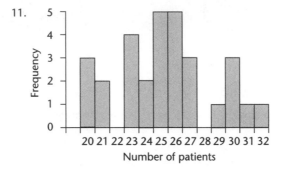

12.

Rating	f	Relative Frequency	Cumulative Frequency	Relative Cumulative Frequency
7	3	.12	25	1.00
6	6	.24	22	.88
5	7	.28	16	.64
4	5	.20	9	.36
3	3	.12	4	.16
2	0	.00	1	.04
1	1	.04	1	.04

13.

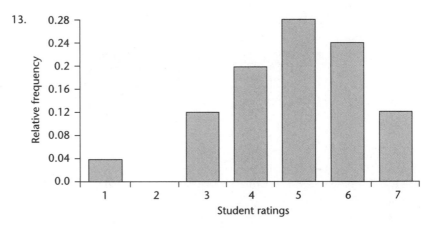

14.

Ethnic Origin	*f*	Relative Frequency
African-American (1)	3	.12
Native American (2)	5	.20
Asian-American (3)	1	.04
Hispanic (4)	4	.16
Caucasian (5)	8	.32
Multiracial (6)	3	.12
Other (7)	1	.04

15.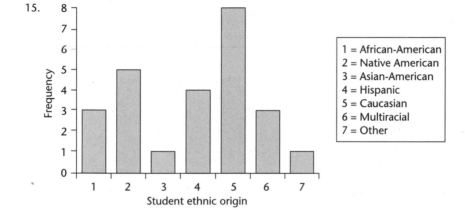

16.

Age	*f*	Relative Frequency	Cumulative Frequency	Relative Cumulative Frequency
12	2	.04	50	1.00
11	3	.06	48	.96
10	5	.10	45	.90
9	11	.22	40	.80
8	19	.38	29	.58
7	6	.12	10	.20
6	4	.08	4	.08

17.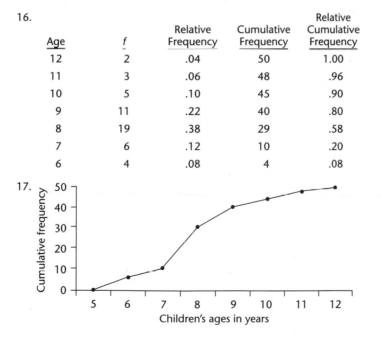

18.

Stem	Leaf							
7	64	90						
7	02	03	10	10	11			
6	67	79	81	94				
6	07	13	13	19	25	32	38	42
5	50	55	73	82	82	83	90	91	94
5	10	12	23	24	29	37	40	
4	59	62	75	83	92	95		
4	16	20	24	38	40			
3	55	70	86	99				

18.

Stem	Leaf									
14	2	4								
13	0	1	5							
12	0	1	2	4	6	7	8			
11	0	2	3	5	7	8	9	9	9	
10	1	2	3	4	4	5	6	6	7	8	9
9	0	2	3	6	8	8				
8	4	7								

20. (A) 5 (B) .20 (C) 20

21. (A) 65–69 (B) 4.0–5.9 (C) 1,500–1,700

22. (A) *LRL* = 69.5, *URL* = 79.5, Mdpt = 74.5 (B) *LRL* = 0.995, *URL* = 1.045, Mdpt = 1.02 (C) *LRL* = 12,500, *URL* = 14,500, Mdpt = 13,500

23.

Stated Limits	LRL	URL	Midpoint
135–139	134.5	139.5	137
130–134	129.5	134.5	132
125–129	124.5	129.5	127
120–124	119.5	124.5	122
115–119	114.5	119.5	117
110–114	109.5	114.5	112
105–109	104.5	109.5	107
100–104	99.5	104.5	102
95–99	94.5	99.5	97
90–94	89.5	94.5	92
85–89	84.5	89.5	87
80–84	79.5	84.5	82
75–79	74.5	79.5	77

24.

Stated Limits	Frequency	LRL	URL	Midpoint
44–45	1	43.5	45.5	44.5
42–43	1	41.5	43.5	42.5
40–41	4	39.5	41.5	40.5
38–39	5	37.5	39.5	38.5
36–37	12	35.5	37.5	36.5
34–35	21	33.5	35.5	34.5
32–33	23	31.5	33.5	32.5
30–31	21	29.5	31.5	30.5
28–29	10	27.5	29.5	28.5
26–27	2	25.5	27.5	26.5

25.

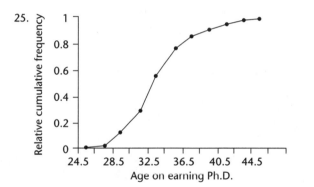

26.

Stated Limits	Frequency	LRL	URL	Midpoint
3.90–3.99	2	3.895	3.995	3.945
3.80–3.89	3	3.795	3.895	3.845
3.70–3.79	4	3.695	3.795	3.745
3.60–3.69	6	3.595	3.695	3.645
3.50–3.59	8	3.495	3.595	3.545
3.40–3.49	9	3.395	3.495	3.445
3.30–3.39	7	3.295	3.395	3.345
3.20–3.29	6	3.195	3.295	3.245
3.10–3.19	3	3.095	3.195	3.145
3.00–3.09	2	2.995	3.095	3.045

27.

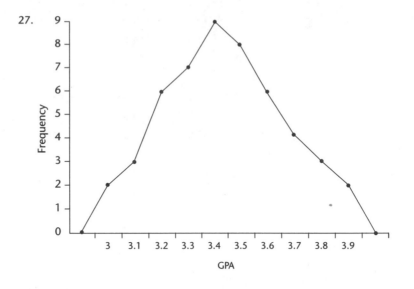

Chapter 4

2. (I) .2964 (II) 2.964 (III) 29.64 (IV) 296.4 (V) 2,964 (VI) 29,640 (VII) 296,400

3. (I) 8.0 (II) 9.0 (III) 8.0 (IV) 80.0

4. (I) 2.73 (II) 27.3 (III) 273

5. (I) 2.65 (II) 2.68 (III) 2.72 (IV) 2.75

8. The mean is the balance point of a distribution. The median is the point below which fall the values of half of the scores. The mode is the most frequently occurring score value.

9. (I) 6.4 (II) 32.9 (III) 510 (IV) 131,700 (V) 1.649 (VI) 0.0544

10. (A) 18 (B) 30 (C) 86 (D) 190 (E) 324 (F) 900

11. (A) 40.6 (B) 5.06 (C) 185.74 (D) 3.23 (E) 1648.36 (F) 25.6036

12. (A) 554 (B) 4,494 (C) 306,916

13. 7.9

14. (I) 3.6 (II) 5.7 (III) 34 (IV) 530 (V) 4.02 (VI) .463

15. (I) 4 (II) 5 (III) 40 (IV) 500 (V) 3.2 (VI) .38

16. (I) 4.0 (II) 5.2 (III) 38 (IV) 520 (V) 3.23 (VI) .380

17. (I) 110.5 (II) 3.12 (III) $14,300

18. (I)

IQ	f	GPA	f	Income	f
115	1	3.5	2	$20,000	2
114	0	3.4	4	19,000	3
113	2	3.3	3	18,000	0

(I) IQ	f	GPA	f	Income	f
112	3	3.2	1	17,000	2
111	3	3.1	2	16,000	0
110	5	3.0	1	15,000	2
109	4	2.9	3	14,000	3
108	1	2.8	2	13,000	0
107	0	2.7	1	12,000	3
106	1	2.6	0	11,000	0
		2.5	1	10,000	3
				9,000	1
				8,000	1

Note: Means are the same as in Exercise 17.

19. Simplified from list: (I) 110 (II) 3.15 (III) $14,000. Simplified from table: (I) 110 (II) 3.15 (III) $14,000

20. Precise method for both list and table: (I) 110.3 (II) 3.15 (III) $14,200

21. Frequency, 30.7; grouped frequency, 30.5

22. Frequency, 31; grouped frequency, 31

23. Frequency, 30.8; grouped frequency, 30.7

24. (I) Simplified and precise: 8 (II) simplified: 8; precise: 7.8 (III) simplified: 40; precise: 43 (IV) simplified: 1.8; precise: 1.78 (V) simplified: 0.06; precise: .058

25. (I) 115 (II) 122.5 (III) major, 110, minor, 135 (IV) 4 (V) major, 3, minor, 6 (VI) Lutheran

26. (I) Mean, because scale is interval and distribution is nearly balanced; (II) median, because even though scale is interval, distribution is skewed; (III) mode, because distribution is bimodal (IV) median, because even though distribution is balanced, scale is ordinal (V) mode, because distribution is bimodal (VI) mode, because scale is nominal

Chapter 5

2. (I) .045 (II) .45 (III) 4.5 (IV) 45 (V) 450 (VI) 4,500 (VII) 45,000

3. (I) 36 (II) 36 (III) 36, (I) 6.5 (II) 10.5 (III) 16.5

4. (I) 2.2 (II) 3.1 (III) 3.1

5. (I) 1.7 (II) 3.4 (III) 17

6. (I) 2.0 (II) 4.0 (III) 20.0

10. (I) 6 (II) 18 (III) 800 (IV) 19,000 (V) .25 (VI) .042

11. (I) 10 (II) 1.1 (III) $13,000

12. (A) (I) 2.0 (II) 0.29 (III) $3,900 (B) (I) 2.0 (II) 0.29 (III) $3,900

13.

Set I: IQ	f	Set II: GPA	f	Set III: Income	f
115	1	3.5	2	20,000	2
113	2	3.4	4	19,000	3
112	3	3.3	3	17,000	2
111	3	3.2	1	15,000	2
110	5	3.1	2	14,000	3
109	4	3.0	1	12,000	3
108	1	2.9	3	10,000	3
106	1	2.8	2	9,000	1
		2.7	1	8,000	1
		2.5	1		

(A) (I) 2.0 (II) 0.29 (III) \$3,900 (B) (I) 2.0 (II) 0.29 (III) \$3,900

14. (A) (I) 2.3 (II) 1.5 (III) 19 (IV) 205 (V) 1.64 (VI) .255 (B) (I) 2.3 (II) 1.5 (III) 19 (IV) = 205 (V) 1.64 (VI) .255

15. (A) (I) 9.2 (II) 9.6 (III) 11.8 (B) (I) 9.2 (II) 9.6 (III) 11.8

16. (A) 4.5 (B) $Q_1 = 27.5$, $Q_2 = 31$, $Q_3 = 34$, $Q = 3.25$ (C) $Q_1 = 27.5$, $Q_2 = 30.8$, $Q_3 = 34.2$, $Q = 3.35$

17. (A) 14.0 (B) $Q_1 = 92$, $Q_2 = 102$, $Q_3 = 112$, $Q = 10.0$ (C) $Q_1 = 93.5$, $Q_2 = 102.5$, $Q_3 = 113.0$, $Q = 9.75$

Chapter 6

2. (A) $\mu = 18$, $\sigma = 5$ (B) $\mu = 60$, $\sigma = 20$ (C) $\mu = 72$, $\sigma = 20$

3.

I. X	z	II. X	z	III. X	z	IV. X	z
7	1.42	9	1.42	9	1.42	70	1.42
6	0.71	7	0.71	8	0.71	60	0.71
5	0.00	5	0.00	7	0.00	50	0
4	−0.71	3	−0.71	6	−0.71	40	−0.71
3	−1.42	1	−1.42	5	−1.42	30	−1.42

$\mu_I = 5.0$ $\mu_{II} = 5.0$ $\mu_{III} = 7.0$ $\mu_{IV} = 50$
$\sigma_I = 1.4$ $\sigma_{II} = 2.8$ $\sigma_{III} = 1.4$ $\sigma_{IV} = 14$

4. (A) $\mu_X = 6.0$, $\sigma_X = 2.0$ (B) $z_{X=8} = 1.00$, $z_{X=6} = 0$, $z_{X=4} = -1.00$, $z_{X=2} = -2.00$ (C) $\mu_z = 0.0$, $\sigma_z = 1.0$

5.

(I) X	Percentile Rank	(II) X	Percentile Rank	(III) X	Percentile Rank
50	95th	50	95th	100	95th
45	85th	45	85th	90	85th
40	75th	40	75th	80	75th
35	65th	35	65th	70	65th
30	55th	30	55th	60	55th

(I)	X	Percentile Rank	(II)	X	Percentile Rank	(III)	X	Percentile Rank
	25	45th		25	45th		50	45th
	20	35th		20	35th		40	35th
	15	25th		15	25th		30	25th
	10	15th		10	15th		20	15th
	5	5th		5	5th		10	5th

7. (A) (i) 1.40 (ii) −0.80 (iii) 0.00 (iv) −2.10 (v) 1.80 (vi) −0.10, (B) (i) 85 (ii) 58 (iii) 94 (iv) 100 (v) 56 (vi) 75

8. (A) (i) 1.60 (ii) 2.40 (iii) −1.20 (iv) 0.80 (v) −2.40 (vi) 0.40, (B) (i) 430 (ii) 350 (iii) 440 (iv) 460 (v) 360 (vi) 400

9. (A) (i) 0.07 (ii) 0.60 (iii) −1.07 (iv) 2.13 (v) −1.00 (vi) −1.73, (B) (i) 11.0 (ii) 14.9 (iii) 10.0 (iv) 16.1 (v) 15.5 (vi) 12.5

10. (A) (i) −2.33 (ii) −1.47 (iii) −0.53 (iv) 0.40 (v) 1.73 (vi) 2.80, (B) (i) 70 (ii) 75 (iii) 93 (iv) 100 (v) 125 (vi) 130

11. (A) (i) −1.75 (ii) −0.35 (iii) −0.01 (iv) 0.01 (v) 1.33 (vi) 2.00, (B) (i) 245 (ii) 304 (iii) 425 (iv) 500 (v) 650 (vi) 733

12. (A) (i) 500 (ii) 600 (iii) 300 (iv) 580 (v) 413 (vi) 760, (B) (i) 85 (ii) 123 (iii) 81 (iv) 141 (v) 100 (vi) 101

13. (A) $\mu = 32.0$, $\sigma = 4.0$, (B) (i) 1.00 (ii) 0.00 (iii) −1.00 (iv) −2.00, (C) (i) 60 (ii) 50 (iii) 40 (iv) 30

14. (A) (i) 0.75 (ii) −0.25 (iii) −1.25, (B) (i) 0.97 (ii) −0.07 (iii) −1.10, (C) (i) 1.21 (ii) 0.18 (iii) −0.59, (D) (i) 113 (ii) 111 (iii) 106, (E) (i) 3.5 (ii) 3.0 (iii) 2.7, (F) (i) $17,000 (ii) $14,000 (iii) $8,000

15. (A) Simplified: (i) 113 (ii) 110 (iii) 109, precise: (i) 113.0 (ii) 109.8 (iii) 109.0, (B) Simplified: (i) 3.45 (ii)3.0 (iii) 2.85, precise: (i) 3.45 (ii) 2.99 (iii) 2.85, (C) Simplified: (i) $19,500 (ii)$12,000 (iii) $10,000, precise: (i) $19,500 (ii)$12,300 (iii) $10,200

16. (A) (i) 78th (ii) 43d (iii) 8th, (B) (i) 80th (ii) 45th (iii) 15th, (C) (i) 83d (ii) 60th (iii) 33d

17. (A) (i) 99th (ii) 96th (iii) 93d (iv) 88th (v) 81st (vi) 73d (vii) 62d (viii) 48th (ix) 34th (x) 22d (xi) 11th (xii) 4th (xiii) 1st, (B) (i) 124 (ii) 116 (iii) 111 (iv) 106 (v) 103 (vi) 99 (vii) 96 (viii) 91 (ix) 86

18. (A) (i) 2.36 (ii) 2.00 (iii) 1.64 (iv) 1.29 (v) 0.93 (vi) 0.57 (vii) 0.21 (viii) −0.14 (ix) −0.50 (x) −0.86 (xi) −1.21 (xii) −1.57 (xiii) −1.93, (B) (i) 132 (ii) 125 (iii) 118 (iv) 111 (v) 104 (vi) 97 (vii) 90 (viii) 83 (ix) 76, (C) (i) 1.43 (ii) 0.86 (iii) 0.50 (iv) 0.14 (v) −0.07 (vi) −0.36 (vii) −0.57 (viii) −0.93 (ix) −1.29

Chapter 7

7. (A) 15.87% (B) 97.72% (C) 2.28% (D) 95.25% (E) 4.75% (F) 68.26% (G) 84.13% (H) 90.50% (I) 97.72% (J) 13.59% (K) 95.25% (L) 45.25% (M) 84.13% (N) 47.72%

8. (A) 34.13% (B) 43.32% (C) 91.98% (D) 4.95% (E) 2.50% (F) 99.02%

9. (A) 1.04 (B) 1.65 (C) −0.84 (D) −1.28 (E) ±0.67 (F) 1.96

10. (A) 9.18% (B) 15.96% (C) 90.82% (D) 11.12% (E) 80.78% (F) 49.72% (G) 3.07%

11. (A) 110 (B) 90 (C) 119 (D) 125 (E) 116 (F) 75

12. (A) 68.26% (B) 4.56% (C) 27.18% (D) 6.68% (E) 0.62% (F) 8.02%

13. (A) .5000 (B) .9772 (C) .0668 (D) .1915 (E) .0116 (F) .3721 (G) .3085 (H) .0819
(I) .0918

14. (A) 567 (B) 628 (C) 416 (D) 665 (E) 475 (F) 372

15. (A) .1587 (B) .2743 (C) .7881 (D) .4207 (E) .8848 (F) .3050 (G) .1156 (H) .0779

16. (A) 1.8 (B) 0.9 (C) 0.7 (D) 1.5

17. (A) 100 (B) 125 (C) 90 (D) 82

18. (A) 98th (B) 91st (C) 50th (D) 23d (E) 5th (F) 1st

Chapter 8

2. (A) I. 1.00 II. .80 III. .00 IV. −.80 V. −1.00

3. (B) I. 1.00 II. 0.80 III. 0.00 IV. −0.80 V. −1.00

5. (I) 1.00. (II) 0.50 (III) 0.00 (IV) −0.50 (V) −1.00 (VI) 0.58 (VII) 0.58 (VIII) −0.58
(IX) −0.58

6. (A)

Political Party	Men	Women	
Democrat	30	20	50
Republican	60	40	100
Total	90	60	

$\phi = 0.00$

(B)

Political Party	Men	Women	
Democrat	0	50	50
Republican	90	10	100
Total	90	60	

$\phi = -.87$

8. (A) Study time and grade: $r = 0.97$; test time and grade: $r = 0.47$; study time and
test time $r = 0.51$

9. (A) Strictness and nurturing $\rho = -0.87$; strictness and time spent with child
$\rho = -0.26$; nurturing and time spent with child $\rho = 0.36$

10. 0.80

11. 0.87

12. −0.68

13. −0.70

14. 0.49

15. −0.13

Chapter 9

2. (A) age 9, $4.00; age 8, $2.00; age 7, $0.00; best guess: 9; (B) age 9, $3.00; payoff age 8, $3.20; age 7, $3.00; best guess: 8; (C) age 9, $4.12; age 8, $4.42; age 7, $4.52; best guess: 7

4. (C) (I) 1.00, (II) 0.50, (III) 0.00, (IV) −0.50, (V) −1.00 (D) (I) $Y' = -1.7 + .04X$, (II) $Y' = .9 + .02X$, (III) $Y' = 3.5$, (IV) $Y' = 6.1 - .02X$, (V) $Y' = 8.7 - .04X$

5. (I) (i) 3.9 (ii) 3.7 (iii) 3.5 (iv) 3.3 (v) 3.1, (II) (i) 3.7 (ii) 3.6 (iii) 3.5 (iv) 3.4 (v) 3.3, (III) (i) 3.5 (ii) 3.5 (iii) 3.5 (iv) 3.5 (v) 3.5, (IV) (i) 3.3 (ii) 3.4 (iii) 3.5 (iv) 3.6 (v) 3.7, (V) (i) 3.1 (ii) 3.3 (iii) 3.5 (iv) 3.7 (v) 3.9

6. (I) (i) 3.78 (ii) 3.54 (iii) 3.42 (iv) 3.26, (II) (i) 3.64 (ii) 3.52 (iii) 3.46 (iv) 3.38, (III) (i) 3.5 (ii) 3.5 (iii) 3.5 (iv) 3.5, (IV) (i) 3.36 (ii) 3.48 (iii) 3.54 (iv) 3.62, (V) (i) 3.22 (ii) 3.46 (iii) 3.58 (iv) 3.74

7. (I) $Y' = 42.5 + 25X$, (II) $Y' = 86.25 + 12.5X$, (III) $Y' = 130 + 0X$, (IV) $Y' = 173.75 - 12.5X$, (V) $Y' = 217.5 - 25X$

8. (I) (i) 140 (ii) 135 (iii) 130 (iv) 125 (v) 120, (II) (i) 135 (ii) 132.5 (iii) 130 (iv) 127.5 (v) 125, (III) (i) 130 (ii) 130 (iii) 130 (iv) 130 (v) 130, (IV) (i) 125 (ii) 127.5 (iii) 130 (iv) 132.5 (v) 135, (V) (i) 120 (ii) 125 (iii) 130 (iv) 135 (v) 140

9. (I) (i) 138 (ii) 133 (iii) 128 (iv) 123, (II) (i) 134 (ii) 131 (iii) 129 (iv) 126, (III) (i) 130 (ii) 130 (iii) 130 (iv) 130, (IV) (i) 126 (ii) 129 (iii) 131 (iv) 134, (V) (i) 123 (ii) 128 (iii) 133 (iv) 138

10. $s_{\text{GPA|IQ}}$: (I) 0 (II) 0.17 (III) 0.2 (IV) 0.17 (V) 0
    $s_{\text{IQ|GPA}}$: (I) 0 (II) 5.3 (III) 6.1 (IV) 5.3 (V) 0

11. (A) (I) $Y' = -167 + 6.67X$, (II) $Y' = -33 + 5.33X$, (III) $Y = 100 + 4.0X$, (IV) $Y' = 233 + 2.67X$, (V) $Y' = 367 + 1.33X$, (VI) $Y' = 500 + 0X$

12. (I) (i) 700 (ii) 600 (iii) 500 (iv) 400 (v) 300, (II) (i) 660 (ii) 580 (iii) 500 (iv) 420 (v) 340, (III) (i) 620 (ii) 560 (iii) 500 (iv) 440 (v) 380, (IV) (i) 580 (ii) 540 (iii) 500 (iv) 460 (v) 420, (V) (i) 540 (ii) 520 (iii) 500 (iv) 480 (v) 460, (VI) (i) 500 (ii) 500 (iii) 500 (iv) 500 (v) 500

13. (A) (i) 1.00 (ii) .80 (iii) .60 (iv) .40 (v) .20 (vi) 0, (B) (i) −1.00 (ii) −.80 (iii) −.60 (iv) −.40 (v) −.20 (vi) 0

14. (i) 0 (ii) 60 (iii) 80 (iv) 92 (v) 98 (vi) 100

15. (A) 637 (B) 478 (C) 532 (D) 446 (E) 500 (F) 500

16. (A) 68 (B) 88 (C) 84 (D) 94 (E) 57 (F) 92

17. (A) $Y' = 3.67 + 1.19X$ (B) 2 weeks: 6.05; 7 weeks: 12.0 (C) 1.3 (D) .8281

18. (A) $Y' = 143 - 3X$ (B) 10.5 months: 112; 11.5 months: 109 (C) 15.01 (D) .09

Chapter 10

2. (A) and (B)

Number of Questions	Probability	Frequency
10	.0010	10
9	.0098	98
8	.0439	439
7	.1172	1,172
6	.2051	2,051
5	.2461	2,461
4	.2051	2,051
3	.1172	1,172
2	.0439	439
1	.0098	98
0	.0010	10

(C) $\mu = 5.0$, $\sigma = 1.58$

3. (A) .0547 (B) .3770 (C) .0108 (D) .0547 (E) .0020

4. (A) and (B)

Number of Questions	Probability	Frequency
10	.0000	0
9	.0000	0
8	.0004	4
7	.0031	31
6	.0162	162
5	.0584	584
4	.1460	1,460
3	.2503	2,503
2	.2816	2,816
1	.1877	1,877
0	.0563	563

5. (B)

Number of Heads	Probability
5	.0312
4	.1562
3	.3125
2	.3125
1	.1562
0	.0312

(D) $\mu = 2.5$, $\sigma = 1.12$

6. (A) .25 (B) .0010 (C) .0781

7. (A) .15 (B) .85 (C) .0001 (D) .0244

8. (A) .1536 (B) .0035 (C) .9965 (D) .4531 (E) .0490

9. (A) .1746 (B) .4114 (C) .3980 (D) .3280 (E) .1074

10.

Number Correct	Binomial Probability
20	.0000
19	.0000
18	.0000
17	.0000
16	.0000
15	.0000
14	.0000
13	.0002
12	.0008
11	.0030
10	.0099
9	.0271
8	.0609
7	.1124
6	.1686
5	.2023
4	.1897
3	.1339
2	.0669
1	.0211
0	.0032

Chapter 11

6. (A) .1762 (B) .0207 (C) .0059 (D) .2632 (E) .8238

7. (A) (1,1) (1,2) (1,3) (1,4) (1,5) (2,1) (2,2) (2,3) (2,4) (2,5) (3,1) (3,2) (3,3) (3,4) (3,5) (4,1) (4,2) (4,3) (4,4) (4,5) (5,1) (5,2) (5,3) (5,4) (5,5)

(B)

$\overline{X}$	f
1.0	1
1.5	2
2.0	3
2.5	4
3.0	5
3.5	4
4.0	3
4.5	2
5.0	1

8. (A) .12 (B) .24 (C) .76

9. (A) $\mu = 3.0$, $\sigma = 1.4$ (B) $\mu_{\bar{X}} = 3.0$, $\sigma_{\bar{X}} = 1.0$ (C) $\mu_{\bar{X}} = 3.0$, $\sigma_{\bar{X}} = 1.0$

10. (A) .1587 (B) .5000 (C) .9050 (D) .0456

11.

n	$\sigma_{\bar{X}}$	p
4	50.0	.6892
9	33.3	.5486
16	25.0	.4238
25	20.0	.3174
36	16.7	.2302
49	14.3	.1616
64	12.5	.1096
81	11.1	.0718
100	10.0	.0456

12. (A) .1335 (B) .0228 (C) .0475 (D) .0150

13. (A) 54.9%, 61.1% (B) 53.9%, 62.1% (C) 43.3%, 50.7% (D) 42.1%, 51.9%

14. (A) 545, 605 (B) 539.3, 610.7 (C) 528.0, 612.0

15. (A) 505.4, 544.6 (B) 936.1, 983.9 (C) 1825.1, 1874.9

Chapter 12

3. p(0 red in 6 candies given 50% red) = .0156; p(3 green in 3 candies given 5% green) = .0001; p(6 blue in 12 candies given 0% blue) = 0; p(6 orange of 10 candies given 15% orange) = .0012; p(3 black in 15 candies given 0% black) = 0

4. (A) $z_{\bar{X}} = -1.07$, $p = .1423$ (B) $z_{\bar{X}} = -1.26$, $p = .1038$ (C) $z_{\bar{X}} = -1.67$, $p = .0475$ (D) $z_{\bar{X}} = -3.29$, $p = .0006$

6. H_0: $\mu_{\text{w/refined carbohydrates}} \geq 100$
H_1: $\mu_{\text{w/refined carbohydrates}} < 100$

12. (A) H_0: $\mu_{\text{reading program}} \leq 89$
H_1: $\mu_{\text{reading program}} > 89$

(B) H_0: $\mu_{\text{w/pets}} \geq 37$
H_1: $\mu_{\text{w/pets}} < 37$

(C) H_0: $\mu_{\text{infants w/alcoholic mothers}} \geq 7.8$ pounds
H_1: $\mu_{\text{infants w/alcoholic mothers}} < 7.8$ pounds

(D) H_0: $\mu_{\text{discs from new system}} = 3.5$ inches
H_1: $\mu_{\text{discs from new system}} \neq 3.5$ inches

(E) H_0: $\mu_{\text{college students}} \geq 8$ hours
H_1: $\mu_{\text{college students}} < 8$ hours

13. (A) unidirectional (B) unidirectional (C) unidirectional (D) bidirectional (E) unidirectional

14. (A) $z_{\text{critical .05}} = 1.65$, $z_{\text{critical .01}} = 2.33$ (B) $z_{\text{critical .05}} = -1.65$, $z_{\text{critical .01}} = -2.33$ (C) $z_{\text{critical .05}} = -1.65$, $z_{\text{critical .01}} = -2.33$ (D) $z_{\text{critical .05}} = \pm 1.96$, $z_{\text{critical .01}} = \pm 2.58$ (E) $z_{\text{critical .05}} = -1.65$, $z_{\text{critical .01}} = -2.33$

17. (A) $z_{\bar{x}} = 2.68$, $p < .05$ (B) $z_{\bar{x}} = -2.06$, $p < .05$ (C) $z_{\bar{x}} = 1.79$, $p > .05$ (D) $z_{\bar{x}} = -2.83$, $p < .05$ (E) $z_{\bar{x}} = -1.90$, $p < .05$

19. $z_{\bar{x}} = -3.98$ $p < .05$. Reject the null hypothesis.

20. $z_{\bar{x}} = 1.31$ $p > .05$. Do not reject null hypothesis.

Chapter 13

10. (A) $t_{\text{critical}} = \pm 2.145$ (B) $t_{\text{critical}} = -2.821$ (C) $t_{\text{critical}} = 1.717$ (D) $t_{\text{critical}} = \pm 2.750$

11. (A) $z_{\text{critical}} = \pm 1.96$ (B) $z_{\text{critical}} = -2.33$ (C) $z_{\text{critical}} = 1.65$ (D) $z_{\text{critical}} = \pm 2.58$

12. $t_{29} = 3.651$, $p < .05$. Reject the null hypothesis.

13. $z = 2.74$, $p < .05$. Reject the null hypothesis.

14. $z = 0.89$, $p > .05$. Do not reject null hypothesis.

15. $t_{19} = 2.136$, $p > .01$. Do not reject null hypothesis.

16. $t_{14} = 2.789$, $p < .05$. Reject the null hypothesis.

17. $z = -0.625$, $p > .05$. Do not reject null hypothesis.

Chapter 14

3. (A) $z = -0.54$, $p = 0.5892$ (B) $z = -1.42$, $p = 0.1556$ (C) $z = 1.89$, $p = 0.0588$ (D) $z = 3.03$, $p = 0.0024$

9. (A) $z_{\text{critical}} = \pm 1.96$ (B) $z_{\text{critical}} = -2.33$ (C) $z_{\text{critical}} = 1.65$ (D) $z_{\text{critical}} = \pm 2.58$

10. $z = 0.88$, $p > .05$. Do not reject the null hypothesis.

11. (A) $t = 1.763$ (B) $t = 0.831$ (C) $t = 2.435$ (D) $t = -4.283$

12. (A) $t_{\text{critical}} = \pm 2.120$ (B) $t_{\text{critical}} = -2.457$ (C) $t_{\text{critical}} = 1.771$ (D) $t_{\text{critical}} = \pm 2.807$

13. $t_{50} = 1.479$, $p > .05$. Do not reject the null hypothesis.

14. (A) $t_{14} = 2.546$ (B) $t_7 = 4.68$

15. $t_8 = 4.045$, $p < .05$. Reject the null hypothesis.

16. (A) $r_{\text{critical}} = \pm .6319$ (B) $r_{\text{critical}} = -.5155$ (C) $r_{\text{critical}} = .4409$ (D) $r_{\text{critical}} = \pm .5368$

17. $r_{\text{SAT} \cdot \text{GPA}} = 0.80$, $p < .05$. Reject the null hypothesis.

18. $z = 1.37$, $p > .05$. Do not reject the null hypothesis.

19. $t_{27} = 2.639$, $p < .05$. Reject the null hypothesis.

20. $t_{11} = 5.455$, $p < .05$. Reject the null hypothesis

21. $r_{\text{time studying} \cdot \text{test scores}} = 0.896$, $p < .05$. Reject the null hypothesis.

Chapter 15

1. (A) Sum of ranks $= \dfrac{n(n + 1)}{2} = \dfrac{7(8)}{2} = \dfrac{54}{2} = 28$. For all combinations of T_1 and T_2, sum of ranks $= 28$.

(B)   Set 1, minimum = 6; Set 2, minimum = 10. (C) Set 2, maximum = 18;
Set 2, maximum = 22.

(D) and (E)

	Sample 1		Sample 2		
	Sum of Ranks	U_1	Sum of Ranks	U_2	$U_1 + U_2$
	6	12	22	0	12
	7	11	21	1	12
	8	10	20	2	12
	9	9	19	3	12
	10	8	18	4	12
	11	7	17	5	12
	12	6	16	6	12
	13	5	15	7	12
	14	4	14	8	12
	15	3	13	9	12
	16	2	12	10	12
	17	1	11	11	12
	18	0	10	12	12

(G)

Sum of Ranks	f	p
0	2	.0286
1	2	.0286
2	4	.0571
3	6	.0857
4	8	.1143
5	8	.1143
6	10	.1428
7	8	.1143
8	8	.1143
9	6	.0857
10	4	.0571
11	2	.0286
12	2	.0286

2. (A) $p(U = 0) = .0286$ (B) $p(U = 12) = .0286$ (C) $p(U \leq 2) = .1143$
(D) $p(U \geq 10) = .1143$

3. (B)

$\Sigma(+ranks)$	$\Sigma(-ranks)$	f	p
15	0	1	.03125
14	1	1	.03125
13	2	1	.03125
12	3	2	.06250
11	4	2	.06250
10	5	3	.09675
9	6	3	.09375

$\Sigma(+\text{ranks})$	$\Sigma(-\text{ranks})$	f	p
8	7	3	.09375
7	8	3	.09375
6	9	3	.09375
5	10	3	.09375
4	11	2	.06250
3	12	2	.06250
2	13	1	.03125
1	14	1	.03125
0	15	1	.03125

4. (A) $p[\Sigma(-\text{ranks}) = 0] = .03125$ (B) $p[\Sigma(+\text{ranks}) = 0] = .03125$
(C) $p[\Sigma(-\text{ranks}) = 15] = .03125$ (D) $p[\Sigma(-\text{ranks}) \leq 3] = .15625$

8. (A) $U_{\text{critical}} = 14$ and 56 (B) $U_{\text{critical}} = 169$ (C) $U_{\text{critical}} = 34$ (D) $U_{\text{critical}} = 73$ and 227
(Note: All critical values of U are for sample 1.)

9. $U = 41$, $p > .05$. Do not reject the null hypothesis.

10. $z_U = 2.34$, $p < .05$. Reject the null hypothesis.

11. (A) One of the samples must have a value of W of 8 or less. (B) Sample 2 must
have a value of W of 69 or less. (C) Sample 1 must have a value of W of 110 or less.
(D) One of the samples must have a value of W of 291 or less.

12. The value of W for the negative ranks is 7, $p < .05$. Reject the null hypothesis.

13. (A) critical $r_S = .522$ (B) critical $r_S = -.392$ (C) critical $r_S = .353$ (D) critical $r_S = .794$

14. $\rho = -.72$, $p < .05$. Reject the null hypothesis.

15. $U = 3.5$, $p > .01$. Do not reject the null hypothesis.

16. W for negative ranks $= 3$, $p = .05$. Reject the null hypothesis.

17. $\rho = -.70$, $p < .05$. Reject the null hypothesis.

Chapter 16

2. (A) Set I: $s_1 = 3.2$, $s_2 = 3.2$; Set II: $s_1 = 0$, $s_2 = 0$; Set III: $s_1 = 3.2$, $s_2 = 3.2$
(B) Set I: $t = 0$; Set II: $t = \infty$; Set III: $t = 2.00$

3.

	Set I				Set II				Set III		
X	Within	Between	Total	X	Within	Between	Total	X	Within	Between	Total
10	4	0	4	4	0	−2	−2	8	4	−2	2
8	2	0	2	4	0	−2	−2	6	2	−2	0
6	0	0	0	4	0	−2	−2	4	0	−2	−2
4	−2	0	−2	4	0	−2	−2	2	−2	−2	−4
2	−4	0	−4	4	0	−2	−2	0	−4	−2	−6
$\bar{X}_1$ 6				4				4			

	Set I				Set II				Set III		
X	Within	Between	Total	X	Within	Between	Total	X	Within	Between	Total
10	4	0	4	8	0	2	2	12	4	2	6
8	2	0	2	8	0	2	2	10	2	2	4
6	0	0	0	8	0	2	2	8	0	2	2
4	−2	0	−2	8	0	2	2	6	−2	2	0
2	−4	0	−4	8	0	2	2	4	−4	2	−2
$\overline{X}_2$ **6**				**8**				**8**			
$\overline{X}_T$ **6**				**6**				**6**			

4.

	Set I				Set II				Set III		
X	Within	Between	Total	X	Within	Between	Total	X	Within	Between	Total
10	16	0	16	4	0	4	4	8	16	4	4
8	4	0	4	4	0	4	4	6	4	4	0
6	0	0	0	4	0	4	4	4	0	4	4
4	4	0	4	4	0	4	4	2	4	4	16
2	16	0	16	4	0	4	4	0	16	4	36
$\Sigma(X-\overline{X}_1)^2$ **40**	**0**	**40**		**0**	**20**	**20**		**40**	**20**	**60**	
10	16	0	16	8	0	4	4	12	16	4	36
8	4	0	4	8	0	4	4	10	4	4	16
6	0	0	0	8	0	4	4	8	0	4	4
4	4	0	4	8	0	4	4	6	4	4	0
2	16	0	16	8	0	4	4	4	16	4	4

5. (A) $df_{between} = 1$, $df_{within} = 8$, $df_{total} = 9$

6. (A) $s_T^2 = 13.33$ (B) $MS_{between} = 40.00$, $MS_{within} = 10.00$ (C) $F = 4.00$

11. (A)

Source	SS	df	MS	F
Between	40	1	40.00	6.96
Within	46	8	5.75	
Total	86	9		

(B)

Source	SS	df	MS	F
Between	40	1	40.00	6.96
Within	46	8	5.75	
Total	86	9		

(C)

Source	SS	df	MS	F
Between	40	1	40.00	2.19
Within	146	8	18.25	
Total	186	9		

(D)

Source	SS	df	MS	F
Between	10	1	10.00	1.74
Within	46	8	5.75	
Total	56	9		

12. (A)

Source	SS	df	MS	F
Between	1,572	3	524.00	42.60*
Within	246	20	12.30	
Total	1,818	23		

$*p < .05$ ($F_{critical} = 3.10$)

(B) $t_{protein\ vs.\ balanced} = 2.469*$, $t_{protein\ vs.\ carbs} = 6.914*$, $t_{protein\ vs.\ none} = 10.371*$, $t_{balanced\ vs.\ carbs} = 3.951*$, $t_{balanced\ vs.\ none} = 7.408*$, $t_{carbs\ vs.\ none} = 3.457*$; $t_{critical}$ with 10 *df* and α of .05 is 2.228. All comparisons with asterisks are significant.

13. (A)

Source	SS	df	MS	F
Between	170	4	42.50	19.32*
Within	44	20	2.20	
Total	214	24		

$*p < .05$ ($F_{critical} = 2.78$)

(B) $t_{D\ vs.\ S} = 2.132$, $t_{D\ vs.\ E} = 5.330*$, $t_{D\ vs.\ none} = 6.396*$, $t_{D\ vs.\ PR} = 7.462*$, $t_{S\ vs.\ E} = 3.198*$, $t_{S\ vs.\ none} = 4.264*$, $t_{S\ vs.\ PR} = 5.330*$, $t_{E\ vs.\ none} = 1.066$, $t_{E\ vs.\ PR} = 2.132$, $t_{none\ vs.\ PR} = 1.066$, $t_{critical}$ with 8 *df* and $\alpha = .05$ is 2.306. Comparisons marked with asterisks are significant.

14. (A)

Source	SS	df	MS	F
Between	170.0	4	42.50	50.00*
Subjects	30.4	4	7.60	
Within	13.6	16	0.85	
Total	214.0	24		

$*p < .05$ ($F_{critical} = 3.01$)

(B) $t_{D\ vs.\ S} = 3.430*$, $t_{D\ vs.\ E} = 8.575*$, $t_{D\ vs.\ none} = 10.290*$, $t_{D\ vs.\ PR} = 12.049*$, $t_{S\ vs.\ E} = 5.145*$, $t_{S\ vs.\ none} = 6.860*$, $t_{S\ vs.\ PR} = 8.575*$, $t_{E\ vs.\ none} = 1.715$, $t_{E\ vs.\ PR} = 3.430*$, $t_{none\ vs.\ PR} = 1.715$, $t_{critical}$ with 8 *df* and $\alpha = .05$ is 2.306. Comparisons marked with asterisks are significant.

15. (A)

Source	SS	df	MS	F
Between	378	2	189.00	54.00*
Subjects	48	8	6.00	
Within	56	18	3.50	
Total	482	27		

$*p < .05$ ($F_{critical} = 3.55$)

(B) $t_{Mozart\ vs.\ Stones} = 3.402*$, $t_{Mozart\ vs.\ Sinatra} = 10.205*$, $t_{Stones\ vs.\ Sinatra} = 6.803*$, $t_{critical}$ with 16 *df* and $\alpha = .05$ is 2.120. Comparisons marked with asterisks are significant.

Chapter 17

2. (A) 400 (B) 0 (C) 200

4. (A) Set V (B) Set II (C) Set VI (D) Set III (E) Set IV (F) Set I

5.

Source	SS	df	MS	F
A	1,040	2	20.00	4.00
B	90	3	30.00	6.00
$A \times B$	60	6	10.00	2.00
Within	1,140	228	5.00	
Total	1,330	239		

6. (A)

Source	SS	df	MS	F
A	80	1	80.00	32.00
B	20	1	20.00	8.00
$A \times B$	0	1	0.00	0.00
Within	40	16	2.50	
Total	140	19		

(B)

Source	SS	df	MS	F
A	80	1	80.00	32.00
B	20	1	20.00	8.00
$A \times B$	0	1	0.00	0.00
Within	40	16	2.50	
Total	140	19		

(C)

Source	SS	df	MS	F
A	180	1	180.00	72.00
B	0	1	0.00	0.00
$A \times B$	20	1	20.00	8.00
Within	40	16	2.50	
Total	240	19		

(D)

Source	SS	df	MS	F
A	80	1	80.00	6.40
B	20	1	20.00	1.60
$A \times B$	0	1	0.00	0.00
Within	200	16	12.50	
Total	300	19		

7. Set I: $SS_A = 160$, $SS_B = 160$, $SS_{A \times B} = 40$; Set II: $SS_A = 120$, $SS_B = 60$, $SS_{A \times B} = 120$; Set III: $SS_A = 2,000$, $SS_B = 180$, $SS_{A \times B} = 120$

8. Set I: $df_A = 1$, $df_B = 3$, $df_{A \times B} = 3$, $df_{within} = 48$, $df_{total} = 55$; Set II: $df_A = 4$, $df_B = 2$, $df_{A \times B} = 8$, $df_{within} = 45$, $df_{total} = 59$; Set III: $df_A = 2$, $df_B = 5$, $df_{A \times B} = 10$, $df_{within} = 162$, $df_{total} = 179$; Set IV: $df_A = 1$, $df_B = 2$, $df_{A \times B} = 2$, $df_{within} = 78$, $df_{total} = 83$

9. Set I: Variable A, $F_{.05} = 4.08$, $F_{.01} = 7.31$. Variable B, $F_{.05} = 2.84$, $F_{.01} = 4.31$. Interaction, $F_{.05} = 2.84$, $F_{.01} = 4.31$. Set II: Variable A, $F_{.05} = 2.61$, $F_{.01} = 3.83$. Variable B, $F_{.05} = 3.23$, $F_{.01} = 5.18$. Interaction, $F_{.05} = 2.18$, $F_{.01} = 2.99$. Set III: Variable A, $F_{.05} = 3.07$, $F_{.01} = 4.78$. Variable B, $F_{.05} = 2.29$, $F_{.01} = 3.17$. Interaction, $F_{.05} = 1.90$, $F_{.01} = 2.47$. Set IV: Variable A, $F_{.05} = 3.98$, $F_{.01} = 7.01$. Variable B, $F_{.05} = 3.13$, $F_{.01} = 4.92$. Interaction, $F_{.05} = 3.13$, $F_{.01} = 4.92$.

10.

Source	SS	df	MS	F
A	20	1	20.00	8.89*
B	45	1	45.00	20.00*
$A \times B$	5	1	5.00	2.22
Within	36	16	2.25	
Total	106	19		

*$p < .05$.

11.

Source	SS	df	MS	F
Type of music	740	2	370.00	49.89*
Type of student	30	1	30.00	4.05
Music $\times$ student	260	2	130.00	17.53*
Within	178	24	7.42	
Total	1,208	29		

*$p < .05$.

Levels of music among traditional students: $t_{critical} = 2.306$, 8 df. $t_{Stones-Sinatra} = 10.448$, $t_{Stones-Mozart} = 3.483$; $t_{Mozart-Sinatra} = 6.965$. Levels of music among nontraditional students: $t_{Mozart-Sinatra} = 4.644$, $t_{Mozart-Stones} = 2.322$, $t_{Stones-Sinatra} = 2.322$.

12.

Source	SS	df	MS	F
Exercise	180	2	90.00	49.09
Sex	30	1	30.00	16.36
Exercise $\times$ sex	0	2	0.00	0.00
Within	44	24	1.83	
Total	254	29		

Comparisons of levels of exercise: $t_{critical} = 2.306$, 8 df. $t_{high-moderate} = 4.959$, $t_{high-low} = 9.918$, $t_{medium-low} = 4.959$.

Chapter 18

3. Professor I: $\chi^2 = 72.00$, $\phi' = .85$; Professor II: $\chi^2 = 18.00$, $\phi' = .42$, Professor I: $\chi^2 = 0$, $\phi' = 0$; Professor IV: $\chi^2 = 18.00$, $\phi' = .42$; Professor V: $\chi^2 = 72.00$, $\phi' = .85$ (A) Professor III (B) Professors I and V

6. (A) $df = 6$, $\alpha = .05$, critical $\chi^2 = 12.59$ (B) $df = 1$, $\alpha = .01$, critical $\chi^2 = 6.64$ (C) $df = 4$, $\alpha = .05$, critical $\chi^2 = 9.49$ (D) $df = 10$, $\alpha = .01$, critical $\chi^2 = 23.21$

7. $df = 1$, $\chi^2 = 23.645$, $p < .05$.

8. $df = 1$, $\chi^2 = 1.2698$, $p > .05$.

9. $df = 3$, $\chi^2 = 27.861$, $p < .05$.

10. $df = 8$, $\chi^2 = 61.25$, $p < .05$.

11. $df - 4$, $\chi^2 - 18.00$, $p < .05$.

12. $df = 1$, $\chi^2 = 1.33$, $p > .05$.

13. $df = 4$, $\chi^2 = 9.85$, $p < .05$.

14. $df = 11$, $\chi^2 = 12.52$, $p > .05$.

Glossary of Statistical Terms

The numbers in parentheses represent the number of the chapter in which the term is first introduced.

abscissa   the horizontal axis of a graph; also called the X–axis (3)

absolute zero   a property of a ratio measurement, in which the value of zero represents the absence of the thing being measured (2)

a posteriori probability   a probability based on a set of scores drawn from observations that have actually been made in the real world (10)

a priori probability   a probability derived from a theoretical distribution, a distribution based on a mathematical theory rather than on a set of scores drawn from empirical observations (10)

alternate hypothesis (H_1)   in a statistical test, the hypothesis that asserts that there is a relationship in a population of scores between the variables being studied and that the sample results were caused by that relationship (12)

analysis of variance   a hypothesis test used to assess whether the means of two or more levels of a factor are significantly different; the analysis of variance can be conducted on one or more factors simultaneously (16)

assumptions   conditions presumed to be true during a hypothesis test (12)

average absolute deviation from the mean   the average of the absolute distance of each score from the mean (5)

bar graph   a graph in which bars are used to represent the frequency that the score values of a discrete, qualitative variable occur in a distribution (3)

between-groups source of variance   in an analysis of variance, a factor or interaction of factors that causes the scores to differ between the groups tested (17)

between-groups sum of squares   the sum of the squared deviations of each sample mean from the grand mean in an analysis of variance, which is a measure of the variation between the sample means, assumed to be attributable to the factor being studied (16)

between-subjects factor   a factor in which different subjects are tested under each level or treatment, such that each subject is tested in only one group for the factor (16)

between-subjects test   a statistical test in which two or more different, unrelated samples of subjects are tested, each sample under one level of the variable under consideration (14)

bidirectional test   for a parametric test, a statistical test in which the alternate hypothesis predicts that a parameter of one population will be different from the same parameter in another population but does not specify in which direction that difference will occur (12)

bimodal distribution   a distribution that has two clusters of scores and thus two peaks in its graph (4)

binomial distribution   the set of probabilities for X successes in N events, with X taking on values from 0 to N, and where the probability of a success on any one event is known (10)

bivariate descriptive statistics   statistics that are used to describe the relationship between two groups of scores, representing two variables (8)

blind guess   a prediction made without the aid of any relevant information (9)

cell   a group of scores tested under one combination of levels of all the factors in an analysis of variance (17); also the frequency of subjects in a contingency table in one combination of the levels of two variables (18)

central limit theorem   the proposition that distributions of sample means become increasingly normal in form as the size of the samples increases (11)

central tendency   the point on a measurement scale that represents the center of a distribution of scores or that represents the score that is most typical or representative of the distribution (4)

chi square (χ^2)   a measure of the degree of relationship between two variables whose values can be listed in a contingency table with r rows (representing one variable) and c columns (representing the other variable) (18)

chi square (χ^2) test   a hypothesis test to determine whether the relationship between two variables differs significantly from what would be expected if there were no relationship; also a hypothesis test to determine whether an observed frequency distribution differs from a set of theoretical or a priori predictions (18)

coefficient of determination   the proportion of variability in the predicted variable Y accounted for by variability in the predictor variable X, which is equal to r^2 (9)

coefficient of nondetermination   the proportion of variability in the predicted variable Y that is not accounted for by variability in the predictor variable X, which is equal to $1 - r^2$ (9)

confidence interval   the segment of the number line between the lower and upper confidence limits (11)

confidence limits the score values between which a population parameter is expected to lie, with a given probability, as predicted by a sampling distribution. The given probability is called the level of confidence (11)

constant a characteristic of a population for which only one value occurs in that population (2)

contingency table a table that shows the frequency of subjects in each combination of levels of two variables (18)

continuous variable a variable for which the unit of measurement can be infinitely divided into smaller and smaller units (2)

correlation a description of the relationship between scores representing two different variables. It is a description of the degree to which the values of those two variables are related or covary (8)

correlation coefficient a number that measures the strength of the relationship between two variables, usually on a scale from -1 to $+1$ (8)

critical value in a statistical test, the value of the statistic being tested that falls at the boundary in the sampling distribution between rejecting and not rejecting the null hypothesis. The critical value of the statistic has α beyond it in the relevant tail(s) of the sampling distribution (12)

cross product in measures of correlation, the product of two scores, each representing a different variable (8). In the analysis of variance, the product of the deviation of a cell mean from the two main effect sample means to which that cell contributes (17)

cumulative frequency table a table that shows the number of subjects who score at or below each score value in a distribution (3)

curvilinear relationship the relationship in a set of pairs of scores representing two variables that can be described by a curved line on a scatterplot (8)

data a set of measurements obtained from a group of subjects on a given variable (2)

datum a measurement of one subject on a given variable. The plural of *datum* is *data* (2)

decision rule a statement in a hypothesis test of the conditions under which the null hypothesis will and will not be rejected (12)

degree of precision the degree of accuracy in which a variable is measured (2)

degrees of freedom (*df*) the number of values that are free to vary in the sample(s) used in a statistical test, given certain restrictions (13)

descriptive statistics procedures used to describe the characteristics of a set of scores or to describe the relationship between sets of scores (1)

deviation the distance that a score lies from a given point (5)

deviation from the mean the distance that a score lies from the mean of the distribution (5)

directional test *see* unidirectional test

discrete variable   a variable which cannot be infinitely divided into smaller units without changing the essential nature of the characteristic being measured (2)

distribution   a set of score values and the frequency with which those values occur (3)

effect size   a measure of the effect that one variable has on another variable. In a statistical test, given that the alternate hypothesis is true, that there is a relationship between two variables, the greater the effect of one of those variables on the other, the more powerful the statistical test is (13)

empirical probability   a probability based on a set of scores drawn from observations that have actually been made in the real world (10)

empirical sampling distribution   a sampling distribution constructed by drawing actual samples from a population and computing the specified statistic (11)

equal intervals   a property of interval and ratio measurement scales, in which the size of the interval in which scores are measured is known and constant across the entire scale (2)

expected frequency   the number of subjects expected to have a given score value or combination of score values if there is no relationship between the variable(s) under study or as predicted theoretically (18)

factor   a variable whose values are used to divide the subjects into groups (16)

first quartile (Q_1)   the point on the number line that has 25 percent of the scores below it (5)

frequency distribution   a set of scores that actually did occur when a set of observations was made (3)

frequency table   a tabular presentation of a frequency distribution showing the number of subjects who receive each score value (3)

goodness of fit   the degree to which the observed frequencies in a contingency table conform to theoretical predictions (18)

grand mean   the mean of all of the scores in an analysis of variance (16)

group interval   a segment of a scale of measurement that contains more than one score value (3)

grouped frequency distribution   a set of groups of score values and the frequencies of the score values in each group (3)

homogeneity of variance   an assumption of parametric hypothesis tests that the variance of the populations from which the samples being tested were drawn is equal (16)

hypothesis   a testable assertion about the relation between variables in a population of scores (12)

independent events   two or more events such that the outcome of one event has no influence whatsoever on the outcome of the other events (10)

independent sample a sample selected such that the selection of any one member of the population for inclusion in the sample does not affect the probability that any other member of the population will be selected (11)

inferential statistics statistical techniques that use scores from a sample to make inferences about the population from which the sample was drawn (1)

insignificant difference in an inferential statistical test, a difference between the sample statistic(s) and the value predicted by the null hypothesis that is not large enough to reject the null hypothesis (12)

interaction in an analysis of variance, a condition in which the effect of one factor on scores differs between levels of the other factor (17)

interquartile range the distance between the first and third quartiles of a distribution (5)

interval the segment of a number line represented by a single value of a continuous variable (2)

interval scale of measurement a scale which has equal distances between adjacent numbers (equal intervals), as well as ordinality (2)

interval size the width of the segment on the number line represented by a score value, which is always equal to the unit of measurement (2)

least-squares criterion defines the accuracy of prediction as the sum of the squared differences between true scores and predicted scores, a sum which is lowest when the predicted scores are on the regression line (9)

level of confidence the probability that the population parameter will lie within the confidence interval (11)

level of significance (α) the probability criterion selected as a basis for rejecting the null hypothesis (12)

levels the values of a variable measuring a subject characteristic that divide the subjects into groups in an analysis of variance (16)

linear relationship the relationship in a set of pairs of scores representing two variables that can be described by a straight line on a scatterplot (8)

lower real limit the lowest point on the number line that can be assigned to a particular score value (2)

lower real limit of a group interval the point on the number line that is one-half the original interval size below the lower stated limit of the group interval (3)

lower stated limit of a group interval the lowest score value in the group interval (3)

magnitude a property of ordinal, interval, and ratio measurement scales in which the size of the score value reflects an amount of the thing being measured and thus the order of the score values is meaningful (2)

main effect the overall influence on the scores of one of the factors in an analysis of variance (17)

major mode the score value that has the highest frequency in a distribution (4)

Mann-Whitney *U* test   a nonparametric statistical test for the difference between two between-subjects samples of scores measured on an ordinal, interval, or ratio scale (15)

marginal value   the number of subjects in a given level of one variable in a contingency table across all of the levels of the other variable represented in the table (18)

mean   the arithmetic average of a distribution; it is the balance point of a group of scores, the value for which the sum of the distances of scores from that value is zero (4)

mean square   in an analysis of variance, the ratio of the sum of squares for a source of variance divided by the degrees of freedom for that source (16)

measure of central tendency   a descriptive statistic that describes the center point(s) of a set of scores, indicating where on a number line a set of scores is centered (3); also, a number that describes the center of a distribution of scores (4)

measure of relative standing   a transformation of a distribution of scores resulting in score values that indicate the location of each score relative to the other scores in the distribution (6)

measure of skewness   a descriptive statistic that describes the degree to which a set of scores is not symmetrical about the center point of the set and thus in which there are more scores at one end of the distribution than at the other (3)

measure of variability   a descriptive statistic that describes the degree to which a set of scores is spread out over the number line (3); also, a number that indicates the degree to which the scores in a distribution vary from the center point (5)

measurement   the process of using a rule to assign values to subjects on the characteristic being observed (2)

median   the value on the number line for which half of the scores in the distribution have lesser values and half of the scores have greater values (4)

midpoint of a group interval   the point on the number line that is halfway between the lower and upper stated limits, which is also halfway between the lower and upper real limits (3)

minor mode   in a distribution with more than one peak, the score value(s) that has the highest frequency in each peak, except for the highest peak (4)

mode   the score value that most frequently occurs in a distribution (4)

multimodal distribution   a distribution that has more than two clusters of scores and thus more than two peaks in its graph (4)

multiplication rule of probability   if the outcomes of two or more events are independent, the probability of a given outcome occurring for all events is the product of their individual probabilities: $P(A$ and B and C and . . .$) = P(A)P(B)P(C)$ . . . (10)

mutually exclusive events   two or more events that cannot occur simultaneously (10)

negative correlation   a relationship between two variables in which positive or large values on one variable tend to go with negative or small values on the other variable (8)

negatively skewed   a distribution in which the lower tail is longer than the upper tail (3)

negative relationship   a relationship between the values of two variables such that high values on one variable tend to occur with low values of the other variable (8)

nominal scale of measurement   a scale in which numbers are used solely to label, classify, identify, or otherwise differentiate values of the characteristic being measured (2)

nondirectional test   *see* bidirectional test

nonparametric statistical test   a hypothesis test in which the null and alternate hypotheses do not predict the value of a specific population parameter (12)

normal distribution   a symmetric, unimodal, bell-shaped probability distribution, used as a theoretical distribution to describe many physical and psychological variables (7)

null correlation   a zero or lack of relationship between the values of two variables, so that positive or high values on one variable occur just as frequently with positive, high values as with negative, low values on the other variable (8)

null hypothesis (H_0)   in a statistical test, the hypothesis that asserts that there is no relationship in a population of scores between the variables being studied, that the sample results were due solely to chance sampling (12)

observed frequency   the number of subjects actually observed in a study to have a given score value or combination of score values (18)

one-tailed test   a unidirectional test in which the rejection region lies in only one tail of the sampling distribution predicted by the null hypothesis (12)

operational definition   defining a variable by the procedures or operations used to measure the variable (2)

ordinal scale of measurement   a scale in which numbers are used to indicate the rank order of values of the characteristic being measured (2)

ordinate   the vertical axis of a graph; also called the Y–axis (3)

p   in a statistical test, the probability of obtaining the value of the sample statistic from the sampling distribution predicted by the null hypothesis (12)

parameter   a numeric summary calculated from the scores of a population, generally represented by Greek letters (2)

parametric statistical test   a hypothesis test in which the null and alternate hypotheses predict the value of a population parameter (12)

partition the sum of squares   to divide the total sum of squares into parts, each part attributable to a different source of variability (16)

Pearson's product-moment correlation coefficient (r)   a measure of the degree of relationship between two interval or ratio variables. The value of r ranges from -1.00 to $+1.00$. The value ± 1.00 represents a perfect relationship, while a value of 0 represents the absence of any relationship (8)

percentile   the score value that has a specified percent of the scores in a distribution below it (6)

percentile rank   the percent of scores in a distribution at or below a specified score value (6)

***phi* (ϕ) coefficient**   a measure of the correlation, or degree of relationship, between two dichotomous nominal variables (8)

***phi'* (ϕ') coefficient**   a measure of the correlation, or degree of relationship, between two dichotomous nominal variables (18)

pooled standard deviation   a combination of the standard deviations from two or more samples, hypothetically all drawn from the same population in order to provide a more stable estimate of the standard deviation of that population (14)

population   a group of subjects or events that have a common set of characteristics of interest in an experiment (2)

positive correlation   a relationship between two variables in which positive or large values on one variable tend to go with positive or large values on the other variable, while negative or small values on one variable tend to go with negative or small values on the other variable (8)

positively skewed   a distribution in which the upper tail is longer than the lower tail (3)

power   the probability of rejecting the null hypothesis when in fact there is a relationship in the population between the variables being studied. The power of a statistical test is $1 - \beta$ (12)

predicted variable   the variable, usually labeled Y', that a regression equation predicts (9)

prediction   a guess about what value an event drawn from a specified population will have on a given variable (9)

predictor variable   the variable in a regression equation, usually labeled X, that gives relevant information to help predict a value on another variable (9)

probability   a quantitative expression of the likelihood that an event will occur. An event whose probability is 1 is certain to occur, while an event whose probability is 0 is certain not to occur (10)

quartile   one of three points that divide a distribution into fourths (5)

random assignment   the process of assigning subjects to groups or treatment conditions in an experiment in such a way that a subject has an equal likelihood of being assigned to each of the groups or conditions (11)

random sample   a subgroup of a population in which each member of the population has an equal chance of being included (2)

random sampling   the process of drawing a sample from a population in such a way that each member of the population has an equal likelihood of being included in the sample (11)

range   the distance that a distribution of scores covers on the number line; that is, the distance between the lower real limit of the lowest score value and the upper real limit of the highest score value (5)

rank sum   the sum of the ranks assigned to the scores in the sample when those scores are rank-ordered (15)

ratio scale of measurement   a scale which has an absolute zero point, as well as equal distance between adjacent numbers and ordinality (2)

raw scores   scores expressed in the measurement scale that was originally used to measure and record the scores (6)

real limits   the upper and lower points of an interval on the number line represented by a given value (2)

regression equation   expresses the relationship between the known value of a predictor variable, X, and the predicted value of variable, Y, based on the correlation between the two variables. A linear regression equation has the form $Y' = a + bX$ (9)

regression toward the mean   the tendency, when the correlation between the predictor and predicted variables is less than perfect, for the value of the predicted variable to be closer to the mean, measured in standard deviations, than the corresponding value of the predictor variable (9)

rejection region   in a statistical test, the values of the statistic being tested that lie in the tail(s) of the sampling distribution beyond the critical value. If the sample statistic falls in the rejection region, then the probability of drawing that sample from the sampling distribution is less than α, and the null hypothesis is rejected (12)

relative cumulative frequency table   a table that shows the proportion of subjects who score at or below each score value in a distribution (3)

relative frequency table   a table that shows the proportion of subjects who receive each score value in a distribution (3)

sample   a subgroup of a population (2)

sampling distribution   a distribution of a given statistic, calculated from independently collected samples of size n, all drawn from the same population (11)

scatterplot   a graph of the relationship between two variables. The X-axis represents the values of variable X, the Y-axis represents the values of variable Y, and paired values of X and Y are represented on the graph by dots (8)

second quartile (Q_2)   the point that has 50 percent of the scores below it; the same point as the median (5)

semi-interquartile range (Q)   the average of the distance between the first and second quartiles and between the second and third quartiles (5)

significant difference   in an inferential statistical test, a difference between the sample statistic(s) and the value predicted by the null hypothesis that is large enough to reject the null hypothesis (12)

skewed   the shape of a distribution that is not symmetrical about the center, such that the frequencies of scores in the upper and lower halves of the distribution are not equal (3)

slope   the degree to which a line in a graph varies from horizontal, which reflects the degree of change in the values on the Y-axis relative to changes in the values on the X-axis. In the regression equation, $Y' = a + bX$, the value b represents the slope (9)

source of variance   a variable that causes the scores in a distribution to vary in value from each other (17)

Spearman's rank-order correlation coefficient (ρ)   a measure of the degree of relationship between two variables that can be ordered by rank. The value of r_s ranges from -1.00 to $+1.00$. The value ± 1.00 represents a perfect relationship, while a value of 0 represents the absence of any relationship (8)

standard deviation   the square root of the variance and thus the square root of the average squared deviation of scores from the mean (5)

standard error   the standard deviation of a sampling distribution (11)

standard error of a difference between means   the standard deviation of a distribution of the differences between the means of independent samples (14)

standard error of estimate   a measure of the degree to which the true value of scores will vary from the predicted values generated by a regression equation (9)

standard error of a mean difference   the standard deviation of a distribution of the mean difference between the scores in two samples (14)

standard error of the mean   the standard deviation of a distribution of sample means (11)

standard error of a proportion   the standard deviation of a distribution of sample proportions (12)

standard score   a measure of relative standing in which a score's location in a distribution is indicated as a ratio between the score's deviation from the mean and the standard deviation (6)

statistic   a numeric summary calculated from the scores of a sample, generally represented by roman letters (2)

stem-and-leaf display   a way of depicting a distribution of scores by separating the digits of each score into two parts, a stem composed of the leftmost digit(s) and a leaf composed of the rightmost digit(s); the leaves are then grouped by the stem values (3)

subject   a person or animal observed or tested in an experiment (2)

sum of squares   the sum of the squared deviations of scores from the center of a set of scores (16)

***t* test**   a parametric statistical test comparing the difference between two sample statistics or of a sample statistic from a given value, in which the standard error is estimated from the sample value (13)

theoretical distribution   the set of scores that would occur if a set of observations were made, based on theoretical predictions (3); also, a set of score values and the frequencies that would occur, as predicted by a theory (7)

theoretical probability   a probability derived from a theoretical distribution, a distribution based on a mathematical theory rather than on a set of scores drawn from empirical observations (10)

theoretical sampling distribution   sampling distribution constructed based on the characteristics of a mathematical theory, such as the binomial distribution or normal distribution (11)

third quartile (Q_3)   the point that has 75 percent of the scores below it (5)

total variance   a measure of the degree to which the scores in a distribution vary from the grand mean (16)

transformed score   score that has been changed by one or more mathematical operations from the original measurement scale to a new scale that has a different center point or degree of variability, or both (6)

treatments   the values of a variable in which subjects are divided into groups according to the way they are treated in the experiment (16)

two-tailed test   a bidirectional test in which there are rejection regions in both tails of the sampling distribution predicted by the null hypothesis (12)

Type I error   in hypothesis testing, a decision error in which the null hypothesis is rejected when in fact there is no relationship in the population between the variables being studied. The probability of a Type I error occurring is α, the level of significance (12)

Type II error   in hypothesis testing, a decision error in which the null hypothesis is not rejected when in fact there is a relationship in the population between the variables being studied. The probability of a Type II error is β (12)

unidirectional test   for a parametric test, a statistical test in which the alternate hypothesis predicts that a parameter of one population will be either less than or greater than the same parameter in another population (12)

unimodal distribution a distribution that has only one apparent cluster of scores and thus only one peak in its graph (4)

unit of measurement the quantity selected to serve as the unit with which to measure a variable (2)

univariate descriptive statistic a statistic that is used to describe a group of scores measured on one variable (8)

upper real limit the point immediately above the highest point on the number line that can be assigned to a particular score value. The upper real limit of one score value is equal to the lower real limit of the next higher score value (2)

upper real limit of a group interval the point that is one-half the original interval size above the upper stated limit of the group interval (3)

upper stated limit of a group interval the highest score value in the group interval (3)

variable a characteristic of a population for which more than one value occurs in that population (2)

variance the average of the squared deviations of scores from the mean (5)

Wilcoxon ranked-sums test a nonparametric statistical test for the difference between two within-subjects samples of scores measured on an ordinal, interval, or ratio scale (15)

within-groups source of variance in an analysis of variance, the variance in scores that is caused by random variation in scores among the subjects within each group (17)

within-groups sum of squares the sum of the squared deviations of each score from the mean of the sample containing that score, which is a measure of the variation of the scores within the samples, assumed to be attributable to random variation (16)

within-subjects factor a factor in which the same or related subjects are tested under each level or treatment (16)

within-subjects test a statistical test in which either one sample of subjects is tested under two or more levels of a variable or different but related samples of subjects are tested under each level of the variable (14)

X-axis the horizontal axis of a graph; also called the abscissa (3)

Y-axis the vertical axis of a graph; also called the ordinate (3)

Y-intercept the point that a line on a graph crosses the Y-axis. In the regression equation, $Y' = a + bX$, the value a represents the Y-intercept (9)

Glossary of Statistical Symbols

The numbers in parentheses represent the number of the chapter in which the symbol is first introduced.

Greek Letters

α Greek *alpha,* the level of significance in a hypothesis test; also the probability of a Type I error; pronounced "al-phuh" (12)

β Greek *beta,* the probability of a Type II error; rhymes with "data" (12)

χ^2 Greek *chi* square, a statistic used in tests of nominal variables; pronounced "ki," rhyming with "eye" (18)

ϕ Greek *phi,* a measure of the correlation between nominal variables; pronounced "fie," rhyming with "pie" (8)

ϕ' *phi',* also called Cramer's statistic (18)

μ Greek *mu,* the mean of the scores in a population; pronounced "mew," rhyming with "pew" (4)

μ_p mean of a distribution of sample proportions (11)

$\mu_{\bar{X}}$ mean of a distribution of sample means (11)

ρ_S Greek *rho,* Spearman's rank-order correlation coefficient for the relationship between two variables in a population of scores; pronounced "row" (15)

ρ_{XY} Greek *rho,* Pearson's product-moment correlation coefficient for the relationship between two variables in a population of scores; pronounced "row" (14)

σ Greek lower-case *sigma,* the standard deviation of the scores in a population; pronounced "sig-muh," where "sig" rhymes with "pig" (5)

σ^2 variance of the scores in a population (5)

σ_P standard error of a proportion (11)

$\sigma_{\bar{X}}$ standard error of the mean (11)

$\sigma_{\bar{X}_1 - \bar{X}_2}$ standard error of the difference between sample means (14)

Σ Greek upper-case *sigma,* the mathematical operation of summation (4)

ΣX	sum of the scores labeled X (4)
ΣX^2	sum of the squares of the scores labeled X (4)
ΣXY	sum of the cross products of scores on variables X and Y (8)

Roman Letters

a	Y-intercept of a regression line (9)
b	slope of a regression line (9)
C	a constant (6)
CL	confidence limit (11)
df	degrees of freedom (13)
f	frequency of scores (3)
F	statistic calculated in the analysis of variance (16)
f_b	frequency of scores with values lower than the value being considered (4)
f_w	frequency of scores with value being considered (4)
H_0	null hypothesis (12)
H_1	alternate hypothesis (12)
i	interval size (3)
LRL	lower real limit (4)
Md	median (4)
MS	mean square (16)
n	the number of scores in a sample (3)
N	number of scores in a population (4)
p	probability of specified outcome occurring in one event (10)
P	proportion of a score value in a sample of scores (11)
p	probability, in a hypothesis test, of obtaining the observed result if the null hypothesis is true (12)
$P(A)$	probability of event A occurring (10)
Q	semi-interquartile range (5)
Q_1	first quartile (5)
Q_2	second quartile (5)
Q_3	third quartile (5)
r	Pearson's product-moment correlation coefficient (8)
r_S	Spearman's rank-order correlation coefficient (8)
r_{XY}	Pearson's product-moment correlation coefficient between variables X and Y (9)
s	standard deviation of the scores in a sample (5)
s^2	variance of the scores in a sample (5)
SS	sum of squares (16)
$s_{\bar{X}}$	unbiased estimate of the standard error of the mean (11)
$s_{\bar{X}_1 - \bar{X}_2}$	standard error of the difference between sample means (14)
$s_{\bar{X}_D}$	standard error of a mean difference (14)
$s_{Y|X}$	standard error of estimate in predicting score value on variable Y from score value on variable X (9)

$t_{\overline{X}}$	statistic calculated in the t test for a sample mean (13)
$t_{\overline{X}_1 - \overline{X}_2}$	statistic calculated in the t test for a difference between sample means (14)
$t_{\overline{X}_D}$	statistic calculated in the t test for a mean difference (14)
U	statistic calculated in the Mann-Whitney U test (15)
W	statistic calculated in the Wilcoxon ranked-sums test (15)
X	a score (3)
$\overline{X}$	mean of the scores in a sample (4)
Y	a score (3)
Y'	score value on variable Y predicted by a regression equation (9)
z	a standard score (6)
z_P	statistic calculated in the z test for a sample proportion (13)
$z_{\overline{X}}$	statistic calculated in the z test for a sample mean (12)

Index

A posteriori probability. *See* Empirical probability
A priori probability. *See* Theoretical probability
Achievement tests, 149
Addition rule in probability, 261–262, 264–265
Alternate hypotheses
bidirectional tests, 323–325
chi square tests, 538–539, 541, 544
explained, 313–315
interaction of two factors, 493–495
main effects of two factors, 492–493
Mann-Whitney U test, 421–424, 427, 429
Pearson's product-moment correlation, 397–400
Spearman's rank-order correlation, 437
t tests, 350, 387, 388–389, 392–395
unidirectional tests, 323–325
Wilcoxon signed-ranks test, 432
z tests, 329, 353, 355
See also Hypothesis testing
American Psychological Association, 5
Analysis of variance
among scores, 449–457
between-subjects and within-subjects tests compared, 476–478
between-subjects factor, 457–466
F statistics, 456–457
one-factor, 457–460
partitioning the degrees of freedom, 454–455
partitioning the sum of squares, 450–454
posttests, 466–468
t test for a difference between sample means, 449–450, 466–468
total variance, 455–457
value of F, 464–465

within-subjects, 468–476
See also Two-factor analysis of variance
ANOVA. *See* Analysis of variance
Arithmetic mean. *See* Mean
Average absolute deviation, 111–113
Average deviation, 111

Bar graphs, 48
Between-groups sum of squares, 453
Between-groups variance, 456, 491–492
Between-subjects factors, 459–460, 488–506
Between-subjects tests, 377–389
analysis of variance, 457–468
compared to within-subject tests, 476–478
Mann-Whitney U test, 419–429
t test for a difference between means, 378–389
Biased estimate of standard error, 295
Bidirectional inferential tests, 323–325
Bimodal distribution, 93
Binomial distribution, 265–272
binomial equation, 267
defined, 265
mean and standard deviation of, 270–272
relevance of, 272
table of binomial probabilities, 268–269, 282–283
See also Distributions; Probability
Bivariate descriptive statistics, 192
Blind guessing, 225–228

Causation
correlation and, 213–214
regression and, 248
Cells,
in the analysis of variance, 492
in a contingency table, 525

Central tendency, measures of, 65, 74
See also Mean; Median; Mode
Characteristics
distribution, 552–554
measurement, 18–20
Chi square, 523–545
comparing tests, 545
computing, 528–530
defined, 524
goodness of fit, 543–545
hypothesis testing, 535–545
as measure of strength of a relationship, 531–534
measuring the significance of, 534–535
null and alternate hypotheses, 538–539, 541, 542–543, 544, 545
observed and expected frequencies, 525–528
test of association, 535–539
test of independence, 540–543
Coefficients
correlation coefficient, 192
determination and nondetermination, 247–248
Pearson's product-moment correlation, 198–200, 395–401
phi, 212–213
phi', 530–535
Spearman's rank-order correlation, 206–207, 436–439
Cohen, Jacob, 366, 367, 368
Computational formulas for variance and standard deviation, 117–119
Confidence, levels of, 298–301
Confidence intervals, 295–301
Constants, 137–141
defined, 17–18
differentiating from variables, 17
Contingency tables, 524–528, 534
Continuous variables, 20–21, 24

Converting units of measurement, 137–145
Correlation, 191–214
    causation and, 213–214
    correlation coefficient, 192
    Cramer's statistic, 530–535
    curvilinear relationship, 196–198
    defined, 192–195
    linear relationship, 196–198
    methods of measuring, 197–198
    negative correlation, 195
    null correlations, 196
    Pearson's product-moment correlation, 198–206, 395–401
    perfect correlation, 195–196
    phi coefficient, 212–213, 530–535
    positive correlation, 195
    regression and, 248
    scatterplots, 193–195
    significant *vs.* meaningful, 400–401
    Spearman's rank-order correlation, 206–211, 436–439
    using chi square to measure two variables, 530–535
    See also Prediction
Cramer's statistic, 530–535
Critical values
    chi square tests, 539, 541, 544–545
    of *F*, 464–465
    Mann-Whitney *U* test, 422, 429
    Pearson's product-moment correlation, 399
    Spearman's rank-order correlation, 438
    t tests, 351, 388, 394
    Wilcoxon signed-ranks test, 433–434
    z tests, 329–330, 355
Cumulative frequency tables, 42–43
Curvilinear relationship, 196–198

Data, 18
Decision rule in hypothesis testing, 320
Definitional formulas for variance and standard deviation, 112–117
Degree of precision, 22–23
Degrees of freedom, 347–348, 454–455, 463–464, 474, 502–503
Describing distribution of scores, 126–128
Descriptive statistics
    bivariate, 192
    defined, 9
    univariate, 192
Determination, coefficient of, 247
Deviation
    average absolute deviation, 111–113
    average deviation, 111

defined, 110
    from the mean, 110–112, 141–144
    partitioning the deviation, 452
    variance, 112
    See also Standard deviation
Discrete variables, 20–21
Distributions
    characteristics of, 65–67, 552–554
    comparing scores between, 140–146
    defined, 38–39
    finite, 171–172
    mean difference, 378–381, 389–391
    measures of central tendency, 65
    measures of skewness, 65–67
    measures of variability, 65, 107–128
    range, 108–110
    rank sums, 413–419
    of scores, 285–286, 555
    shape of, 553–554
    symmetrical *vs.* unsymmetrical, 553–554
    unimodal *vs.* multimodal, 554
    See also Binomial distribution; Frequency distributions; Normal distribution; Sampling distributions; Theoretical distributions

Educational tests, 159
Effect size and power of a statistical test, 364–367
Empirical distributions of sample means, 285–288
Empirical probability, 258–261
Empirical sampling distribution, 281–282, 283–285
Error
    calculating, using sample standard deviation, 294–295
    prediction and, 228, 244–246
    standard error of a distribution of sample means, 380–381
    standard error of estimate, 244–246
    standard error of the mean, 290, 294–295
    type I and II errors, 333–336, 357–368, 448
Estimates, sample statistics as, 16
Ethical Principles of Psychologists and Code of Conduct, 5
Ethics, 5–6
Events and probability, 261
Expected frequencies, 525–528
Experiments
    describing distribution of scores, 126–128
    psychological research, 6–9
    structure of, 14–18

F, values of, 464–465, 474–475, 495–506
Factors, 457–460, 486–488
Finite distributions, 171–172
Formulas, 77–78
Frequencies, observed and expected, 525–528
Frequency distributions
    advantages of frequency tables, 40
    bar graphs, 48
    calculating mean from frequency tables, 81–82
    calculating the median, 85–89
    calculating quartiles, 121–124
    constructing frequency tables, 39–44, 45
    constructing graphs, 44–55
    cumulative, 42–43
    defined, 38, 39–40
    frequency histograms, 48
    frequency ogives, 51
    frequency polygons, 50–52
    grouped, 55–65
    mode, 94–96
    relative, 41–42
    relative cumulative, 43–44
    using summation sign in, 76–77

General addition rule of probability, 262
General multiplication rule of probability, 263
Given proportions under the normal curve and corresponding scores, 181–186
Goodness of fit, 543–545
Gosset, William, 348
Grand mean, 450–454
Graphs
    bar graphs, 48
    basic structure of, 45–47
    binomial distribution, 269
    chi square tests, 539, 541, 545
    constructing, 53
    frequency distribution, 44–55, 94–96
    frequency polygons, 50–52
    histograms, 48
    interaction between factors, 486–488, 494
    Mann-Whitney *U* test, 422–424
    mode and, 94–96
    normal distribution, 168–169
    Pearson's product-moment correlation, 399
    regression line, 233–237
    sampling distributions, 290–293, 330
    scatterplot, 193–195, 229–230
    slope, 230–232

Spearman's rank-order correlation, 438
straight line, 229–233
t tests, 351, 388–389, 394–395
Wilcoxon signed-ranks test, 434
Y-intercept, 230–237
z test for a sample proportion, 355
Group intervals, 55–62
Grouped frequency distribution
calculating the mean, 81–82
calculating the median, 89
modes, 95–96
percentile ranks, 156
standard deviation, 116–117
tables, 55–65, 156
Guessing, blind, 225–228

Histograms, frequency, 48
Hypothesis testing
bidirectional tests, 323–325
Chi square, 535–545
decision making, 331–336, 357–368
decision rule, 320
differences between statistical tests, 439–440
inferring the value of the population mean, 309
population, 368–370
possible values of population mean, 310–311
power of a statistical test, 335, 357–368
as purpose of statistic, 557
sampling distribution and, 315–323
significant and insignificant difference in, 321–322
Type I and Type II errors, 333–336, 357–368, 448
unidirectional tests, 323–327
value of *p*, 322–323
z test for a sample mean, 320–322, 327–332
See also Alternate hypotheses; Null hypotheses

Independent events and probability, 262–263
Independent samples, 280–281
Inferential statistics, 278, 308
defined, 9
See also Hypothesis testing
Insignificant difference in hypothesis testing, 321–322
Intelligence tests, 148–149
Interaction between factors, 486–488
null and alternate hypotheses, 493–495

posttests, 508–515
sum of squares, 499–500
Intervals, 23–24
interval scales of measurement, 29–30, 98, 412, 553
interval size, 24–26, 108–109

*k*th percentile, 150–156

Least-squares criterion and regression, 242–244
Level of significance. *See* Significance, level of
Levels, 458
Levels of confidence. *See* Confidence, levels of
Linear relationship, 196–198
Lower real limits, 24–26, 63–64
Lower stated limits of group intervals, 62–63

Main effects
in analysis of variance, 492–493
posttests for, 506–508
Major modes, 94
Mann-Whitney *U* test, 419–429
Marginal value in a contingency table, 526
Math phobia, 2–3
Maximum rank sum, 416–417
Mean
average absolute deviation from the, 112
as balance point of a distribution, 83–84
of binomial distribution, 270–272
calculating, 79–82
comparing median, mode and, 96–98
converting scores, 138–140
defined, 79
deviation from the, 110–112, 141–144
difference, 389–395
formula for calculating, 77
interpreting, 82–84
of a population, 80–81
proportion of scores between the, and a *z* score, 175–177
regression to the, 239–242
regression as predictor of the, 238–239
sample means, distributions of, 285–295
of samples, 80–81
of standard scores, 144–145
t test comparing more than two means, 449–450, 466–468

t test of a mean difference, 389–395
t test for a difference between means, 378–395
t test for a sample mean, 345–352
using, as a prediction, 227–228
Mean squares, 503
Meaningful correlations, 400–401
Measurement
characteristics and number lines, 18–20
continuous and discrete variables, 20–21
converting units of, 137–145, 147
defined, 18
degree of precision, 22–23
interval scales, 29–30, 98, 412, 553
nominal scales, 27, 97, 412–413, 552–553
operational definitions, 18
ordinal scales, 27–29, 97–98, 412–413, 553
ratio scales, 30, 98, 412, 553
real limits, 24–26
scales of, 26–32, 97–98, 412–413, 552–553
units of, 20, 22–23, 24
Median
comparing mean, mode and, 96–98
computing, 84–89
defined, 84
interpreting, 89–92
Midpoints
calculating means using, 81–82
of group intervals, 65
Minimum rank sum, 416
Minor modes, 94
Misuse of statistics, 5–6
Mode
bimodal distribution, 93
comparing mean, median and, 96–98
defined, 92
of grouped distributions, 93
multimodal distribution, 93, 554
Multimodal distribution, 93, 554
Multiplication rule of probability, 262–265
Mutually exclusive outcomes in probability, 261–262

Negative correlation, 195
Nominal scales of measurement, 27, 97, 412–413, 552–553
Nominal variables, 524
Nondetermination, coefficient of, 248
Nonparametric inferential tests, 412–440
Nonparametric statistics, 308

Nonparametric tests
　　Mann-Whitney *U* test, 419–429
　　parametric tests *vs.*, 440
　　sampling distribution of ranks, 413–419
　　sampling distribution of *U*, 417–419
　　Spearman's rank-order correlation, 436–439
　　Wilcoxon signed-ranks test, 430–436
Normal distribution
　　characteristics, 169–171
　　defined, 168–169
　　determining proportion of scores under the normal curve, 174–181
　　given proportions under the normal curve and corresponding scores, 181–186
　　graphs, 169–171, 173–174
　　intelligence tests and, 171
　　proportion of scores under normal curve, 174–181
　　relevance of, 186–187
　　tables, 170–171, 173–174
　　as theoretical distribution, 171–173
Notation system in two-factor analysis of variance, 491–492
Null correlations, 196
Null hypotheses, 313–314
　　analysis of variance for a between-subjects factor, 464–466
　　bidirectional and unidirectional tests, 324–325
　　chi square tests, 538–539, 541, 542–543, 544, 545
　　critical values in eliminating, 318–320
　　explained, 314–315
　　interaction of two factors, 493–495
　　level of significance in eliminating, 317–318
　　logic of hypothesis testing, 314–315
　　main effects of two factors, 492–493
　　Mann-Whitney *U* test, 421–424, 427, 429
　　Pearson's product-moment correlation, 397–400
　　rejecting, 331–336, 357–368
　　sampling distribution predicted by, 315–323
　　Spearman's rank-order correlation, 437, 439
　　t tests, 350, 352, 381, 387, 388–389, 392–395
　　type I and II errors in rejection of, 333–336, 357–368
　　Wilcoxon signed-ranks test, 432, 435

z tests, 327–332, 329, 353–355, 356
　　See also Hypothesis testing
Number lines, 18–20

Observed frequencies, 525–528
One-factor analysis of variance, 448–478
One-sample parametric tests. *See* Parametric tests for one sample
Operational definitions, 18
Ordinal scales of measurement, 27–29, 97–98, 412–413, 553

p, value of, in hypothesis testing, 322–323
Parameters, definition of, 16
Parametric statistics, 308
Parametric tests
　　interval or ratio scales and, 412
　　nonparametric tests *vs.*, 440
　　understanding, 401–402
Parametric tests for one sample
　　power of a statistical test, 357–368
　　t test for a sample mean, 345–352
　　testing hypotheses about a population, 368–370
　　z test for a sample mean, 352–357
Parametric tests for two samples
　　between-subjects tests, 377–389
　　overview, 376–377
　　Pearson's product-moment correlation, 395–401
　　t tests, 378–395
　　within-subjects tests, 377–378
　　z test for a difference between means, 385
Partitioning the degrees of freedom, 454–455
Partitioning the sum of squared deviations, 452–453
Pearson's product-moment correlation, 198–206, 395–401
　　calculating, 201–203
　　direction of the relationship, 198–201
　　factors that affect size of, 203–206
　　interpreting, 198
　　magnitude of the relationship, 201
Percentile ranks, 151, 153–154, 156
Percentiles, 78–79, 150–159
Perfect correlation, 195–196
Phi coefficient, 212–213, 530–534
Polygons, frequency, 50–52
Pooled standard deviation, 381–385
Population
　　defined, 14–15
　　differentiating from samples, 15
　　mean, 80–81, 309, 310–311

standard deviation, 113–114
testing hypotheses, 368–370
Positive correlation, 195
Posttests
　　analysis of variance, 466–468
　　interaction between factors, 508–515
　　main effects, 506–508
　　for two-factor analysis of variance, 506–516
　　within-subject factor, 475–476
Power of a statistical test, 335, 359–367
Precise method of finding percentiles, 154–156
Predicted variables, 229
Prediction
　　blind guessing, 225–228
　　correlation and causation, 248
　　defined, 224–225
　　error and, 228, 244–246
　　graphs, 229–238
　　least-squares criterion, 242–244
　　predicting *X* from *Y*, 237
　　predicting *Y* from *X*, 233–236
　　predictor variables, 229
　　as purpose of statistic, 556
　　regression lines, 233–237
　　relevant variables, 228–229
　　second regression line, 237
　　standard error of estimate, 244–246
　　straight line graphs, 229–233
　　See also Correlation; Probability; Regression
Probability
　　addition rule, 261–262
　　combination of events, 264–265
　　defined, 256
　　empirical and theoretical probability, 258–261
　　multiplication rule, 262–264
　　proportion and, 256–258
　　using addition and multiplication rules, 264–265
　　See also Binomial distribution; Prediction
Proportion, probability and, 256–258
Proportion of scores under the normal curve, 174–181
Psychological testing
　　percentiles, 159
　　standard scores in, 148–149
Psychological theories, 6–7
Psychology
　　research and, 6–9
Purpose of statistics, 554–557

Quartiles, 121–126

Random assignment, 281
Random sampling, 15, 281
Range, 108–110
Rank sums, distribution of, 413–419
Ranks
    percentile, 151, 153–154, 156
    Wilcoxon signed-ranks test, 430–436
Ratio scales of measurement, 30, 98,
    412, 553
Raw scores, 136
Real limits, 24–26, 63–64
Regression
    coefficient of determination and non-
      determination, 247–248
    correlation, causation and, 248
    defined, 239–242
    least-squares criterion, 242–244
    predicting X from Y, 237
    predicting Y from X, 233–236
    as predictor of the mean, 238–239
    regression lines, 233–237
    regression to the mean, 241–242
    second regression line, 237
    standard error of estimate, 244–246
    See also Prediction
Relationship between variables, 555–
    556
Relative cumulative frequency tables,
    43–44
Relative frequency tables, 41–42
Relative standing, measures of
    percentiles, 150–159
    standard scores, 137–150
Rounding, 78–79

Sample means, 378–381
Sample size and power of a statistical
    test, 363–364
Samples
    defined, 14
    differentiating from populations, 15
    means of, 80–81
    random, 15
    standard deviation, 113–115
Sampling distributions
    characteristics of distributions of
      sample mean, 288–290
    confidence intervals, 295–301
    constructing distribution of sample
      means, 285–288
    criteria, 280–281
    distributions of sample means, 285–
      295
    eliminating null hypotheses, 315–323
    exactness of parameter estimates,
      295–301
    graphing, 290–293, 330
    independent samples, 280–281

mean of distribution of sample
    means, 289–290
methods of sampling, 281
Pearson's product-moment correla-
    tion, 395–396
of ranks, 413–419
sample means, 285–295, 327–332,
    345–352
sample proportions, 279–285, 292–
    293, 352–356
shape of distribution of sample
    means, 288–289
standard deviation of distribution of
    sample means, 290
standard error of the mean, 290
t test for a sample mean, 345–352
theoretical sampling, 281–285
of U, 417–419
unbiased estimate of standard error,
    294–295
using normal distribution to con-
    struct, 290–293
z test for a sample mean, 327–332,
    345–346
z test for a sample proportion, 352–
    356
Scales of measurement, 26–32, 552–
    553
Scatterplots, 193–195, 200, 229–230
Scientific method, 6
Second regression line, 237
Semi-interquartile range, 124–126
Significance, level of
    chi square, 524–535, 539, 541, 544
    F in between-subjects analysis of vari-
      ance, 504–506
    in hypothesis testing, 317–318
    Mann-Whitney U test, 422, 428
    Pearson's product-moment correla-
      tion, 396–401
    Spearman's rank-order correlation,
      437
    t test for a difference between means,
      388
    t test for a mean difference, 394
    Wilcoxon signed-ranks test, 433
    z test for a sample mean, 329
    z test for a sample proportion, 355
Significant correlations, 400–401
Significant differences in statistical tests,
    321–322, 367–368
Simplified method for finding percen-
    tiles, 150–153
Skewness, measures of, 65–67
Slope, 230–232
Sources of variance, 489–491
Spearman's rank-order correlation, 206–
    211, 436–439

calculating, 207–210
interpreting, 210–211
Standard deviation
    of binomial distribution, 270–272
    calculating standard error using
      sample standard deviation, 294–
      295
    characteristics, 119–121
    converting scores, 138–140
    of distribution of sample means, 288–
      289, 290
    formulas, 112–119
    pooled standard deviation, 381–385
    proportion of scores relative to, 180–
      181
    relationship with power of a statistical
      test, 361–363
    of standard scores, 144–145
    t test for a sample mean, 351–352
    See also Deviation
Standard error
    calculating using sample standard de-
      viation, 294–295
    of a distribution of sample means,
      380–381
    of estimate, 244–246
    of the mean, 290, 294–295
    of a proportion, 293
Standard scores, 137–150
    appropriate use of, 149–150
    converting back to original units of
      measurement, 147
    converting scores to, 140–145
    as measures of relative standing, 145–
      146
    Pearson's product-moment correla-
      tion, 201
    proportion of scores and, 175–180
Standardized tests, 148–149, 159
Stated limits of group intervals, 62–63
Statistical procedure, 8
Statistical tests
    decision making and, 331–336, 357–
      368
    effect size and power, 364–367
    power of, 335, 359–367
    sample size and power, 363–364
    significant differences, 367–368
    standard deviation and power, 361–
      363
    t test for a sample mean, 345–352
    testing hypotheses about a popula-
      tion, 368–370
Stem-and-leaf displays, 52–55
Straight line graphs, 229–233
Strength of relationship, measures of,
    531–534
Subjects, definition of, 14–16

Subjects sum of squares, 471–473
Sum of squares, 450–454, 461–463
    between-groups, 461, 469–470
    interaction between factors, 499–500
    subject, 471–473
    total, 462, 474, 501–502
    treatment, 471–473
    two-factor between-subjects analysis
        of variance, 495–502
    within-group, 461, 500–501
Summary tables
    between-subjects test, 464
    within-subjects test, 475–476
Summation sign, 74–77
Symmetrical distributions, 553

t tests,
    analysis of variance and, 449–450,
        466–468
    for a difference between means, 378–
        395
    for a mean difference, 389–395
    for a sample mean, 345–352
Tables
    contingency, 524–528, 534
    frequency, 39–44, 45
    grouped frequency, 55–65, 156
Tests of association, 535–539
Tests of independence, 540–543
Theoretical distributions, 38, 39, 168,
    171–173
    relevance of, 186–187, 272–273
    sampling, 282–285
Theoretical probability, 258–261
Total rank sum, 416
Total sum of squares, 474
Total variance, 455–457
Transformed scores, 136, 137–140
Treatment sum of squares, 471–473
Treatments, 458
Two-factor analysis of variance, 486–
    516
    assumptions, 489
    between-groups sources of variance,
        491–492
    between-subjects factors, 488–506

cells, 492
computing values of *F* for two-factor
    between-subjects, 495–506
degrees of freedom, 502–503
interaction between factors, 499–500
interaction of several factors, 515–
    516
main effect, 492
mean squares, 503
notation system in two-factor, 491–
    492
null and alternate hypotheses, 492–
    495
posttests for two-factor, 506–516
significance of *F*, 504–506
sources of variance, 489–491
sum of squares, 495–502
total sum of squares, 501–502
within-groups sources of variance,
    491–492
within-groups sum of squares, 500–
    501
within-subject factors, 515
Two-tailed tests. *See* Bidirectional infer-
    ential tests
Type I and Type II errors, 333–336,
    357–368, 448

U
    alternate method for calculating,
        424–426
    converting to *z*, 429
    Mann-Whitney *U* test, 419–429
    sampling distribution of, 417–419
Unbiased estimate of standard error,
    294–295
Unidirectional inferential tests, 323–327
Unimodal distributions, 93, 554
Units of measurement, 20, 22–23, 24
Univariate descriptive statistics, 192
Unsymmetrical distributions, 553–554
Upper stated limits of group intervals,
    62–63
Upper real limits, 24–26, 63–64

Values of *F*, 464–465, 474–475, 495–
    506

Variability, measures of, 65, 107–128
Variables
    bivariate descriptive statistics, 192
    continuous, 20–21, 24
    defined, 17–18
    describing relationship between, 555–
        556
    differentiating from constants, 17
    discrete, 20–21
    operational definitions, 18
    Pearson's product-moment correla-
        tion, 198–206
    Spearman's rank-order correlation,
        206–211
    univariate descriptive statistics, 192
Variance
    characteristics, 119–121
    formulas, 112–119

W, value of, in Wilcoxon signed-ranks
    test, 434–436
Wilcoxon signed-ranks test, 430–436
Within-groups sum of squares, 453
Within-groups variance, 456, 491–492
Within-subject factors, 459–460, 468–
    476
    analysis of variance, 515
    degrees of freedom, 474
    posttests, 475–476
    value of *F*, 474–475
Within-subjects tests, 377–378
    analysis of variance, 468–477
    compared to between-subject tests,
        476–478
    t test for a mean difference, 389–395
    Wilcoxon signed-ranks test, 430–436

Y-intercept, 230–237

z, converting to value of, 429, 435–436
z scores. *See* Standard scores
z tests, 320–322, 327–332, 345–346,
    352–356, 385
Zero correlation, 196

Grouped Frequency Distribution

3-1 Proportion

$$\text{proportion of scores} = \frac{\text{frequency of scores}}{n}$$

3-5 Distance covered

$$\text{distance} = \text{largest score value} - \text{smallest score value} + i$$

3-5 Number of score values

$$\text{number of score values} = \frac{\text{distance covered on number line}}{\text{interval size}}$$

3-6 Number of groups

$$\text{number of groups} = \frac{\text{total number of score values}}{\text{number of score values per group}}$$

3-7 Size of group interval

$$\text{size} = (\text{unit of measurement}) \times \begin{pmatrix}\text{number of score values} \\ \text{per group}\end{pmatrix}$$

3-10 Lower real limit

$$\text{lower real limit} = \text{lower stated limit} - \frac{\text{interval size}}{2}$$

3-10 Upper real limit

$$\text{upper real limit} = \text{upper stated limit} + \frac{\text{interval size}}{2}$$

3-10 Midpoint

$$\text{midpoint} = \frac{\text{lower stated limit} + \text{upper stated limit}}{2}$$

Central Tendency and Variability

4-1 Population mean

$$\mu = \frac{\Sigma X}{N} \quad \text{or} \quad \mu = \frac{\Sigma Xf}{N}$$

4-1 Sample mean

$$\bar{X} = \frac{\Sigma X}{n} \quad \text{or} \quad \bar{X} = \frac{\Sigma Xf}{n}$$

4-2 Median

$$\text{Median} = \text{LRL} + i\left(\frac{.5n - f_b}{f_w}\right)$$

5-1 Range

$$\text{Range} = \text{highest score value} - \text{lowest score value} + i$$

5-2 Population standard deviation

$$\sigma = \sqrt{\frac{\Sigma(X - \mu)^2}{N}} \quad \text{or} \quad \sigma = \sqrt{\frac{\Sigma(X - \mu)^2 f}{N}}$$

5-3

$$\sigma = \sqrt{\frac{\Sigma X^2 - \frac{(\Sigma X)^2}{N}}{N}} \quad \text{or} \quad \sigma = \sqrt{\frac{\Sigma X^2 f - \frac{(\Sigma Xf)^2}{N}}{N}}$$

5-2 Sample standard deviation

$$s = \sqrt{\frac{\Sigma(X - \bar{X})^2}{n - 1}} \quad \text{or} \quad s = \sqrt{\frac{\Sigma(X - \bar{X})^2 f}{n - 1}}$$

5-3

$$s = \sqrt{\frac{\Sigma X^2 - \frac{(\Sigma X)^2}{n}}{n - 1}} \quad \text{or} \quad s = \sqrt{\frac{\Sigma X^2 f - \frac{(\Sigma Xf)^2}{n}}{n - 1}}$$

5-4 Quartiles

$$Q_k = \text{LRL} + i\left(\frac{qn - f_b}{f_w}\right)$$

5-5 Semi-interquartile range

$$Q = \frac{Q_3 - Q_1}{2}$$

Relative Standing

6-3 Standard (z) score

$$z = \frac{X - \mu}{\sigma} \quad \text{or} \quad z = \frac{X - \bar{X}}{s}$$

6-4 Score converted from z

$$X = z\sigma + \mu \quad \text{or} \quad X = zs + \bar{X}$$

6-5 Percentile rank (simplified)

$$\text{percentile rank} = 100\left(\frac{f_b + .5f_w}{n}\right)$$

6-6 Percentile (precise method)

$$k\text{th percentile} = \text{LRL} + i\left[\frac{.01kn - f_b}{f_w}\right]$$

6-6 Percentile rank (precise method)

$$\text{percentile rank} = \frac{100\left[f_b + f_w\left(\frac{X - \text{LRL}}{i}\right)\right]}{n}$$